MAGILL'S GUIDE TO
MILITARY HISTORY

MAGILL'S GUIDE TO MILITARY HISTORY

Volume 3
Japanese Civil Wars of 1331-1392–
Peloponnesian Wars

Editor
John Powell
Department of History, Cumberland College

Managing Editor
Christina J. Moose

Project Editor
Rowena Wildin

SALEM PRESS, INC.
Pasadena, California   Hackensack, New Jersey

Managing editor: Christina J. Moose
Project editor: Rowena Wildin
Copy editor: Melanie Watkins
Copy editor: Ifsha Rahman
Acquisitions editor: Mark Rehn
Assistant editor: Andrea E. Miller

Research supervisor: Jeffry Jensen
Research assistant: Jeff Stephens
Photograph editor: Philip Bader
Graphics and design: James Hutson
Layout: William Zimmerman
Maps: Ross Castellano

Copyright © 2001, by SALEM PRESS, INC.

All rights in this book are reserved. No part of this work may be used or reproduced in any manner whatsoever or transmitted in any form or by any means, electronic or mechanical, including photocopy, recording, or any information storage and retrieval system, without written permission from the copyright owner except in the case of brief quotations embodied in critical articles and reviews. For information address the publisher, Salem Press, Inc., P.O. Box 50062, Pasadena, California 91115.

∞ The paper used in these volumes conforms to the American National Standard for Permanence of Paper for Printed Library Materials, Z39.48-1992 (R1997).

Library of Congress Cataloging-in-Publication Data

Magill's guide to military history / editor John Powell ; managing editor Christina J. Moose ; project editor Rowena Wildin.
    p. cm.
Includes bibliographical references and index.
    ISBN 0-89356-014-6 (set : alk. paper) — ISBN 0-89356-015-4 (v. 1 : alk. paper) — ISBN 0-89356-016-2 (v. 2 : alk. paper) — ISBN 0-89356-017-0 (v. 3 : alk. paper) — ISBN 0-89356-018-9 (v. 4 : alk. paper) — ISBN 0-89356-019-7 (v. 5 : alk. paper)
    1. Military history—Dictionaries. 2. Generals—Biography—Dictionaries. I. Powell, John, 1954-   .

D25.A2 M34 2001
355'.009—dc21

00-066072

First Printing

PRINTED IN THE UNITED STATES OF AMERICA

Contents

List of Maps xliii

Japanese Civil Wars of 1331-1392 781
Japanese Civil Wars of 1450-1550 782
Japanese Colonial Wars 783
Japanese military 786
Japanese Wars of Unification 788
Java War, Great 789
Javanese Wars of Succession 791
Javelin 792
Jayavarman VII 792
Jellicoe, John 793
Jemappes 793
Jena and Auerstädt 794
Jericho 796
Jerusalem, Siege of 796
Jewish Revolts 798
Jihad 799
Joan of Arc 800
Jodl, Alfred 801
Joffre, Joseph-Jacques-Césaire 802
John I Zimisces 802
John II Comnenus 803
John III Sobieski 803
Johnston, Albert Sidney 804
Johnston, Joseph Eggleston 805
Jomini, Antoine Henri, baron de 805
Jones, John Paul 807
Joseph, Chief 808
Josephus, Flavius 809
Joubert, Petrus Jacobus 809
Joust 810
Juel, Niels 810
Junot, Andoche 810
Just war 811
Justinian I 811
Jutland 812

Kadesh 814
Kalmar Wars 814
Kandahar 816
Kanem-Bornu Sultanate 816
Kangxi 818
Karageorge 818
Kars 819
Kashmir 820
Kearny, Philip 820
Kearny, Stephen W. 821

Keitel, Wilhelm 821
Kesselring, Albert 822
Kett's Rebellion 823
KGB 824
Khair ed-dīn 824
Khālid ibn-al-Walīd 825
Khalkin-Gol 826
Kharkov 826
Khartoum, Siege of 827
Khe Sanh, Siege of 828
Khmer-Cham Wars 829
Khmer-Thai Wars 830
Kiev 832
Kigeri IV 832
Killiecrankie 833
Kim Il Sung 833
Kimberley, Siege of 834
Kimmel, Husband Edward 835
King, Ernest 836
King's Mountain 837
Kinsale, Siege of 838
Kitchener, Lord 838
Kléber, Jean-Baptiste 839
Knights and chivalry 840
Kolchak, Aleksandr 842
Konev, Ivan 843
Könniggrätz 843
Korean (North) military 844
Korean War 845
Kościuszko, Tadeusz 849
Kosovo 851
Kruger, Paul 852
Ksar el-Kebir 853
Kublai Khan 854
Kuropatkin, Aleksei 855
Kursk 855
Kut-al-Amara 857
Kutná Hora 857
Kutuzov, Mikhail Illarionovich 858

La Hogue and Barfleur 860
La Rochelle, Siege of 860
Ladysmith, Siege of 861
Lafayette, marquis de 862
Lake Champlain 863
Lake Erie 863
Lake Trasimene 864
Lannes, Jean 865

Entry	Page
Laotian Civil War	866
Las Navas de Tolosa	868
Laswari	868
Latin American Wars of Independence	869
Latin Empire-Byzantine Wars	871
La Trémoille, Louis II de	873
Laupen	873
Lawrence, T. E.	874
Laws of war	875
Lebanon	878
Lechfeld	880
Lee, Henry	881
Lee, Robert E.	882
Lefebvre, Francis Joseph, duke of Danzig	883
Legion	884
Legnano	884
Leipzig	885
LeMay, Curtis	885
Leningrad, Siege of	886
Leo III	888
Lepanto	888
Lettow-Vorbeck, Paul Emil von	890
Leuctra	890
Leuthen	891
Lexington and Concord	892
Leyte Gulf	893
Li Hongzhang	894
Li Shimin	895
Li Zongren	896
Liberia	896
Liddell Hart, Basil	897
Light Brigade, Charge of the	898
Lin Biao	899
Lincoln, Abraham	899
Lissa	900
Literature, war in	901
Little Bighorn	905
Livonian War	906
Lloyd George, David	908
Lobengula	908
Lodi	909
Logistics	910
Lombard League, Wars of	910
Long Island	912
Long March	912
Longbow	913
Longstreet, James	913
Louis XIV	914
Louisbourg, Siege of	915
Louvois, François-Michel Le Tellier, marquis de	915
Luccan-Florentine War	916
Ludendorff, Erich	917
Lützen	918
Luxembourg	918
Luxembourg, François-Henri de Montmorency-Bouteville, duke of	919
Lyautey, Louis H. G.	919
Lysander	920
MacArthur, Douglas	921
Maccabees, Revolt of the	922
McClellan, George B.	924
McDowell, Irvin	925
Macedonian Wars	926
Machel, Samora	928
Machiavelli, Niccolò	929
Mackensen, August von	929
McNamara, Robert S.	930
Magdeburg, Siege of	930
Maginot Line	932
Magsaysay, Ramón	933
Magyars	934
Mahan, Alfred Thayer	934
Maḥmūd of Ghazna	935
Majorian	936
Malayan Emergency	937
Maldon	939
Mali Empire	939
Malplaquet	940
Malta, Siege of	941
Mamlūk-Ottoman War	942
Mamlūks	943
Manchu Expansion, Wars of	944
Mandalay	946
Mannerheim, Carl Gustaf	946
Manstein, Erich von	947
Mansura	948
Mantinea	949
Manzikert	949
Mao Zedong	950
Maps and cartography	952
Marāṭhā-Mogul Wars	954
Marāṭhā Wars	956
Marathon	957
Marcellus, Marcus Claudius	958
Marcus Aurelius	959
Marengo	960
Marignano	961
Marines	962
Marines, U.S.	962
Marion, Francis	964
Marius, Gaius	965

Entry	Page
Marlborough, first duke of	965
Marne	967
Marshall, George C.	968
Marston Moor	969
Martial law	970
Martinet, Jean	970
Masada, Siege of	971
Masséna, André	971
Masurian Lakes	972
Matthias I Corvinus	973
Mau Mau Rebellion	973
Maurice	975
Maurice of Nassau, Prince	976
Mauryan Empire	977
Maximilian I	978
Mayan Empire	979
Meade, George G.	980
Medici, Giovanni de' (1475-1521)	981
Medici, Giovanni de' (1498-1526)	982
Medicine, military	982
Medieval warfare	985
Megiddo, 1469 B.C.E.	988
Megiddo, 1918	989
Mehmed II	989
Menelik II	990
Mercenaries	991
Meroë, Kingdom of	991
Messenian Wars	992
Metz, Siege of, 1552-1553	994
Metz, Siege of, 1870	994
Meuse-Argonne	995
Mexican-American War	996
Mexican Civil Wars	999
Mexican Revolution	1001
Mexican Wars of Independence	1003
Mexico, U.S. Invasion of	1005
Miani	1006
Midway	1006
Miguelite Wars	1008
Miles, Nelson A.	1009
Militarism	1010
Military academy	1010
Military organization, U.S.	1011
Military theory	1013
Militia	1019
Milvian Bridge	1019
Minamoto Yoshitsune	1020
Minden	1020
Mitchell, Billy	1021
Mithridatic Wars	1022
Mobilization	1024
Mobutu Sese Seko	1024
Mogul Conquest of the Deccan	1025
Mogul-Persian War	1026
Mogul-Sikh Wars	1027
Mogul Wars of Succession	1028
Mohács	1030
Moltke, Helmuth von (1800-1891)	1031
Moltke, Helmuth von (1848-1916)	1032
Monck, George	1033
Mongol Empire	1033
Monitor vs. *Virginia*	1035
Monmouth	1036
Monongahela	1037
Mons Graupius	1037
Montcalm, Louis-Joseph de	1038
Monte Cassino	1038
Montenegrin Wars of Independence	1040
Monterrey	1041
Montgomery, Bernard Law	1041
Montmorency, Anne, duke of	1042
Montrose, James Graham, marquess of	1043
Morat	1044
Moscow	1044
Moscow, Retreat from	1045
Mount Badon	1046
Mountbatten, Louis	1047
Mozambican Civil War	1048
Mozambican War of Independence	1049
Mubārak, Hosnī	1052
Muḥammad Ahmad	1052
Muḥammad ʿAlī Pasha	1053
Muhammad of Ghor	1054
Muhammad of Ghor, conquests of	1055
Muḥammad I Askia	1056
Mühlberg	1056
Mukden	1057
Mulhouse	1058
Munda	1058
Murad I	1059
Murat, Joachim	1059
Mūsā ibn Nuṣayr	1060
Music, martial	1061
Musket	1063
Muslim Civil War of 657-661	1064
Muslim Civil War of 861-870	1065
Muslim Conquests	1067
Muslim unrest in China	1071
Mussolini, Benito	1072
Mustard gas	1074
Muster and review	1074
Mutiny	1074
My Lai Massacre	1074
Mysore Wars	1075

Nādir Shāh	1078	Norman Conquests	1130
Nagashino	1078	Normandy Invasion	1132
Naguib, Muḥammad	1079	North Atlantic	1134
Nagumo, Chuichi	1079	North Atlantic Treaty Organization	
Nahāvand	1080	(NATO)	1135
Namibian War of Independence	1081	Northern Ireland Civil War	1136
Nanjing, Rape of	1083	Northern War	1138
Napier, Charles James	1083	Northumberland, duke of	1139
Napier, Robert	1084	Novgorod, Muscovite Conquest of	1140
Napier, William	1085	Nuclear and atomic weapons	1141
Napoleon I	1085	Nuremberg Trials	1144
Napoleonic Wars	1087	Nurhaci	1144
Narses	1091		
Narva	1092	Oda Nobunaga	1146
Naseby	1093	Offa's Wars	1147
Nashville	1094	Officer	1148
Nasser, Gamal Abdel	1095	Ogatai	1148
National Guard	1096	Okinawa	1149
Naval weapons	1096	Omani Conquest of Eastern Africa	1150
Navarro, Pedro	1100	Omdurman	1152
Navies: Organization and tactics	1100	Ōnin War	1152
Navy	1105	Opium Wars	1153
Navy, U.S.	1105	Orléans, Siege of	1156
Nelson, Horatio	1108	Osaka Castle, Siege of	1157
Německý Brod	1109	Ostend, Siege of	1157
Nero, Gaius Claudius	1109	Ostrogoths	1158
Neutrality	1110	Otto I	1158
Neville's Cross	1110	Ottoman Civil Wars	1159
New Orleans	1111	Ottoman-Druze Wars	1160
Ney, Michel	1112	Ottoman Empire	1162
Nez Perce War	1112	Oudenarde	1163
Nicaragua, Walker's invasion of	1114	Oudinot, Nicolas Charles	1164
Nicaraguan Civil War of 1925-1933	1115		
Nicaraguan Civil War of 1977-1989	1117	Pacific, War of the	1166
Nicephorus II Phocas	1119	Pacifism	1167
Nicholas, Grand Duke	1119	Pānīpat, 1399	1167
Nicopolis	1120	Pānīpat, 1526	1168
Nieuport	1120	Parachute troops	1168
Nigeria-Biafra Civil War	1121	Parma, Alessandro Farnese, duke of	1169
Nimeiri, Gaafer Muhammad al-	1123	Parthian Empire	1169
Nimitz, Chester W.	1123	Patriotism	1170
Nivelle, Robert	1124	Patton, George S.	1171
Nogi, Maresuke	1125	Pavia	1172
Nongovernmental organizations' roles in warfare	1126	Pax Romana	1173
		Pearl Harbor attack	1173
Nördlingen	1128	Peloponnesian Wars	1174
Norman-Byzantine Wars	1129		

List of Maps

VOLUME 1

Alexander's Early Campaign Against
    the Persian Empire, 334-331 B.C.E. 40
Major Sites in the Civil War, 1861-1865 59
Indian Wars in the West, 1840's-1890 68
Major Sites in the American
    Revolutionary War 74
The Anglo-Spanish War 95
Athenian Empire, 5th Century B.C.E. 141
Austerlitz, 1805 147
Early Civilization in the Americas 156
Site of the Battle of Bannockburn 171
Blenheim, 1704 191
British India, 1914 227
Bulge, 1944-1945 238
Byzantine Empire, c. 1250 255
Cannae, 216 B.C.E. 277
Division of Charlemagne's Empire 285
Carolingian Empire 316
Chinese Civil War 329

VOLUME 2

Major Sites in the Crimean War,
    1853-1856 394
Europe and the Byzantine Empire
    During the Crusades 398
Castro's Cuban Revolution 408
Delhi Sultanate, 1236-1398 425
Dutch Provinces That Declared
    Independence from Spain 453
War of 1812: Battles in the South 470
War of 1812: Battles in the North 471
Selected Battle Sites in the English Civil
    War of 1642-1651 484
Africa as of 1914 489
Important Etruscan Cities,
    530-520 B.C.E. 495
Franco-Spanish War 540
Major Battles in the French and Indian
    War, 1754-1763 551

Final Campaign Against Gallic Tribes,
    52 B.C.E. 573
Unification of Germany, 1863-1871 593
Gettysburg, 1863 597
Major Battles Against Darius and
    Xerxes 620
Gulf War, 1991 644
Hastings, 1066 667
Holy Roman Empire 686
Major Sites in the Hundred Years' War 702
Partition of India, 1947 723
Great Irish Rebellion 755
Unification of Italy 771

VOLUME 3

Korean War, 1950-1953 846
Manchuria, c. 1697 945
Marāṭhās in the Mid-Eighteenth
    Century 955
Battle Sites in the Mexican-American
    War 997
Ships Sunk at Midway, June 4, 1942 1007
The Mongol Empire in 1260 1034
Muslim Empire in 760 1068
Selected Battle Sites in the
    Napoleonic Wars 1088
Norman Conquests 1130
Normandy Invasion, 1944 1133
Ottoman Empire in 1566 1162
The Peloponnesian Wars 1176

VOLUME 4

Persian Empire, c. 500 B.C.E. 1186
Third Partition of Poland, 1795 1213
Battles of the Second Punic War,
    218-202 B.C.E. 1249
Iberian Peninsula, c. 1150 1275
The Riel Rebellions, 1869 and 1885 1296
Roman Empire, c. 117 1309

Wars of the Roses, 1455-1485 1322
Russian Civil War of 1918-1921 1328
Russian Empire, 1914 1331
Russo-Japanese War, 1904-1905 1338
Saratoga, October 7, 1777 1372
Seven Years' War 1397
Southeast Asia in the mid-1700's 1410
Six-Day War 1428
South American Independence 1445
Division of Spain, 1936 1455
War of the Spanish Succession 1462
Thirty Years' War, First Ten Years 1528

VOLUME 5

Republic of Turkey, 1923 1573
Vietnam Conflict, 1954-1975 1603
Viking Raids, 790-850 1612
World War I: Western Front,
   1915-1917 1652
World War I: Offensives on the
   Western Front, 1918 1654
World War II: The European Theater 1657
World War II: The Pacific Theater 1658

MAGILL'S GUIDE TO
MILITARY HISTORY

Japanese Civil Wars of 1331-1392

At issue: Control of the Japanese imperial throne
Date: 1331-1392
Location: Japan
Combatants: Emperor vs. Kamakura shogunate; southern emperor vs. northern emperor/Ashikaga shogunate
Principal commanders: *Southern emperor*, Go-Daigo (1288-1339); *Northern emperor*, Shogun Ashikaga Takauji (1305-1358)
Result: The northern emperor won and the Ashikaga shogunate retained power

Background

In 1192, after defeating the emperor Go-Toba's forces, Minamoto Yoritomo became the first shogun, or military ruler of Japan. He set up headquarters at Kamakura about thirty miles south of Tokyo, while the much-weakened emperor remained with his court at Kyoto. At first, the shogun took absolute control only of military matters, but eventually he controlled all aspects of the Japanese government.

When Yoritomo died in 1199, his wife, Hōjō Masako, took control, and power passed from the Minamoto to the Hōjō with the establishment of the Kamakura shogunate. The Hōjō family ruled Japan for more than one hundred years, but many other Japanese families, including the imperial family, resented its power. This resentment, coupled with growing poverty in Japan, caused widespread discontent and constant fighting among the leading daimyo, or feudal barons. In 1331, the emperor Go-Daigo decided to regain control of the Japanese government.

Action

In 1331, fighting broke out between the forces of Emperor Go-Daigo and those of the Kamakura shogunate. The shogunate sent Hōjō general Ashikaga Takauji to fight the emperor's army. However, Ashikaga, seeing more potential power for himself as an ally of the emperor than as an ally of the shogun, switched sides and fought against the shogun. Many generals and samurai followed Ashikaga, and the Kamakura shogunate fell.

Go-Daigo regained power, but the Kemmu Restoration lasted only from 1334 to 1338. In 1336, Ashikaga named himself shogun, and in 1337, he revolted against Emperor Go-Daigo. That year, the emperor fled Kyoto and took his court to Yoshino, where he established a southern court. When leaving Kyoto, Go-Daigo took with him the traditional symbols of the Japanese imperial line, including the sword, the jewel, and the mirror. In 1338, Ashikaga located his government in Muromachi in Kyoto and placed a second emperor on the throne in Kyoto. Japan's imperial powers were split between the northern emperor in Kyoto and the southern emperor in Yoshino.

For more than fifty years, the northern Japanese and southern Japanese empires waged war. The northern emperors hoped to regain the traditional symbols of the Japanese imperial line and, thus, establish themselves as the legitimate imperial house. Although the northern armies were generally stronger, the southern armies were able to invade Kyoto and destroy it regularly.

While the southern and northern emperors battled, the leading families of Japan were also engaged in fighting. Although the various sections of Japan had been relatively independent under the Hōjō, the Ashikaga shogunate centralized power in Japan and created a federation of states. Each state was ruled by a daimyo, who functioned as a military governor. The daimyo, who owned huge estates and were the patriarchs of Japan's leading families, retained samurai, or hired warriors, for the constant battles with each other for land, power, and the possibility of controlling the shogunate.

In 1392, through the diplomacy of Ashikaga Yoshimitsu, the southern empire yielded to the northern empire, and Japan was reunited under the northern emperor Go-Kamatsu and his court.

Aftermath

Although there was constant fighting between the northern and southern empires and between the major families of Japan during the latter part of the fourteenth century, it was a time of relative prosperity and a flowering of the arts. The daimyo received tribute from farmers who grew rice on their lands, and they made arms and armor for the samurai. Merchants began to trade with Chinese and Korean businesspeople. Various regions became known for producing pottery, paper, textiles, and lacquerware. Trade grew between the regions of Japan, and artisan guilds were created. Art forms such as the tea ceremony, Noh drama, and ikebana, or flower arranging, were developed during this period.

However, the most important outcome of the Japanese Civil Wars of the fourteenth century was the determination that the Japanese imperial family would descend from the northern emperors, not the southern ones.

RESOURCES

Friday, Karl F. *Hired Swords: The Rise of Private Warriors: Power in Early Japan*. Stanford, Calif.: Stanford University Press, 1996.

Martin, Peter, and James Melville. *Chrysanthemum Throne: A History of Emperors of Japan*. Honolulu: University of Hawaii Press, 1998.

Mass, Jeffrey B., and William B. Hauser, eds. *The Bakufu in Japanese History*. Stanford, Calif.: Stanford University Press, 1993.

Samurai Japan. Documentary. Films for the Humanities and Sciences, 1999.

Sansom, George B. *A History of Japan, 1334-1615*. Stanford, Calif.: Stanford University Press, 1991.

Sato, Hiroaki. *Legends of the Samurai*. New York: Overlook Press, 1996.

Shogun: The Supreme Samurai. Documentary. A&E Television Networks, 1997.

SEE ALSO: Gempei War; Japanese Civil Wars of 1450-1550; Minamoto Yoshitsune.

Annita Marie Ward

JAPANESE CIVIL WARS OF 1450-1550

AT ISSUE: Control of various Japanese provinces and eventually of the country as a whole
DATE: 1450-1550
LOCATION: Japan
COMBATANTS: Various Japanese daimyo (feudal barons)
PRINCIPAL COMMANDERS: Yamana Mochitoyo, later Yamana Sōzen (1404-1473), Hosokawa Katsumoto (1430-1473), Hōjō Sōun (1432-1519), Hōjō Ujitsuna (1478-1541), Uesugi Kenshin (1530-1578), Takeda Shingen (1521-1573)
PRINCIPAL BATTLES: Odawara, Kuzuryugawa, Edo, Sendanno, Konodai
RESULT: Indecisive; however, developments during this period later led to the consolidation of power on a national scale

BACKGROUND

Between 1153 and 1221, Japan's imperial court fell under the power of the samurai, the nation's emerging warrior class. The imperial court maintained a great deal of prestige, but the administration of the country was divided among military barons who controlled individual districts. By 1450, the *bakufu*, the central military authority, was no longer powerful enough to maintain order. A period of civil war known as the Epoch of the Warring Country resulted. As the daimyo (feudal barons) fought against one another in order to expand their territory and bring more resources under their control, Japan was progressively divided into a large number of autonomous domains ruled over by either the powerful warrior families of old or by ambitious upstarts.

ACTION

The first serious conflict during the Epoch of the Warring Country was the Ōnin War (1467-1477). This decade-long struggle originated with succession disputes involving two of the great daimyo—Yamana Mochitoyo and Hosokawa Katsumoto—and their attempts to dominate the decadent and virtually powerless Ashikaga *bakufu*, which theoretically administered the country in the emperor's name. Most of the fighting took place in and around the city of Kyoto, and much of the ancient capital was destroyed in the fighting. The Hosokawa were the nominal victors and established their dominance over the *bakufu*, but they did not wield enough power to impose their authority on a national scale.

Despite the lack of a national hegemony, some notable warlords were able to expand their domains and dominate entire regions. In 1491, Hōjō Sōun occupied **Odawara** and gained control over Izu province. He then began to consolidate his hold over the strategically important Kanto plain. Sōun was a wandering samurai from an undistinguished family and the fact that he attained such great power shows how chaotic Japanese political life was during this period. Sōun was succeeded by his son, Hōjō Ujitsuna, who further expanded his territory by defeating the powerful Uesugi family at **Edo** (1524). At **Konodai** (1538), Ujitsuna also defeated the forces of Satomi Yoshitaka and Ashikaga Yoshiaki, bringing the power of his family to new heights. The fortunes of the Hōjō continued to rise until after 1550.

Even more striking than Sōun's rise from obscurity to a position of power was the uprising of the Ikko sect. This religious movement seized the province of Kaga from its hereditary governor in 1486. With this victory, the Ikko sect established itself as a major military force in central Japan. The Ikko sect controlled Kaga until the period after 1550 and was forced to defend the province a number of times. Its first serious challenge came at **Kuzuryugawa** (1506), where the sect defeated the forces of Asakura Norikage. The Ikko sect was later attacked by Nagao Tamekage, another ambitious daimyo, but the religious group mounted a successful defense at **Sendanno** (1536).

Takeda Shingen and Uesugi Kenshin are two other famous generals who were active during the Epoch of the Warring Country. Their territories were located next to each other, which put them in continuous conflict. Before 1550, both men struggled to carve out their territory by fighting against other warlords. For example, Takeda seized control of the province of Kai by overthrowing his father in 1541 and spent the rest of the decade fighting against rivals in order to consolidate his gains. Having succeeded in subduing other opposition, both Takeda and Uesugi proceeded to fight five battles against one another on the plain of Kawanakajima.

These examples are just a few of the numerous battles and skirmishes that were fought between rival warlords during this period. The campaigns of the Hōjō and men such as Uesugi and Takeda show the pattern of warfare during this era to be a struggle toward establishing and consolidating regional power.

Aftermath

The period of warfare from 1450-1550 ended the power of the Muromachi *bakufu* and led to the emergence of many powerful and politically independent fiefs throughout the country. The period of civil war did not cease after 1550, as powerful daimyo such as Oda Nobunaga, Takeda Shingen, and Uesugi Kenshin continued to attempt to impose their authority on a national scale. After 1550, however, Western-style firearms, which were introduced in Japan in 1542, became a decisive weapon on the battlefield. This and other developments that occurred between 1450 and 1550 created the conditions that made possible the campaign of national conquest of Oda Nobunaga and his successors.

Resources

Grossberg, Kenneth A. *Japan's Renaissance: The Politics of the Muromachi Bakufu*. Cambridge, Mass.: Harvard University Press, 1981.

Sato, Hiroaki. *Legends of the Samurai*. New York: Overlook Press, 1996.

Turnbull, Stephen. *The Samurai Sourcebook*. London: Arms & Armour Press, 1998.

_____. *Samurai Warfare*. London: Arms & Armour Press, 1996.

See also: Bakufu; Bushido; Oda Nobunaga; Ōnin War; Samurai; Tokugawa Ieyasu; Toyotomi Hideyoshi.

Matthew Penney

Japanese Colonial Wars

At issue: Japan's status as a major Pacific power, European interests in the Far East, and the territorial integrity of China

Date: 1874-1931

Location: Formosa, Korea, China, Manchuria

Combatants: Japanese vs. Chinese, Russians, Germans, and the Formosan and Manchurian peoples

Principal commanders: *Japanese*, Field Marshal Aritomo Yamagata (1838-1922), General Maresuke Nogi (1849-1912), Admiral Heihachirō Tōgō (1848-1934); *Russian*, General Aleksei Nikolaevich Kuropatkin (1848-1925)

Principal battles: Pyongyang, Yalu River, Weihaiwei, Port Arthur, Mukden, Tsushima, Qingdao (Tsingtao), Manchurian Incident

Result: A series of Japanese victories resulted in the formation of a Japanese empire on the Asian mainland

Background

In 1853, American commodore Matthew C. Perry arrived in Japan and pressured the Tokugawa *bakufu* into ending its nearly 250-year-old policy of virtual national seclusion. This event was followed by increased contact between Japan and the nations of the West. The Japanese leadership recognized its military inferiority and had little choice but to enter into a series of unequal treaties with the major Western powers such as the United States, France, Great Britain, and Russia, granting them rights such as extraterritoriality and control over Japanese tariffs. This chain of events led to considerable political upheaval in Japan, and in 1868, the Tokugawa *bakufu* was overthrown and the Emperor Meiji, backed by a new group of influential soldiers and statesmen, was restored to power. The new government was dedicated not only to military and economic modernization but also to making Japan a major power in Asia with the aim of protecting the nation against Western imperialism and encouraging the Western powers to agree to revise the unequal treaties. These ambitions conflicted with those of imperial China, which was trying to establish its control over traditional dependencies such as Korea, and also Russia, which was busy carving out a considerable sphere of influence in Northern China in the late nineteenth century.

Action

In 1874, just one year after the formation of the Imperial Japanese Army and the introduction of conscription, Japan launched its first overseas adventure of the nineteenth century. In December of 1871, aborigines from Formosa attacked a group of fishermen from the Ryūkyū Islands, killing 54. The Ryūkyūs were considered by the Japanese to be a part of their territory, and the government decided to launch an armed expedition in order to punish the Formosan natives. It was hoped that this gesture would help solidify Japan's claim to the Ryūkyū Islands, which were traditionally affiliated with the Chinese. In May, 1874, 3,000 Japanese troops were sent to the island, but they made little headway against the natives and were soon withdrawn. Although the expedition to Formosa was poorly handled, it did allow the Japanese government to claim that it, not the Chinese government, was the rightful governing body in the Ryūkyū Islands. This fighting set the pattern for Japanese colonial warfare as the Japanese government showed that it was willing to use violence to protect its "sphere of influence" and to assert its status as a major power in Asia.

Korea was another area considered essential to Japan's interests. The Korean Peninsula represented the most likely point on the mainland of Asia from which an invasion of Japan could be launched. The potential profit that could be won by exploiting Korea as a colonial dependency was not lost on the Japanese leaders. As early as 1873, influential Japanese generals and statesmen such as Takamori Saigo had called for an invasion of Korea. Other members of the government believed that invading Korea was beyond Japan's power, and the idea was eventually scrapped. However, Japan did force Korea to accept the Treaty of Kanghwa in 1876 and received trade privileges as a result. Korea, like the Ryūkyū Islands, was traditionally a dependency of China. The Chinese were anxious to retain their traditional control and saw the Japanese efforts to gain privileges in Korea as a threat to their own interests. This conflict became more serious throughout the 1880's and 1890's.

When a rebellion threatened the Korean crown in 1894, both China and Japan sent troops to the peninsula. After a series of minor encounters including the sinking of a British ship carrying Chinese troops to Korea, Japan declared war on August 1, 1894, marking the beginning of the Sino-Japanese War. On September 16 of that year, the Japanese army won a major land victory at **Pyongyang**. This battle put an end to Chinese military strength in Korea. On the following day, a naval engagement was fought at the **Yalu River** and ended in a Japanese victory for forces under Aritomo Yamagata. The remainder of the Chinese fleet was defeated at **Weihaiwei** on February 12, 1895. These victories allowed the Japanese to march into Northern China. The Japanese advance resulted in the seizure of the Liaodong Peninsula in Southern Manchuria.

The Chinese had been decisively defeated by the Japanese, and the war ended with the Treaty of Shimonoseki in 1895. The provisions of this treaty clearly demonstrate the colonial motives of Japanese aggression in the Far East. Japan forced China to recognize its interests in Korea and also to transfer Formosa and the Liaodong Peninsula to Japanese control. The Chinese also agreed to pay a large indemnity to Japan. This war also helped the Japanese win the respect of the Western powers and facilitated the renegotiation of the unequal treaties that had offended Japanese nationalists since the 1850's. However, Japan's success in the war against China made several Western nations, including Germany, France, and Russia, concerned about the security of their Asian possessions. These three powers forced Japan to return the Liaodong Peninsula to China in the Tripartite Intervention. Japan, not yet strong enough to challenge the Western powers, had no choice but to comply. The situation became even more unbearable to the Japanese leadership when Russia annexed the Liaodong Peninsula in 1898.

During the Boxer Rebellion in 1900, the Japanese sent troops to Beijing as part of an international force to rescue foreign diplomats in the city. The Japanese government wished to use the Boxer Rebellion as an opportunity to expand its power in Northern China, but the Russian government acted sooner and occupied Manchuria. The Russo-Japanese War (1904-1905) was a product of rival imperialist ambitions in the region. It began on February 9, 1904, when the Imperial Japanese Navy launched a surprise attack against the Russian fleet at Port Arthur. The Russian fleet was tied up in port, giving the Japanese a chance to ferry additional forces to Korea. On May 1, the Japanese army broke through the Russian defensive line at the Yalu River and moved into the Russian-held region of Northern China. By August, Japanese forces under General Maresuke Nogi had laid siege to **Port Arthur** (1904-1905) on the strategically vital Liaodong Peninsula. The fortress fell in January of 1905. This was followed in March by a fierce battle at **Mukden** in which a Japanese force of 250,000 engaged the main body of the Russian forces numbering more than 320,000 in the Far East. The Russians withdrew after ten days of fighting. Both sides were exhausted, and when the Russian Baltic Fleet was destroyed at **Tsushima** (May 27, 1905) by forces under Heihachirō Tōgō, a peace treaty was mediated by U.S. president Theodore Roosevelt. The Treaty of Portsmouth (September 5, 1905) was signed, and Japan won exclusive power in Korea as well as control over Russia's South Manchurian Railway. This established a more significant Japanese presence in Northern China, which was to have a great impact on future relations between the two nations.

In 1914, Japan decided to enter World War I on the side of Britain and its allies. The Japanese government wished to increase its power in China by taking control of Germany's possessions there. The Kiaochow (Jiao Xian) Leased Territory, containing the important port of Qingdao (Tsingtao), was Germany's most important possession in the Far East, and the Japanese coveted it as a way to hasten their economic penetration of China. On September 2, 1914, the Japanese landed troops near **Qingdao** and laid siege to the city. The German garrison surrendered after six weeks. Japan followed this victory by presenting the Chinese government with demands for additional economic and political privileges in the country.

Around the time of World War I, the Japanese government also had ambitions to take control of the Russian Far East. This led to Japan's participation in a joint expedition with U.S. and British troops to rescue a corps of Czechoslovak troops who were trapped in Russia after the Bolshevik Revolution. In 1917, the Japanese government sent 70,000 troops into the Russian Far East, and they remained after the expedition's aims had been accomplished. As many as 50,000 Japanese settlers also entered the region. In 1922, there was fighting between Japanese and Bolshevik troops, and the Japanese government decided to withdraw its forces rather than risk a serious conflict. Japanese troops withdrew from the Russian Far East in June of 1922.

Throughout the 1920's, the Japanese continued to expand their economic interests in China and endeavored to keep Manchuria from falling under the control of the Chinese Nationalist government. The assertion of Chinese power in the region and the gradual buildup of Soviet military power in the Far East over the course of the 1920's caused many officers of the Imperial Japanese Army to call for action.

This action materialized on September 18, 1931, in the form of an unauthorized plot by Japanese troops in Manchuria, known as the **Manchurian Incident**. The Japanese staged a bombing of a railroad near Mukden that they blamed on Chinese troops in the region. This provided the Japanese army with an excuse for the total occupation of Manchuria, which was completed before the end of the year.

Aftermath

The Japanese seizure of power in Manchuria resulted in the formation of the independent nation of Manchukuo in 1932. The government of Manchukuo was dominated by the Japanese, and international public opinion censured the Japanese government for its aggression. In 1933, the League of Nations refused to acknowledge the existence of Manchukuo and condemned Japan for its actions there. As a result, the Japanese withdrew from the league. These developments put Japan at odds with the Western democracies. Japan also continued to expand its economic and military power across the borders of Manchukuo and into Northern China. This evoked a considerable nationalist response from the Chinese, and an exchange of fire between Japanese and Chinese troops near Peking in 1937 precipitated a major war between the two nations, known as the Second Sino-Japanese War (1937-1945). The Japanese military presence in Manchukuo also put them into conflict with Russia, which had its own military interests in Mongolia and the Russian Far East. The Japanese Colonial Wars between 1874 and 1931 created the conditions that led to the eruption of the war in the Far East, which lasted between 1937 and 1945.

Resources

Harries, Meirion, and Susie Harries. *Soldiers of the Sun: The Rise and Fall of the Imperial Japanese Army*. New York: Random House, 1991.

Lone, Stewart. *Japan's First Modern War: Army and Society in the Conflict with China, 1894-1895*. New York: St. Martin's Press, 1994.

Wells, David, and Sandra Wilson, eds. *The Russo-Japanese War in Cultural Perspective, 1904-1905*. New York: St. Martin's Press, 1999.

See also: Bakufu; Bolshevik Revolution; Boxer Rebellion; Hasegawa, Yoshimichi; Hirohito; Japanese military; Mukden; Nogi, Maresuke; Port Arthur, Siege of; Russo-Japanese War; Sino-Japanese War; Tōgō, Heihachirō; Tsushima; World War I; World War II; Yalu River; Yamagata, Aritomo.

Matthew Penney

Japanese Military

At the beginning of the twentieth century, the Japanese military reflected the continuing legacy of the Meiji Restoration (1866-1868). With the destruction of the feudal class system, both the army and navy relied on conscription rather than the traditional samurai class to fill their ranks. Both services also mirrored the new reform government's commitment to Western modernization. The army modeled itself along German lines, and the navy followed the British example. The post-World War II Japanese Self-Defense Forces are a product of Japan's defeat in World War II as well as early Cold War (1945-1991) tension.

Early Twentieth Century

In its first test in the new century—the Russo-Japanese War (1904-1905)—the navy devastated the Russian Far Eastern Fleet in a surprise attack on February 9, 1904, at its home base at Port Arthur. Fifteen months later, on May 27, 1905, Admiral Heihachirō Tōgō again led the fleet to victory, destroying the bulk of the Russian Baltic Fleet in the Tsushima Straits. The army, meanwhile, ejected Russian forces from Korea and secured southern Manchuria with its victory in March, 1905, at Mukden.

During World War I, Japan honored the Anglo-Japanese alliance and committed some 30,000 troops in a campaign, which lasted from September 2 to November 7, 1914, to oust German forces from China's Shandong Peninsula. The navy, meanwhile, occupied Germany's Pacific possessions and conducted patrols in the Mediterranean. Both branches also participated, along with several Western nations, in an anti-Bolshevik intervention during the Russian Civil War of 1918-1921. Japanese marines landed in Vladivostok in April, 1918, and the army, which defied restrictions placed on it by civilian authorities, dispatched in excess of 80,000 men to Siberia.

The army displayed even greater independence on September 18, 1931, when elements of the Guangdong army, acting without orders from either the government or their superiors in Tokyo, undertook the conquest of the Chinese province of Manchuria in what became known as the Manchurian Incident. The following year, the army spearheaded the creation of the Japanese puppet-state of Manchukuo, poisoning relations with China and setting the stage for even greater calamity.

On July 7, 1937, Japanese and Chinese troops clashed near the Marco Polo Bridge on the outskirts of Beijing, sparking the eight-year-long Second Sino-Japanese War (1937-1945). The army quickly established control over most of coastal China and several major interior cities, but continued hostilities and Anglo-American aid to China drew Japan into the Axis alliance and eventually World War II.

Although the Japanese military entered the war divided—the general staffs of both services favored an early beginning to hostilities far more than the respective ministries—the armed forces nonetheless won a series of stunning early victories sweeping Dutch, British, and American forces from Southeast Asia.

Victory proved short-lived, however. On May 8, 1942, the U.S. navy blunted Japan's advance in the Coral Sea, and at Midway on June 4-5, 1942, U.S. carrier-based air attacks destroyed four frontline Japanese aircraft carriers. Both services, now on the defensive, suffered a string of disasters that culminated in crushing defeats in the Mariana Islands from June-August, 1944, and the U.S. reconquest of the Philippines, which began in October, 1944.

Despite the U.S. conquest of Iwo Jima from February 19-March 16, 1945, and Okinawa from April 1-June 22, 1945, both branches stood ready to meet the anticipated U.S. invasion of the home islands. Even with American use of atomic weapons against Hiroshima on August 6 and Nagasaki three days later, army and navy leaders deadlocked the cabinet until Emperor Hirohito compelled the government to accept the Potsdam Declaration.

After World War II

Demilitarization quickly became a hallmark of the U.S.-led occupation of Japan. The International Military Tribunal for the Far East took pains both to document and exorcize the spirit of militarism that many, among victors and vanquished alike, believed had plunged the Far East into ruin. Although Article 9 of Japan's 1947 constitution renounced war as a sovereign right and forbid the possession of any armed forces, the onset of the Korean War led U.S. occupation authorities to press Japan to establish some means for self-defense. Consequently, in July, 1950, Japan established a 75,000-man National Police Reserve. Four years later, Tokyo created the Self-Defense Force (SDF).

Japan's close security relationship with the United States continued following the end of the occupation. Both the 1951 and 1960 security treaties placed Japanese defense firmly in U.S. hands and consequently allowed Japan to limit defense spending to generally less than 1 percent of the annual gross national product. Nonetheless, continued preoccupation with North Korea, China, and the Soviet Union, along with prodding from the United States for Japan to share more equitably its defense burden, contributed to a significant Japanese military buildup from 1986 to 1990 that focused on improved air defense and control of vital sea lanes.

By the mid-1990's, total Self-Defense Force strength had grown to 235,000 men. The Ground Self-Defense Force, some 145,000 troops, are divided into five separate armies designed to counter a limited foreign assault against the home islands. The Maritime Self-Defense Force, with approximately 45,000 sailors and fifty-six major surface ships, including thirty-nine destroyers and seventeen frigates, is divided into four flotillas each designed to protect Japanese sea lanes. The mission of the Air Self-Defense Force, with just more than 45,000 officers and men and 330 frontline attack aircraft, provides primarily air defense, reconnaissance, and ground support. An all-volunteer force, the Self-Defense Force remains, as it has been since its creation, firmly under civilian control. Although the Self-Defense Force was barred from overseas deployment, in 1991, Tokyo dispatched four minesweepers to the Persian Gulf, and the following year, the government approved the International Peace Preservation Law, which opened the way for Japanese participation in United Nations peacekeeping efforts in Cambodia in 1993 and the Golan Heights in 1996.

Resources

Barnhart, Michael A. *Japan and the World Since 1868*. London: Edward Arnold, 1995.

Copley, Gregory R., ed. *Defense and Foreign Affairs Handbook*. Alexandria Va.: International Strategic Studies Association, 1999.

Dolan, Ronald E., and Robert L. Worden. *Japan: A Country Study*. Washington D.C.: United States Government Printing Office, 1992.

LaFeber, Walter. *The Clash: A History of U.S.-Japan Relations*. New York: W. W. Norton, 1997.

SEE ALSO: Coral Sea; Iwo Jima; Leyte Gulf; Midway; Mukden; Okinawa; Pearl Harbor attack; Port Arthur, Siege of; Russian Civil War of 1918-1921; Russo-Japanese War; Tsushima; World War II.

Sidney Pash

JAPANESE WARS OF UNIFICATION

AT ISSUE: Rule of Japan
DATE: 1550-1615
LOCATION: Japan
COMBATANTS: Various daimyo (feudal barons)
PRINCIPAL COMMANDERS: Oda Nobunaga (1534-1582), Toyotomi Hideyoshi (1537-1598), Ishida Mitsunari (1560-1600), Tokugawa Ieyasu (1543-1616)
PRINCIPAL BATTLE: Sekigahara
RESULT: Victorious Ieyasu became shogun of a unified Japan

BACKGROUND

The sixteenth century in Japan was a time of great upheaval and chaos. Continuous fighting raged across the land, creating a class of autonomous regional barons, each seeking to expand his territory by conquering neighboring domains. By the century's end, all had been unified under a single military ruler who imposed peace and instituted a stable political and social system. Unification was the cumulative accomplishment of three great chieftains, each building on the work of his predecessors. The process was begun by Oda Nobunaga, virtually completed by Toyotomi Hideyoshi, and finalized by Tokugawa Ieyasu, who became the first shogun of a unified Japan.

ACTION

The mid-sixteenth century anarchy provided ample opportunity for the strong and ambitious to amass land and gain regional hegemony at the expense of weaker neighbors. Nobunaga, a determined and daring daimyo, or warlord, who first tried to dominate all Japan, gained control of Owari province in 1559 and acquired the Kanto Plain in 1560. Nobunaga next marched westward to establish his power base in Kyoto (then Japan's capital), where he continued to strengthen his position by violently attacking and harshly punishing opposing daimyo.

Nobunaga was a zealous and courageous warrior who took advantage of every opportunity to better his position. He lacked exceptional military talent but was nevertheless extraordinarily successful because of the strict discipline and absolute obedience he demanded from his soldiers. Although he was totally ruthless and barbarously cruel, his energy and determination made him one of Japan's greatest military leaders.

In 1582, while leading his armies against the western provinces, Nobunaga was assassinated by one of his generals. His death was speedily avenged by Hideyoshi, who then assumed Nobunaga's role of unifier. Decisive victories during the next year made Hideyoshi master over most of Honshu (Japan's main island). He next attacked the southern island of Kyushu, where his rule was not recognized. Hideyoshi subjugated the recalcitrant daimyo, but allowed them to retain their lands if they swore obedience. In 1588, Hideyoshi invited the feudal lords to his lavish new residence, where they were required to pledge their loyalty. By 1590, with all Japan under his control, Hideyoshi gazed westward toward Korea. His greed for new lands led him to attack Korea in 1592 and again in 1597. The first invasion, repulsed by Chinese armies, led to an ignominious retreat. The equally unsuccessful second invasion was abandoned in 1598 only because Hideyoshi died.

Hideyoshi, a skilled tactician with a genius for strategy, was arguably the greatest military commander in Japan's long history. He rose from peasant to national overlord by sheer ability and drive. An able administrator who made decisions quickly, he never faltered in pursuing power but realized the importance of careful planning and patience. He was shrewd, passionate, frank, and informal, but his affections and jealousies led to cruel and horrifying excesses.

The power vacuum left by Hideyoshi was soon filled by two great leagues of daimyo who confronted each other for the prize of a unified Japan, which Hideyoshi had secured with great difficulty. Leading one faction was Ieyasu, who had faithfully served Nobunaga and later Hideyoshi (who presented Ieyasu the Kanto Plain as a reward for his loyalty). Ieyasu was the strongest daimyo, but the many enemies he had acquired during his rise to power left him somewhat vulnerable. His chief adversary was Ishida Mitsunari, who was supported by several other major daimyo. On October 20, 1600, the two great armies clashed at the Battle of **Sekigahara**, the most momentous of Japan's civil war battles. With the strategic assistance of several daimyo who changed sides to join the winning faction, Ieyasu routed his rivals and executed Mitsunari. The other opposing daimyo submitted to Ieyasu in the hope of keeping their domains. Ieyasu accepted their submissions but redistributed the fiefs in order to secure his power base. Relatives and consistently loyal daimyo were placed in strategic spots throughout Japan to enable Ieyasu to impose a tightly controlled military government subjugating the country. In 1603, Ieyasu appointed himself shogun and made Edo (later Tokyo) his power base. Although he ceded the title of shogun to his son in 1605, he retained power until his death. Only Nobunaga's young son remained as a possible threat, so in 1614, Ieyasu forced him to commit suicide.

Ieyasu's success was the result of his shrewdness, endurance, and considerable luck. He was a cunning military strategist who could be unscrupulous when it yielded an advantage. As Japan's first shogun, he ruled with firm practicality but without compassion. Although he was not an adept politician, lacked virtue, and was not particularly admired by his subjects, he was one of Japan's greatest leaders.

Aftermath

Under Ieyasu, Japan became a unified feudal state. The Japanese like to say that Nobunaga mixed the dough, and Hideyoshi baked the cake, but it was Ieyasu who ate it. These three men had very different personalities, but each was an ambitious self-made man who achieved dominance by hard work, willful determination, and ruthlessness.

Ieyasu imposed strict rules for conduct under the Tokugawa government. Among other things, licentious behavior was prohibited, building new castles was forbidden, marriages of daimyo had to be authorized, and subjects were expected to dress unostentatiously. Under the strict rule of the Tokugawa regime, Japan's internal wars ceased and the country became a peaceful and prosperous feudal state. To eliminate outside influences that might threaten their power, the Tokugawa closed Japan's borders; no Japanese were allowed to leave and no foreigners were allowed to enter. Under this shogunate, social harmony and economic security lasted for 250 years. These conditions led to a flowering of distinctive Japanese arts and crafts that would not have been possible had the country continued its destructive civil wars.

Resources

Cortazzi, Hugh. *The Japanese Achievement*. New York: St. Martin's Press, 1990.

Sadler, A. L. *The Life of Tokugawa Ieyasu*. Rutland, Vt.: Charles E. Tuttle, 1989.

Schirokauer, Conrad. *A Brief History of Japanese Civilization*. New York: Harcourt Brace Jovanovich, 1993.

See also: Oda Nobunaga; Osaka Castle, Siege of; Sekigahara; Tokugawa Ieyasu; Toyotomi Hideyoshi.

George R. Plitnik

Java War, Great

At issue: Dutch supremacy on Java
Date: 1825-1830
Location: Java, Dutch East Indies
Combatants: Dutch vs. Javanese
Principal commanders: *Dutch*, Lieutenant Governor General Hendrik Merkus, baron de Kock (1779-1845); *Javanese*, Prince Dipo Negara (1785-1855)
Principal battles: Tegal Redjo, Djokjakarta, Soerakarta, Kadilangoe, Magellan
Result: Dutch victory; restoration of Dutch colonial rule

Background

On May 6, 1823, the Dutch colonial government issued an ill-advised decree that made farming-out of nongovernment land illegal. This measure greatly disadvantaged the local nobility, whose earnings were almost exclusively derived from lease fees from European and Chinese planters. It also impoverished the local population, who relied on plantation labor for income. When Dutch indemnity payments proved to be inadequate, the local nobility in turn refused to compensate the planters for the loss of their investments. Tensions ran high when colonial officials intervened and used strong-arm tactics to force these payments.

The 1823 decree particularly soured relations between Prince Dipo Negara, the uncle and legal guardian of the two-year-old fifth sultan of Djokjakarta, and A. H. Smissaert, the Dutch resident of Djokjakarta. After Dipo Negara refused to pay compensation, Smissaert attempted to arrest Dipo but instead was publicly humiliated by the prince. In retaliation, Smissaert repeatedly insulted the local nobleman and ordered Assistant Resident of Djokjakarta F. P. H. de Chevalier to plan a government road straight through Dipo's Tegal Redjo estate. When on July 16, 1825, road workers broke down a house and desecrated two sacred graves at Tegal Redjo, Dipo Negara attacked the highest indigenous official in colonial service, the Rijksbestierder Radu Adipatti Danoe Redjo. On July 18, Dipo Negara refused Smissaert's orders to appear before him. Despite the urging of many to let the matter rest, Smissaert ordered that the prince be taken into custody.

Action

When Chevalier, accompanied by 125 soldiers, tried to arrest Dipo Negara at **Tegal Redjo** (July 20, 1825) he mistook local armed bystanders for Dipo's guards and opened fire. As a result, a mass insurrection ensued forcing the local noblemen (in many cases reluctantly) to choose Dipo Negara's side, thus spreading the revolt over the entire island. For the central colonial government, which was already fighting wars on West Sumatra, Borneo, and Celebes, the insurrection on Java was a surprising and unwelcome development. Therefore, Governor Baron Godert Alexander Gerard Philip van der Capellen hastily deployed Lieutenant Governor General Hendrik Merkus, baron de Kock, to Semarang to repress the rebellion. Kock tried initially to mediate, but Smissaert and Chevalier's actions had made this impossible. Furthermore, Dipo Negara, on advice of the Islamic cleric Kjai Modjo, was now demanding the departure of the Dutch and the implementation of Islamic law on Java. Therefore, Kock had no other choice than to forcefully repress the rebellion.

The rebels initially had the upper hand. Bands numbering well over 1,000 attacked **Djokjakarta** (August 11-24, 1825). With only 200 men at his disposal, Kock held the city by using the Krantons (fortified, walled residences) as defense lines. In answer to the rebels' tactics of hit, run, and hide, Kock erected a total of 161 bentengs, or redoubts, on strategic points on Java. These bentengs would house a total of 7,800 troops and had the task of keeping a region stable once it was pacified. A mobile army, consisting of eight independent columns of 1,000 men each would serve as rapid response forces once rebels were sighted. For manpower, Kock relied on a combination of Dutch officers and indigenous government-friendly troops.

However, Dipo Negara remained elusive. The government troops chased the prince all the way from Dikso to Kapoeren and into the Merapi Mountains. Yet, his followers could threaten the Dutch at any time. Besides numerous small engagements, the Siege of **Soerakarta** (October, 1826) by 4,000 well-armed rebels was only repelled after ten days of ferocious fighting. At **Kadilangoe** (October 3, 1828) a column was ambushed, causing 400 casualties.

However, Kock was able to eventually suppress the insurrection by subduing the local princes one at a time with a combination of force and favorable terms of surrender, thus eroding Dipo Negara's support and resources. Using these princes, Kock was able to force Dipo Negara into negotiations in **Magellan** (March 8-28, 1830). After respecting the prince's observance of Ramadan, Kock arrested Dipo Negara, thus ending the war.

Aftermath

Dipo Negara was banished to Fort Vlaardingen on Menado. Dutch rule on Java was restored.

Resources

Carey, Peter. *The Origins of the Java War (1825-30)*. London: Longmans, 1976.

Knight, G. R. *Narratives of Colonialism: Sugar, Java, and the Dutch.* Huntington, N. Y.: Nova Science, 2000.

Raffles, Stamford, Sir. *The History of Java: Complete Text.* Oxford, England: Oxford University Press, 1994.

Oscar E. Lansen

Javanese Wars of Succession

At issue: Control of Java
Date: 1704-1757
Location: Java, Batavia
Combatants: Dutch and various Mataram family members vs. other Mataram family members
Principal commanders: *Dutch and Mataram,* Pangeran Puger, Pakubuwana II; *Mataram,* Blitar, Purbaya, Chief Mangkubumi; *Mataram, then Dutch and Mataram,* Amung Kurat IV
Principal battles: Demak, Surakarta
Result: Dutch domination of nearly all Java

Background

The Dutch had increasing interest in the Indonesian islands from the seventeenth century onward, leading to struggles against and with the rulers of the central Javanese kingdom of Mataram. In 1620, Sultan Agung of the Mataram laid siege to the main Dutch stronghold at Batavia. Agung's forces eventually withdrew, but the conflict's result was inconclusive and left both sides wary. However, internal strife among the Mataram caused some members to seek Dutch aid. In return for aid in a succession dispute (1674), Amung Kurat I, Agung's successor, as well as Amung Kurat II, gave the Dutch East India Company the Preanger region of western Java. This pattern of giving land for Dutch aid in succession matters would lead to European domination of the region by the 1750's.

Action

The First War of Succession (1704-1705) began after tension grew between Amung Kurat II and his former Dutch allies when he failed to make good on some of his promises, including payment. Amung Kurat III, his successor, squabbled with his uncle, Pangeran Puger, who in turn looked to the Dutch for aid. The Dutch East India Company recognized Puger as Susuhunan Pakubuwana (1704-1719) and headed to meet the main resistance in the coastal area of **Demak**, taken in October and November (1704). The rest of the coastal areas fell in line. In August, 1705, a mixed force of Javanese and Madurse, with Dutch East India Company Europeans, Bugis, Makasarese, Balinese, Malays, Bandanese, Ambonese, and Mardijker (free Portuguese-speaking Indonesian soldiers) marched on Kartasura. Their opposition largely changed sides while they approached, causing Amung Kurat III to flee, and in September Pakubuwana I was installed as the new ruler. For their services, the Dutch received large land concessions, the right to build fortifications anywhere on Java, and permission for a Dutch East India Company garrison to return to man the court at the king's expense.

As financial difficulty and internal divisions wracked the Javanese throne, Pakubuwana I died and left his son Amung Kurat IV a country that hated him. The Second War of Succession (1719-1723) began in June, 1719, when Amung Kurat IV's brothers Blitar and Purbaya, along with their uncle Pangeran Arya Mataram, attempted to assault the king at his court and were repulsed by the Dutch East India Company garrison.

In November, the Dutch East India Company headed to Mataram and drove the rebel princes from their stronghold. The princes fled eastward where rebellion had arisen, and the Dutch East India Company headed east as well. Dutch East India Company forces accumulated victories as rebellion began to coalesce only to be destroyed by disease and battle. Pangeran Arya Mataram surrendered in October, 1719, and other families (Surabaya) followed suit. Blitar died in 1721, and Purbaya was kept in Batavia, the main rebellion being broken by 1723. The cost of the war added continued woe to the throne of Amung Kurat IV.

The Third War of Succession (1749-1757) largely began when Dutch governor general Gustaaf van Imhoff became unnecessarily involved in the dynastic feud of the remaining Mataram. He insisted that King Pakubuwana II not give the powerful chief Mangkubumi certain land destined for the Dutch East India Company, and the resulting indignation meant war. Mangkubumi joined another interested rebel, Mas Said, and both garnered a large following. By

1747, Mangkubumi commanded an estimated 13,000 men, including 2,500 cavalry. The Dutch East India Company forces were in poor shape at the time, able only to maintain their positions on the coast and not able to defeat the rebels inland. In 1748, Mangkubumi and Mas Said attacked the new capital **Surakarta**, nearly taking the court.

The rebels grew in strength as the contested crown passed to Susuhunan Pakubuwana III (1749-1788). Mas Said again attacked Surakarta, inflicting heavy losses on the Dutch East India Company. Prestigious members of the court were soon deserting the king. The fighting continued with little likelihood of either side attaining decisive victory. The Dutch East India Company ventured to broker an end to a war that was bankrupting the company and exhausting its resources. In 1754, Pakubuwana III and Mangkubumi agreed to meet, and hostilities were formally ended with the Treaty of Giyanti of February 13, 1755.

AFTERMATH

Mangkubumi was recognized as sultan and ruler of central Java, but it was essentially under Dutch domination.

RESOURCES

Coolhaas, W. P. *A Critical Survey of Studies on Dutch Colonial History*. The Hague: Nijhoff, 1980.

Ricklefs, M. C. *A History of Modern Indonesia Since c. 1300*. 1981. 2d ed. Stanford, Calif.: Stanford University Press, 1993.

Vlekke, Bernard H. M. *The Story of the Dutch East Indies*. Cambridge, Mass.: Harvard University Press, 1945.

SEE ALSO: Dutch Colonial Wars.

Jason Ridler

JAVELIN

A light spear, designed for throwing. Javelins made of wooden shafts tipped with stone, bone, and even fire-hardened wood were widely used by prehistoric humans for hunting and war. After millennia of use, the javelin reached its technological height in the Roman *pilum*. The *pilum*, which could also double as a thrusting weapon, was five feet long, one-third of that length owing to a point of soft iron. This made the weapon heavy and gave it shorter range, but it also imbued the weapon with greater impact. The long iron head served another purpose: Whether it stuck in human flesh or in an enemy shield, the pilum's long point bent under the weight of the shaft, making it difficult to extract and impossible to return. Javelins were abandoned as a weapon in the sixteenth century.

Jeremiah Taylor

JAYAVARMAN VII

BORN: c.1120; place unknown
DIED: c.1215; place unknown
PRINCIPAL WARS: Khmer-Cham Wars
MILITARY SIGNIFICANCE: Under Jayavarman VII, Kambuja reached its apogee of political power, territorial expansion, and cultural growth.

During the Ankgorian Period (802-1431), the Khmer Empire, by force of arms, extended its commonwealth to encompass vast areas of Southeast Asia. After a voluntary exile over a succession claim, Jayavarman returned to Kambuja in 1178 to help mitigate the damage done by the sack of Angkor by the Khmer Empire's primary adversaries, the Chams from central Vietnam. In 1181, Jayavarman became king and raised an army, as standing armies seldom existed, and subsequently defeated the Cham in a great naval battle. After this first victory, he celebrated his coronation at Angkor. Immediately afterward, however, he was called upon to put down an uprising in the dependent Malyang. Jayavarman's army subdued the rebels, and his commander, who was himself a Cham refugee from his own country, was selected to help him in the total conquest of Champa. In 1190, after exhaustive preparation, Jayavarman launched a great attack on Champa and was victorious. The son of Jayavarman VII, Prince In, was proclaimed king at Vijaya, and Champa became a vassal state of the Khmer Empire. Rebellions against the new regime were ubiquitous, but in 1203 the Khmer armies drove out the insurgents, and for seventeen years, 1203-1220, Champa was under Khmer domination. Although the death of Jayavarman VII is shrouded in mystery, he is thought to have died about 1215.

RESOURCES

Hall, D. G. E. *A History of South-East Asia.* London: Macmillan, 1981.

Harrison, Brian. *South-East Asia: A Short History.* London: Macmillan, 1966.

Ross, Russell R., ed. *Cambodia: A Country Study.* 3d ed. Washington, D.C.: Library of Congress, 1987.

SEE ALSO: Champa Kingdom; Khmer-Cham Wars.
Aaron Plamondon

JELLICOE, JOHN

FULL NAME: John Rushworth Jellicoe, First Earl
ALSO KNOWN AS: Admiral of the Fleet First Earl Jellicoe
BORN: December 5, 1859; Southampton, Hampshire, England
DIED: November 20, 1935; London, England
PRINCIPAL WAR: World War I
MILITARY SIGNIFICANCE: Jellicoe commanded the British fleet at the 1916 Battle of Jutland, a strategic victory for the British.

In the first part of his career, John Jellicoe was an impressive naval officer who was groomed in the early 1910's by Admiral Lord John Fisher for higher command. Jellicoe became commander of the Grand Fleet of the Royal Navy when World War I began. He commanded the British fleet at the Battle of Jutland in 1916. This battle, a strategic victory for the British that the Germans also declared a victory, maintained the hegemony of the British fleet. Although Jellicoe's leadership at Jutland later came into question, he was promoted to first sea lord of the Admiralty. Statesman Winston Churchill observed that as commander of the Grand Fleet, Jellicoe was the only person who could lose the war in an afternoon. He was dismissed in 1917 partly because of perceived failures in the campaign against German U-boats, which the Germans increasingly used after the Battle of Jutland. After the war, he toured India, Australia, New Zealand, and Canada, formulating policies for imperial defense.

RESOURCES

Bacon, R. H. S. *Life of John Rushworth, Earl Jellicoe.* London: Cassell, 1936.

Jellicoe, John. *The Crisis of Naval War.* London: Cassell, 1920.

_____. *The Grand Fleet, 1914-1916: Its Creation, Development, and Work.* London: Cassell, 1919.

Marder, Arthur J. *From Dreadnought to Scapa Flow: The Royal Navy in the Fisher Era, 1904-1919.* 5 vols. London: Oxford University Press, 1961-1978.

Patterson, A. Temple. *Jellicoe: A Biography.* London: Macmillan, 1969.

_____, ed. *The Jellicoe Papers: Selections from Private and Official Correspondence.* 2 vols. *Publications of the Navy Records Society.* London: Navy Records Society, 1966-1968.

Winton, John. *Jellicoe.* London: Joseph, 1981.

SEE ALSO: Fisher, John; Jutland; World War I.
Eugene L. Rasor

JEMAPPES

TYPE OF ACTION: Ground battle in the War of the First Coalition
DATE: November 6, 1792
LOCATION: Jemappes, Austrian Netherlands
COMBATANTS: 40,000 French vs. 14,000 Austrians
PRINCIPAL COMMANDERS: *French*, General Charles François Dumouriez (1739-1823); *Austrian*, Duke Albert of Saxe-Teschen (1738-1822)
RESULT: French defeat of Austrian forces

On November 6, 1792, General Charles François Dumouriez's Army of the North, advancing toward Mons, encountered the forces of Duke Albert of Saxe-Teschen. The latter could concentrate only some 14,000 troops and deployed them in positions along a ridge running through the village of Jemappes. The French opened with an artillery barrage of some three hours and then, about noon, attacked in tight columns that deployed into line formation at close range. Although repulsed several times, the French troops were rallied by Dumouriez. By two o'clock, the Austrian lines collapsed, and the troops fled from Jemappes. Each side suffered between 4,500 and

7,000 casualties. French numbers and revolutionary ardor had carried the day.

Significance

Jemappes was of great strategic importance. It was the first real field victory by the French revolutionary armies and, coupled with Valmy (September 20, 1792), saved the revolution. Within a week, Brussels had fallen to the French and, within a month all the Austrian Netherlands. However, the euphoria of victory caused French volunteers, who had signed on for one campaign, to go home in droves, and the home front was likewise lulled. This disintegration set the stage for the disastrous French defeats in 1793.

Resources

Blanning, T. C. W. *The French Revolutionary Wars, 1787-1802*. London: Arnold, 1996.

Lynn, John A. *Bayonets of the Republic: Motivation and Tactics in the Army of Revolutionary France, 1791-1794*. Urbana: University of Illinois Press, 1984.

Scott, Samuel F. *From Yorktown to Valmy: The Transformation of the French Army in an Age of Revolution*. Niwot: University Press of Colorado, 1998.

See also: French Revolution; French Revolutionary Wars; Valmy.

James K. Kieswetter

Jena and Auerstädt

Type of action: Simultaneous ground battles in the Napoleonic Wars
Date: October 13-14, 1806
Location: Saale River valley, Thuringia, Germany
Combatants: 148,500 French vs. 111,500 Prussians and Saxons
Principal commanders: *French*, Emperor Napoleon I (1769-1821), Marshal Louis Davout (1770-1823); *Prussian*, King Frederick William III (1770-1840), Field Marshal Charles William

Napoleon (center), accompanied by Louis Alexandre Bertheir (behind Napoleon) and Joachim Murat (behind Bertheir) looks at a group of French soldiers at the Battle of Jena. (Library of Congress)

Ferdinand, duke of Brunswick (1735-1806); *Prussian and Saxon*, General Friedrich Ludwig Hohenlohe (1746-1818)

Result: Complete French victory opened the way to Berlin

Napoleon Bonaparte created the Confederation of the Rhine (July 12, 1806) to bring the plethora of German states under French control. Emperor Francis II disbanded the Holy Roman Empire (August 6). Prussia, under King Frederick William III, resisted Napoleon, but mostly without allies, except for a few Saxon states and, nominally, Russia.

By the evening of October 13, General Francis Joseph Lefebvre's 15,000 infantry of the Imperial Guard had occupied Jena, and Napoleon had personally inspected the town. General Jean-Baptiste-Jules Bernadotte's First Corps with 20,000 men was just south of Naumburg. Marshal Louis Davout's Third Corps with 26,000 men was at Kösen, between Naumburg and Auerstädt. The 18,000 men of Marshal Nicolas Jean de Dieu Soult's Fourth Corps were about evenly divided between Jena and Eisenberg. Marshal Jean Lannes's Fifth Corps held firm with 20,500 men a mile north of Jena. Marshal Michel Ney, southeast of Jena, sent 4,500 of his Sixth Corps to Jena and the remaining 15,000 to Roda. Marshal Pierre François Charles Augereau, southeast of Jena with 16,500 men, separated his Seventh Corps into thirds, directing groups northwest toward Jena, east-southeast toward the Saale, and west toward Magdala. Marshal Joachim Murat split his cavalry reserves, sending 6,000 east of Bernadotte and 7,000 southeast of Ney.

The 63,500 men under Charles William Ferdinand, duke of Brunswick, marched east toward Auerstädt. Friedrich Ludwig Hohenlohe commanded 35,000 men northwest of Jena, just beyond Lannes, and was beginning to deploy toward the southwest and northeast. General Ernst Friedrich Wilhelm Philipp von Rüchel had 13,000 infantry in reserve at Weimar. The Prussian army was well drilled but tactically conservative.

The duke of Brunswick and Davout engaged frontally mid-morning of October 14 about halfway between Auerstädt and Kösen. Brunswick squandered his chances by failing to take advantage of superior numbers. Davout wore the Prussians down with artillery, then seized an opportunity to sweep one division around on his left to crush Brunswick's right flank. Brunswick was mortally wounded. Soon the French were able to create the classic pincer attack. The Prussians broke and ran, back through Auerstädt and southwest.

Meanwhile, Bernadotte and the part of Murat's cavalry attached to him rushed southwest to check Hohenlohe's left flank. Lannes held the center while Soult attacked Hohenlohe's left and Augereau his right. Murat's cavalry made random assaults. Napoleon took full advantage of the skill of his generals to deploy his troops in multifaceted, flexible formations that confused and eventually ensnared the Germans. Hohenlohe could not effectively counter the swift maneuvers of the French. Soult and Lannes routed their enemy by mid-afternoon. Augereau mastered first Hohenlohe's Saxons, then Rüchel's reinforcements.

French casualties were about 6,000 at Jena and 7,100 at Auerstädt. German casualties were about 12,000 killed or wounded and 15,000 taken prisoner at Jena, 10,000 killed or wounded and 3,000 taken prisoner at Auerstädt, plus about 20,000 more taken prisoner within the next few days as the French pursued. The French captured 112 guns at Jena and 115 at Auerstädt.

Significance

The German philosopher G. W. F. Hegel, living in Jena at the time of the battle, wrote that by seeing Napoleon he had seen the world-soul on a horse. Conquering Prussia was indeed the high tide of Napoleon's empire. The embarrassing defeat forced Prussia to reinvent its army. Within fifty years, it became a stunning military power.

Resources

Chandler, David G. *Jena 1806: Napoleon Destroys Prussia*. London: Osprey Military, 1993.

Hourtoulle, F. G. *Jena-Auerstaedt: The Triumph of the Eagle*. Paris: Histoire & Collections, 1998.

Maude, F. N. *The Jena Campaign 1806*. London: Greenhill, 1998.

Napoleon I. *The Jena Campaign*. Reno, Nev.: Physical Studies, 1967.

Petre, F. Loraine. *Napoleon's Conquest of Prussia. 1806.* London: Greenhill, 1993.

SEE ALSO: Blücher, Gebhard Leberecht von; Brunswick, Charles William Ferdinand, duke of; Davout, Louis; Lannes, Jean; Murat, Joachim; Napoleon I; Napoleonic Wars; Ney, Michel; Soult, Nicolas Jean de Dieu.

Eric v. d. Luft

JERICHO

TYPE OF ACTION: City siege in biblical account of Israelite conquest of Canaan
DATE: c. 1400 B.C.E.
LOCATION: Southern Jordan River Valley of Palestine
COMBATANTS: Israelites vs. Canaanites
PRINCIPAL COMMANDERS: *Israelite*, Joshua
RESULT: Destruction of Jericho; inhabitants massacred

The siege and destruction of Jericho by the Israelites under Joshua is known only from the biblical account (Joshua 6). After espionage, Israel besieged Jericho by the unusual method of marching around the city once for six consecutive days. On the seventh day, the army marched around Jericho seven times and, at the sound of trumpets, shouted—following which, the city walls collapsed. Various interpreters explain these actions as purely ceremonial in conjunction with a miraculous earthquake, a ruse to relax defenses through repetition, followed by a sudden attack, or a trick whereby the unusual activity of day seven brought all the besieged inhabitants to an assumed casemate wall, which then collapsed under their excessive weight. Most biblical scholars, however, regard the story as etiological.

Excavation results at the site of Jericho, Tell es-Sultan, hamper attempts to reconstruct Joshua's conquest. In the 1930's, excavator John Garstang concluded that the city suffered destruction about 1400 B.C.E., consistent with a then-popular chronology for the Exodus and Joshua's campaigns. He further related a fallen mudbrick wall to the work of Joshua. Re-excavation of Jericho by Kathleen Kenyon in the 1950's conclusively reassigned Garstang's wall to an earlier period and redated the final destruction of Canaanite Jericho to about 1550 B.C.E., implying there was no city at Jericho for Joshua to have destroyed a century and a half later.

A careful reevaluation of Kenyon's work by Bryant Wood attempts to reestablish a 1400 B.C.E. date for the destruction of Canaanite Jericho. Scholarly consensus, however, has moved the horizon for Israel's emergence—and thus the period of Joshua—to about 1200 B.C.E., making any connection between Joshua and known remains at Jericho hardly possible.

SIGNIFICANCE
If an actual event, Jericho's fall marks the spearhead of Joshua's invasion and conquest of Canaan. If etiological, the story provides the basis for "holy war" in ancient Israel.

RESOURCES
Garstang, John, and J. B. E. Garstang. *The Story of Jericho.* London: Hodder & Stoughton, 1940.
Kenyon, Kathleen M. *Digging Up Jericho.* London: Benn, 1957.
Wood, Bryant G. "Did the Israelites Conquer Jericho?" *Biblical Archaeology Review* 16/2 (March/April, 1990): 44-59.

SEE ALSO: Ancient warfare; David; Religion and war.

Daniel C. Browning, Jr.

JERUSALEM, SIEGE OF

TYPE OF ACTION: Siege in the First Crusade
DATE: July 15, 1099
LOCATION: Near the summit of the Judaean Hills (in modern-day Israel), close to the junction of two valleys, the Hinnom and the Kidron
COMBATANTS: Crusaders vs. Fatimid Egyptians
PRINCIPAL COMMANDERS: *Crusader*, Godfrey of Bouillon (1061?-1100), Raymond of Toulouse (d. 1105); *Fatimid*, Iftikhar ad-Dawla
RESULT: Crusaders seized the city and established the kingdom of Jerusalem, which Europeans ruled from 1099 to 1187 and from 1229 to 1243

The fortified city of Jerusalem, the site of Christ's death and resurrection and the holiest city in

The Crusaders retreat from the city of Jerusalem, which they would subsequently enter using siege towers. (Library of Congress)

heat and thirst, were thrown back. They proceeded to construct two huge siege towers and in several weeks were ready to make another assault. Godfrey of Bouillon led the successful breakthrough. He was riding one of the towers when it was pushed to the weakest part of the city walls. The crusaders ran beams from the tower to the ramparts to make a bridge and charged across. Once inside the city walls, the Franks massacred Muslims and Jews (who were thought to have helped the Fatimids).

With their goal achieved, the crusaders chose a ruler for the city. After much discussion, Godfrey of Bouillon agreed to rule but refused to be crowned king of Jerusalem. Instead, he chose the title Defender of the Holy Sepulchre in honor of Christ's burial place. Godfrey did not rule long, however. He died of a fever a year later. His successors, beginning with Baldwin, did rule as kings. They set up a feudal organization known as the Latin Kingdom of Jerusalem. It consisted of four parts: the county of Edessa, the principality of Antioch, the county of Tripoli, and the royal territories.

Christendom, had been under Muslim control since the 600's. Its liberation was one of the main goals of the First Crusade. The Frankish crusaders, Godfrey of Bouillon and Raymond of Toulouse, advanced on Jerusalem in the spring of 1099 following their successful conquest of the city of Antioch and the founding of a principality there under the rule of Bohemund. On the 400-mile march south, the crusaders kept to the Mediterranean coast where they could count on English and Genoese ships and supplies. The Franks were able to advance through Muslim territory without serious opposition and arrived at the walls of Jerusalem on June 7, ready to launch an all-out attack against its Fatimid Egyptian defenders led by Iftikhar ad-Dawla, the governor of the city. The crusaders assaulted the walls but, lacking scaling ladders and suffering from the

SIGNIFICANCE

The conquest of the Holy City of Jerusalem by the leaders of the First Crusade saw the establishment of the Latin Kingdom of Jerusalem within the Muslim-controlled Middle East. At the peak of its power, the kingdom included parts of northern Mesopotamia, the entire Syrian-Palestine coast, Palestine, and parts of Jordan extending south to the gulf of Aqaba.

RESOURCES

Armstrong, Karen. *Jerusalem: One City, Three Faiths*. New York: Alfred A. Knopf, 1996.
Baldwin, Marshall W., ed. *The First Hundred Years*. Vol. 1 in *A History of the Crusades*, edited by Kenneth M. Setton. Madison: University of Wisconsin Press, 1969.

The Crusades. Documentary. A&E Home Video, 1995.

Gates of Jerusalem: History of the Holy City. Documentary. Questar, 1996.

Riley-Smith, Jonathan, ed. *The Oxford Illustrated History of the Crusades.* New York: Oxford University Press, 1997.

Runciman, Steven. *A History of the Crusades.* Vol. 1. Cambridge, England: Cambridge University Press, 1953.

SEE ALSO: Alexius I Comnenus; Antioch; Crusades.

Adriane Ruggiero

JEWISH REVOLTS

AT ISSUE: Jewish rebellion against Roman rule
DATE: 66-135 C.E.
LOCATION: Roman province of Judea in the land of Palestine, especially the city of Jerusalem
COMBATANTS: Romans vs. Jews
PRINCIPAL COMMANDERS: *Jewish*, Simon bar Giora (d. 70 C.E.), Flavius Josephus (37-100 C.E.), Bar Kokhba (d. 135 C.E.); *Roman*, Vespasian (9-79 C.E.), Titus (39-81 C.E.), Julius Severus (d. after 135 C.E.), Hadrian (76-138 C.E.)
PRINCIPAL BATTLES: Beth Horon Pass, Jerusalem, Siege of Masada, Bethar
RESULT: Roman victory; destruction of Jerusalem and the Jewish temple; banishment of the Jews from their holy city and dispersion throughout the empire (the Diaspora)

BACKGROUND

The First and Second Jewish Revolts (66-74 C.E. and 132-135 C.E.) resulted from long-standing Jewish antagonisms toward Roman overlordship. In 63 B.C.E., the Roman general Pompey the Great invaded Palestine and put an end to an autonomous Jewish commonwealth that been ruled by the Hasmonean Dynasty for almost one hundred years. The Jewish people living in Roman Palestine became vassals of the Roman Republic (later the Roman Empire).

During the decades following this humiliation, an Idumean ruler named Herod the Great (r. 37- 4 B.C.E.) gradually acquired power and gained the favor of Roman leaders, who ultimately bestowed on him the titles of king and governor. At the same time, leadership of the Jerusalem priesthood became more or less hereditary within a powerful family tied to the conservative religious party, the Sadducees, who supported the political status quo or even inclined toward collaboration with the Romans. Roman rule was viewed by the populace as harsh, especially after Herod's sons and grandsons succeeded him.

Economic burdens from excessive taxation, acts of brutality, and a series of corrupt Roman governors who replaced Herod's successors aggravated an explosive situation. Revolutionary groups such as the Zealots emerged calling for armed revolt, believing that God supported them.

ACTION

In the summer of 66 C.E., after the Roman governor Gessius Florus confiscated money from the temple treasury in Jerusalem, the Jews of Judea combined to expel the Romans from the city. In autumn of that year, the Romans sent a punitive force under the command of Cestius Gallus, the imperial legate in Syria, to subdue the Jews. Jewish rebel troops led by Simon bar Giora overwhelmed the Romans at the **Beth Horon Pass** north of Jerusalem, resulting in a disaster for the Romans. The Jews established a provisional revolutionary government that ended up promoting civil war in Jerusalem. During this time a revolutionary group called the *Sicarii* ("dagger men" or assassins) fled to Herod's old mountain stronghold named Masada.

In 67 C.E., the Emperor Nero sent Rome's best general, Vespasian, to crush the rebellion. He enjoyed great success but was replaced by his son Titus in 68 C.E. so he could return to Rome to become emperor. The Roman armies first conquered the northern district of Galilee, where the Jewish general, but soon to be historian, Flavius Josephus, was in command. After the fall of the fortress Jotapata, Josephus surrendered and offered his services as chronicler to the Romans. In the summer of 69 C.E, Titus laid siege to **Jerusalem** with four battle-hardened legions possessing names like Fretensis ("the boiling one") and Fulminata ("the thundering one"). The Siege of Jerusalem was protracted and resulted in great horrors, as described by Josephus in his work *Bellum Judaicum* (75-79 C.E.; *The Jewish War*, 1847). On the ninth day of the Jewish month of Av, Jerusalem finally fell, the temple was destroyed, and blood flowed in the streets of the upper city. Archaeologists have uncovered grim evidence of the disaster.

From 71 C.E. onward, the Roman Tenth Legion was garrisoned in Jerusalem, and surviving Jews lived in conditions of poverty and hardship. In 73 C.E., at the rock fortress of **Masada** south of Jerusalem, Roman troops finally stormed the defense walls of the *Sicarii* holdouts, only to find that some 960 people had committed suicide rather than be taken captive by the Romans.

In 132 C.E., Jewish rebels again fought against Roman dominion when the emperor Hadrian attempted to assimilate the Jews through a policy of Hellenization that included establishing Jerusalem as the Roman colony of Aelia Capitolina. Led by Bar Kokhba, the Second Jewish Revolt (also called the Bar Kokhba Revolt) was supported by one of the leading rabbis of the time, Akiba ben Joseph, who gave to Simeon bar Kosiba the title Bar Kokhba ("son of the star"), a messianic reference. The suddenness of the revolt and swift attack on Jerusalem forced the Romans to evacuate the city. Bar Kokhba attempted to extend the rebellion to the Galilee region where some battles were fought, but many Galilean Jews did not join the rebel effort. However, the war became so serious in Judea that the emperor Hadrian came from Rome to Palestine and called in the general Julius Severus to lead Roman forces. Severus advanced slowly and deliberately, conquering position after position in order to avoid the fate of the Twenty-second Legion, which had advanced rashly and been virtually wiped out. Ultimately, Bar Kokhba and his rebels were forced to abandon Jerusalem and were driven to the fortress of **Bethar**, where they were surrounded and killed.

Aftermath

The Jewish Revolts were an unmitigated disaster for the Jewish people. According to Josephus, the First Jewish Revolt claimed the lives of 1.1 million Jews. For the Second Revolt, the Roman historian Dio Cassius reported that fifty fortresses were captured, 985 villages destroyed, and 580,000 Jews killed, although the Roman army also suffered irreparable damage. After 135 C.E., the Jews were forbidden to enter Jerusalem upon penalty of death, and the great dispersion of the Jewish people, the Diaspora, begun in 70 C.E., was confirmed and extended.

Resources

Cornfeld, Gaalya, ed. *Josephus: The Jewish War*. Grand Rapids, Mich.: Zondervan, 1982.

Hadas-Lebel, Mereille. *Flavius Josephus: Eyewitness to Rome's First-Century Conquest of Judea*. New York: Maxwell Macmillan, 1993.

Jagersma, Henk. *A History of Israel from Alexander the Great to Bar Kokhba*. Philadelphia, Pa.: Fortress Press, 1986.

Price, Jonathan T. *Jerusalem Under Siege: The Collapse of the Jewish State, 66-70 C.E.* New York: Brill, 1992.

Rhoads, David M. *Israel in Revolution 6-74 C.E.* Philadelphia, Pa.: Fortress Press, 1976.

Smallwood, E. Mary. *The Jews Under Roman Rule: From Pompey to Diocletian*. Leiden, the Netherlands: E. J. Brill, 1981.

Yadin, Yigael. *Bar-Kokhba: The Rediscovery of the Legendary Hero of the Last Jewish Revolt Against Imperial Rome*. New York: Random House, 1971.

See also: Hadrian; Josephus, Flavius; Vespasian.

Andrew C. Skinner

Jihad

An Arabic word often translated as "holy war," but which literally means "striving." While many Muslims have interpreted jihad in a spiritual sense—that it entails a figurative moral "warfare"—numerous early authorities discussed it as a literal war against infidels or apostates. Most manuals of Islamic law regulate jihad in minute terms. For example, participants in a jihad must not wantonly kill women and children or torture enemies. Matters such as the opening, interruption, and cessation of hostilities are also thoroughly covered by Islamic law.

The historical jihad began in the lifetime of Muhammad (c. 570-632 C.E.) with campaigns against the pagans of Arabia. It spread, during the wars of conquest, into the rest of the Middle East, much of south and central Asia, North Africa, and sections of southeastern and southwestern Europe. European reaction to jihad ultimately led to the Crusades (1095-1272), a series of European Christian "holy wars" against the Muslims.

Jeremiah Taylor

Joan of Arc

Also known as: Joan the Maid, Jehanne or Jeanne la Pucelle, Jeanne d'Arc
Born: c. 1412; Domrémy, France
Died: May 30, 1431; Rouen, France
Principal war: Hundred Years' War
Principal battle: Orléans (1429)
Military significance: Joan of Arc led troops that forced British forces to abandon their seven-month siege of the city of Orléans. This was the turning point in the Hundred Years' War and ultimately led to the driving of English forces out of France.

A defining event of the Hundred Years' War was the defeat of French forces by the British, led by English King Henry V, at Agincourt on August 25, 1415. The French, demoralized by military losses and decimated by epidemics of plague that lasted from 1348 until Joan's girlhood, were also divided by factional disputes. These led to the Treaty of Troyes in 1420, which named Henry V as heir to the throne of France and disinherited the dauphin (crown prince), the future Charles VII.

In 1428, British troops, aided by Burgundian allies, besieged the city of Orléans, a city critical to control of the south of France. At this crisis, Joan of Arc, daughter of a prosperous farmer father and devoutly religious mother, left the village of Domrémy, claiming voices from God had ordered her to lift the siege. Although illiterate, she convinced first an uncle and then a regional authority, Robert de Baudricourt, to allow her to go to the dauphin at Chinon, where she was received by Charles on March 6, 1429. Wearing short-cropped hair and men's apparel in defiance of the social codes and religious edicts of her time, she led the troops Charles assigned to her, fighting despite a serious injury. The English fled Orléans on May 8, 1429. She went on to victories at Jargeau, Meung, Patay, Auxerre, and Troyes; a demoralized British force vacated the Beaugency area without a battle. She then convinced the dauphin to legitimatize his reign and escorted him to Rheims, where he was crowned Charles VII on July 17, 1429.

She next wanted to capture Paris, but Charles, without her knowledge, chose negotiation and, on August 28, 1429, signed a truce with Philip III the Good of Burgundy. Charles was deceived; the truce gave the Burgundians time to fortify Paris. Joan fought, failed, and again was wounded. Despite Joan's protests, Charles ordered her to desist on September 9 and disbanded her army on September 21. Joan was sent to battle a mercenary captain, Perrinet Gressart, at Saint-Pierre-le-Moutier. She won and moved on to help the people of Compiègne resist recapture by the Burgundians.

There, on May 23, 1430, Joan was captured by Burgundian forces. Charles made no attempt to rescue or ransom her. The Burgundians sold her to the British, who had her convicted as heretic and idolator by an ecclesiastical court after a long imprisonment. She was turned over to secular British forces and was burned at the stake in the marketplace of Rouen. In 1456, after the French had retaken Normandy (1450) and the last battle

Joan of Arc. (Library of Congress)

of the Hundred Years' War was fought at Castillon (1453), Charles, in part to secure his hold on the throne, caused her to be retried. This rehabilitation or nullification trial, held at Rouen, overturned the results of the 1431 trial. In 1920, Joan was canonized a saint of the Roman Catholic Church. By then, she had long since become a symbol of moral and physical courage.

RESOURCES

Devries, Kelly. *Joan of Arc, A Military Leader*. Phoenix Mill, England: Sutton, 1999.

Joan of Arc: Virgin Warrior. Documentary. A&E Entertainment, 1998.

Margolis, Nadia. *Joan of Arc in History, Literature, and Film: A Select, Annotated Bibliography*. New York: Garland, 1990.

Pernoud, Régine, and Marie-Véronique Clin. *Joan of Arc, Her Story*. Translated and revised by Jeremy duQuesnay Adams. New York: St. Martin's Press, 1998.

Warner, Marina. *Joan of Arc: The Image of Female Heroism*. Berkeley: University of California Press, 1981.

SEE ALSO: Agincourt; Archery; Armor; Franks and Burgundians; Henry V; Hundred Years' War; Knights and chivalry; Medieval warfare; Mercenaries; Orléans, Siege of; Sieges and siege weapons.

Betty Richardson

JODL, ALFRED

BORN: May 10, 1890; Wurzburg, Germany
DIED: October 16, 1946; Nuremberg, Germany
PRINCIPAL WARS: World War I, World War II
PRINCIPAL BATTLES: Polish Campaign (1939), France (1940), Soviet Union (1941)
MILITARY SIGNIFICANCE: A loyal Nazi and follower of Adolf Hitler, Jodl served as German chief of the Armed Forces Operational Staff from 1939 until 1945. He was one of the few professional German officers who thought that Hitler understood history and had genius as a military leader.

Alfred Jodl joined the Fourth Bavarian Field Artillery Regiment in 1910 and served in active duty

Alfred Jodl. (Archive Photos/Hulton Getty Collection)

throughout World War I. After the war, he continued to serve in the German army (*Reichswehr*) from 1921 to 1935. In 1929, he was assigned to the General Staff. Along with Generals Wilhelm Keitel and Walter Warlimont, Jodl opposed the Prussian old guard that dominated the German General Staff. As Adolf Hitler rose to power in 1933, Jodl embraced the philosophy of Nazism and recognized Hitler as a gifted leader. By 1935, he was head of the National Defense Office and, within three years, rose to the rank of major general. Throughout World War II, Jodl served as Hitler's closest adviser and most staunch military supporter. A supporter of Hitler's concept of total war, Jodl directed overall German military operations on both the western and eastern fronts throughout the war in Europe. He surrendered the German armies in the west on May 7, 1945, at Reims. He was convicted for war crimes at Nuremberg and executed by hanging on October 16, 1946.

RESOURCES

Barnett, Correlli, ed. *Hitler's Generals*. New York: Grove Weidenfeld, 1989.

Downing, David. *The Devil's Virtuosos: German*

Generals at War, 1940-1945. New York: Dorset, 1993.

Kershaw, Ian. *Hitler.* New York: Longman, 1991.

_____. *Hitler, 1889-1936: Hubris.* London: Allen Lane, 1998.

Lukacs, John. *The Hitler of History.* New York: Alfred A. Knopf, 1997.

The Wannsee Conference. Fiction feature. Infafilm GMBH Munich, Manfred Korytowski, Austrian Television, and the Bavarian Broadcasting Corporation, 1984.

SEE ALSO: Hitler, Adolf; War crimes; World War I; World War II.

William T. Walker

JOFFRE, JOSEPH-JACQUES-CÉSAIRE

BORN: January 12, 1852; Rivesaltes, France
DIED: January 3, 1931; Paris, France
PRINCIPAL WAR: World War I
PRINCIPAL BATTLES: Marne (1914), Verdun (1916), Somme (1916)
MILITARY SIGNIFICANCE: Joffre served as the commander of all French forces from December, 1915, until December, 1916.

Joseph-Jacques-Césaire Joffre was a civil engineer who served in the French army from 1870 until 1920. He was actively involved in construction projects in France's African colonies and won impressive victories in various colonial wars in Africa. Just before the outbreak of World War I in 1914, Joffre became a major general. He led French forces in repulsing the German advance during the Battle of the Marne in September, 1914, and forced German soldiers to retreat. Historians generally agree that General Joffre's decisive victory in this battle prevented the Germans from reaching an early victory in World War I.

In December, 1915, Joffre became the commander of all French forces. General Joffre hoped to launch attacks both from the western and eastern fronts against Germany, but 1916 did not go well for the French and British forces. There were massive losses during the Battles of Verdun and the Somme. Joffre was promoted to marshal in December, 1916, but he no longer played a central role in commanding allied forces against the Germans. He died in Paris in 1931 and his *Memoires du marechal Joffre* (1932; *The Personal Memoirs of Joffre, Field Marshal of the French Army*, 1932) were published posthumously in 1932.

RESOURCES

Barnett, Correlli. *The Swordbearers: Supreme Command in the First World War.* New York: William Morrow, 1964.

Fyfe, Albert J. *Understanding the First World War.* New York: Peter Lang, 1988.

Kirchberger, Joe H. *The First World War.* New York: Facts on File, 1992.

SEE ALSO: Foch, Ferdinand; Marne; Somme; Verdun; World War I.

Edmund J. Campion

JOHN I ZIMISCES

ALSO KNOWN AS: John Tzimisces
BORN: 925; Chozana, Armenia
DIED: January 10, 976; Constantinople
PRINCIPAL WARS: Bulgarian-Byzantine Wars, Conquest of Lebanon-Galilee
PRINCIPAL BATTLES: Preslav (971), Dristra (971), Baalbek (975), Tripoli (975)
MILITARY SIGNIFICANCE: Emperor John I evicted the Russians from Bulgaria, drove the Egyptian Fatimids out of Syria, and revived Byzantine military power in Europe and Asia.

A nobleman and experienced soldier, John I Zimisces assassinated the reigning emperor, Nicephorus II Phocas, to seize the Byzantine throne. The Byzantines accepted his regicide because serious military dangers imperiled them. In Europe, Russian prince Svjatoslav had conquered Bulgaria and boldly threatened to march on Constantinople. In the Middle East, the Fatimids had surrounded Antioch in 971 and seemed poised to conquer Byzantine Syria.

In April, 971, John launched into southern Bulgaria with 40,000 troops. Simultaneously, he sealed the Danube delta with troops and three hundred ships to prevent the Russians escaping northward. The Byzantines routed Svjatoslav's forces, stormed the Bulgarian capital at Preslav, and chased the humiliated prince to Dristra. At

Dristra, John encircled and decimated the Russian defenders, forcing Svjatoslav to surrender. Vindicated, the emperor allowed the prince and his survivors to straggle home.

With Bulgaria annexed, John turned south. After reinforcing Antioch in 974, he began full campaigning in 975. Apamea, Baalbak, and Beirut fell quickly, and Damascus opened its gates to avoid siege. Acre, Tiberius, Sidon, Caesarea, and Nazareth all became tributaries, but the Fatimid port of Tripoli denied John full control of the Lebanese coast. John died of typhus in 976 without achieving his professed dream of taking Jerusalem.

RESOURCES

Ostrogorsky, George. *History of the Byzantine State*. New Brunswick, N.J.: Rutgers University Press, 1969.

Treadgold, Warren. *A History of the Byzantine State and Society*. Stanford, Calif.: Stanford University Press, 1997.

Wittow, Mark. *The Making of Byzantium, 600-1025*. Los Angeles: University of California Press, 1996.

SEE ALSO: Bulgarian-Byzantine Wars; Byzantine Empire; Byzantine-Muslim Wars; Nicephorus II Phocas.

Weston F. Cook, Jr.

JOHN II COMNENUS

BORN: September 13, 1087; possibly Constantinople
DIED: April 8, 1143; place unknown
PRINCIPAL WARS: Serb Revolt, Danishmendid War, Cilician War, Anatolia-Black Sea coast campaigns
PRINCIPAL BATTLES: Laodicea (1119), Beroea (1122), Haram (1128), Anazarbus (1137), Antioch (1137), Aleppo (1138), Trebizond (1141)
MILITARY SIGNIFICANCE: Ruler of Byzantium from 1118 to 1143, John II reversed the empire's military decline, recovering several important territories.

John II Comnenus inaugurated his reign by attacking the Turks in the Meander River region of southeast Anatolia, capturing Laodicea in 1119. In 1121, the nomadic Pecheneg (Patzinak) tribes of the Danube renewed their plundering incursions into the Balkans, throwing European Byzantium into turmoil. Emboldened by these incursions, several Serbian chieftains, backed by the king of Hungary, revolted against Constantinople. The emperor retaliated swiftly. In 1122, near Beroea, he smashed the Pechenegs so totally they never endangered Byzantium again. After several more years, John crushed the Serb Revolt and, at the Battle of Haram (1128), drove the Hungarians back across the Danube.

Europe pacified, John returned to Anatolia, battering the Danishmendid sultan of central Anatolia from 1130 to 1136. In 1137, he then turned south into Cilicia and besieged Anazarbus, the capital of Little Armenia. Anazarbus secured, the emperor forced the Crusader states at Antioch and Odessa to acknowledge his lordship. Cowed, Raymond of Antioch paid homage to Constantinople and joined John against the sultan of Aleppo. However, the Aleppo (1138) campaign failed. Toward the end his life, John conquered the coastline of northern Anatolia, subduing the city of Trebizond and restoring Byzantine authority eastward to the Caucasus Mountains.

RESOURCES

Norwich, John Julius. *Byzanium: The Decline and Fall*. New York: Alfred A. Knopf, 1996.

Ostrogorsky, George. *History of the Byzantine State*. New Brunswick, N.J.: Rutgers University Press, 1969.

Treadgold, Warren T. *A History of the Byzantine State and Society*. Stanford, Calif.: Stanford University Press, 1997.

SEE ALSO: Alexius I Comnenus; Bogomils' Revolt and Pecheneg-Byzantine War; Byzantine Empire; Byzantine-Seljuk Wars; Crusades.

Weston F. Cook, Jr.

JOHN III SOBIESKI

ALSO KNOWN AS: Jan Sobieski
BORN: August 17, 1629; Olesko, Poland
DIED: June 17, 1696; Castle Wilanów, near Warsaw, Poland
PRINCIPAL WARS: Khmelnytsky's Cossack Revolt,

Polish-Swedish Wars, Russo-Polish Wars of 1499-1667, Turkish Wars of European Expansion

PRINCIPAL BATTLES: Chocim (1673), Zorawano (1676), Vienna (1683)

MILITARY SIGNIFICANCE: John III was the allied commander at the relief of the Siege of Vienna on September 12, 1683. The Ottoman army of Kara Mustapha was soundly defeated and the final Turkish thrust to Central Europe was broken once and for all.

John III Sobieski was raised in a patriotic Polish family. Sobieski's grandfather was Hetman Stanisław Zolkiewski, who died in battle fighting the Ottoman army, and his father, Jakub, became the castellan of Kraków. Sobieski joined the Polish army in 1648 and fought in Khmelnytsky's Cossack Revolt, which began in that same year. He was sent as a military attaché to Istanbul, where he learned Turkish and Tatar. Sobieski became one of the high commanders of the anti-Swedish forces in the Polish-Swedish Wars (1654-1660) and, from 1655 to 1667, participated in the Russo-Polish Wars of 1499-1667. In 1655, Sobieski became grand marshal of Poland and in 1668, he was named grand hetman. He was put in charge of conducting military operations against the Turks and Cossacks in the eastern part of the Polish Commonwealth. In 1673, Sobieski defeated the Turks at Chocim in one of two Turkish Wars. The victory won him great fame, and he was elected king of Poland in 1674. He continued operations against the Turks in 1675 with the goal of regaining the region of Podolia. In 1676, his forces held out for two weeks against massive Turkish forces led by Ibrāhīm Pasha at Zorawano.

When the Turkish army moved on Vienna in 1683, Sobieski was approached to lead an allied army to save the city. He routed the army of Kara Mustapha in one mighty charge by his heavy cavalry, his winged Hussars. He tried to organize a unified pursuit of the remnants of the Turkish army, but national interests destroyed the allied coalition. Despite this setback, the Turkish thrust into Central Europe was now in decline.

RESOURCES

Franaszek, Antoni. *The Relief of Vienna: 1683*. Cracow, Poland: Drukarnia Wydawnieza, 1984.

Laskowski, Otto. *Sobieski: King of Poland*. Glasgow: Polish Library, 1944.

Morton, J. B. *Sobieski: The King of Poland*. London: Payot, 1932

Palmer, Alicia. *Authentic Memoirs of John Sobieski*. London: Longman, 1815.

Stefancic, David. "The Siege of Vienna, 1683." In *Events That Changed the World in the Seventeenth Century*, edited by Frank W. Thackeray. Westport, Conn.: Greenwood Press, 1999.

SEE ALSO: Polish-Swedish Wars for Livonia; Russo-Swedish Wars of 1590-1658.

David R. Stefancic

JOHNSTON, ALBERT SIDNEY

BORN: February 2, 1803; Washington, Kentucky

DIED: April 6, 1862; Shiloh battlefield, near Pittsburg Landing, Tennessee

PRINCIPAL WARS: Black Hawk War, Texan War of Independence, Mexican-American War, Mormon Expedition, American Civil War

PRINCIPAL BATTLES: Monterrey (1846), Shiloh (1862)

MILITARY SIGNIFICANCE: In 1861, Confederate president Jefferson Davis appointed Johnston to command Confederate Department No. 2, encompassing the entire region west of the Appalachian Mountains.

In the fall of 1821, Albert Sidney Johnston became a cadet at the United States Military Academy. After graduating in 1826, he fought in the Black Hawk War (1832) with the Sixth U.S. infantry and in the Texan War of Independence (1835-1836). In 1837, he served as brigadier general in the Army of the Republic of Texas. In 1838, he became the secretary of war for the Republic of Texas. In 1845, General Zachary Taylor recommended Johnston for command of the U.S. Army's First Texas Infantry. After six months, he became inspector general of the army. He fought at Monterrey (1846) during the Mexican-American War (1846-1848). He resigned from the army in 1846.

Johnston returned to military service in October, 1849, as army paymaster for the Department of Texas. In March, 1855, he became commander of the Second U.S. Cavalry and in 1856 commanded the Department of Texas. In 1857, as a breveted brigadier general, he led an army expedition to Utah to deal with the Mormon rebellion. Briefly in 1861, he commanded the Department of the Pacific.

On September 10, 1861, after the American Civil War (1861-1865) began, he again resigned from the U.S. Army and became a major general in command of the Confederate western district. He died in battle at on the battlefield at Shiloh, Tennessee, on April 6, 1862.

Resources
Johnston, William Preston. *The Life of Albert Sidney Johnston: Embracing His Service in the Armies of the United States, the Republic of Texas, and the Confederate States*. 1878. Reprint, New York: Da Capo Press, 1997.

Roland, Charles P. *Albert Sidney Johnston: Soldier of Three Republics*. 1964. Reprint. Austin: University of Texas Press, 1994.

See also: American Civil War; Mexican-American War; Monterrey; Shiloh; Texan War of Independence.

Stacy W. Reaves

Johnston, Joseph Eggleston

Born: February 3, 1807; near Farmville, Virginia
Died: March 21, 1891; Washington, D.C.
Principal war: American Civil War
Principal battles: First Bull Run (1861), Seven Pines (1862), Bentonville (1865)
Military significance: Johnston was one of the most able practitioners of defensive tactics on either side during the American Civil War (1861-1865) but was limited as a commander by his lack of strategic planning and his poor communication skills.

Joseph Eggleston Johnston joined Confederate service in June, 1861, and was promoted to full general following his successful defense of the Shenandoah Valley and a crucial victory at the First Battle of Bull Run. He commanded the South's principal field army for nearly a year after Bull Run, guarded the road to Richmond, and delayed a Union advance on that city for nearly two months. He fought an action at Seven Pines in which he was badly wounded on May 31, 1862.

Following his recovery, Johnston assumed control of the Army of Tennessee in December, 1863. The following year, he oversaw the rebuilding of that force and undertook the defense of Georgia and its vital rail junction at Atlanta against a numerically superior force. Johnston made good use of terrain to delay his opponent, William T. Sherman, and inflicted more casualties than he took. However, he was removed from command on June 17 because he ignored the preservation of vital area resources, was unable to exploit his victories, and did not take the offensive against Sherman.

Seven months later, with Sherman driving through the Carolinas, Johnston was recalled. He consolidated scattered forces and surprised Sherman at Bentonville, North Carolina, on March 19, 1865. His failure to win a victory there led to the surrender of his army a month later.

Resources
Castel, Albert. *Decision in the West*. Lawrence: University of Kansas, 1992.

Hughes, Nathaniel. *Bentonville*. Chapel Hill: University of North Carolina, 1996.

Johnston, Joseph E. *Narrative of Military Operations*. New York: Appleton, 1874.

Symonds, Craig. *Joseph E. Johnston*. New York: W. W. Norton, 1992.

See also: American Civil War; Atlanta; Bull Run, First; Sherman, William T.

Louis P. Towles

Jomini, Antoine Henri, baron de

Full name: Antoine Henri Jomini
Born: March 6, 1779; Vaud, Switzerland
Died: March 22, 1869; Brussels, Belgium
Principal wars: Napoleonic Wars
Principal battles: Austerlitz (1805), Jena (1806), Eylau (1807), Lützen (1813), Bautzen (1813), Varna (1828)
Military significance: Jomini was the first military writer to codify and explain the precepts of

Napoleonic warfare. His writings were published throughout the world and widely read by generations of military officers.

Antoine Henri, baron de Jomini, joined the French-sponsored Swiss army in 1798, and by 1800, he had relocated to Paris to pursue the career of a military theorist/writer. This brought him to the attention of Marshal Michel Ney, who invited him to join his staff in 1805, and Jomini participated in the Ulm and Austerlitz campaigns, winning much praise. In 1806, Napoleon Bonaparte was sufficiently impressed to allow him to join his personal staff, and he witnessed the Battles of Jena (1806) and Eylau (1807) as a colonel.

In 1808, Jomini transferred back to Ney's staff and accompanied him to Spain. Serious disagreements between the two men led to his resignation, but Napoleon, eager to maintain his services, allowed him to simultaneously hold a commission in the Russian army. Jomini subsequently served under the emperor's personal secretary, Marshal Louis Alexandre Berthier, who resented his talents. Nevertheless, Jomini continued publishing, and in 1810, he commenced his classic study *Histoire critique et militaire des guerres de la Révolution* (1819-1824; history of the revolutionary war), which was not completed until 1824. When Napoleon invaded Russia in 1812, Jomini, who was openly sympathetic to Czar Alexander I, was assigned rear area duties only. In the spring of 1813, he rejoined Ney's staff and fought at the Battles of Lützen and Bautzen. Ney recommended him for promotion to major general, but Berthier had him arrested for a minor technicality. At this juncture, Jomini switched sides and joined the Russian service as aide-de-camp to the czar. He witnessed the defeat of Napoleon at Leipzig and the ensuing campaign in France in 1814. The following year, he returned to Paris after Waterloo and unsuccessfully pleaded with King Louis XVIII not to execute his old friend Ney.

Jomini returned to Russia in 1816 and spent the next several decades as a high-ranking military adviser. In 1827, he served as aide-de-camp to the new Czar Nicholas II and the following year rendered useful service against the Turkish forces at Varna. He also labored hard to establish the Russian General Staff College in 1832. However, in 1838, Jomini published his most influential work,

Antoine Henri Jomini. (Library of Congress)

his *Précis de l'art de la guerre* (1838; *Summary of the Art of War*, 1854). In it he claimed to have distilled Napoleon's secret for military success. To Jomini, military victory was predicated upon the principles of mass, surprise, and concentration. These, when coupled with decisive blows at the enemy's weak points, should result in a crushing victory. Jomini's work exerted profound influence on military thinking in its day and was translated into several languages. It was especially important in the United States and formed the basis of strategy and tactics used by both sides during the American Civil War (1861-1865).

In 1854, Jomini served as the czar's military adviser during the Crimean War (1853-1856). For many years thereafter, he alternated between St. Petersburg and Brussels, writing no less than thirty volumes on the art of war. By the time of his death, he was regarded as the most important military writer and theorist of his day. However, Jomini erred in misunderstanding one essential point of warfare, namely, that the key to victory is the destruction of an enemy's army. This was something that Prussian military writer Carl von

Clausewitz emphasized strongly, and for that reason, his writings have largely supplanted Jomini's as the basis for modern military instruction.

RESOURCES

Alger, John. *Antoine-Henri Jomini: A Bibliographic Survey.* West Point, N.Y.: United States Military Academy, 1975.

Earle, Edward M., ed. *Makers of Modern Strategy: Military Thought From Machiavelli to Hitler.* Princeton, N.J.: Princeton University Press, 1960.

Handel, Michael I. *Masters of War: Sun Tzu, Clausewitz, and Jomini.* London: Frank Cass, 1991.

Howard, Michael. *The Theory and Practice of War.* Bloomington: Indiana University Press, 1975.

Paret, Peter, ed. *Makers of Modern Strategy: From Machiavelli to the Nuclear Age.* Princeton, N.J.: Princeton University Press, 1986.

SEE ALSO: Alexander I; Austerlitz; Berthier, Louis Alexandre; Clausewitz, Carl von; Jena and Auerstädt; Leipzig; Lützen; Military theory; Napoleon I; Ney, Michel; Waterloo.

John C. Fredriksen

JONES, JOHN PAUL

ALSO KNOWN AS: John Paul
BORN: July 6, 1747; Arbigland Estate, Kirkbean, Kirkcudbright, Scotland
DIED: July 18, 1792; Paris, France
PRINCIPAL WARS: American Revolution, Russo-Turkish Wars
PRINCIPAL BATTLES: Flamborough Head (1779), Liman (1788)
MILITARY SIGNIFICANCE: In 1779, at Flamborough Head, off the east coast of Yorkshire, Jones and his ship *Bonhomme Richard* prevailed against the British frigate *Serapis*. His victory was a remarkable triumph for the fledgling U.S. Navy.

John Paul grew up in Scotland of lower-middle-class parentage. In 1759, he emigrated to the Caribbean, where he became a merchant captain. In 1773, he killed a sailor who tried to mutiny against his command. To escape the notoriety of this act, he added "Jones" to his name. Jones moved to Virginia, where his brother lived. When the American colonies began to rebel against Britain in 1775, Jones volunteered for command in the Continental navy. As captain of the *Alfred*, he mounted a successful raid on Halifax, Nova Scotia, in late 1776. Despite his lack of diplomacy in relating to the Continental Congress during the American Revolution, he was given a more prominent command. In 1777, Jones received command of the sloop of war *Ranger*. He raided the northwest English port city of Whitehaven, accomplishing the rare feat of bringing a foreign war to English soil. In April, 1778, the *Ranger* swept down upon St. Mary's Isle, near Jones's Scottish boyhood home, and departed with some valuable silver from the house of the Earl of Selkirk. He also captured several British ships.

By this time, the American rebels had entered into alliance with France. The French helped equip Jones's next expedition and provided a ship, which Jones refitted and renamed the *Bonhomme Richard*. On September 23, 1779, Jones engaged in the climactic battle off Flamborough Head with the *Serapis*, commanded by Captain Richard Pearson. Jones was accompanied by two other ships, one commanded by a French admiral who bafflingly fired at both allied and enemy ships, and the *Bonhomme Richard* struggled alone. Glory and bloodshed went hand in hand. It was a battle of attrition, in which both ships were crippled. When the British commander thought Jones was ready to surrender, inquiring "Sir, do you strike?" Jones replied, "I have not begun to fight." In the end, Jones's forces managed to board the *Serapis* just before the *Bonhomme Richard* itself was too damaged to continue fighting.

Jones's victory stunned the world, yet he was hobbled throughout the war by personal quarrels with Congress and with American and French naval commanders, which often left him idle and unable to fight for months or even years. Frustrated in his attempts to undertake further commands in the U.S. Navy, Jones settled in Paris where he became involved in aristocratic social life. He became a mercenary, though a very exalted one. In this capacity, he was hired by the Russian empress Catherine the Great to lead the Russian Navy against the Turks at the Liman estuary of the Dnieper River in 1788 to gain access to the Black Sea. Jones was prevented from total success by the intrigue of rival Russian officers.

He soon returned to Paris, where he died of pneumonia in 1792.

Despite being the first great American naval hero, Jones spent relatively little of his short life within the borders of the United States. Nonetheless, his primary allegiance was to his adopted American home.

RESOURCES

Gardiner, Robert, ed. *Navies and the American Revolution, 1775-1783*. Annapolis, Md.: United States Naval Institute, 1997.

John Paul Jones. Fiction feature. Warner Brothers, 1959.

John Paul Jones: Captain of the High Seas. Documentary. A&E Biography Video, 1996.

Lutz, Norma Jean. *John Paul Jones: Father of the U.S. Navy*. New York: Chelsea House, 1999.

Mackay, James. *I Have Not Yet Begun to Fight: A Life of John Paul Jones*. Edinburgh, Scotland: Mainstream, 1998.

Morison, Samuel Eliot. *John Paul Jones: A Sailor's Biography*. Annapolis, Md.: United States Naval Institute, 1999.

Nicastro, Nicholas. *The Eighteenth Captain*. Ithaca, N.Y.: McBooks, 1999.

Walsh, John Evangelist. *Night on Fire: The First Complete Account of John Paul Jones' Greatest Battle*. New York: McGraw-Hill, 1978.

SEE ALSO: American Revolution; Navy, U.S.; Russo-Turkish Wars.

Nicholas Birns

JOSEPH, CHIEF

FULL NAME: Joseph the Younger, Chief
ALSO KNOWN AS: Young Joseph; Heinmot Tooyalakekt ("Thunder Rolling in the Mountains")
BORN: c. 1840; Lapwai Preserve, Wallowa Valley, northeastern Oregon
DIED: September 21, 1904; Colville Indian Reservation, Washington
PRINCIPAL WAR: Nez Perce War
PRINCIPAL BATTLES: White Bird Canyon (1877), Clearwater (1877), Big Hole (1877), Bear Paws (1877)
MILITARY SIGNIFICANCE: In an attempt to find refuge in Canada, Chief Joseph led six hundred Nez Perce on a seventeen-hundred-mile march from Oregon, defeating U.S. military forces along the way and surrendering only fifty miles from freedom.

Young Joseph was in his mid-thirties when he became chief of the Nez Perce. In the face of pressure from white settlers, Chief Joseph, opposed to war, reluctantly agreed to move his people to the Lapwai Reservation in Idaho. In June, 1877, before the move was completed, renegade Nez Perce warriors killed some settlers, and the U.S. military moved in swiftly.

A peace-loving man, Chief Joseph proved a remarkable general. He assembled 600 Nez Perce, only 155 of whom were warriors, and left the Wallowa Valley in Oregon, seeking refuge in Canada. The group of Nez Perce fought their way seventeen hundred miles across Idaho and into Montana. In a number of battles, including White Bird Canyon (June 17, 1877) and Clearwater River (July 11-12), they outwitted the military and suffered few losses. At Big Hole (August 9-10), the Nez Perce were ambushed and suffered losses of more than 90 people. They reached Bear Paws Mountain, about fifty miles from Canada, in October. However, fresh calvary troops arrived, and with most of his warriors now dead and many of his people starving and freezing, Chief Joseph surrendered on October 5, 1877, declaring, "I will fight no more forever."

RESOURCES

A Clash of Cultures: "I Will Fight No More Forever." Documentary. Discovery Channel, 1993.

Hook, Jason. *American Indian Warrior Chiefs: Tecumseh, Crazy Horse, Chief Joseph, Geronimo*. New York: Sterling, 1989.

Malinowski, Sharon, ed. *Notable Native Americans*. Detroit, Mich.: Gale Research, 1995.

Sacred Journey of the Nez Perce. Documentary. Idaho Public Television, 1996.

Scott, Robert Alan. *Chief Joseph and the Nez Percés*. New York: Facts on File, 1993.

Warburton, Lois. *The Importance of Chief Joseph*. San Diego, Calif.: Lucent Books, 1992.

SEE ALSO: American Indian wars; Miles, Nelson A.; Nez Perce War.

Lisa A. Wroble

Josephus, Flavius

Also known as: Joseph ben Matthias
Born: 37/38 C.E.; Jerusalem, Palestine
Died: c. 100 C.E.; probably in Rome
Principal war: First Jewish Revolt
Principal battles: Siege of Jotapata (67 C.E), Siege of Jerusalem (70 C.E)
Military significance: Josephus unsuccessfully defended Galilee as a rebel commander, then defected and aided the Romans in the Siege of Jerusalem. His main significance, though, is as a military historian.

Born into a wealthy family of priests, Flavius Josephus was appointed rebel governor of the Galilee in November or December, 66 C.E. Despite his claim of training an army of 60,000 in the Roman fashion, Josephus's forces probably consisted of militia, some mercenaries, and a small bodyguard, a few thousand men at most. Other rebel units were independent and often hostile. In the spring of 67 C.E., Vespasian quickly overran most of the Galilee. Josephus defended Jotapata, which fell after a forty-seven-day siege. Then, defecting to the Romans, he became a translator for Titus, Vespasian's son and successor as military commander in Judaea. At the Siege of Jerusalem (70 C.E.), Josephus aided in interrogating prisoners and exhorted the surrender of rebel forces.

After the First Jewish Revolt (66-73 C.E.), Josephus was granted Roman citizenship, moved to Rome and devoted himself to writing. His *Bellum Judaicum* (75-79 C.E.; *The Jewish War*, 1847) is the best surviving account of the early imperial army at war. In addition to his own experience and other eyewitness accounts, he used the war diaries of Vespasian and Titus.

Resources

Bohrmann, Monette. *Flavius Josephus, the Zealots, and Yavne: Towards a Rereading of the War of the Jews*. Bern, Switzerland: Lang, 1994.
Cohen, Shaye. *Josephus in Galilee and Rome*. Leiden, the Netherlands: Brill, 1979.
Feldman, Louis, and Gohei Hata. *Josephus, Judaism, and Christianity*. Detroit, Mich.: Wayne State University Press, 1986.

See also: History, military; Jewish Revolts; Roman Empire, Wars of the; Vespasian.

Jonathan P. Roth

Joubert, Petrus Jacobus

Also known as: Piet Joubert
Born: January 20, 1831; near Prince Albert, Cape Colony
Died: March 27, 1900; Pretoria, South Africa
Principal wars: Boer Wars
Principal battles: Laing's Nek (1881, 1899), Majuba (1881), Siege of Ladysmith (1899-1900)
Military significance: Joubert was a popular leader around whom the Boers rallied against the British.

Born on the family farm, Petrus Jacobus Joubert was six when his parents took him to Natal. Later he settled in Transvaal. He was always at heart a farmer and had a kindly, diplomatic nature. He was successful in farming, law, business, and politics. His original popularity was purely civilian.

Joubert had almost no military experience when he was elected commandant general at the start of the First Boer War, but his victories over British General Sir George Colley at Laing's Nek (1881, 1899) and Majuba (1881) liberated Transvaal and made him a national hero. Nevertheless, he lost presidential elections to Paul Kruger (1888, 1893, and 1898). In the 1880's and 1890's, he enlarged and improved the Boer artillery.

In the Second Boer War, especially during the Siege of Ladysmith (1899-1900), he was ineffective because he cared too much about making peace. His victories over British Lieutenant General Sir George Stuart White, before Ladysmith, were caused more by White's mistakes than by Joubert's tactics.

Two days after Joubert was disabled by a fall from his horse, he was succeed by Louis Botha as commandant general.

Resources

Bateman, Philip. *Generals of the Anglo-Boer War*. Cape Town: South African Historical Mint, 1977.
Coetzer, Owen. *The Anglo-Boer War: The Road to Infamy, 1899-1900*. London: Arms and Armour, 1996.

Meintjes, Johannes. *The Commandant-General: The Life and Times of Petrus Jacobus Joubert of the South African Republic, 1831-1900*. Cape Town, South Africa: Tafelberg-Uitgewers, 1971.

SEE ALSO: Boer Wars; Botha, Louis; Buller, Redvers Henry; Cetshwayo; Kruger, Paul; Ladysmith, Siege of.

Eric v. d. Luft

JOUST

In medieval western Europe, a mock battle between two horsemen who attempted to unhorse each other by charging with leveled lances. Jousting reached its height in the fifteenth century, when it largely replaced the *melee* (a mock battle between bodies of horsemen) at tournaments. Jousts served a dual purpose of diversion and combat training. Even practice and pageant could be deadly: In 1559, King Henry II of France was accidentally killed in a joust tournament. By the end of the sixteenth century, jousting was passé. However, it survived in another form: "tilting at the rings," a game in which a horseman tries to put a lance through a series of metal rings while riding at full speed.

Jeremiah Taylor

JUEL, NIELS

ALSO KNOWN AS: Niels Juul
BORN: May 8, 1629; Christiania (later Oslo), Norway
DIED: April 8, 1697; Copenhagen, Denmark
PRINCIPAL WAR: Scanian War
PRINCIPAL BATTLES: Gotland (1676), Öland (1676), Köge Bay (1677)
MILITARY SIGNIFICANCE: A most distinguished Scandinavian admiral of the era, Juel was a talented tactician whose victories served as models for future admirals.

In his youth, Niels Juel served in the Dutch fleet under both Michiel de Ruyter and Maarten Tromp and rose to the rank of captain. Returning to Denmark, he distinguished himself as a squadron commander during the defense of Copenhagen (1659).

In 1675, the Scanian War (1675-1679) erupted. Juel received command of the Danish fleet and launched an attack that captured the island of Gotland (1676). A Danish-Dutch squadron under Juel and Cornelius Tromp subsequently met the Swedes at the Battle of Öland (1676). The fleets were evenly matched, but the Swedish flagship capsized in heavy winds, and the allied fleet inflicted a stunning defeat on the Swedes.

The next year, a Swedish squadron of twenty-five ships of the line encountered Juel's fleet of nineteen ships in Köge Bay (1677). The Swedish forces became disordered when one ship ran aground. Juel split his fleet and succeeded in breaking the Swedish line. Juel pursued the Swedish fleet into the night, and the Danes ultimately sank or captured ten Swedish ships of the line, without losing a single vessel of their own. As a result of this victory, the Danish fleet controlled the Baltic for the balance of the war.

RESOURCES
Jesperson, Knud V. "Warfare and Society in the Baltic: 1500-1800." In *European Warfare: 1453-1815*, edited by Jeremy Black. New York: St. Martin's Press, 1999.
Pemsel, Helmut. *A History of War at Sea*. Annapolis, Md.: Naval Institute Press, 1989.

SEE ALSO: Anglo-Dutch Wars; Danish-Swedish Wars; Kalmer Wars; Northern War; Scandinavian War; Tromp, Maarten.

Reid J. Rozen

JUNOT, ANDOCHE

FULL NAME: Jean Andoche Junot, duke of Abrantès
BORN: October 23, 1771; Bussy-le-Grand, France
DIED: July 29, 1813; Montbard, France
PRINCIPAL WARS: French Revolutionary Wars, Napoleonic Wars
PRINCIPAL BATTLES: Vimeiro (1808), Borodino (1812)
MILITARY SIGNIFICANCE: Junot served under Napoleon Bonaparte in Italy, Egypt, the Peninsula, and Russia and was his trusted friend and aide.

Andoche Junot first became a friend and administrative aide to Napoleon Bonaparte during the French Revolutionary Wars (1792-1802). In Egypt, he revealed to Napoleon that Josephine Bonaparte had been an unfaithful wife, an incident that many historians believe caused a significant depressive change in Napoleon's personality.

In 1807, Napoleon assigned Junot to military and political command over Portugal after it violated the continental system trade boycott against England. On August 21, 1808, 14,000 British under Arthur Wellesley, future duke of Wellington, decisively defeated Junot's 13,000 French at the Battle of Vimeiro near Lisbon. French losses were 2,000 dead and wounded. The resulting Convention of Cintra armistice removed all of the French from Portugal.

During the 1812 Russian campaign, Junot commanded an entire army corps with a minor role and was in reserve at the Battle of Borodino. He committed suicide in 1813 after being assigned to an obscure political governorship.

RESOURCES
Chandler, David. *The Campaigns of Napoleon*. New York: Macmillan, 1996.
Elting, John. *Swords Around a Throne: Napoleon's Grand Armée*. New York: Da Capo Press, 1997.

SEE ALSO: Borodino; French Revolutionary Wars; Napoleon I; Napoleonic Wars; Wellington, duke of.
Alan Prescott Peterson

JUST WAR

In medieval Europe, the concept that a ruler could wage a war of "justice" outside of his own jurisdiction—in short, a boundless crusade to punish the wicked, avenge the wronged, or defend the defenseless. Waging war for a just cause is an idea as old as Saint Augustine (354-430 B.C.E.) and one espoused by the Dutch jurist and scholar Hugo Grotius in the seventeenth century. While such "sentimental" views of war have largely been dispelled by realpolitik and the great destruction caused by industrial warfare, the concept of just war was somewhat revived in the twentieth century. Some nations argued that international peace-keeping was just cause for military intervention outside one's own borders.
Jeremiah Taylor

JUSTINIAN I

FULL NAME: Flavius Petrus Sabbatius Justinianus
BORN: 483; Illyria
DIED: November 14, 565; Constantinople (later Istanbul, Turkey)
PRINCIPAL WARS: First Persian War, Vandal War, Gothic War, Second Persian War, Bulgar-Slav Invasion
PRINCIPAL BATTLES: Callinicum (531), Rome (536), Ravenna (538-539), Taginae (552), Mons Lactarius (553)
MILITARY SIGNIFICANCE: Justinian's numerous wars and conquests resulted in partial or temporary recovery of Rome that had been lost to barbarians and regained some of the Roman Empire's former glory.

Born from Latin-speaking peasant stock, Justinian had an uncle who advanced in the military to become Justin I, Byzantine emperor, in 518. Justin adopted his nephew and made him commander of the home troops. Shortly before his death in 527, Justin named his nephew co-emperor and successor.

As a Roman, Justianian desired to rebuild the empire. Rome once had professionally trained legions, 500,000 strong, stationed throughout the empire and supported by excellent communications, but a series of barbarian invasions in the third and fourth centuries had reduced the army's power. Justinian had to use this reduced military system to defend the east against the Persians and reconquer the west from the barbarian kings. Warlike tribes—some of whom, including the horse-riding archers from the steppes, had special skills—were enlisted as *foederati*, or "special troops." Commanders formed their own elite troops, the *bucellarii*, to achieve superiority of mass and maneuverability. Soldier-settlers, *limitanei*, protected frontiers. Support from Constantinople was inadequate, and Justinian was slow to allocate reinforcements. The dissolution of the imperial relay postal system hurt communications. Religious divisions made the Christian clergy a muddy source of intelligence. The navy, based on regional shipyards, remained dependable.

As a commander, Justinian knew soldiering and chose his subordinates well, some of whom, particularly Belisarius, had been his *bucellarii*. He was aided in retaining their loyalty by his consort, Theodora, particularly in the Nika riots in the capital in 532.

Belisarius threw back the Persian attacks at the beginning of Justinian's reign through his victory at the fortress of Dara in 530, and though beaten at Callinicum (531), he concluded the Perpetual Peace of 532. This freed Justinian for the reconquest of Vandal North Africa (533-534). His forces may have exceeded 100,000 men at the time; however, typically only a fraction was available for any particular operation. Belisarius landed unexpected and unopposed on the North African coast. King Gelimer, engaged inland against the Berbers and an uprising of his Roman population and weakened by having sent his major force against his governor on Sardinia in revolt, lost his kingdom.

Success in North Africa encouraged Justinian to "reconquer" Italy, where the Gothic king Theodoric had since 489 built a kingdom depending on Constantinople and effectively governed by a joint Gothic military and Roman civil administration. Succession problems since the death of Theodoric in 526 suggested that it might be possible to return Italy to direct Roman rule, but Justinian's timing and strategy were ill conceived. Instead of waiting for a further deterioration of the ruling caste and then occupying the Gothic capital of Ravenna with the aid of the navy, Justinian ordered Belisarius to land on Sicily in 535. In 536, Belisarius crossed over to the mainland and occupied Rome. Alerted, the Goths elected a strong new king, Witiges, and Justinian was saddled with a reconquest that dragged on for seventeen years. Besieged, Belisarius broke out and drove the besiegers back to Ravenna (538-539), in part thanks to his archers decimating the Goths' cavalry. In 540, he entered Ravenna through deceit and sailed with Witiges to Constantinople. The Goths replaced their abdicated king with the resourceful Totila.

After the death of Theodora in 548, Justinian, who was often jealous of Belisarius, replaced Belisarius with a new commander in chief, the eunuch Narses, who swept across the Po Valley from Dalmatia and destroyed Totila's army at Taginae (552). Totila's navy had been sunk off Senigallia. With Totila mortally wounded at Taginae, the Goths elected their last king, Teias. They lost their king and their kingdom at Mons Lactarius (553).

By 554, Justinian held southeasternmost Spain and the Straits of Gibraltar, reclaiming much of what had been the Western Roman Empire. In the east, his Second Persian War resulted in a new "permanent" stand-off three years before his death. In 559, Justinian called Belisarius out of retirement to repulse a Bulgar-Slav invasion of Thrace. In 562, he imprisoned Belisarius, accusing him of treason, but he released him a year later.

RESOURCES

Amory, Patrick. *People and Identity in Ostrogothic Italy, 489-554*. New York: Cambridge University Press, 1997.

The End of the Ancient World A.D. 100-A.D. 600. Documentary. Landmark, 1985.

Garland, Lynda. *Byzantine Empresses: Women and Power in Byzantium,* A.D. *527-1204*. New York: Routledge, 1999.

Lee, A. D. *Information and Frontiers: Roman Foreign Relations in Late Antiquity*. Cambridge, England: Cambridge University Press, 1993.

Moorhead, John. *Justinian*. London: Longman, 1994.

Treadgold, Warren. *Byzantium and Its Army, 284-1081*. Stanford, Calif.: Stanford University Press, 1995.

SEE ALSO: Belisarius; Byzantine Empire; Byzantine-Persian Wars; Gothic War; Goths; Narses; Taginae; Vandals.

Reinhold Schumann

JUTLAND

TYPE OF ACTION: Naval battle in World War I
DATE: May 31-June 1, 1916
LOCATION: In the North Sea due west of the entrance to the Skagerrak and west of Jutland bank off the coast of Denmark
COMBATANTS: 28 battleships, 9 battle cruisers, 34 cruisers, and 80 destroyers of the British Grand Fleet vs. 22 battleships, 5 battle cruisers, 11

Smoke billows from a battleship hit during the Battle of Jutland. (Archive Photos/Hulton Getty Collection)

cruisers, and 63 destroyers of the German High Seas Fleet

PRINCIPAL COMMANDERS: *British*, Admiral John Jellicoe (1859-1935), Admiral David Beatty (1871-1936); *German*, Admiral Reinhard Scheer (1863-1928), Admiral Franz von Hipper

RESULT: A tactical victory for the Germans and a strategic victory for the British

The German High Seas Fleet, led by Admirals Reinhard Scheer and Franz von Hipper, came out early on May 31, 1916, and the British Grand Fleet, led by Admirals John Jellicoe and David Beatty, came down from its base at Scapa Flow. Advance battle cruiser squadrons met first, then the main fleet. The weather was poor, and the main confrontation occurred late in the afternoon, followed by confused and violent night action. British losses were 3 battle cruisers, 3 cruisers, 8 destroyers, 6,945 casualties; German were 2 battleships, 4 cruisers, 5 destroyers, and 3,058 casualties.

Debate over the battle, its leadership (especially that of Admiral Jellicoe), deficiencies, consequences, and implications continued for decades. Both sides were deficient in leadership, intelligence, communication, navigation, staff planning, and ability to handle night operations. In addition, there were flaws in warship and weapons design, optics, and fire control systems. The Germans immediately declared a victory, and although the battle was a strategic victory for the British, the initial announcement was factual, subdued, and depressing. That assessment persisted, exaggerating German accomplishments.

SIGNIFICANCE

Though many believed the naval battle at Jutland would be decisive, the strategic situation of British naval hegemony and German naval isolation remained unchanged. The British Grand Fleet was operational and ready for battle on June 1; the High Seas Fleet was crippled, only ten capital ships being operational on June 1. The fact that three British battle cruisers blew up caused agonizing reappraisal of British capital ship design.

RESOURCES

Campbell, N. John M. *Jutland: An Analysis of the Fighting*. London: Conway, 1986.

Corbett, Julian S., and Henry Newbolt. *Naval Operations: History of the Great War*. 5 vols. London: Longman, 1920-1940.

Frost, Holloway H. *The Battle of Jutland*. Annapolis, Md.: Naval Institute, 1970.

Marder, Arthur J. *From Dreadnought to Scapa Flow: The Royal Navy in the Fisher Era, 1904-1919*. 5 vols. London: Oxford University Press, 1961-1970.

Rasor, Eugene L. *The Battle of Jutland: A Bibliography*. Westport, Conn.: Greenwood Press, 1991.

SEE ALSO: Jellicoe, John; Navies: Organization and tactics; World War I.

Eugene L. Rasor

K

Kadesh

Type of action: Ground battle in the Egyptian-Hittite War
Date: c. 1274 B.C.E.
Location: Tel Nebi Mend on the Orontes river, northwestern Syro-Palestine
Combatants: Egyptians vs. 47,500 Hittites
Principal commanders: *Egyptian*, Pharaoh Ramses II (1292-1225 B.C.E.); *Hittite*, King Muwatallish
Result: Hittites retain Kadesh, but avoid another major confrontation with Egypt

In late May of 1274 B.C.E., during his fifth regal year, Ramses II approached Kadesh with four divisions. South of Kadesh, two bedouin reported that the Hittites waited at Aleppo. Ramses and the army of Amun advanced to camp northwest of Kadesh. Two captured Hittites then informed Ramses that the Hittites were behind Kadesh. Hittite king Muwatallish sent 2,500 chariots across the Orontes, scattering the second Egyptian army and attacking Ramses' camp.

Countercharges by Ramses slowed the Hittites, allowing the Egyptians to regroup. Muwatallish committed a further 1,000 chariots, and Ramses urged the army of Ptah to hasten north (the army of Seth was still distant). As the Hittites looted Ramses's camp, a fifth force, the Neʿarin, arrived. The Hittites fled in panic, many drowning in the Orontes (attacking chariots were still fording the river when the retreat created deadly confusion).

Significance

Kadesh revealed different approaches to chariot warfare. Egypt employed the two-manned chariot with rear axle as an archery platform, as had the Hittites earlier in battle against Ramses's father Seti I. At Kadesh, the Hittites abandoned light chariots for heavy infantry transport vehicles with central axles and three men, carrying infantry weapons.

The Hittites retained Kadesh but were badly mauled. Within six years, Ramses had thwarted Hittite activity in Moab and outflanked Kadesh with the conquest of Dapur. Under Egyptian and Assyrian pressure, the Hittites sought a treaty with Egypt.

Resources

Goedicke, Hans, ed. *Perspectives on the Battle of Kadesh*. Baltimore, Md.: Halgo, 1985.
Kitchen, Kenneth A. *Pharaoh Triumphant: The Life and Times of Ramses II*. Warminster, England: Aris and Philips, 1982.
Murnane, William J. *The Road to Kadesh*. Chicago: Oriental Institute, 1990.
Santosuosso, Antonio. "Kadesh Revisited: Reconstructing the Battle Between the Egyptians and the Hittites." *Journal of Military History* 60 (July, 1996): 423-444.

See also: Assyrian Empire; Egyptian Empire; Hittite Empire.

John Coleman Darnell

Kalmar Wars

At issue: Swedish independence
Date: 1409-1613
Location: Denmark and the Scandinavian peninsula
Combatants: Danes vs. Swedes
Principal commanders: *Danish*, Christian II (1481-1559); *Swedish*, Gustavus I Vasa (1496?-1560)
Principal battles: Brunkeberg, Lake Äsunden, Axtorna, Bornholm
Result: Sweden achieves independence

Background

In 1388, Queen Margaret of Denmark succeeded to the throne of Norway, and in the same year, the Swedish nobility, after enduring decades of domestic instability and a series of weak rulers, elected Margaret as queen of Sweden. This personal union of the three kingdoms was transformed into a formal federation in 1397 by the Union of Kalmar. Although each kingdom retained a great deal of control over internal matters, Copenhagen would remain the center of power for the union, and Sweden became increasingly disaffected under Danish rule.

ACTION

The first major challenge to the Union of Kalmar came in the 1430's. King Erik of Pomerania had engaged in a costly and ultimately unsuccessful war with the dukes of Holstein and the Hanseatic League (1422-1435). Erik's attempts to raise taxes in order to finance his aggressive foreign policy led to a revolt in Sweden. The revolt, begun in 1434, spread quickly to Norway and eventually to Denmark. In 1439, the nobles of the three kingdoms deposed Erik and chose his nephew, Christopher of Bavaria, as ruler.

Christopher died in 1448, leaving no heirs, and the Danish nobility chose Christian of Oldenburg to succeed to the throne. In Sweden and Norway, however, Karl Knutsson was crowned king as Charles VIII, and a period followed in which both Christian and Karl contended for control and Sweden became embroiled in a confused civil war. After Karl's death in 1470, Christian led a campaign to take Stockholm but was defeated by a Swedish army under Sten Sture at **Brunkeberg** (1471). As a result of this battle, Sten became the effective ruler of Sweden, although he did not formally end the Union of Kalmar.

Christian I's successor, John, continued the struggle with Sten, and, in 1497, succeeded in driving him from Sweden. Sten returned in 1501, taking advantage of John's preoccupation with a conflict on Denmark's southern frontier, and another period of domestic turmoil ensued, continuing until 1512.

The tranquility that followed did not last long. John's son, Christian II, attempted to reassert Danish predominance in Sweden, where Sten Sture the Younger, held sway as guardian of the realm. In 1520, Christian invaded Sweden and defeated Sten's forces at the Battle of **Lake Äsunden**. Christian then seized Stockholm and, in what became known as the Stockholm Bloodbath, he quickly ordered the executions of more than eighty rebel leaders.

The brutality of Christian's measures sparked a widespread Swedish revolt, led by Gustavus Vasa. Meanwhile, Christian faced opposition in Denmark, where the nobility resisted the monarch's attempts at centralization. In 1523, Christian fled to the Netherlands, and his uncle, Frederick I, was proclaimed king. In June of that year, Gustavus I was elected king of Sweden, which effectively ended the Union of Kalmar.

In the years immediately following the union's demise, a shared fear of the exiled Christian II led to an alliance that temporarily suspended the struggle between the two rivals. In 1533, both states were drawn into a war against Lübeck, which merged with a Danish civil war known as the Count's War (1533-1536). An allied naval force crushed the Lübecker fleet at the Battle of the Little Belt (1535). Lübeck agreed to peace the next year.

In 1563, the struggle between Sweden and Denmark resumed with the Seven Years' War. Erik XIV had instituted reforms of the Swedish army and navy, but the war initially went badly for Sweden. The Danes captured the important fortress town of Älvsborg at the outset of the war and later defeated the Swedish army at the Battle of **Axtorna** (1565). Swedish forces advanced into central Norway in 1564; although they were initially successful, it proved impossible to hold these conquests. A subsequent invasion of southern Norway led to the capture of Oslo (1567), but this too was retaken by the Danes.

Denmark's navy held the Swedes in check until the Swedish fleet, led by Klas Kristersson Horn, defeated the Danes at **Bornholm** (1565). The Swedish Navy, from that point on, dominated the Baltic. Sweden, however, could not extract more advantages from this success because an internal revolt, sparked by Erik's growing insanity, erupted in 1568. The next year, Erik was deposed and replaced by his brother, John III, who negotiated a peace with Denmark that restored the prewar status quo.

In the four decades following this conflict, Sweden became preoccupied with territorial expansion in the eastern Baltic and waged war against both Russia and Poland. In 1611, taking advantage of this situation, Christian IV declared war on Sweden. The Kalmar War of 1611-1613 took its name from the Swedish fortress that became the focus of Denmark's war effort. The fortress held out against a vigorous Danish siege, and the young Gustavus II Adolphus led a series of diversionary actions that kept the Danes off balance. In 1612, Denmark took Älvsborg, and a Danish force landed near Stockholm. These troops withdrew, however, when Gustavus Adolphus rushed troops to defend the capital. The two sides agreed to English mediation, and the Peace of Knäred (January, 1613) ended the war.

Aftermath

The Danish-Swedish wars ended the dream of a Scandinavian union forever. Although Denmark retained control over the sound and the lucrative tolls on Baltic trade, Sweden had achieved its independence and would soon gain the upper hand in its struggle with Denmark over supremacy in the Baltic.

Resources

Jesperson, Knud V. "Warfare and Society in the Baltic: 1500-1800." In *European Warfare: 1453-1815*, edited by Jeremy Black. New York: St. Martin's Press, 1999.

Oakley, Stewart. "War in the Baltic 1550-1790." In *The Origins of War in Early Modern Europe*, edited by Jeremy Black. Edinburgh, Scotland: J. Donald, 1987.

Roberts, Michael. *The Early Vasas: A History of Sweden, 1523-1611*. Cambridge, England: Cambridge University Press, 1968.

See also: Danish-Swedish Wars; Gustavus II Adolphus; Livonian War; Polish-Swedish Wars for Livonia; Russo-Swedish Wars of 1590-1658; Scandinavian War.

Reid J. Rozen

Kandahar

Type of action: Ground battle in the Second Anglo-Afghan War
Date: September 1, 1880
Location: Kandahar, Afghanistan (300 miles southwest of Kabul)
Combatants: 9,986 British and native troops vs. unknown number of Afghani tribesmen
Principal commanders: *British*, Lieutenant General Frederick Sleigh Roberts (1832-1914); *Afghani*, Ayub Khan (1855-1914)
Result: Successful British relief of besieged force

Following a decisive British defeat at Maiwand, in which a brigade under Brigadier General George Burrows was nearly annihilated, news arrived in Kabul that 4,000 men under Major General James Primrose were being besieged in the southern Afghanistan city of Kandahar. On August 8, Lieutenant General Frederick Sleigh Roberts was dispatched from Kabul with 9,986 British and native troops to relieve the besieged force.

After completing the 320-mile march on August 31, Roberts found the British force in Kandahar to be in little danger, with ample stores and ammunition and situated behind thick walls. The Afghani tribesmen, under the able leadership of Ayub Khan, had abandoned the siege upon Roberts's approach and had established camp nearby at Mazra. On September 1, Roberts hastened to engage the Afghani forces in battle and won a decisive victory. The Afghani force was routed, and all of its artillery captured. The British casualties amounted to 40 dead and 210 wounded, and the Afghani dead were estimated at greater than 600.

Significance

Despite the victory at Kandahar, the British withdrew their forces from Afghanistan. The greatest significance of the operation was that it propelled Roberts to international fame.

Resources

Farwell, Byron. *Eminent Victorian Soldiers: Seekers of Glory*. New York: W. W. Norton, 1985.

_____. *Queen Victoria's Little Wars*. New York: W. W. Norton, 1972.

Hannah, W. H. *Bobs, Kipling's General: The Life of Field-Marshal Earl Roberts of Kandahar, V.C.* London: Lee Cooper, 1972.

See also: British Colonial Wars; Roberts, Frederick Sleigh.

Leo Blanken

Kanem-Bornu Sultanate

Date: Ninth to eleventh centuries
Location: West Africa between the Niger River

and Lake Chad, bordering the Hausa states of Nigeria and the Songhai Empire

Principal military action: Expansion throughout western Sudan

Military significance: The Kanem-Bornu Empire paved the way for the rise of the Fulani kingdoms throughout western Sudan.

Kanem was the first state in the northern Sudan to be well documented. Thanks to Arab historians, the history of Bornu is well documented from about the ninth century onward. Lake Chad, much larger at the time, attracted large populations around its basin and acted as a stimulus for trade.

A pastoral group, ancestors of the Kanuri, established a centralized state over those referred to collectively as the Bulala, or Sao. By 1000, the Kanuri, originally a loose confederation of tribes, had settled in Kanem. Initially, Kanem established trading links as far east as Egypt and the Nile Valley. Kanem appears to have made contact and established ties with the Christian kingdoms of Nubia. These ties ended when Muslims took control of Kanem, including its ruling family, in the eleventh century. The new rulers used Islamic law to consolidate and strengthen their power. Under their Muslim rulers, Kanem dominated areas to the south and west of the lake. Although successful in trade, the Kanem Empire failed to maintain a long period of peace. By the twelfth century, they came under attack from the Sao and moved their capital to the region west of Lake Chad, losing control of most of the original territory of Kanem.

In the thirteenth century, the Kanuri began to conquer the surrounding areas. Conquest, marriage, and ties to Islam helped enlarge the empire. Mai (Emperor) Dunama Dibbalemi was the first of the Kanuri to convert to Islam. Dibbalemi then used his conversion to declare a jihad, or "holy war," against surrounding chieftaincies. This jihad led to a long period of conquest in the region. At its height, under Mai Idris Alooma, the Kanem Empire was a major power in the eastern Sudan. Using firearms obtained from the Ottoman Turks, it controlled the major eastern Saharan routes to Egypt.

In the fourteenth century, the Kanuri moved to the Bornu area, leaving Kanem to fall to the southern Bulala people. In Bornu, in northeastern Nigeria, the Kanuri mixed with the indigenous people. They then returned to Chad and conquered lands the Saifawas had lost. The Kanuri founded the ruling dynasty of the empire, setting its capital at Njimi. The empire, like all in the region, was based on trans-Saharan trade. Using Islam as a basis for legal and military organization, the empire expanded west to the Niger River, east to Wadai, and north to Fezzan.

From its new center, the kingdom of Kanem-Borno became the dominant power in the central Sudan, including much of Hausaland. The rulers of Bornu were Muslims but kept the traditional structure of the monarchy, with the queen mother and other female officials exercising considerable power. Traditional means of determining the succession prevailed, as did other pre-Islamic practices. The king posted members of the royal family away from the capital to govern the frontiers. Kings kept people of slave origin around themselves to govern as royal guards and officials, seeing in them no threat to the monarchy.

By the early sixteenth century, Bornu had recaptured Kanem and made it a protectorate. Under Mai Idris Alawma, Kanem-Bornu reached its height. In the nineteenth century, the Fulani conquered Kanem-Bornu. After a brief period of independence, the empire fell first to the Fulani in the late nineteenth century and then to the British, who restored the sultanate.

Resources

Botting, Douglas. *The Knights of Bornu*. London: Hodder and Stoughton, 1961.

Cohen, Ronald. *The Kanuri of Bornu*. New York: Holt, Rinehart, and Winston, 1967.

Fartua, Ibn Ahmed. *History of the First Twelve Years of the Reign of Mai Idris Alooma of Bornu: 1571-1583*. London: Frank Cass, 1970.

Government of Northern Nigeria. *Gazetteers of the Northern Provinces of Nigeria*. Vol.1. London: Frank Cass, 1972,

Hall, Augustin F. *The Diwan Revisited*. New York: Columbia University Press, 2000.

Koslow, Philip. *Kanem-Bornu: A Thousand Years of Splendor*. New York: Chelsea House Publishers, 1995.

Nachtiqal, Gustav. *Sahara and Sudan: Bornu, Kanem, Borku, Ennedi*. New York: Barnes & Noble, 1970.

Palmer, H. R. *The Bornu Sahara and Sudan.* New York: Negro University Press, 1970.

Schultze, Arnold. *The Sultanate of Bornu.* London: Frank Cass, 1968.

SEE ALSO: Jihad.

Frank A. Salamone

KANGXI

ALSO KNOWN AS: K'ang-Hsi
BORN: May 4, 1654; Beijing, China
DIED: December 20, 1722; an imperial estate outside Beijing, China
PRINCIPAL WARS: War of the Three Feudatories, Dzungar War
MILITARY SIGNIFICANCE: Kangxi consolidated Manchu rule, creating a long period of peace and prosperity.

A Manchu, Kangxi ascended the Chinese throne at the age of six and took complete control of the government in 1669, personally running it energetically and skillfully until his death. To complete the conquest of China, the emperor launched the War of the Three Feudatories (1673-1681) to destroy three virtually independent feudal states ruled by Chinese generals in southern China. After defeating the three states, Kangxi's forces seized the island of Taiwan in 1683. Kangxi then sent forces to stop Russian encroachment from Siberia into the Amur region. After destroying Russian fortifications there, China concluded its first treaty with a European power, the Treaty of Nerchinsk (1689), which recognized Chinese control of the area. In the Dzungar War (1690-1696), Chinese forces spent a number of years in border skirmishes with the Dzungars, then Kangxi led a force of 80,000 across Mongolia to victory against the Dzungar chieftain at Chao-Modo (1696). In 1683, the Manchus annexed Taiwan. In 1720, Kangxi sent his troops to expel the Western Mongols from Tibet, thereby adding this territory to China. Besides his military accomplishments, Kangxi undertook several massive inspection tours of his empire to monitor his reign. A patron of the arts and a scholar, Kangxi used Jesuit missionaries to cast cannons, teach him Western math and science, and act as interpreters.

RESOURCES

Forbidden City: The Great Within. Documentary. The Discovery Channel, 1995.

Kessler, Lawrence. *K'ang-hsi and the Consolidation of Ch'ing Rule, 1661-1684.* Chicago: University of Chicago Press, 1978.

Lux, Louise. *The Unsullied Dynasty and the K'ang-hsi Emperor.* Philadelphia: Mark One Printing, 1998.

Spence, Jonathan. *Emperor of China: Self Portrait of K'ang-hsi.* New York: Alfred A. Knopf, 1974.

Wu, Hsiu-liang. *Passage to Power: K'ang-hsi and His Heir Apparent, 1661-1722.* Cambridge, Mass.: Harvard University Press, 1979.

SEE ALSO: Chinese Imperial Wars; Manchu Expansion, Wars of.

Gregory C. Ference

KARAGEORGE

FULL NAME: Karageorge Petrovich
ALSO KNOWN AS: George Petrovich; Karadjordje; Djordje Petrovič
BORN: November 14, 1762; Višavac, Serbia, Ottoman Empire
DIED: July 25, 1817; Radovanje, Serbia
PRINCIPAL WARS: Austro-Turkish War of 1787-1791, Serbo-Ottoman Conflict
PRINCIPAL BATTLES: Belgrade (1806)
MILITARY SIGNIFICANCE: In 1804, Karageorge organized and led the first modern Balkan revolt against the Ottoman Empire, resulting in autonomous Serbia.

Karageorge, a chieftain of Serbia and founder of the Karageorgevich Dynasty, was first a successful swine herder. Karageorge fought with the Austrians as a sergeant in the Austro-Turkish War of 1787-1791. Later he organized the Serbs to aid the Turkish governor fighting renegade Janissaries (1802). The Janissaries, with the aid of a neighboring warlord, murdered the governor and beheaded more than seventy Serbs. Karageorge then led the Serbs in a revolt for independence, the Serbo-Ottoman Conflict, beginning in 1804. The Serbs drove the Turks into a few fortresses that Karageorge ordered besieged. The sultan declared a holy war against the Serbs, and Karageorge responded with brilliance and force. His commanders led guerrilla attacks against the Turkish forces on the periphery while he used his central position with the bulk of his forces to bolster weak positions. He drove the Turks from Belgrade (1806), then cleared them from the other fortresses (summer, 1807). However, when he refused an Ottoman offer of autonomy and instead threw in his lot with Russia hoping for complete independence, his fortunes changed. When Napoleon Bonaparte invaded Russia in 1812, the Russians deserted the Serbs. Austria and France rejected Karageorge's overtures. Dispirited, he deserted his troops and fled to Austria, and the Turks reconquered Serbia. When he returned in 1817, the new Serbian leader Miloš Obrenović had him executed.

RESOURCES
Dakic, Mile. *The Serbian Krayina: Historical Roots and Its Birth.* Knin: Iskra, 1994.
Ivic, Pavle, et al. *The History of Serbian Culture.* Translated by Randall A. Major. Edgware, Middlesex, England: Porthill, 1995.
Meriage, Lawrence P. *Russia and the First Serbian Insurrection: 1804-1813.* New York: Garland, 1987.
Petrovich, Michael Boro. *A History of Modern Serbia, 1804-1918.* New York: Harcourt Brace Jovanovich, 1976.
Vucinich, Wayne S., ed. *The First Serbian Uprising: 1804-1813.* Boulder, Colo.: Social Science Monographs, 1982.

SEE ALSO: Austro-Turkish Wars; Janissaries; Napoleon I; Napoleonic Wars; Ottoman Empire; Serbo-Ottoman Conflict.

Frederick B. Chary

This London News *illustration shows the Ottoman Turks using heavy cannons to defend Kars against the Russians.* (Archive Photos/Hulton Getty Collection)

KARS

TYPE OF ACTION: Ground battle in the Russo-Turkish War
DATE: November 17-18, 1878
LOCATION: City in northeastern Turkey
COMBATANTS: 70,000 Russians vs. 24,000 Turks
PRINCIPAL COMMANDERS: *Russian*, General Count Mikhail Tarielovich Loris-Melikov (1825?-1888); *Turkish*, Hussein Pasha
RESULT: Successful Russian capture of Kars

Russia's war with Turkey in 1877-1878 was signified by battles in southeastern Europe and Asia Minor. While much European attention was directed toward the Russian Siege of Plevna in Bulgaria and the eventual march on Constantinople, a second front was established in Asia Minor to put greater pressure on the Ottomans.

Commanding a powerful column that had pushed through the Caucasus Mountains, Mikhail Tarielovich Loris-Melikov stormed Kars on the night of November 17. Savage fighting resulted in the capitulation of the fortresses protecting the eastern side of the city, with Russian forces entering Kars itself. The southern and western forts held out until November 18, when Turkish commander Hussein Pasha attempted to cut his way through enemy lines. Only a few officers, including Hussein Pasha, escaped successfully.

The victory at Kars resulted in 2,273 Russians killed and wounded. Turkish forces, however, were decimated in the attack. More than 2,500 were killed, with 5,000 more wounded. In addition, 17,000 Turkish soldiers were taken prisoner.

SIGNIFICANCE

The loss of Kars helped convince Turkey to develop peaceful relations with Russia. Following the Treaty of San Stefano (1878) signed with Turkey, and the subsequent Congress of Berlin, Kars remained in Russian hands.

RESOURCES

Furneaux, Rupert. *The Breakfast War*. New York: Crowell, 1968.

Greene, V. R. *Report on the Russian Army and Its Campaigns in Turkey, 1877-1878*. 1878. Reprint. Nashville, Tenn.: Battery Press, 1996.

SEE ALSO: Plevna, Siege of; Russo-Turkish Wars.

Kenneth P. Czech

KASHMIR

A former princely state in southern Asia, Kashmir is administered in two sections: Jammu and Kashmir by India and Azad Kashmir by Pakistan. In the fourteenth century, Kashmir was conquered by Muslims, who converted most of the Hindu and Buddhist population. Despite the large Islamic presence, the British planted seeds of unrest by installing a Hindu ruler there in 1846. When India was partitioned in 1947, Pakistani-backed Muslims revolted against Kashmir's Hindu government. India reacted by sending in troops. After a United Nations cease-fire in 1949, the district was divided between India and Pakistan. The control of Kashmir has remained a point of violent contention since that time, and has sparked armed conflicts between Pakistan and India, such as the Indo-Pakistani Wars (1965-1971). In the 1990's, the two nations even exchanged fire over control of Siachen Glacier, an area incapable of supporting human life.

Jeremiah Taylor

KEARNY, PHILIP

BORN: June 1, 1814; New York, New York
DIED: September 1, 1862; Chantilly, Virginia
PRINCIPAL WARS: Mexican-American War, American Civil War
PRINCIPAL BATTLES: Solferino (1859), Williamsburg (1862), Second Bull Run (1862), Chantilly (1862)
MILITARY SIGNIFICANCE: Kearny was a student of the uses of the cavalry and the values of reconnoitering.

Philip Kearny enlisted in 1837 as a second lieutenant in the First United States Dragoons, serving in the West. Sent to France to study cavalry tactics, he fought with distinction with the French in Algiers in 1840. Upon his return to the United States, he became an aide-de-camp to General Winfield Scott, commander in chief of the U.S. Army.

Kearny resigned his commission in 1846 but rejoined the army when the Mexican-American War (1846-1848) began. His lost his left arm in battle but remained in the Army until 1851. He served in 1859 on the French army staff and fought under Napoleon III at the Battle of Solferino. He returned to the United States at the outbreak of the American Civil War (1861-1865) to serve as a brigadier general in charge of the cavalry with the Army of the Potomac.

During the American Civil War, Kearny fought in at least a dozen battles in the Virginia campaign, including Williamsburg (1862) and the Second Battle of Bull Run (1862). He was shot and killed on September 1, 1862, while reconnoitering in preparation for the Battle of Chantilly. Adored by his troops for his bravery and gallantry, Kearny was described by General Scott as "the most perfect soldier he ever knew."

RESOURCES

De Peyster, J. Watts. *Personal and Military History of Philip Kearny, Major-General United States Volunteers*. New York: Rice and Gage, 1869.

Kearny, Philip. *Letters from the Peninsula: The Civil*

War Letters of General Philip Kearny. Kearny, N.J.: Belle Grove, 1988.
Kearny, Thomas. *General Philip Kearny, Battle Soldier of Five Wars, Including the Conquest of the West*. New York: G. P. Putnam, 1937.
Werstein, Irving. *Kearny, The Magnificent: The Story of General Philip Kearny, 1814-1862*. New York: John Day, 1962.

SEE ALSO: American Civil War; Mexican-American War; Scott, Winfield.

Robert L. Patterson

KEARNY, STEPHEN W.

FULL NAME: Stephen Watts Kearny
ALSO KNOWN AS: The Pathfinder
BORN: August 30, 1794; Newark, New Jersey
DIED: October 31, 1848; St. Louis, Missouri
PRINCIPAL WARS: War of 1812, Mexican-American War
PRINCIPAL BATTLES: Santa Fe (1846), San Pasqual (1846), San Diego (1846), Los Angeles (1847)
MILITARY SIGNIFICANCE: Kearny held several commands in the West and was instrumental in creating the territories of New Mexico and California.

Stephen W. Kearny joined the U.S. Army as a lieutenant and fought in the War of 1812. He was injured at Queenston Heights, captured, paroled, and then made a captain. He saw no further action in that war. Kearny remained in the army after the war, serving in Missouri. Accompanying Henry Atkinson on his Yellowstone Expedition in 1819, Kearny began his long service in the West.

He maintained peace with the Native Americans and was responsible for several treaty negotiations with them. Promoted to colonel in 1836, he became commander of the First Dragoon Regiment, and later the commander of the Third Military District. His last expedition was along the Oregon Trail in 1845. Afterward, he was promoted to brigadier general and appointed commander of the western army.

During the Mexican-American War, Kearny moved against Santa Fe in August, 1846, and took the city by peaceful means, establishing New Mexico as a territory under civil government. Moving his troops to California, he met heavy resistance and was nearly defeated at San Pasqual. However, Kearny captured San Diego in December, 1846, and Los Angeles in January, 1847, with the assistance of naval forces under Commodore Robert Field Stockton. Kearny and Stockton struggled over control of the new territory. Stockton named John C. Frémont governor. Frémont refused to obey Kearny's orders, so Kearny had the governor arrested and court-martialed. Frémont eventually resigned.

Kearny moved on to Baja California, then took his forces back to Fort Leavenworth. He later served temporarily as governor general of Veracruz and Mexico City. He died in St. Louis of complications from the yellow fever he contracted in Mexico City.

RESOURCES
Bauer, K. Jack. *The Mexican War 1846-1848*. New York: Macmillan, 1974.
Clarke, Dwight L. *Original Journals of Henry Smith Turner, with Stephen Watts Kearny to New Mexico and California 1846-1847*. Norman: University of Oklahoma Press, 1966.
Wilkes, Homer D. *Kearny on the Gila*. Scottsdale, Ariz.: H. D. Wilkes, 1990.

SEE ALSO: Mexican-American War.

Ken Willingham

KEITEL, WILHELM

BORN: September 22, 1882; Helmscherode, Braunschweig, Germany
DIED: October 16, 1946; Nuremberg, Germany
PRINCIPAL WARS: World War I, World War II
MILITARY SIGNIFICANCE: As chief of the newly created Supreme Command of the Armed Forces, Keitel ratified Adolf Hitler's instructions, which included numerous criminal orders.

The son of a small estate owner, Wilhelm Keitel entered the army in 1901. During World War I, he served as an officer in an artillery regiment in Belgium and France until selected for General Staff work in 1915. In 1925, he continued his staff duties in the Truppenamt, the new name for the banned General Staff. In August, 1935, War Minister Werner von Blomberg appointed him head of the Wehrmachtsamt, which was responsible for the war ministry's administrative work. After Nazi leader Adolf Hitler abolished the war ministry in early 1938, he selected Keitel to head his new central planning staff, the Supreme Command of the Armed Forces.

Wilhelm Keitel, who became known as "Hitler's Lackey," trusted Hitler's judgment and faithfully supported his decisions, which resulted in massive deaths in Poland and in the Soviet Union. He also issued the Nacht und Nebel (Night and Fog) decrees that permitted the secret arrest of anyone endangering German security. Keitel did not participate in Hitler's decision-making process, although in tactical discussions he supported Hitler's views against those of his fellow officers. He was tried, convicted, and hanged in Nuremberg for war crimes in 1946.

RESOURCES
Hitler's Henchmen: Keitel. Documentary. History Channel, 1998.
Keitel, Wilhelm. *The Memoirs of Field Marshal Keitel*. London: William Kimber, 1965.
Mitcham, Samuel W. *Hitler's Field Marshals and Their Battles*. Chelsea, Mich.: Scarborough House, 1990.
Mueller, Gene. *The Forgotten Field Marshal: Wilhelm Keitel*. Durham, N.C.: Duke University Press, 1979.
Schneller, Helmut. *Hitler and Keitel: An Investigation of the Influence of Party Ideology on the Command of the Armed Forces in Germany Between 1938-1945*. Fort Hays: Kansas State College, 1970.

SEE ALSO: Hitler, Adolf; War Crimes; World War II.
Johnpeter Horst Grill

KESSELRING, ALBERT

ALSO KNOWN AS: "Smiling Albert"
BORN: November 20, 1885; Marktsteft, Bavaria, Germany
DIED: July 16, 1960; Bad Nauheim, West Germany
PRINCIPAL WARS: World War I, World War II
PRINCIPAL BATTLES: Tunisia (1942-1943), Cassino (1943-1944)

MILITARY SIGNIFICANCE: Between 1933 and 1939, Kesselring played a key role in developing Adolf Hitler's air force. He later supported Erwin Rommel's operations in North Africa and skillfully held up the Allied advance in Italy in the Battle of Cassino.

The son of a teacher, Albert Kesselring joined a Bavarian artillery regiment in 1904 and served with his unit in World War I until he was transferred to general staff duties in 1917. After 1918, he remained in the army until 1933 when he was transferred to the new German air force (Luftwaffe). By 1936, Kesselring was chief of the general staff of the air force. As commander of an air fleet he participated in the Polish, French, and Russian campaigns.

In November, 1941, he was transferred to Sicily and named commander of the south, supporting Erwin Rommel's forces in North Africa. In late 1942, Kesselring urged Nazi leader Adolf Hitler to hold Tunisia as a bridgehead, which resulted in the capture of the German army group in Africa in May, 1943. He was more successful in transferring German troops in Sicily across the Straits of Messina and establishing defensive positions near the monastery of Cassino. Kesselring repulsed repeated Allied assaults on Cassino in the winter of 1943-1944 until he was defeated by the Allies in May, 1944. After he was injured in a car accident, he left the Italian front and did not reappear again until March, 1945, as commander in chief west. A British military court sentenced him to death in 1947 for war crimes involving the Ardeatine Caves massacre of 320 Italian prisoners. His sentence was reduced to life imprisonment; he was released from prison because of ill health in 1952 and died eight years later.

RESOURCES
Barnett, Correlli, ed. *Hitler's Generals*. New York: Grove Weidenfeld, 1989.
Battle for the Boot. Masters of War Series. Documentary. Perpetual Motion Film Production, 1993.
Graham, D., and S. Bidwell. *Tug of War: The Battle for Italy 1943-1945*. London: Hodder and Stoughton, 1986.
Kesselring, Albert. *The Memoirs of Field Marshal Kesselring*. Mechanicsburg, Pa.: Stackpole Books, 1997.

Macksey, K. *Kesselring: The Making of the Luftwaffe*. London: Batsford, 1978.

SEE ALSO: Hitler, Adolf; Rommel, Erwin; War crimes; World War I; World War II.

Johnpeter Horst Grill

KETT'S REBELLION

AT ISSUE: Peasant grievances against the landed gentry
DATE: June-August, 1549
LOCATION: Norfolk, East Anglia, England
COMBATANTS: East Anglian peasants and farmers vs. the government of King Edward VI
PRINCIPAL COMMANDERS: *Peasant*, Robert Kett (d. 1549); *English government*, Sir William Parr, marquis of Northampton; John Dudley, earl of Warwick, later duke of Northumberland (1502?-1553)
PRINCIPAL BATTLES: St. Martin-at-Palace-Gate Plain, Dussindale
RESULT: The earl of Warwick's successful use of cavalry and mercenary troops in the rebellion increased his prestige in the council and provided an important basis for his subsequent rise to power through a *coup d'état* against the government of Edward Seymour, first duke of Somerset

BACKGROUND

In May, 1549, Norfolk peasants and farmers began antienclosure agitation that by summer culminated in a rebellion led by the Wymondham tanner Robert Kett against the landed gentry. The summer uprising began in Wymondham, where the Feast of Saint Thomas (July 7) brought together a large crowd. The gathering provided a public forum for the discussion of multiple grievances of the peasants against the local gentry, and from these talks emerged the determination to force open enclosed lands. The peasants and farmers chose Kett, a landed gentleman, as their leader.

ACTION

On July 9, Kett's horde moved to Norwich. Having failed to obtain permission to march through its streets, they set up headquarters at Mount Surrey in Mousehold Heath to the east of the town where they maintained camp for six weeks (July 12-August 26). When the mayor and a number of Norwich gentry saw that several of the town's malcontents had gone over to the rebel camp, they tried to reason with Kett and even endorsed his list of grievances. Meanwhile, the Mousehold camp was joined by other camps from the shire.

On July 21, Kett rejected an overture of peace from London, and the city authorities mounted a defense. However, the next day, the insurgents forced their way into Norwich through Bishop's Gate and captured the mayor and other town leaders. The council in London sent an expeditionary force of 1,500 men including some mercenaries under the command of Sir William Parr, the marquis of Northampton, a courtier with little military experience. On July 30, his army entered the city, and Kett withdrew to Mousehold. Northampton unwittingly closed the city and held it against the camp, thereby diverting his forces to defend a sprawling site that could have provided them maneuverability. The next day Northampton's army repelled a determined attack from the camp but was defeated on August 1 in the Battle of **St. Martin-at-Palace-Gate Plain** and withdrew to Cambridge. The rebels captured Norwich and unsuccessfully attempted to take Yarmouth on August 17. The same day, John Dudley, the earl of Warwick (and later duke of Northumberland), was appointed commander of the government force for the Norfolk uprising.

Warwick marched via Cambridge, Thetford, and Wymondham, receiving reinforcement on the way, and arrived at Intwood, three miles from Norwich, on August 23. His force included five peers, three sons of peers, and several experienced soldiers and administrators. After an initial attempt at negotiation failed, his army broke through St. Stephen's Gate, the Brazen Doors, and St. Benedict's Gate and took control of the city on August 24. Street fighting ensued with the rebels who had remained within the city walls. Numerous rebels were captured and 49 of them executed. However, they set fire to Conisford Street and their camp at Mousehold during the night of August 25 and moved to Dussindale. Their dispersal enabled Warwick to use his cavalry. On August 27, he chased them with all his horses and about 100 mercenary foot soldiers, leaving the English troops to guard the city. Following an unsuccessful offer of pardon, the earl's professionals charged through the rebel ranks, ignoring their screen of gentlemen prisoners. More than 3,000 insurgents were slain in **Dussindale** on the afternoon of Tuesday, August 27, and the rebellion came to an end.

AFTERMATH

Kett was captured and sent to London for trial along with his elder brother William. The two condemned rebels were brought back to Norfolk for execution. On December 7, Robert was hanged at Norwich Castle and William from Wymondham steeple.

RESOURCES

Bindoff, Samuel T. *Kett's Rebellion*. 1949. Reprint. London: Historical Association, 1968.
Cornwall, Julian. *Revolt of the Peasantry*. London: Routledge & Kegan Paul, 1977.
Fletcher, Anthony. *Tudor Rebellion*. 1968. 3d ed. London: Longman, 1992.
Land, Stephen K. *Kett's Rebellion: The Norfolk Rising of 1549*. Ipswich, England: Boydell Press, 1977.
MacCulloch, Diarmaid. "Kett's Rebellion in Context." *Past and Present* 84 (1979).
Sotherton, Nicholas. *The Commoyson in Norfolk 1549*. Stibbard, England: Larks Press, 1987.

SEE ALSO: Anglo-French Wars; Anglo-Scottish Wars of 1513-1560.

Narasingha P. Sil

KGB

In full, *Komitet gosudarstvennoi Bezopasnosti*, or "Committee for State Security." The KGB was the primary intelligence/counterintelligence agency and political police of the former Soviet Union from 1954 until 1991. The last and most enduring of a long line of similar agencies (beginning with the Cheka in 1917), the KGB operated in domestic circles as well as in the world of international espionage. In the four decades following World War II (1939-1945), the KGB engaged in more espionage activity than any of its Western counterparts, and infiltrated the ranks of every major intelligence agency in the world, save the CIA. In the Soviet Union, it served as an instrument of social and political control—as the Communist Party's national monitor. The KGB also controlled approximately 300,000 troops, with artillery, armor, and naval vessels. This force, under the Border Guards Chief Directorate, was charged with keeping the Soviet Union's borders impregnable—to foreigners wishing to illegally enter and to citizens wanting to slip out. Just prior to the fall of the Soviet Union in 1991, the KGB was stripped of military and many domestic functions.

Jeremiah Taylor

KHAIR ED-DĪN

ALSO KNOWN AS: Khizr; Barbarossa
BORN: c. 1483; Greece
DIED: 1546; Istanbul
PRINCIPAL WARS: War of the Holy League, Third and Fourth Valois-Habsburg Wars
PRINCIPAL BATTLES: Tunis (1534), Preveza (1538)
MILITARY SIGNIFICANCE: Created a powerful fleet, making the Ottoman Empire the dominant sea power in the Mediterranean for most of the sixteenth century.

The youngest of four sons, Khair ed-dīn began as a pirate, operating from the island base of Jerba, off the coast of Tunisia, around 1504. His red beard and fearsome reputation earned him the nickname Barbarossa. Moving to Djidjelli in 1512, he used it as a base for capturing towns on the Algerian coast in 1517. In the following year, Khair ed-dīn paid homage to Ottoman sultan Selim I, who made him governor (*bey*) of Algiers and provided troops, in return for efforts against Spain. In 1519, Khair ed-dīn temporarily captured Algiers from the Spanish. While armies under Süleyman I extended Ottoman influence in the Balkans and Hungary, he consolidated Ottoman control of the eastern Maghrib (Barbary coast), improving the economy of Algiers, raiding the coasts of southern Italy and Sicily, and capturing Tunis, in 1534. Charles V (king of Spain and Holy Roman emperor) sent Genoese admiral Andrea Doria and a fleet of 600 ships to stop Khair ed-dīn's depredations. Khair ed-dīn was defeated off the coast of Tunis, leading to a sack of the city by a Spanish army and the establishment of a Spanish protectorate there.

In 1533, Khair ed-dīn was made an admiral by Süleyman I and proved his worth by fashioning a Turkish navy from a collection of Barbary pirate fleets, requiring better training and discipline, and building larger and more heavily armed galleys. In the war with the Holy League (Spain, the Papacy, Venice), he pillaged Italian coastal cities (May-August, 1537), and though driven off in his Siege of Corfu (August-September, 1537), attacked the Venetian garrisons at Nauplia and Malvasia, raided Crete, and captured the Venetian islands of Patmos, Aegina, Ios, Paros, and Skyros. (October, 1537-July, 1538). After a nominal but indecisive Turkish victory at Preveza (1538), in which Doria lost seven galleys, Venice sued for peace in 1539, recognizing Aegean losses, giving up footholds in northern Greece, and establishing Ottoman dominance in the Mediterranean.

During the Fourth Valois-Habsburg War in which France allied itself with the Ottomans, Khair ed-dīn joined forces with a French fleet in attacks against Catalonia, southern France, and northwestern Italy. In 1543, a combined fleet under his command besieged and sacked imperial Nice. Following the Treaty of Crépy (September 18, 1544), he served at the sultan's court in Istanbul until his death in 1546.

RESOURCES
Bradford, Ernle. *The Sultan's Admiral: The Life of Barbarossa*. New York: Harcourt, Brace & World, 1973.
Guilmartin, Francis. *Gunpowder and Galleys: Changing Technology and Military Warfare at Sea in the Sixteenth Century*. Cambridge, England: Cambridge University Press, 1974.
Kunt, Metin, and Christine Woodhed, eds. *Süleyman the Magnificent and His Age*. New York: Longman, 1995.
Shaw, Stanford J. *History of the Ottoman Empire and Modern Turkey*. Cambridge, England: Cambridge University Press, 1976.

SEE ALSO: Doria, Andrea; Mohács; Selim I; Süleyman I; Valois-Habsburg Wars.

John Powell

KHĀLID IBN-AL-WALĪD

ALSO KNOWN AS: Sīf Allāh; Sayf Allāh
BORN: Late sixth century; probably Mecca, Arabia
DIED: 642; Location disputed (either Hims, Syria or Medina, Arabia)
PRINCIPAL WARS: Medinese-Meccan War, Ridda Wars, Muslim Conquests of Iraq and Syria
PRINCIPAL BATTLES: Uḥud (625), Siege of Mecca (630), March to Syria (634)
MILITARY SIGNIFICANCE: Among the finest of the early Muslim generals, ibn-al-Walīd helped consolidate Muslim control over the Arabian peninsula, Iraq, and Syria.

Born into the powerful Meccan Quraysh tribe and a contemporary of Muḥammad, Khālid ibn-al-Walīd was initially among the pagan oligarchy that bitterly opposed Islam. After Muḥammad's emigration to Medina in 622, the Muslims began to systematically attack Meccan commercial activities in the Medinese-Meccan War (622-630). Ibn-al-Walīd led a retaliatory assault on Medina in 625, winning a tentative victory at the Battle of Uḥud. Sensing the Muslims' advantage, ibn-al-Walīd converted to Islam in 629 and assisted Muḥammad in the invasion of Mecca in 630.

In 632, the caliph Abū Bakr commissioned ibn-al-Walīd to suppress an anti-Muslim tribal revolt known as the Ridda Wars (632-634), in which he came under criticism for killing fellow Muslims in the course of battle. In 633, Abū Bakr sent ibn-al-Walīd into Iraq, where he contested Persian control of several cities along the Euphrates River. He was then ordered to Syria, where—after a legendary trek across the desert in 634—he engaged the Byzantines and participated in the conquest of Bostra, Damascus, and Hims.

Seeking to promote early Muslim converts into key government positions at the expense of the old Quraysh aristocracy, the caliph ʿUmar relieved ibn-al-Walīd of command in 634, relegating him to only marginal roles in future conquests.

RESOURCES
Donner, Fred McGraw. *The Early Islamic Conquests*. Princeton, N.J.: Princeton University Press, 1981.
Kennedy, Hugh. *The Prophet and the Age of the Caliphates*. Reprint. London: Longman Group, 1999.

Watt, W. Montgomery. *Muhammad: Prophet and Statesman*. London: Oxford University Press, 1961.

See also: ʿAmr ibn al-ʿĀṣ; Byzantine-Muslim Wars; Muslim Conquests.

Timothy L. Wood

Khalkin-Gol

Type of action: Ground battle in Second Sino-Japanese War
Date: May-September, 1939
Location: Manchuko, outer Mongolian border between the Khalkin-Gol River and the village of Nomonhan
Combatants: 57,000 Russians with 844 armored vehicles vs. 30,000 Japanese with 92 armored vehicles
Principal commanders: *Russian*, General Georgy Zhukov (1896-1974); *Japanese*, Lieutenant General Michitaro Komatsubara
Result: After the Japanese attacks were stopped, the Russian counterattack encircled and nearly annihilated the Japanese forces

Disputes over primacy in Mongolia led the Japanese into a series of punitive attacks. On May 28, 1939, the Japanese, under Lieutenant General Michitaro Komatsubara, launched a major assault. Stout Russian resistance frustrated the Japanese into ordering stronger attacks between July 3 and July 17. Strong Russian defenses inflicted terrible losses, and the stymied Japanese dug in.

On August 20, 1939, General Georgy Zhukov launched a classic double envelopment attack. Overwhelmed by superior Russian artillery and tanks, Japanese forces resorted to bayonet attacks and Molotov cocktails to stop the Russians. Although Russian attacks demonstrated considerable skill in combined arms tactics, they often were too direct and very costly. By August 30, the Russians had surrounded the Japanese, but heavy Russian casualties and major events in Europe reduced Mongolia to a sideshow, so in September, both sides decided on a cease-fire. During the fighting, the Japanese suffered more than 17,000 casualties, and the Russians admitted to some 10,000.

Significance
Although many Japanese officers sought to expand Japan's possessions, the severe losses at Khalkin-Gol, also known as the Nomonhan Incident, convinced them to look elsewhere. With the United States unprepared for war and the British fighting Nazi leader Adolf Hitler, Khalkin-Gol persuaded the Japanese that Pearl Harbor, the Philippines, the Dutch East Indies, and Malaysia would be easier, less costly conquests.

Resources
Coox, Alvin D. *Nomonhan: Japan Against Russia*. Stanford, Calif.: Stanford University Press, 1985.
Drea, Edward J. *Nomonhan: Japanese-Soviet Tactical Combat, 1939*. Fort Leavenworth, Kans.: Combat Studies Institute, 1981.
Snow, Philip. "Nomonhan: The Unknown Victory." *History Today* 40, no. 7 (July, 1990): 22-27.

See also: Russo-Japanese War; World War II; Zhukov, Georgy.

Kevin B. Reid

Kharkov

Type of action: Series of ground battles in World War II
Date: 1942-1943
Location: Kharkov, Soviet Union (later Karkiv, Ukraine)
Combatants: Germans vs. Russians
Principal commanders: *German*, Field Marshal Erich von Manstein (1887-1973); *Russian*, Marshal Semyon Timoshenko (1895-1970), Marshal Nikolai Vatutin (1901-1943)
Result: The Germans stopped the Russian winter offensive and prepared the way for an attack on Kursk

In October, 1941, the Germans had seized the Soviet railway center of Kharkov. On May 12, 1942, the Russians, under Marshal Semyon Timoshenko, decided to cross the Donetz River in order to encircle and liberate Kharkov. However, the Germans encircled the Russian forces, and the offensive ended on May 30, with the rout of three Russian armies. Timoshenko had lost 1,200 tanks and more than 200,000 troops.

German soldiers take cover outside a burning house near Kharkov. (Archive Photos/Hulton Getty Collection)

In early 1943, Russian commanders prepared for a counteroffensive. The Russian force levels in the region were 640,000 men, 1,200 tanks, 13,000 field guns and mortars, and 926 planes; the Germans had 636,000 men, 1,000 tanks, 16,000 field guns and mortars, and 1,220 planes. On February 11, Soviet marshal Nikolai Vatutin crossed the Donetz near Kharkov and encircled the city on February 16. On February 19, German forces under Field Marshal Erich von Manstein launched a counterattack. On March 9, the Germans reached the city, and their tanks rolled into the city. On March 15, the Germans closed off Kharkov, defeated the last pocket of Russian resistance, and occupied the city.

SIGNIFICANCE

The fall of Kharkov stopped the Soviet winter offensive and freed the German general staff to prepare for major offensive operations in the Kursk theater.

RESOURCES

Carruthers, Bob, and John Erickson. *The Russian Front, 1941-1945*. New York: Sterling, 1999.

Mellenthin, F. W. *Panzer Battles: A Study in the Employment of Armor in the Second World War*. Norman: University of Oklahoma Press, 1955.

The War in Europe. The War Chronicles: World War II series. Documentary. A&E Home Video, 1983.

Winchester, Charles. *Ostfront: Hitler's War on Russia, 1941-1945*. Oxford, England: Osprey, 1998.

SEE ALSO: Kursk; Tanks; World War II.

Michael J. Siler

KHARTOUM, SIEGE OF

TYPE OF ACTION: Siege in the Mahdist Uprising
DATE: 1884-1885
LOCATION: Khartoum, Sudan
COMBATANTS: Egyptians and British vs. Mahdists (Sudanese and Africans)
PRINCIPAL COMMANDERS: *Mahdist*, Muḥammad Ahmad (1844-1885); *British*, General Charles George Gordon (1833-1885)
RESULT: The fall of Khartoum strengthened Muḥammad Ahmad's control of the Sudan

In early 1884, the khedive (viceroy) of Egypt appointed Charles George Gordon as the governor general of the Sudan, requesting that he restore good government and peacefully evacuate from Khartoum all European and Egyptian persons because of the grave danger posed by the jihad (holy war) declaration by Muḥammad Ahmad, who had declared himself the Madhi (messiah).

In mid-February, General Gordon arrived in Khartoum without troops or credibility. His earlier attempt to negotiate with the Madhi failed, and his decision to release to the public the khedive's order to peacefully evacuate Khartoum stunned its inhabitants. Faced with an untenable situation, matters were made worse with ill-informed statements, which suggested that a British expedition was coming to save Khartoum and that Indian troops would crush the Madhi's armies. On March 13, the British government denied these statements.

Meanwhile, the Madhi's armies overran the province of Berber, cutting off the city's links with the outside world. In April, the Madhi's advanced guard occupied positions around Khartoum. In late October, the Madhi arrived, giving orders to lay siege. In January, 1885, a relief expedition was ordered by the British government, but it was too late. On January 26, the Madhi ordered a final assault of Khartoum, and its exhausted defenders were killed, including General Gordon.

SIGNIFICANCE

The fall of Khartoum signaled the end of direct British influence in the Sudan.

RESOURCES

Featherstone, Donald F. *Khartoum 1885: General Gordon's Last Stand*. London: Osprey, 1998.

Holt, P. M. *The Mahdist State in the Sudan*. Oxford, England: Clarendon Press, 1970.

Holt, P. M., and M. W. Daly. *The History of the Sudan: From the Coming of Islam to the Present Day*. Boulder, Colo.: Westview Press, 1979.

SEE ALSO: Abu Klea; British Colonial Wars; Gordon, Charles George; Muḥammad Aḥmad; Religion and war.

Michael J. Siler

KHE SANH, SIEGE OF

TYPE OF ACTION: Ground and air battle in the Vietnam Conflict
DATE: January 21-April 6, 1968
LOCATION: Marine air base at Khe Sanh in northern province of South Vietnam
COMBATANTS: 3,500 Marines and 2,100 South Vietnamese soldiers vs. 22,000 North Vietnamese troops
PRINCIPAL COMMANDERS: *United States*, General William Westmoreland (1914-   ); *North Vietnam*, General Vo Nguyen Giap (1911-   )
RESULT: Although U.S. firepower clearly overwhelmed the North Vietnamese, General Giap refused to admit defeat, claiming the battle was a deliberate diversionary tactic

As part of the Tet Offensive, in January, 1968, North Vietnamese troops directed by General Vo Nguyen Giap attacked the marine air base at Khe Sanh, scoring an early direct hit on the base's main ammunition dump, which detonated more than 1,500 tons of explosives. With little food and a precarious water supply, marines and other soldiers were besieged for seventy-seven days. The United States retaliated with massive round-the-clock air strikes, one of the most concentrated aerial bombardments in the history of warfare.

General William Westmoreland, seeking a decisive set-piece battle, placed the defense of Khe

A Sikorsky S-64 Skycrane lifts the air cavalry and its equipment to the Khe Sanh landing zone. (Archive Photos/Hulton Getty Collection)

Sanh over all other military operations, with an estimated five tons of artillery and aerial munitions deployed for every North Vietnamese soldier. During the siege, 205 U.S. Marines and an estimated 10,000 to 15,000 North Vietnamese were killed in action. After the battle, Khe Sanh reverted to its previous status as a strategically unimportant site.

SIGNIFICANCE

Although the United States claimed victory, the siege at Khe Sanh brought about serious debate on U.S. military strategy in Vietnam. Soon after, General Westmoreland was relieved of his command.

RESOURCES

Hammel, Eric. *Khe Sanh: Siege in the Clouds, An Oral History.* Pacifica, Calif.: Pacifica Press, 2000.
Pisor, Robert. *The End of the Line: The Siege of Khe Sanh.* New York: Ballantine Books, 1982.
Prados, John, and Ray W. Stubbe. *Valley of Decision: The Siege of Khe Sanh.* Boston: Houghton Mifflin, 1991.

SEE ALSO: Hue; Tet Offensive; Vietnam Conflict; Vo Nguyen Giap; Westmoreland, William.

Margaret Boe Birns

KHMER-CHAM WARS

AT ISSUE: Khmer territorial expansion and political control over Champa
DATE: 1050-1203
LOCATION: Cambodia and Champa
COMBATANTS: Cambodians vs. Chams
PRINCIPAL COMMANDERS: *Cambodian,* Suryavarman II (r. 1113-1150) and Jayavarman VII (c. 1120-c. 1215); *Cham,* Harivarman IV (r. 1074-c. 1100)
PRINCIPAL BATTLES: Vijaya, Tonle Sap, Yasoharapura
RESULT: Khmer-Cham wars are inconclusive but do contribute to the eventual decline of both powers at the hands of the Thai and Vietnamese

BACKGROUND

During the first half of the eleventh century, the Khmer Empire approached its zenith under Suryavarman I. The empire extended to the Burmese-Malay frontier, encompassed most of modern-day Thailand and Laos, and extended to the mouth of the Mekong River. In the east, meanwhile, the neighboring Champa Dynasty, located roughly between Hue and the northern border of the Mekong River delta, began a nearly five-hundred-year-long, intermittent conflict with its newly independent neighbor, the kingdom of Vietnam. Adding to Cham concerns, Cambodian forces launched a limited invasion against the Nha Trang region in 950. Suryavarman, however, anxious to expand Khmer authority in the Me Nam valley to the east, made peace with the Chams. With his death in 1050, however, the period of Khmer-Cham peace ended.

ACTION

From 1050-1066, during the reign of Udayadityavarman II, the loose skein of Khmer-Cham peace unraveled. Not until 1074, however, during the reign of the Khmer king Harshavarman III, did Champa attempt a major invasion of Cambodia. While the historical sources are incomplete, it is believed that the Cham, led by King Harivarman IV, defeated the Khmer forces. Meanwhile, the heir to the Cham throne also defeated the Khmer in the south and took the city of Sambor along the Mekong River. While this fighting went against the Khmer, it remained far from decisive, and it did not prevent the rival empires from briefly joining China in 1076 in an ill-fated campaign against Vietnam.

During the reign of ancient Cambodia's greatest king, Suryavarman II, the Khmer Empire launched a series of wars against its western neighbors. In 1127, a 20,000-man Khmer army invaded Vietnam only to be repulsed. Three years later, the Cham joined their former Khmer enemies in yet another invasion of Vietnam. In a final attack against Vietnam, in 1150, Khmer forces struck deep into the heart of the Red River Valley. The Cham, however, who refused to support the Khmer after 1131, were themselves attacked by Cambodia in 1138. In 1145, yet another Cambodian invasion led to the capture of the Cham capital at **Vijaya** and Khmer occupation for the next four years. By the time of Suryavarman's death in 1150, however, near constant warfare had begun to sap Khmer strength and contributed to rebellions in various parts of the empire. Perhaps distracted by Mon uprisings, the Khmer were unable to stifle a successful Cham revolt in 1158.

Between 1177 and 1203, Khmer-Cham fighting reached new heights. In 1177, a Cham fleet sailed up the Mekong and into the great **Tonle Sap** itself. There the victorious Cham took, then destroyed **Yasoharapura**, the Khmer capital. Under the leadership of a new monarch, Jayavarman VII, Khmer forces expelled the Cham. Jayavarman first recruited dissident Chams living in Cambodia, who along with Thai soldiers tipped the balance of power in Cambodia's favor. In 1181, the Khmer navy bested its Cham opponents. Nine years later, Jayavarman's forces began the first of many invasions of the Cham homeland. Finally, in 1203, organized Cham resistance collapsed.

AFTERMATH
For nearly twenty years, Champa remained under direct Khmer control. Jayavarman's decision to permanently garrison Champa proved effective but draining for the empire as a whole. When continued Mon rebellions forced the withdrawal of Khmer forces from Champa, Cambodia quickly lost control over its vassal. In 1223, the Chams regained their independence. Champa continued to exist as an independent state until finally succumbing to the Vietnamese in 1471. Though more successful in maintaining their independence, Khmer decline also set in after 1220, accelerated by the rise of powerful Thai and Vietnamese states to the east and west.

RESOURCES
Cady, John F. *Southeast Asia: Its Historical Development*. New York: McGraw-Hill, 1964.
_____. *Thailand, Burma, Laos, and Cambodia*. Englewood Cliffs, N.J.: Prentice-Hall, 1966.
Cœdès, G. *The Making of South East Asia*. Berkeley: University of California Press, 1969.
Jumsai, Manich. *History of Thailand and Cambodia: From the Days of Angkor to the Present*. Bangkok: Chalermnit, 1970.
SarDesai, D. R. *Southeast Asia: Past and Present*. Boulder, Colo.: Westview, 1997.

SEE ALSO: Champa Kingdom; Jayavarman VII; Vietnamese-Cham Wars.

Sidney Pash

KHMER-THAI WARS

AT ISSUE: Siamese attempts to exert political dominance over Cambodia
DATE: 1352-1434
LOCATION: Northern Cambodia
COMBATANTS: Cambodians vs. Siamese
PRINCIPAL COMMANDERS: *Siam*, King Ramadhipati I (r. 1351-?); *Cambodia,* Ponhea-Yat (c. 1405-c. 1467)
PRINCIPAL BATTLE: Siege of Angkor
RESULT: Political and territorial decline of the Khmer Empire

BACKGROUND
By the middle of the fourteenth century, the once-great Khmer Empire, which at its height encompassed much of modern Laos, Vietnam, and Thailand, was in the midst of an agonizing centuries-long decline. The Mongol conquest of China during the thirteenth century transformed what had been a slow southern migration of the Thai people from Yunnan to Southeast Asia into a mass exodus. The refugees soon established large Thai communities in the northern reaches of the Khmer Empire. The favorable climate and rich soil of the Me Nam River basin soon produced sufficient surplus for the Thai newcomers to build formidable armies with which to defend their new lands and expand at the expense of the increasingly beleaguered Khmer. Beginning in 1287, Rama Khamheng transformed the tiny Thai kingdom of Sukhothai into a regional power at Khmer expense. In 1351, Ramadhipati I established a rival Thai dynasty at Phra Nakhon Si Ayutthaya, which, like its rival, came to dominate the declining Khmer Empire. For most of the next century, from the 1350's to the 1430's, Cambodia and the Siamese of Phra Nakhon Si Ayutthaya remained locked in a near-continuous struggle for territory from which Siam emerged the dominant regional power.

ACTION
Within a year of founding Phra Nakhon Si Ayutthaya, Ramadhipati sent two separate armies against Cambodia in an attempt to subjugate the Khmer Empire. While successful along the frontier, the Thai forces, apparently exhausted as they neared the Khmer capital at Angkor, were

surprised and overwhelmed. Rather than pursue their foe, however, the Khmer focused on taking war booty and prisoners and allowed the remnants of the Thai army to escape. In December, 1351, Thai forces under the command of King Ramadhipati again invaded and shortly began a devastating sixteen-month Siege of **Angkor**. During the invasion of the capital, Siamese forces turned back repeated Khmer attempts to break the siege. Eventually, Siamese forces broke through the city's eastern gate and took control of the magnificent Khmer capital and its 100,000 inhabitants. During the siege, the Khmer king, Lampong, died either in battle or from illness. His brother, who had directed Khmer forces to victory in 1351, also perished. Though most of the city's treasure fell into Siamese hands, a small band of Khmer troops managed to fight their way through Siamese lines and, in the process, spirit away the royal regalia. Following their capture of Angkor, a Siamese garrison of 10,000 men occupied the town and Ramadhipati placed his son Batas on the throne. Nearby provinces also succumbed to Siamese forces and were administered by Thai governors. The outer provinces, however, remained independent.

In 1354, the Khmer prince Soryotei, who had attempted to relieve Angkor during the Thai siege only to be driven back into Laos, raised a new army and retook the capital. Crowned king in 1357, Soryotei fought a series of intermittent wars with Siam for the next dozen years. While ultimately inconclusive, Khmer forces regained the bulk of the territory lost during the 1350's.

During the final decade of the fourteenth century, Thai forces once again attacked the Khmer Empire in force. After a seven-month siege of Angkor, Siamese forces took the city in 1393. Various sources argue that Thai troops, who had earlier sought refuge with the Cambodians, opened the city's gates for their compatriots, thus allowing for the rapid capture of the capital. Other sources, however, note that traitorous Khmer generals opened the city gates for the besieging Thai troops. In any event, after taking Angkor, the Siamese took the royal regalia and left behind a permanent garrison of some 5,000 troops.

In 1430, the Siamese king, Boromaraja II sent an army to retake Angkor from Ponhea-Yat, heir to the Khmer throne. After yet another seven-month siege, Siamese forces retook and once again looted the glorious Khmer capital. Boromaraja's son, Intaburi, stayed behind to govern Angkor, but his rule proved short-lived. A month after his installment, Ponhea-Yat's emissaries came to the capital ostensibly to pay homage to their new Siamese ruler. Once in striking distance, however, they murdered Intaburi. Ponhea-Yat then attacked and retook Angkor, whose populace joined in slaughtering the bulk of the Siamese.

Ponhea-Yat soon discovered that Angkor had suffered mortal damage during the latest Thai siege. The vast system of canals that brought sufficient water from the Tonle Sap to irrigate some 12.5 million acres of land sustained sufficient damage to severely undermine agricultural production in the Angkor region. In 1434, Suryavarman III moved his capital south beyond the Tonle Sap to present day Phnom Penh.

AFTERMATH

During the remainder of the fifteenth century, the Khmer and Siamese empires fought a series of wars in which Siam attempted to secure Khmer submission as a tributary state, while the Khmer, with intermittent success, attempted to regain their lost territory and independence. As the century drew to a close, the Siamese of Phra Nakhon Si Ayutthaya completed the political integration of the Thai people and went on to establish Siam as a great regional power. From their new capital at Lovek, meanwhile, Khmer leaders played the occasional role of spoiler, frequently siding with Phra Nakhon Si Ayutthaya's enemies. They were, however, never able to reestablish Khmer power to anything near its thirteenth century greatness.

RESOURCES

Charnvit, Kasetsiri. *The Rise of Ayudhya: A History of Siam in the Fourteenth and Fifteenth Centuries*. Kuala Lumpur, Malaysia: Oxford University Press, 1976

Jumsai, Manich. *History of Thailand and Cambodia: From the Days of Angkor to the Present*. Bangkok: Chalermnit, 1970.

SarDesai, D. R. *Southeast Asia: Past and Present*. Boulder Colo.: Westview, 1997.

SEE ALSO: Siamese-Cambodian Wars.

Sidney Pash

KIEV

TYPE OF ACTION: Ground battle in World War II
DATE: September 16-26, 1941
LOCATION: Kiev, Ukraine, Soviet Union
COMBATANTS: 710,000 Germans vs. 680,000 Soviets
PRINCIPAL COMMANDERS: *German*, Field Marshal Gerd von Rundstedt (1875-1953); *Soviet*, Colonel General Mikhail Petrovich Kirpanos
RESULT: German annihilation of Soviet southwestern front

On September 16, 1941, 680,000 Soviet troops of Colonel General Mikhail Petrovich Kirpanos's southwestern front were encircled in the "Kiev pocket" (130 miles in width and depth) when German armored forces advancing from Smolensk in the north linked up with German armored forces advancing from Kremenchug in the south at Lokhvitsa (125 miles east of Kiev). For the next ten days, soldiers of six trapped Soviet armies, the entire strength of southwestern front, struggled to break their encirclement, while German forces, coordinated by Field Marshal Gerd von Rundstedt, fought to reduce the pocket.

Although some 15,000 Soviet troops ultimately escaped, Kirpanos's armies did not possess sufficient power to achieve a large-scale breakout against an enemy who enjoyed numerical superiority and command of the skies. Kiev fell on September 20. Six days later, Soviet resistance inside the pocket ended. Four Soviet armies were entirely destroyed; two others were severely emasculated. According to German statistics, the Battle of Kiev cost the Soviets 665,000 prisoners, 824 tanks, 3,018 guns, and 418 antitank guns.

SIGNIFICANCE

The annihilation of Soviet southwestern front in the Battle of Kiev allowed Rundstedt's forces to advance farther on the southern part of the eastern front, capturing central and eastern Ukraine and most of the Crimea in the last months of 1941.

RESOURCES

Boog, Horst, et al. *Germany and the Second World War*. Vol. 4 in *The Attack on the Soviet Union*. Oxford, England: Clarendon Press, 1998.
Glantz, David, and Jonathan House. *When Titans Clashed: How the Red Army Stopped Hitler*. Lawrence: University of Kansas Press, 1995.
Ziemke, Earl F., and Magna E. Bauer. *Moscow to Stalingrad: Decision in the East*. Washington, D.C.: U.S. Army Center for Military History, 1987.

SEE ALSO: Rundstedt, Gerd von; Smolensk; World War II

Bruce J. DeHart

KIGERI IV

FULL NAME: Kigeri Rwabugiri
BORN: Date unknown; Rwanda
DIED: 1895; Kigali, Rwanda
PRINCIPAL WARS: Invasions into Uganda and Tanzania
MILITARY SIGNIFICANCE: Kigeri IV united the kingdom of Rwanda and built a professional army, successfully resisting imperialist pressures.

Kigeri IV was the last precolonial king of Rwanda and was responsible for enlarging the kingdom to its farthest extent. The aristocratic Tutsi based their wealth on cattle, and from the 1400's they had gradually extended their primacy over the Hutu, an agricultural people. Kigeri ruled from 1865 to 1895 and completed this process.

Pressed by population increases that generated competition for scarce land, Kigeri reorganized and centralized authority in the kingdom and abolished hereditary appointments. Having created a bureaucracy at court and local officials who were loyal to him and not competitors for power, he then built up an army of Hutu conscripts under Tutsi officers and equipped it with firearms. Reinforcing the Tutsi definition of wealth, regiments fostered social cohesion by identifying with their regimental cattle and were known by the name of their herd. This force subdued the last Hutu chieftains and assured the hegemony of the Tutsi, who became the dominant group economically and socially, reducing the Hutu to little more than serfs. Farm plots were reallocated to cattle raising. Disadvantaged Tutsi often were absorbed into the Hutu or crossed the borders to tend cattle for other tribes, if they had none of their own. More successful Hutu moved upward into Tutsi society. The caste system was maintained strictly, however, in the army.

Kigeri's reign was one of almost constant warfare. He extended the kingdom's sovereignty into what later became Uganda and Tanzania, as well as Hutu territories of Burundi. He was able to complete Rwandan expansion by subjugating the last Hutu chiefdoms. He was also able to resist European imperialism because cattle remained the basis of wealth, and trade goods were not desired. Firearms were the only trade goods freely admitted to the kingdom.

RESOURCES
Newbury, Catherine. *The Cohesion of Oppression*. N.Y.: Columbia University Press, 1988.
Rennier, J. K. "The Pre-Colonial Kingdom of Rwanda." *Transafrican Journal of History* 2 (1972): 11-54.

SEE ALSO: Rwanda and Burundi, Civil Wars of.
Norbert Brockman

KILLIECRANKIE

TYPE OF ACTION: Ground battle during the War of the Grand Alliance
DATE: July 27, 1689
LOCATION: Killiecrankie Pass (thirty-six miles northwest of Dundee, Perth and Kinross, Scotland)
COMBATANTS: 1,900 Scottish Highlanders vs. 3,500 English government troops
PRINCIPAL COMMANDERS: *Highland*, John Graham of Claverhouse, First Viscount Dundee (1649?-1689); *Government (William III)*, Major General Hugh Mackay of Scourie
RESULT: A Pyrrhic victory for the Highland army

During the Jacobite Rebellions, part of the War of the Grand Alliance in which the Scottish expressed their opposition to William III, the English Williamite army came out of Killiecrankie Pass around midday and saw the approach of John Graham, Viscount Dundee, and his army from around a hill. Major General Hugh Mackay's men, on low ground, turned quickly to face the Highland army and formed three ranks. However, Dundee waited until the sun was out of his eyes before giving the order to charge. Despite their orders, many of Dundee's men fired their weapons on the run with little effect, then threw away their firearms continuing their rush with broadswords.

The charge of Dundee's Highlanders was a terrifying spectacle for the Williamite soldiers who had already fired but, failing to halt the charge, had no time to reload. Although some of the government's forces stood their ground and were killed, many of Mackay's battalions broke and ran back through Killiecrankie Pass. Dundee charged with his cavalry but in the smoke and confusion lost contact with his army and fell mortally wounded to a musket ball. In the end, Mackay lost about 1,200 men, and the Highland army suffered 700 dead.

SIGNIFICANCE
The battle was a tactical success for the Highlanders, but replacing their losses was more difficult. Dundee's death was most catastrophic as his personality and inspiration united the Highlanders' divergent interests.

RESOURCES
Gooch, Leo. *The Desperate Faction? The Jacobites of North-east England, 1688-1745*. Hull, England: University of Hull Press, 1995.
Hesketh, Christian, and Magnus Linklater. *For King and Conscience*. London: Weidenfeld & Nicolson, 1989.
Hill, James Michael. *Celtic Warfare, 1595-1763*. Edinburgh, Scotland: John Donald, 1986.
Lenman, Bruce. *The Jacobite Risings in Britain, 1689-1746*. Reprint. Aberdeen, Scotland: Scottish Cultural Press, 1995.

SEE ALSO: Boyne; Grand Alliance, War of the; Jacobite Rebellions.
C. E. Wood

KIM IL SUNG

ALSO KNOWN AS: Kim Song Ju; Kim Sung Chu
BORN: April 15, 1912; Pyongyang, North Korea
DIED: July 8, 1994; Pyongyang, North Korea
PRINCIPAL WARS: Sino-Japanese War, Korean War
PRINCIPAL BATTLES: Putianbao (1937), Seoul (1950)

MILITARY SIGNIFICANCE: As the founder and builder of the Korean Communist armed forces, Kim transformed the Korean People's Army from a farmer and refugee guerrilla army into a Soviet-style conventional army.

From 1925 to 1941, Kim Il Sung (born Kim Song Ju) lived in Manchuria, where he joined the Korean Communist Workers' Party in 1931 and established the Korean People's Anti-Japanese Army in 1932. In 1934, he renamed his army the Korean People's Army (KPA) and joined the Chinese Communist Northeast Anti-Japanese Allied Army. He served as a battalion, regiment, and division commander, and won the Battle of Putianbao in 1937. After the allied army failed, he led 600 remaining Korean soldiers into Russia in 1941 and became a battalion commander in the Soviet Red Army's Eighty-eighth Brigade of the First Far East Army Corp. On August 9, 1945, he returned to Korea with the Red Army. During the Soviet occupation, Kim founded the Democratic People's Republic of Korea (DPRK) and became the republic's premier and supreme commander in 1948. On June 25, 1950, Kim ordered 100,000 KPA troops to cross the thirty-eighth parallel, and in a few months, he had occupied most of South Korea, including Seoul. Douglas MacArthur landed the United Nations Forces at Inchon and pushed the fight back to the north. China's intervention in the conflict helped Kim by stabilizing the front along the thirty-eighth parallel. After the truce was signed in 1953, he continued his communist movement and made the KPA, 1.2 million strong by his death, the fourth largest army in the world with possession of nuclear weapons.

RESOURCES
Buzo, Adrian. *The Guerrilla Dynasty: Politics and Leadership in North Korea.* Boulder, Colo.: Westview Press, 1999.
Jung, Walter, and Xiaobing Li. *Korea and Regional Geopolitics.* New York: University Press of America, 1998.
Seiler, Sydney A. *Kim Il Sung, 1941-1948: The Creation of a Legend.* New York: University Press of America, 1994.
Yang, Sung-Chul. *Korea and Two Regimes: Kim Il Sung and Park Chung Hee.* Cambridge, Mass.: Schenckman, 1981.

SEE ALSO: Inchon Landing; Korean War; MacArthur, Douglas; Mao, Zedong; Pusan Perimeter.
Xiaobing Li

Kim Il Sung. (National Archives)

KIMBERLEY, SIEGE OF

TYPE OF ACTION: Siege in the Boer Wars
DATE: October 14, 1899-February 15, 1900
LOCATION: Diamond mining town in Cape Colony, four miles west of the Orange Free State border
COMBATANTS: 4,600 British vs. 4,000 Boers
PRINCIPAL COMMANDERS: *British*, Lieutenant Colonel R. G. Kekewich (1854-1914); *Boer*, Commandant General J. Wessels
RESULT: Successful British defense of a frontier town, the headquarters of the DeBeers Company

On October 14, 1899, the Siege of Kimberley began when Boer forces, under General J. Wessels, cut the lines of communication connecting the frontier town with Cape Town. Defending the town was a garrison of about 4,600 troops includ-

Many buildings, including the interior of the Exchange, were damaged during the Siege of Kimberley. (Archive Photos/Hulton Getty Collection)

ing 600 British regulars, 500 Cape police, and a large number of local volunteers. This garrison faced a Boer force of approximately 4,000 and held out for 126 days. The siege was lifted on February 15, 1900, when troops under the command of Frederick Sleigh Roberts relieved the city.

The Boers never directly attacked Kimberley, preferring instead to try to starve its inhabitants into submission. The major conflict during the siege was between Cecil John Rhodes, the managing director of DeBeers Company, and Lieutenant Colonel R. G. Kekewich. Only 21 inhabitants of the town were killed by shelling, but 1,500 died of disease.

SIGNIFICANCE

With the relief of Kimberley, the British forces kept the town out of the hands of the Boers. To relieve Kimberley, Lord Roberts had to delay a planned invasion of the Orange Free State. Rhodes gained international renown as the "defender of Kimberley."

RESOURCES

Farwell, Byron. *The Great Anglo-Boer War*. New York: W. W. Norton, 1990.

Gardner, Brian. *The Lion's Cage*. London: Arthur Barker Limited, 1969.

Pakenham, Thomas. *The Boer War*. New York: Random House, 1994.

Rhodes. Documentary. Twentieth Century Fox, 1997.

Roberts, Brian. *Kimberley: Turbulent City*. Cape Town, South Africa: D. Philip, 1985.

SEE ALSO: Boer Wars; Roberts, Frederick Sleigh; Sieges and siege weapons.

John David Rausch, Jr.

KIMMEL, HUSBAND EDWARD

BORN: February 26, 1882; Henderson, Kentucky
DIED: May 14, 1968; Groton, Connecticut
PRINCIPAL WAR: World War II

PRINCIPAL BATTLE: Pearl Harbor (1941)
MILITARY SIGNIFICANCE: Admiral Kimmel was commander in chief of the Pacific Fleet when the Japanese attacked Pearl Harbor.

Although he hoped to attend the U.S. Military Academy at West Point, Husband Edward Kimmel was unable to secure an appointment. When his congressman suggested the U.S. Naval Academy at Annapolis, he accepted. Shortly after graduation, he participated in the cruise of the Great White Fleet. He specialized in naval gunnery, and during World War I, he taught the British Royal Navy new targeting techniques.

During the period between the wars, he served at sea and ashore. In 1933, he attained command of the battleship *New York* and, a year later, became chief of staff to the commander of battleships. After a stint ashore as the U.S. Navy's budget officer, he attained the rank of rear admiral and command of a cruiser division. In 1939, he became commander of cruisers, a rank he held until promoted to command of the Pacific Fleet in 1941.

He held that post when the Japanese attacked Pearl Harbor on December 7, 1941. Blamed for the disaster caused by the surprise attack, Kimmel was relieved of command on December 17. He testified in numerous inquiries but was never officially found at fault for the naval forces' lack of preparedness. His relief of command and subsequent disgrace became a major point of controversy.

RESOURCES
Beach, Edward L. *Scapegoats: A Defense of Kimmel and Short at Pearl Harbor.* Annapolis, Md.: Naval Institute Press, 1995.
Prange, Gordon W. *At Dawn We Slept: The Untold Story of Pearl Harbor.* New York: Penguin, 1981.
Stinnett, Robert B. *Day of Deceit: The Truth about FDR and Pearl Harbor.* New York: Free Press, 1999.
Toland, John. *Infamy: Pearl Harbor and Its Aftermath.* New York: Berkley, 1991.
Tora! Tora! Tora! Documentary. CBS Fox Video, 1970.

SEE ALSO: Japanese military; Pearl Harbor attack; Short, Walter C.; World War II.

Leigh Husband Kimmel

KING, ERNEST

FULL NAME: Ernest Joseph King
BORN: November 23, 1878; Lorain, Ohio
DIED: June 25, 1956; Portsmouth, New Hampshire
PRINCIPAL WAR: World War II
MILITARY SIGNIFICANCE: Admiral King directed all U.S. Navy strategy during World War II.

Following the Pearl Harbor attack in 1941, Ernest King, who had been in command of the Atlantic Fleet, was placed in charge of the entire U.S. Navy. He found that the Navy was poorly prepared for war despite the fact that war had already begun in Europe. His first task was to get the best fighting admirals into key fleet positions.

Much of King's work involved arranging for the construction of new ships and deciding which ships should be assigned where. The latter decision was complicated because the United States was fighting Germany in the Atlantic and Japan in the Pacific. The admiral participated in numer-

Ernest King. (Library of Congress)

ous conferences with world leaders to plan major strategy.

Under King's direction, the U.S. Navy helped win the Battle of the North Atlantic against the German submarine force. Other major battles against Germany included the invasions of North Africa and of Normandy, France. In the Pacific, King's fleet fought the Japanese at Coral Sea, Midway, and Leyte Gulf. Leyte almost became a disaster because King did not provide good coordination between two independent task forces.

On December 15, 1944, King, Chester W. Nimitz, and William Leahy became the first men appointed to the new rank of fleet admiral.

Resources
Buell, Thomas B. *Master of Sea Power*. Boston: Little, Brown, 1980.
Keegan, John. *The Price of Admiralty: The Evolution of Naval Warfare*. New York: Penguin, 1990.
King, Ernest J., and Walter Muir Whitehill. *Fleet Admiral King: A Naval Record*. New York: W. W. Norton, 1952.

See also: Leyte Gulf; MacArthur, Douglas; Nimitz, Chester W.; North Atlantic.

Edwin G. Wiggins

King's Mountain

Type of action: Ground battle in the American Revolution
Date: October 7, 1780
Location: King's Mountain, South Carolina (forty miles west-southwest of Charlotte, N.C.)
Combatants: 1,100 British Loyalist militia and regulars vs. about 1,400 American patriot militia
Principal commanders: *British*, Major Patrick Ferguson (1744-1780); *American*, Colonel William Campbell (1745-1781)
Result: Americans destroyed Ferguson's force

On October 7, 1780, British forces subduing the south suffered a major defeat when American patriot militia under Colonel William Campbell from the Carolinas, Virginia, and the Tennessee region combined forces at King's Mountain. There, the Americans annihilated Major Patrick Ferguson's Loyalists, protecting General Charles Cornwallis's left flank as he advanced toward Charlotte, North Carolina. The American militia trapped Ferguson's force atop King's Mountain, an open plateau rising sixty feet with steep, heavily wooded sides. The rifle-armed Americans advanced up the mountain, using terrain well, and attacked about three in the afternoon. Ferguson's troops, using musket and bayonet charges, drove attackers back only to face repeated assaults from regrouped riflemen. With his force steadily cut down by deadly frontier rifle fire and his position hopeless, Ferguson and a few followers attempted a breakthrough. A hail of bullets felled the British commander, ending the battle although Americans continued firing briefly at the despised, surrendering Loyalists. British casualties included about 200 killed, 160 wounded and about 700 prisoners. Americans lost 28 killed and 62 wounded.

Significance
American victory at King's Mountain, which ended a string of British victories, forced Cornwallis to abandon his move into North Carolina and retreat to Winnsborough. It became a turning point of the revolution in the south.

Resources
Bailey, J. D. *Commanders at King's Mountain*. Greenville, S.C.: A Press, 1980.
Draper, Lyman C. *King's Mountain and Its Heroes: A History of the Battle of King's Mountain, October 7, 1780, and the Events Which Led to It*. Baltimore, Md.: Genealogical Publishing, 1997.
Liberty: The American Revolution. Documentary. Middlemarch Films, 1997.
Lumpkin, Henry. *From Savannah to Yorktown: The American Revolution in the South*. New York: Paragon House, 1981.
Ward, Christopher. *The War of the Revolution*. 2 vols. New York: Macmillan, 1952.
White, Katherine Keogh. *The King's Mountain Men: The Story of the Battle, With Sketches of the American Soldiers Who Took Part*. Baltimore, Md.: Genealogical Publishing, 1998.

See also: American Revolution; Camden; Cornwallis, First Marquess; Cowpens.

W. Calvin Smith

Kinsale, Siege of

Type of action: Siege of a walled town in the Anglo-Spanish War
Date: October 17, 1601-January 2, 1602
Location: Kinsale, Ireland
Combatants: 12,000 English and naval squadron vs. 5,000 Irish and 4,500 Spanish
Principal commanders: *English*, Charles Blount, Baron Mountjoy (1563-1606); *Irish*, Hugh O'Neill, earl of Tyrone (1540?-1616); *Spanish*, General Don Juan del Aguila
Result: Irish and Spanish defeated; fall of O'Neill as Irish leader

In the later stages of the Tyrone Rebellion (1594-1603)—a rebellion by native Irish against English rule—Charles Blount, Baron Mountjoy, began effectively to ring in the powerful northern Irish warlord Hugh O'Neill with forts and alliances. When a pro-Irish Spanish army of about 3,500 under Don Juan del Aguila landed at Kinsale harbor at the far south of Ireland in September, 1601, Mountjoy raced to hem them in. He arrived with about 4,300 men and promises of reinforcements and took the high ground around the town. O'Neill was forced to march three hundred miles to relieve and join with the Spanish. He reacted cautiously, however, slogging through the dreadful fall weather with about 3,700 irregular infantry and 670 mounted men.

Meanwhile, the English force swelled to nearly 12,000 by mid-November and seized two important forts in Kinsale harbor. The English bombarded the town, and the Spanish conducted several bloody sorties to prevent too close an English advance. On December 5, about 700 Spanish reinforcements under Pedro de Zubiar landed thirty miles away at Castlehaven. Three days later, O'Neill's men began to invest the woods around Mountjoy's positions and cut the roads, isolating Mountjoy's now dissipating force by December 13. On December 17, O'Neill grudgingly decided to attack, and on December 24, the English succeeded in breaking the Irish line; the English cavalry scattered the entire army into the muddy countryside. The Spaniards were allowed to withdraw on January 2, 1602; O'Neill sailed for Spain to seek unsuccessfully more aid.

Significance
The dream of an Irish-Spanish defeat of Queen Elizabeth's armies was shattered. The English grip on Ireland grew ever tighter, and in 1603, the English suppressed the rebellion, ending the Nine Years' War.

Resources
Morgan, Hiram. *Tyrone's Rebellion*. Woodbridge, England: Boydell & Brewer, 1993.
O'Faolain, Sean. *The Great O'Neill*. Cork, Ireland: Mercier and Dufour, 1997.
Silke, J. J. *Kinsale*. New York: Fordham University Press, 1970.

See also: Anglo-Spanish War; Armada, Spanish; Irish Rebellion, Great; Sieges and siege weapons; Yellow Ford.

Joseph P. Byrne

Kitchener, Lord

Full name: Horatio Herbert Kitchener
Also known as: Horatio Herbert, first earl of Kitchener, Khartoum, and Broome
Born: June 24, 1850; near Listowel, County Kerry, Ireland
Died: June 5, 1916; off the Orkney Islands, Scotland
Principal wars: Second Boer War, World War I
Principal battles: Atbara (1898), Omdurman (1898)
Military significance: Kitchener, a popular British military hero, headed the War Office from 1914 to 1916.

English parents, an Irish boyhood, a Swiss education, and two years at Woolwich brought Lord Kitchener to his commission in the Royal Engineers. Surveying in Palestine gave him a command of Arabic, which led to assignments in Egypt, eventually leading to the post of commander ("sirdar") for his 1896-1899 conquest of the Sudan, which included the Battle of Atbara (1898) and a victory at Omdurman (1898), which restored the Sudan to Egypt in 1898.

Kitchener peacefully eliminated the French presence at Fashoda on the Nile River in 1898 and brought the Second Boer War (1900-1902) to a suc-

Lord Kitchener. (Library of Congress)

cessful conclusion in 1902. Later, in India, he reformed the Indian army officers' training, and his subsequent administration of Egypt was capable. Tall, taciturn, and abrupt, Field Marshal Kitchener was Britain's symbol of military success, when, with the outbreak of World War I, he was appointed secretary of state for war.

Kitchener did not reform the War Office, organize an effective staff, efficiently use the Territorial Reservists, break the deadlock in France, or understand the Gallipoli operation. On the other hand, he was unique in forecasting the scope, duration, manpower, supply, and equipment demands of the war. Kitchener's methods were flawed, but initially he was indispensable. By 1916, his cabinet prestige was falling, but his public reputation was still high when he was drowned en route to Russia by the sinking of the cruiser HMS *Hampshire*.

Resources

Cassar, George H. *Kitchener: Architect of Victory.* London: William Kimber, 1977.

Magnus, Sir Philip. *Kitchener: Portrait of an Imperialist.* New York: E. P. Dutton, 1959.
Pollock, John. *Kitchener: The Road to Omdurman.* London: Constable, 1999.
Royal, Trevor. *The Kitchener Enigma.* London: Michael Joseph, 1985.
Smithers, A. J. *The Fighting Nation: Lord Kitchener and His Armies.* London: L. Cooper, 1994.
Warner, Philip. *Kitchener.* New York: Atheneum, 1986.

See also: Boer Wars; Omdurman; World War I.

K. Fred Gillum

Kléber, Jean-Baptiste

Born: March 9, 1754; Strasbourg, Alsace
Died: June 14, 1800; Cairo
Principal wars: French Revolutionary Wars
Principal battles: Fleurus (1794), Mount Tabor (1799), Heliopolis (1800)
Military significance: A talented commander and effective administrator, Kléber was noted for his dedication to republican ideals.

Though Alsatian, Jean-Baptiste Kléber received his military education in Bavaria and served as an officer in the Austrian army. In 1783, he returned to France and civilian life. Upon the outbreak of the French Revolution in 1789, he joined the national guard and later served against the rebels of the Vendée. Promoted to divisional command in 1794, he distinguished himself at the Battle of Fleurus (1794) and served in the Rhineland and Netherlands.

In 1798, Kléber took command of one of the five divisions of Napoleon's expeditionary force for Egypt. Severely wounded in the capture of Alexandria, Kléber served as governor of that city while recuperating. In Palestine in 1799, he was particularly instrumental in the Battle of Mount Tabor, in which a large Ottoman army was scattered before it could begin to advance against Egypt.

When Napoleon secretly left for France in August, 1799, he appointed Kléber to command the French remaining in Egypt. Kléber opened negotiations with the Ottoman grand vizier, and in January, 1800, signed the Convention of al-Arish,

Jean-Baptiste Kléber. (Library of Congress)

which established terms for French withdrawal. Kléber began to reposition his troops in the coastal towns preparatory to evacuation, and the grand vizier's army moved into Lower Egypt to restore Ottoman control. However, when London disavowed the convention, Kléber quickly organized his troops, inflicted a sharp defeat on the Ottomans at the Battle of Heliopolis (1800), and drove them out of Egypt. He then suppressed a major popular insurrection in Cairo. Kléber was assassinated in Cairo on June 14, 1800.

RESOURCES
Dykstra, Darrell. "The French Occupation of Egypt, 1798-1801." In Vol. 2 of *The Cambridge History of Egypt*, edited by M. Daly. Cambridge, England: Cambridge University Press, 1998.

SEE ALSO: French Revolutionary Wars; Napoleon I; Napoleonic Wars.

Darrell I. Dykstra

KNIGHTS AND CHIVALRY

Mention of knighthood can be traced as far back as the first century C.E., when young Germans were initiated into manhood as warriors. A mix of German military custom and Christian influences, the concept of knighthood arrived at a time when the cavalry was becoming more and more important to the armies of the Middle Ages. The word "knight" is derived from the Old English *cniht* meaning "boy" or "servant." Knighthood, now awarded as an honor for services rendered, was originally used to describe a formerly professional calvaryman. Chivalry was the gallant and honorable behavior expected of a knight. Eventually, the term was used in the general sense of "courtesy."

ANCIENT HISTORY

As Europe emerged from the Dark Ages, after the fall of Rome to the barbarians, people longed for security. Villagers banded together under one leader. They built fortresses and defended themselves from roaming bands who plundered and burned villages and anything else in their path. Eventually abler, stronger men rose above the rest. These men became nobles, who controlled certain areas of land, or *fiefs*. Peasants farmed the fiefs while the nobles and their vassals defended the land. The nobles and vassals became professional soldiers, as did their sons and relatives after them.

A wealthy noble who desired to increase the number of his armies could offer land, or fiefs, to nobles of lesser status in exchange for military service. Knights were free men, but they were obligated to serve anywhere from twenty to sixty days as payment. Little more was expected of the knight than that he respect the laws of the Roman Catholic Church, be loyal to his feudal or military superiors, and preserve his personal honor on and off the battlefield.

EARLY MIDDLE AGES: 500 TO 1100

The importance of knighthood can be seen as early the eighth century, as indicated by records of Charlemagne *girding* (presenting with a sword) his son Louis the Pious in 791, and of Louis in turn girding his son Charles II the Bald in 838. It is also recorded in the *Anglo-Saxon Chronicle* (hand-copied books, earliest version ends c. 899, the latest c. 1114) that William I the Conqueror's son was dubbed into knighthood in 1085.

The pinnacle of knighthood was the tenth through twelfth centuries with the onset of the

Crusades. At the request of the Roman Catholic Church, knights gathered to rescue the holy land of Palestine from Muslim control during the tenth century. In exchange for their services, knights were awarded certain protections and privileges by the Church. They were exempt from paying penances and were offered one-tenth of all Church revenues. A knight, in turn, was expected to vow service to God. Military orders and brotherhoods, such as the Knights Templar, were formed to guard the city and protect pilgrims visiting the Holy Land.

It was during this period that the concept of chivalry was introduced. Displeased with the violence and bloodshed of war, the Church encouraged chivalric customs. Although there was no actual written "code" of chivalry, there was an understanding between knights of a certain courtesy toward one another. Knights strove for justice, courage, loyalty, and prowess.

The romanticism of chivalry was heightened by the creation of the legend of King Arthur and his Roundtable. This piece of literature and others like it encouraged a more gentlemanly way of life during the long intervals of war. Women were seen in a different light, as a hand to be won rather than a way to obtain land. Chivalry was also a means of separation between the nobility and the common people. Only the wealthy could afford the banquets, hunting, and tournaments that were becoming popular.

LATE MIDDLE AGES: 1300 TO 1500

By the fourteenth and fifteenth centuries, with the conclusion of the Crusades and the development of artillery, the necessity of knighthood began to wane. To protect himself against the *crossbow* and the *longbow*, a knight had to increase his protection. His armor became too heavy, making it easy for him to be knocked off his horse and difficult for him to get up.

Also at this time, chivalry began to lose its religious aspect. A nobleman now vowed service to a lady, often another man's wife, instead of the Church. A knight took part in fewer wars and in more tournaments and banquets full of pageantry. Chivalry became a mere court service. The science of heraldry and genealogy were created. A noble now distinguished himself by his coat of arms, not his accomplishments in battle.

The onset of the sixteenth century saw knighthood reduced to a title of honor that sovereigns could award as they pleased. As early as the 1600's, women began to be accepted into the Orders of Knighthood, because many women were in their own right powerful nobles and wished to gain admission in the prestigious Orders of Chivalry.

THE MAKING OF A KNIGHT

A young boy often began his training for the knighthood by the age of seven. As a *varlet*, he learned horsemanship, how to use a *crossbow, light sword*, and *lance* in mock combat. At the age of fifteen, he became a *page* and was sent to the castle of a relative or friend to begin serious training, often under the wing of an elderly knight. There he learned battle tactics and knightly duties, courtesy to other knights and their ladies, and respect for the Church. A page could only carry his master's helmet, and he never went into battle.

By the age of eighteen, a page became a *squire*, earning the right to wear silver spurs. After a time, a squire was appointed *squire-of-the-body* and accompanied the knight into battle. When the master felt it was time, the squire was knighted. Often a great feast was planned with family and friends to celebrate the ceremony, or *dubbing*.

The night before his dubbing, a young knight's sponsor presented him with golden spurs. Relatives would give him his armor, weapons, horse with saddle, and lance with *pennon* embroidered with his own crest.

A bachelor knight served and fought under the banner of another knight. A *banneret* was a knight who fought under his own banner. A *knight errant* was a nobleman who gave up thoughts of selfish gain to ride the country helping others.

A knight accused of treason, or other serious charges, was brought before a jury of his peers. If found guilty, his sword was broken, his golden spurs taken away, and water thrown in his face. This action was called *degradation*.

Wealth was an important factor in becoming a knight. Poor squires who could not afford their own equipment were often refused knighthood. Such a person could hire himself out to a rich noble or join one of the great military orders such as the Knights Hospitaller. Some knights who did not like to fight could pay another to take their place in battle. This custom was called *scutage*.

The jousting tournament was the high point of a knight's life outside of battle. A joust was the only way a knight could practice in peacetime. It was also a way for an inexperienced knight to learn the skill to keep him alive in battle. With the introduction of chivalry, the joust evolved into an event of pageantry.

Military Orders

At the request of the Church, knights gathered to rescue the holy places of Palestine from Muslim control during the tenth century. These wars were called the Crusades. After the conquest of Jerusalem, the knights remained in the Holy City to protect it from invasion. These knights formed military orders, which vowed to dedicate their lives to serving God and helping others in times of sickness. A few such orders were the Knights Templar, Knights Hospitaller, Knights of Our Lady of Montjoie, and the Teutonic Knights.

Resources

Bouchard, Constance Brittain. *Strong of Body, Brave and Noble: Chivalry and Society in Medieval France.* Ithaca, N.Y.: Cornell University Press, 1998.

Burman, Edward. *The Templars, Knights of God.* Rochester, Vt.: Crucible, 1986.

Corbin, Carole Lynn. *Knights.* New York: Franklin Watts, 1989.

Holmes, George. *The Oxford Illustrated History of Medieval Europe.* New York: Oxford University Press, 1988.

Kaeuper, Richard W. *Chivalry and Violence in Medieval Europe.* Oxford, England: Oxford University Press, 1999.

Laing, Lloyd Robert. *Medieval Britain: The Age of Chivalry.* New York: St. Martin's Press, 1996.

Strickland, Matthew. *War and Chivalry: The Conduct and Perception of War in England and Normandy, 1066-1217.* New York: Cambridge University Press, 1996.

Wright, Nicholas. *Knights and Peasants: The Hundred Years War in the French Countryside.* Woodbridge, Suffolk, England: Boydell Press, 1998.

See also: Charlemagne; Crusades; Feudalism; Hundred Years' War; Medieval warfare; Religion and War; Teutonic Knights.

Maryanne Barsotti

Kolchak, Aleksandr

Full name: Aleksandr Vasilyevich Kolchak
Born: November 16, 1874; St. Petersburg, Russia
Died: February 7, 1920; Irkutsk, Siberia
Principal wars: World War I, Russian Civil War of 1918-1921
Principal battle: Siberia (1918)
Military significance: Kolchak commanded the Russian Black Sea Fleet during World War I and organized anti-Bolshevik forces in Siberia during the Russian Civil War of 1918-1921.

Aleksandr Kolchak, a Russian naval officer, rose to prominence in World War I (1914-1918). A flag officer of the Baltic Fleet, he took command as admiral of the important Black Sea Fleet in 1916. When the czar abdicated in March, 1917, Kolchak resigned his commission. However, the Bolshevik Revolution in November, 1917, brought Kolchak back into service. He quickly became a leader among the various anti-Bolshevik "White" forces scattered across Russia.

In November, 1918, Kolchak staged a *coup d'état*

Aleksandr Kolchak. (Library of Congress)

against the Siberian federation government in Omsk, taking power as a virtual dictator. He received financial and material support from the United States and Great Britain, but his attempts to defeat the Bolsheviks failed, not so much because of the strength of the Red Army but rather because of Kolchak's inability to suppress the infighting among his own forces. Bolshevik forces captured Omsk in November, 1919, forcing Kolchak to retreat to Irkutsk. In January, 1920, he was victim of a *coup d'état*. The Bolsheviks captured Kolchak soon after and executed him, taking all Siberia in the process.

Resources
Connaughton, R. M. *The Republic of Ushakova: Admiral Kolchak and the Allied Intervention in Siberia, 1918-1920*. London: Routledge, 1990.
Smele, Jonathon. *Civil War in Siberia: The Anti-Bolshevik Government of Admiral Kolchak, 1918-1920*. New York: Cambridge University Press, 1996.

See also: Bolshevik Revolution; Russian Civil War of 1918-1921; World War I.

William Allison

Konev, Ivan

Full name: Ivan Stepanovich Konev
Born: December 28, 1897; Lodeino, Russia
Died: May 21, 1973; Moscow, Soviet Union
Principal wars: Russian Civil War of 1918-1921, Kronstadt Rebellion, World War II
Principal battles: Moscow (1941-1942), Kursk (1943), Korsun (1944), Polish Campaign (1944), Berlin (1945)
Military significance: One of the great Soviet marshals of World War II (1939-1945), Konev played an important role in many of the eastern front's fierce battles.

A reserved former peasant, Ivan Konev joined the Bolshevik Party in 1918. He fought in the Red Army during the Russian Civil War of 1918-1921. After participating in the suppression of the mutineers in the Kronstadt Rebellion in 1921, he graduated from Frunze Military Academy in 1926.

Attaining the rank of general before the Soviet Union became involved in World War II in 1941, Konev became known for his ability to launch counterattacks against the Germans. Having participated in Marshal Georgy Zhukov's defense of Moscow in 1941, Konev also played an important role at Kursk in 1943, when his troops recaptured the city of Kharkov. After his victory at Korsun in early 1944, Konev was promoted to marshal. This promotion, made in spite of Konev's history of difficulties with Soviet leader Joseph Stalin, was Stalin's acknowledgment of the new marshal's talents.

In 1944, Konev led Soviet forces across Poland and, in 1945, he played a key role in the storming of Berlin. After the war, Konev, replacing his rival Zhukov, rose to supreme command of all Soviet ground forces in 1946. Konev later held the top military post in the Warsaw Pact alliance, and he commanded Soviet forces in Germany during the 1961-1962 Berlin Crisis.

Resources
Bialer, Seweryn. *Stalin and His Generals*. New York: Penguin, 1969.
Konev, Ivan. *Year of Victory*. Moscow: Progress, 1984.
Shukman, Harold. *Stalin's Generals*. New York: Weidenfeld, 1993.

See also: Berlin; Kursk; Moscow; Russian Civil War of 1918-1921; Russian military; Stalin, Josef; Zhukov, Georgy.

Mark Orsag

Könniggrätz

Type of action: Ground battle in the Austro-Prussian War
Date: July 3, 1866
Location: Near the village of Sadowa, northwest of the town of Könniggrätz, Bohemia, Austrian Empire (later Sadová and Hradec Králové, respectively, the Czech Republic)
Combatants: 240,000 Austrians and Saxons vs. 245,000 Prussians
Principal commanders: *Austro-Saxon*, Austrian General Ludwig von Benedek (1804-1881); *Prussian*, General Helmuth von Moltke (1800-1891)
Result: Decisive Prussian victory

General Helmuth von Moltke grouped three Prussian armies spread along more than a two-hundred mile front in an attempt to encircle the combined Austro-Saxon forces that General Ludwig von Benedek joined into a single army. The Prussians, armed with breech-loading needleguns, attacked their muzzle-loading opponents in the morning. Superior Austrian artillery repulsed the uncoordinated Prussian assault. Von Benedek, however, did not follow up this advantage with his cavalry, which allowed the second Prussian attack to begin in the mid-afternoon and turned the tide in favor of the Prussians. Only a skillful retreat by von Benedek, covered by his artillery, kept the defeat from becoming a complete rout. Austrian casualties amounted to about 43,000, of whom around half were captured, and the Saxons lost approximately 1,500 men. The Prussians suffered about 9,000 losses.

Significance

Könnigrätz, the largest European land battle before World War I, determined the outcome of the Austro-Prussian War (also known as the Seven Weeks' War). Austria's loss resulted in its diminished role as a great power and exclusion from German affairs. This contributed to the Prussian unification of Germany by 1871.

Resources

Bonnal, Henri. *Sadowa: A Study.* London: Hugh Rees, 1913.

Craig, Gordon A. *The Battle of Könnigrätz: Prussia's Victory over Austria, 1866.* Westport, Conn.: Greenwood Press, 1975.

Wawro, Geoffrey. *The Austro-Prussian War: Austria's War with Prussia and Italy in 1866.* Cambridge, England: Cambridge University Press, 1996.

See also: German Wars of Unification; Moltke, Helmuth (1800-1891).

Gregory C. Ference

Korean (North) military

North Korea's military forces are ranked fifth in the world in terms of size, while North Korea is ranked as one of the most heavily armed nations in the world. The North Korean army consists of 16 corp commands, 2 special forces operations, and 9 military district commands, which are commanded by the Ministry of the People's Armed Forces. The North Korean army combat unit consists of 153 brigades and divisions, which includes 60 infantry brigades, 25 mechanized infantry brigades, 13 tank brigades, 25 special operations forces, and 30 artillery brigades. The North Korean army also has more than 600 amphibious vehicles and 2,000 floating bridge sections. Initially modeled along the Chinese and Soviet army models, the North Korean army consists of about 1 million active duty personnel, including 30 infantry divisions, 1 mobile truck division, and between 20 and 25 reserve divisions, 18 reserve brigades, 15 armored brigades, 20 mechanized brigades, and 4 infantry brigades. The army is equipped with approximately 2,000 rocket launchers, 3,500 tanks, 4,000 personnel carriers, and 6,000 artillery pieces.

The North Korean navy has two fleets, maintaining operations in eight locations along the east and west coast of North Korea. The North Korean navy had 60,000 personnel, 24 submarines, 1 frigate, and 388 patrol and coastal-landing craft.

The North Korean air force has 82 Soviet- and Chinese-made bombers and a variety of Soviet-made MiG-23/Floggers, MiG-29/Fulcrums, and SU-25/Frogfoots, numbering about 200 aircraft in total. North Korea had "friendship treaties" with the former Soviet Union and the People's Republic of China to provide training and military assistance.

The North Korean regime of Kim Jong Il claims that it is the sole legitimate government of the Korean Peninsula and thus engages in military competition with South Korea. The existence of rival political regimes is seen as a threat to each country's security; therefore, North Korea deals seriously with threats, perceived or real, and justifies its policies by inculcating the populace with propaganda designed to ensure loyalty and obedience.

Organization Structure

The Korean Worker's Party exercises complete control over the military through its political corps, the Ministry of the People's Armed Forces, which is responsible for the management and control of the armed forces. The North Korean military is made up of the People's Armed Forces, which consists of the Korean People's Army, the Korean People's Air Force, and the Korean People's Navy as well as specialized military units such as Escort Command and Pyongyang Defense Command. Paramilitary units such as Korean People's Security Units, the Peasant-Worker Red Guard Militia, and the Red Youth Militia form the core of military reserve. The Ministry of the People's Armed Forces consists of several departments, each of which ensures loyalty to the state political structure. Political and policy guidance resides in the Central Military Committee, and the National Defense Commission controls the military and administrative functions. The General Staff Department has effective operational control and is under a unitary, unified military command structure in which the Office of the General Staff of the Korean People's Army asserts command over the different branches in a unified manner.

Resources

Bae, Myong Oh. "Development Process of North Korea's Military Strategy." *Vantage Point* 5 (1982): 1-11.

Chung Bong-ik, ed. *A Handbook on North Korea*. Seoul: Naewoo Press, 1998.

Committee on International Relations. *North Korean Military and Nuclear Proliferation Threat*. Washington, D.C.: U.S. Government Printing Office, 1996.

Lee, Suck-Ho. *Party-Military Relations in North Korea: A Comparative Analysis*. Seoul: Seoul Computer Press, 1989.

North Korea: The Foundations for Military Strength. Washington, D.C.: Defense Intelligence Agency, 1996.

Savado, Andrea Matles, ed. *North Korea: A Country Study*. Washington, D.C.: U.S. Government Printing Office, 1994.

Yang, Sung-Chul. *The North and South Korean Political Systems: A Comparative Analysis*. Boulder, Colo.: Westview Press, 1994.

See also: Kim Il Sung; Korean War.

Keith A. Leitich

Korean War

AT ISSUE: Reunification of Korea
DATE: June 25, 1950-July 27, 1953
LOCATION: Korea
COMBATANTS: North Korea and China vs. South Korea, the United States, and fifteen members of the United Nations
PRINCIPAL COMMANDERS: *North Korea*, Choe Yong Gun (1900-1976); *United States*, Douglas MacArthur (1880-1964); *United Nations*, Matthew B. Ridgway (1895-1993)
PRINCIPAL BATTLES: Kaesong, Seoul (1950), Osan, Taejon, Pusan Perimeter, Inchon Landing, Seoul (1951), Bloody Ridge, Heartbreak Ridge, Pork Chop Hill
RESULT: Military stalemate and restoration of prewar status quo

Background

The division of Korea in 1945 after World War II at the thirty-eighth parallel into U.S. and Soviet zones of military occupation resulted in the creation of two separate governments. The determination of both the Republic of Korea (ROK) in the south and the Democratic People's Republic of Korea (DPRK) in the north to reunify the country ignited the Korean War.

After its creation in September, 1948, North Korea had focused on supporting southern guerrillas, holding its army in reserve, and allowing South Korea to initiate most of the clashes along the thirty-eighth parallel. Starting in May, 1949, North Korea escalated its retaliation, resulting in major fighting. After Soviet arms deliveries tilted the balance in its favor, North Korea committed its regular army in August, 1949, to a campaign that drove ROK forces from salients north of the parallel. Except for a brief clash on the Ongjin Peninsula, there were few serious border incidents for the next ten months, as South Korea avoided fights it could no longer win. However, the clashes persuaded the United States to limit South Korea's offensive military capability, denying it tanks, planes, and much heavy artillery, while bolstering North Korea's argument to Moscow that only conquest of South Korea would remove future threats to its survival.

ACTION

Soviet leader Joseph Stalin gave his reluctant consent to North Korea's invasion plan in April, 1950. At dawn on June 25, 1950, the North Korean People's Army (NKPA), led by Choe Yong Gun, launched assaults at seven points along the parallel, while staging amphibious landings on the east coast. Composed of roughly 135,000 well-trained troops, it had about 150 Soviet-built T-34 tanks, 110 combat planes, and abundant heavy artillery. The South Korean army consisted of eight combat divisions totaling 65,000 soldiers plus 33,000 support troops, with only flat-trajectory antitank guns and rocket-launching bazookas. The North Korean army's main offensive thrust sent four of seven infantry divisions and 120 tanks toward **Kaesong** (June 25, 1950), seizing the city after just three hours. Early the next day, the North Korean forces crushed South Korea's counterattacking Seventh Division, and fleeing South Korean soldiers abandoned countless mortars, howitzers, machine guns, and antitank guns. The North Koreans occupied **Seoul** on June 28, 1950. Meanwhile, in the center of the peninsula, South Korean forces mounted a spirited defense against two Northern Korean divisions and thirty tanks for five days, then withdrew to avoid being flanked from the west. Isolated on the east coast, the South Korean Eighth Division fought well and delayed the North Korean advance.

KOREAN WAR, 1950-1953

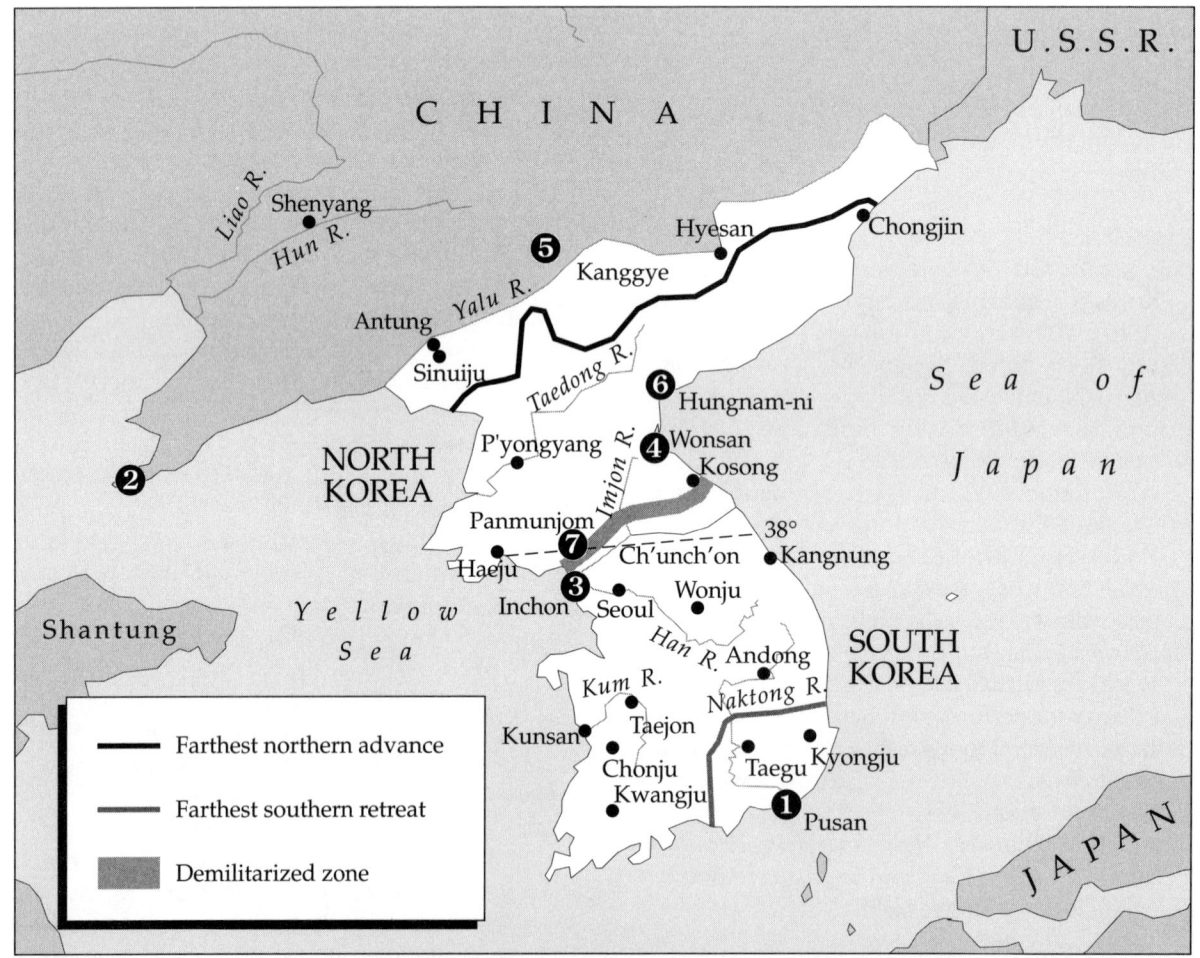

(1) Main U.N. base. (2) Russian-Chinese naval installation. (3) Sept. 15, 1950, U.N. forces land. (4) Oct. 8, 1950, U.N. forces land. (5) Nov. 26, 1950, Chinese attack. (6) Dec. 9, 1950, U.N. forces evacuate. (7) July 27, 1953, armistice signed.

North Korea's attack surprised the United States, although intelligence reports that spring had indicated that North Korea was evacuating civilians and staging a military buildup just north of the parallel. Following existing plans, President Harry S. Truman secured resolutions at the United Nations (U.N.) authorizing military assistance to South Korea. He ordered U.S. naval and air support for South Korean forces on June 25 but did not commit ground troops until five days later, approving the urgent request of General Douglas MacArthur, the occupation commander in Japan. Reorganized remnants of the South Korean army delayed the North Korean advance south of the Han River until July 3. At the Battle of **Osan** (July 5, 1950), the North Korean forces, in their first engagement with understrength, poorly equipped, and ill-trained U.S. forces, easily swept aside Task Force Smith. A United Nations resolution created the U.N. Command, and Truman named MacArthur commander. After **Taejon** (July 16-20, 1950) fell, North Korea pushed U.N. forces back to the **Pusan Perimeter** (July 29-September 19, 1950) in the southeastern corner of Korea. By August, the North Korean army had grown to ten divisions with the addition of South Koreans who either had been impressed into service or had voluntarily enlisted. It faced five reorganized South Korean divisions and the U.S. Twenty-fourth and Twenty-fifth Infantry Divisions and First Cavalry Division.

The Tenth Corps' amphibious assault at the port of **Inchon** (September 15, 1950), thirty miles west of Seoul, met only slight resistance. The next morning, the U.S. First Marines moved eastward, with the Seventh Infantry Division protecting its right flank. Recapture of Seoul (September 26, 1950) was more difficult even after linking up with the U.S. Eighth Army that had broken out of the Pusan Perimeter, but once accomplished, United Nations forces on September 29 pushed the remnants of the North Korean forces out of South Korea.

After the United States sent its Seventh Fleet into the Taiwan Strait, the People's Republic of China feared that U.S. destruction of the North Korean army would threaten not only its security, but its image as the leader in Asia. In July, China reorganized its Thirteenth Army Corps into the Northeastern Border Forces and deployed it along the Yalu River. On October 2, Mao Zedong persuaded his reluctant colleagues to approve sending troops to fight in Korea as "volunteers." Beijing made a final effort to avoid entry when on October 3, Premier Zhou Enlai told India's ambassador that if U.S. forces crossed the parallel, China would react. Most U.S. officials thought Beijing was bluffing.

In fact, the Truman administration had decided in August to invade North Korea, finalizing plans for forcible reunification on September 11 and giving MacArthur almost a free hand in advancing to the Yalu River. On October 8, both United Nations and Chinese forces moved into North Korea. Major engagements early in November confirmed China's intervention, but MacArthur viewed full Chinese participation as unlikely. He launched his Home-by-Christmas Offensive on November 24 to force North Korea to capitulate. The Eighth Army and the Tenth Corps were to strike northward separately before linking to crush the North Korean forces. The U.N. forces encountered little resistance initially, then China counterattacked in force, sending its enemy into rapid retreat. Only a harrowing withdrawal from the Chongjin Reservoir and a miraculous evacuation at Hungnam rescued the Tenth Corps from annihilation. MacArthur pressed for a naval blockade and military attacks against China, but Truman refused to widen the war, despite publicly hinting in December that he was considering using atomic weapons.

General Matthew B. Ridgway, who became commander of U.N. ground forces in December, halted the retreat after Chinese forces recaptured **Seoul** early in January, 1951. He then implemented a strategy to inflict maximum casualties on the enemy, providing for the use of long-range artillery coupled with air attacks using napalm and rockets before ground troops with support of tanks advanced with heavy machine-gun and mortar fire. Beginning in February, Ridgway employed this "meat-grinder" strategy in Operation Killer and then in Operations Ripper and Courageous. Within three months, the U.N. forces had returned to the parallel. However, on April 22, the Chinese initiated a final effort to destroy the U.N. forces and reunite Korea. The primary target of this offensive was Seoul, with a secondary thrust at Kapyong to the east. The Chinese assault, relying as before on night attacks and superior numbers to overwhelm the enemy, was costly and ineffective against well-prepared U.N. forces, although the South Korean Sixth Division collapsed.

Despite suffering huge casualties, the Chinese redeployed eastward in May and sent thirty divisions against U.N. lines. South Korean units again broke under pressure, but reinforcements blocked a breakthrough. A U.N. counteroffensive soon threatened Chinese forces with envelopment, forcing them to retreat in disarray. China's Fifth Phase Offensive gained nothing, and its forces sustained the worst losses of the war. By confirming the U.N. forces' ability, through superior organization and firepower, to overcome tactics relying on massed manpower, the offensive hastened a military stalemate, thus opening the way to truce talks on July 10. By then, smaller contingents of military forces from Australia, Belgium, Canada, Colombia, Ethiopia, France, Greece, Luxembourg, the Netherlands, New Zealand, Philippines, Thailand, Turkey, South Africa, and Britain had joined South Korea and the United States. However, to maintain the multinational character of the U.N. forces, the United States had to comply when its allies opposed military escalation.

U.N. forces maintained battlefield pressure to achieve a quick armistice, seizing key positions north of the parallel in the Battles of **Bloody Ridge** (August, 1952) and **Heartbreak Ridge** (September, 1952). To force concessions, the United States dropped dummy atomic bombs and intensified B-29 bombing raids on North Korea, but communist MiG fighters, often with Soviet pilots, inflicted heavy damage, climaxing in the Battle of Namsi (1952). When negotiators agreed to a cease-fire line in November, the U.N. forces adopted active defense as the basis for ground strategy. The Eighth Army would undertake no major offensives and limit the scope of operations to capturing outposts in terrain suitable for temporary defense. Thereafter, a pattern emerged of patrolling and small-scale fighting, with U.N. forces merely reacting to enemy contacts. Peng Dehuai, commander of Chinese forces, followed suit, causing Korea to develop into a war of attrition resembling World War I, with a static battlefield and armies depending on barbed wire, trenches, artillery, and mortars. Because both sides placed a priority on achieving an early armistice, they emphasized gaining and maintaining defense in depth, increasing troops, and stockpiling equipment behind the front line.

U.S. military leaders proposed plans for offensive action but were unable to gain approval for implementation from either the administration of Presidents Truman or Dwight D. Eisenhower. However, the United States did expand the air war in the spring of 1952, attacking North Korean targets of economic importance to China and the Soviet Union. That summer, the U.N. forces bombed power installations along the Yalu and Tumen Rivers, such as the huge Suiho plant. This strategy extended to attacking targets of political significance, especially Pyongyang, using napalm as well as high explosives, with the aim of undermining enemy morale and raising to an unacceptable level the costs of stalling the truce talks. Despite the raids, the North Koreans remained inflexible, resulting in suspension of the talks in October. Both sides continued to sustain huge losses in protracted ground engagements in the spring of 1953 at Triangle, Whitehorse, and **Pork Chop Hill**. By then, U.S. planners had gained approval for attacks against the dams supplying water for rice cultivation in North Korea, the first attacks taking place in May.

President Eisenhower later credited the armistice ending the Korean War to convincing the North Koreans and Chinese that the alternative was a wider war, employing atomic weapons. Atomic coercion may have played a role in China's accepting voluntary repatriation on June 4, 1953, thus opening the way to an armistice, but domestic economic pressures in the communist states, the Soviet bloc's growing desire for peaceful coexistence, and the death of Stalin were more important. The communists then launched new military thrusts to gain the propaganda value of a symbolic military victory at the end of the war. China also focused attacks on South Korean forces to persuade South Korea's government to endorse and respect the armistice agreement. Despite more than a year of U.S. effort to train and equip an enlarged South Korean army capable of postwar self-defense, only U.S. troops from the Third and Twenty-fourth Divisions, and commitment of the 187th Regimental Combat Team from Japan, halted the offensive. A U.N. counteroffensive on July 17 restored a position six miles south of the original battle line. On July 27, 1953, signing of an armistice ended fighting in the Korean War. More than 2 million Koreans died during the war, and China sustained an estimated 360,000 casualties. U.N. forces casualties totaled 159,000, which included 33,629 U.S. combat deaths.

Aftermath

Conflict between South Korea and North Korea continued into the twenty-first century, making the demilitarized zone that separates the two Koreas one of the world's most heavily fortified and dangerous boundaries. Chinese forces withdrew, but the United States retained troops in South Korea. Periodic incidents kept alive fears of renewed war.

Resources

Blair, Clay. *The Forgotten War: America in Korea, 1950-1953*. New York: Times Books, 1987.
Chen, Jian. *China's Road to the Korean War: The Making of the Sino-American Confrontation*. New York: Columbia University Press, 1994.
Cumings, Bruce. *The Origins of the Korean War*. 2 vols. Princeton, N.J.: Princeton University Press, 1990.
Foot, Rosemary. *The Wrong War: American Policy and the Dimensions of the Korean Conflict, 1950-1953*. Ithaca, N.Y.: Cornell University Press, 1985.
Goncharov, Sergei, John W. Lewis, and Xue Litai. *Uncertain Partners: Stalin, Mao, and the Korean War*. Stanford, Calif.: Stanford University Press, 1993.
James, D. Clayton. *Refighting the Last War: Command and Crisis in Korea, 1950-1953*. New York: Free Press, 1993.
Kaufman, Burton I. *The Korean War: Challenges in Crisis, Credibility, and Command, 1950-1953*. Philadelphia, Pa.: Alfred A. Knopf, 1986.
Korea: The Forgotten War. Documentary. A Lou Red Production, 1987.
Korea: The Unknown War. Documentary. Thames Television, 1988.
MacDonald, Callum A. *Korea: The War Before Vietnam*. New York: Free Press, 1986.
Matray, James I., ed. *Historical Dictionary of the Korean War*. Westport, Conn.: Greenwood Press, 1991.
Merrill, John. *Korea: The Peninsular Origins of the War*. Newark: University of Delaware Press, 1989.
Sandler, Stanley. *The Korean War: No Victors, No Vanquished*. Lexington: University of Kentucky Press, 1999.
Stueck, William W., Jr. *The Korean War: An International History*. Princeton, N.J.: Princeton University Press, 1995.
Zhang, Shu Guang. *Mao's Military Romanticism: China and the Korean War, 1950-1953*. Lawrence: University of Kansas Press, 1995.

See also: Imjin River; Inchon Landing; MacArthur, Douglas; Pork Chop Hill; Pusan Perimeter.

James I. Matray

Kościuszko, Tadeusz

Full name: Tadeusz Andrezj Bonawentura Kościuszko
Born: February 4, 1746; Mereczowszczyzna, Poland (later Belarus)
Died: October 15, 1817; Solothurn, Switzerland
Principal wars: American Revolution, Russian Invasion of Poland, Wars of Polish Partition
Principal battles: Saratoga (1777), Siege of Ninety-Six (1781), Zielence (1792), Dubienka (1792), Raclawice (1794), Siege of Warsaw (1794), Maciejowice (1794)
Military significance: Kościuszko, a foreign volunteer during the American Revolution, designed fortifications and fought in sieges. He later served Poland in battles against Russia.

Tadeusz Kościuszko attended the newly formed Knights School in Warsaw in 1746 and studied in France in 1769. He returned to Poland but was unhappy with conditions there and decided to leave and offer his services to the American Continental Army in the American Revolution. He was commissioned by the Continental Congress on October 19, 1776, as a colonel of engineers. His first assignments were to design and build Fort Mercer on the Delaware River. He was then assigned to General Horatio Gates's army. He built the fortifications at Saratoga, which contributed greatly to the American victory there in 1777. His next assignment was to design and construct the first

Catherine II offers a sword to Tadeusz Kościuszko after the failure of a rebellion that led to the partition of Poland. (Library of Congress)

fortifications at West Point. Kościuszko went on to serve under General Nathanael Greene on the southern front. Greene made him chief of transport and expanded his duties to include cavalry commander and a stint as an intelligence officer. He served at the Siege of Ninety-six (1781) and Charleston, South Carolina. He ended the war as a brigadier general.

Kościuszko returned to Poland in 1784. He was given the rank of major general and led Polish troops against invading Russians in 1792, fighting at Zielence and Dubienka (both 1792). Kościuszko resigned his commission when the Polish king ordered an end to the Polish resistance. He left Poland for France but returned in March, 1794, to head a Polish insurrectionary army to resist further attacks by Russian, Prussian, and Austrian forces. The Polish army was hastily raised and poorly equipped; the army had an abundance of artillery but lacked muskets. Despite these shortcomings, Kościuszko's forces trounced a large Russian force at Raclawice on April 4, 1794. Following his victory, he moved to Warsaw (1794), pursued by Russian and Prussian forces. He conducted a successful two-month defense of the city against the Russo-Prussian besiegers. In an attempt to prevent a massive assault on the city, in October, Kościuszko led a preemptive strike on the Russian army at Maciejowice. He did not receive support that was promised to him and wound up facing a Russian army twice the size of his. The Polish assault failed. Kościuszko was wounded and taken prisoner. He was to spend two years in a Russian prison. The defeat at Maciejowice led to the defeat of the insurrection and the final partition of Poland in 1795.

He eventually settled in retirement outside of Paris and then in Switzerland. While in retirement, General William Davie asked him to write the book, *Manouvers of Horse Artillery* (1808), for the U.S. Army in 1800, and it was used at West Point. He was approached by Napoleon to come to the duchy of Warsaw and later by Czar Alexander I to come to the Congress Kingdom. He said he would return only to a free Poland. He died in exile in 1817.

Resources

Gardner, Monica. *Kościuszko*. New York: Scribners, 1920.

Gronowicz, Antoni. *The Gallant General*. New York: Scribners, 1947.

Haiman, Miecislaus. *Kościuszko in the American Revolution*. New York: Kościuszko Foundation, 1975.

_____. *Kościuszko: Leader and Exile*. New York: Kościuszko Foundation, 1977.

Pula, James S. *Thaddeus Kościuszko: The Purest Son of Liberty*. New York: Hippocrene Books, 1999.

Szymczak, Robert. "Tadeusz Kościuszko." *Mankind* 5, no. 6 (1976): 33-35, 60-63.

See also: American Revolution; Polish Partition, Wars of; Polish Rebellion of 1830-1831.

David R. Stefancic

Kosovo

Type of action: Ground battle in Turkish Wars of European Expansion
Date: June 15, 1389
Location: Kosovo, Serbia
Combatants: Serbians (and other European nationalities) vs. Ottomans
Principal commanders: *Serbian*, Prince Lazar (d. 1389); *Ottoman*, Sultan Murad I (1326?-1389)
Result: Ottoman victory; Turks seize the Balkans and encircle the Byzantine Empire

After the demise of the Crusades, the Ottoman Empire (the most powerful force in the Islamic world) began its westward probe. The empire, controlled by Turkey, had two primary goals: to push up the Danube River valley and capture Vienna, capital of the rival Habsburg Dynasty, and to encircle and then overrun the thousand-year-old Byzantine Empire. To accomplish either goal, the Ottomans had to conquer the states bordering on the Balkan mountain range. Orthodox, proud, and determined, the independent state of Serbia took the lead in stopping the advancing Muslims. Murad I, a consummate opportunist, took advantage of Byzantine internal dissension (a chronic problem) and the frequent feuds and rivalries of the Slavic states to extend Ottoman control of the Balkan Peninsula.

The stakes were enormous and clearly understood. A European victory would end the immediate threat to the Balkans and reinforce the Byzantine Empire and might even encourage the Western Europeans to restart the Crusades. Conversely, an Ottoman victory would mean abject disaster for the Christian forces. Only the Habsburgs would stand in the way of possibly millions of Muslims flooding into central and western Europe. Prince Lazar, the strongest Serbian leader, was put in charge of the combined defensive group. Although Serb-dominated, the defenders also consisted of Bosnians, Bulgars, Croats, Vlachs, Albanians, Magyars, and even Poles. Kosovo, also known as "the field of blackbirds," was known for its rivers and mountains and thereby seemed to be a logical place to fortify and await the nearing Ottomans.

Blessed by religious fervor and a string of capable leaders after 1300, the Turks crossed the straits connecting the Mediterranean and Black Seas in 1354 and began moving north. Following river valleys, the Islamic invaders captured Serres (1383), Sofia (1385), and Nish (1386), before attacking Kosovo on June 15, 1389. These victories were largely the product of vastly superior Ottoman infantry and cavalry units, composed mostly of Christian Janissary forces. The Turks were also outstanding administrators, which meant they did not need to allocate huge numbers of troops to maintain control of previously conquered areas.

Early in the battle, Prince Lazar's forces did well. Fighting a defensive war on familiar terrain, the Serbs rebuffed the initial Ottoman advances. Then a nearly miraculous act occurred that seemed to seal victory for the Europeans. A Serbian nationalist named Miloš Obilić pretended to be a deserter and, through a combination of bluff and good fortune, found his way into the sultan's tent and fatally stabbed him with a hidden poisoned dagger. As might be expected, chaos ensued in the Islamic camp and when word of

Obilić's audacious act drifted back to the Serbs and their allies, many believed that the assassination was an act of God to save and preserve Christian Europe.

The Ottomans soon recovered, however. Murad's son, Bayezid, was quickly installed as the new sultan, and he acted forcefully and resolutely. The assassin was summarily executed as Bayezid I consolidated his power. He then launched an immediate offensive with the goals of surprising the still celebrating defenders and surrounding their forces. The new sultan succeeded on both counts, and the Europeans suffered tremendous defeat. Prince Lazar was captured and executed as all resistance came crumbling to an end. The Ottoman Empire gained control of southeastern Europe.

Significance

As feared, central Europe was besieged and attacked by Ottoman forces. Although Hungary and most of the area would be conquered, Vienna survived the Turkic invasion and would remain the ruling city of the Habsburg Dynasty until 1918. The Byzantine Empire, however, was not as fortunate, falling to Ottoman sultan Mehmed II in 1453.

Resources

Judah, Tim. *The Serbs: History, Myth, and the Destruction of Yugoslavia*. New Haven, Conn.: Yale University Press, 1997.

Malcolm, Noel. *Kosovo: A Short History*. New York: New York University Press, 1998.

Singleton, Frederick Bernard. *A Short History of the Yugoslav Peoples*. New York: Cambridge University Press, 1988.

See also: Byzantine-Ottoman Wars; Crusades; Mehmed II; Murad I; Ottoman Empire; Religion and war; Turkish Wars of European Expansion.

Thomas W. Buchanan

Kruger, Paul

Full name: Stephanus Johannes Paulus
Also known as: Oom Paul
Born: October 10, 1825; Colesberg, Cape Colony, South Africa

Paul Kruger. (Library of Congress)

Died: July 14, 1904; Clarens, Switzerland
Principal wars: Wars of Boer Expansion, Boer Wars
Military significance: Kruger's military and political leadership helped forge an independent Boer state in the Transvaal region of southern Africa.

As a boy of 10, Paul Kruger accompanied his parents on the Great Trek, as Boers (descendants of Dutch farmers) migrated north of the Orange River to escape British control. Growing up on the frontier, he had little education except for Bible study but became proficient at hunting and fighting. Before the age of fourteen, when his family moved north of the Vaal River, he had already participated in battles against the Ndebele (1836) and the Zulus (1838). As one of the founding citizens of the Transvaal state, Kruger was soon pressed into military and public service. At the age of seventeen, he was made an assistant field cornet. Three years later, he was promoted to full field cornet and, by age twenty-seven, became the leader of an expedition against the Bechuanaland.

A staunch Boer nationalist, Kruger joined a group that unsuccessfully tried to force a union between the Transvaal and the Orange Free State. In 1864, he was elected commandant general of the Transvaal military. He resigned in 1873, after a number of difficult campaigns against tribes in the northern Transvaal but regained his prominent position in public affairs after the British forced the Transvaal into a South African confederation in 1877. His campaign for Boer independence culminated in the First Boer War, in which the Transvaal regained its independence, though under the nominal suzerainty of Great Britain. Though considered narrow by many and presiding over governments involved in considerable corruption, Kruger was elected president of the Transvaal Republic four times. Too old to go on commando when the Second Boer War erupted, he went to Europe to lobby for diplomatic support. He died in Switzerland, but his body was returned to South Africa and buried at Pretoria.

RESOURCES

Meintjes, Johannes. *President Paul Kruger: A Biography*. London: Cassell, 1974.

Pakenham, Thomas. *The Boer War*. London: Folio Society, 1999.

Schreuder, D. M. *Gladstone and Kruger: Liberal Government and Colonial "Home Rule": 1880-1885*. London: Routledge and Kegan Paul, 1969.

SEE ALSO: Boer Wars; Botha, Louis; Joubert, Petrus Jacobus; Smuts, Jan Christian.

John Powell

KSAR EL-KEBIR

TYPE OF ACTION: Land battle in the Portuguese Colonial Wars
DATE: August 3-4, 1578
LOCATION: Ksar el-Kebir, Morocco
COMBATANTS: 10,000 Portuguese, 3,000 Castilians, 3,000 German, Italian, Walloon, and English mercenaries, and 1,000 Moroccans vs. 70,000 Moroccans
PRINCIPAL COMMANDERS: *Portuguese*, King Sebastian (1554-1578); *Moroccan*, Sultan ʿAbd al-Malik (d. 1578)
RESULT: Moroccans crush Portuguese invasion, ending more than a century of struggle

By 1570, Portugal's long dominance in Morocco was crumbling against the Saʿdīan Dynasty. However, the dynasty seemed to split after ʿAbd al-Malik deposed his nephew, Muḥammad al-Mutawakkil in 1576. When Muḥammad sought Portuguese troops to wrest the sultanate back, King Sebastian hoped to restore him as Lisbon's puppet. In July, 1578, Sebastian landed at Arzila with 20,000 Portuguese troops and diverse European mercenaries, mostly mismatched infantry, some cavalry, and thirty cannons. Muḥammad provided 1,000 horsemen. Marching inland, the Portuguese encountered ʿAbd al-Malik at the Wādī al-Makhāzin River. The sultan had assembled 30,000 infantry and cavalry (including *sipahis*, who fired arquebus rifles from horseback), thirty cannons, and 35,000 tribal irregulars. Their backs to the river, Sebastian's disjointed units formed a defensive square behind his cannons. Moroccan forces responded with a crescent formation, maneuvering cavalry and *sipahis* for a double enfilade. Eventually, Saʿdīan superior tactics, firepower, and numbers smashed the Portuguese formation. Sebastian, Muḥammad, and ʿAbd al-Malik all died in this engagement, sometimes called "The Battle of the Three Kings," and Aḥmad al-Manṣūr (ʿAbd al-Malik's brother) became sultan of a unified Morocco.

SIGNIFICANCE

Saʿdīan victory secured Moroccan independence for three centuries. With Sebastian's death, Spain annexed Portugal, claimed Lisbon's colonies, and thereby intensified European fears of Spanish imperialism.

RESOURCES

Bovill, E. W. *The Battle of Alcazar*. London: Batchworth Press, 1952.

Cook, Weston F., Jr. *The Hundred Years War for Morocco*. Boulder, Colo.: Westview Press, 1994.

Trim, David. "Early-Modern Colonial Warfare and the Campaign of Alcazarquivir, 1578." *Small Wars and Insurgencies* 8, no. 1 (Spring, 1997): 1-34.

SEE ALSO: Portuguese Colonial Wars.

Weston F. Cook, Jr.

Kublai Khan

BORN: September 23, 1215; Mongolia
DIED: February 18, 1294; Dadu (later Beijing)
PRINCIPAL WARS: Chinese conquest, Japanese invasions
PRINCIPAL BATTLES: Diaoyu Shan (1265), Xiangyang (1268-1273), Kyushu Island (1274, 1281)
MILITARY SIGNIFICANCE: Kublai Khan, the grandson of Genghis Khan, brought the Mongol Empire to the peak of its power after he conquered China. He moved the Great Khan capital from Mongolia to Beijing in 1264 and founded the Yuan Dynasty in 1271.

The first significant campaign for Kublai Khan was to bring the Chinese kingdom of Tali under Mongol jurisdiction. His assault in October of 1253 was successful. The Great Khan, his brother Mangu, next asked Kublai to lead one of his four armies into southern China against the Song Dynasty. The dense forest and heat posed special challenges for the Mongol invaders accustomed to hit-and-run cavalry operations in the cool and dry climate of the north. Siege warfare with heavy artillery and, ultimately, naval operations would be necessary. In the summer of 1258, Kublai's force of some 90,000 was directed to cross the Yangtze at Wuchang in modern-day Hubei.

In 1259, just as the campaign was really getting started, however, Mangu died. Reports vary as to whether he succumbed to dysentery or an arrow wound. The struggle for succession pitted Kublai against his younger brother, Arigböge, who finally conceded the title of Great Khan to Kublai in 1264.

His first major battle with the Song took place in Sichuan province near Diaoyu Shan in early 1265. Kublai Khan was victorious and reportedly captured 146 ships, showing his awareness of the need to build a navy.

The crucial battle in the Mongol conquest of China was a siege against the garrisons at Xiangyang and Fancheng, which sat on either side of the Han River and controlled access to the Yangtze River basin. Kublai Khan assembled a multiethnic force including Chinese, Koreans, Jurchens, and Muslims from the Middle East. The amphibious siege lasted from 1268, with some interruptions, until Fancheng was overrun and Xiangyang surrendered in 1273. The key to victory was the design and construction of a vastly improved catapult system by two Muslim engineers.

Then Kublai appointed his old friend, Bayan, as field commander, and the Mongol forces moved toward Hangzhou, which fell in 1276. The last of the Song pretenders drowned off the island of Yaishan while under Mongol naval attack in 1279.

As the founder of a new Chinese dynasty, Kublai Khan inherited traditional Chinese ambitions with respect to Japan. To subjugate the Japanese and exact tribute would help greatly to consolidate his position as the head of the Yuan Dynasty.

In 1274, a multiethnic force of nearly 30,000 sailed from friendly Korea and established bases on the islands of Tsushima and Iki. The Mongols fought the Japanese at Kyushu and baffled them with novel battle formations and techniques. With victory seemingly in their grasp, however, a terrible storm (known as kamikaze, or "divine wind" in Japan) hit and destroyed most of the

Kublai Khan. (Library of Congress)

Mongol fleet, killing some 13,000. The second attempted invasion of Japan in 1281 was nearly a replay of the first. The Mongol force was almost twice as large and again established itself on Tsushima and Iki. The Mongols engaged the Japanese in a series of land and sea battles off north Kyushu, but mother nature intervened in the same deadly fashion. The Mongols and allies were cut off from supplies, and only a few managed to survive.

The disasters in Japan aside, Kublai Khan was very successful in adapting Mongol military experience to new conditions. This flexibility enabled him to rule China with success and to establish a foreign dynasty that lasted a hundred years. Unfortunately, it also caused suspicion among more traditionalist Mongols such as his cousin Khaidu, who challenged Kublai in their homeland. Perhaps it also facilitated his weakness for fine Chinese food and drink, leading to a conspicuous decline in his later years.

RESOURCES
Dramer, Kim. *Kublai Khan*. Broomall, Pa.: Chelsea House, 1990.
Keegan, John. *A History of Warfare*. Toronto: Vintage, 1994.
Perkins, Dorothy. *Encyclopedia of China*. New York: Roundtable Press, 1999.
Rossabi, Morris. *Khubilai Khan: His Life and Times*. Berkeley: University of California Press, 1988.

SEE ALSO: Chinese Imperial Wars; Genghis Khan; Mongol Empire.

Steven Lehman

KUROPATKIN, ALEKSEI

FULL NAME: Kuropatkin, Aleksei Nikolaevich
BORN: April 10, 1848; Pskov District, Russia
DIED: January 25, 1925; Shemchurino, Soviet Union
PRINCIPAL WAR: Russo-Japanese War
PRINCIPAL BATTLES: Liaoyang (1904), Mukden (1905)
MILITARY SIGNIFICANCE: Kuropatkin served as Russian minister of war and commander of Russian field forces in Manchuria during the Russo-Japanese War.

Aleksei Kuropatkin experienced his baptism of fire in a series of skirmishes in Turkestan in the 1860's and during the Russo-Turkish War (1877-1878). Rising through the ranks, he was appointed minister of war (1898) by Czar Nicholas II (ruled 1894-1917) and was influential in urging the government to occupy Port Arthur on the Liaodong Peninsula (1898), forcing China to grant Russia a thirty-six-year lease.

When war broke out with Japan over territorial rights in Manchuria in 1904, Kuropatkin assumed command of Russian field forces in the region. Though he recognized Russian unpreparedness and anticipated Japan's drive to obtain an early victory, he was saddled with long supply lines, bureaucratic ineptness, and generally poor reconnaissance efforts. Suffering enormous losses at Liaoyang (1904) and Mukden (1905), the Russian army was forced to retreat as morale plummeted. Blamed for the defeats, Kuropatkin was dismissed in 1905. He sought personal vindication through his publication of *Zapiski Generala Kuropatkina o Russko-Iaponskoi Voine* (1909; *The Russian Army and the Japanese War*, 1909).

RESOURCES
Martin, Christopher. *The Russo-Japanese War*. New York: Abelard-Schuman, 1967.
Menning, Bruce W. *Bayonets Before Bullets: The Imperial Russian Army, 1861-1914*. Bloomington: Indiana University Press, 1992.
Walder, David. *The Short Victorious War: The Russo-Japanese Conflict 1904-1905*. New York: Harper & Row, 1973.
Warner, Denis, and Peggy Warner. *The Tide at Sunrise: A History of the Russo-Japanese War, 1904-1905*. New York: Charterhouse, 1974.
Westwood, J. N. *Russia Against Japan, 1904-1905: A New Look at the Russo-Japanese War*. London: Macmillan, 1986.

SEE ALSO: Mukden; Russo-Japanese War; Russo-Turkish Wars.

Kenneth P. Czech

KURSK

TYPE OF ACTION: Ground battle in World War II
DATE: July 5-15, 1943

The Soviets employed Katyusha multiple rocket launchers at Kursk. (Archive Photos/Hulton Getty Collection)

LOCATION: Kursk (approximately 250 miles northeast of Kiev, Ukraine)
COMBATANTS: 700,000 Germans vs. 1.3 million Russians
PRINCIPAL COMMANDERS: *German*, Field Marshal Erich von Manstein (1887-1973), Field Marshal Günther von Kluge (1882-1944); *Soviet*, General of the Army Konstantin Rokossovsky (1896-1968), General of the Army Nikolai Vatutin (1900-1944)
RESULT: The German forces failed to eliminate the Kursk salient and had to stop their offensive

The German offensive at Kursk, led by Erich von Manstein and Günther von Kluge, was intended to demonstrate to the Allies that even after the losses at Stalingrad, the German army was still capable of mounting a major offensive. On the first day, German forces, including several Schutzstaffel (SS) divisions, attacked on two fronts. The well-prepared defenders enjoyed numerical superiority in armor, support aircraft, and field pieces. Although the Germans managed to break through the first of several lines of Soviet defenses, they found themselves slowed down by unexpectedly strong Soviet resistance. Although the Red Army, led by Konstantin Rokossovsky and Nikolai Vatutin, sustained severe losses, it enjoyed the advantage of greater reserves. By the third day of the battle, the German advance had bogged down. On July 12, some 1,200 tanks were involved near Prokhorovka in what was the largest tank battle of the war. On the following day, Adolf Hitler called off the offensive.

SIGNIFICANCE
The Battle of Kursk was a turning point of the war. It was the last major offensive mounted by the German forces against the Red Army.

RESOURCES
Dunn, Walter S., Jr. *Kursk: Hitler's Gamble, 1943.* Westport, Conn.: Prager, 1997.
Glantz, David M., and Jonathan M. House. *The Battle of Kursk.* Modern War Studies Series. Lawrence: University of Kansas Press, 1999.

Piekalkiewicz, Janusz. *Operation "Citadel." Kursk and Orel: The Greatest Tank Battle of the Second World War.* Novato, Calif.: Presidio Press, 1987.

The War in Europe. The War Chronicles: World War II series. Documentary. A&E Home Video, 1983.

SEE ALSO: Hitler, Adolf; Russian military; Stalingrad; Tanks; World War II.

Helmut J. Schmeller

KUT-AL-AMARA

TYPE OF ACTION: Siege in World War I
DATE: December 8, 1915-April 29, 1916
LOCATION: On the banks of the Tigris River, Mesopotamia, one hundred miles south of Baghdad
COMBATANTS: 12,000 Anglo-Indians vs. 12,000 Turks
PRINCIPAL COMMANDERS: *British*, Major General Sir Charles Townshend (1861-1924); *Turkish*, Colonel Nur-ed-Din, with German adviser General Kolmar von der Goltz (1843-1916)
RESULT: Unsuccessful British defense of a town on the Tigris River

While making his drive toward Baghdad, Sir Charles Townshend and his Indian Sixth Division (having twice as many Asian Indians as Britons) were besieged in the small town of Kut-al-Amara. With 10,000 able-bodied men (2,000 being sick or wounded), he fortified his position on the banks of the Tigris, hoping to survive a brief siege. When a Turkish assault failed with heavy casualties, the Turks, led by Colonel Nur-ed-Din with German adviser General Kolmar von der Goltz, shifted their focus to thwarting British relief attempts. Three attempts to break the siege were repelled with heavy losses.

Without hope for relief, the British offered to ransom the survivors but this offer was rejected. Starvation and sickness forced Townshend to surrender unconditionally to Khalil Pasha, the new Turkish commander.

SIGNIFICANCE

The surrender of nearly 10,000 men was the greatest surrender of British troops ever and was surpassed only by the surrender of Singapore in 1942. Although the siege and surrender at Kut-al-Amara was strategically insignificant to the outcome of the war, it did have serious ramifications for British influence in the Middle East. This ignominious defeat, following on the heels of the Gallipoli fiasco, signaled the beginning of the end of British supremacy in the region.

RESOURCES

Barker, A. J. *The Bastard War: The Mesopotamian Campaign of 1914-1918.* New York: Dial, 1976.

_____. *Townshend of Kut: A Biography of Major-General Sir Charles Townshend K.C.B., D.S.O.* London: Cassell, 1967.

Gilbert, Martin. *The First World War: A Complete History.* New York: Henry Holt, 1994.

Townshend, Sir Charles Vere Ferres, Major General. *My Campaign.* 2 vols. New York: James A. McCann, 1920.

SEE ALSO: Baghdad; Gallipoli Campaign; World War I.

José E. Alvarez

KUTNÁ HORA

TYPE OF ACTION: Ground battle in Hussite Wars
DATE: December 21-22, 1421
LOCATION: Kutná Hora, Czech Republic (about ten miles from Kolín)
COMBATANTS: 12,000 Hussites vs. 30,000 Germans and Hungarians
PRINCIPAL COMMANDERS: *Czech*, Jan Žižka (1360-1424); *German-Hungarian*, King Sigismund of Hungary (1367-1437), Pipo Spano (c. 1370-1430)
RESULT: Sigismund's forces take a crucial city in Eastern Bohemia

In December, 1421, King Sigismund launched a crusade from Hungary against Bohemia, directed at Kutná Hora. On December 21, German-Hungarian forces engaged a Hussite force under Jan Žižka to the north of the city. Hussite artillery repulsed repeated frontal attacks throughout the day, but the city to Žižka's rear let in elements of Sigismund's army and the Kutnohorian Germans began massacring the local Czechs. Pipo Spano placed a ring around the small Hussite force, preparing for a mini siege. However, Žižka made use of his cannons in a night attack and breached the German-Hungarian line by charging Sigismund's camp. He managed to flee with his troops to Kaňk Hill, and then to Kolín, leaving Sigismund in command of Kutná Hora.

Significance

Kutná Hora was the German-Hungarian high tide. After Žižka's retreat, Sigismund placed troops in the surrounding area, with a detachment placed at Nebovidy. Little did he know that Žižka's reprovisioned army would lash out from Kolín in January, 1422, in a multiday campaign that would destroy his army and run him out of Bohemia completely.

Resources

Bartos, F. M. *The Hussite Revolution, 1424-1437*. New York: Columbia University Press, 1966.

Heymann, Frederick. *John Žižka and the Hussite Revolution*. Princeton, N.J.: Princeton University Press, 1955.

Kaminsky, Howard. *A History of the Hussite Revolution*. Berkeley: University of California Press, 1967.

See also: Hungarian-Turkish Wars; Hussite Wars; Německý Brod; Turkish Wars of European Expansion; Žižka, Jan.

Matt Schumann

Kutuzov, Mikhail Illarionovich

Full name: Mikhail Illarionovich Golenishchev-Kutuzov (prince of Smolensk)
Born: September 16, 1745; St. Petersburg, Russia
Died: April 28, 1813; Bunzlau, Silesia (later Boleslawiec, Poland)
Principal wars: Russo-Turkish Wars, Napoleonic Wars
Principal battles: Siege of Ochakov (1789), Izmail (1790), Durrenstein (1805, Austerlitz (1805), Borodino (1812), Maloyaroslavets (1812), Smolensk (1812), Berezina River (1812)
Military significance: Kutuzov's leadership spelled disaster in Russia for Napoleon Bona-

Mikhail Illarionovich Kutuzov. (Library of Congress)

parte's Grand Army in 1812, leading to Napoleon's downfall and preserving the political structures of Europe.

The son of a general, Mikhail Illarionovich Kutuzov was trained in the St. Petersburg Engineering and Artillery School. Commissioned in 1761, he fought in Poland during the Russian Intervention of 1764-1769 but was transferred to the Crimea, where he fought in the first Russo-Turkish War. At the Battle of Alushta (1774), he was severely wounded and lost sight in his right eye. He fought as a major general under his mentor General Aleksandr V. Suvorov in the second Russo-Turkish War. He was wounded again at the Siege of Ochakov (1789) but recovered to participate in the taking of Izmail in 1790.

From 1792 to 1805, Kutuzov held a number of administrative posts, including ambassador to Constantinople and governor of Finland. He retired from the military but was recalled to command the Russian contingent of coalition forces against Napoleon in 1805. He won a delaying action at Durrenstein but was defeated, together with his Austrian allies, at Austerlitz. Czar Alexander I relieved Kutuzov of command but later appointed him military governor of Kiev, then of Vilnius. In 1811, Kutuzov was selected as the commander of the Russian army in Moldavia, where his troops destroyed the Turkish army at Rushchuk, enabling the Russian annexation of Bessarabia.

When Napoleon invaded Russia in 1812, Kutuzov supported a strategy of falling back before the French forces, preserving the Russian troops until attrition and supply line problems weakened the French. In August, 1812, he replaced General Barclay de Tolley as Russian commander and, from September 7-8, gave battle at Borodino, one of the bloodiest conflicts of the Napoleonic Wars. After the battle, Napoleon's troops occupied Moscow, but Russia did not surrender, and Kutuzov's army had not been destroyed. In subsequent 1812 battles—Maloyaroslavets, Vyazma, Smolensk, and the Berezina River—following Napoleon's withdrawal from Moscow in October, Kutuzov's troops, aided by partisan activity and by the Russian winter climate, decimated the Grand Army such that only 30,000 of the original 440,000 left Russian soil alive. Kutuzov continued his pursuit of the French through Poland and into Prussia, where he died of exhaustion.

RESOURCES

Brett-James, Antony, ed. and trans. *1812: Eyewitness Accounts of Napoleon's Defeat in Russia*. London: Macmillan, 1966.

Duffy, C. *Borodino: Napoleon Against Russia, 1812*. London: Sphere, 1972.

Kazakov, N. I. "Kutuzov, Mikhail Illarionovich." In *Great Russian Encyclopedia*. Vol. 14. New York: Macmillan, 1976.

Parkinson, Roger. *The Fox of the North: The Life of Kutuzov, the General of War and Peace*. New York: David McKay, 1976.

War and Peace. Fiction feature. Paramount, 1956.

SEE ALSO: Berezina River; Borodino; Napoleon I; Napoleonic Wars; Suvorov, Aleksandr V.

Lee B. Croft

L

La Hogue and Barfleur

TYPE OF ACTION: Naval battle in the War of the Grand Alliance
DATE: May 28-June 2, 1692
LOCATION: The English Channel, northwest of the Cotentin peninsula
COMBATANTS: 39,000 Anglo-Dutch and 88 ships vs. 30,000 French and Irish and 44 ships
PRINCIPAL COMMANDERS: *Anglo-Dutch*, Admiral Edward Russell (1653-1727); *French*, Admiral Anne-Hilarion de Cotentin de Tourville (1642-1701)
RESULT: Defeat of the French fleet and prevention of a French-Jacobite invasion

France collected a force of 30,000 French and Irish soldiers for a descent on Ireland, and Paris dispatched orders to the fleet to cover the invasion. Admiral Anne-Hilarion de Cotentin de Tourville's fleet, ultimately totalling 44 ships of the line, was to be augmented by a squadron of sixteen ships of the line from Toulon.

Under orders to attack, Tourville sought out the opposing fleet even though the Toulon squadron had not arrived. On May 29, Tourville closed with the Anglo-Dutch forces, under Admiral Edward Russell. The opposing fleets fought for eight hours, with neither side losing any ships. The allies threatened to envelop the outnumbered French, but a mist formed, and Tourville managed to extricate his fleet.

During the night, the French fleet became dispersed. Although most of the French vessels eluded the allies, fifteen ships of the line were forced to seek refuge in the harbors of Cherbourg and La Hogue, where they were burned by the allies.

SIGNIFICANCE
The defeat placed the French fleet on the defensive for the remainder of the war.

RESOURCES
Lynn, John A. *The Wars of Louis XIV 1667-1714*. London: Longman, 1999.
Pemsel, Helmut. *A History of War at Sea*. Annapolis, Md.: Naval Institute Press, 1989.
Symcox, Geoffrey. *The Crisis of French Seapower 1688-1697*. The Hague: M. Nijhoff, 1974.

SEE ALSO: Bart, Jean; Grand Alliance, War of the.
Reid J. Rozen

La Rochelle, Siege of

TYPE OF ACTION: Siege of fortified city in the French Wars of Religion
DATE: 1572-1573
LOCATION: La Rochelle, on the coast of France
COMBATANTS: Citizens of La Rochelle vs. Royalist army
PRINCIPAL COMMANDER: *Royalist*, Henry, duke of Anjou (1551-1589)
RESULT: Royalist forces fail to take the town; peace negotiations conclude the siege

Following the Protestant Reformation in Germany, the ideas behind it spread to France, where the movement was led by John Calvin, a Frenchman who established headquarters in Geneva, Switzerland. His ideas appealed to many members of the rising middle class in France and some among the nobility. These Protestants, or Huguenots, were seen as a threat to the power of the king as well as of the French Catholic Church, which sought to suppress the movement militarily.

The result was the French Wars of Religion (1562-1598). The high point of Huguenot power was reached by 1570, when the Huguenots controlled numerous walled towns, including La Rochelle, a port on the Atlantic coast. When La Rochelle refused to accept the royal governor appointed by the French king, Charles IX, he declared war on the city (November, 1572) and sent an army to besiege it. The besieging army, was, however, unable to organize an effective siege, largely as a result of conflicts among its commanders, who included Henry, duke of Anjou. The besiegers suffered many casualties, and although the walls of the city were battered, the siege was lifted in the summer of 1573.

Significance

During the Fourth War of Religion (1572-1573), the Protestants gained political and military control over much of southwest France. Moderate Catholics, including those involved in the Siege of La Rochelle, formed a political party that made concessions to the Protestants for the sake of national unity.

Resources

Holt, Mack P. *The French Wars of Religion: 1562-1629*. Cambridge, England: Cambridge University Press, 1995.

Sutherland, N. M. *The Huguenot Struggle for Recognition*. New Haven, Conn.: Yale University Press, 1980.

Wood, James B. *The Army of the King: Warfare, Soldiers, and Society During the Wars of Religion in France, 1562-1676*. Cambridge, England: Cambridge University Press, 1996.

See also: French Wars of Religion; Religion and war.

Nancy M. Gordon

Ladysmith, Siege of

Type of action: Siege in the Boer Wars
Date: November 2, 1899-February 28, 1900
Location: Ladysmith, Natal, South Africa
Combatants: 13,000 British vs. 2,000-3,000 Boers
Principal commanders: *British*, Lieutenant General Sir George Stuart White (1835-1912), Redvers Henry Buller (1839-1908); *Boers*, General Petrus Jacobus Joubert (1831-1900)
Result: Of this siege it is commonly said that both sides lost

After Lieutenant Colonel Frank Carleton's surrender to Commandant Christiaan De Wet at Ni-

Members of the Boer army load their artillery before battle at Ladysmith. (Archive Photos/Hulton Getty Collection)

cholson's Nek and Sir George Stuart White's loss to General Petrus Jacobus Joubert at Modderspruit (both on October 30, 1899, "Mournful Monday"), White retreated to the town of Ladysmith with nearly all the remaining British forces in Natal. Among those who escaped on the last trains out of Ladysmith before it was surrounded were ambulance volunteer Mohandas K. Gandhi, Major General John French, and Colonel Douglas Haig.

Except for several relief attempts by General Sir Redvers Henry Buller, Ladysmith was a remarkably inactive siege. Both Joubert and White seemed willing to wait it out. The Boers' constant shelling with "Long Tom" guns from the heights of Bulwana, Platrand, Pepworth, and other nearby hills kept the British hemmed in but inflicted few casualties.

When Buller finally broke through from the Tugela River, the garrison was starving and had lost 3,500 dead, mostly from disease.

Significance

Buller was a short-term hero, but his indecision after he relieved Ladysmith resulted in a series of setbacks for the British. Ladysmith was the popular Joubert's last action. He died of natural causes and was succeeded as commandant general by Louis Botha.

Resources

Childs, Lewis. *Ladysmith, Colenso, Spion Kop: Boer War*. London: Leo Cooper, 1998.

_____. *Ladysmith: The Siege*. Barnsley, South Yorkshire: Pen and Sword, 1999.

Farwell, Byron. *The Great Anglo-Boer War*. New York: Harper and Row, 1976.

Pakenham, Thomas. *The Boer War*. New York: Random House, 1979.

Watt, Steve. *Battle-Siege of the Ladysmith, 2 November 1899-28 February 1900*. Johannesburg, South Africa: Ravan, 1999.

See also: Boer Wars; Botha, Louis; Buller, Redvers Henry; Churchill, Winston; Colenso; French, John; Haig, Douglas; Joubert, Petrus Jacobus; Kimberley, Siege of.

Eric v. d. Luft

Lafayette, Marquis de

Full name: Marie Joseph Paul Yves Roch Gilbert du Motier de Lafayette
Born: September 6, 1757; Chavaniac, Auvergne, France
Died: May 20, 1834; Paris, France
Principal wars: American Revolution, French Revolution
Principal battles: Brandywine (1777), Monmouth (1778), Yorktown (1781), Paris (1789)
Military significance: Lafayette served with distinction in the American Revolution, leading American forces to several victories. He served France by endeavoring to smooth political transitions created by the French Revolution.

The marquis de Lafayette studied at the Military Academy in Versailles and became a captain in the French cavalry at age sixteen. He sailed to America in 1777 to participate in the American Revolution (1775-1783) and was assigned to the staff of George Washington. He became a great friend of Washington and a trusted field officer.

After performing well in battles against the British in Pennsylvania (Brandywine, 1777) and

Marquis de Lafayette. (Library of Congress)

New Jersey (Monmouth, 1778), he was given command of his own division of American troops. In 1779, he returned to France and obtained financial and military aid for the Americans. After returning to America in 1780, he played a vital role in the entrapment and surrender of Lord Charles Cornwallis at Yorktown in 1781.

Returning to France in 1782, Lafayette participated in the French Revolution (1789-1792), serving as commander of the French National Guard. In 1830, he became the leader of a revolution that dethroned the Bourbon kings of France.

RESOURCES
Fritz, Jean. *Why Not, Lafayette?* New York: Putnam, 1999.
Izerda, Stanley, and Robert R. Crout. *Lafayette in the Age of the American Revolution.* Ithaca, N.Y.: Cornell University Press, 1981.
Kramer, Lloyd S. *Lafayette in Two Worlds.* Greensboro: University of North Carolina Press, 1996.
Liberty. Six-part documentary. Norwest Corporation and KTCA-TV, 1997.
Neely, Sylvia. *Lafayette and the Liberal Ideal, 1814-1824.* Carbondale: Southern Illinois University Press, 1991.

SEE ALSO: American Revolution; Brandywine; Cornwallis, First Marquess; French Revolution; French Revolutionary Wars; Monmouth; Washington, George; Yorktown and Virginia Capes.
Alvin K. Benson

LAKE CHAMPLAIN

TYPE OF ACTION: Naval battle in the War of 1812
DATE: September 11, 1814
LOCATION: Plattsburgh Bay, New York
COMBATANTS: 937 British vs. 882 Americans
PRINCIPAL COMMANDERS: *British*, Captain George Downie; *American*, Master Commandant Thomas Macdonough (1783-1825)
RESULT: Surrender of the British squadron to the Americans

After the defeat of Napoleon I in early 1814, the British government sent the duke of Wellington's veterans to Canada and instructed Governor General Sir George Prevost to conquer the Lake Champlain Valley for incorporation into the British empire. British shipbuilding efforts on the lake slightly outmatched those of the Americans. However, the recently arrived Captain George Downie had little time to create unit cohesion among his hastily assembled crews. Master Commandant Thomas Macdonough's squadron lay anchored with spring lines to each vessel's anchor cables so each could be turned 180 degrees within its mooring lines. There were four major vessels on each side, and the British had eleven row galleys and gunboats and the Americans ten. The principal combatants were Downie's thirty-seven-gun *Confiance* and Macdonough's twenty-six-gun *Saratoga*. Downie fell early in the battle, leaving his fleet leaderless. With the outcome in doubt, Macdonough wound his ship so the port guns could be employed, and this fresh broadside allowed him to destroy resistance on the British flagship. Only a few gunboats escaped. Macdonough lost 52 killed and 58 seriously wounded. British casualties included 54 dead, 116 wounded, and the remainder prisoners of war. Also captured were a frigate, a brig, two sloops of war, and several gunboats.

SIGNIFICANCE
Because the British lacked naval superiority, Prevost withdrew his ground forces back to Canada. This defeat contributed to the British decision to end the war and restore territory to its prewar status.

RESOURCES
Everest, Allan S. *The War of 1812 in the Champlain Valley.* Syracuse, N.Y.: Syracuse University Press, 1981.
Sweetman, Jack, ed. *Great American Naval Battles.* Annapolis, Md.: Naval Institute Press, 1998.
Turner, Wesley B. *British Generals in the War of 1812: High Command in the Canadas.* Montreal: McGill-Queen's University Press, 1999.

SEE ALSO: 1812, War of.
David Curtis Skaggs

LAKE ERIE

TYPE OF ACTION: Naval battle in the War of 1812
DATE: September 10, 1813

LOCATION: Lake Erie, west of Put-in-Bay, Ohio
COMBATANTS: 562 British vs. about 500 Americans
PRINCIPAL COMMANDERS: *British*, Commander Robert H. Barclay (1785-1837); *American*, Master Commandant Oliver Hazard Perry (1785-1819)
RESULT: Surrender of the British squadron to the Americans

Following the surrender of Detroit in 1812, U.S. officials sought to reclaim their control of the Old Northwest by first gaining naval dominance of Lake Erie. The U.S. Navy ordered Master Commandant Oliver Hazard Perry to Erie, Pennsylvania, where he supervised the construction of an American squadron. By August, 1813, his efforts provided the U.S. Navy superiority in vessels and firepower over its foe. Commander Robert H. Barclay, operating out of the small, isolated Detroit River port of Amherstburg, Ontario, could not match the American shipbuilding effort.

A shift in the wind gave Perry the advantage and allowed him to close with the British and bring his short-range carronades to bear. His squadron lagged behind the flagship, the *Lawrence*, and the British concentrated their fire on that vessel, rendering her useless. Perry transferred his flag to the advancing brig *Niagara* and ordered its commander to bring up the other vessels. *Niagara* crossed the British line, and the trailing vessels raked the six Royal Navy ships. This bloodiest naval engagement of the war saw 41 British killed and 94 wounded. Perry lost 27 dead and 96 wounded.

SIGNIFICANCE
Perry's victory opened the way for American ground forces to reclaim Detroit and drive the British and their Indian allies out of Michigan's lower peninsula and southwestern Ontario.

RESOURCES
Skaggs, David Curtis, and Gerard T. Altoff. *A Signal Victory: The Lake Erie Campaign, 1812-1813*. Annapolis, Md.: Naval Institute Press, 1997.
Welsh, William Jeffrey, and David Curtis Skaggs, eds. *War on the Great Lakes*. Kent, Ohio: Kent State University Press, 1991.

SEE ALSO: 1812, War of; Harrison, William Henry; Perry, Oliver Hazard; Tecumseh.

David Curtis Skaggs

LAKE TRASIMENE

TYPE OF ACTION: Ground battle in the Second Punic War
DATE: June 24, 217 B.C.E.
LOCATION: Lake Trasimene in Umbria
COMBATANTS: Romans vs. Carthaginians
PRINCIPAL COMMANDERS: *Roman*, Gaius Flaminius (d. 217 B.C.E.); *Carthaginian*, Hannibal (247-182 B.C.E.)
RESULT: Roman army destroyed in ambush

Together with Cannae (216 B.C.E.), the Battle of Lake Trasimene establishes Hannibal as one of the greatest military strategists. After crossing the Alps with elephants and an army of Gauls, Africans, and Spaniards, Hannibal defeated the Romans at the Trebia River. In response, Rome sent its consuls, Servilius Geminus and Gaius Flaminius, with two legions each, to guard the eastern and western routes respectively. Hannibal's strategy was to break up the Italian confederation by getting the allies to rebel against Rome. He headed for Etruria by way of the swampy Arno Valley toward Faesulae and then Arretium (Arezzo), where Flaminius was encamped. Many of Hannibal's elephants and horses perished along the way, and Hannibal lost an eye to disease.

In an attempt to lure Flaminius out of Arretium, Hannibal burned the villages along the way to Cortona. Instead of waiting for reinforcements, Flaminius and an army of 30,000 pursued the Carthaginians to the point where the hills almost reach Lake Trasimene. Here the consul encamped just before sunset, intending to follow the enemy into the valley north of the lake; he hoped to do battle or at least to push Hannibal into the other Roman army moving across the Apennines. During this respite, Hannibal prepared his ambush.

Roman historians Livy and Polybius differ on some battle details, and modern historians have placed the battle at four sites: the plain between Cortona and the hills north of the lake, the edge of the lake (the level of which was probably much higher than it is today) from just west of Tuoro to almost Passignano, the narrow pass on the eastern side of the lake near Torricella, and the valley and pass between Mount Gualandro and Tuoro, where the road from Cortona enters the lake. The last location is the most traditional interpretation and the one that seems to be closest to the Roman sources. No version fits the sources completely, and the archeological evidence for all theories is weak.

During the night, Hannibal positioned his slingers behind the Tuoro hill, his African and Spanish infantry and javelin throwers on the north hill, and his Carthaginian and Numidian cavalry near the entrance to the valley. The following dawn, the Romans rounded Mount Gualandro and turned north into the defile, shrouded in heavy mist, without having first reconnoitered it. When the Roman columns reached the end of the pass, they were attacked on all sides, their rear assailed by cavalry. Only the vanguard of 6,000 managed to escape, and even these were captured the next day. About 15,000 Romans were killed, some of whom were driven into the lake and drowned. The Roman survivors were sold into slavery, but the allies were permitted to return to their homes. Afterward, Hannibal defeated Geminus's relief force coming from the northeast.

SIGNIFICANCE

The battle at the lake was a major win in a series of victories for Hannibal and a major defeat for Rome. It led Rome to adopt Quintus Fabius Maximus's strategy of avoiding open battle with Hannibal, to recruit many more legions, to increase efforts to forge closer bonds with its Italian allies, and to accelerate movement toward the Romanization of Italy.

RESOURCES

Bagnell, Nigel. *The Punic Wars*. London: Hutchinson, 1990.
Briscoe, J. "The Second Punic War." In *Cambridge Ancient History*. Vol. 8 Cambridge, England: Cambridge University Press, 1989.
Cottrell, L. *Hannibal: Enemy of Rome*. New York: Holt, Rinehart, and Winston, 1960.
Lazenby, J. *Hannibal's War*. Warminster, England: Aris and Phillips, 1991.
Livy. *The War with Hannibal*. Baltimore, Md.: Penguin Books, 1965.

Polybius. *The Rise of the Roman Empire*. New York: Penguin Books, 1979.

SEE ALSO: Ancient warfare; Cannae; Fabius Maximus, Quintus; Hannibal; Punic Wars; Scipio Africanus; Trebia, The; Zama.

Thomas Renna

LANNES, JEAN

FULL NAME: Jean Lannes, duke of Montebello, prince of Sievers
BORN: April 10, 1769; Lectoure, France
DIED: May 31, 1809; Vienna, Austrian Empire
PRINCIPAL WARS: French Revolutionary Wars, Napoleonic Wars
PRINCIPAL BATTLES: Arcola (1796), Acre (1799), Aboukir (1799), Montebello (1800), Marengo (1800), Friedland (1807), Tudela (1808), Siege of Saragossa (1808-1809), Ratisbon (1809), Aspern-Essling (1809)
MILITARY SIGNIFICANCE: A courageous and brilliant commander, Lannes often won battles against great odds. Honest and outspoken, he was a true friend to Napoleon, who wept openly at his death.

A Gascon farmer's son, Jean Lannes was briefly educated by his brother, a priest, before becoming a dyer. Joining the army in 1792, he rose through the ranks during several campaigns. At Arcola in 1796, he was wounded when his horse slid into a bog as he was protecting Napoleon Bonaparte, this act of bravery established a friendship between them. In 1799, he was shot in the head and left for dead during the Siege of Acre and wounded at Aboukir. The following year, his performance at Montebello and Marengo also was noted by Napoleon.

Realizing that courage could not replace education and self-control, Lannes developed his tactical skills, sought to master his temper, and assumed increasingly important responsibilities. As ambassador to Portugal (1801-1804), he negotiated a commercial treaty with that historically pro-British nation. In 1804, he became one of fourteen active marshals of the empire. His talents helped ensure many of France's greatest victories, including those at Friedland (1807), Tudela

(1808), Siege of Saragossa (1808-1809), and Ratisbon (1809). Lannes's death from wounds sustained at Aspern-Essling (1809) deprived the army of one of its most charismatic leaders. He was the first marshal killed in action. Napoleon lost a comrade who could not be replaced.

Resources

Arnold, James R. *Crisis on the Danube: Napoleon's Austrian Campaign of 1809*. New York: Paragon House, 1990.

Dunn-Pattison, R. P. *Napoleon's Marshals*. London: Methuen, 1909. Reprint. Wakefield, England: EP, 1977.

Elting, John R. *Swords Around a Throne: Napoleon's Grande Armée*. New York: Free Press, 1988.

Haythornthwaite, Philip J. *The Napoleonic Source Book*. New York: Facts on File, 1990.

Horward, Donald D. "'Roland of the Army'— Lannes." In *Napoleon's Marshals*, edited by David G. Chandler. New York: Macmillan, 1987.

See also: Aboukir; French Revolutionary Wars; Friedland; Junot, Andoche; Lodi; Marengo; Murat, Joachim; Napoleon I; Napoleonic Wars; Ney, Michel; Oudinot, Charles; Saragossa.

Dorothy T. Potter

Laotian Civil War

At issue: Political identity of postcolonial Laos
Date: Spring, 1953-February 21, 1973
Location: Laos
Combatants: Royalists/United States vs. Communists/Pathet Lao/Viet Minh vs. Neutralists
Principal commanders: *Royalist/pro-Western*, Colonel Phoumi Nosavan (1920-1985), General Vang Pao (1931-   ); *Neutralist*, Kong Le (1934-   ), Colonel Deuane Sunnalath; *Communist/Pathet Lao*, Prince Souphanouvong (1890-?)
Principal battles: Sam Neua, Plain of Jars, Nam Tha, Phou San, Paksong
Result: Withdrawal of foreign military forces and creation of a neutral coalition government

Background

During most of World War II, Laos was officially ruled by a pro-Vichy French administration. Under special agreements reached during 1940, however, Japanese military forces were stationed throughout the country. There was little effective anti-Japanese resistance. Allied policy called for French reoccupation of Laos following Japan's surrender in 1945. By then, however, a fledgling Free Lao movement had developed under a French-educated Laotian prince, Souphanouvong, who was supported by the communist-led Viet Minh in Vietnam. French troops decisively defeated a small Free Lao force in March, 1946, forcing nationalist and communist leaders to flee to Thailand. King Sisavang Vong was restored to his throne, and French colonial rule reestablished.

In 1950, the exiled Free Lao leaders split into two factions, both seeking independence from France but in different manners. The Neutralists planned a peaceful transition to nonalignment, but the other group, led by Souphanouvong, was committed to establishing Communist Party rule. With political and tactical support from the Viet Minh, Souphanouvong created a Free Lao party, a skeletal guerrilla organization, and an all-Indochina alliance with Vietnamese and Cambodian Communists. When the focus of the Viet Minh's war against the French shifted to northwestern Vietnam, near the Vietnam-Laos border, in 1953, Laos became embroiled in Vietnam's anticolonial war.

Action

In early 1953, Viet Minh armed divisions crossed the border into northeastern Laos and occupied most of two provinces, Phong Saly and Sam Neua. They encountered and defeated a small French garrison at the provincial seat, the town of **Sam Neua** (spring, 1953). The move denied the French the use of this strategically important area in their war against the Viet Minh and allowed Souphanouvong's Free Lao party to establish its capital at Sam Neua. In late December, 1953, Viet Minh troops from central Vietnam launched a successful attack against several French posts in central Laos, dividing the French in Laos into northern and southern sections. Souphanouvong's Pathet Lao (PL) guerrilla units harassed the French in northern and central Laos while Viet Minh troops countered French activities in northwestern Vietnam. The Geneva peace agreement, which followed the French surrender at Dien Bien Phu (1954), allowed Souphanouvong's followers to retain control of the two northern provinces seized in 1953, while a neutral Royal Laotian Government (RLG) governed the rest of the country from Vientiane.

Negotiations on national reunification elections between the Pathet Lao and Royal Laotian Government failed, and small-scale military clashes took place at the end of 1955. Meanwhile, Communist organizers developed a complete civil administration in Phong Saly and Sam Neua as Pathet Lao guerrilla forces grew. The United States increased its military aid to the Royal Laotian Government in 1956-1957, and Pathet Lao forces began receiving weapons, supplies, and training from both the Viet Minh in North Vietnam and the Chinese Communists. In November, 1957, the Pathet Lao joined a coalition government at Vientiane, and in February, 1958, 1,500 Pathet Lao soldiers were integrated into the Royal Laotian Government Army, and 4,200 others were disarmed and demobilized. The Pathet Lao force inside the Royal Army retained its own command structure, however, and the disbanded Pathet Lao forces hid thousands of weapons and tons of supplies in secret caches in the northeast.

When the coalition government collapsed, it was replaced by a pro-Western cabinet in which Colonel Phoumi Nosavan, an experienced anticommunist officer, served as secretary of defense. Phoumi ordered a purge of Pathet Lao forces from the Royal Army. One former Pathet Lao battalion complied, but the other defied Phoumi's order and was attacked by royalist forces near the **Plain of Jars** (May, 1959). With tactical assistance and supplies provided by North Vietnam, Pathet Lao units were reactivated and a counterattack was launched, but the offensive was suspended when Souphanouvong was arrested by the increasingly pro-U.S. government.

A coup in 1960 by neutralist paratrooper Colonel Kong Le began a round of inconclusive clashes involving the Royal Army, Kong Le's troops, and the Pathet Lao. The Geneva Conference was reconvened. To improve the Communists' negotiating position, Pathet Lao forces breached the temporary cease-fire agreement by attacking Royal Army troops at **Nam Tha** (May 6, 1961). As a result, Souphanouvong was released and admitted to the new coalition government established by the conference. A political assassination in 1963 shattered the coalition, however, and Pathet Lao ministers fled to northeastern Laos, where Pathet Lao military strength had grown to 20,000 men armed with Chinese and Soviet weaponry. Neutralist forces split, with one faction under Kong Le supporting the royalists and another led by Colonel Deuane Sunnalath supporting the Communists. Pathet Lao troops attacked Kong Le at **Phou San** (April 27, 1964), shattering his forces and seizing control over much of eastern central Laos. The Communists controlled this area for the remainder of the war, establishing a complex of trails used to transport supplies from North Vietnam to Communist guerrillas in the South.

U.S. military aid to Laotian anticommunists grew in the late 1960's. An important recipient was General Vang Pao, who organized a guerrilla army among ethnic minorities. U.S. policy saw Pao's forces as a surrogate for direct U.S. involvement in the war in Laos. Pao's efforts were undermined by corruption, and Communist forces continued to grow. By 1970, Pathet Lao troops numbered at least 48,000. Main-force units cooperating with North Vietnamese regulars captured **Paksong** (May 15, 1971), bolstering Communist control over the trail complex.

Souphanouvong followed South Vietnamese Communist forces in negotiating with the United States in 1971-1972. Just weeks after the Paris Peace Accords on Vietnam, a separate agreement was signed in Vientiane in February, 1973, providing for the withdrawal of all foreign military forces. A protocol established a new coalition government in which Souphanouvong headed the principal policy-making assembly.

AFTERMATH

As Cambodia and southern Vietnam were conquered by Communist military forces in the spring of 1975, neutralists were removed from the ruling coalition in Vientiane, and a Communist government was established.

RESOURCES

Brown, MacAlister, and Joseph J. Zasloff. *Apprentice Revolutionaries: The Communist Movement in Laos, 1930-1985*. Palo Alto, Calif.: Hoover Institution Press, 1986.

Conboy, Kenneth J. *War in Laos, 1954-1975*. Carrollton, Tex.: Squadron/Signal Publications, 1994.

Dommen, Arthur J. *Laos: Keystone of Indochina*. Boulder, Colo.: Westview Press, 1985.

Stuart-Fox, Martin. *A History of Laos*. Cambridge, England: Cambridge University Press, 1997.

SEE ALSO: Cambodian Civil War; Cold War; Indochina War; Vietnam Conflict.

Laura M. Calkins

LAS NAVAS DE TOLOSA

TYPE OF ACTION: Ground battle in the Reconquest of Spain
DATE: July 16, 1212
LOCATION: Southern Castile
COMBATANTS: Christian crusaders vs. Almohad Muslims
PRINCIPAL COMMANDERS: *Christian*, King Alfonso VIII of Castile (d. 1214); *Muslim*, Muḥammad al-Nāṣir (d. 1213)
RESULT: Rout of Muslims left Al-Andalus open to further Christian gains, but pestilence and lack of supplies prevented immediate exploitation

Muslim victories over the Knights of Calatrava in September, 1211, spurred Alfonso VIII of Castile to send Archbishop of Toledo Ximénes de Rada to Rome to ask Pope Innocent III to endorse a Spanish crusade. Ximénes preached the crusade in Italy, Germany, and France, and 70,000 northerners joined Alfonso's 60,000 Spanish troops at Toledo in spring, 1212. Diego López de Haro led the northern vanguard out of Toledo on June 20. King Pedro II and his Aragonese followed, and Alfonso's Castilian troops and members of the military orders brought up the rear. They took Malagón (June 24) and Calatrava (July 1) before most of the northern troops returned northward. Heat, disease, and disgust with humane treatment of the Muslims (no plunder) by the Spanish drove them off. This loss was compensated in part by the arrival of Sancho VII of Navarre and his troops. After taking several more strongholds, the force reached Las Navas de Tolosa on July 13, where they were blocked by the army of Muḥammad al-Nāṣir, the emir of Morocco. The weakened López de Haro held the Christian center, with Pedro on the left and Sancho on the right. Alfonso held his large force in reserve. On July 16, Pedro and Sancho acted as pincers, while Alfonso crushed the Muslim center. Muḥammad al-Nāṣir fled, leaving untold thousands of Muslim dead. His tent and standard were sent to Pope Innocent.

SIGNIFICANCE
One of the greatest battles of the Reconquest of Spain, Las Navas de Tolosa shifted the balance of power to the Christians and proved to be the beginning of the end of Almohad power in Spain.

RESOURCES
Kennedy, Hugh. *Muslim Spain and Portugal*. London: Addison-Wesley, 1996.

Lourie, Elena. *Crusade and Colonisation*. Aldershot, Hampshire, England: Variorum, 1990.

Powers, James F. "Townsmen and Soldiers." *Speculum* 46 (1971): 641-655.

SEE ALSO: Alfonso VIII; Crusades; Reconquest of Spain.

Joseph P. Byrne

LASWARI

TYPE OF ACTION: Ground battle in the Second Marāṭhā War
DATE: November 1, 1803
LOCATION: Laswari, India
COMBATANTS: 10,000 British and Indians vs. 14,000 Marāṭhās
PRINCIPAL COMMANDERS: *British*, General Gerard Lake (1744-1808); *Marāṭhā*, Daulat Rāo Shinde
RESULT: British victory, forcing Shinde's submission

Britain's growing conquest of India and the need to parry Napoleon I's influence in the region mingled with growing resentment of the large armies of the Marāṭhās. At Laswari, British primacy in India would be marked by decisive victory.

General Gerard Lake and his 10,000 troops, mostly British East India Company native troops with a small English contingent, had occupied Aligarh, defeated the French at Delhi, then taken Āgra (September 5-October 17, 1803). He then faced Daulat Rāo Shinde's 9,000 infantry and 5,000 cavalry at Laswari.

The Marāṭhā army drew itself up behind a line of cannons, chained together by the wheel, as Lake's cavalry charged over the lines. The Marāṭhā veteran infantry rallied against the assault, but Lake's troops, who had covered sixty-eight miles in forty-eight hours, arrived just in time to destroy the Marāṭhā forces, who had held their ground nobly until 7,000 of their number had fallen. With victory impossible, the Marāṭhā laid down their arms, handing over seventy-two guns and large stores of ammunition. The British suffered about 800 killed. Later that month, Lake took Farrnkhabad.

SIGNIFICANCE

Coupled with the victories at the Deccan of General Arthur Wellesley, later duke of Wellington, the Battle of Laswari forced Shinde into submission.

RESOURCES:

Barnett, Correlli. *Britain and Her Army, 1509-1970*. Harmondsworth, England: Penguin, 1974.

Bhatia, H. S., ed. *Military History of British India, 1607-1947*. New Delhi, India: Deep and Deep, 1977.

Pitre, K. G. *The Second Anglo-Maratha War, 1802-1805*. Poona, India: Dastane Ramchandra, 1990.

SEE ALSO: British Colonial Wars; Marāṭhā Wars.

Jason Ridler

LATIN AMERICAN WARS OF INDEPENDENCE

AT ISSUE: Latin American independence from Spain
DATE: 1808-1826
LOCATION: Mexico, Chile, Peru, Colombia, Venezuela, Ecuador
COMBATANTS: Royalists vs. insurgents; Spanish vs. Spanish American revolutionaries
PRINCIPAL COMMANDERS: *Royalist*, General Félix María Calleja del Rey (1755?-1828); *Insurgent*, Father Miguel Hidalgo y Costilla (1753-1811), Father José María Morelos y Pavón (1765-1815); *Revolutionary*, Simón Bolívar (1783-1830), José de San Martín (1778-1850), Antonio José de Sucre (1795-1830), Bernardo O'Higgins (1778-1842)
PRINCIPAL BATTLES: Guanajuato City, Las Cruces, Aculco, Calderón, Zitácauro, Cuautla Amilpas, Oaxaca City, Acapulco, Valladolid, Chacabuco, Boyacá, Carabobo, Mount Pichincha, Ayacucho
RESULT: Regional instability; political life dominated by charismatic military leaders known as *caudillos*; victory by the revolutionaries and the end of Spanish colonial rule in the Americas

BACKGROUND

Three elements created the conditions for Latin America's independence movements. The first was a growing nationalism among creoles (elite of European descent), characterized by extreme dislike of peninsular officials sent to rule them. The second was the spread of Enlightenment philosophies; the third was the inspiration of the American Revolution. Support for independence was dampened by deep-seated loyalty to the Crown, revulsion at the excesses of the French Revolution, and fear of a Haitian-style slave insurrection. Indeed, the Napoleonic Wars were the necessary catalyst of independence, and it is unlikely the colonies would have pursued it otherwise.

When Napoleon Bonaparte closed European ports to English shipping, Portugal refused to cooperate with his continental system. In 1807, Napoleon invaded Portugal through the territory of his ally, King Charles IV of Spain. Portuguese emperor João VI fled with his court to Brazil. Meanwhile, Spaniards attacked French garrisons and rioted in Madrid, forcing Charles to abdicate in favor of his son, Ferdinand VII. When, in 1808, Napoleon was forced to abdicate in favor of his brother, Joseph Bonaparte, the Spanish resisted and established loyalist juntas allied with England. By 1810, Napoleon's army held most of the peninsula, although the Spanish were still conducting guerrilla war. In Cádiz, the Regency Council and Cortes (parliament), meeting under British protection, enacted a liberal constitution in 1812, creating a limited monarchy and inviting colonial participation in government. With Napoleon's defeat, Ferdinand returned, restored absolutism, and dispatched troops to the colonies. In 1820, the army revolted, forcing Ferdinand to reinstate the constitution and accept radical reforms. Although royalist forces still held New Spain (Mexico) and Peru, the revolt made Latin American independence inevitable.

Action

The events of 1808 led peninsular Spaniards to oust New Spain's pro-creole viceroy in anticipation of the arrival of Viceroy Francisco Javier de Venegas. Mexico City's creole aristocracy accepted the peninsular action, but regional creole elites, such as Father Miguel Hidalgo y Costilla, did not. On September 16, 1810, warned of his imminent arrest, Hidalgo summoned his followers and gave a famous speech, known as "El Grito de Dolores," in which he said, "Death to bad government; long live King Ferdinand and the Virgin of Guadalupe!" As Hidalgo's army mushroomed to 60,000, the movement became less creole and more mestizo and Indian.

Heading south toward the capital, Hidalgo's horde sacked **Guanajuato** (September 28, 1810), executing its *gachupín* residents. Creoles, fearing a race war, left the movement. Armed mostly with homemade lances, slings, and machetes, Hidalgo's forces moved on Mexico City. At the Battle of **Las Cruces** (October 30, 1810), 2,500 royalist troops with muskets and cannons inflicted 2,000 casualties. The insurgents held the field, but 40,000 deserted. The following weeks saw royalist victories at **Aculco** (1810) and Guanajuato. Hidalgo was routed at **Calderón** (January 11, 1811) and fled northward, where he was captured, tried, and shot.

The focus shifted southward, where insurgents commanded by another radical priest, José María Morelos y Pavón, fortified the towns of **Zitácauro** (1812) and **Cuautla Amilpas** (1812). Royalist general Félix María Calleja del Rey easily took the first, but the Siege of Cuautla lasted seventy-two days before Morelos y Pavón evacuated on May 1, 1812. Morelos y Pavón rebuilt his forces, took control of the countryside between Veracruz and Mexico City, and captured **Oaxaca City** (November, 1812). Now in control of the south, Morelos y Pavón took **Acapulco** in the summer of 1813. Meanwhile Calleja del Rey, who became viceroy in March, 1813, reorganized royalist forces and, beginning with the Battle of **Valladolid** (December, 1813), inflicted a series of defeats on Morelos y Pavón culminating in his capture on November 5, 1815. From 1816 to 1820, a stalemate existed. Royalists held the cities, and insurgents held the countryside. In 1820, however, rebels in Spain imposed a constitution abolishing the privileges for which Mexican royalists had fought. Thus, General Agustín de Iturbide sought out insurgent leader Vicente Guerrero. On February 24, 1821, the two joined forces under the Plan de Iguala, promising an independent monarchy, the supremacy of the Catholic Church, and civil equality for native and Spanish-born. In September, Iturbide proclaimed Mexican independence, and in May, 1822, the new Mexican congress proclaimed him emperor of Mexico.

In South America, the wars of independence proceeded on three fronts: the viceroyalties of La Plata (Buenos Aires), Peru (Lima and Potosí), and New Granada (Bogotá, Quito, and Caracas). Peru, having put down an Inca rebellion in 1782, was a royalist bastion, dragged into independence by the patriot movements of Buenos Aires and New Granada.

As Napoleon's army threatened Cádiz in 1810, the citizens of Buenos Aires (known as *porteños*) forced the viceroy to hold an open municipal meeting, deposed him, and established a junta. *Porteño* patriot armies sent to liberate the interior provinces were resisted not only by royalists but also by regional *caudillos* (strongmen), who wanted independence from Buenos Aires as well as from Spain. José Gervasio Artigas's *gaucho* cavalry maintained Uruguayan autonomy, and in Paraguay, creoles led by José Gaspar Rodríguez de Francia turned back the *porteños*, then expelled the Spanish.

In Peru, the *porteño* army defeated royalists at Suipacha (November 7, 1810) and seized silver-rich Potosí only to be driven back to Tucamán at the Battle of Huaqui (June 20, 1811), near Lake Titicaca. Patriot general Manuel Belgrano riposted in 1813 but was forced out of Potosí again. José de San Martín, seeing that the royalists were prepared for attacks by the usual route, equipped an army to cross the Andes to link up with Chile's patriot forces, which had continued as guerrillas after their defeat at the Battle of Rancagua (October 1-2, 1814). In January, 1817, accompanied by Chilean general Bernardo O'Higgins, San Martín swept down from mountain passes to defeat royalist forces at **Chacabuco** (February 12, 1817). Beaten at Cancha Rayada (March, 1818), San Martín recovered to win a decisive victory at Maipo (April 15, 1818), near Santiago. O'Higgins became dictator of Chile, and San Martín prepared to attack Lima by sea with the help of British naval officer Thomas Cochrane. In August, 1820, Cochrane, along with his fleet of seven warships and eighteen transports, blockaded the port, landed his army, and forced a Spanish evacuation by June, 1822. A large royalist army from the interior then forced San Martín to withdraw to Guayaquil, where he met Simón Bolívar.

Bolívar, known as the Liberator, rose to power with the Caracas creole junta. After the junta deposed Spanish officials, Bolívar was sent to London to request British assistance. There he encountered exiled revolutionary Francisco de Miranda and brought him back to lead Venezuela's patriot army. On March 26, 1812, an earthquake destroyed the patriot-held region but did not affect Spanish-held regions. It was, said royalist clergy, divine punishment of the revolutionaries. Venezuela's patriot cause collapsed. Bolívar gave up the key fortress of Puerto Cabello (July 6, 1812), and Miranda surrendered Caracas (July 15, 1812). Bolívar joined the Colombian forces and launched his Campaña Admirable (1813). After retaking Caracas (August 6, 1812), he ruled as military dictator, alienating many former supporters, most significantly the *llaneros* (cowboys), who formed lancer units that pushed Bolívar from Caracas (July, 1814). The Liberator retreated to Cartagena, then Jamaica, and then Haiti, just ahead of a large Spanish expeditionary force dispatched by Ferdinand to retake New Granada. Bolívar traded promises to abolish slavery and institute equal rights for the races in return for Haitian assistance. He renewed his campaign at Angostura (September, 1816), on the Orinoco River. Seeking a more diverse base, he recruited people of color and, with British loans, hired a legion of British veterans. Proceeding up river, he crossed the Andes, scattered the royalists at **Boyacá** (August 7, 1819) and entered Bogotá unopposed. After a brief armistice, Bolívar destroyed a Spanish army at **Carabobo** (June 24, 1821). Linking up with San Martín's troops, his lieutenant, Antonio José de Sucre, defeated a Spanish army at **Mount Pichincha** (May 24, 1822) incorporating Ecuador into Great Colombia. After disagreeing with Bolívar at Guayaquil over the future of government of the region, San Martín retired. Bolívar entered Peru and routed royalist forces at Junín Lake (August 6, 1824), and Sucre finished the last Spanish army at **Ayacucho** (December 9, 1824).

Aftermath

Power vacuums and instability followed the wars, giving rise to decades of Liberal-Conservative conflict and to charismatic military leaders known as *caudillos*, who dominated Latin American political life well into the twentieth century.

Resources

Bethell, Leslie, ed. *The Independence of Latin America*. New York: Cambridge University Press, 1988.

Lynch, John. *The Spanish American Revolutions, 1808-1826*. New York: W. W. Norton, 1973.

McFarlane, Anthony, and Eduardo Posada-Carbo, eds. *Independence and Revolution in Spanish America: Perspectives and Problems*. London: Institute of Latin American Studies, 1999.

Rodriguez O., Jaime E. *The Independence of Spanish America*. New York: Cambridge University Press, 1998.

See also: Bolívar, Simón; Central American Federation Civil Wars; Mexican Wars of Independence; San Martín, José de; South American Wars of Independence.

William Schell, Jr.

Latin Empire-Byzantine Wars

At issue: Byzantine recovery of capital and lands from crusaders
Date: 1204-1261
Location: Greece and Thrace around Constantinople
Combatants: Latin Empire of Constantinople and republic of Venice forces vs. empire of Nicea, despotate of Epirus, and Second Bulgarian Empire forces
Principal commanders: *Nicean*, Emperor John

III Vatatzes (1193-1254), Emperor Michael VIII Palaeologus (1234-1282); *Epirote*, Despot Theodore Doukas, Despot Michael II Doukas; *Bulgar*, Czar Kalojan (d. 1207)

PRINCIPAL BATTLES: Adrianople, Poimaneon, Pelagonia

RESULT: Empire of Nicea recovers Constantinople and reestablishes the Byzantine Empire; Latin Empire ends

BACKGROUND

Bitterness and mistrust grew in the twelfth century between the Greek Christians of the Byzantine Empire and the Latin Christians of Western Europe as the closer contact of the Crusades showed them how much they had come to diverge culturally.

In 1202, the knights gathered at Venice to participate in the Fourth Crusade (1198-1204) found that they could not pay for the ships to take them to their planned target of Egypt. A pretender to the Byzantine throne offered to give them the money for the ships if they would make him emperor. In June, 1203, a crusading army composed half of feudal knights and half of Venetian citizen-sailors appeared by ship at Constantinople. The current emperor fled without fighting in July, and the Byzantines accepted the pretender. In January, 1204, he was killed by a court conspiracy, and the crusaders decided to seize the city for themselves. On April 13, 1204, after a few days of unsuccessful assault, they got in through an undefended postern gate, and the upper classes simply fled, leaving the common people to surrender.

The crusaders elected Baldwin of Flanders the new emperor of the Latin Empire of Constantinople. Meanwhile, two Byzantine nobles fled in opposite directions and established the despotate of Epirus in western Greece and the empire of Nicea in Asia Minor. The leader of Nicea, Theodore Lascaris, proclaimed himself emperor in 1206.

ACTION

During the rest of 1204, the crusaders captured much Byzantine territory in Greece and Thrace. They set up localized feudal rule, including a kingdom of Thessalonica in the north and a principality of Achaia in the Peloponnesus, in place of the Byzantines' strong central government. Therefore, the Latin Empire had effective power only in Constantinople and environs, and the rest of Greece became and remained radically decentralized.

The Latin Empire was mortally wounded at the start by the resurgence of the Second Bulgarian Empire. At **Adrianople** (April, 1205), the Latin army was slaughtered by the Bulgars under Czar Kalojan, and the Emperor Baldwin disappeared, leaving the empire leaderless and too weak to fight the Byzantine governments in exile. When Henry of Flanders, Baldwin's brother, invaded the empire of Nicea in 1211, Theodore Lascaris easily held his own against the Latins and their Seljuk Turkish allies and secured his frontiers in Asia Minor by 1214.

The despotate of Epirus's best leader, Theodore Doukas, captured Thessalonica in 1224 before being captured by the Bulgars in 1230. The next Nicean Emperor, John III Vatatzes, won against the Latin Empire forces at **Poimaneon** in 1224 and crossed into Europe to take most of Thrace from them without a battle in 1225. He failed to take Constantinople in 1234-1236 because of the Venetian fleet, but he took Thessalonica from the Epirotes in 1246. This gave him a common border with the despotate, and the two Byzantine states fought each other through the 1250's for the privilege of despatching the weak Latin Empire.

In January, 1259, a Nicean nobleman who had proved himself in battle against Epirus in 1257 usurped the throne as the Emperor Michael VIII Palaeologus. The despot Michael II Doukas, fearing his potential strength, gathered an unnatural coalition of Greeks and Latin feudal rulers—not including the Latin emperor—to fight Nicea at the most important battle of the war, **Pelagonia** (September, 1259). The despot was driven off, his son defected to Nicea, and Michael VIII crushed or captured the Latin forces. He was now free to attack the Latin Empire directly.

The end of the Latin Empire was as much a fluke as its beginning. While fighting Epirus again in 1261, Michael sent a force of 800 past Constantinople on a related errand. Hearing from local civilians that the defending forces were away from the city, these men scaled the walls and got in on the spur of the moment. The Latins evacuated by ship without a fight, and Byzantine rule was reestablished.

Aftermath

The Byzantine Empire survived for another two hundred years and took the despotate of Epirus in 1339 but did not succeed in ending the feudal decentralization of Greece; therefore, it remained much weaker than it was before 1204.

Resources

Angold, Michael, *A Byzantine Government in Exile: Government and Society Under the Laskarids of Nicaea (1204-1261)*. London: Oxford University Press, 1975.

Geanakoplos, Deno John. "Greco-Latin Relations on the Eve of the Byzantine Restoration: The Battle of Pelagonia, 1259." *Dumbarton Oaks Papers* 7 (1953): 99-141.

Nicol, Donald M. *The Despotate of Epiros*. Oxford: Oxford University Press, 1957.

Wolff, Robert Lee. *Studies in the Latin Empire of Constantinople*. London: Variorum, 1976.

See also: Bulgarian-Byzantine Wars; Byzantine Empire; Crusades.

Jane Bishop

La Trémoille, Louis II de

Full name: Louis II de La Trémoille, viscount of Thouars
Born: March 20, 1460; La Trémoille, Poitou, France
Died: February 24, 1525; Pavia, Italy
Principal wars: Franco-Austrian War, Italian Wars
Principal battles: Saint-Aubin-du-Cormier (1488), Novara (1513), Marignano (1515), Pavia (1525)
Military significance: La Trémoille was the principal French commander during the French invasions of Italy

From prominent French nobility, Louis II de La Trémoille gained a reputation at an early age as an effective captain. In 1487, he was given command of the French army sent into Brittany to crush the revolt of Louis of Orléans (the future Louis XII). He won a brilliant victory at Saint-Aubin-du-Cormier (July 29, 1488). Ten years later, Louis became king and forgave La Trémoille for defeating him. Louis used him extensively as a commander in the Italian Wars (1494-1559), in which, unfortunately for the French, La Trémoille failed to appreciate the significance of the innovations made in the Spanish infantry by Gonzalo Fernández de Córdoba. In May, 1513, he laid siege to the Swiss-held fortress of Novara near Milan. A Swiss relief army surprised him by marching all night to give battle at dawn (June 6, 1513). After this defeat, La Trémoille retreated to France where he had to defend Dijon against the Swiss (September, 1513). He was forced to sign a humiliating treaty, but it was never implemented because the Swiss withdrew. Under Francis I, he served as royal chamberlain, participating in the Battle of Marignano (September, 1515). He was with the king in the Battle of Pavia (February 5, 1525), in which he was killed.

Resources

Baumgartner, Frederic. *Louis XII*. New York: St. Martin's Press, 1994.

Hall, Bert. *Weapons and Warfare in Renaissance Europe*. Baltimore, Md.: The John Hopkins University Press, 1997.

Taylor, Frederick. *The Art of War in Italy, 1494-1529*. Westport, Conn.: Greenwood Press, 1973.

See also: Fernández de Córdoba, Gonzalo; Franco-Austrian War; Italian Wars; Marignano; Pavia.

Frederic J. Baumgartner

Laupen

Type of action: Ground battle in Swiss Wars of Independence
Date: June 21, 1339
Location: Laupen, Switzerland
Combatants: 4,000 militia of Fribourg and Lords of Little Burgundy and 1,200 knights vs. 5,000 militia of Bern and 1,000 Swiss of the "Forest Cantons"
Principal commanders: *Burgundian*, Rudolf von Nidau, Gerard von Valengin; *Bernese and Swiss*, Rudolf von Erlach
Result: Swiss victory, Siege of Laupen lifted

On June 21, 1339, the Bernese and Swiss arrived to relieve Laupen from assault by a league of feudal lords and the Fribourgers. Rudolf von Erlach drew up his forces on Bramburg Hill, with three Bernese divisions on the right and the Swiss on the left. Seeking favorable ground for cavalry operations, the Burgundian knights deployed opposite the Swiss; the Fribourgers and the levies occupied the left. The heavily armored knights intended, as was customary in central Europe, to ride down all opposition and scatter the enemy.

Erlach allowed the Burgundians, led by Rudolf von Nidau and Gerard von Valengin, to begin the ascent of the hill, then launched the Swiss down in thick columns. As the baronial cavalry charged, the Swiss formed the hedgehog, a dense square that bristled with the halberd, a pole with a heavy axe-shaped head, the Swiss national weapon. The knights charged again and again but could not break the formation.

The main mass of the Bernese, despite the rout of their rear division by a flanking movement, attacked downhill, completely dispersing the Fribourgers. Erlach then turned them on the knights, who, already exhausted from their ordeal with the hedgehog formation, charged the Bernese once and rode off with heavy losses.

SIGNIFICANCE

The Swiss phalanx's repulse of the aristocratic knights had a great effect on morale and delivered a heavy blow to the supremacy of cavalry in central Europe.

RESOURCES

Delbrück, Hans. *Medieval Warfare*. Vol. 3 in *History of the Art of War*. Lincoln: University of Nebraska Press, 1990.

Oman, Sir Charles. *A History of the Art of War in the Middle Ages: 1278-1485 A.D.* London: Greenhill Books, 1998.

SEE ALSO: Austro-Swiss Wars; Sempach.

Bart L. R. Talbert

LAWRENCE, T. E.

FULL NAME: Thomas Edward Lawrence
ALSO KNOWN AS: Lawrence of Arabia
BORN: August 16, 1888; Tremadoc, Laenarvonshire, Wales

T. E. Lawrence. (Library of Congress)

DIED: May 19, 1935; Bovington, near Cloud Hill, Dorset, England
PRINCIPAL WAR: World War I
PRINCIPAL BATTLE: Damascus (1918)
MILITARY SIGNIFICANCE: From 1916 to 1918, Lawrence led a loose coalition of Arab tribes against the flanks of the Turkish forces in Arabia and Palestine.

During World War I, various tribes in the Middle East rose up against the occupying Turkish (Ottoman) army, then allied with Germany and the Austro-Hungarian Empire. Initially, the Arabs remained neutral, but the threat to the holy city of Mecca mobilized the tribes. At first, the Arabs were defeated by the better-equipped and superior Ottoman troops, but as Arab resistance increased, the British realized that a guerrilla force behind enemy lines would be of strategic value to the advance on Damascus.

T. E. Lawrence, an inexperienced junior officer with considerable knowledge of the Arab peoples and their land, took command and helped funnel equipment and money to the insurgents. He also helped train and organize an army from various, often hostile, Arab tribes. The exploits of this irregular force proved useful to British military efforts, especially in destroying the Turkish supply lines along the Hejaz Railway that linked Medina with Damascus in 1918.

Lowell Thomas, a Chicago newspaperman covering the war, popularized the story of Lawrence of Arabia through his postwar illustrated speaking tours about his experiences as a correspondent.

RESOURCES

Crawford, Fred D. *Richard Aldington and Lawrence of Arabia: A Cautionary Tale*. Carbondale: Southern Illinois University Press, 1998.

Falls, Cyril, and A. F. Becke, eds. *Military Operations in Egypt and Palestine*. Vol. 2 in *History of the Great War*. London: His Majesty's Stationery Office, 1930.

Lawrence, T. E. *Revolt in the Desert*. New York: Doren, 1927.

Lawrence of Arabia. Fiction feature. Columbia Pictures, 1962.

Thomas, Lowell. *With Lawrence in Arabia*. New York: Century, 1924.

SEE ALSO: Allenby, Lord; Megiddo, 1918; World War I.

Charles L. P. Silet

LAWS OF WAR

Laws of war are the body of international law that deals with the inception, conduct, and termination of warfare. They include limitations and restrictions placed on use of armed force and other methods of warfare. Laws of war are also referred to as laws of armed conflict and concern the code or rules that govern the rights and duties of *belligerents* or warring states, and the initiation and conduct of hostilities. They chiefly affect prisoners, spies, traitors, private property, blockades, and rights of capture. Their primary purpose is to make war or armed conflict (regardless of whether there is a formal declaration of war) more humane by regulating what weapons may be used, defining legitimate military targets, and aiming at minimizing the impact of war on civilians.

The laws of war approach their primary goal emphasizing humanity by recognizing that every individual, no matter how that person is classified (for example, prisoner of war, enemy, captured person, or detainee) is still a human being and, as such, is entitled to humane treatment. No unnecessary suffering or destruction is to be inflicted; everyone is to be treated humanely. Orders requiring commission of criminal acts in violation of the laws of war are unlawful and punishable. The laws of war have been broken repeatedly during armed conflicts. Even in war, however, many international laws are observed, such as laws governing the treatment of prisoners of war.

The laws of war have had difficulty keeping up with rapid changes brought about by technology, which has created newer weapons and more advanced warfare, resulting in damage to the natural environment and requiring constant supplements to earlier treaties.

The laws of war should be distinguished from "martial law," the law based on necessity or policy that is applied to all persons and property in occupied territory during an invasion or occupation. Martial law also refers to military rule exercised by a nation or state over its citizens in an emergency situation.

INTERNATIONAL LAWS OF WAR

An elaborate, well-developed body of international law functions to specify the rights and obligations of belligerents and the rights of neutrals and noncombatants. The constraints are based on the principles of military necessity and humanity, requiring that use of force be limited so that military goals are achieved with the least possible destruction and expenditure of life and resources. Nations and states act in accordance with international mandates, often without coercion, desiring to be perceived as acting according to international norms and standards of civility. Twentieth century societies also provide themselves with police as a supplement to the incentives of acting honorably and according to civil norms.

The international environment is characterized by anarchy because there is no supreme law enforcer. The World Court relies on the voluntary submission of parties to its rulings and the voluntary submission of parties to appear before it. There is no international police force to compel countries to obey international law. A Permanent Court of Arbitration was established in 1899 at The Hague, Netherlands. Members of the court serve as arbitrators. In 1920, the League of Nations created the Permanent Court of International Justice, renamed by the United Nations in 1946 as the International Court of Justice. Nations are not required to use the court, but they must accept its decisions if they decide to use it.

Nations at War

The laws of war are partly self-enforcing; that is, they are effective because it is in the best interest of the belligerents to obey the rules of conduct. When nations are at war, a major constraint on their behavior is the likelihood that the enemy will retaliate for unlawful behavior. This threat of *reprisal* helps to deter the use of weapons and tactics in violation of international law. The international law of war provides legitimate grounds for applying force by one state against another in retaliation for a violation. Threatened retaliation can also function as a restraint against misbehavior.

Wars have been fought for various reasons throughout history. A primary motivating factor has been potential gains associated with the *annexation* of foreign territory as well as the appropriation of wealth in the other country. To the extent that wars are fought by states seeking to maximize their revenues, governments are encouraged to minimize the costs of war to those nations involved.

Technological change has profoundly affected the waging of war. The invention of the bow, chariot, and gunpowder all significantly altered the nature of warfare. Starting in the sixteenth century, widespread use of guns in religious and political wars led to higher casualty rates than those of medieval wars. More efficient weapons often require adoption of new rules and adaptation of existing doctrines in order to maintain the objectives of the law. The invention of the submarine, pervasive use of strategic air power, and atomic weaponry are examples of military technology that grew faster than the law regulating it.

Historical Overview

In ancient times, war was not subject to any control other than that exercised by the combatants themselves. Any limitations placed on their actions on the battlefield would have been due to military necessity rather than any belief that what they were doing was wrong or illegal. The Vikings of the eleventh century attacked and pillaged at will. No treaties prohibiting brutal acts in battle had been negotiated between the states, and no uniform practice existed that avoided such conduct. Neither were the Crusades controlled by anything similar. The precepts of Christianity began to pervade conduct on the battlefield during the Middle Ages and the Renaissance. In 1625, Dutch lawyer Hugo Grotius wrote *De jure belli ac pacis* (1625; *The Law of War and Peace*, 1925) in which he explored the basic principles of humanitarian treatment of the victims of war. Physicians and theologians laid down principles of the just war, *jus ad bellum*, which have endured: War must be waged by a legitimate authority and for a just cause (to make reparation for an injury or to restore what had been wrongly seized) with the intention of advancing good or avoiding evil. There had to be a reasonable prospect of victory, and every attempt should have been made to reconcile the differences by peaceful means. Immunity was granted to noncombatants, especially priests and pilgrims. Another facet of immunity involved *double effect* or *collateral damage*, a concept often used to justify inflicting incidental harm on innocent bystanders if the harm occurs as a by-product of an attack on a legitimate military target. The amount of force was not to be disproportionate to the goal to be achieved.

Laws regulating the conduct of war were a secular creation developed to suit the needs of a stratified social order privileged to bear arms. A significant development that occurred in the early modern period, after the religious wars in Europe, was the abandonment of the concept of the just war. War became a natural or necessary element in international politics and pragmatic necessity rather than abstract principles shaped it. Generally, noncombatants within a battle zone had no rights or immunities, and had none until the twentieth century. There were, however, ethical considerations that began to surround their treatment. The goodwill of the local populace was

Landmark War Laws of the Twentieth Century

Law and Year	Description
Hague Conferences 1899 and 1907	Implemented by the Fourth Hague Convention. Recognized the following as established custom: To preserve human lives and rights, military attacks must be strictly necessary to a legitimate military aim; destruction and loss of life must be minimized; captured prisoners cannot be killed; captured towns cannot be pillaged; and weapons used must not cause unnecessary suffering.
Geneva Conventions 1929	Implemented after World War I. Expanded and complemented 1907 Hague Conventions.
Geneva Conventions 1949 • Convention for the Amelioration of the Condition of the Wounded, Sick in Armed Forces in the Field • Convention for the Amelioration of the Condition of the Wounded, Sick, and Shipwrecked Members of the Armed Forces at Sea • Convention Relative to the Treatment of Prisoners of War • Convention Relative to the Protection of Civilian Prisoners in Time of War	Implemented after World War II. Protected war victims. Drew 132 parties to these conventions; became binding on the United States when ratified by the Senate in 1956.
Protocols I and II to the Geneva Conventions of 1949 December 12, 1977	Implemented after the Vietnam Conflict. Established principles of humanity and dictates of public conscience; right of self-determination against domination; mandatory policing of conduct during hostilities; stronger standards of treatment of prisoners of war. Placed greater humanitarian obligation on parties; additional protections accorded children and noncombatant families.
International Covenant on Civil and Political Rights March, 1976	Implemented by the United Nations General Assembly resolution. Sought to preserve fundamental human rights during war and peace.

considered a necessity. Historians generally consider the French Revolution (1789-1792) the end of limited and the beginning of total war. The English fought with a ruthlessness that became apparent in accounts of the American Revolution (1775-1783). George Washington's standards of professionalism were in sharp contrast to the lack of control of the opposition.

The nineteenth century revealed growth of a bourgeois culture uneasy with the brutality of war, although the growing range and power of weapons were increasing the destructive nature of warfare. A consensus was evolving, holding that although war might still be a necessary element of international politics, it should be waged with humanity. A common code of conduct existed among the peoples of the Western nations during the first two decades of the twentieth century. Recognition of the adversary as a human being possessing certain fundamental rights is at the root of the humanist attempts to constrain war. The Nuremberg trials after World War II (1939-1945) had to take account of Nazi war crimes of a kind and on a scale that could not have been imagined.

The insurgency movements of the twentieth century, which received international recognition because they epitomized a particular cause, placed insurgents and incumbent authorities on equal footing before the law and imposed the additional obligation on the insurgents to observe the Geneva Conventions (1864-1949) fully.

Resources

Anderson, Gary M., and Adam Gifford, Jr. "Order Out of Anarchy: The International Law of War." *The Cato Journal* 15, no. 1 (Spring/Summer 1995): 25-38.

Bishop, Joseph W., Jr. *Justice Under Fire: A Study of Military Law*. New York: Charterhouse, 1974.

Howard, Michael, George J. Andreopoulos, and Mark R. Shulman, eds. *Constraints on Warfare in the Western World*. New Haven, Conn.: Yale University Press, 1994.

Reisman, W. Michael, and Chris T. Antoniou, eds. *The Laws of War: A Comprehensive Collection of Primary Documents on International Laws Governing Armed Conflict*. New York: Vintage, 1994.

Roberts, Adam, and Richard Guelff, eds. *Documents on the Laws of War*. Oxford, England: Clarendon Press, 1989.

Schmitt, Michael N., and Leslie C. Green, eds. *The Law of Armed Conflict: Into the Next Millennium*. Newport, R.I.: Naval War College, 1998.

See also: American Revolution; Chemical and biological warfare; Crusades; French Revolution; Geneva Conventions; Martial law; Religion and war; Vikings; War crimes; Washington, George; World War II.

Marcia J. Weiss

Lebanon

At issue: Control of Lebanon
Date: 1958-2000
Location: Eastern Mediterranean Sea, north of Israel, west of Syria
Combatants: Muslims vs. Christian Lebanese; Palestine Liberation Organization (PLO) members vs. Israelis
Principal commanders: *Lebanese Christian*, General Michel Aoun (1935-   ), Camille Chamoun (1900-1987); *American*, Dwight D. Eisenhower (1890-1969), Ronald Reagan (1911-   )
Result: PLO negotiation for a peace settlement, bringing the Lebanese Civil War to an end in 1990

Background

Domestic and international crises brought about civil war in Lebanon from 1975 to 1990. A French protectorate until 1945, Lebanon was placed under a coalition government. The president was a Maronite Christian, the prime minister was a Sunni Muslim, and the speaker of the National Assembly was a Shī'ite Muslim. Maronite Christians attempted to maintain control of the government, although the Muslim population was growing at a faster rate than the Christian population.

Action

In 1958, after trying to amend the Lebanese constitution to allow himself to run again for the presidency, Lebanese President Camille Chamoun asked U.S. President Dwight D. Eisenhower to send in military forces to assist him in putting down an Islamic rebellion. Eisenhower was probably concerned about Arab nationalism and suspected that the Soviet Union was involved in the uprising. On July 14, the king of Iraq was overthrown and his family was murdered, egged on by Radio Cairo. The next day, 5,000 U.S. Marines, supported by the U.S. Sixth Fleet, landed in Lebanon and helped secure Beirut and the airport. U.S. Army and Air Force personnel supplemented the Marines, bringing the total U.S. contingent to 14,000. U.S. forces were withdrawn that October.

The establishment of the Palestine Liberation Organization (PLO) in Lebanon increased tensions between Muslim and Christian factions. On April 13, 1975, full-scale civil war broke out. War continued in the region throughout the remainder of the decade and into the 1980's. The PLO conducted raids into Israel and used long-range artillery and rockets to shell Israeli territory.

The United States became directly involved in Lebanon again during the administration of President Ronald Reagan. On June 6, 1982, Israeli Defense Force (IDF) units launched the Peace for Galilee Operation, an attempt to create a buffer zone in South Lebanon and deprive forces of the PLO of their sanctuaries in that region. IDF forces then drove north on Beirut, and Reagan sent special envoy Philip C. Habib to negotiate a cease-fire. PLO guerrillas were evacuated under combined French, Italian, and U.S. operations.

The U.S. Marines deployed in Lebanon left on September 10, 1982, but soon returned. On September 14, president-elect Bashir Gemayel was assassinated. On the evening of September 17, Christian Phalangists entered two Palestinian refugee camps at Sabra and Shatila and killed 700-800 refugees, including women and children, while Israeli soldiers reportedly watched from nearby rooftops. (The Israeli government later issued a statement condemning the atrocities and said they assumed the Phalangists were targeting guerrillas, not noncombatants.) U.S. Marines returned on September 29 as part of a peacekeeping contingent.

Multinational peacekeeping forces were redeployed in Beirut during September 20-22, 1982. The U.S. Marine position was just east of the airport; the Italian contingent was farther north, closer to Beirut, and the French contingent was still farther north. The French contingent was later joined by a British contingent of about 150 men.

The Marine presence did not deter the violence, and the Marines themselves became targets. On April 18, 1983, the U.S. embassy in Beirut

U.S. Marines drive by the remains of the barracks that was destroyed by a terrorist bomb in 1983. (U.S. Navy)

was bombed, killing 63 people. (Among the 17 U.S. dead were several Central Intelligence Agency officials.) By October 17, snipers had killed 6 Marines. On October 23, a suicide bomber drove a van into the Marine compound and detonated the equivalent of 12,000 pounds of dynamite, killing 220 Marines and an additional 21 Navy medical personnel. This constituted the highest loss of Marines in a single day since the Iwo Jima campaign of 1945. In another bombing at about the same time, 58 French peacekeepers were killed.

Like Eisenhower in 1958, Reagan blamed the attacks on Moscow. The Soviet Union supported violence, Reagan said, "through a network of surrogates and terrorists." After nonbinding resolutions calling for U.S. withdrawal from Lebanon passed the House and Senate, Reagan announced on February 7, 1984, that he was "redeploying" the Marines to ships off the coast of Lebanon. Attacks on U.S. citizens did not end though, and on September 20, 1984, the U.S. embassy was bombed again, killing 24. From February 7 to March 31, 1984, multinational peacekeeping forces withdrew from Lebanon.

In 1990, two Christian militia units fought for control of Beirut. The Christian forces under General Michel Aoun were forced to capitulate after their supply of arms from Saddam Hussein's Iraq was cut off because of the arms embargo against Baghdad. The PLO negotiated a peace settlement between the two parties. This brought the Lebanese Civil War to an end. From 1975 to 1990, the conflict claimed 144,000 dead, 17,415 missing, and 200,000 wounded.

Aftermath

On May 24, 2000, twenty-two years after they had first invaded, Israeli forces pulled out of southern Lebanon. The South Lebanon Army (SLA), Israel's ally in the occupation, sought refuge in Israel as Shīʿite Hezbollah ("Party of God") forces filled the vacuum left by the departure of the Israeli forces.

Resources

AbuKhalil, Asʿad. *Historical Dictionary of Lebanon*. Lanham, Md.: Scarecrow Press, 1998.

Ambrose, Stephen E. *Eisenhower* (Vol. II). New York: Simon & Schuster, 1983.

Ambrose, Stephen E., and Douglas G. Brinkley. *Rise to Globalism: American Foreign Policy Since 1938*. 8th ed. New York: Penguin Books, 1997.

Frank, Benis M. *U.S. Marines in Lebanon: 1982-1984*. Washington, D.C.: U.S. Marine Corps, 1987.

Gailey, Harry A. *Historical Dictionary of the United States Marine Corps*. Lanham, Md.: The Scarecrow Press, 1998.

Korbani, Agnes G. *U.S. Intervention in Lebanon, 1958 and 1982: Presidential Decisionmaking*. New York: Praeger, 1991.

Millett, Allan R. *Semper Fidelis: The History of the United States Marine Corps*. New York: Free Press, 1991.

Moskin, J. Robert. *The U.S. Marine Corps Story*. 3d ed. Boston: Little, Brown, 1992.

O'Ballance, Edgar. *Civil War in Lebanon: 1975-1992*. New York: St. Martin's Press, 1998.

U.S. Foreign Policy: The Reagan Imprint. Washington, D.C.: Congressional Quarterly, 1986.

Woodward, Bob. *Veil: The Secret Wars of the CIA, 1981-1987*. New York: Simon & Schuster, 1987.

See also: Arafat, Yasir; Dayan, Moshe; Israeli military; Marines, U.S.; Rabin, Yitzhak; Sharon, Ariel.

John T. Donovan

Lechfeld

Type of action: Ground battle in the Magyar invasions
Date: August 10, 955
Location: Lechfeld, outside Augsburg, Germany
Combatants: Germans vs. Magyars, Hungarians
Principal commander: *German*, Otto I (912-973)
Result: The defeat of the Magyars stopped their raids of central Europe and resulted in their peaceful settlement on the plains of Hungary.

The Battle of Lechfeld was the greatest victory of Otto I, the founding emperor of the First German Reich. In 895, the Magyars, a restless nomadic people, had taken possession of the ancient Roman province of Pannonia, from which they raided central Europe for half a century. In 955, some of Otto's domestic enemies encouraged them to invade Germany. The Hungarian hordes, confident of success because of their sheer numerical strength (estimated at 100,000 horsemen by contemporaries), laid siege to the city of Augsburg, which was heroically defended by its bishop. With only dilapidated walls to protect the city, defeat of the badly outnumbered Augsburg forces appeared immanent. When Otto learned of the Magyar invasion, he hastily assembled an army from all parts of Germany and hurried to Augsburg. The decisive Battle of Lechfield took place on August 10, 955, outside of Augsburg on the Lech River.

In the scorching heat, three waves of Bavarians, followed by a wave of Franks, a fifth wave of elite Saxon troops led by the king himself, followed by five lines of Swabians and a rear guard composed of Bohemians charged the Hungarians. At first, the Hungarians were able to avoid the direct attack and even caused havoc by falling into the rear of Otto's army. Valor saved the day. Otto himself, sword in hand, fought in the thick of battle. As the tide of battle turned, many of the Hungarians drowned trying to escape across the Lech River. The rest of the Magyar invaders were routed and killed. Contemporary sources state that 100,000 Hungarians died.

SIGNIFICANCE

After the tremendous defeat, the Magyars gave up their restless wandering, accepted Christianity, and peacefully settled on the plains of Hungary, eventually becoming allies of the Holy Roman Empire.

RESOURCES
Falco, Giorgio. *The Holy Roman Empire*. Westport, Conn.: Greenwood Press, 1980.
Fichtenau, Heinrich. *Living in the Tenth Century: Mentalities and Social Order*. Chicago: University of Chicago Press, 1991.
Reuter, Timothy. *Germany in the Early Middle Ages*. London: Longman, 1991.

SEE ALSO: Holy Roman Empire; Magyars; Otto I.
Herbert Luft

LEE, HENRY

ALSO KNOWN AS: Light Horse Harry
BORN: January 29, 1756; near Dumfries, Prince William County, Virginia
DIED: March 25, 1818; Cumberland Island, Georgia
PRINCIPAL WAR: American Revolution
PRINCIPAL BATTLES: Paulus Hook (1779), Guilford Courthouse (1781), Eutaw Springs (1781)
MILITARY SIGNIFICANCE: An accomplished horseman and fearless cavalryman, Lee successfully commanded a legion of cavalry and infantry during the American Revolution. His victory at Paulus Hook was one of the most impressive feats of the war.

A Virginian, Henry Lee initially served in the American Revolution (1775-1783) as captain of a troop of cavalrymen under General George Washington. His natural abilities as a scout and leader led, in 1778, to his promotion to major and the command of three troops of cavalry and three companies of infantrymen, collectively known as Lee's Legion. In 1779, Lee and his troops surprised the British at Paulus Hook near New York, in a brilliant maneuver that resulted in the capture of nearly 160 of the enemy. In 1780, Lieutenant Colonel Lee joined General Nathanael Greene in the southern campaign, where his cavalry conducted several crucial raids and covered Greene's army as they retreated through North Carolina. Thwarted by Lee and his Legion, British cavalry were unable to break through to stop Greene and his men.

Although Lee's Legion fought valiantly in several battles, including Guilford Courthouse and Eutaw Springs, both in the 1781 southern campaign, their primary role was to harass the British in skirmishes, provide cover for the ground troops, and act as scouts. At such, Lee was brilliant.

In 1782, Lee resigned from the army to become a planter and politician. He also published his memoirs and fathered several children, including Robert E. Lee, the Confederate general.

RESOURCES
Gerson, Noel Bertram. *Light Horse Harry: A Biography of Washington's Great Cavalryman, General Henry Lee*. Garden City, N.Y.: Doubleday, 1966.
Lee, Henry. *The Revolutionary War Memoirs of General Henry Lee*. Edited by Robert E. Lee. New York: Da Capo Press, 1998.
Royster, Charles. *Light Horse Harry Lee and the Legacy of the American Revolution*. Baton Rouge: Louisiana State University Press, 1994.

SEE ALSO: American Revolution; Greene, Nathanael; Lee, Robert E.; Washington, George.
Jane Marie Smith

LEE, ROBERT E.

FULL NAME: Robert Edward Lee
BORN: January 19, 1807; Stratford Hall, Westmoreland County, Virginia
DIED: October 12, 1870; Lexington, Virginia
PRINCIPAL WARS: Mexican-American War, American Civil War
PRINCIPAL BATTLES: Chancellorsville (1863), Gettysburg (1863)
MILITARY SIGNIFICANCE: As commander of the Confederacy's Army of Northern Virginia from 1862 to 1865, Lee executed the offensive component of the Confederacy's strategy. His battlefield successes kept the Confederacy militarily viable, preserving its prospects for independence.

The son of Henry Lee, a war hero of the American Revolution, Robert E. Lee graduated from the U.S. Military Academy at West Point in 1829, then served with distinction in the peacetime army and the Mexican-American War (1846-1848) and as superintendent of West Point. The secession of eleven Southern states created a quandary for Lee, a slaveholder and a Virginian but a veteran soldier, whose father helped found the United States. Offered command of the volunteer army raised to quell secession and restore those states—including Virginia—to the Union, Lee sided instead with the Old Dominion.

The first year of the American Civil War (1861-1865) did little to enhance his prewar reputation. First, he was unsuccessful in securing control of western Virginia. He found himself advising Confederate President Jefferson Davis on military matters, not assuming another field assignment until the Union army approached the gates of Richmond, Virginia, in May, 1862, and the Confederate field commander, Joseph Eggleston Johnston, was wounded. Assuming command, Lee attacked his powerful nemesis and, in a series of successive battles styled the Seven Days' Battles, induced Union commander George B. McClellan to withdraw his forces to the Chesapeake.

Moving swiftly northward, Lee led his army to a smashing victory at the Second Battle of Bull Run on August 29-30, 1862, and then moved his army into Maryland, where it fought the Union army to a bloody draw at Antietam on September 17, 1862. Lee retreated with his army intact and assumed defensive positions at Fredericksburg, athwart the Union line of advance to Richmond. From this position, Lee's army repulsed the Army of the Potomac on December 13, 1862. Although Lee had not destroyed the Union army, his bold conduct cost three Union generals their commands and created the impression in the minds of many Northerners that the Civil War was futile.

In May, 1863, Lee firmly etched his name in the pantheon of military greatness by smashing the Army of the Potomac at Chancellorsville. Eschewing conventional military wisdom, Lee divided his forces in the face of a numerically superior enemy, sending Stonewall Jackson's corps to surprise the Union right flank. Although Jackson was mortally wounded, costing Lee his most able field general, the Army of the Potomac withdrew. In its wake, Lee invaded Pennsylvania.

Robert E. Lee. (Corbis)

The Army of Northern Virginia and the Army of the Potomac next came together at Gettysburg, where from July 1 to 3, Lee's generalship was put to the most extreme test. Critics have found fault with Lee's indirect orders for battle on July 2, which cost his army control of Little Round Top, although the blame might more correctly lay with James Longstreet, who was delinquent in bringing his corps into battle. Critics have also wondered why on July 3, Lee ordered a frontal assault, known as Pickett's Charge, on the Union center. Lee's defenders note that this offensive mind set had yielded success at the Seven Days' Battles and, given the uncertain nature of the command structure within the Army of the Potomac, Lee's decision seemed at least as reasonable as rash. However, the Union center held, and Lee retreated to Virginia.

During May and June, 1864, Lee defended Richmond from hammer-like assaults aimed at opening the road to the capital. Responding to a rapid flanking maneuver, Lee moved his army south to prevent the Army of the Potomac from capturing Petersburg, which sat across the railroad lines to Richmond. Using his skills as an engineer and his great gifts to inspire, Lee kept the Union at bay until April 1, 1865, when the Army of the Potomac seized the railroads to Richmond and threatened Lee's army with encirclement. Badly outnumbered and lacking in supplies, Lee surrendered his army.

RESOURCES

Gallagher, Gary W. *Lee and His Generals in War and Memory*. Baton Rouge: Louisiana State University Press, 1998.

———. *Lee the Soldier*. Lincoln: University of Nebraska Press, 1996.

Roland, Charles P. *Reflections on Lee: A Historian's Assessment*. Mechanicsburg, Pa.: Stackpole, 1995.

Thomas, Emory M. *Robert E. Lee: A Biography*. New York: W. W. Norton, 1995.

SEE ALSO: American Civil War; Antietam; Bull Run, Second; Chancellorsville; Fredericksburg; Gettysburg; Jackson, Stonewall; Johnston, Joseph Eggleston; Longstreet, James; McClellan, George B.; Pickett, George E.; Seven Days' Battles.

Edward R. Crowther

LEFEBVRE, FRANCIS JOSEPH, DUKE OF DANZIG

FULL NAME: Pierre-François-Joseph Lefebvre, duc de Dantzig
BORN: October 25, 1755; Rouffach, France
DIED: September 14, 1820; Paris, France
PRINCIPAL WARS: French Revolutionary Wars, Napoleonic Wars
PRINCIPAL BATTLES: Fleurus (1794), Danzig (1807), Durango (1808), Eckmühl (1809), Borodino (1812), Dresden (1813), Champaubert (1814), Montmirail (1814)
MILITARY SIGNIFICANCE: Lefebvre was known as an able commander, a good tactician, a strict disciplinarian, and a devoted, entrusted military leader under Napoleon Bonaparte.

The son of the town constable, Francis Joseph Lefebvre joined the French Guards at the age of seventeen. By 1788, he had risen to first sergeant and entered the National Guards in 1789. Promoted to general of the brigade, he fought with great bravery at Fleurus (1794), where his troops beat back three Austrian attacks led by Prince Charles.

In 1799, Lefebvre was appointed commander of the Seventeenth Military Division in Paris and played a vital role in helping Napoleon seize power. In return, Napoleon appointed Lefebvre a senator in 1800 and gave him command of the Imperial Guard Infantry in 1806. For his successful Siege of Danzig in 1807, Lefebvre was named duke of Danzig on September 10, 1808. He fought at Durango (1807) during the Spanish campaign before returning to Germany to fight at Eckmühl (1809). After a three-year rest, he fought at Borodino (1812) in the Russian campaign. During the German campaign in 1813, he led the Imperial Guard at Dresden and Leipzig. He also led the guard in successful engagements at Champaubert and Montmirail in the campaign in France in 1814. Reluctantly, he participated in pressuring Napoleon to abdicate.

RESOURCES

Chandler, David G. *Waterloo: The Hundred Days*. London: Osprey, 1980.

O'Brian, Patrick. *The Hundred Days*. New York: W. W. Norton, 1998.

Whaley, Leigh Ann. *The Impact of Napoleon, 1800-1815*. Lanham, Md.: Scarecrow Press, 1997.

SEE ALSO: Borodino; Dresden; French Revolution; French Revolutionary Wars; Jena and Auerstädt; Napoleon I; Napoleonic Wars.

Alvin K. Benson

LEGION

The largest permanent unit in the ancient Roman military. Legions, ideally composed of 6,000 soldiers, were divided into ten cohorts. Each cohort contained six *centuria*, each composed of approximately 100 men. Legionaries were armed with a seven-foot javelin called a *pilum* and a heavy thrusting sword with a twenty-inch blade called a *gladius*, and protected by a helmet, convex shield, and cuirass. The infantry was supported by varying numbers of cavalry, archers, slingers, and, if concentrating upon defense or siege, catapults and ballistae. By the fourth century C.E., the proportion of cavalry to infantry had significantly increased, because the Roman army needed more mounted soldiers to combat mobile barbarian raiders.

In the modern times, the term "legion" has come to mean a body of mercenaries or foreign troops in the service of another country. The French Foreign Legion (1831-2000), composed of foreign volunteers under French officers, is most famous of these.

Jeremiah Taylor

LEGNANO

TYPE OF ACTION: Ground battle in the Wars of the Lombard League
DATE: May 29, 1176
LOCATION: Legnano, sixteen miles northwest of Milan
COMBATANTS: 3,000 troops of the Holy Roman Empire vs. 3,500 of the Lombard League
PRINCIPAL COMMANDERS: *Holy Roman Empire*, German emperor Frederick I Barbarossa (c. 1123-1190); *Lombard League*, rectors
RESULT: League victory brought about the Peace of Venice (1177)

German reinforcements crossed Lukmanier Pass into the Lake Como region in April, 1176. Frederick I Barbarossa rode secretly from Pavia along the Ticino River to meet them and to lead them to a joint operation with his main force. At Como, Italian imperialist troops increased the reinforcements to about 3,000. To intercept them, the Milanese and the Lombard League placed about 3,500 men near the west bank of the Olona across approaches from Como to the Ticino. The infantry around the Milanese war cart, the *carroccio*, stood in a hastily fortified position at Borsano. One wing of cavalry stretched from there two and one-half miles east-northeast to Legnano on the Olona and the other wing one and one-half miles north to Busto Arsizio.

At dawn, the rectors sent a reconnaissance force of 700 horsemen north. The emperor had crossed the Olona and was marching south from Cairate, five miles north-northeast of Busto Arsizio. The reconnaissance group engaged the emperor's vanguard but was routed and fled beyond Borsano when his main army pushed on. Frederick's knights turned on the infantry. However, the fleeing reconnaissance troops met knights from Brescia, and jointly they hit the German knights at the *carroccio* from the rear. Frederick's horse fell, and as he was believed killed, his troops fled, pursued to the Ticino by the league cavalry. The booty and numbers of prisoners taken were immense.

SIGNIFICANCE
Prompt Milanese coordination and strong infantry blocking defeated Frederick's hasty engagement from the march. The league's victory proved its superior military leadership and resulted in the favorable Peace of Venice (1177).

RESOURCES
Carson, Thomas, ed. *Barbarossa in Italy*. New York: Italica, 1994.
Morazzoni, Joseph. *The Majolicas and the Ancient Weapons of Legnano*. Milan, Italy: Associazione Amatori Armi Antiche, 1950.
Munz, Peter. *Frederick Barbarossa: A Study in Medieval Politics*. London: Eyre & Spottiswoode, 1969.
Otto I, Bishop of Freising. *The Deeds of Frederick Barbarossa*. Toronto: University of Toronto Press, 1994.

Pacaut, Marcel. *Frederick Barbarossa*. London: Collins, 1970.

See also: Frederick I Barbarossa; Lombard League, Wars of.

Reinhold Schumann

Leipzig

Type of action: Ground battle in the Napoleonic Wars
Date: October 16-19, 1813
Location: Leipzig, Saxony (Germany)
Combatants: 195,000 French, Bavarians, and Saxons vs. 365,000 Austrians, Prussians, Russians, and Swedes, also known as the Sixth Coalition
Principal commanders: *French*, Napoleon I (1769-1821); *Allied*, Prince Karl Philipp Schwarzenberg (1771-1820), Field Marshal Gebhard Leberecht von Blücher (1742-1819), Prince Jean-Baptiste-Jules Bernadotte (1763-1844)
Result: Decisive victory for the armies of the Sixth Coalition

Leipzig was a series of engagements, fought in and near Leipzig, a city in the German state of Saxony. In terms of the number of soldiers involved, it was the largest battle of the Napoleonic Wars. The battle developed when the armies of the Sixth Coalition—Prince Karl Philipp Schwarzenberg's Army of Bohemia, Field Marshal Gebhard Leberecht von Blücher's Army of Silesia, and Prince Jean-Baptiste-Jules Bernadotte's Army of the North—converged on Napoleon I's forces near Leipzig.

In the initial engagements, fought north and south of the city on October 16, Napoleon fought Schwarzenberg and Blücher to a draw. October 17 was a day of reinforcement and redeployment for both combatants, the major development being the arrival of Bernadotte's army from the east. October 18 turned out to be the decisive day, with Napoleon defending his position against attacks by each of his enemies' armies. After nine hours of intense combat, the emperor ordered a phased withdrawal through Leipzig and over the Elster River.

During the retreat, which continued through October 19, some 20,000 French troops deployed as a rear guard were lost when the only bridge over the Elster was destroyed while Napoleon's Bavarian and Saxon allies switched sides. Although the emperor extricated more than 100,000 soldiers, Napoleon lost nearly 75,000 men, casualties that he could no longer afford.

Significance

The decisive battle of the Napoleonic Wars, Leipzig cost Napoleon control of Germany and guaranteed his ultimate defeat, which came in the campaign of France in early 1814.

Resources
Chandler, David G. *The Campaigns of Napoleon*. New York: Macmillan, 1966.
Hofschroer, Peter. *Leipzig 1813*. London: Osprey, 1993.
Nafziger, George. *Napoleon at Leipzig*. Chicago, Ill.: Emperor's Press, 1996.

See also: Blücher, Gebhard Leberecht von; Napoleon I; Napoleonic Wars.

Bruce J. DeHart

LeMay, Curtis

Full name: Curtis Emerson LeMay
Born: November 15, 1906; Columbus, Ohio
Died: October 1, 1990; March Air Force Base, California
Principal war: World War II
Military significance: A controversial figure throughout his military career, LeMay was also one of the finest combat commanders in U.S. history and the youngest to make full general after only Ulysses S. Grant.

Curtis LeMay was commissioned in the army in 1928 through the Reserve Officers Training Corps program at Ohio State University and became both a navigator and a pilot. He received command of the 305th Bombardment Group in April, 1942, and of the Third Bombardment Division in June, 1943. In March, 1944, he was promoted to major general and led the Twentieth Bomber Command in China. After being named head of the Twenty-first Bomber Command on Guam in January, 1945, he developed successful new tactics for B-29 raids against Japan. In July, he became commander of the Twentieth Air Force.

Curtis LeMay. (Library of Congress)

After the war, LeMay was promoted to lieutenant general in the new U.S. Air Force and played a key role in the 1948-1949 Berlin Airlift. From 1948 to 1957, he headed the Strategic Air Command. Promoted to general in 1951, he became Air Force vice chief of staff in 1957 and served as chief of staff from 1961 to 1965. LeMay was at odds with the administrations of both Presidents John F. Kennedy, Jr., and Lyndon B. Johnson over the shift from massive retaliation to flexible response, whether to develop the XB-70, and the conduct of the Vietnam Conflict. He favored massive bombing of North Vietnam and believed victory could be achieved through strategic bombing.

LeMay retired in 1965. In 1968, he was a candidate for vice president on George Wallace's American Independent Party ticket.

RESOURCES

Coffee, Thomas M. *Iron Eagle: The Turbulent Life of General Curtis E. LeMay.* New York: Crown, 1986.

LeMay, Curtis E. *America Is in Danger.* New York: Funk & Wagnalls, 1968.

LeMay, Curtis E., and MacKinlay Kantor. *Mission with LeMay: My Story.* New York: Doubleday, 1965.

SEE ALSO: Berlin Blockade; Guam; World War II.

Spencer C. Tucker

LENINGRAD, SIEGE OF

TYPE OF ACTION: Siege in World War II
DATE: 1941-1944
LOCATION: Leningrad, Soviet Union
COMBATANTS: Soviets vs. Germans
PRINCIPAL COMMANDERS: *Soviet*, Georgy Zhukov (1896-1974); *German*, Wilhelm von Leeb (1876-1956)
RESULT: Soviet victory; blockade lifted

A major goal in Adolf Hitler's war plan was Operation Barbarossa, a surprise invasion of the Soviet Union. The German forces attacked along an eight-hundred-mile front with the northern army, led by Wilhelm von Leeb, aimed at Leningrad (June 22, 1941). Only hours after entering Soviet territory, the German Luftwaffe (air force) had annihilated most of the Russian front-line aircraft. Ground troops, unsupported and poorly led, retreated, and many surrendered. To assist in the defense of Leningrad, reserve troops, workers' battalions, and student battalions were mobilized. Hundreds of thousands of civilians were ordered to dig anti-tank ditches, trenches, and other defenses.

The bombing attacks on Leningrad targeted industrial sites, communications and transportation centers, bridges on the Neva River, air bases, and naval ports.

After weeks of intense air raids failed to bring about the collapse of the city, the Nazi leadership decided to encircle it and starve the population into submission. By September, 1941, three million people were trapped and isolated from the rest of the Soviet Union. This blockade would last nine hundred days.

General Georgy Zhukov was ordered by Joseph Stalin to take command in the defense of Leningrad. Under his leadership, German advances were halted, additional regular troops were brought to resist the Wermacht, and a system of organization for civilian life in the city was established.

In January, 1942, a mass evacuation of civilians began, consisting primarily of children and the elderly. The route of escape took them across the frozen ice road of Lake Ladoga and then east into rural Russia, where the majority would later succumb to starvation and freezing.

The principal concern of the city authorities was maintaining a food supply. The possibility of aid from the outside was negligible because of the blockade. Furthermore, the air attacks had destroyed much of the city's reserves. The decision was made to issue each citizen a ration card to be used each day to obtain food. Through the winter of 1941-1942, the rations were cut five times as supplies dwindled.

In addition to food shortages, a fuel shortage ensued as both oil and coal supplies were used up. The daily life of the residents of Leningrad was marked by a lack of food, light, and heat and by continual air attacks. In November, 1941, more than 11,000 died; in January, 1942, between 3,500 and 4,000 died daily from starvation and freezing. By January, the water mains and sewers had frozen and broken, causing water shortages and epidemics.

In spite of such dire privations, morale was sustained in several ways. Theatrical performances, cinemas, poetry readings, schools, and many factories continued on as best they could.

The ice road across Lake Ladoga brought slight relief to the starving civilians. Food supplies, although meager, were brought in by motor transports. A petrol pipeline was also laid to bring more fuel into the city.

With the coming of spring (1942 and 1943), Leningrad residents planted vegetables throughout the city. A more somber duty was the disposal of the dead in mass graves. Thousands had died on the streets and in homes. Too weak to bury their dead or to carry them to cemeteries, many just left family members along the streets.

The long nightmare for Leningrad ended in January, 1944, with the arrival of a large Soviet force that met up with the troops of the Leningrad front. The counteroffensive lasted only a few days as the Germans began to retreat to Estonia. The blockade was lifted on January 27, 1944.

Significance

After nine hundred days, a city of 3 million was reduced to 600,000. Never in history had a city suffered such a loss of civilian life.

Resources

Barber, John, and Mark Harrison. *The Soviet Home Front, 1941-1945*. London: Longman, 1991.

Salisbury, Harrison E. *The Nine Hundred Days: The Siege of Leningrad*. New York: Harper & Row, 1969.

Volkogonov, Dimitri. *Stalin, Triumph and Tragedy*. New York: Grove Weidenfeld, 1991.

See also: Hitler, Adolf; Stalin, Joseph; World War II; Zhukov, Georgy.

LaRae Larkin

Milestones in the Siege of Leningrad

June, 1941	German forces attack the Soviet Union, headed for Leningrad.
September, 1941	Siege of Leningrad begins, isolating 3 million people.
November, 1941	More than 11,000 Leningrad residents die from starvation and cold.
January, 1942	Mass evacuation of civilians, mostly children and the elderly, begins. Many die from the cold and lack of food after arriving in rural Russia; meanwhile, Leningrad residents are dying at the rate of 3,500 to 4,000 per day.
Spring, 1942	Leningrad residents plant vegetables in an effort to obtain food.
January 15-19, 1944	Soviet army attacks German forces besieging Leningrad, freeing the city.
January 27, 1944	Blockade on Leningrad is lifted.

Leo III

Full name: Emperor Leo III the Isaurian
Born: c. 680; Germanikeia, Commagene, Syria
Died: June 18, 741; Constantinople
Principal wars: Byzantine-Muslim Wars
Principal battles: Siege of Constantinople (717-718), Akroinon (740)
Military significance: After breaking an Arab siege of Constantinople, Leo stabilized the Byzantine state, reorganized the empire's military defenses, and fought successfully against perennial Arab raids in eastern and central Asia Minor.

Leo III's early years were spent as a diplomat and soldier in the northeastern Byzantine Empire. After being appointed military governor (*strategos*) of the military district of Anatolikon in Asia Minor (715), he overthrew Byzantine emperor Theodosius III, entering Constantinople on March 25, 717. This ended two decades of anarchy and civil war during which seven rulers rose and fell violently. Although Leo had been emperor for only a short time, Constantinople was prepared for the Arab attack of July, 717, when about 120,000 men and 1,800 ships under the leadership of Maslamah ibn ʿAbd al-Malik and Caliph Sulaymān. Greek fire, a petroleum mixture, kept the Muslim fleet at bay, and the naval blockade failed. The Arab army suffered through a harsh winter outside the city's great walls and from the attacks of Bulgarians that Leo had rallied. The siege was lifted in August, 718.

From 720 to 740, Leo fought against Arab raids in eastern Asia Minor and Armenia, and against Cyprus (725). Caesarea was sacked in spring, 726. Leo reorganized the empire's eastern military defenses and allied himself with the Bulgarian Khazars. He also invoked divine aid by outlawing religious images (*iconoclasm*), forcibly baptizing Jews, and updating the legal code. His last victory, at Akroinon (740), over 20,000 Arabs, temporarily halted their raids.

Resources

Scott, Roger, ed. *The Chronicle of Theophanes Confessor*. Oxford: Clarendon Press, 1997.
Treadgold, Warren. *Byzantium and Its Army, 284-1081*. Stanford, Calif.: Stanford University Press, 1995.
Whittow, Mark. *The Making of Byzantium, 600-1025*. Berkeley: University of California Press, 1996.

See also: Ancient warfare; Byzantine Empire; Byzantine-Muslim Wars; Constantinople, Siege of, 717-718.

Joseph P. Byrne

Lepanto

Type of action: Sea battle in Cyprus War
Date: October 7, 1571
Location: Mediterranean Sea in the Gulf of Corinth off Lepanto (the Italian name for what later became the Greek port of Návpaktos)
Combatants: Christian fleet of 208 galleys and 6 galleasses vs. Turkish fleet of 250 galleys and 40 galliots
Principal commanders: *Christian*, Don Juan de Austria (1547-1578); *Turkish*, Ali Pasha
Result: A decisive victory for the Christian forces

In response to Turkish threats in the eastern Mediterranean and especially the attack on the Venetian-held island of Cyprus, a naval force was organized through the efforts of Pope Pius V. Don Juan de Austria, half brother of King Philip II of Spain, was placed in supreme command. Spain and Venice supplied most of the ships. There was also a Genoese squadron under the command of Andrea Doria and a small squadron from the Papal States commanded by Marc Antonio Colonna. The fleet consisted mostly of galleys—light fast ships propelled by oars.

The force gathered at Messina in Sicily from which it departed in the summer of 1571 to seek out and destroy the Turkish fleet. At Corfu, reconnaissance galleys were dispatched under the command of Gil de Andrade, who located the Turkish fleet in the harbor at Lepanto. Aware of the presence of a Christian fleet in the area but not knowing its size, the Turkish commander, Ali Pasha, sent a message to Sultan Selim I suggesting that it might be advisable for the Turkish fleet to remain in port under the guns of shore batteries. This would give the Turks a defensive advantage and safety in the event the enemy fleet was a superior force. The sultan replied in sharp terms that his previous order to seek out and destroy the Christian fleet stood and that the next message he expected to receive from his admiral was the happy news of the total destruction of the Christian fleet. The Turkish fleet, accordingly, left port to confront the Christian fleet.

In preparation for the battle, Don Juan ordered that battering rams be removed from the ships to give the bow-mounted cannons a clear field of fire. This was a departure from the conventional naval tactic of the day of ramming the enemy's ships before grappling and boarding them. All galley slaves who were not Muslim prisoners of war were unchained. They were given weapons and promised their freedom if the Christian fleet proved victorious. Triple rations of wine were then issued to all hands.

Although the fleets were almost equally matched in the number of galleys, the six galleasses that the Christians placed in front of their squadrons delivered considerable firepower for that era. These were much larger and sturdier ships than a galley but lacked maneuverability. Each carried about forty or more cannons as against the five or six of a fragile galley.

At first the Turks did not attempt to grapple and board, as their deadly arrows proved more effective than the crude firearms of the Christians. Eventually the arrows were exhausted, however, and the conventional boarding and hand-to-hand fighting took place. Don Juan personally led an attack on Ali Pasha's flagship. Before the two could engage in personal combat, Ali Pasha was shot in the head. He fell into the rowing benches, where a Christian slave grabbed a scimitar and cut off his head. The admiral's head was then mounted on a pike for all to see.

The battle was over by four o'clock in the afternoon. The Christian losses were 7,000 to 8,000 killed and 10 to 15 ships destroyed. About 10,000 Christian galley slaves were liberated and 117 ships captured intact. On the Muslim side, more than 25,000 were killed. Fewer than 50 Turkish ships escaped, and most of these were later burned as unseaworthy.

Significance

The decisive victory at Lepanto left the Turks without a navy. Although it was replaced within a year, Turkish expansion into western Mediterranean was halted and the myth of Turkish invincibility overcome.

Resources

Beeching, Jack. *The Galleys at Lepanto*. New York: Charles Scribner's Sons, 1982.

Bryer, Anthony, and Michael Urskins, eds. *Manzikert to Lepanto: The Byzantine World and the Turks 1071-1571: Papers Given at the Nineteenth Spring Symposium of Byzantine Studies, Birming-*

Turkish sailors cling to the remains of their ship during a battle off Lepanto. The Christian fleet led by Don Juan de Austria among others would eventually triumph over the Turkish fleet. (Library of Congress)

ham, March, 1985. Amsterdam: A. M. Hakkert, 1991.

Fuller, J. F. C. *A Military History of the Western World: From the Earliest Time to the Battle of Lepanto*. Vol. 1. New York: Funk and Wagnalls, 1954.

Marx, Robert F. *The Battle of Lepanto: 1571*. Cleveland, Ohio: World, 1966.

Natkiel, Richard, and John Pimlott. *Atlas of Warfare*. New York: Gallery Books, 1988.

SEE ALSO: Byzantine Empire; Byzantine-Ottoman Wars; Don Juan de Austria; Famagusta, Siege of; Selim I; Turkish Wars of European Expansion.

Gilbert T. Cave

LETTOW-VORBECK, PAUL EMIL VON

ALSO KNOWN AS: The Hero of German East Africa
BORN: March 20, 1870; Saarlouis, Germany
DIED: March 9, 1964; Hamburg, Germany
PRINCIPAL WAR: World War I
PRINCIPAL BATTLES: Tanga (1914), Mahiwa (1917)
MILITARY SIGNIFICANCE: During World War I in eastern Africa, Lettow-Vorbeck led a successful guerrilla campaign against the British, French, Belgians, and Portuguese, tying down nearly one million men and remaining undefeated throughout the war.

Paul Emil von Lettow-Vorbeck entered the cadet corps in Potsdam in 1881 and later graduated from the Main Cadet Academy at Groß-Lichterfelde near Berlin, where he received the unusual honor of being allowed to take an imperial oath. Following further study at the Military Academy, he was attached to the German general staff, took part in the suppression of the Boxer Rebellion in China (1900-1901) and the Herero, Hottentot, and Nama Uprisings in German South West Africa (1904-1907).

In 1914, before the outbreak of World War I, he was given command of the Schutztruppe (defense force) in German East Africa. At the Battles of Tanga (November 2-4, 1914) and Mahiwa (October 15-18, 1917), he decisively defeated the British. On November 25, 1918, Lettow-Vorbeck surrendered his troops at Abercorn, south of Lake Tanganyika, on orders from the German high command. He was regarded as an extremely able colonial soldier, even by his foes. Following conclusion of hostilities, Lettow-Vorbeck became a protagonist and symbolic figure for German colonial revisionists. He participated in a failed coup in Hamburg involving right-wing conservatives and represented the German National People's Party in the Reichstag as the successor of Grand Admiral Alfred von Tirpitz from 1928 to 1930.

RESOURCES

Farwell, Byron. *The Great War in Africa, 1914-1918*. New York: W. W. Norton, 1986.

Hoyt, Edwin P. *Guerrilla: Colonel von Lettow-Vorbeck and Germany's East African Empire*. New York: Macmillan, 1981.

Rooney, David. "A German Guerrilla Chief in Africa." *History Today* 49, no. 11 (November, 1999): 28-34.

SEE ALSO: Boxer Rebellion; German Colonial Wars; Guerrilla warfare.

Gregory Weeks

LEUCTRA

TYPE OF ACTION: Ground battle in the Wars for Greek Hegemony
DATE: July, 371 B.C.E.
LOCATION: Leuctra, near Thebes (Boeotia, Greece)
COMBATANTS: 12,100 Spartans and their allies vs. 9,000 Thebans
PRINCIPAL COMMANDERS: *Spartan*, King Cleombrotus (380-371 B.C.E.); *Theban*, Epaminondas (410-362 B.C.E.)
RESULT: Theban victory resulting in the deaths of 500 Spartans and 300 Thebans

In 371 B.C.E., a Spartan army led by King Cleombrotus invaded Boeotia, seeking to prevent Theban dominance over the region. The Spartans met the Theban army under Epaminondas on the plains of Leuctra. Cleombrotus arranged the Spartans in a shallow crescent formation, twelve ranks deep across the battle line. Facing numerical superiority, Epaminondas made his phalanx advance in oblique formation, loading his left wing with fifty ranks of hoplites (heavy infantrymen) while retaining the traditional eight ranks in his center

The Spartans form a crescent in preparation for their battle against the Theban forces at Leuctra. (Library of Congress)

and right. The battle began with the Theban cavalry and the Sacred Band (a Theban elite corps composed of 300 hoplites) driving back the Spartan cavalry facing the Theban left. As the two opposing phalanxes continued their advance, the massive Theban left wing clashed with the Spartan right. While the Theban cavalry prevented a Spartan outflanking maneuver, the Spartan right was shattered and the battle line was broken. After Cleombrotus and a great number of officers were killed, the Spartans and their allies withdrew to their camp with the Theban cavalry in pursuit. The Theban victory was achieved without Epaminondas's right wing ever engaging the enemy's left.

Significance

Epaminondas's victory at Leuctra proved the effectiveness of his revolutionary military tactics and shattered the myth of Spartan invincibility. In the aftermath of the battle, Epaminondas launched a series of invasions into the Peloponnese, disrupting the system of Spartan alliances in that region. Leuctra marked the end of Spartan hegemony and the beginning of Theban ascendancy in Greek political and military affairs.

Resources

Buckley, John. *The Theban Hegemony*. Cambridge, Mass.: Harvard University Press, 1980.

Hanson, U. D. *The Soul of Battle: From Ancient Times to the Present Day*. New York: Free Press, 1999.

Keegan, John. *A History of Warfare*. New York: Alfred A. Knopf, 1994.

Plutarch. "Life of Pelopidas." In *Plutarch's Lives*. New York: Modern Library, n.d.

Warry, John. *Warfare in the Classical World*. New York: Salamander Books, 1993.

See also: Epaminondas; Spartan Empire.

Gilmar E. Visoni

Leuthen

Type of action: Battle in the Seven Years' War
Date: December 5, 1757
Location: Silesia
Combatants: 33,000 Prussian vs. 65,000 Austrian troops
Principal commanders: *Prussian*, Frederick the Great (1712-1786); *Austrian*, Prince Charles Alexander of Lorraine (1712-1780)
Result: Prussian victory that led to reconquest of Silesia in 1757

After his victory at Rossbach (1757), Frederick the Great turned to Silesia, where a strong Austrian army, under Prince Charles Alexander of Lorraine, had taken Schweidnitz and the capital,

Breslau. Learning of Frederick's approach, the Austrians left their fortified camp near Breslau to oppose the Prussians near the village of Leuthen.

Because Frederick and his generals were familiar with the territory around Leuthen—the site of Prussian peacetime autumn maneuvers—Frederick's instructions throughout the battle were of extraordinary clarity and precision. With his vastly inferior troops, he feigned an attack on the Austrian right wing, while the bulk of his infantry executed a concealed march under ground cover toward the Austrian left wing. The Austrian commander, convinced of an impending attack on his right flank, strengthened it with his reserves. Meanwhile, the main Prussian thrust fell against the Austrian left flank about four miles to the south, forcing the Austrians to regroup their left and center. Frederick's execution of the attack formed a textbook example of the "oblique order of battle" that he perfected at Leuthen.

The massive Prussian infantry attack on the Austrian left wing was ably assisted by mobile batteries of heavy guns. Soon, the whole Austrian army had to be wheeled from its original south-north into a new south-facing front. After the failure of an Austrian cavalry charge to relieve its embattled infantry, the Austrians fled in confusion, assisted by the descending darkness of the short winter day, which made an immediate pursuit unfeasible. The Austrian losses of 22,000 exceeded Prussian casualties more than threefold.

SIGNIFICANCE

The high morale of Prussian troops, mostly native Pomeranians and Brandenburgers, Frederick's familiarity with and shrewd exploitation of the terrain, the unhurried pace of the attack, and the extraordinary mobility of Prussian artillery, all combined to make Leuthen one of the most decisive victories of the century.

RESOURCES

Duffy, Christopher. *Frederick the Great: A Military Life*. Routledge: London, 1985.

Showalter, Dennis. *The Wars of Frederick the Great*. Longman: London, 1996.

SEE ALSO: Frederick the Great; Hochkirch; Minden; Plassey; Rossbach; Seven Years' War; Torgau.

Hermann H. Beck

LEXINGTON AND CONCORD

TYPE OF ACTION: Ground battle in the American Revolution

DATE: April 19, 1775

LOCATION: Lexington and Concord (fifteen and twenty miles, respectively, northwest of Boston, Massachusetts)

COMBATANTS: 3,500 Americans vs. 1,700 British

PRINCIPAL COMMANDERS: *American*, Lexington, Captain John Parker (1729-1775), Concord, Colonel James Barrett; *British*, Lexington and Concord, Lieutenant Colonel Francis Smith (1723-1791)

RESULT: British companies subjected to heavy fire from American militiamen during excursion from Boston

On the evening of April 18, 1775, General Thomas Gage, commander of the British forces in Boston, dispatched a detail of 700 grenadiers and light infantrymen, under the command of Lieutenant Colonel Francis Smith, to Concord. Their objective was to confiscate the Americans' military arms and ammunition stored there. Gage's plan depended heavily on secrecy. News of the plan, however, soon leaked, and the Americans were informed of the advancing British military party.

Around 4:30 on the morning of April 19, the detail reached Lexington, where it was met by the Lexington Militia Company—seventy-seven volunteers under the command of Captain John Parker—mustered on Lexington Green. British major John Pitcairn ordered the militiamen to disperse. As the colonists were reluctantly obeying Pitcairn's order, a shot was fired. Neither side accepted responsibility for the shot. When order was finally restored, eight Americans lay dead. The British column continued its march to Concord. As news of the Lexington skirmish spread throughout the countryside, thousands of Minutemen rushed toward Concord.

The British arrived in Concord around 7:00 in the morning. Three infantry units proceeded through the town to the home of Colonel James Barrett, where the munitions were supposedly housed. The remaining infantry units were posted on the North Bridge, located just outside of Concord proper, while the grenadiers searched houses, taverns, shops, and other buildings in Concord.

The searches produced very little. The Americans, having been informed of the impending British advance, had hidden the arms. During the search, however, a fire erupted. Determined to prevent the Redcoats from destroying their homes, the militiamen fired into the ranks of the British infantry units deployed on the North Bridge.

After the brief encounter on the North Bridge, the British party regrouped and began the march back to Boston. The first mile was relatively uneventful. However, at Merriam's Corner, where the British had to cross a narrow bridge, they reencountered the militiamen, and the battle—sixteen miles of running skirmishes—was on. The battlefield was, in reality, a gauntlet through which the British soldiers were forced to travel. The militiamen, hiding behind rocks, trees, fences, and buildings, unleashed a constant barrage of fire on the entrapped British column, easily visible in their bright red coats. After the column had passed, the militiamen would traverse the countryside and be ready to fire upon the Redcoats farther up the road.

Around 2:30 in the afternoon, after two hours of this onslaught, British brigadier general Sir Hugh Percy arrived in Lexington with a relief brigade of 1,000 troops. The combined British forces re-formed on the Lexington Green, then set out for Boston. When the party reached Menotomy, about two and one-half miles from Lexington, it encountered a fresh band of militiamen. More than 5,000 men engaged in the battle here, the most vicious and deadly of the entire day's skirmishes. The British column continued its march to Boston and to safety, arriving in Charleston shortly after sunset.

The British suffered 273 casualties: 73 dead, 174 wounded, and 26 missing. The Americans endured 94 casualties: 49 dead, 40 wounded, and 5 missing.

Significance

The Battle of Lexington and Concord was the first hostile action of the American Revolution. Although the battle was of little strategic significance, it indicated to the British that the American colonists were indeed committed to securing their rights, by force if necessary. The rebellion obviously ran deeper than many in the British ministry had suspected.

Resources

Andrews, Joseph L., Jr. *Revolutionary Boston, Lexington and Concord: The Shots Heard Round the World*. Concord, Mass.: Concord Guides Press, 1999.

April Morning. Fiction feature for television. Hallmark Hall of Fame, 1988.

Fischer, David Hackett. *Paul Revere's Ride*. New York: Oxford University Press, 1994.

Liberty: The American Revolution. Documentary. Middlemarch Films, 1997.

Malcolm, Joyce Lee. *The Scene of the Battle, 1775*. Boston: Division of Cultural Resources, National Park Service, U.S. Department of the Interior, 1985.

Road to Revolution. Documentary. National Park Service, 1999.

Tourtellot, Arthur Bernon. *Lexington and Concord: The Beginning of the War of the American Revolution*. New York: W. W. Norton, 1963.

See also: American Revolution; Gage, Thomas.

Richard A. Glenn

Leyte Gulf

Type of action: Air and sea battle in World War II
Date: October 23-26, 1944
Location: In and around Leyte Gulf, in the Philippines
Combatants: U.S. Navy vs. Imperial Japanese Navy
Principal commanders: *United States*, Admiral William F. Halsey (1882-1959); *Japanese*, Vice Admiral Jisaburo Ozawa (1886-1966)
Result: Decisive defeat of Japanese fleet

Japan risked most of the Imperial Navy trying to defeat the American landing on Leyte. Early efforts to slip forces through the Sibuyan Sea and Suriagao Strait were unsuccessful, but when Vice Admiral Jisaburo Ozawa's decoy force lured Admiral William F. Halsey's Third Fleet away from the landing beaches, the stage was set for a Japanese victory. Vice Admiral Takeo Kurita slipped through the San Bernardino Strait and headed for Leyte Gulf, only to encounter lightly armored escort carriers and escorts under the command of Rear Admiral Clifton Sprague. U.S. forces fought

General Douglas MacArthur leads U.S. troops in this October, 1944, landing at Leyte. (Digital Stock)

a heroic delaying action against the heavy Japanese warships until Kurita decided to withdraw because of fatigue, furious U.S. surface and air attacks, and concerns over fuel supplies. His decision prevented a slaughter on the American beaches.

Japan lost more than 10,500 sailors, four aircraft carriers, nine cruisers, twelve destroyers, three battleships, and hundreds of aircraft. U.S. losses included three light aircraft carriers, two destroyers, one destroyer escort, and one submarine.

Significance

Leyte Gulf was the largest naval battle in history and marked the debut of large numbers of Japanese kamikaze (suicide planes). The U.S. victory accelerated the end of World War II by destroying much of the Japanese fleet and ensuring the successful completion of the Philippines campaign.

Resources

Cutler, Thomas J. *The Battle of Leyte Gulf, 23-26 October 1944.* New York: HarperCollins, 1994.

Falk, Stanley L. *Decision at Leyte.* Norwalk, Conn.: Easton Press, 1989.

Masters of War: The Battle for Leyte Gulf. Documentary. U.S. News Video, 1998.

Showdown at Leyte Gulf. Documentary. A&E Home Video, 1993.

Solberg, Carl. *Decision and Dissent: With Halsey at Leyte Gulf.* Annapolis, Md.: Naval Institute Press, 1995.

See also: Halsey, William F.; World War II.

Lance Janda

Li Hongzhang

Also known as: Li Hung-chang
Born: February 15, 1823; Hefei, Anhui, China

DIED: November 7, 1901; Tianjin, China
PRINCIPAL WARS: Taiping Rebellion, Sino-Japanese War, Boxer Rebellion
MILITARY SIGNIFICANCE: Statesman Li advocated the adoption of Western technology to modernize and strengthen China.

Scholar-official Li Hongzhang came to prominence during the Taiping Rebellion (1850-1864) by organizing resistance to the Taipings. Appointed governor of Jiangsu province, he suppressed the rebels by cooperating with foreign and foreign-trained troops of the Ever Victorious Army led by Charles George "Chinese" Gordon. Gordon's success convinced Li of the need to adopt Western technology in the Self-Strengthening Movement. After the defeat of the Taipings, Li held such high posts as governor general of Chihli province, superintendent of trade for northern ports, and grand secretary to the imperial court. In such positions, and as the leader of the Self-Strengthening Movement after 1872, he built railways, telegraph lines, and Western-style arsenals and shipyards; founded technical and military schools; and sent youths to study abroad. As China's chief diplomat, he parleyed with Japan, France, and Great Britain. He attempted to maintain Chinese influence in Korea, leading to the Sino-Japanese War (1894-1895) in which the Japanese destroyed Li's northern fleet. Forced to negotiate the humiliating Treaty of Shimonoseki (1895), Li survived an assassination attempt in Japan. During a visit to Europe in 1896, he concluded a secret alliance with Russia. Li died shortly after being forced to negotiate another humiliating treaty after the Boxer Rebellion (1900-1901).

RESOURCES
Bland, John O. P. *Li Hung-chang*. Freeport, N.Y.: Books for Libraries Press, 1971.
Chu, Samuel C., and Kwang-Ching Liu, eds. *Li Hung-chang and China's Early Modernization*. Armonk, N.Y.: M. E. Sharpe, 1994.
Spector, Stanley. *Li Hung-chang and the Huai Army*. Seattle, Wash.: University of Washington Press, 1964.

SEE ALSO: Boxer Rebellion; Gordon, Charles George; Sino-Japanese War; Taiping Rebellion.
Gregory C. Ference

LI SHIMIN

ALSO KNOWN AS: Li Shi-min; Tang Taizong (T'ang T'ai-tsung)
BORN: 600; China
DIED: 649; China
PRINCIPAL WARS: Sino-Turkic War, Third Sino-Korean War
MILITARY SIGNIFICANCE: Although Li's campaigns against Koguryo failed to achieve their objectives, his defeat of the eastern Turks changed the balance of power in North and Central Asia.

Emperor Li Shimin is known mainly for his benevolent rule, although the talented commander is also famous for his military exploits. The most formidable international challenge he had to face on coming to power in 626 was the dominant presence of the eastern Turks on the northern frontier, extending from Central Asia, Mongolia, to Manchuria. In the first year of the Sino-Turkic War (629-630), Li began to attack Xueli, the *qaghan* (king) of the eastern Turkic khanate south of the Gobi Desert. Li's generals Li Jing and Li Shiji, commanding an army 100,000 strong, overran Xueli's camp. Xueli was captured and brought to the Tang capital Changan in 630.

After this historic victory, Li was crowned the "heavenly *qaghan*" by the leaders of various ethnic groups across Central Asia. By 640, Li had conquered the key outpost of the Western Regions, Gaochang (Turfan), and was on his way to incorporate the area into Tang China. Overcoming dissenting opinions from his chief ministers, an overconfident Li launched three military operations against the northeastern neighbor Koguryo in the Third Sino-Korean War (645-648). All failed after sustaining great losses.

RESOURCES
Pan Yihong. *Son of Heaven and Heavenly Qaghan: Sui-Tang China and Its Neighbors*. Bellingham, Wash.: Center for East Asian Studies, Western Washington University, 1997.
Twitchett, Denis. *Sui-Tang China, 589-906, Part I*. Vol. 3 in *The Cambridge History of China*. Cambridge, England: Cambridge University Press.

SEE ALSO: Chinese Imperial Wars; Sino-Korean Wars; Turks.

Victor Xiong

LI ZONGREN

ALSO KNOWN AS: Li Tsung-Jen; Te-lin
BORN: 1890; Guilin, Guangxi, China
DIED: 1969; China
PRINCIPAL WARS: Second Sino-Japanese War, Chinese Civil War
PRINCIPAL BATTLE: Taierhchuang (1938)
MILITARY SIGNIFICANCE: The Guangxi army, led by Li, helped the Nationalists under Chiang Kai-shek defeat the warlords and unify China in 1928, then fought against the Chiang-led central government in 1929-1930, the Japanese during the Second Sino-Japanese War, and the Communists in the Chinese Civil War (1926-1949).

After fighting in various local civil wars during the early republican period, Li Zongren joined Sun Yat-sen's Nationalist cause in 1923. By 1925, he had emerged as leader of the so-called Guangxi clique and would remain so until the communist victory in China in 1949.

Li participated in the victorious Nationalist Northern Expedition led by Chiang Kai-shek between 1926 and 1928. Li's Guangxi army expanded Chiang's forces to 300,000 men and helped garrison parts of central and northern China. Jealous of Chiang's national leadership, Li led revolts against the central government in 1929 and 1930. Both times, he was defeated and driven back to Guangxi, which remained semiautonomous. Li was commander of the Fifth War Zone during the Second Sino-Japanese War (1937-1945). His men played an important part in inflicting heavy casualties on the Japanese at the Battle of Taierhchuang in March, 1938. Li was elected vice president of China in 1948 against Chiang's candidate and became acting president when Chiang resigned in early 1949. Li unsuccessfully attempted to prosecute the war against the communists and to negotiate a peace with them. He refused to join the Nationalist government on Taiwan. He left for the United States, remaining there until 1965, when he returned to the People's Republic of China. The Guangxi army and clique disintegrated in 1949; some leaders went to Taiwan.

RESOURCES
Ch'i Hsi-sheng. *Warlord Politics in China, 1916-1928*. Stanford, Calif.: Stanford University Press, 1976.
Lary, Diana. *Region and Nation: The Kwangsi Clique in Chinese Politics, 1925-1937*. New York: Cambridge University Press, 1974.
Li, Tsung-jen. *Memoirs of Li Tsung-jen*. Boulder, Colo.: Westview Press, 1979.
Liu, F. F. *A Military History of Modern China, 1924-1949*. Princeton, N.J.: Princeton University Press, 1956.

SEE ALSO: Chiang Kai-shek; Chinese Civil War.

Jiu-Hwa Lo Upshur

LIBERIA

AT ISSUE: Control of Liberia
DATE: 1989-1997
LOCATION: Liberia, West Africa
COMBATANTS: National Patriotic Front of Liberia (NPFL) vs. Armed Forces of Liberia (AFL), Independent National Patriotic Front of Liberia (INPFL), Economic Community of West African States (ECOWAS), Cease-Fire Monitoring Group (ECOMOG)
PRINCIPAL COMMANDERS: *NPFL*, Charles Taylor (1948-   ), General Roosevelt Johnson (1924-   )
PRINCIPAL BATTLE: Operation Octopus
RESULT: Precarious peace agreement; presidential elections; electoral victory for chief warlord Taylor

BACKGROUND
Established in 1821 as a home for freed American slaves, Liberia became an independent republic on July 26, 1847. Despite the existence of numerous powerful tribes, the country was ruled until 1980 by descendants of African American settlers. The last of these rulers, President William R. Tolbert, was assassinated during a coup led by twenty-eight-year-old Master Sergeant Samuel Doe, who went on to impose a brutal dictatorship from 1980 to 1990. In December, 1989, a few hun-

dred National Patriotic Front of Liberia (NPFL) fighters, led by Charles Taylor, launched an invasion from the Ivory Coast into northern Liberia in an attempt to overthrow Doe. The NPFL assault, which quickly garnered support, was met with a ruthless counterinsurgency effort by government troops—Armed Forces of Liberia (AFL)—and a vicious ethnic war erupted.

ACTION

Initially, the NPFL contained only a couple hundred fighters, but with increasing popular support, it evolved into a large irregular army of approximately 25,000 combatants, which controlled about 80 percent of the country. The NPFL enjoyed the active support of Libya, Burkina Faso, and the Ivory Coast, particularly in the early years of the war. Most of its members were initially drawn from the Gio and Mano ethnic groups of northern Liberia.

In July, 1990, the NPFL split into two, with the breakaway Independent National Patriotic Front of Liberia (INPFL), under the leadership of Prince Yormie Johnson, capturing strategic points in Monrovia. During the same month, the AFL massacred 600 displaced people (many of whom were Gio and Mano) who had taken refuge in a Lutheran church in the capital. August witnessed the first involvement of the Economic Community of West African States (ECOWAS). The Cease-Fire Monitoring Group (ECOMOG), which fluctuated between 4,000-15,000 troops, was a regional military force in Liberia mandated by the ECOWAS alternatively for both peacekeeping and the more controversial "peace enforcement."

The ECOMOG launched a major offensive against the NPFL, preventing them from capturing Monrovia and facilitating the establishment of an interim civilian government under Amos Sawyer. At the end of 1990, the United Nations estimated that 150,000 people had been killed in the conflict and half a million displaced.

In October, 1992, the NPFL launched Operation Octopus, an assault on Monrovia, but the advance was repulsed by a combination of ECOMOG and AFL forces, now acting in open alliance. The ECOMOG offensive severely weakened the NPFL, though it failed to annihilate it. Despite a United Nations embargo on arms sales, weapons continued to flow into Liberia, and a plethora of new factions of varying sizes and longevities emerged. After many false starts, a tentative peace process between the main warring factions was established, culminating with the formation of a new five-member council of state to replace the largely ineffective interim government in September, 1994. There was, however, a brief but intense return to fighting in Monrovia (April 6-20, 1996), when an attempt was made to arrest one of the chief warlords, Roosevelt Johnson.

Estimates on fatalities during the seven-year conflict vary greatly, though it is probable that about 250,000 people were killed. In addition, two million of the country's three million inhabitants were driven from their homes. The widespread use of child soldiers was one of the many unsavory aspects of the conflict, and the United Nations estimated that up to 20,000 children had directly participated in acts of violence.

AFTERMATH

On July 19, 1997, Taylor emerged as the clear victor in national presidential elections, taking 72 percent of the vote.

RESOURCES

Alao, Abiodun, John MacKinlay, and Funmi Olonisakin. *Peacekeepers, Politicians, and Warlords: The Liberian Peace Process*. New York: United Nations University Press, 2000.

Ellis, Stephen. *The Mask of Anarchy: The Destruction of Liberia and the Religious Dimension of an African Civil War*. New York: New York University Press, 1999.

Huband, Mark, and Stephen Smith. *The Liberian Civil War*. Portland, Ore.: F. Cass, 1998.

SEE ALSO: Civil war; Genocide/ethnic cleansing.

Donnacha Ó Beacháin

LIDDELL HART, BASIL

FULL NAME: Basil Henry Liddell Hart
BORN: October 31, 1895; Paris, France
DIED: January 29, 1970; Marlow, Buckinghamshire, England
PRINCIPAL WARS: World War I, World War II
MILITARY SIGNIFICANCE: British military historian Liddell Hart's views on the use of mechanized

armor were appreciated by the Germans during the 1930's and contributed to their early success in World War II.

British historian Basil Liddell Hart's personal experiences on the western front during World War I and his serious study of the military calamities of the struggle led him to develop revolutionary military strategy and tactics for future wars. Through a series of publications (including *The Real War*, 1930, and *The Ghost of Napoleon*, 1933) Liddell Hart developed a reputation as an innovative military thinker and historian. By the late 1930's, he was influential but encountered difficulty with the publication of *The Defence of Britain* in July, 1939; he was forced to resign as a correspondent for *The Times* and did not hold any position of influence throughout World War II.

After the war, Liddell Hart interviewed and studied the defeated German generals and published four major works: *The Other Side of the Hill* (1948), *The Rommel Papers* (1953), *The Tanks* (1959), and *History of the Second World War* (1970). Liddell Hart has been applauded as a regimental historian but many scholars have criticized his failure to recognize the political and societal aspects of war.

RESOURCES
Bond, Brian. *Liddell Hart: A Study of His Military Thought*. New Brunswick, N.J.: Rutgers University Press, 1977.
Mearsheimer, John J. *Liddell Hart and the Weight of History*. Ithaca, N.Y.: Cornell University Press, 1988.
Reid, Brian Holden. *Studies in British Military Thought: Debates with Fuller and Liddell Hart*. Lincoln: University of Nebraska Press, 1998.
Swain, Richard M. "B. H. Liddell Hart and the Creation of a Theory of War, 1919-1933." *Armed Forces and Society* 17 (Fall, 1990): 35-51.

SEE ALSO: Military history; Military theory; Tanks; World War I; World War II.

William T. Walker

LIGHT BRIGADE, CHARGE OF THE

TYPE OF ACTION: Cavalry vs. artillery engagement in the Battle of Balaklava, Crimean War
DATE: October 25, 1854
LOCATION: North Valley between Fedioukine Heights and Causeway Heights, Crimean peninsula
COMBATANTS: 675 British vs. 25,000 Russians
PRINCIPAL COMMANDERS: *British*, Fitzroy James Henry Somerset, Baron Raglan (1788-1855), Brigadier General James Thomas Brudenell, seventh earl of Cardigan (1797-1868)
RESULT: Suicidal cavalry charge blunted Russian advance

Fitzroy James Henry Somerset, Baron Raglan, the allied commander in chief at Balaklava, routinely deferred tactical decisions to staff and field officers not in communication with one another or with him. Baron Raglan wanted to recover British guns the Russians had captured on Causeway Heights. Colonel Richard Airey wrote Raglan's order as follows: "Lord Raglan wishes the Cavalry to advance rapidly to the front, follow the Enemy & try to prevent the Enemy carrying away the guns. Troop Horse Attily may accompany. French Cavalry is on yr left. Immediate." The imprecision of this order has sparked many theories of who was at fault for the disaster.

Captain L. E. Nolan carried the order to General George Charles Bingham, third earl of Lucan, nominal commander of all British cavalry, who gave it to Brigadier General James Thomas Brudenell, seventh earl of Cardigan. Cardigan, believing that Raglan meant the Russian guns, merely obeyed, leading his Light Brigade a mile and a quarter between two large Russian batteries toward a third at the eastern end of the valley. About half the original force reached the objective. Only about 200 returned.

SIGNIFICANCE
British skill and valor confused and demoralized the Russians. British propaganda made much of this event.

RESOURCES
Adkin, Mark. *The Charge: Why the Light Brigade Was Lost*. London: Leo Cooper, 1996.
Compton, Piers. *Cardigan of Balaclava*. London: Hale, 1972.
Harris, John. *The Gallant Six Hundred: A Tragedy of Obsessions*. London: Hutchinson, 1973.

Mollo, John, and Boris Mollo. *Into the Valley of Death: The British Cavalry Division at Balaclava, 1854.* London: Windrow & Greene, 1991.

Woodham-Smith, Cecil. *Reason Why.* New York: McGraw-Hill, 1954.

SEE ALSO: Alma; Balaklava; Crimean War; Inkerman; Sebastopol, Siege of.

Eric v. d. Luft

LIN BIAO

ALSO KNOWN AS: Lin Piao; Lin Yu-rong
BORN: December 5, 1907; Huanggang County, Hubei Province, China
DIED: September 13, 1971; near Öndörhaan, Mongolia
PRINCIPAL WARS: Second Sino-Japanese War, Chinese Civil War
PRINCIPAL BATTLES: Liao-Shen (1948), Ping-Jin (1949)
MILITARY SIGNIFICANCE: In 1948-1949, Lin turned the Chinese Civil War from a Communist defense to a strategic offense by winning the Liao-Shen and Ping-Jin campaigns, which ensured a Communist victory in China.

Lin Biao enrolled in Whampoa Military Academy and joined the Chinese Communist Party in 1925. He served as a battalion, regiment, division, and army commander in the Red Army in 1928-1935 and president of the Red Army Academy in 1935-1937. During the Second Sino-Japanese War (1937-1945), he was the commander of the 115th Division of the Eighth Route Army. From 1946 to the end of the Chinese Civil War (1926-1949), he was commander and political commissar of the Chinese Communist Party Northeast Military Region and the Fourth Field Army of the People's Liberation Army. He turned the war effort from a defensive to an offensive strategy. His Liao-Shen (1948) and Ping-Jin (1949) campaigns eliminated one million Nationalist troops and made him one of the top Communist Party leaders. After the founding of the People's Republic of China in 1949, Lin became the defense minister, vice premier, and vice chairman of the Central Military Commission. He was one of the ten marshals in 1955 and vice chairman of the Chinese Communist Party Central Committee in 1959-1971. He was killed in a plane crash in a Mongolian desert on September 13, 1971, and accused of forming an "anti-revolutionary clique," conducting a military coup, planning assassinations of Mao Zedong, and betraying his country.

RESOURCES

Ginneken, Jaap van. *The Rise and Fall of Lin Piao.* New York: Avon Books, 1972.

Kau, Michael Y. M., ed. *The Lin Biao Affair: Power Politics and Military Coup.* White Plains, N.Y.: International Arts and Science Press, 1975.

Swaine, Michael. *The Military and Political Succession in China.* Santa Monica, Calif.: Rand, 1992.

SEE ALSO: Chinese Civil War; Korean War; Mao Zedong.

Xiaobing Li

Lin Biao. (AP/Wide World Photos)

LINCOLN, ABRAHAM

ALSO KNOWN AS: Honest Abe
BORN: February 12, 1809; near Hodgenville, Kentucky

Abraham Lincoln. (Library of Congress)

DIED: April 15, 1865; Washington, D.C.
PRINCIPAL WAR: American Civil War
MILITARY SIGNIFICANCE: As president of the United States, Lincoln directed the Northern war effort during the American Civil War. His abilities and unshakable commitment to preserving the Union mark him as one of the nation's greatest leaders.

Abraham Lincoln made full use of his vast war powers as commander in chief throughout the American Civil War (1861-1865), perhaps most notably with the Emancipation Proclamation (January 1, 1863). Recognizing that the war would be a protracted struggle, Lincoln formulated a strategy designed to utilize most effectively the North's superior resources. Despite his lack of military experience, he had a clearer conception of Union strategy than the officers he commanded. He constantly urged them to use all their men in battle, to advance simultaneously, and to focus on fighting opposing armies rather than capturing places. Most Union military leaders, schooled in Jominian doctrines, ignored his advice.

Early on, Lincoln deferred too readily to his generals; however, by late 1862, he resolved he would change commanders until he had the men who would bring him victories. He still made mistakes in his appointments, but in 1864, he found a man to lead his armies who shared his strategic views and would without complaint implement them, Ulysses S. Grant. In the final year of the war, with Grant acting as a doggedly relentless general in chief, chief of staff Henry W. Halleck serving as an effective military-civilian liaison, and Lincoln continuing as an aggressive commander in chief, the North created a modern command system that ensured victory. Lincoln constantly acted to fulfill his solemn determination to restore the Union.

RESOURCES
Donald, David Herbert. *Lincoln.* New York: Simon & Schuster, 1995.
Williams, Kenneth P. *Lincoln Finds a General: A Military Study of the Civil War.* 5 vols. New York: Macmillan, 1949-1959.
Williams, T. Harry. *Lincoln and His Generals.* New York: Alfred A. Knopf, 1952.

SEE ALSO: American Civil War; Grant, Ulysses S.; Halleck, Henry W.; McClellan, George B.

Ralph L. Eckert

LISSA

TYPE OF ACTION: Naval battle in the Austro-Prussian War
DATE: July 20, 1866
LOCATION: Near the island of Lissa in the Gulf of Venice in the Adriatic Sea
COMBATANTS: Ten Italian ironclad and twenty-two wooden warships vs. seven smaller Austrian ironclads and fourteen wooden warships
PRINCIPAL COMMANDERS: *Italian*, Admiral Count Carlo de Persano (1806-1883); *Austrian*, Admiral Wilhelm von Tegetthoff (1827-1871)
RESULT: The smaller Austrian fleet defeated the Italian fleet

Allying themselves with the Prussians against Austria, the Italians hoped to regain the province of Venetia. In an attempt to control the Adriatic

Sea, the Italian fleet of ironclads, commanded by Admiral Count Carlo de Persano, attacked the Austrian fortress on the island of Lissa (July 19). A stubborn defense by Austrian troops forced the Italian vessels to withdraw out of range for the night.

By morning (July 20), Admiral Wilhelm von Tegetthof's combined fleet of ironclads and wooden vessels approached the Italian flotilla. Though badly outgunned, the Austrian admiral formed his fleet into a series of wedges and ordered his ironclads to ram the Italian ships. As the battle began to develop, Persano suddenly changed his flagship from the *Re d'Italie* to the new *Affondatore*. The movement left the Italian fleet confused and unable to bring their superior firepower to bear. In the confused fighting, Tegetthoff's flagship *Ferdinand Max* rammed and sank the *Re d'Italie* and the *Palestro*. Persano withdrew his battered fleet, leaving the Austrians controlling the sea.

Significance

Lissa was the first battle of sea-going ironclads in history. Tegetthof's effective use of the ram would influence naval experts and shipbuilders for the next twenty years.

Resources

Gray, Edwyn. "Battered Beyond Repair." *Military History* 8, no. 4 (December, 1991): 38-44.

Sondhaus, Lawrence. *The Hapsburg Empire and the Sea: Austrian Naval Policy, 1797-1866*. Lafayette: Purdue University Press, 1989.

Wawro, Geoffrey. *The Austro-Prussian War: Austria's War with Prussia and Italy, in 1866*. Cambridge, England: Cambridge University Press, 1996.

See also: Italian Wars of Unification.

Kenneth P. Czech

Literature, war in

War is surprisingly inconspicuous among the topics of early Western literature. Most of the wars and battles featured in literature before 1800—including the Siege of Troy in Homer's *Iliad* (c. 800 B.C.E.; English translation, 1616), the First Crusade in *Gerusalemme liberata* (1581; *Jerusalem Delivered*, 1600) by Torquato Tasso, and the Battle of Agincourt in William Shakespeare's *Henry V* (produced c. 1598-1599)—were historically distant to their authors and approached legendary status.

Hans Jakob Christoffel von Grimmelshausen was the one of the first writers to incorporate his own war experience—he was press-ganged into the Thirty Years' War at the age of thirteen—into a major literary work, the satirical novel *Der abenteuerliche Simplicissimus* (1669; *The Adventurous Simplicissimus*, 1912). In one of the supplements to this work, Bertolt Brecht found the story that inspired the bitter and brutal *Mutter Courage und ihre Kinder* (pr. 1941; *Mother Courage and Her Children*, 1941); however, Grimmelshausen's demolition by mockery of the guiding myths of aristocratic warfare—duty, chivalry and heroism—stood alone for more than a century.

Such retrospective analyses became common only when the era of political warfare began, and the slow spread of democratic responsibility began to engage whole populations—at least tacitly—in matters of diplomatic propriety. That was the context in which Napoleon Bonaparte became a legend in his own lifetime; his charisma rubbed off on everyone who fought for and against him.

The Napoleonic and Crimean Wars

Although it was the Russian winter of 1812 rather than Lord Nelson or the duke of Wellington that ruined Napoleon's ambitions, the English never stopped congratulating themselves for their role in his downfall. The celebratory note struck by Thomas Campbell in such poems as "Hohenlinden" (1803) and "Ye Mariners of England" (1809) recurs in countless nineteenth century works that exult in the expansion of the British Empire. The same tone permeates popular romances of the twentieth century by such writers as C. S. Forester and Patrick O'Brian, which nostalgically regard the Napoleonic era to be the most recent into which a contemporary writer can plausibly insert an authentic military hero—a contention deftly subverted by the subtle comedies of George MacDonald Fraser. The most notable dramatic account of the 1815 Battle of Waterloo—*La Chartreuse de Parme* (1839; *The Char-*

terhouse of Parma, 1895)—was, however, written by Stendhal, a Frenchman.

The business and representation of war were irrevocably altered by the Crimean War of 1853-1856, which was the first to be extensively reported. The highly critical running commentary provided by the London *Times* mobilized popular opinion so successfully that the public became intoxicated by its newly discovered right of censure and laid virtual siege to Parliament. Alfred Lord Tennyson wrote the popular poem "The Charge of the Light Brigade" (1854) in response to a newspaper account of the Battle of Balaklava. The combatants in the Crimea included Russian Leo Tolstoy, who preferred to look back to a conflict in which his own side had emerged victorious in compiling his massive pseudosociological study *Voyna i mir* (1865-1869; *War and Peace*, 1886), and British writer G. A. Henty, who became the archetypal author of jingoistic British "boys' books."

The delusions entertained and promoted by celebratory accounts of war received little opposition in Britain until the end of the century, when they were lampooned in such works as George Bernard Shaw's *Arms and the Man* (produced 1894). Even the significant subgenre of future war stories, launched in 1871 by George T. Chesney's ingeniously alarmist *The Battle of Dorking* (1871), was dominated by saber-rattling imperialist fantasies such as Louis Tracy's *The Final War* (1896).

THE AMERICAN CIVIL WAR

The American Civil War (1861-1865) was reported even more conscientiously than the Crimean War, with the additional luxury of illustrative photography. Such reportage provided the imaginative kindling for the genre of contemporary war poetry, although the vast majority of the works subsequently collected in such volumes as Herman Melville's *Battle-Pieces and Aspects of the War* (1866) and William Gilmore Simms's anthology *War Poetry of the South* (1867) were written by civilians reacting to the news rather than by combatants. The first novel representing battle as a uniquely challenging and self-revealing species of personal experience, Stephen Crane's *The Red Badge of Courage* (1895), has a Civil War setting, but its author was born in 1871. It was not until the Civil War was safely and distantly embedded within the United States' creation mythology—carefully bracketed by the American Revolution and World War I—that literary analysis of its epochal significance could be pioneered by works such as Stephen Vincent Benet's epic poem *John Brown's Body* (1928), MacKinlay Kantor's trilogy of novels begun with *The Jaybird* (1932), and Margaret Mitchell's best-selling *Gone with the Wind* (1936).

The Civil War provided one of the most significant stimuli to the development of modern alternative history fiction, which had been pioneered in France with novels of a victorious Napoleon. Many writers explored the possible consequences of Southern victory in their novels. A similar phenomenon would occur after World War II, when numerous writers penned accounts of worlds that might have developed following a German-Japanese victory.

WORLD WAR I

World War I (1914-1918) was the first war to have been loudly and lavishly written about in advance of its occurrence. The future war subgenre had suggested that some kind of settlement between the British Empire and German imperialistic ambitions was inevitable and that the world would be its stage. The slogans by which World War I was marketed to the men who had to fight it emerged from this futuristic fiction, most notoriously its representation as "the war to end war." The avidity with which poets responded to the war's outbreak was amazing; the British poet laureate, William Watson, published sixteen war poems in the first three weeks. A bibliography compiled by Catherine Reilly lists 2,225 British war poets, although only 417 of them were on active service. The number of war poems produced by German writers in the first six months of hostilities is said to have run into the millions. Novelists were, of necessity, slower off the mark, but the first classic account of trench warfare, Henri Barbusse's *Le Feu: Journal d'une esconade* (1916; *Under Fire: The Story of a Squad*, 1917), appeared two years after war broke out.

The impact that new technology would have on the fighting of World War I was anticipated by works such as Wilhelm Lamszus's *Menschenschlachthaus* (1912; *The Human Slaughterhouse*, 1913) but not fully understood. Once experience of the new high-tech warfare and such side-effects as battle neurosis had been fully digested, however,

Twenty Classics of War in Literature

Work	Author	War
Iliad (c. 800 B.C.E.; English translation, 1616)	Homer	Trojan War
Henry V (produced c. 1598-1599)	William Shakespeare	Agincourt
"The Star-Spangled Banner" (1857)	Francis Scott Key	American Revolution
Voyna i mir (1865-1869; *War and Peace*, 1886)	Leo Tolstoy	Napoleonic War
Arms and the Man (produced 1894)	George Bernard Shaw	Napoleonic War
The Red Badge of Courage (1895)	Stephen Crane	American Civil War
Le Feu: Journal d'une esconade (1916; *Under Fire: The Story of a Squad*, 1917)	Henri Barbusse	WWI
"Anthem for Doomed Youth" (written 1918)	Wilfred Owen	WWI
John Brown's Body (1928)	Stephen Vincent Benét	American Civil War
Im Westen nichts Neues (1929, 1968; *All Quiet on the Western Front*, 1929, 1969)	Erich Maria Remarque	WWI
Long Remember (1934)	MacKinlay Kantor	Gettysburg
For Whom the Bell Tolls (1940)	Ernest Hemingway	Spanish Civil War
Mutter Courage und ihre Kinder (pr. 1941; *Mother Courage and Her Children*, 1941)	Bertolt Brecht	Thirty Years' War
"Death of the Ball Turret Gunner" (1945)	Randall Jarrell	WWII
The Naked and the Dead (1948)	Norman Mailer	WWII
Shadow on the Hearth (1950)	Judith Merril	Future War
Wo Warst du, Adam? (1951; *Adam, Where Art Thou?*, 1955)	Heinrich Böll	WWII
Doktor Zhivago, (1957; *Doctor Zhivago*, 1958)	Boris Pasternak	WWI, Russian Revolution
Catch-22 (1961)	Joseph Heller	WWII
The Bamboo Bed (1969)	William Eastlake	Vietnam Conflict

the response to its horrors was extreme. Although there was a marked hiatus for a decade, the war was still fairly raw in living memory when Ernest Hemingway's *A Farewell to Arms* (1929) and Erich Maria Remarque's *Im Westen nichts Neues* (1929, 1968; *All Quiet on the Western Front*, 1929, 1969) were published and R. C. Sherriff's play *Journey's End* (1930) was first produced.

The United States' reluctance to get involved in World War I is reflected in the American literary response, whose most notable rapid product came from members of the ambulance corps such as Hemingway, John Dos Passos, and E. E. Cummings. Dos Passos published *Three Soldiers* in 1921, and Cummings's *The Enormous Room* (1922) was a study of valiant individual struggle against insane but relentless authority, a theme that would recur in American literary accounts of war.

World War I was the first conflict in which literary writers were consulted as to how enemy propaganda might be countered. Within weeks of the outbreak, the British government had convened an assembly including Thomas Hardy, Arnold Bennett, H. G. Wells, G. K. Chesterton, John Galsworthy, Arthur Conan Doyle, and J. M. Barrie. In the beginning, the overwhelming mass of published war poetry was intended to boost morale. However, the tide of antiwar sentiment could not be stemmed by censorship once Siegfried Sassoon had made a public appeal for the war to be ended in 1917. Sassoon's gesture proved a key inspiration to many contemporary writers, including Robert Graves and Wilfred Owen, and continues to haunt the imagination in the work of such writers as Pat Barker. The war left behind an exceedingly bitter legacy among the survivors on both sides, many of whom felt that their dead comrades and relatives had been betrayed by politicians and generals who had botched its termination as badly as its strategy. That acute sense of betrayal became both the cause and context of its sequel.

World War II

Like its predecessor, World War II was widely anticipated in Europe even before the outbreak of its prelude, the Spanish Civil War. British futuristic war fiction of the 1930's was frankly apocalyptic, insisting that air fleets armed with poison gas, high explosives, and incendiaries could obliterate civilization. Such representations probably encouraged Adolf Hitler's belief that blitzkrieg would demolish British morale, as well as his reluctance to introduce poison gas into the arena.

The immediate literary response to the war was relatively muted. The necessity of maintaining morale was generally accepted, and the literary legacy of World War I was seen as an obstacle rather than a model—an attitude that persisted in Europe after 1945. The United States was not so heavily burdened, and the attack on Pearl Harbor licensed an indignation that was soon plowed back into retrospective literary analyses. The influence of such works was exaggerated by the facility with which James Michener's *Tales of the South Pacific* (1947) was converted into a Broadway musical hit and such novels as Norman Mailer's *The Naked and the Dead* (1948) and James Jones's *From Here to Eternity* (1951) became successful Hollywood movies. From a more distant retrospect, however, the war came to seem like an absurd waste, and continuing preoccupation with the tension between the individual and military authority was exaggerated to surreal extremes in such acrid black comedies as Joseph Heller's *Catch-22* (1961), Kurt Vonnegut's *Slaughterhouse-Five: Or, The Children's Crusade, a Duty-Dance with Death* (1969), and Thomas Pynchon's *Gravity's Rainbow* (1973). It is no coincidence that these novels became popular while the United States' long-term military involvement in Southeast Asia was becoming deeply problematic.

The manner of World War II's ending reanimated the future war genre, which was dominated by lurid depictions of nuclear holocaust for the next half-century. The horrible plausibility of such accounts was fed by the Cold War confrontation of the United States and the Soviet Union, which also fueled the further development of the spy novel and the technothriller—popular subgenres that had made their first appearances as spinoffs of pre-World War I future war fiction.

Vietnam and Beyond

Television made every American a spectator in the Vietnam Conflict, and this immediacy was reflected in the literary response. So prompt was the recognition that the war was something requiring literary interpretation that it was the subject of fourteen novels published in 1966 and twenty-two in 1967. *The Green Berets* (1965), written by advertising executive Robin Moore, set the commercial pace, launching a new subgenre of machismo-soaked novels about elite forces. Many correspondents delegated to cover the Vietnam War—some of them, such as Gustav Hasford, author of *The Short Timers* (1967; filmed as *Full Metal Jacket*, 1987) seconded from military units—subsequently wrote novels based on their reportage. In addition, soldiers who fought in the war wrote fictionalized accounts of their experiences. Tim O'Brien, an infantryman in the Vietnam War, established his reputation as one of the foremost fiction writers about the war with the highly acclaimed *The Things They Carried* (1990), a linked group of stories about soldiers in Vietnam.

Resources

Beidler, Philip D. *American Literature and the Experience of Vietnam*. Athens: University of Georgia Press, 1982.

Clarke, I. F. *Voices Prophesying War, 1763-1984*. London: Oxford University Press, 1966.

Ferguson, John. *War and the Creative Arts: An Anthology.* London: Macmillan, 1972.

Franklin, H. Bruce. *War Stars: The Superweapon and the American Imagination.* Oxford: Oxford University Press, 1988.

Fussell, Paul. *The Great War and Modern Memory.* London: Oxford University Press, 1975.

Harvey, A. D. *A Muse of Fire: Literature, Art, and War.* London: Hambledon Press, 1998.

Miller, Wayne Charles. *An Armed America: A History of the American Military Novel.* New York: New York University Press, 1970.

SEE ALSO: Films, war in; Propaganda, military.

Brian Stableford

LITTLE BIGHORN

TYPE OF ACTION: Ground battle in Sioux Wars
DATE: June 25, 1876
LOCATION: Montana Territory (near modern-day Crow Agency, Montana)
COMBATANTS: 617 Seventh U.S. Cavalry vs. 1,800 Sioux, Cheyenne, Arapaho
PRINCIPAL COMMANDERS: *United States*, Lieutenant Colonel George A. Custer (1839-1876), Major Marcus Reno (1834-1889), Captain Frederick Benteen (1834-1898); *Sioux*, Crazy Horse (1842?-1877), Gall (c. 1840-1894), Sitting Bull (1831-1890); *Cheyenne*, Lame White Man, Two Moon (c. 1847-c. 1917)
RESULT: Stunning but short-lived Indian victory

On June 25, 1876, the Seventh U.S. Cavalry under command of Lieutenant Colonel George A. Custer suffered one of the worst defeats in U.S. military history when approximately 1,800 Sioux, Cheyenne, and Arapaho repelled the soldiers, killing all 210 men under Custer as well as about 90 other troopers, Indian scouts, and civilians.

In early summer, 1876, three columns of U.S. troops were ordered to round up free-roaming Native Americans and force them into the bounds of the Great Sioux Reservation in Dakota Territory. Custer commanded the Seventh Cavalry, and on the morning of June 25, 1876, he was alerted to a large Indian camp to the south. Custer advanced, and as he crossed the divide between the Rosebud and Little Bighorn Rivers, he split his

The Indians decisively defeated the Seventh U.S. Cavalry under command of Lieutenant Colonel George A. Custer at Little Bighorn. (Library of Congress)

command in three. Captain Frederick Benteen and three companies headed south to block the Indian retreat. Custer ordered Major Marcus Reno and three additional companies to cross the Little Bighorn River and attack the village. Custer and his command of five companies headed north, probably intending to strike the village from the north. Custer, however, had not yet seen the Indian encampment and did not know the terrain. Ultimately from the vantage point atop bluffs, Custer saw a large village of about 7,000 people in a three-mile swath along the river.

Reno's command, 175 soldiers plus Indian scouts, was embroiled in a fierce battle against warriors, many from Sitting Bull's camp. Reno's troops dismounted and fought about ten minutes, then retreated into the timber along the river. After approximately thirty minutes, Reno led a retreat to bluffs east of the river. Many Sioux pursued the soldiers and pinned them on a hill. Reno lost 40 men in the attack and retreat.

As the Native Americans drove Reno's soldiers across the river, they saw other soldiers approaching the far end of the village. Warriors, Hunkpapa under Gall and Cheyenne under Lame White Man and Two Moon, drove the soldiers north to a high ridge. Another force, mostly Oglala under Crazy Horse, doubled back from the north. Custer's troops were surrounded, and Indians struck from all directions. Many of the soldiers dismounted and were picked off quickly. Within a brief span of time, probably less than an hour, Custer and all 210 soldiers under him were dead. Benteen joined Reno, soon followed by the pack train, swelling the troops to 368 men on the hill. From this position, the soldiers could not see Custer or penetrate the warriors, so they dug in on the hill and fended off Indian attacks until late afternoon the next day. Some 13 soldiers died in this area.

Native American accounts list a total of about 100 dead. Most deaths occurred during the Reno and Custer assaults. Late in the afternoon of June 26, 1876, the warriors withdrew and accompanied their people as they moved southwest toward the Bighorn Mountains.

Significance

The Battle of the Little Bighorn was a big Indian victory, but it quickly brought many recriminations and strict federal policies upon all Plains Indians. This battle shocked and outraged Americans. Soldiers flooded into Indian country to round up those free-roaming Native Americans and force them into the bounds of the reservations. This battle gave leverage to settle the impasse over the Black Hills, which were annexed from the Great Sioux Reservation in October, 1876. The battle itself, not key in military annals, nonetheless had considerable emotional impact on the American public and colored Native American policy for many years.

Resources

Fox, Richard Allan. *Archeology, History, and Custer's Last Battle*. Norman: University of Oklahoma Press, 1998.

Libby, Orin Grant, et al., eds. *The Arikara Narrative of Custer's Campaign and the Battle of the Little Bighorn*. Norman: University of Oklahoma Press, 1998.

Michno, Gregory F. *Lakota Noon: The Indian Narrative of Custer's Defeat*. Tennessee: Mountain Press, 1999.

Rankin, Charles E. *Legacy: New Perspectives on the Battle of the Little Bighorn*. Helena: Montana Historical Society Press, 1996.

Utley, Robert, and Brian Dippie. *Custer and the Great Controversy: The Origin and Development of a Legend*. Lincoln: University of Nebraska, 1998.

See also: American Indian wars; Crazy Horse; Custer, George A.; Sioux Wars; Sitting Bull.

Carole A. Barrett

Livonian War

At issue: Control of eastern Baltic; ascendancy in struggle between Poland and Russia
Date: 1557-1582
Location: Modern-day Estonia, Latvia, and Lithuania
Combatants: Poles vs. Russians
Principal commanders: *Polish*, Stefan Batory (1533-1586), Krzysztof Radziwill (1547-1603); *Russian*, Ivan the Terrible (1530-1584)
Principal battle: Pskov
Result: Polish victory, establishing Poland as a major power

Background

Livonia, essentially modern-day Estonia and Latvia, was intermittently controlled by the Livonian Knights after about 1230. The rise of a powerful Polish-Lithuanian state after 1386 and the increasing power of Muscovy caused the knights to turn to the Teutonic Knights of Prussia for protection. However, the latter collapsed in 1525 and passed under nominal Polish control. Sweden and Denmark, rivals for Baltic predominance since the end of the Union of Kalmar in 1523, were also interested in replacing the fading Livonian Knights in this strategic territory. The chief threat, however, came from Russia, which in 1514 had captured the vital Polish outpost of Smolensk and had designs on the Baltic coast.

Action

Unable to maintain their independence in the face of the Danish, Swedish, and Russian menace, the Livonian Knights accepted Polish suzerainty in 1557. This provoked an attack by Ivan the Terrible of Russia, who saw this strategic territory passing under Polish control. The initial Russian invasion was stopped at the Battle of Kiesia (1558), but Russian gains, which included the strategic asset of Polock, left a standing threat to Wilno. The new Polish king, the Transylvanian soldier Stefan Batory, determined that the moment for a showdown with the Russians had arrived. After lengthy preparation, he gathered a force of 20,000-30,000 and launched a major counterthrust—the First Livonian campaign (1579) designed to end the threat to Wilno and to assume the strategic initiative in Livonia. Maneuvering brilliantly, Batory crossed the Dvina by pontoon bridge and besieged the Russians at Polock, which was soon again in Polish hands. Batory won a string of victories in a series of battles involving maneuvers and sudden attacks on Russian positions, thereby demoralizing the far more numerous enemy. By year's end, the Russian invasion force of perhaps 100,000 had been routed.

In 1580, Batory launched the second Livonian campaign, a two-pronged offensive against Pskov and Smolensk. The main target was Wielkie Łuki, the nerve center of the entire Russian military position in the northeast. The Polish attack was complex in its development, designed to sever Russian efforts at relief and preclude any coordinated defense. Wielkie Łuki fell after a few days and was burned. A Russian effort to regain the initiative was crushed by a brilliant cavalry attack by Krzysztof Radziwill, who pursued the Russians far enough to threaten Moscow. The fall of Wielkie Łuki ended the Russian threat to the area; it was time to pass to the offensive.

In 1581, Batory again collected about 30,000 men, this time with Pskov as his main goal. Again Radziwill played a central role when he intercepted a Russian attack from Smolensk, routed it, and followed with an astonishing cavalry campaign, driving the Russians back in a series of defeats from the upper Dnieper to the approaches to Novgorod. Having paralyzed Ivan IV, Radziwill circled back to join Batory before Pskov. The Siege of **Pskov** (1581-1582) was an arduous operation that stretched into winter, costing the Poles enormous casualties. Though the city did not fall, the desperate Russians accepted Polish terms on January 15, 1582, signing the Treaty of Jan Zapolski. The result netted Poland control over all of Livonia as well as the key city of Polock.

Aftermath

Batory's victories over the Russians, won despite the enemy's huge numerical superiority, were the result the radical reorganization of Polish forces and brilliant generalship as well as Russian strategic blundering. Only Batory's failure to retake Smolensk prevented the Livonian War from being a complete Polish victory. As it was, it represented the establishment of Polish predominance in this region for more than a generation and Polish strategic advantage over Russia until the middle of the seventeenth century.

Resources

Davies, Norman. *God's Playground: A History of Poland*. Vol. 1. New York: Columbia University Press, 1982.

Martin, Janet. *Medieval Russia, 980-1584*. New York: Cambridge University Press, 1995.

Tiberg, Erik. *Moscow, Livonia, and the Hanseatic League, 1487-1550*. Stockholm, Sweden: Almqvist & Wiksell International, 1995.

See also: Ivan the Great; Polish-Swedish Wars for Livonia; Polish Wars of Expansion; Russo-Polish

Wars of 1499-1667; Russo-Swedish Wars of 1590-1658.

M. B. B. Biskupski

Lloyd George, David

ALSO KNOWN AS: Earl Lloyd-George of Dwyfor
BORN: January 17, 1863; Manchester, England
DIED: March 26, 1945; Ty Newydd, near Llanystumdwy, Wales
PRINCIPAL WAR: World War I
MILITARY SIGNIFICANCE: During World War I, Lloyd George served as minister of munitions, then as Britain's prime minister.

Born in England and raised in Wales, David Lloyd George established a successful law career and entered Parliament as a Liberal. Known for his radical views and abilities as a speaker, Lloyd George rose to hold a series of government offices in the Liberal governments of Sir Henry Campbell-Bannerman and Herbert Henry Asquith.

David Lloyd George. (Library of Congress)

At first opposed to Britain's entry into World War I, Lloyd George changed his mind following the German violation of Belgian neutrality. In 1915, he was appointed minister of munitions in a coalition government. In this position, he made probably his greatest contribution to the war. With great energy, Lloyd George mobilized Britain's resources to increase munition and armament production. He became increasingly critical of the higher direction of the war and of the generals.

In December, 1916, with Conservative support, Lloyd George replaced Asquith as prime minister. Under his dynamic leadership, the cabinet was reduced from twenty-three members to a small war cabinet of five. Ministries of labor, food, and shipping were established. Lloyd George favored greater Allied cooperation and unity of the military command structure. Never satisfied with the attrition warfare on the western front, Lloyd George favored attacking the Central Powers at their weakest points. Following the November, 1918, armistice, he led the British delegation at the Paris Peace Conference (1919).

RESOURCES

Adams, R. J. Q. *Arms and the Wizard: Lloyd George and the Ministry of Munitions, 1915-1916.* London: Cassell, 1978.
Bourne, J. M. *Britain and the Great War, 1914-1918.* London: Edward Arnold, 1989.
Constantine, Stephen. *Lloyd George.* New York: Routledge, 1992.
Woodward, D. R. *Lloyd George and the Generals.* London: Associated University Presses, 1983.

SEE ALSO: World War I.

Van Michael Leslie

Lobengula

FULL NAME: Lobengula Khumalo
BORN: c. 1836; Mosega, Transvaal, South Africa
DIED: January, 1894; near Bulawayo, Matabeleland (later in Zimbabwe)
PRINCIPAL WARS: Ndebele Civil War, Matabele War
PRINCIPAL BATTLES: Zwangendaba Kraal (1870), Shangani (1893), Bembesi (1893)

MILITARY SIGNIFICANCE: Lobengula's ill-fated war with the British South Africa Company (1893) marked the end of the Ndebele (Matabele) nation and its domination of the land between the Limpopo and Zambezi Rivers (modern Zimbabwe).

Lobengula succeeded Mzilikazi, founder and first king of the Ndebele nation, in 1870. A military faction opposed Lobengula because his mother was not of royal birth. He crushed the rebellion in a brief but bloody clash at Zwangendaba Kraal in June, 1870.

Lacking his father's leadership, demanding discipline, and martial spirit, Lobengula presided over the decline of the vaunted Ndebele regiments. A treaty with Cecil John Rhodes's British South Africa Company opened the territory to white settlement (1890). In 1893, armed conflict (Matabele War) erupted with the settlers. Two major battles at the Shangani and Bembesi Rivers, resulted in an Ndebele defeat. However, in an ill-advised effort to capture Lobengula, a small British South Africa Company force was annihilated by Ndebele warriors (Shangani Patrol). The king died the next month while attempting to flee across the Zambesi River.

Lobengula's defeat resulted from a failure to modify the Zulu-inspired tactics long used by his regiments. Referred to as the "chest-and-horns" formation, they called for massed infantry, carrying short stabbing spears, to make a frontal assault ("chest") while other units enveloped from the flanks ("horns"). Ndebele discipline, training, and esprit usually carried the day against African tribal opponents using similar weaponry but were ineffective against modern firearms. Failure to adapt to the new military technology, especially the Maxim gun, led to the downfall of Lobengula and the Ndebele.

RESOURCES
Bhebe, Ngwabi. *Lobengula of Zimbabwe*. London: Heinemann Educational Books, 1977.
Dods, Glen Lyndon. *The Zulus and Matabele: Warrior Nations*. London: Arms and Armour, 1998.
Gann, Lewis H. *A History of Southern Rhodesia: Early Days to 1934*. Reprint. New York: Humanities Press, 1969.
Glass, Stafford. *The Matabele War*. Harlow, Essex, England: Longmans, 1968.
Hole, Hugh Marshall. *The Passing of the Black Kings*. Reprint. Bulawayo, Rhodesia: Books of Rhodesia, 1978.
Rasmussen, R. Kent, and Steven C. Rubert. *Historical Dictionary of Zimbabwe*. Metuchen, N.J.: Scarecrow Press, 1990.
Summers, Roger, and C. W. Pagden. *The Warriors*. Cape Town, South Africa: Books of Africa, 1970.
Vickery, Paddy. "The King and the Cleric." *Southern African Encounter* 3 (1996): 16-19.
Wills, W. A., and L. T. Collingridge. *The Downfall of Lobengula*. Reprint. Bulawayo, Rhodesia: Books of Rhodesia, 1971.

SEE ALSO: Tribal warfare.

Anthony P. DiPerna

Lodi

TYPE OF ACTION: Ground battle in the War of the First Coalition
DATE: May 10, 1796
LOCATION: Lodi, Lombardy
COMBATANTS: 16,000 French vs. 9,000 Austrians
PRINCIPAL COMMANDERS: *French*, General Napoleon Bonaparte (1769-1821); *Austrian*, General Johann Peter Beaulieu (1725-1819)
RESULT: Austrian evacuation of Lodi and French crossing of the Adda River

Lodi was an effort by Napoleon Bonaparte to prevent the Austrians from escaping across the Adda River at Lodi. Napoleon ordered a forced march to seize the two-hundred-yard-long bridge. However, when the French advance guard arrived about 11:00 A.M. on May 10, the main body of the Austrian army, led by General Johann Peter Beaulieu, had already crossed. Their rear guard then crossed the bridge, destroyed part of it, and entrenched on the opposite bank. The French cavalry forded the river two miles upstream and rode to outflank the Austrians, as Napoleon supervised the aiming of artillery to bombard them. When charges by French grenadiers faltered in the face of stiff opposition, officers such as André Masséna and Louis Alexandre Berthier rallied the troops. Masséna led the final charge that forced the Austrians into retreat, just as the French cavalry arrived. Fatalities were estimated at 350 French and 153 Austrians. The main body of the Austrian army then retreated toward Mantua.

SIGNIFICANCE

The military significance of Lodi was minimal. The battle was costly for the French, and the Austrians were withdrawing and would have been gone within twenty-four hours. Furthermore, the main body of the Austrian army had again eluded Napoleon. Although Masséna played the decisive role, Napoleon's dispatches glorified his own role and thus greatly enhanced his image at home.

RESOURCES

Chandler, David G. *The Campaigns of Napoleon*. New York: Macmillan, 1966.

Connelly, Owen. *Blundering to Glory: Napoleon's Military Campaigns*. Wilmington, Del.: Scholarly Resources, 1990.

Ferrero, Guglielmo. *The Gamble: Bonaparte in Italy, 1796-1797*. London: Walker, 1961.

Muir, Rory. *Tactics and the Experience of Battle in the Age of Napoleon*. New Haven, Conn.: Yale University Press, 1998.

The Napoleonic Wars. Documentary. Films for the Humanities and Sciences, 2000.

SEE ALSO: Berthier, Louis Alexandre; French Revolutionary Wars; Masséna, André; Napoleon I; Napoleonic Wars.

James K. Kieswetter

LOGISTICS

The art or science of moving and supplying armed forces. For millennia, armies lived off the land, devouring all before their path. This crude method had, however, great limitations—particularly, when campaigns were undertaken in hostile climates, in bad growing seasons, or in areas purposely decimated by opposing forces. While horses and other draft animals relieved soldiers by carrying preserved food and other bulky supplies, there was still the problem of feeding the animals. In the early modern era, European armies only campaigned during the growing season, as sufficient food could not be found for their horses in winter and late fall. By the late eighteenth century, armies were being supplied from designated stations, but this provided another problem: Delicate supply lines were inviting targets for the enemy and limited the movements of the army being thus supplied. Though a succession of new inventions—for example, efficient rail transport, internal combustion engines, and airplanes—have significantly simplified logistics, it still remains a foremost consideration for commanders. Its importance is well conveyed in an old axiom: "Amateurs study tactics, but professionals study logistics."

Jeremiah Taylor

LOMBARD LEAGUE, WARS OF

AT ISSUE: Autonomy of the North Italian cities within the Holy Roman Empire
DATE: February/March, 1167-June 25, 1183
LOCATION: Kingdom of Lombardy
COMBATANTS: Lombard League and Pope Alexander III vs. Holy Roman Empire forces
Principal commanders: *Holy Roman Empire*, German emperor Frederick I Barbarossa (c. 1123-1190), Rainald of Dassel (c. 1118-1167); *Lombard League*, rectors
PRINCIPAL BATTLES: Carcano, Legnano
RESULT: Legitimacy of the Lombard League, the free government of its cities under consuls, and their retention of the royal revenue, the *regalia*

BACKGROUND

In the kingdom of Lombardy, German emperor Frederick I Barbarossa enforced the collection of the *regalia*, or royal revenue, which the cities had been keeping for themselves. Although the cities had agreed to the revenue's collection at a congress, the Diet of Roncaglia, in 1158, the harsh manner in which it was gathered by the imperial chancellor for Italy, Rainald of Dassel, bred resentment. The city of Milan resisted, defeating the emperor when he and a small group of followers became separated from his main force at the castle of **Carcano**, east of Como, in August, 1160. Frederick destroyed the city and dispersed its inhabitants in March, 1162. The Papacy feared similar royal repercussions in the lands of the Catholic

Church, leased in part to another German house rivaling Frederick's, the Welf house. At the death of an accommodating pope, Adrian IV, the anti-imperialists elected a new pope, Alexander III, and the imperialists adhered between 1159 and 1178 to three successive antipopes.

Action

Early in 1164, Verona, Vicenza, and Padua agreed to resist the German (Holy Roman) emperor. In 1166 this Veronese League blocked Frederick's return to Italy at the Chiusa di Verona. Frederick, in revenge, descended the Val Camonica and devastated the countryside between the Alps and the Po River. In February-March, 1167, Brescia, Bergamo, Cremona, Mantua, and Lodi allied in defense in the Lombard League. On April 7, this league, growing with further members, met at Pontida, between Milan and Bergamo, and resolved to rebuild Milan. Frederick took up the challenge by installing his antipope, Victor III, in Rome, but a plague destroyed his army and many of its leaders, including Rainald, and the Welf heir. Frederick escaped to Germany.

In the absence of Frederick, the Lombard League expanded throughout the Po Valley, obtaining the adherence of major vassals of the emperor such as Marquis Obizo Malaspina. It absorbed the Veronese League in December, 1167, and gave itself a constitution with rectors at a congress at Lodi in May, 1168. By then, a new fortress-town named in honor of the pope, Alessandria, had been created in order to block Frederick's entry into Italy from his wife Beatrix's Burgundian kingdom. Genoa and Montferrat had remained imperial under pressure from Christian of Mainz, Frederick's lieutenant in Italy. Marquis William of Montferrat, too close to Alessandria for comfort, was besieged in his castle of Montebello and on June 19, 1172, forced to adhere to the league.

By 1174, Frederick had gathered a new army to return to Italy. He destroyed Susa, forced Asti to surrender, and besieged Alessandria. Christian, after exploits in the south and central areas, attacked the Bolognese castle of San Casciano. The league protected Bologna and made Frederick raise the Siege of Alessandria. Frederick had met his match and opened negotiations for a truce and possible peace. However, the negotiations, formalized at Montebello on April 16, 1175, broke down, with the emperor hoping to act once more from strength if only he could obtain reinforcements from Germany. A year later, he met these reinforcements and new Italian supporters on Lake Como to lead them to a union with his troops at Pavia. However, the Milanese prevented the union, in a manner similar to that employed at Carcano, by destroying his reinforcements at **Legnano** (May 29, 1176). Frederick asked Alexander III to mediate, recognizing him as the true pope in the Treaty of Anagni in October, 1176. The result was the truce agreement with all parties at Venice in July, 1177,

Milestones in the Lombard League Wars

Date	Event
1166	Emperor Frederick I launches an expedition into Italy, installing his antipope in Rome.
February-March, 1167	Brescia, Bergamo, Cremona, Mantua, and Lodi form the Lombard League to defend themselves against the German emperor.
Spring, 1168	Frederick is forced to return to Germany when an illness devastates his army.
1168-1174	Lombard League gains strength and followers.
1174	Frederick returns to Italy, defeating Susa and Asti and besieging Alessandria.
May, 1175	Lombards defeat Frederick's forces at Legano, driving them from the field.
July, 1177	Truce signed in Venice.
June, 1183	Treaty of Constance, a permanent peace agreement, is signed.

with a permanent peace to be concluded within seven years. This was the Treaty of Constance, on Lake Constance, of June 25, 1183.

AFTERMATH

All parties gained. The Church gained unity, the cities of the league their rights, revenues, and a permanent peace organization, the emperor freedom to pursue the Welf inheritance in central lands and the Norman succession in southern Italy and Sicily. Frederick's son Henry married Constance, the heiress of the Norman kingdom, in the cathedral of Milan in 1186.

RESOURCES

Carson, Thomas, ed. *Barbarossa in Italy*. New York: Italica, 1994.

The Holy Roman Empire. Documentary. Coronet, 1961.

Otto I, Bishop of Freising. *The Deeds of Frederick Barbarossa*. Toronto: University of Toronto Press, 1994.

SEE ALSO: Frederick I Barbarossa; Holy Roman Empire-Papacy Wars; Legnano; Sicilian-Byzantine Wars.

Reinhold Schumann

LONG ISLAND

TYPE OF ACTION: Ground battle in the American Revolution
DATE: August 27-30, 1776
LOCATION: Brooklyn, New York
COMBATANTS: 32,000 British vs. 19,000 Americans
PRINCIPAL COMMANDERS: *British*, General Sir William Howe (1732-1786); *American*, General George Washington (1732-1799)
RESULT: General Washington's army retreated across the East River to Manhattan

George Washington moved his troops to Manhattan in March, 1776, convinced that the British would attack. Fortifications were constructed around Manhattan. On June 29, British ships moved toward Staten Island. On August 12, British reinforcements arrived, consisting of more than four hundred transport ships protected by thirty warships.

These ships, with a total of 10,000 sailors, brought 32,000 soldiers to Staten Island. After learning of this troop movement, General Washington, realizing that he must confront the British in Brooklyn at the western extreme of Long Island, sent 7,000 troops there, increasing the number of American troops there to 19,000. These troops fortified Brooklyn Heights, establishing an outer defensive position behind their fortifications, which had a weak spot at Jamaica Pass.

On August 27, one British contingent attacked the American troops while another body of troops swarmed in through the Jamaica Pass, completely overwhelming Washington's forces. The Americans suffered 1,012 casualties, whereas the British incurred 392. Capitalizing on stormy weather that kept British warships at bay, Washington led a retreat to Manhattan.

SIGNIFICANCE

Victorious in Brooklyn, the British held Long Island until 1783. The Battle of Long Island, however, prevented General William Howe's forces from capturing Manhattan. The British victory was bittersweet.

RESOURCES

Johnston, Henry P. *The Campaign of 1776 Around New York and Brooklyn*. New York: Da Capo Press, 1971.

Liberty: The American Revolution. Documentary. Middlemarch Films, 1997.

Millett, Allan Reed. *For the Common Defense: A Military History of the United States of America*. New York: Free Press, 1994.

Nickerson, Hoffman. *The Turning Point of the Revolution*. Port Washington, N.Y.: Kennikat Press, 1967.

SEE ALSO: American Revolution; Howe, William; Washington, George; White Plains.

R. Baird Shuman

LONG MARCH

TYPE OF ACTION: Long march during Chinese Civil War
DATE: October, 1934-December, 1935
LOCATION: Western China from Jiangxi to Shaanxi

COMBATANTS: Nationalist Party forces vs. Communist Party forces
PRINCIPAL COMMANDERS: *Nationalist*, Chiang Kai-shek (1887-1975); *Communist*, Mao Zedong (1893-1976), Lin Biao (1907-1971)
RESULT: A deeply wounded Chinese Communist Party survived the onslaughts of the Nationalists and regrouped in the northwest

Beginning in 1934, Chiang Kai-shek, leader of the Nationalist government in China, launched a series of encirclement campaigns around the armies of Mao Zedong, who had formed a separatist state in Jiangxi province. Trapped within the state, the Communists made a desperate move to break out in October, 1934. Their success prompted the beginning of a long flight to the northwest region, a one-year trek involving at least fifteen military encounters. From November 25 to December 3, 1934, a battle raged as the Communist army crossed the Xiang River. Communist General Lin Biao directed the troops and the crossing, suffering high casualties. The next major battle was near Tucheng, at the Red River. Here the Sichuan provincial army defeated them in battle, but the Communists successfully made the crossing at Tucheng on January 28-29, 1935. On May 27, 1935, the famous contest for the Liuding Bridge took place across the Dadu River when a hero named Yang Chengwu led his battalion across the bridge under heavy gunfire. Behind him were other comrades replacing the planks so that the other troops could safely cross. After six thousand miles, the Communist armies arrived in Wuqi, Shaanxi, and the Long March was completed. Mao established a new political center in Yenan by December, 1935. Of the original 86,000 troops that left Jiangxi, only 4,000 arrived in Shaanxi. Many were killed, some deserted, and others simply stayed behind.

SIGNIFICANCE

The surviving forces in Shaanxi provided the nucleus for rebuilding the Communist state that challenged Chiang after the Japanese were expelled in 1945.

RESOURCES
Lindesay, William. *Marching with Mao: A Biographical Journey*. London: Hodder & Stoughton, 1993.
Salisbury, Harrison E. *The Long March: The Untold Story*. New York: Harper & Row, 1985.
Tuten, Frederic. *The Adventures of Mao on the Long March*. New York: Marion Boyars, 1997.

SEE ALSO: Chiang Kai-shek; Chinese Civil War; Mao Zedong.

John D. Windhausen

LONGBOW

Though of Welsh origin, the primary English missile weapon from the fourteenth and well into the sixteenth century. The longbow, about six feet tall, was made of a well-seasoned stave of choice yew or elm and strung with hemp whipped with linen cord. Its arrows were about thirty-seven inches long, tipped with a small lozenge-shaped head, and fletched with halves of goose feathers. An archer had to be a man of some strength, for it required about 100 pounds of pull to draw the string and let fly an arrow. The longbow was accurate at a range of 250 yards, but could fire an arrow as far as 350 yards. The weapon was perhaps at its height of effectiveness during the Hundred Years' War (1337-1457). Of particular note and fame is the role of the longbow in the Battle of Crécy. There, on August 6, 1346, the power, accuracy, and rapid rate of fire of the English longbow triumphed over the slower, clumsier crossbows wielded by Italian mercenaries.

Jeremiah Taylor

LONGSTREET, JAMES

ALSO KNOWN AS: Pete Longstreet; Lee's Old War Horse
BORN: January 8, 1821; Edgefield District, South Carolina
DIED: January 2, 1904; Gainesville, Georgia
PRINCIPAL WARS: Mexican-American War, American Civil War
PRINCIPAL BATTLES: First Bull Run (1861), Gettysburg (1863)
MILITARY SIGNIFICANCE: Longstreet, Robert E. Lee's second in command for most of the war, obeyed Lee and ordered a charge on Cemetery

Ridge at Gettysburg, which was driven back at great cost to the Confederates and ended the battle.

James Longstreet served in the U.S. Army during the Mexican-American War (1846-1848). When the American Civil War (1861-1865) started, Longstreet resigned his commission in the U.S. Army and offered his services to the Confederacy. By the Battle of the First Bull Run (1861), he had been promoted to the rank of brigadier general. He became the senior lieutenant general under Robert E. Lee and commanded the First Corps of the Army of Northern Virginia.

Longstreet's reputation suffered in the South after the war for several reasons. First, he criticized Lee's decision to assault Cemetery Ridge at Gettysburg in 1863. Against his better judgment, Longstreet ordered General George E. Pickett and some 15,000 troops to charge Cemetery Ridge, the center of the Union line. The assault was repulsed and the Confederate Army suffered great losses, ending the Battle of Gettysburg in defeat. His subsequent federal appointments as minister to Turkey (1880), U.S. marshal for Georgia (1881), and U.S. railroad commissioner (1898) further damaged his reputation among southerners.

RESOURCES
Freeman, Douglas Southall. *Lee's Lieutenants: A Study in Command*. 3 vols. New York: Charles Scribner's Sons, 1942-1944.
Longstreet, James. *From Manassas to Appomattox: Memoirs of the Civil War in America*. Bloomington: Indiana University Press, 1960.
Wert, Jeffry D. *General James Longstreet: The Confederacy's Most Controversial Soldier*. New York: Simon & Schuster, 1993.

SEE ALSO: American Civil War; Bull Run, First; Gettysburg; Lee, Robert E.

Ken Willingham

LOUIS XIV

FULL NAME: Louis XIV, king of France
ALSO KNOWN AS: The Sun King
BORN: September 5, 1638; Château de Saint-Germain, Saint-Germain-en-Laye, France
DIED: September 1, 1715; Palace of Versailles, Paris
PRINCIPAL WARS: War of Devolution, Dutch War, War of the Grand Alliance, War of the Spanish Succession
MILITARY SIGNIFICANCE: The War of Spanish Succession made Louis XIV determined to break the ring of Habsburg power in Europe and forced him to face the most serious decision of his reign—to push the claim of his grandson for the throne of Spain.

Known as the Sun King, Louis XIV (ruled 1661-1715) is considered one of the greatest military figures in seventeenth century European history. Although seldom seen within range of a battlefield, Louis was nevertheless an aggressive king whose ambitions were related to the aggrandizement of France. He saw himself as the personification of the greatness of the crown that he wore. Having inherited a well-established and directed military, Louis had the advantage of the military strength and readiness necessitated by his military ambitions and desires. His primary targets were the Habsburg Empire and the Dutch, his traditional foe, whose strength and determination he often underestimated. His wars included the War of Devolution (1667-1668), the Dutch War (1672-1678), War of the Grand Alliance (1688-1697), and War of the Spanish Succession (1701-1714). Louis found that he was able to direct foreign affairs in England by financing the economic needs of his cousin Charles II, newly restored to the English throne in 1660. The French king was determined to control European foreign affairs, secretly if necessary, as in the case of the Treaty of Dover (1670) in which he committed his armies to reestablish Roman Catholicism in England when the king determined the appropriate time.

RESOURCES
Behrens, C. B. A. *The Ancien Regime*. New York: W. W. Norton, 1989.
Lewis, W. H. *The Splendid Century*. Prospect Heights: Waveland, 1997.
The Man in the Iron Mask. Fiction feature. United Artists, 1998.
Wolf, John B. *Louis XVI*. New York: W. W. Norton, 1967.

SEE ALSO: Grand Alliance, War of the; Spanish Succession, War of the.

Pamela M. Gross

LOUISBOURG, SIEGE OF

TYPE OF ACTION: Ground battle in the French and Indian War
DATE: June 8-July 26, 1758
LOCATION: Cape Breton Island in the Gulf of St. Lawrence
COMBATANTS: 11,442 British soldiers and 14,005 British sailors vs. 3,500 French soldiers and 2,400 French sailors
PRINCIPAL COMMANDERS: *British*, Major General Jeffrey Amherst (1717-1797), Vice Admiral Edward Boscawen (1711-1761); *French*, Governor Augustin de Boschenry de Drucour (d. 1762)
RESULT: British capture Louisbourg on Cape Breton Island

On May 28, 1758, Vice Admiral Edward Boscawen's 140-ship fleet sailed from Halifax, Nova Scotia, carrying Major General Jeffrey Amherst's army and arrived off Louisbourg on June 2. The French garrison numbered 3,500, supported by 0ten warships in the fortress's harbor. Brigadier General James Wolfe led the British landing on June 8. Over the next seven weeks, Amherst conducted a formal siege, with Boscawen's assistance. British soldiers and sailors steadily advanced trenches, erected batteries, and bombarded the fortress. Governor Augustin de Boschenry de Drucour's abandonment of some of his outer defenses early in the siege further aided them. On the night of July 9, the French sortied but were repulsed after a sharp fight. Amherst relentlessly continued his operations, and on July 26, Drucour surrendered with the town in rubble and his fleet destroyed. British losses were approximately 500 killed and wounded.

SIGNIFICANCE

The fall of Louisbourg marked a turning point in the French and Indian War; Britain achieved great success during the conflict's final stage. Furthermore, it opened the St. Lawrence River to attack, but this would not occur until 1759, as Drucour's stubborn defense consumed much of the summer. Finally, the siege marked the emergence of Amherst and Wolfe as able leaders.

RESOURCES

Gipson, Lawrence Henry. *The British Empire Before the American Revolution*. Vol. 7. New York: Alfred A. Knopf, 1965.
Hitsman, J. Mackay, and C. C. J. Bond. "The Assault Landing at Louisbourg, 1758." *Canadian Historical Review* 35 (December, 1954): 314-330.
Williams, Noel St. John. *Redcoats Along the Hudson: The Struggle for North America, 1754-1763*. London: Brassey's, 1997.

SEE ALSO: French and Indian War; Pitt, William; Quebec; Wolfe, James.

Michael P. Gabriel

LOUVOIS, FRANÇOIS-MICHEL LE TELLIER, MARQUIS DE

BORN: January 18, 1639; Paris, France
DIED: July 16, 1691; Versailles, France
PRINCIPAL WAR: War of the Grand Alliance
MILITARY SIGNIFICANCE: Louvois, as war minister to Louis XIV, played a key role in building up and administering the largest European army since the fall of Rome. This huge army permitted the king of France to bid for European hegemony in a series of wars.

As the son of Michel Le Tellier, war minister of France beginning in 1643, François-Michel Le Tellier, marquis de Louvois, was destined for high office by the bureaucratic dynasticism that was characteristic of old regime France. From 1662 to 1677, he shared joint control of the war department with his father; thereafter, Louvois enjoyed sole control of that office until his death. Gifted with a brutal, energetic personality, Louvois enjoyed the confidence of the king and dominated the administration of the French army.

During his tenure of office, the peacetime strength of the army rose from 72,000 to about 165,000. Its peak wartime strength has been conservatively estimated at 340,000, far larger than any forces previously fielded by France and not significantly exceeded until after the French Revolution. Louvois used his talents not only to increase the size of the army, but also to make major improvements in its discipline and logistical support.

RESOURCES

Lynn, John A. *Giant of the Grand Siècle: The French Army, 1610-1715*. Cambridge, England: Cambridge University Press, 1997.

_____. "The Quest for Glory: The Formation of Strategy Under Louis XIV, 1661-1715." In *The Making of Strategy: Rulers, States, and War*, edited by Williamson Murray, MacGregor Knox, and Alvin Bernstein. Cambridge, England: Cambridge University Press, 1994.

Martin, Ronald. "The Army of Louis XIV." In *The Reign of Louis XIV*, edited by Paul Sonnino. Atlantic Highlands, N.J.: Humanities Press International, 1990.

SEE ALSO: Grand Alliance, War of the; Louis XIV; Vauban, Sébastien Le Prestre de.

Mark S. Lacy

LUCCAN-FLORENTINE WAR

AT ISSUE: Ghibelline or Guelph domination of Tuscany
DATE: 1320-1328
LOCATION: Tuscany, Lunigiana
COMBATANTS: Luccans vs. Florentines
PRINCIPAL COMMANDERS: *Luccan*, Castruccio Castracani (1281-1328); *Florentine*, Guido dalla Petrella, Marquis Spinetta Malaspina, Raymond of Cardona
PRINCIPAL BATTLE: Altopascio
RESULT: Major setback for Ghibellines in Tuscany

BACKGROUND

Guelph, propapal, and Ghibelline, proimperial, city-groups had been in conflict, usually over territorial and commercial advantages, since the death of the last strong German emperor in Italy, Frederick II, in 1250. Emperors promoted by opposing parties in Germany made only sporadic appearances in Italy. The Luccan-Florentine War fell between the death of Emperor Henry VII near Siena in 1313 and the imperial coronation of Louis the Bavarian in Rome in 1328. Lucca, under the lordship of a local strongman, Castruccio Castracani, since 1316, vied for Ghibelline hegemony in Tuscany, and Florence, staunchly propapal since 1302, supported Guelph hegemony. The expansion of the two rival textile cities was at stake, and both Florence and Lucca wanted to annex Pisa, which had been in decline for some time. On a European scale, a Guelph northern and central Italy would protect the French Angevin royal house of Naples, favored by the popes then residing at Avignon, against its enemies from across the Alps.

ACTION

When, in 1320, a French commander, Philip of Valois, entered Lombardy to attack the Ghibelline Visconti in Milan, the Florentines sent their troops to aid him. Castruccio Castracani had himself named vicar of the empire in Tuscany by one of the rival emperors, Frederick the Handsome of Habsburg, and in this capacity, he marched on Florence, forcing the city to recall its force from Lombardy. Philip, unsupported, returned to France. The Florentines, with the enemy at their gates, hired a professional soldier, Guido dalla Petrella, as their commander. Petrella occupied the Val di Nievole as far as Altopascio, eight miles from Lucca. In 1321, the Florentines allied themselves with an old enemy of Castruccio, Marquis Spinetta Malaspina, in the Lunigiana, the coastal area bordering on Tuscany. Malaspina attacked Castruccio from the rear, but Castruccio occupied Pontremoli in his flank and controlled the passage from Lombardy to the coast over the Cisa pass.

Harassed Pistoia hoped to maintain its neutrality by placing itself under the rule of an abbot. However, the abbot's nephew, Filippo Tedici, ousted him in 1323, and two years later sold Pistoia to Castruccio for 10,000 florins. The Florentines responded by hiring a new commander recommended by the pope, Raymond of Cardona. On September 23, 1325, Cardona engaged Castruccio in battle at **Altopascio**. However, Castruccio, reenforced at the last moment by Visconti cavalry, beat him. Guelphism could no longer depend on Florence. In May-July, 1326, the king of Naples sent his trusted lieutenants Walter of Brienne and Duke Charles of Calabria with 1,400 horsemen to take over temporarily the government of Florence and fight Castruccio.

The conflict escalated. Louis the Bavarian prepared an Italian campaign, and on September 1, 1327, Castruccio welcomed him at Pontremoli. He then left Lucca to join the emperor at Viterbo and Rome with plans for an attack on Naples. His absence triggered the occupation of Pistoia by the vicar of Charles of Calabria, Filippo di Sangineto, on January 27, 1328. Castruccio, with his usual energy, rushed back from Rome, besieged Pistoia and forced it to surrender on August 5. As protagonist of the imperial party, he saw himself as the future lord of Florence. However, his sudden death from malaria on September 3 ended his hopes and the war.

AFTERMATH

A peace accord between Florence and Pistoia in 1329 paved the way for placing the town permanently under Florentine control. The Guelph-Ghibelline balance in Tuscany tipped in favor of the Guelphs, but the strife continued for years to come.

RESOURCES

Blomquist, Thomas W., and Maureen F. Mazzaoui, eds. *The "Other Tuscany."* Kalamazoo, Mich.: The Medieval Institute, 1994.

Herlihy, David. *Medieval and Renaissance Pistoia*. New Haven, Conn.: Yale University Press, 1967.

SEE ALSO: Florentine Wars; German Civil War of 1314-1325.

Reinhold Schumann

LUDENDORFF, ERICH

FULL NAME: Erich Friedrich Wilhelm Ludendorff
BORN: April 9, 1865; Posen, Prussia (later Poznan, Poland)
DIED: December 20, 1937; Munich, Germany
PRINCIPAL WAR: World War I
PRINCIPAL BATTLES: Tannenberg (1914), Ludendorff Offensive (1918)
MILITARY SIGNIFICANCE: After early successes against the Russians in World War I, Ludendorff used his growing prestige to develop an influential theory of total war that nearly brought Germany victory.

Before the outbreak of World War I, Erich Ludendorff, head of the general staff's mobilization and deployment section, argued for a greatly expanded German army. His contribution to Germany's World War I effort began in August, 1914, when he helped mastermind the capture of the important fortress of Liege in eastern Belgium. Before the end of the year, he was transferred to the eastern front, where he won credit (shared with General Paul von Hindenburg) for the victory over the Russians at Tannenberg in east Prussia.

Continued success on the eastern front allowed Ludendorff and Hindenburg to assume virtual supreme military control of Germany's war effort in August, 1916. Until the end of the war, Ludendorff hoped to guarantee Germany's eventual victory through the total mobilization of the country's remaining resources. Ludendorff's belief in the possibility of winning a decisive military victory led him to approve of the tactic of unrestricted submarine warfare, a decision that would result in the United States' entry into the war in 1917. After eliminating Russia's threat to

Erich Ludendorff (left of center) speaks with a German officer while attending a funeral. (Library of Congress)

Germany in the east, Ludendorff engaged in a final gamble to defeat Germany's remaining enemies in France. After some initial successes, the Ludendorff Offensive (March, 1918) in the west eventually failed, forcing Germany to ask for an armistice. After the war, Ludendorff became an initial supporter of the Nazi cause.

RESOURCES
Asprey, Robert B. *The German High Command at War: Hindenburg and Ludendorff and the First World War*. London: Warner, 1994.

SEE ALSO: Hindenburg, Paul von; Tannenberg; World War I.

Mark R. Polelle

LÜTZEN

TYPE OF ACTION: Ground battle in the Thirty Years' War
DATE: November 16, 1632
LOCATION: Lützen, ten miles north of Leipzig in Saxony (north central Germany)
COMBATANTS: 18,000 Swedish Protestants vs. 28,000 Imperialist Catholics
PRINCIPAL COMMANDERS: *Swedish/Protestant*, Swedish king Gustavus II Adolphus (1594-1632); *Imperial/Catholic*, General Albrecht Wenzel von Wallenstein (1583-1634)
RESULT: A tactical victory for the Swedes that forced Wallenstein to retreat to Bohemia

Having already sent his army into winter quarters, General Albrecht Wenzel von Wallenstein learned on November 15, 1632, that the Swedish army was approaching. He quickly recalled his scattered forces and prepared a defensive line with his right anchored on the town of Lützen and his line behind hastily erected fortifications. When the Swedish army of 18,000 attacked in a thick fog at 8 A.M. on November 16, visibility was virtually nonexistent. The Swedish right pushed Imperial forces back, but the recalled Imperialists arrived in time to stabilize that flank. On the Swedish left, Gustavus II Adolphus rode forward to encourage his troops but was killed when he rode into an enemy formation. News of the king's death resulted in a savage onslaught by Swedish forces, and Wallenstein was driven from the field. The Swedish army suffered about 10,000 casualties while inflicting about 12,000 on the Imperial army.

SIGNIFICANCE
Although Lützen was a Swedish (Protestant) victory, the death of Gustavus left Protestant forces bereft of dynamic leadership. Lack of a strategic vision led to Imperial success and to direct French intervention in the Thirty Years' War.

RESOURCES
Fuller, J. F. C. "The Battles of Breitenfeld and Lützen, 1631 and 1632." In *The Decisive Battles of the Western World*. Vol. 2. London: Eyre & Spottiswoode, 1961.
Parrott, D. A. "Strategy and Tactics in the Thirty Years' War: The Military Revolution." *Militärgeschichtliche Mitteilungen* 18, no. 2 (1985): 7-25.
Roberts, Michael. *Gustavus Adolphus*. 2 vols. 2d ed. New York: Longman, 1992.

SEE ALSO: Gustavus II Adolphus; Thirty Years' War; Wallenstein, Albrecht Wenzel von.

William S. Brockington, Jr.

LUXEMBOURG

TYPE OF ACTION: Ground battle for Luxembourg independence in the War of the Reunions
DATE: June 7, 1684
LOCATION: Fortress of Luxembourg
COMBATANTS: French vs. Dutch armies
PRINCIPAL COMMANDERS: *French*, François-Henri de Montmorency-Bouteville, duke of Luxembourg (1628-1695); *Dutch*, William of Orange (William III) (1650-1702)
RESULT: French occupation of Luxembourg

Throughout its history, the duchy of Luxembourg had been a province of France, Spain, Austria, Denmark, or Burgundy. After many years of fighting and raids, France, Spain, the Holy Roman Empire, Denmark, and Brandenburg agreed to terms of peace. However, William of Orange of the Netherlands (who later became king of England) felt betrayed by the truce signed between

Holland and France and attacked France while it was in control of Luxembourg. The fortress of Luxembourg was taken from the French, led by François-Henri de Montmorency-Bouteville, duke of Luxembourg, after a five-week battle during the War of the Reunions.

SIGNIFICANCE

Louis XIV of France and William of Orange both wanted control of the land in the Low Countries, along the Rhine, and on the Mediterranean Sea, including Luxembourg.

RESOURCES

Eggenberger, David. *A Dictionary of Battles from 1479 to the Present*. New York: Thomas Y. Crowell, 1967.

McDonald, George. *Frommer's Belgium, Holland, and Luxembourg*. New York: Simon & Schuster, 1997.

SEE ALSO: Louis XIV; Luxembourg, François-Henri de Montmorency-Bouteville, duke of.

Maryanne Barsotti

LUXEMBOURG, FRANÇOIS-HENRI DE MONTMORENCY-BOUTEVILLE, DUKE OF

BORN: January 8, 1628; Paris, France
DIED: January 4, 1695; Versailles, France
PRINCIPAL WARS: Franco-Dutch War, War of the Grand Alliance
PRINCIPAL BATTLES: Saint-Denis (1678), Fleurus (1690), Leuze (1691), Steenkerke (1692), Neerwinden (1693)
MILITARY SIGNIFICANCE: The duke of Luxembourg, one of Louis XIV's ablest commanders, enjoyed a string of victories over the armies of the Grand Alliance.

François-Henri de Montmorency-Bouteville, duke of Luxembourg, scion of a great noble house, served under the Great Condé in the Wars of the Fronde and in the War of Devolution. He first held independent command in the Franco-Dutch War. His retreat from Utrecht to Maastricht in 1673 against heavy odds demonstrated his mastery of the art of maneuver. Made a marshal of France in 1675, Luxembourg defeated William of Orange (later William III of England) at Saint-Denis (1678). He later fell out of the king's favor and was not immediately employed in the War of the Grand Alliance. However, in 1690, Louis XIV, desperate for more effective generals, recalled Luxembourg to active duty. He won a series of victories over members of the Grand Alliance, including Fleurus (1690), Leuze (1691), Steenkerke (1692), and Neerwinden (1693).

RESOURCES

Childs, John. *The Nine Years' War and the British Army 1688-1697: The Operations in the Low Countries*. Manchester, England: Manchester University Press, 1991.

Lynn, John. *Giant of the Grand Siècle: The French Army, 1610-1715*. Cambridge, England: Cambridge University Press, 1997.

Weigley, Russell *The Age of Battles: The Quest for Decisive Warfare from Breitenfeld to Waterloo*. Bloomington, Ind.: Indiana University Press, 1991.

SEE ALSO: Condé, the Great; Fronde, Wars of the; Grand Alliance, War of the; Louis XIV; Louvois, François-Michel Le Tellier, marquis de.

Mark S. Lacy

LYAUTEY, LOUIS H. G.

FULL NAME: Louis Hubert Gonzalve Lyautey
BORN: November 17, 1854; Nancy, France
DIED: July 21, 1934; Thorey, France
PRINCIPAL WARS: World War I, Riff War
PRINCIPAL BATTLES: Bou Denib Oasis (1908), Fez (1912)
MILITARY SIGNIFICANCE: Lyautey was France's most successful colonial administrator and was noted for his application of the principles of "slow penetration," which he first employed in Indochina and Madagascar and brought to fruition as resident general of Morocco.

A graduate of Saint-Cyr, Louis H. G. Lyautey was first stationed abroad in Algeria in 1880, then in Indochina in 1894, where he adopted the ideas of his superior, Joseph-Simon Galliéni, regarding indirect rule, respect for native institutions, and the civilizing mission of the French army regarding the colonial population. In 1897, Lyautey was appointed to command the turbulent northwest sector of Madagascar, where he successfully defused native resistance and within two years had pacified the region.

Lyautey's transfer to Algeria in 1904 led to his appointment as commandant at Oran in 1906 and his victory over the clans of the Eastern High Atlas Mountains at the Battle of Bou Denib Oasis (1908). Lyautey was posted to the Morocco protectorate in 1912 and served as resident general until 1916 and again from 1917-1925. Although confined in Fez (1912) during a siege, he brought order to the region and expanded French control. His respect for indigenous customs, traditions, and institutions and willingness to govern through local dignitaries contributed materially to the consolidation of French authority over the hinterlands.

Lyautey served as French war minister from 1916 to 1917 during World War I and was promoted to marshal in 1921. During the Riff War (1921-1925), Lyautey successfully defended Fez against Abd el-Krim but was replaced by Marshal Henri-Philippe Pétain in 1925.

RESOURCES

Hoisington, William A., Jr. *Lyautey and the French Conquest of Morocco*. New York: St. Martin's Press, 1995.

Jones, Archer. *The Art of War in the Western World*. New York: Oxford University Press, 1989.

Scham, Alan. *Lyautey in Morocco: Protectorate Administration, 1912-1925*. Berkeley: University of California Press, 1970.

SEE ALSO: Abd el-Krim; Galliéni, Joseph-Simon; Pétain, Henri-Philippe.

Raymond Pierre Hylton

LYSANDER

BORN: Date unknown; Sparta
DIED: 395 B.C.E.; Haliartos
PRINCIPAL WARS: Peloponnesian Wars, Corinthian War
PRINCIPAL BATTLES: Notium (407-406 B.C.E.), Aegospotami (405 B.C.E.), Haliartus (395 B.C.E.)
MILITARY SIGNIFICANCE: Lysander won the first major naval battle against the Athenians in the Peloponnesian Wars and ended the fighting after victory at Aegospotami.

Though Lysander's family claimed descent from Heracles (also known as Hercules), his father was apparently too poor to afford his son the usual Spartan military education. A royal connection may have furnished the money. After 433 B.C.E., Lysander developed an intimate relationship with Agesilaus II, son of Archidamus II. This may partly explain his sudden emergence as admiral of the fleet in 408-407, during the Peloponnesian Wars. He skillfully secured war funds from the Persian prince Cyrus and in 407-406 B.C.E. won a major naval battle against the Athenians at Notium.

During this period, he began to lay the groundwork for a personal empire through diplomacy with conquered Greek cities. In 406, his successor as admiral was defeated at Arginusae. Returning in 405, technically as second in command, Lysander defeated the Athenians at Aegospotami. After a naval blockade, he imposed a final settlement in 404. For his exploits, the island of Samos granted him divine status.

Fueled by his own personal ambition, Lysander became the principal architect of a harsh Spartan imperialism after the war. Even Agesilaus, whom Lysander helped to the throne, became suspicious and sought to diminish his status after Lysander accompanied him on a military expedition to Asia Minor in 396. Sent home, he died at the Battle of Haliartus (395 B.C.E.) in central Boeotia during the Corinthian War.

RESOURCES

Cartledge, Paul. *Agesilaos*. Baltimore, Md.: The John Hopkins University Press, 1987.

Shipley, D. R. *A Commentary on Plutarch's Life of Agesilaos*. Oxford: Clarendon Press, 1997.

SEE ALSO: Aegospotami; Agesilaus II; Peloponnesian Wars.

David J. Ladouceur

M

MacArthur, Douglas

Born: January 26, 1880; Little Rock, Arkansas
Died: April 5, 1964; Washington, D.C.
Principal wars: World War I, World War II, Korean War
Principal battles: Pusan Perimeter (1950), Inchon Landing (1950)
Military significance: MacArthur commanded Allied forces in the Southwest Pacific during World War II and was instrumental in defeating Japan. After commanding the occupation of Japan, he led United Nations forces in the Korean War until relieved of his command following a public controversy.

Douglas MacArthur was the son of General Arthur MacArthur, the highest ranking officer in the U.S. Army from 1906 to 1909. He attended West Point, graduating in 1903 with the highest marks ever recorded there. He rose rapidly through the ranks, becoming a captain in 1908, major in 1915, and colonel in 1917. In World War I, he earned numerous medals and emerged as a brigadier general. During three years as West Point commander, he broadened the curriculum and raised standards. In 1930, President Herbert Hoover named MacArthur chief of staff. His five-year term was marred in 1932 when he used the army to drive bonus marchers, World War I veterans seeking relief from the Depression, out of the capital because of unfounded fears of communist influence. In 1935, President Franklin D. Roosevelt appointed him military adviser to the Philippines. Philippine president Manuel Quezon named MacArthur field marshal in 1936, leading to his resignation from the U.S. Army in December, 1937.

With war clouds looming over the Pacific, Roosevelt recalled MacArthur to active duty in July, 1941, as commander of U.S. Army forces in the Far East. The general, operating out of the Philippines, inexplicably allowed the Japanese to destroy his air forces on the ground ten hours after Pearl Harbor. Then he engineered a retreat to Bataan Peninsula and Corregidor Island before Roosevelt ordered him to Australia in March, 1942, where he famously proclaimed, "I shall return." Commanding U.S. and Australian troops in the liberation of New Guinea and neighboring islands over the next two years, MacArthur, though a late convert to the idea, made "island hopping" famous, bypassing strong Japanese defensive positions to save lives. On October 20, 1944, MacArthur landed on Leyte Island in the Philippines and began the liberation he had promised. The general, with numerous tours of duty in the Philippines, opposed the Allied strategy of defeating Germany before Japan—to him the Pacific was paramount. In December, 1944, he was awarded his fifth star, and he received the Japanese surrender in Tokyo Bay on board the battleship *Missouri* on September 2, 1945.

After the war, President Harry S. Truman appointed MacArthur head of the Allied occupation of Japan. For almost five years, he directed the reconstruction of the nation and implemented a surprisingly liberal reform program involving demilitarization, land reform, women's rights, and a new constitution, earning him enduring affection in Japan. When North Korea invaded South Korea on June 25, 1950, Truman appointed MacArthur commander of United Nations (U.N.) forces resisting the invasion. He commanded the forces in battles such as the Pusan Perimeter (1950). A daring landing at Inchon on September 15 turned the tide, and with Truman's permission, MacArthur pushed north of the thirty-eighth parallel that had divided the two Koreas in a move to unite the country. Brushing aside warnings that the new communist regime in China might intervene, MacArthur was shocked by a massive Thanksgiving invasion of Chinese soldiers that pushed the U.N. forces well below the thirty-eighth parallel before they could halt the advance. The frustrated general began calling for the bombing of Chinese bases, rejecting the novel concept of a limited war advanced by the president. When his criticisms became more strident

Douglas MacArthur. (Digital Stock)

and public, Truman fired him in April, 1951. He returned to a hero's welcome, along with Senate hearings into his views. Chief of Staff Omar N. Bradley's famous testimony that war with China would be the "wrong war, at the wrong place, at the wrong time, and with the wrong enemy" became the conventional wisdom, and MacArthur, now too old for his conservative Republican presidential aspirations to bear fruit, faded away from the political scene.

RESOURCES

Imparato, Edward T. *MacArthur, Melbourne to Tokyo.* Shippensburg, Pa.: Burd Street Press, 1997.

James, D. Clayton. *The Years of MacArthur: 1880-1941.* New York: Houghton Mifflin, 1970.

_____. *The Years of MacArthur: 1941-1945.* New York: Houghton Mifflin, 1975.

_____. *The Years of MacArthur: Triumph and Disaster, 1945-1964.* New York: Houghton Mifflin, 1985.

MacArthur. Documentary. PBS Home Video. Warner Home Video, 1999.

Manchester, William. *American Caesar: Douglas MacArthur, 1880-1964.* Boston: Little, Brown, 1978.

Perret, Geoffrey. *Old Soldiers Never Die: The Life of Douglas MacArthur.* New York: Random House, 1996.

Return to the Philippines. Documentary. MCA Distributing, 1988.

Spanier, John. *The Truman-MacArthur Controversy and the Korean War.* New York: W. W. Norton, 1965.

Victory. America at War series. Documentary. Bridgestone Multimedia Group, 1995.

SEE ALSO: Bradley, Omar N.; Inchon Landing; Korean War; Leyte Gulf; Pearl Harbor attack; Pusan Perimeter; Roosevelt, Franklin D.; World War II.

John R. M. Wilson

MACCABEES, REVOLT OF THE

AT ISSUE: Jewish religious and political independence

DATE: 168-143 B.C.E.

LOCATION: Judea and the southern Levant

COMBATANTS: Jews vs. Syrians (Seleucids)

PRINCIPAL COMMANDERS: *Jewish*, Mattathias (d. ?166 B.C.E.), Judas Maccabeus (d. 160 B.C.E.), Jonathan (d. 143/142 B.C.E.), Simon (d. 135/134 B.C.E.); *Syrian*, Antiochus IV Epiphanes (c. 215-164 B.C.E.), Lysias (d. 162 B.C.E.), Bacchides (fl. second century B.C.E.), Tryphon

PRINCIPAL BATTLES: Ascent of Lebonah, Beth Horon, Emmaus, Bethsura, Beth Zachariah, Elasa

RESULT: Jewish victory; creation of independent Hasmonean Jewish state

BACKGROUND

After a Roman victory in 192 B.C.E., the Seleucid rulers of Syria struggled to pay a heavy annual indemnity to Rome. Taxes were levied and the temples of subject peoples were raided. When Antiochus IV Epiphanes inherited the Syrian throne (175 B.C.E.), he used the right to confirm the title of high priest to raise funds by selling the position to the highest bidder. Eventually, a man who was not qualified under Jewish law was confirmed as the Jewish high priest, an act that enraged the religious sensibilities of many in Judea.

Following Antiochus IV's unsuccessful attempt to conquer Egypt (168 B.C.E.), the historical record blurs. He may have provoked a revolt by the Jewish inhabitants of Judea while returning to Syria, or they may have seen an opportune moment, emboldening them to revolt. In either case, Antiochus moved quickly to suppress the developing revolt. Upon reaching Jerusalem, he desecrated the Jewish temple by entering the holiest place and then offering a sow upon the great altar of sacrifice. Subsequently, all residents of Judea were ordered to honor a particular Greek god (perhaps Zeus, Dionysius, or Ba'al Zaphon). To enforce this, altars were erected, and Syrian soldiers were sent into every Judean village.

ACTION

At Modi'in (167 B.C.E.), with the villagers assembled, Mattathias, a member of a Jewish priestly family, was asked by the Syrian soldiers to lead a ceremony honoring the Greek god. When he and his sons refused, another man offered to do so. Mattathias and his sons seized the soldiers' weapons, killing that man and the Syrian soldiers. Unable to remain in their village, Mattathias and his sons sought refuge in the Judean hills as they moved from village to village overturning the foreign altars and rousing the people to revolt (167 B.C.E.). After the death of his father, Judas Maccabeus assumed command of the revolt, organizing those who had joined them into an irregular military force suited for action in a mountainous environment.

During the ensuing four years, Maccabean Jewish forces commanded by Judas continually frustrated Syrian efforts to reinforce their soldiers. At the **Ascent of Lebonah** (167 B.C.E.), an entire Syrian unit was destroyed. An army of 5,000 Syrian soldiers subsequently attempted to reach Jerusalem from the northwest via **Beth Horon** (166 B.C.E.) and later by **Emmaus** (165 B.C.E.). Finally, the Syrian commander, Lysias, brought an army through Idumea, which was loyal to Syria, to **Bethsura** (164 B.C.E.), only again to be defeated by Judas's forces. Having effectively sealed off all routes to Jerusalem, the Maccabeans repaired the temple in Jerusalem (December, 164 B.C.E.), cleansed its precincts, and restored the traditional services.

Numerous campaigns followed these initial successes, both with neighboring peoples who feared the rising power of Judea and with the Syrians who continued to attempt to suppress the revolt. However, the death of Antiochus IV in 163 B.C.E. led into a lengthy succession struggle, undermined Syrian unity, and disrupted Syrian

MILESTONES IN THE REVOLT OF THE MACCABEES

Date	Event
167 B.C.E.	Jewish priest Mattathias and his sons revolt against Syrians.
167 B.C.E.	After his father's death, Judas Maccabeus assumes leadership.
167 B.C.E. - 164 B.C.E.	Judas wins battles at Ascent of Lebonah, Beth Horon, Emmaus, and Bethsura.
164 B.C.E.	Maccabeans repair temple in Jerusalem.
162 B.C.E.	Syrian regent Lysias defeats the Jews at Bethsura and Beth Zachariah.
162 B.C.E.	Syrian general Bacchides defeats Judas and drives him from Jerusalem.
161 B.C.E.	Judas defeats Syrians at Adasa; Judas is defeated and killed in battle at Elasa; his brother Jonathan takes command.
155 B.C.E.	Jonathan occupies a fortress at Beth-Basi, resulting in a negotiated peace that gives him control over most of Judea.
143 B.C.E.	Jonathan falls into a trap and is captured and executed at Ptolemais.
142 B.C.E.	Jonathan's brother Simon becomes king of newly independent Judea; he and his descendants found the Hasmonean kingdom.

attempts to subdue the Jewish revolt. After two quick campaigns, at Bethsura and **Beth Zachariah** (162 B.C.E.), victories by Lysias enabled the Syrians to reach Jerusalem and reinforce Syrian control. Lysias, however, had to return quickly to Syria because there arose a rival claimant to the throne, Demetrius I Soter. Bacchides, commander under Demetrius, appointed as high priest in Jerusalem Alcimus, a man whom the religious leaders accepted as legitimate under Jewish law (161 B.C.E.). Except for Alcimus's treachery toward some of his own people, this would have removed the religious motivation for continuing the revolt. Instead, continued revolt resulted in further Syrian efforts to suppress the Maccabean forces. At **Elasa** (161 B.C.E.), in perhaps the most serious defeat of the Jewish forces by Syria, Judas was killed and Syria regained control over Judea. The Jewish forces took refuge in the Judean hills and elected Judas's brother, Jonathan Maccabeus, to succeed him as commander.

After an interval of five years, Jonathan moved to recover Judea from Syrian control by occupying a fortress at Beth-Basi (155 B.C.E.), an act immediately met by Syrian action. However, the ensuing siege by Bacchides ended in a negotiated peace that allowed Jonathan to extend his control over virtually all of Judea except Jerusalem and Bethsura. Jonathan was thereafter in a position to act as a power broker in the Syrian succession struggle, with great benefit for Judea. The claimant to the Syrian throne, Alexander Balas, appointed Jonathan high priest (152 B.C.E.), while Demetrius offered him three districts in Samaria with Jewish populations. Still later, Balas appointed Jonathan a commander, and the governor of Judea (150 B.C.E.). In 147 B.C.E., Syrian rivals added to Jonathan's control contiguous territories west of Judea. Successful campaigns by Jonathan in Transjordan added further territory in 144 B.C.E., which Syrian officials acknowledged. At Ptolemais (143 B.C.E.), another claimant to the Syrian throne, Tryphon, used deceit to lure Jonathan into a trap, but was unable to turn that into a Syrian victory over the Maccabean forces partly because of a snowstorm. As the Syrian forces retreated, Jonathan was executed, while Jonathan's brother Simon was elected commander by the Jews. Simon sided with a rival of Tryphon, who granted Judea independence in 142 B.C.E.

Aftermath

Simon and his descendants established the Hasmonean kingdom, which would eventually encompass most of the territory of ancient Israel as it was under King David. For a brief time, other claimants to the Syrian throne attempted unsuccessfully to reassert control over some part of the Hasmonean kingdom, but these efforts subsided as the succession struggle weakened and consumed the Syrians and their rulers.

Resources

Aharoni, Yohanan, and Michael Avi-Yonah. *The Modern Bible Atlas*. London: George Allen & Unwin, 1982.

Baumgarten, Albert I. *The Flourishing of Jewish Sects in the Maccabean Era*. New York: Brill, 1997.

Derfler, Steven Lee. *The Hasmonean Revolt: Rebellion or Revolution*. Lewiston, N.Y.: E. Mellen Press, 1990.

Harrington, Daniel J. *The Maccabean Revolt: Anatomy of a Biblical Revolution*. Wilmington, Del.: Michael Glazier, 1988.

Mindlin, Valerie, and Gaalyahu Cornfeld. *The Epic of the Maccabees*. New York: Macmillan, 1962.

Sievers, Joseph. *The Hasmoneans and Their Supporters: From Mattathias to the Death of John Hyrcanus I*. Atlanta: Scholars Press, 1990.

See also: David; Religion and war; Syrian-Egyptian Wars.

Richard A. Bennett

McClellan, George B.

Full name: George Brinton McClellan
Born: December 3, 1826; Philadelphia, Pennsylvania
Died: October 29, 1885; Maywood, Orange Mountain, New Jersey
Principal war: American Civil War
Principal battles: Peninsular Campaign (1862), Antietam (1862)
Military significance: Although McClellan was unsuccessful in destroying Confederate armies or capturing Richmond, his victory at Antietam permitted the issuance of the Eman-

cipation Proclamation in 1863, and he helped make the Army of the Potomac a potent fighting force.

Long considered the "problem child" of the American Civil War (1861-1865), George B. McClellan was a talented, if flawed, general. Following initial success in the Ohio Valley, he was elevated to command of the Army of the Potomac and, during the fall of 1861, directed the operations of all Union armies. He transformed the Army of the Potomac from a volunteer fighting force into a professional army, but did not lead it to ultimate victory. Adored by his troops, he nonetheless proved reluctant to take risks, retreating from Richmond in 1862, the object of his Peninsular Campaign, rather than engaging the Confederate army in a slugfest. Although he badly bloodied the Army of Northern Virginia at Antietam (1862), he did not attack quickly when he knew his foe was divided and then did not give vigorous pursuit when the Army of Northern Virginia retreated. Further, his personal loathing for President Abraham Lincoln created policy problems for the Union over issues such as slavery and war aims. Cashiered in November, 1862, McClellan unsuccessfully ran for president against Lincoln in 1864.

RESOURCES

Roland, Thomas J. *George B. McClellan and Civil War History: In the Shadow of Grant and Sherman*. Kent, Ohio: Kent State University Press, 1998.

Sears, Stephen W. *Controversies and Commanders: Dispatches from the Army of the Potomac*. Boston: Houghton Mifflin, 1999.

_____. *George B. McClellan: The Young Napoleon*. New York: Tickenor & Fields, 1988.

SEE ALSO: American Civil War; Antietam; Lincoln, Abraham.

Edward R. Crowther

George B. McClellan. (Corbis)

McDowell, Irvin

BORN: October 15, 1818; Columbus, Ohio
DIED: May 4, 1885; San Francisco, California
PRINCIPAL WARS: Mexican-American War, American Civil War
PRINCIPAL BATTLES: First Bull Run (1861), Second Bull Run (1862)
MILITARY SIGNIFICANCE: McDowell commanded the Union Army at First Bull Run.

Born in Ohio, Irvin McDowell was first educated in France and then at West Point. He graduated in 1838 and was assigned to the artillery. During the Mexican-American War (1846-1848), he was breveted for his actions at Buena Vista (1847).

Between the Mexican-American War and the American Civil War (1861-1865), McDowell worked in the adjutant general's department, rising to the rank of major and serving as assistant adjutant general.

When the American Civil War erupted, officers with battle experience were at a premium in both armies. Promoted to brigadier general and charged with the defense of the capitol, McDowell was under political pressure to strike the Confederates at the Battle of the First Bull Run (1861). The result was a disaster for the Union Army. Their retreat was known as the "the great skedaddle." Days later, President Abraham Lincoln replaced McDowell with General George B. McClel-

Irvin McDowell. (Library of Congress)

lan, and McDowell became a division commander under McClellan.

Later, McDowell was placed in command of the First Corps. He was to join forces with McClellan, then in the midst of his Peninsula Campaign, and move on to Richmond. However, McDowell's forces had to contend with Stonewall Jackson in the Shenandoah Valley, and the move on Richmond was averted.

McDowell also commanded the Third Corps at Second Bull Run. Partially blamed for the defeat of the Union Army at that battle, McDowell requested a court of inquiry and was eventually cleared of any responsibility for the defeat. He was later assigned command of the Department of the Pacific.

After the war, McDowell commanded the Departments of the South and West and retired in 1882. Little has been written about his life.

RESOURCES
Longacre, Edward G. "Fortune's Fool." *Civil War Times Illustrated* 18 (May, 1979): 20-31.
Robertson, James I., Jr. *Stonewall Jackson: The Man, The Soldier, The Legend.* New York: Macmillan, 1997.

SEE ALSO: American Civil War; Buena Vista; Bull Run, First; Bull Run, Second; McClellan, George B.; Mexican-American War.

Ken Willingham

MACEDONIAN WARS

AT ISSUE: Hegemony over Greece
DATE: 215-146 B.C.E.
LOCATION: Balkans
COMBATANTS: Romans vs. Macedonians
PRINCIPAL COMMANDERS: *Macedonian,* King Philip V (238-179 B.C.E.), King Perseus (c. 213-c. 165 B.C.E.), Andriscus (fl. second century B.C.E.); *Roman,* Titus Quinctius Flamininus (c. 227-174 B.C.E.), Lucius Aemilius Paulus Macedonicus (229?-160 B.C.E.), Quintus Caecilius Metellus Macedonicus (d. 46 B.C.E.)
PRINCIPAL BATTLES: Cynoscephalae, Pydna
RESULT: Dissolution of the Macedonian monarchy; establishment of Roman hegemony over Greece

BACKGROUND
The Argead Macedonian monarch King Philip II established Macedonian rule over Greece with his victory over a coalition of Athens and other Greek states at Chaeronea in Boeotia in 338 B.C.E. His son, Alexander the Great, further strengthened Macedonian control over the Greek city-states before launching his successful mission of conquest of the Persian Empire. Thereafter, the Antigonid Dynasty, which succeeded the Argead, continued to hold an uneasy Macedonian sway over the Greek city-states throughout the third century B.C.E. The Greek city-states, and especially Athens, with its proud traditions and glorious past, never fully acquiesced to Macedonian rule and were ever ready to seize any opportunity to throw off the Macedonian yoke. In the course of the third century B.C.E., two confederations of Greek states, the Achaean and Aetolian Leagues, managed to maintain a certain degree of autonomy from the Macedonian monarchs.

By 300 B.C.E., the Roman Republic controlled peninsular Italy through various sorts of treaties and alliances with the Italian states, in which Rome was the dominant party and invariably required its allies to contribute an annual quota of troops to the Roman military machine. Throughout much of the third century B.C.E., Rome was preoccupied with its great nemesis Carthage, a mercantile imperial power near modern-day Tunis, and Rome's imperial expansion in this period was principally to its immediate north and south, Cisalpine Gaul and Sicily, respectively. In the great struggle against the Carthaginian leader Hannibal, Rome came to realize that the contest was for control of the western province of Spain, rich in manpower and mines.

In 229 B.C.E., marauding activities of the Illyrians interfered with Italian maritime trading, leading to Rome's first military operations to the east. Illyria served as a buffer zone between Rome and Macedonia, and a Roman presence across the Adriatic Sea created new tension between the two superpowers. This tension led to a series of wars between Rome and Macedonia. At the beginning of these conflicts, Rome's aims were no more than establishing stability in the Greek world and curtailing the power of Macedonia. By the end of the Romano-Macedonian wars, the former kingdom of Macedonia was incorporated into the Roman Empire as part of Roman provincial territory.

Action

In the course of Rome's war against Hannibal, Rome and Macedonia first came into conflict. The Macedonian king Philip V struck an alliance with Hannibal in the aftermath of the latter's crushing victory over the Romans at Cannae (216 B.C.E.), and this event led to the beginning of the First Macedonian War (215-205 B.C.E.). Rome's efforts in the Greek theater were half-hearted; the Republic relied on its new ally, the Aetolian League, to keep Philip in play while it brought the war against Carthage to its conclusion. The war died of inanition in the Peace of Phoenice (205 B.C.E.).

Once Rome had decisively defeated Carthage at Zama (202 B.C.E.), it began to settle accounts with Philip V, thus commencing the Second Macedonian War (200-196 B.C.E.). The Roman elite had a hard time persuading the popular assembly to vote for war against Philip, as the rank and file were war weary from the long struggle against Hannibal. In the first two years of the war, Roman troops had difficulty penetrating the Balkan mountain passes and defiles into Macedonia; they were somewhat more effective in their propaganda war in Greece, where they proclaimed that they had come as liberators of Greeks from Macedonian domination. The Roman commander Titus Quinctius Flamininus brought the war to an end by defeating Philip at **Cynoscephalae** (197 B.C.E.) in Thessaly, thereby demonstrating the superiority of the Roman legion over the Macedonian phalanx.

King Perseus, Philip V's successor, attempted to strengthen and consolidate Macedonian power, while at the same time remaining on friendly terms with Rome. Roman imperialism, however, hardened in the course of the second century B.C.E., and the Roman Senate was determined to eliminate Macedonia as a serious rival. The Third Macedonian War (172-167 B.C.E.) in general replicated the second: After some early Macedonian successes, the Roman legions crushed the Macedonian phalanx in a decisive battle. The Roman commander Lucius Aemilius Paulus Macedonicus met Perseus's forces at **Pydna** (June 22, 168 B.C.E.) on the northeast coast of Greece. Here the terrain was ultimately a disadvantage to the phalanx formation, and the Roman maniples were able to infiltrate the formation and carry the day.

In 149 B.C.E., Andriscus, a pretender to the Macedonian throne, invaded Macedonia from Thrace. He briefly aroused great hopes in Macedonia, demonstrating the strong anti-Roman sentiment there at this time. After defeating a Roman praetorian army, he was crushed in 148 B.C.E. by the Roman praetor Quintus Caecilius Metellus Macedonicus.

Aftermath

At the conclusion of the Third Macedonian War, the Macedonian kingdom ceased to exist after being divided into four separate republics by the Romans. Shortly after the defeat of Andriscus, in 146 B.C.E., Rome annexed Macedonia as imperial territory. Rome thereby departed from its longstanding policy of serving as hegemonial adviser and avoiding direct annexation in the Greek east.

Resources

Badian, Ernst. *Foreign Clientelae (264-70 B.C.).* Oxford: Clarendon Press, 1958.

Errington, R. M. *The Dawn of Empire: Rome's Rise to World Power.* Ithaca, N.Y.: Cornell University Press, 1972.

Gruen, Erich S. *The Hellenistic World and the Coming of Rome.* Berkeley: University of California Press, 1984.

Habicht, Christian. *Athens from Alexander to Antony.* Cambridge, Mass.: Harvard University Press, 1997.

Harris, William V. *War and Imperialism in Republican Rome.* Oxford: Clarendon Press, 1979.

SEE ALSO: Alexander the Great; Alexander's Wars of Conquest; Ancient warfare; Athenian Empire; Cannae; Chaeronea, 338 B.C.E.; Cynoscephalae; Hannibal; Philopoemen; Zama.

Craige B. Champion

MACHEL, SAMORA

FULL NAME: Samora Moisès Machel
BORN: September 29, 1933; Chilembene, Mozambique
DIED: October 19, 1986; Mbuzini, near Komatipoort, Lebombo Mountains, South Africa
PRINCIPAL WAR: Mozambican War of Independence

Samora Machel. (AP/Wide World Photos)

MILITARY SIGNIFICANCE: Machel served as military commander of the Mozambique Liberation Front during the anticolonial war in Mozambique.

Originally trained as a nurse, Samora Machel was one of the early members of the Mozambique Liberation Front (FRELIMO). His mentor was Eduardo Mondlane, FRELIMO's founder. In 1963, after going to Tanzania to join FRELIMO, Machel was sent to Algeria for military training. He then established the first FRELIMO camp, and within a year had prepared 250 trained men. Proving himself in guerrilla combat, Machel rose to commander in 1968. He joined the ruling council when Mondlane was assassinated the following year and was elected president in 1970. Under his leadership, the rural areas were liberated from Portuguese control, which was replaced with a civil administration. He received arms from the Soviet Union and was a Marxist most of his life.

In 1974, the Portuguese army mutinied and brought down the government, largely in response to the military successes of FRELIMO and other colonial movements. In 1975, Machel became president of an independent Mozambique after authority was transferred to FRELIMO. He faced daunting economic and social problems, but the military situation remained the major trouble spot. Apartheid South Africa funded and supported a right-wing guerrilla movement, the Mozambique National Resistance (RENAMO), which harassed the new Mozambican army, destroyed crops, and terrorized the countryside. Machel in turn provided sanctuary and support for the military wing of the African National Congress and Rhodesian liberation forces. Machel surprised many by signing the Nkomati Accord with South Africa in 1984, agreeing to deny bases to the African National Congress (ANC), while South Africa agreed to withdraw support to RENAMO.

Machel was returning from a visit to Zambia two years later when his plane crashed along the South African-Mozambican border. The cause was never explained satisfactorily.

RESOURCES
Cann, John P. *Counterinsurgency in Africa: The Portuguese Way of War, 1961-1974.* Westport, Conn.: Greenwood Press, 1997.

Christie, Iain. *Samora Machel*. Atlantic Highlands, N.J.: Panaf, 1989.

SEE ALSO: Mozambican Civil War; Mozambican War of Independence; Portuguese Colonial Wars.

Norbert Brockman

MACHIAVELLI, NICCOLÒ

FULL NAME: Niccolò di Messer Bernardo Machiavelli
BORN: May 3, 1469; Florence, Italy
DIED: June 21, 1527; Florence, Italy
PRINCIPAL WARS: Pisan War, War of the Holy League
PRINCIPAL BATTLE: Prato (1512)
MILITARY SIGNIFICANCE: Machiavelli was dismissed from government service after the fall of Florence to a papal-Spanish army; after dismissal, he wrote several works on war and politics.

Niccolò Machiavelli began working for the republican government of Florence in 1498. His duties included acting as civil servant responsible for the supervision of military operations. In 1507, he was charged with administering the citizen militia of Florence in the Pisan War. He commanded the militia against Pisa, leading to that city's surrender in 1509. He also played a part in the preparations for the War of the Holy League (1510-1511). On August 29, 1512, the rout of the Florentine militia at the hands of a papal-Spanish army at Prato humiliated Machiavelli, as almost half of his fleeing troops were hand picked by him for valor. The subsequent collapse of the Florentine Republic led to his dismissal from government service.

After his years of service, Machiavelli wrote the works that made him famous, including *Dell' arte della guerra* (1521; *The Art of War*, 1560). Most of this work is a detailed discussion of military management, training, order of battle, and leadership. However, the central thrust of the work contains themes found in his more well-known books, *Il principe* (1532; *The Prince*, 1640) and the *Discorsi sopra la prima deca di Tito Livio* (1531; *Discourses on the First Ten Books of Titus Livius*, 1636). According to Machiavelli, military and political affairs are interdependent, and the art of war is contingent on the art of politics. Good laws must accompany strong armies. A ruler should rely only on his own arms, and that means a virtuous citizen army rather than mercenaries. The best military strength is found in a stable city with solid republican institutions that its patriotic citizens are ever ready to defend.

RESOURCES
Bayley, C. C. *War and Society in Renaissance Florence*. Toronto: University of Toronto Press, 1961.
Hale, J. R. *War and Society in Renaissance Europe, 1450-1620*. New York: St. Martin's Press, 1985.
Mansfield, Harvey C. *Machiavelli's Virtue*. Chicago: University of Chicago Press, 1996.
Viroli, Maurizio. *Machiavelli*. Oxford: Oxford University Press, 1998.
Wood, Neal. *Introduction to Machiavelli's "The Art of War."* Indianapolis, Ind.: Bobbs Merrill, 1965.

SEE ALSO: Holy Roman Empire; Italian Wars.

Donald G. Tannenbaum

MACKENSEN, AUGUST VON

BORN: December 6, 1849; Haus Leipnitz, Saxony (now in Germany)
DIED: November 8, 1945; Celle, Germany
PRINCIPAL WAR: World War I
PRINCIPAL BATTLES: Tannenberg (1914), Gorlice-Tarnow (1915), Serbia (1915), Romania (1916)
MILITARY SIGNIFICANCE: Architect of several German victories in the east, Mackensen served as a troubleshooter for the German army. He drove the Russians back from the German border, defeated the Serbian army, and conquered Romania.

The son of a businessman, August von Mackensen began his military career in the cavalry. He rose through the ranks, briefly serving as military tutor to Kaiser William II. However, his rise to prominence came during the Battle of Tannenberg (1914). Mackensen led the Seventeenth Corp, which surrounded and destroyed the invading Russian army. His success there earned him command of the Eleventh Army, which led the offensive to conquer Russian Poland. His "Mackensen wedge" involved a brief but heavy artillery bombardment on a narrow front. His attack focused on the enemy trenches and artillery and was followed by a rapid infantry assault. Mackensen's tactics were successful against the Russians at Gorlice and Tarnow (1915) and led to the Russian abandonment of Poland.

With the Russians at bay, Mackensen traveled to the Serbian front. He led a mixed Austrian and German army against the Serbs and with timely aid from the Bulgarians was able to overrun the country in 1915.

In 1916, the Romanian declaration of war against the Central Powers resulted in Mackensen's move to Bulgaria. There he worked with a German and Bulgarian force to attack the Romanian capital of Bucharest and eventually drove the Romanian army into Russia. In 1917, Mackensen returned to Russia. His attacks against the newly formed Soviet Union drove deep into its territory and forced the Soviet leadership to sue for peace.

RESOURCES

Herwig, Holger. *The First World War*. London: Arnold, 1997.
Keegan, John. *The First World War*. New York: Alfred A. Knopf, 1999.
Lincoln, W. Bruce. *Passage Through Armageddon*. New York: Simon & Schuster, 1986.

SEE ALSO: Gorlice-Tarnow; Tannenberg; World War I.

Douglas Clouatre

MCNAMARA, ROBERT S.

FULL NAME: Robert Strange McNamara
BORN: June 9, 1916; San Francisco, California
PRINCIPAL WARS: World War II, Vietnam Conflict
MILITARY SIGNIFICANCE: McNamara brought to the U.S. Defense Department the administrative techniques of modern business.

Recruited by Colonel Charles B. Thornton to establish a statistical control system for the Eighth Air Force in World War II, Robert S. McNamara and his aides, known as the Whiz Kids, were brought into the Ford Motor Company in 1946 to revitalize its corporate structure. McNamara rose to the presidency of the company and was recruited by President John F. Kennedy, Jr., in 1961 to bring his management skills to the Pentagon.

McNamara centralized the management of the Defense Department, ending the old system in which the three military branches operated under independent budgeting programs. McNamara also increased the size of the military and adopted a policy of "flexible response" to replace the "massive retaliation" policy of the previous administration.

Remaining with the administration of President Lyndon B. Johnson following the assassination of Kennedy in 1963, McNamara at first supported the increasing involvement of the United States in the Vietnam Conflict but by 1967 began to question the efficacy of the war and lost his influence in the administration. He left the Defense Department in April, 1968, to take a position as the head of the World Bank.

RESOURCES

Hendrikson, Paul. *The Living and the Dead: Robert McNamara and Five Lives of a Lost War*. New York: Alfred A. Knopf, 1996.
McNamara, Robert S., James G. Blight, and Robert K. Brigham. *Argument Without End: In Search of Answers to the Vietnam Tragedy*. New York: Public Affairs, 1999.
Shapley, Deborah. *Promise and Power: The Life and Times of Robert McNamara*. Boston: Little, Brown, 1993.
Trewitt, Henry L. *McNamara*. New York: Harper & Row, 1971.

SEE ALSO: Vietnam Conflict; World War II.

Robert L. Patterson

MAGDEBURG, SIEGE OF

TYPE OF ACTION: Ground battle in the Thirty Years' War
DATE: May 18-20, 1631
LOCATION: North central Germany on Elbe River
COMBATANTS: 20,000 Catholics vs. Protestants
PRINCIPAL COMMANDERS: *Imperial/Catholic*, Count Johan Tserclaes Tilly (1559-1632), General

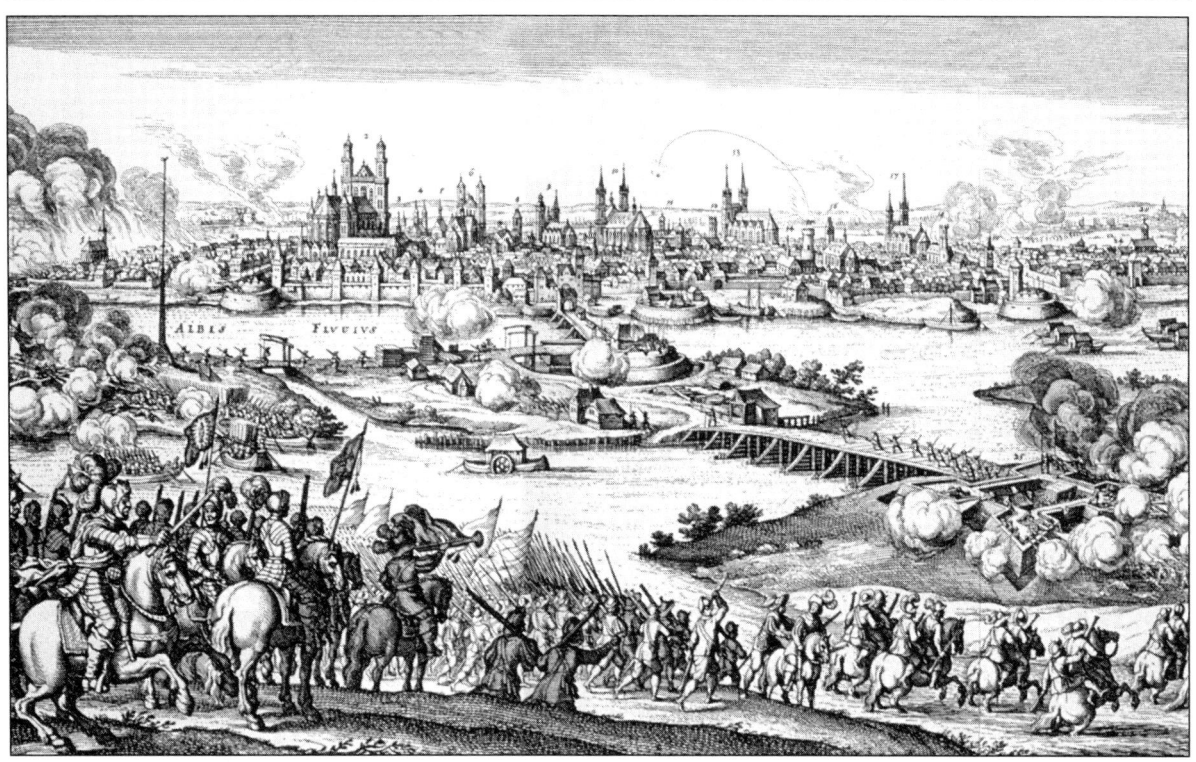

Imperial commanders Count Johan Tserclaes Tilly and Count Gottfried H. zu Pappenheim besieged the city of Magdeburg. (Library of Congress)

Count Gottfried H. zu Pappenheim (1594-1632); *Protestant*, Dietrich von Falkenberg
RESULT: The city fell to the besieging Imperial forces after only minimal resistance

Count Johan Tserclaes Tilly and Count Gottfried H. zu Pappenheim, the Imperial commanders, had hoped to secure the important trading city of Magdeburg largely to provision their troops. King Gustavus II Adolphus of Sweden, a leader of the Protestant forces in Germany, wished to retain a valuable ally. He sent his lieutenant Dietrich von Falkenberg to organize Magdeburg's defenses until he could arrive with his army.

Gustavus's actions were made too late. Beginning on May 18, Tilly and Pappenheim lay siege to the city. The burghers of the city were no match for the battle-hardened Imperial forces. The walls were breached at the end of the second day; fires began simultaneously in several parts of the largely wooden city, turning it into a furnace. Those whom the fires did not destroy were massacred. An estimated 20,000 to 30,000 perished.

SIGNIFICANCE

The Protestants turned the siege and destruction of Magdeburg into a major propaganda event. Tracts and graphic woodcut prints were distributed all over Germany, warning citizens what treatment they could expect from the vengeful Catholic emperor. Heretofore wavering supporters rallied to the Protestant cause, prolonging and intensifying an already brutal war.

RESOURCES

Asch, R. G. "Sack of Magdeburg." In *The Thirty Years War*. London: Macmillan Press, 1997.

Malleson, G. B. "Breitenfeld." In *The Battlefields of Germany*. Westport, Conn.: Greenwood Press, 1971.

Wedgwood, C. V. "Siege of Magdeburg." In *The Thirty Years War*. Gloucester, Mass.: Peter Smith, 1969.

SEE ALSO: Gustavus II Adolphus; Thirty Years' War; Tilly, Count Johan Tserclaes.

Nis Petersen

Maginot Line

Date: Constructed from 1930 to 1935
Location: Along France's northeastern border with Germany, following the Rhine from Basel, Switzerland to Hagenau in the Vosges then west to Longuyon to the southeast corner of Belgium
Principal military action: France
Military significance: This static line of fortifications complemented and determined French military strategy during the 1930's.

In 1925, the decision to construct a line of permanent fortifications along France's eastern and northern frontiers took shape when Minister of War Paul Painlevé established the Commission de Defense des Frontiers (commission for the defense of the frontiers). However, it was not until five years later, under Painlevé's successor, André Maginot, that construction on the Maginot Line began in earnest. French military planners had been impressed by the ability of fixed fortifications, such as those at Verdun, to withstand assault and many saw in such defenses the means to protect the country against a sudden, surprise attack from Germany. This fear was acute in 1930 when Allied occupation troops were pulled out of the Rhineland five years ahead of schedule. In addition, during World War I, more than 1.3 million French died, creating a dip in the birth rate. The resulting manpower shortage caused the length of compulsory military service to be reduced in 1927 to one year, making offensive action against Germany less likely. A static line of permanent reinforced-concrete fortifications seemed the perfect way to compensate for such French weakness.

The Maginot Line was made strongest in its northeastern sector where it consisted of three interdependently fortified girdles. These contained antitank traps, pillboxes, casemates with interlocking fields of fire, and large subterranean forts (*ouvrages*) that contained living quarters, power supplies, magazines, and service areas. The forts were connected with other areas of the line by tunnels, often serviced by underground trains. In addition to the technical problems of maintaining an army in such living conditions, the Maginot Line posed real problems for French foreign policy insofar as the line's defensive nature undermined the commitments that France had made to Poland and Czechoslovakia with which it had treaties promising aid in case of German attack. Another apparent problem was an absence of extended fortifications along the Belgian frontier, the route of invasion in 1914. French military planners were aware of this omission but had argued that the fortified regions in Alsace-Lorraine would serve as support for a war on the western plains. However, the streamlining of tactics and organization to make such a strategy viable was never accomplished, much to France's detriment.

In 1940, German armies advanced through the lightly defended Ardennes sector, flanked the Maginot Line and quickly rolled up the French and British armies that had advanced into Bel-

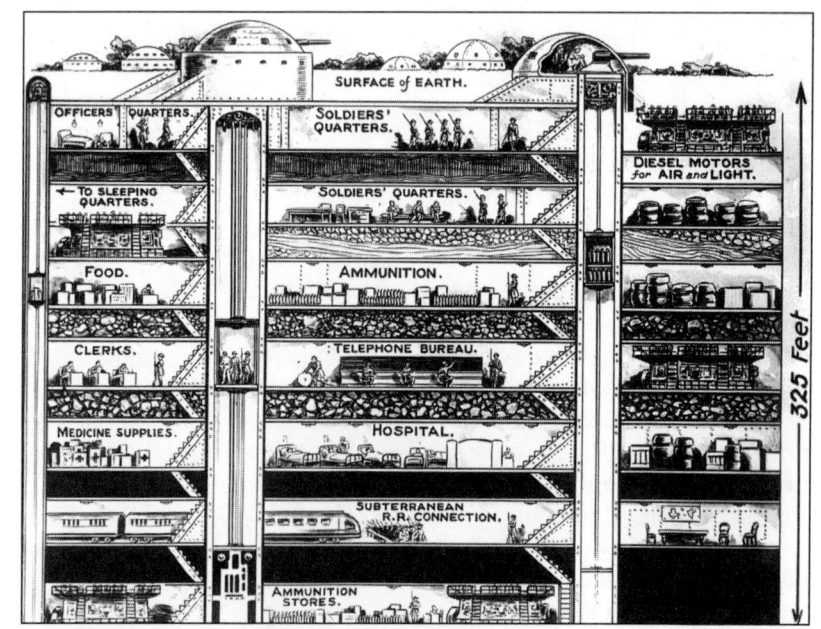

The Maginot Line, shown in this sectional drawing, was built to protect against German invasion. (Archive Photos/Hulton Getty Collection)

gium, forcing a British evacuation and a French surrender in June, 1940. It was small consolation that the Maginot Line had not been breached.

RESOURCES
Hughes, Judith. *To the Maginot Line: The Politics of French Military Preparation in the 1920's.* Cambridge, Mass.: Harvard University Press, 1971.
Kaufman, J. E. *The Maginot Line: None Shall Pass.* Westport, Conn.: Praeger, 1997.
Kemp, Anthony. *The Maginot Line: Myth and Reality.* New York: Stein and Day, 1982.
Rowe, Vivian. *The Great Wall of France: The Triumph of the Maginot Line.* London: Putnam, 1959.

SEE ALSO: Blitzkrieg; France; World War II.

Wm. Laird Kleine-Ahlbrandt

Magsaysay, Ramón

BORN: August 31, 1907; Iba, Zambales province, Luzon Island, Philippines
DIED: March 17, 1957; Cebu, Philippines
PRINCIPAL WARS: World War II, Hukbalahap Revolt
MILITARY SIGNIFICANCE: During World War II, Magsaysay organized guerrilla forces to fight against the Japanese; after the war, he successfully put down the Hukbalahap Revolt.

Ramón Magsaysay received a bachelor of science degree in commerce from José Rizal College in 1932. He started as a mechanic, then became branch manager of a transportation company. During the war with Japan, the U.S. Army requisitioned the transportation company's trucks and engaged Magsaysay as their expert mechanic. After Bataan fell (December, 1941-April, 1942) and the Americans surrendered at Corregidor (May, 1942), Magsaysay organized the western Luzon guerrilla forces and for three years fought with the guerrillas against the Japanese in the mountains of Zambales province. After U.S. troops liberated the province in 1945, General Douglas MacArthur, who was impressed with Magsaysay's accomplishments, appointed him military governor of his native province. He later was elected representative from Zambales to the Philippine legislature.

Serving as secretary of defense under President Elpidio Quirino in 1950, Magsaysay fought the Hukbalahaps (also known as Huks or the People's Anti-Japanese Army), a guerrilla group organized by nationalist communists during the war with Japan that had not been incorporated into the postwar Philippine government. He broke up the Huk organization with guerrilla tactics, offering land and tools to those who surrendered and fighting vigorously against those who continued to resist, and reorganized the Philippine constabulary and army.

On December 30, 1953, Magsaysay was inaugurated as the third president of the Philippine Republic, succeeding Quirino. Early in the morning of Sunday, March 17, 1957, he died in an airplane crash in a mountain in Cebu. Magsaysay's sudden death occurred before much of the program for rural improvement that he advocated had been put into action. However, during his administration, he organized the National Rehabilitation and Resettlement Administration and rehabilitated agricultural dissidents in the Philippine Armed Forces Economic Development Corps settlements. On March 18, 1957, Vice President Carlos P. Garcia became the fourth president of the Philippine Republic, completing Magsaysay's unexpired term in 1957.

RESOURCES
Golay, Frank H. *The Philippines: Public Policy and National Economic Development.* Ithaca, N.Y.: Cornell University Press, 1961.
Mahajani, Usha. *Philippine Nationalism: External Challenge and Filipino Response, 1965-1946.* St. Lucia, Queensland: University of Queensland Press, 1971.
Romulo, Carlos P. *The Philippines Presidents: Memoirs of.* Quezon City: New Day Publishers, 1988.
Vaughan, Josephine Budd. *The Land and People of the Philippines.* New York: J. B. Lippincott, 1956.
Waddell, J. R. E. *An Introduction to Southeast Asian Politics.* New York: John Wiley & Sons, 1972.

SEE ALSO: Hukbalahap Revolt; MacArthur, Douglas; World War II.

Ceferina Gayo Hess

Magyars

Date: 895-1038
Location: Carpathian basin and Danubian river banks
Principal military action: Augsburg
Military significance: King Stephen created a strong, centralized Catholic Hungary that was to serve as a buffer between the Habsburg Dynasty to the west and the Ottoman Turks to the east.

The Magyars were people of Finno-Urgian heritage who left their home on the steppes north of the Black Sea and migrated across the Carpathian Mountains around the year 895. During their first two centuries in their new home, the Magyars were nomadic cattle traders and raiders who attacked weaker neighbors and sold them as slaves to the Turks. The Magyars terrorized central Europe and expanded throughout the area until finally being stopped by Holy Roman emperor Otto the Great in 910 outside Augsburg.

Stephen I István, from the dominant Arpádian clan, created the first modern Hungarian state. He reconciled with the Holy Roman Empire and married a Bavarian princess. He embraced Catholicism and made it the established faith, despite the proselytizing efforts of Orthodox and Islamic representatives. Defeating rival claimants in battles between 997 and 1038, he created a powerful, national state. Stephen embraced the political and educational ideas of the Franks and largely destroyed clan identity while freeing his own slaves and encouraging others to do the same. By the standards of his time, his reign was considered enlightened.

Resources
McGuigan, Dorothy Gies. *The Habsburgs*. Garden City, N.Y.: Doubleday, 1966.
Sisa, Stephen. *The Spirit of Hungary: A Panorama of Hungarian History and Culture*. Morristown, N.J.: Vista Books, 1990.
Teleky, Richard. *Hungarian Rhapsodies: Essays on Ethnicity, Identity and Culture*. Seattle: University of Washington Press, 1997.

See also: Franks and Burgundians; Hungarian War with the Holy Roman Emperor; Otto I.

Thomas W. Buchanan

Mahan, Alfred Thayer

Born: September 27, 1840; West Point, New York
Died: December 1, 1914; Washington, D.C.
Principal wars: American Civil War, Spanish-American War
Military significance: Mahan's monumental work *The Influence of Sea Power upon History 1660-1805*, published in 1890, argued the case for sea power as a decisive factor in history.

Alfred Thayer Mahan was born at West Point, New York, where his father, a noted authority on field fortifications and siege warfare, taught engineering at the military academy. Mahan graduated from the U.S. Naval Academy at Annapolis, Maryland, in 1859. As a young lieutenant, he served as executive officer aboard the USS *Pocahontas* during the early part of the American Civil War. Mahan's lack of attention on duty resulted in his ship colliding with another Union ship at anchor. Such accidents became characteristic of Mahan's subsequent commands. While at sea, he was in a constant state of anxiety and very much preferred a life on land—in the classroom or pursuing a writing career. It was clear that his abilities did not suit him for work as a naval officer in command but as a strategist and historian.

After teaching at the newly formed Naval War College for a few months, he became president of the college in 1886. In 1890, Mahan published his electrifying and renowned work *The Influence of Sea Power upon History 1660-1805*, which was based largely on his lectures at the college. In this major work, Mahan stressed the large and even decisive effect of sea power on the course of history and the prosperity of nations. No previous writer or strategist had placed such emphasis on naval might. Mahan's work initially received a more enthusiastic response in Europe than in the United States, especially in naval circles. It provided the Royal Navy and the British government the best possible arguments for continuing and strengthening a strong navy policy. In Germany, the kaiser was much impressed and ordered the dissemination of the work among his naval officers. It has been claimed that the writing of Mahan was instrumental in creating the naval rivalry between Great Britain and Germany that contributed to the outbreak of World War I. Great

Britain would accept German military might but not a threat to her naval superiority. It is more likely that Mahan's popularity within the two countries was a symptom of the rivalry rather than the cause.

In 1893, Mahan was ordered to sea and given command of the new cruiser *Chicago*. It was dispatched to Europe to return the visits of European warships to the United States in commemoration of the discovery of America. In Europe, Mahan was welcomed as a celebrity in a triumphal procession through European ports and was presented to Queen Victoria and William II, the kaiser. Returning home, Mahan found that his fame had grown immensely. Future president Theodore Roosevelt and Senator Henry Cabot Lodge could be counted among his supporters. The relationship between Roosevelt and Mahan, both personally and professionally was especially close.

Mahan retired from the U.S. Navy in 1896 with the rank of rear admiral after having served close to forty years. Much of his time in retirement was spent writing books and serialized magazine articles that were later published in book form. He returned to the Navy temporarily in 1898 during the Spanish-American War to serve on the Naval War Board.

Resources

Mahan, Alfred Thayer. *The Influence of Sea Power upon History 1660-1805*. 1890. New York: Gallery Books, 1980.

Sumida, Jon Tetsuro. *Inventing Grand Strategy and Teaching Command: The Classic Works of Alfred Thayer Mahan Reconsidered*. Washington, D.C.: Woodrow Wilson Center Press, 1997.

Turk, Richard W. *The Ambiguous Relationship: Theodore Roosevelt and Alfred Thayer Mahan*. Westport, Conn.: Greenwood Press, 1987.

See also: American Civil War; Navy, U.S.; Spanish-American War.

Gilbert T. Cave

Maḥmūd of Ghazna

Full name: Yamin Al-Daula Abu'l-Qasim Maḥmūd Ibn Sebüktigin

Born: November 1, 971; place unknown
Died: April 21, 1030; Ghazna
Principal wars: Wars against Kanauj, Khajuraho, Gwalior, Kathiawar
Principal battle: Somnāth (1024)
Military significance: Maḥmūd of Ghazna plundered Indian cities and temples and set the example for later Muslim dynasties in India.

Maḥmūd, sultan of Ghazna in south Afghanistan, is considered a central figure in the spread of Islam in South Asia. Maḥmūd had no intention of establishing an empire in India, but his example of conquest in India led to empire building by successive Muslim dynasties.

Leaving his principality in eastern Afghanistan, which he won from his younger brother, Ismail, in around 997, he embarked on seventeen devastating raids between the year 1000 and 1025 to attack Hindu temple cities in India and to extend his rule to the Punjab in India. He started his raids in the dry season in October and returned to Afghanistan before the hot weather began and the monsoon rains made the rivers difficult for his plunder-laden armies to cross. His sway extended from central Asia through Afghanistan to eastern Persia and western India.

Several factors contributed to his military success. His cavalry consisted of specially trained slaves who had practically been raised on horseback and were subject to constant training. They would charge toward the enemy and, at a certain moment, rein their horses to a halt, turn them so the horses' heads were not in the way, and then let go a coordinated volley of arrows. They would then ride off to attack elsewhere before they could be the subject of assault. Maḥmūd's army also benefitted from the refusal of the Hindu rulers to cooperate with each other, either on or off the battlefield, even in the face of Maḥmūd s attacks. Islamic society was also more egalitarian than Hindu communities, and anyone of military ability could join Maḥmūd's army and gain rapid advancement. This attracted talented volunteers from distant places who sought glory and fortune.

Maḥmūd took enormous amounts of wealth and innumerable slaves as well as Indian craftsmen back to Afghanistan from India, and he destroyed numerous temples, killing tens or hundreds of thousands of Hindus in the name of Islam. With his plunder, he made his capital city of Ghazna one of the finest in the world. From the Punjab, the Muslims later expanded deeper into India, establishing Muslim dynasties in the north of India from 1175 and converting Indians to Islam.

Maḥmūd attacked the Gurjura Pratiharas of Kanauj in 1019, capturing their seven forts in one day; the Chandellas of Khajuraho in 1019 and 1021-1022; and the Rājput rulers of Gwalior, all of whom were defeated and their territories plundered. The defeat of the Gurjura Pratiharas was especially important because it gave him easy access to the northern plains of India. Maḥmūd targeted the Hindu holy places, destroying and looting the holy places of Thaneswar, Mathura, and Kanauj. The pinnacle of his onslaught on the "pagan" Hindus came about in 1024 with his onslaught by some 30,000 horsemen of the Shiva temple at Somnāth on the south coast of Kathiawar in Gujarat. He destroyed the Shiva lingam with his own hands and then returned to Afghanistan with more than six tons of gold. Many of his troops did not survive the difficult journey through the desert. As an orthodox Muslim, he did not spare a Muslim ruler, Daud, who was a follower of the heterodox Muslim sect, the Ismailis. He attacked him twice, the second time killing many Muslims who had not kept their promise to convert to the Orthodox Sunni faith. A highly capable general, Maḥmūd was also a patron of Muslim learning and literature, art, and architecture.

Resources

Habib, Muhammad. *Politics and Society During the Early Medieval Period*. New Delhi: Peoples Publishing House, 1981.

_____. *Sultan Mahmud of Ghazni*. New Delhi: S. Chand, 1951.

Lal, K. S. *Early Muslims in India*. New Delhi: Books and Books, 1984.

Wink, Andre. *Al-Hind: The Making of the Indo-Islamic World Seventh-Eleventh Centuries*. Reprint. New York: Brill, 1997.

See also: Muslim Conquests; Religion and war.

Roger D. Long

Majorian

Full name: Julius Valerius Majorianus
Born: c. 420; Danubian provinces
Died: August 7, 461; Tortona, Italy
Principal wars: Barbarian wars
Principal battles: Vicus Helena (c. 448), Piacenza (456), Elche (460)
Military significance: The last emperor of the Western Roman Empire to have significant successes against the barbarians and to offer hope that the empire could be restored.

As a youth, Majorian served with Aetius, along with the Gallic Aegidius and the barbarian Ricimer. He fought against the Franks at the Battle of Vicus Helena (c. 448). After the murder of Aetius in 454, he was made count of the domestics by Emperor Valentinian III. He retained this position under Petronius Maximus and Eparchius Avitus. When Avitus's popularity in Italy waned in 456, Majorian and Ricimer, now a military count, revolted, defeating and deposing Avitus at Piacenza.

On February 28, 457, Majorian was named master of soldiers by the Eastern Roman emperor Leo I. In this capacity, he sent Count Burco against Alamanni, who had invaded Italy. The resultant victory led to Majorian's acclamation as emperor on April 1. Majorian spent his entire reign attempting to consolidate his authority. In 458, he defeated a Vandal party raiding Campania. Soon thereafter, Majorian marched into Gaul. The Visigoths were driven away from Arles, and Majorian made his old friend Aegidius master of soldiers of Gaul. The Burgundians were defeated, and Lyon was besieged and captured. In 459, Majorian reoccupied much of Spain, which he wanted to use as a base to attack the Vandals in Africa. However, the following year, his fleet was destroyed through treachery at Elche, near Cartagena. He then returned to Italy, and on August 7, 461, he was beheaded by Ricimer at Tortona. With him died the last hope of reviving the Western Roman Empire.

Resources

Clover, Frank M. *The Late Roman West and the Vandals*. Brookfield, Vt.: Variorum, 1993.

Hodgkin, Thomas. *Italy and Her Invaders*. 8 vols. Oxford: Clarendon Press, 1880-1899.

Mathisen, Ralph W. "Resistance and Reconciliation: Majorian and the Gallic Aristocracy After the Fall of Avitus." *Francia* 7 (1979): 597-627.

SEE ALSO: Aetius; Roman Empire; Roman Empire, Wars of the; Vandals; Visigoths.

Ralph W. Mathisen

Malayan Emergency

AT ISSUE: Political identity of postcolonial Malaya
DATE: June 16, 1948-July, 1960
LOCATION: Malayan Peninsula
COMBATANTS: Commonwealth and Malayan forces vs. Malayan Communist Party guerrillas
PRINCIPAL COMMANDERS: *British*, Lieutenant General Sir Harold Briggs, General Sir Gerald Templer; *Communist*, General Secretary Chen Ping, Deputy General Yeung Kwo, Commander Lau Yew, Siu Mah
PRINCIPAL BATTLES: Kajang, Kuala Krau, Semenyih
RESULT: Elimination of Communist-led military forces in peninsular Malaya

Background

The Malayan Communist Party directed extensive guerrilla warfare activities against the Japanese during World War II. Its principal strategist was Chen Ping, an ethnic Chinese with ties in the international Communist movement. His forces received arms and training from the British, and at the Japanese surrender in August, 1945, the party controlled 4,000 armed guerrillas, 6,000 organized support personnel, and widespread caches of arms, ammunition, and supplies. After the war, the Communist Party emerged as the principal political organization of the ethnic Chinese population. In late 1945, food shortages, unemployment, and the return of a British colonial administration caused a wave of unrest that was compounded by assassinations and strikes. Britain's preference for training ethnic Malays to administer postcolonial Malaya exacerbated traditional tensions between the Malay and Chinese populations.

When the formation of the quasi-independent Malayan Union was announced on February 1, 1948, the Communist Party, led by Chen, adopted a policy of using armed force to achieve Communist-led independence. The Malayan Communist guerrillas were organized into battalion-sized units, which in late February, 1948, initiated a series of assaults against Malay and British civil and military targets and attacks on European plantation managers and their families. As strikes and violence spread, the British resolved to eliminate the Communist threat before granting full independence to Malaya.

Milestones in the Malayan Emergency

Date	Event
February 1, 1948	Federation of Malaya is formed from former British colonies.
February-May, 1948	Communists, many of whom are of Chinese ethnicity, revolt.
June 16, 1948	Malayan government declares a state of emergency as guerrilla warfare escalates; troops from Great Britain, New Zealand, and Australia come to the government's aid.
February, 1952	British forces led by General Sir Gerald Templer launch anti-insurgency campaign.
February, 1954	British forces announce that the communist leaders have withdrawn and moved to Sumatra.
August 31, 1957	Federation of Malaya becomes a constitutional monarchy, staying within the Commonwealth.
July 31, 1960	Malayan government announces official end of emergency, in which 6,705 communist rebels and 2,384 government troops lost their lives.

Action

By mid-June, 1948, a full-scale insurrection had developed, with Communists leading both strikes and violence in urban areas and an armed guerrilla movement based in the rural hinterland. The government of the Malayan Union declared a state of emergency on June 16 and formally requested British military assistance. British, Indian, and other Commonwealth military forces quickly joined local Malayan forces in antiguerrilla operations. Martial law was declared on July 5, 1948. That month, British-led special forces ambushed a Communist command post south of Kuala Lumpur at **Kajang** (July 16, 1948), killing Lau Yew, commander of the Malayan Races Liberation Army, as the guerrilla organization was known. Nonetheless, Communist forces launched an offensive in September, 1948. One attack, at the town of **Kuala Krau** (September 11, 1948), resulted in the deaths of hundreds of civilians and scores of government soldiers and police.

In April, 1950, Lieutenant General Harold Briggs took command of all pro-government forces and introduced the Briggs Plan, which was to isolate the enemy from its sources of supply and from the general populace by containing it in mountain and jungle bases, which could then be attacked using paratroopers and main-force units. Peasants, squatters, and ethnic Chinese who supported the Communist rebellion were forcibly removed from their communities into government-built New Villages encircled by barbed wire and overseen by Malayan police. By 1952, 461,000 people had been relocated into more than five hundred New Villages. The resettlement program proved effective in denying food, supplies, and new recruits to the Communist insurgents. Briggs was forced by failing health to leave his command, and British interests suffered another loss when High Commissioner for Malaya Sir Henry Gurney was killed in 1951 in a Communist ambush led by guerrilla commander Siu Mah. In mid-1952, General Gerald Templer assumed both the military and civilian posts previously held by Briggs and Gurney. Templer focused on improving antiguerrilla tactics while conducting sweeps of Communist jungle bases.

The Communist leadership sought but failed to attract military aid from the People's Republic of China. This, plus Britain's military effectiveness under Templer and the reduced civilian assistance available to the Communists under the Briggs Plan, led to a shift in the Communists' tactics. Large-unit attacks on military and police targets were abandoned, and greater emphasis was placed on political propaganda and low-level guerrilla warfare.

In October, 1953, Templer launched a drive against the Communist Party's command structure based in Pahang, driving its principal leaders across the border into Thailand. British forces succeeded in driving a wedge between the main Communist armed units in the northern and southern sectors of the Malayan Peninsula. Paratroops were then employed in attacks on isolated guerrilla bases in mountainous central Malaya. With the success of the offensive, martial law was ended in some areas in late 1953. Further offensives against guerrilla strongholds forced Communist leaders to agree to cease-fire talks at the end of 1955.

The talks collapsed when Chen refused to agree to the dissolution of the Malayan Communist Party although the party's active guerrilla force had been reduced to around 1,000 ill-equipped men in several small, isolated bases. British intelligence, aggressive tactics, and superior mobility wore down the remaining insurgents. During an attack on a Communist base in southern Selangor, at **Semenyih** (April, 1956), British special forces killed Yeung Kwo, leader of the Communists' political propaganda program.

Satisfied that the Communist insurgency was under control, Britain granted Malaya full independence in 1957. The new government offered amnesty for Communist Party members and guerrillas. Defections increased, and terrorist attacks dropped off sharply. By this time, the Communist Party had lost most of its influence with Malaya's ethnic Chinese population, which turned increasingly to commerce and to more conservative political parties.

Aftermath

By offering the Chinese population full participation in the political process, independent Malaya undermined the Communists' appeal to traditional ethnic antagonisms between the Malay and Chinese communities. Popular support for the Chinese-led Malayan Communist Party dropped significantly after 1957, and by 1960, virtually all armed insurgent activity had ceased, although the Communist Party leadership did not renounce its commitment to armed struggle tactics. In July, 1960, the government of Malaya ended the state of emergency.

RESOURCES
Coates, John. *Suppressing Insurgency: An Analysis of the Malayan Emergency, 1948-1954*. Boulder Colo.: Westview Press, 1992.
Jackson, Robert. *The Malayan Emergency: The Commonwealth's Wars, 1948-1966*. London: Routledge, 1991.
Kheng, Cheah Boon. *Red Star over Malaya: Resistance and Social Conflict During and After the Japanese Occupation of Malaya, 1941-1946*. Singapore: Singapore University Press, 1983.

SEE ALSO: Burmese Civil Wars; Guerrilla warfare; Laotian Civil War.

Laura M. Calkins

MALDON

TYPE OF ACTION: Ground battle in a Viking raid on England
DATE: 991
LOCATION: Beside the Panta (Blackwater) River, near Maldon (in Essex, England)
COMBATANTS: Nearly 3,000 English vs. about 3,000 Vikings from 93 ships
PRINCIPAL COMMANDERS: *English*, Byrhtnoth, earl of Essex (926?-991); *Viking*, Sweyn I Forkbeard of Denmark (d. 1014)
RESULT: Viking victory

In 991, Vikings, led by Sweyn I Forkbeard, landed on Northey Island, at the mouth of the Panta River, and tried unsuccessfully to extort gold from the English. A causeway that was submerged at high tide ran between the Vikings and local troops led by Byrhtnoth, the earl of Essex, restricting the two forces to shooting arrows. As the tide ebbed, the English thwarted a Viking advance, but the narrowness of the causeway allowed little room for fighting. To keep the Vikings from raiding elsewhere on the coast and to show martial pride, Byrhtnoth had his troops withdraw up the slope away from the river and allow the Vikings to cross the causeway so that a decisive battle could occur. In the ensuing combat, Byrhtnoth died and some of the English fled. Many of his retainers, however, fought until they too perished.

SIGNIFICANCE
After the English defeat, King Æthelred II the Unready began bribing the Vikings and consequently imposing on his English countrymen a tax called the "Danegeld." Yet from heroism in defeat came the Old English poem "The Battle of Maldon," which celebrates the Anglo-Saxon warrior's code of honor.

RESOURCES
Cooper, Janet, ed. *The Battle of Maldon: Fiction and Fact*. London: Hambledon, 1993.
Graham-Campbell, James, ed. *Cultural Atlas of the Viking World*. New York: Facts on File, 1994.
Trapp, J. B. "Introduction to 'The Battle of Maldon.'" In *The Oxford Anthology of English Literature*, edited by Frank Kermode, et al. Vol. 1. New York: Oxford University Press, 1973.

SEE ALSO: Angles, Saxons, and Jutes; Brunanburgh; Clontarf; Literature, war in; Stamford Bridge; Viking Raids; Vikings.

Victor Lindsey

MALI EMPIRE

DATE: Thirteenth to sixteenth century
LOCATION: Sudan region of West Africa
PRINCIPAL MILITARY ACTION: Kirina
MILITARY SIGNIFICANCE: Through a series of successful military campaigns, the emperors of Mali created a massive kingdom stretching across a vast section of West Africa.

The Mali Empire in West Africa was founded by the Sosso, members of a tributary state in ancient Ghana. Under the leadership of Sumanguru of the Kante clan, the Sosso established a new state independent of ancient Ghana. The Sosso state was built mainly through raids and military conquests in which the Sosso killed rulers of neighboring lands and seized tributes.

During the early 1220's, Sumanguru's army raided the Malinke to the south and attacked the northern Soninke of ancient Ghana, sacking the capital in about 1224. A Malinke survivor, Sundiata of the Keita clan, organized a resistance. In 1235, he led a Malinke army against the Sosso, defeating Sumanguru at the Battle of Kirina. After his victory, Sundiata took control of the Soninke people who had been conquered by the Sosso and whose lands included much of former Ghana. This was the genesis of the vast Mali Empire. The capital was located at Niani. As a result of Sundiata's subsequent military operations, the empire's boundaries extended to encompass vast areas of the West African Sudan.

Sundiata, the creator of the Mali kingdom, took the title of mansa, Malinke for ruler. He was resourceful and powerful. The wealth of the empire derived from the gold trade, taxes, tributes, and agriculture. The mansa and his military commanders controlled their own state farms where servants were mobilized to produce food for the army and the king's court. After Sundiata, most of the mansas of Mali were Muslim. The mansas of Mali kept a large standing army. The battalion commanders were among the more important officials of the state. Each army battalion consisted of a small elite corps of horsemen and a large body of foot soldiers/infantry armed with bows, arrows, and spears. The military was used to protect the empire from external attack, to patrol trading routes, and to ensure that the district chiefs paid their tributes to the king.

The Mali Empire reached the height of its power and fame in the fourteenth century. The strength and success of the empire depended on the personal power of the rulers. Toward the end of the thirteenth century, a series of dynastic disputes and brief reigns temporarily weakened the power of the monarchy. However, in the fourteenth century, the monarchy recovered with the reigns of very effective rulers, notably Mansa Mūsā (1312-1337). He brought Mali to the notice of the rest of the world with his lavish pilgrimage to Mecca from 1324 to 1325. He encouraged the development of Islamic learning. By the end of his reign, Tombouctou had become an important center for trade and scholarship. In the fourteenth century, Mali was so well known that it was noted on maps made by European cartographers.

In the fifteenth century, the power of the Mali rulers waned as a result of increasing instability in the regime. The outlying provinces took advantage of the reduction in central authority to assert their independence. Tuareg nomads attacked Tombouctou, capturing it in 1433. The fall of this important center demonstrated the military decline of the Mali Empire that would eventually enable the Songhai to gain power of the region. By 1500, the Mali Empire had dwindled down to its Malinke core. However, the notion that the Mali Empire might be resurrected inspired many people well into the nineteenth century.

RESOURCES

The Ancient Africans. Documentary. International Film Foundation, 1985.

Chu, Daniel, and Elliott Skinner. *A Glorious Age in Africa: The Story of Three Great African Empires.* Trenton, N.J.: Africa World Press, 1991.

Mann, Kenny. *The Western Sudan: Ghana, Mali, Songhay.* Parsippany, N.J.: Silver Burdett Press, 1995.

Wisniewski, David. *Sundiata: Lion King of Mali.* New York: Clarion Books, 1992.

SEE ALSO: Almoravid Empire; Ghanaian Empire; Songhai Empire; Sundiata.

Kwasi Sarfo

MALPLAQUET

TYPE OF ACTION: Ground battle in the War of the Spanish Succession
DATE: September 11, 1709
LOCATION: Village of Malplaquet, France, ten miles south of Mons
COMBATANTS: 100,000 allies (British, Dutch, and Austrians) vs. 90,000 French
PRINCIPAL COMMANDERS: *British*, John Churchill, first duke of Marlborough (1650-1722); *Austrian*, Prince Eugene of Savoy (1663-1736); *French*, Marshal Claude-Louis-Hector, duc de Villars (1653-1734), Marshal Louis-François, duc de Boufflers (1644-1711)
RESULT: Allied victory, although the French suffered fewer losses and conducted an orderly withdrawal from the field without being pursued

On September 11, 1709, 100,000 allied troops forced 90,000 defending French troops from the field, both suffering huge losses. The British-Dutch-Austrian allies had besieged the fortress at Mons on September 4. To break the siege, Marshal Claude-Louis-Hector, duc de Villars, massed 90,000 troops in nearby Malpaquet. To remove this threat to their siege operation, the allies advanced against the well-entrenched French.

Eugene of Savoy's infantry attacked the French left flank, while that of John Churchill, the first duke of Marlborough, attacked the right. To reinforce his right, Villars had to weaken his center. Marlborough then directed the 30,000 allied cavalry against the weakened French center and suffered very heavy losses. Louis-François, duc de Boufflers, now in command, counterattacked with his reserves and reestablished the French line. After attack and counterattack, the allies finally broke through the center. The French withdrew in good order, but the allies were too weakened to pursue. The allies had 22,000 casualties (6,500 killed), and the French lost 12,000 (4,500 killed).

Significance

With victory in the bloodiest battle of the war, the allies were finally able to capture Mons on October 24.

The Knights of St. John defend Malta against the Turks. (Library of Congress)

Resources

Belloc, Hilaire. *British Battles: Malplaquet*. London: Swift, 1911.

Chandler, David. *Marlborough as Military Commander*. London: Batsford, 1973.

Churchill, Winston. *Marlborough, His Life and Times*. Vol. 4. London: Harrap, 1938.

Hugill, J. A. C. *No Peace Without Spain*. Oxford: Kensal Press, 1991.

Taylor, Frank. *The Wars of Marlborough, 1702-1709*. Vol. 2. Oxford, Blackwell, 1921.

See also: Denain; Eugene of Savoy; Marlborough, first duke of; Oudenarde; Ramillies; Spanish Succession, War of the.

Thomas McGeary

Malta, Siege of

Type of action: Siege war in the Turkish Wars of European Expansion
Date: May 18-Sept. 8, 1565
Location: Malta, a Mediterranean island south of Sicily
Combatants: 9,000 Christians vs. 40,000 Ottoman soldiers
Principal commanders: *Christian/Knights of Malta*, Jean Parisot La Valette (1494-1568); *Ottoman*, Mustafa Pasha
Result: Failed siege by Ottomans

In 1522, the Knights of St. John at Rhodes were forced by overwhelming Ottoman forces to surrender their island fortress after a six-month siege. The Ottoman emperor Süleyman I, impressed by the courage of the knights, spared their lives. They were given the island of Malta by Emperor Charles V (1530), became known as the Knights of Malta, and resumed their Rhodesian practice of raiding Ottoman shipping.

Süleyman, regretting his benevolence to the knights, amassed his empire's forces to destroy them. The Ottomans, led by Mustafa Pasha, landed in May, expecting a speedy victory. However, the ferocious courage of the knights, led by Jean Parisot La Valette, combined with the strength of their star-shaped fortifications, made for a long, grueling siege. Ottoman advances were paid for in horrifying losses and bogged down before the harbor forts. Late in the summer, about 7,000 Spaniards slipped past the Turks and bolstered the remaining several hundred defenders of Malta. Süleyman's forces, faced with a strengthened enemy, the threat of further Spanish aid, and the approach of winter, lifted the siege and withdrew home.

Significance

The triumph of the Knights of Malta was Süleyman's bitterest defeat. His losses were staggering—some 30,000 slain—and his designs on Western Europe were halted.

Resources

Bradford, Ernie. *The Great Siege: Malta, 1565*. London: Wordsworth Editions, 1999.
Prata, Nicholas C. *Angels in Iron*. Huntingdon Valley, Pa.: Evolution, 1997.
Sire, H. J. A. *The Knights of Malta*. New Haven, Conn.: Yale University Press, 1996.
Soldiers of God. Documentary. RPM Media, 1999.

See also: Knights and chivalry; Rhodes, Siege of; Süleyman I; Turkish Wars of European Expansion.

Paul John Chara, Jr.

Mamlūk-Ottoman War

At issue: Control over Egypt and the western Middle East
Date: May, 1485-April 13, 1517
Location: Southern Anatolia, Syria, and Egypt
Combatants: Mamlūks vs. Ottomans
Principal commanders: *Mamlūk*, al-Ashraf Kāʾit Bāy, Kāṣawh al-Ghawrī, Tūmānbāy; *Ottoman*, Sultan Bayezid II (c. 1447-1512), Sultan Selim I (1470-1520)
Principal battles: Tarsus, Adana, Ayas, Payas (Bab al-Malik), Aga-Cayiri, Damascus, Raydāniyya, Cairo
Result: Ottoman Empire annexed Syria, Palestine, Egypt, and Arabia

Background

Two decades of mutual mistrust and friction along ill-defined frontiers between Mamlūk Syria and Ottoman Anatolia caused the Mamlūk-Ottoman War. After their epic conquest of Constantinople, the Ottomans had arrogantly declared themselves the leaders of Islam. The Mamlūks of Cairo, who controlled Egypt, Syria, Palestine, and the holy cities of Mecca and Medina, regarded such posturing as a veiled demand for submission. In defiance, the Mamlūks had supported revolts against the new Ottoman sultan, Bayezid II, in 1481, and routinely obstructed Ottoman access to India. In 1485, when the ruler of a Syrian border town (Elbistan) in Mamlūk Syria tried to switch to the Ottoman side, Bayezid decided to intervene by force.

Action

The Mamlūk-Ottoman War was actually two wars, divided by twenty-five years of uneasy peace. The first war, confined to Cilicia and northern Syria, ran from 1485 until 1491. This phase ended in a *status quo ante bellum* treaty. The second war broke out in 1516, ending in the complete conquest of the Mamlūk states by the Ottoman Empire.

In May, 1485, Bayezid sent an expedition south and captured the cities of **Tarsus** and **Adana**, the keys to northern Syria. Awaiting reinforcements, Mamlūk Aleppo responded only with reconnaissance probes. Finally, in April, 1486, a Mamlūk army of 15,000 lured the Turkish garrisons into the field and devastated them. Unable to hold Tarsus and Adana, the Ottomans retreated. However, food shortages and troop mutinies prevented the Mamlūk sultan from following up his success. The next year, Bayezid reinforced his expedition with Janissary infantry, *sipahi* cavalry, cannoneers, and other professionals. Once again, Tarsus was stormed and became the Ottoman operational center (June, 1487).

The second Ottoman offensive began in April, 1488, with the conquest of Adana and the port of **Ayas**. To meet this thrust, Mamlūk sultan al-Ashraf Kāʾit Bāy amassed 40,000 troops at Aleppo. Aiming at a quick strike, an Ottoman joint land and naval force attempted to entrap the forward elements of Kāʾit Bāy's army at **Payas** (Bab al-Malik) (July 12, 1488). However, an unexpected storm wrecked the Turkish fleet and the Mamlūks broke loose, inflicting severe casualties on Ottoman troops. Eventually, the main armies collided at **Aga-Cayiri** (August 16, 1488), and although outnumbered, the Mamlūks routed the invaders. Again, the Ottomans withdrew, returning Tarsus to Mamlūk control (October, 1488). Serious clashes did not occur again until March, 1490, when Mamlūk cavalry poured into Ottoman Anatolia. This expedition proved fruitless and finally slouched home in August, its ranks thinned by desertions.

In 1491, the war sputtered into a peace treaty. New threats from Spain, Portugal, and Hungary suddenly appeared more dangerous to Istanbul than the Mamlūks. The Mamlūks, bedeviled by economic exhaustion, urban unrest, and a rash of local mutinies, also needed peace. The treaty worked until 1514, when an aggressive new Ottoman sultan, Selim I, upset the regional balance of power by defeating the Safavids of Iran and seizing more Anatolian lands. Alarmed, the Mamlūk sultan Ḳāṣawh al-Ghawrī feared he would be next.

In 1516, anticipating an Ottoman march on Aleppo, al-Ghawrī led 20,000 Mamlūks north. Selim intercepted him at Mardj Dābiḳ (August 24, 1516) with 60,000 Ottoman troops and field guns, and shattered the out-gunned Mamlūks. With al-Ghawrī dead, the Ottomans plunged south and took **Damascus** (September 27, 1517). The new Mamlūk sultan, Tūmānbāy, tried to appease Selim, but hostilities resumed in December. Sweeping through the Sinai, the Ottomans crushed the Mamlūks again at **Raydāniyya** (January 22, 1517) and blasted their way into **Cairo**. The Ottomans captured Tūmānbāy, hanged him in public on April 13, 1517, and extinguished Egyptian independence.

Aftermath

Selim eliminated the Mamlūk leaders but integrated the lower ranks into his regime. Syria, Lebanon, Palestine, Egypt, and Arabia became provinces in the Ottoman Empire and remained so until 1918.

Resources

Har-el, Shai. *Struggle for Domination in the Middle East: The Ottoman-Mamlūk War*. Leiden: E. J. Brill, 1995.

Holt, P. M. "Mamlūk." *Encyclopedia of Islam*. 2d ed. Leiden: E. J. Brill, 1991.

Petry, Carl F. *Protectors or Praetorians? The Last Mamluk Sultans and Egypt's Waning as a Great Power*. New York: State University of New York Press, 1994.

SEE ALSO: Mamlūks; Mehmed II; Ottoman Empire; Selim I.

Weston F. Cook, Jr.

Mamlūks

DATE: Ninth through nineteenth centuries
LOCATION: Islamic Africa, Near East, and Asia
MILITARY SIGNIFICANCE: Throughout the Islamic world, mamlūks (military slaves) were recruited into elite regiments, forming a mainstay of military power for many medieval Muslim dynasties.

Mamlūk is a technical Arabic term meaning "military slave" (also called *ghulam*). Large-scale institutionalized recruitment of slaves as soldiers began in the 800's under the ʿAbbāsid caliph al-Muʿtaṣim, who formed a Turkish Mamlūk regiment to counteract the power of disloyal factions. Mamlūks were soon appointed as military commanders and governors for the ʿAbbāsids. Following the breakup of the ʿAbbāsid caliphate in the late ninth century, Mamlūk regiments appeared in many successor states.

With rigorous training and high *esprit de corps*, Mamlūk soldiers were among the finest in the medieval world. As members of elite royal regiments, they played key roles in power politics and succession, often manipulating weak rulers and sometimes even usurping power, creating "slave dynasties." The most famous are the Mamlūks of Egypt (1250-1517), who drove the crusaders from the Holy Land and regularly bested the Mongols in battles such as ʿAyn Jāhlūt (1260) and Hims (1280). Mamlūk dynasties were also found among the Muslim sultanates of northern India.

Because Islamic law forbade enslaving Muslims, most Mamlūks were drawn from the surrounding populations of Central Asia, Africa, and Europe. In the form of the Janissaries of the Ottoman Empire, mamlūk institutions continued until the early nineteenth century.

RESOURCES
Amitai-Preiss, Reuven. *Mongols and Mamluks*. Cambridge, England: Cambridge University Press, 1995.
Ayalon, David. *Islam and the Abode of War*. Aldershot: Variorum, 1994.
_____. *Studies on the Mamluks of Egypt*. London: Variorum Reprints, 1977.
Crone, Patricia. *Slaves on Horseback*. Cambridge, England: Cambridge University Press, 1980.
Holt, P. *The Age of the Crusades*. London: Longman, 1986.
Irwin, Robert. *The Middle East in the Middle Ages*. Carbondale: Southern Illinois University Press, 1986.
Pipes, David. *Slave Soldiers and Islam*. New Haven, Conn.: Yale University Press, 1981.

SEE ALSO: Janissaries; Ottoman Empire.
William J. Hamblin

MANCHU EXPANSION, WARS OF

AT ISSUE: Establishment and consolidation of the Qing Dynasty
DATE: c. 1600-1683
LOCATION: Manchuria
COMBATANTS: Manchu leaders vs. Ming loyalists
PRINCIPAL COMMANDERS: *Manchu and allies*, Nurhaci (1559-1626), Abahai (1592-1643), Dorgon (1612-1650), Kangxi (1654-1722); *Rebel*, Li Zicheng (1606-1645); *Ming*, Zheng Chenggong (1624-1662); *Ming/Manchu*, Wu Sangui (1612-1678)
PRINCIPAL BATTLES: Mukden, Beijing, Chao-Modo
RESULT: Manchurian victories create a larger country and create the Qing Dynasty

BACKGROUND
The Manchus were initially nomads of the Jurchid group. Their ancestors founded the Jin Dynasty that ruled parts of northern China. During the Ming Dynasty, they lived in southern Manchuria intermixed with the Han Chinese, from whom they learned the ways of sedentary life.

ACTION
The rise of the Manchus began under Nurhaci, who, between 1600 and 1615, conquered most of the Jurchid tribes and formed them into the eight banners (military and administrative units). As Manchu power expanded, eight Mongol and eight Han Chinese banners were added, and bannermen were able to concentrate on fighting and governing, leaving farming to conquered subject peoples. In 1616, Nurhaci proclaimed himself emperor of the Later Jin Dynasty. In 1618, he began to fight the Ming. The Manchus captured **Mukden** (1621) but were defeated by the Ming near the Great Wall in 1623.

In 1627, Nurhaci was succeeded by his son Abahai, who continued his father's work. He changed his tribal name from Jurchid to Manchu and the dynastic name from Ming to Qing in 1835 (although his son, not Abahai, is generally regarded as the first Qing emperor). He set up a Chinese-style civil administration employing Chinese and Mongols in addition to Manchus in a pattern that would persist to the end of the Qing Dynasty. Abahai subdued Korea (1636-1637) but did not make sustained efforts to attack the passes along the Great Wall, which were heavily defended by Ming armies. In 1643, Abahai was succeeded by his five-year-old son Fulin with his uncle Prince Dorgon as regent.

In 1644, rebels led by Li Zicheng seized the Ming capital of **Beijing**, and the last Ming emperor committed suicide. Whereupon General Wu Sangui, commander of Ming forces at the eastern terminus of the Great Wall, invited the Manchus to help him against the rebels. The joint forces ousted the rebels from the capital, and while Wu chased them to complete defeat, Dorgon restored order in the capital, buried the emperor with honors, proclaimed his nephew Fulin as Emperor Shun Zhi, and moved the Qing capital to Beijing.

Between 1644 and 1683, the Qing Dynasty battled Ming loyalists who proclaimed several emperors in the southern capital of Nanjing and controlled several provinces in southern China. Although most of these loyalists were ineffective, Zheng Chenggong, a member of a pirate family, was able to sustain the Ming cause until 1663, first along the southern coastal provinces, then in Taiwan, which he captured from the Dutch East India Company.

Manchuria, c. 1697

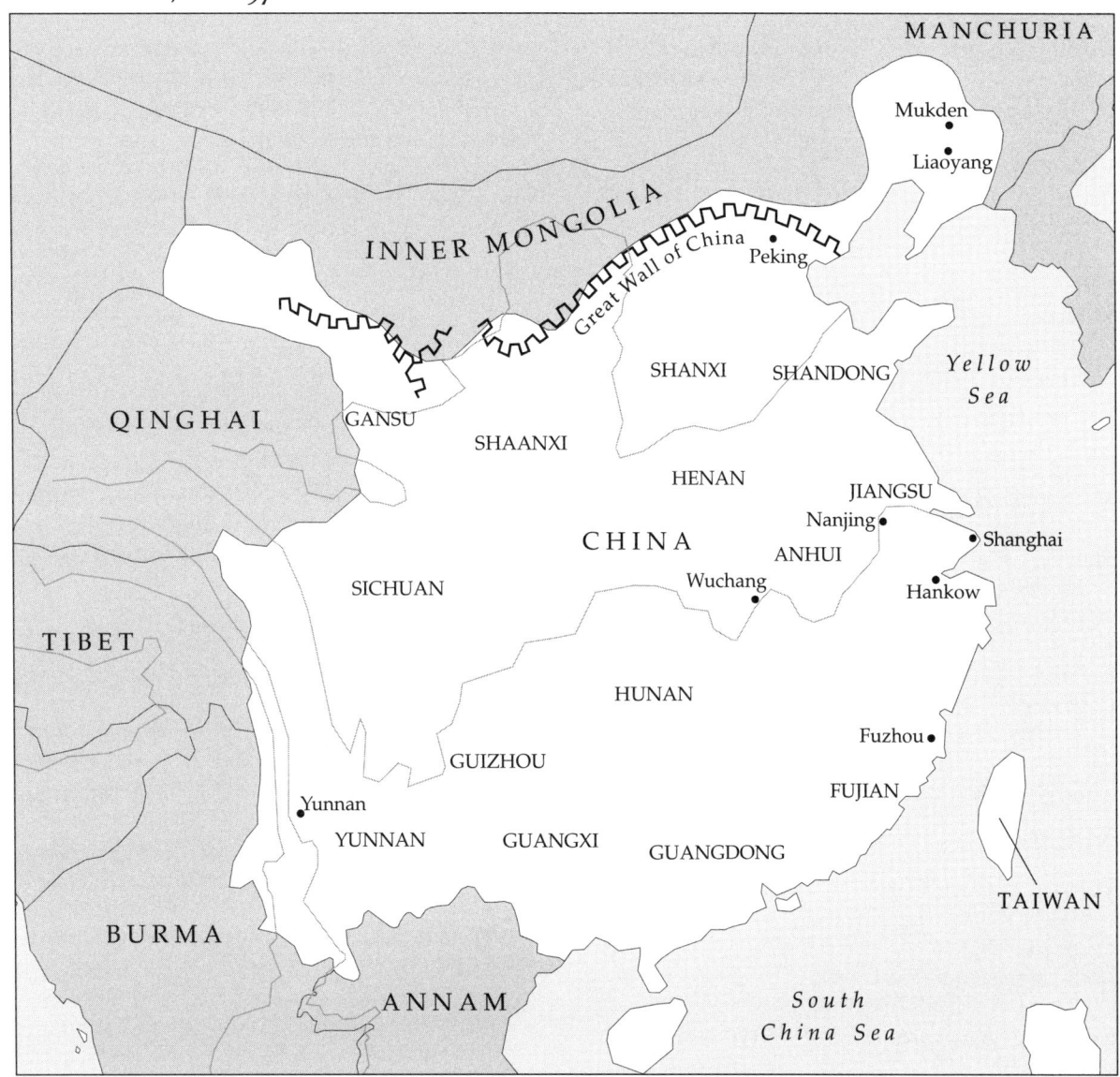

Shun Zhi's early death led to the enthroning of Kangxi, who then was less than eight years old. He would become the longest reigning emperor since the first century in the common era and one of the greatest in Chinese history. Assuming personal power at age twelve, Kangxi completed the conquest begun by his ancestors. He suppressed the War of the Three Feudatories (1673-1681), a rebellion led by Wu Sangui and two other Chinese generals, whose defection to the Manchus in 1644 had enabled the establishing of the Qing. These three generals had been rewarded with princely titles and given semi-independent powers in several southern provinces. In 1696, Kangxi defeated a Dzungar chieftain at **Chao-Modo** in Mongolia to end the Dzungar War, started in 1690. In addition, Kangxi annexed Taiwan in 1683 and Tibet in 1720.

Aftermath

By 1683, the Qing Dynasty had become well established and essentially at peace, although there were boundaries to be settled with the expanding Russian Empire in the Treaty of Nerchinsk in 1689 (further defined in the Treaty of Kaikhta in 1727) and other campaigns under Kangxi's successors to subdue Mongol and Turkic tribes.

RESOURCES
Chan, Albert. *The Glory and Fall of the Ming Dynasty*. Norman: University of Oklahoma Press, 1982.
Fang, Chaoying. "A Technique for Estimating the Numerical Strength of the Early Manchu Military Forces." *Harvard Journal of Asiatic Studies* 13 (1950): 192-215.
Kessler, Lawrence D. *K'ang-hsi and the Consolidation of Ch'ing Rule, 1664-1684*. Chicago: University of Chicago Press, 1976.
Michael, Franz. *The Origin of Manchu Rule in China*. Baltimore, Md.: The Johns Hopkins Press, 1942.
Spence, Jonathan D. *The Emperor of China: Self-Portrait of K'ang-hsi*. New York: Vintage Books, 1974.

SEE ALSO: Chinese Imperial Wars; Chinese military; Kangxi; Zheng Chenggong.

Jiu-Hwa Lo Upshur

MANDALAY

TYPE OF ACTION: Diversionary ground action in World War II
DATE: March, 1945
LOCATION: Mandalay, Burma
COMBATANTS: British vs. Japanese
PRINCIPAL COMMANDERS: *British*, William Joseph Slim (1891-1970); *Japanese*, various unit commanders
RESULT: The British successfully used an attack on Mandalay to draw Japanese forces away from other targets in Burma, then took Mandalay itself; the Japanese lost one-third of their fighting forces and the Allies gained control of the area and the Burma Road

After the Japanese victories in 1942, the Burma Road, the major allied supply route in Asia, was closed. The allied forces realized that if the Japanese were to be defeated, control of Burma and the Burma Road had to be regained. Lieutenant General Daniel Sultan directed a three-pronged effort to regain Burma. Field Marshal William Joseph Slim drove to seize the various crossings of the Chindwin River and then to drive toward Mandalay. When Slim became aware of the Japanese plans to move their forces away from the river, he decided that the most advantageous move would be to take Meiktila, then a Japanese communication center. In order to mask his real intentions, General Slim sent a portion of his troops on to take the city of Mandalay and to draw Japanese troops away from their ever-dwindling army. This strategy worked, and British forces took Meiktila on March 3, 1945, and Mandalay itself on March 13, 1945.

SIGNIFICANCE
General Slim's plan to use Mandalay as a distraction for the Japanese forces while other targets were hit led to the British regaining control of all Burma.

RESOURCES
Allen, Louis. *Burma, The Longest War 1941-1945*. London: Dent, 1984.
Grant, Ian Lyall. *Burma 1942: The Japanese Invasion*. Chichester, England: Zampi, 1999.
McEnery, John H. *Epilogue in Burma*. Tunbridge Wells, England: Spellmount, 1990.
Prasad, Bisheswar, ed. *The Retreat from Burma 1941-1942*. Calcutta: Orient Longmans, 1954.

SEE ALSO: Slim, William Joseph.

Thomas B. Frazier

MANNERHEIM, CARL GUSTAF

FULL NAME: Carl Gustaf Emil Mannerheim, also known as Baron von Mannerheim
BORN: June 4, 1867; Villnäs, Finland
DIED: January 27, 1951; Lausanne, Switzerland
PRINCIPAL WARS: World War I, Russo-Finnish Winter War, World War II
MILITARY SIGNIFICANCE: Mannerheim defeated Finnish and Russian Bolsheviks (1918), skillfully attacked and retreated from Soviet aggressive forces (1939-1940, 1941-1944), and was the principal architect of Finnish post-World War II independence.

Finnish marshal Carl Gustaf Mannerheim (left) speaks with German air general Hans-Jürgen Stumpff. (Library of Congress)

Carl Gustaf Mannerheim served as a Russian army cavalry lieutenant during the Russo-Japanese War (1904-1905) and was a lieutenant general and a corps commander in World War I (1914-1918). After the Russian Revolution began in 1917, Mannerheim aided Finland, commanded anti-Bolshevik forces, defeated Finnish Bolsheviks, and repulsed their Soviet allies in 1918.

Mannerheim chaired Finland's defense council and supervised construction of the Mannerheim Line fortifying his country against possible Soviet aggression from Leningrad. As commander in chief, he defended Finland against Soviet attacks during the Russo-Finnish Winter War (1939-1940), was defeated by overwhelming enemy forces, on which the Finns inflicted almost incredible casualties, but was required to accept harsh peace terms.

When Germany attacked the Soviet Union in 1941 during World War II (1939-1945), Mannerheim commanded the Finnish army alongside initially victorious German units, was appointed marshal of Finland in 1942, and retreated from massive Soviet forces in 1944. He served as president of Finland from 1944 to 1946. One of his first duties was to arrange an armistice with the Soviets including severe reparations. The friendship treaty of 1948 resulted in Finland's careful neutrality in dealing with the Soviet Union until the Soviet dissolution in 1991.

Mannerheim suffered from ill health later in life. He partly completed an autobiography and history of Finland before dying of an ulcer and stomach surgery.

Resources
Jägerskiöld, Stig. *Mannerheim: Marshal of Finland*. London: C. Hurst, 1986.
Tillotson, H. M. *Finland at Peace and War: 1918-1993*. Wilby, Norwich: Michael Russell, 1993.
Trotter, William R. *A Frozen Hell: The Russo-Finnish Winter War of 1939-1940*. Chapel Hill, N.C.: Algonquin Books, 1991.

See also: World War I; World War II.

Robert L. Gale

Manstein, Erich von

Also known as: Erich von Lewinski
Born: November 24, 1887; Berlin, Germany
Died: June 10, 1973; Irschenhausen, near Munich, West Germany
Principal wars: World War I, World War II
Principal battles: France (1940), Sevastopol (1942), Stalingrad (1942-1943), Kursk (1943)
Military significance: Manstein developed the strategy for trapping the British and French armies in Belgium, commanded the siege forces around the fortress of Sevastopol, and extricated the German army from southern Russia during the Battle of Stalingrad.

Coming from a family of military men, Field Marshal Erich von Manstein rose quickly through the ranks of the German army. Serving briefly in World War I and in the 1939 invasion of Poland, Manstein rose to prominence with his proposal for the German army to attack through the Ardennes Forest, which would cut off the British and French armies in Belgium. His plan led to the fall of France (1940) after six weeks of war. He was rewarded with command of the Fifty-sixth Pan-

Erich von Manstein (front) leads two military men on an inspection tour in Russia. (Library of Congress)

zer Corps during the 1941 invasion of Russia. His troops opened the road to Leningrad but could not capture the city. He was sent south to clear the Crimean Peninsula. In the spring of 1942, Manstein's Eleventh Army captured Sevastopol.

In November, 1942, Manstein took command of Army Group Don. Manstein held back the Soviet armies, extricated the German army from the Caucasus region, and attempted to rescue the Sixth Army trapped in Stalingrad. After the Sixth Army surrendered in February, 1943, Manstein launched a counteroffensive and stabilized the southern front.

In July, 1943, Manstein commanded the southern prong of the attack on the Kursk salient. After the attack failed, Manstein retreated through the Ukraine. His defensive tactics angered Nazi leader Adolf Hitler, who relieved him of command in March, 1944.

Resources

Beevor, Antony. *Stalingrad: The Fateful Siege*. New York: Penguin, 1999.

Manstein, Erich von. *Lost Victories*. New York: Presidio, 1958.

Ziemke, Earl, and Magna Bauer. *Moscow to Stalingrad*. New York: Military Heritage Press, 1985.

SEE ALSO: France; Hitler, Adolf; Kursk; Leningrad, Siege of; Stalingrad; World War II.

Douglas Clouatre

Mansura

TYPE OF ACTION: Ground battle in the Seventh Crusade
DATE: December, 1249-April 6, 1250
LOCATION: Nile delta, Egypt
COMBATANTS: Crusaders vs. Egyptians
PRINCIPAL COMMANDERS: *French*, Louis IX (1214-1270), Robert of Artois
RESULT: The Ayyūbids of Egypt decisively defeated the Seventh Crusade

Responding to the sack of Jerusalem in 1244, Louis IX of France invaded Egypt with a large crusader army, capturing Damietta on June 6, 1249. Summer flooding of the Nile delayed his planned advance to Cairo, allowing the Egyptians to muster reinforcements at Mansura on the south side of the Bahr al-Saghir branch of the Nile.

When the inundation had receded, the crusaders marched for Cairo, reaching the Muslim army at Mansura on December 21. For six weeks, the crusaders attempted to build an earthen bridge to cross the Bahr al-Saghir but were repeatedly thwarted by strong Egyptian resistance with Greek fire projected from trebuchets.

Discovering a ford downstream, the crusaders crossed the river undetected on February 8, 1250. Instead of waiting for the entire army, Robert of Artois, commander of the vanguard, launched a charge in hope of catching the Egyptians by surprise. He succeeded, but the Egyptians drew his knights into an ambush in the narrow streets of Mansura, where they were massacred. When Louis's main force crossed the river, the Egyptians rallied, fighting the crusaders to a standstill in a fierce battle. For eight weeks, the stalemate continued, until the reinforced Egyptian Navy cut the crusaders' river supply lines in late March.

His army overcome by dysentery, typhoid, and famine, Louis made the decision to retreat. After a day's march under severe pressure from the Egyptians, the crusader army surrendered on April 6, 1250.

SIGNIFICANCE

The defeat of the Europeans by the Egyptians ended major European intervention in the Near East and paved the way for Muslim reconquest of the Holy Land.

RESOURCES

Maqrizi. *A History of the Ayyubid Sultans of Egypt*. Boston: Twayne, 1980.

Richard, J. *Saint Louis*. Cambridge, England: Cambridge University Press, 1992.

Thorau, Peter. *The Lion of Egypt: Sultan Baybars I*. London: Longman, 1987.

SEE ALSO: Acre; Crusades.

William J. Hamblin

MANTINEA

TYPE OF ACTION: Ground battle in the war between Tegea and Mantinea
DATE: 362 B.C.E.
LOCATION: Mantinea, Northern Peloponnese (Greece)
COMBATANTS: 23,000 Spartans, Athenians, Mantineans and allies vs. 33,000 Thebans and allies
PRINCIPAL COMMANDERS: *Spartan*, King Agesilaus II (c. 444-360 B.C.E.); *Theban*, Epaminondas (410-362 B.C.E.)
RESULT: Theban victory eclipsed when Epaminondas died of his wounds after the battle

When a dispute arose between the Peloponnese cities of Tegea and Mantinea, two rival coalitions were formed. Sparta and Athens joined the Mantineans, and Thebes and its Boeotian allies came to the assistance of Tegea. After failing to capture Sparta by surprise, Epaminondas, at the command of the Boeotian force, marched on Mantinea. The road to the city was blocked by an allied force under King Agesilaus II of Sparta. Agesilaus had assembled his troops across a mile-long plain flanked by steep ridges on both sides. When Epaminondas came upon this force, he ordered his men to march across the front and ground arms, giving the impression that he would not present battle that day. Suddenly, however, the Boeotian force attacked, with the phalanx advancing in oblique formation. Epaminondas's loaded left wing (fifty ranks deep) crashed against the enemy right (twelve ranks deep), and Theban cavalry and peltasts (light troops) pinned down the enemy left and exposed the right flank. The Mantineans and their allies fled, but Epaminondas was mortally wounded. As news of Epaminondas's death spread through the battlefield, the Thebans abandoned the pursuit of the enemy, thus failing to consolidate their victory.

SIGNIFICANCE

Epaminondas's victory at Mantinea confirmed his military genius, but his death demoralized the Thebans who, without a capable leader, soon lost their commanding position in Greek affairs. Ironically, Epaminondas's brilliant victory at Mantinea marked the beginning of his city's military and political decline.

RESOURCES

Buckley, John. *The Theban Hegemony*. Cambridge, Mass.: Harvard University Press, 1980.

Hanson, U. D. *The Soul of Battle: From Ancient Times to the Present Day*. New York: Free Press, 1999.

Warry, John. *Warfare in the Classical World*. New York: Salamander Books, 1993.

SEE ALSO: Agesilaus II; Epaminondas; Leuctra; Spartan Empire.

Gilmar E. Visoni

MANZIKERT

TYPE OF ACTION: Ground battle in the Byzantine-Seljuk Wars
DATE: August 19, 1071
LOCATION: Near Lake Van in Anatolia, between the

fortress of Manzikert and Turkish-held Akhlat
COMBATANTS: 35,000 Byzantines vs. 50,000 Seljuk Turks
PRINCIPAL COMMANDERS: *Byzantine*, Romanus IV Diogenes (d. 1072); *Seljuk Turkish*, Alp Arslan (c. 1030-1072)
RESULT: Romanus's Byzantine army was defeated, leaving most of Anatolia open to Turkish occupation

In the spring of 1071, the Byzantine emperor Romanus IV Diogenes mounted a major campaign to drive the Seljuk Turks out of the eastern part of his domains. While moving toward Akhlat with the main Byzantine field army in mid-August, he unexpectedly encountered Alp Arslan's force of about 50,000 men.

Normally, Byzantium's disciplined heavy cavalry (cataphracts), which effectively combined missile-fire and shock tactics, outmatched the Seljuk light cavalry. However, Romanus's efforts at Manzikert were consistently undermined by treason. Alp Arslan's unforeseen appearance at Akhlat occurred because Romanus's advance formation withdrew without notifying him of the Turkish army's presence. When Romanus retreated toward Manzikert in order to consolidate his position, his mercenary light cavalry deserted. At a crucial point during the Battle of Manzikert, while he was leading a counterattack, his second in command, Andronicus Ducas, failed to come to his aid. When Andronicus withdrew roughly half of the Byzantine force from the battlefield, the emperor's unsupported troops became disorganized and were enveloped and massacred.

SIGNIFICANCE

The defeat at Manzikert sparked a decade-long series of rebellions and civil wars within the empire. During that time, the Turks overran most of Anatolia, permanently undermining Byzantine power.

RESOURCES
Friendly, Alfred. *The Dreadful Day: The Battle of Manzikert, 1071*. London: Hutchinson, 1981.
Kaegi, Walter E. *Byzantium and the Early Islamic Conquests*. New York: Cambridge University Press, 1992.
Treadgold, Warren. *Byzantium and Its Army, 284-1081*. Stanford, Calif.: Stanford University Press, 1995.

SEE ALSO: Alp Arslan; Byzantine Empire; Byzantine-Seljuk Wars.

Michael J. Fontenot

MAO ZEDONG

ALSO KNOWN AS: Mao Tse-tung
BORN: December 26, 1893; Shaoshan, Hunan Province, China
DIED: September 9, 1976; Beijing, China
PRINCIPAL WARS: Chinese Civil War, Second Sino-Japanese War, Korean War
PRINCIPAL BATTLE: Long March (1934-1935)
MILITARY SIGNIFICANCE: Mao led the Chinese Communist Party to victory in a successful re-

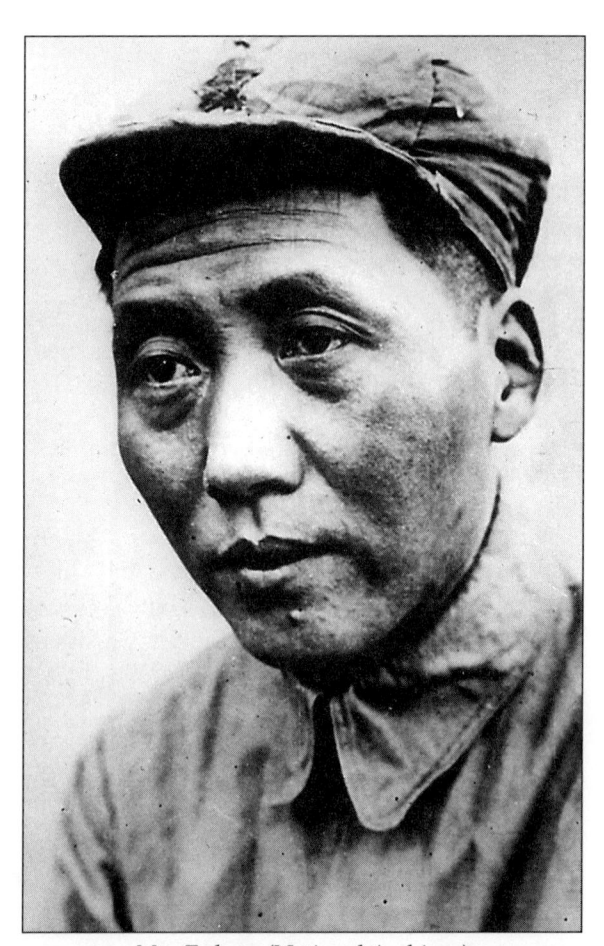

Mao Zedong. (National Archives)

volt against the Nationalists and established a Communist government.

Mao Zedong became the paramount Chinese Communist Party leader and one of the most important theorists and strategists in Chinese military history. He began his military career by organizing rural-centered, armed revolts in his home province in 1927 and establishing the first Communist base in Jinggangshan in 1928. In this remote mountainous region in South China, he became the first political commissar of the Chinese Red Army and the chairman of the Chinese Soviet Republic in 1931. He transformed the revolt begun with the Chinese Revolution from an urban working-class struggle to a rural-based peasant armed rebellion. He led the Long March in 1934-1935 to save the Red Army from destruction by Chiang Kai-shek's Nationalist (Guomindang) Army, emerging as the unquestionable top man in the Chinese Communist Party. In the Second Sino-Japanese War (1937-1945), his successful strategy of cooperating with Chiang and mobilizing guerrilla warfare behind Japanese lines increased Chinese Communist Party members from 40,000 in 1937 to more than one million in 1945 with nearly two million regular troops and two million militia. He was elected chairman of the Chinese Communist Party Central Military Commission in 1937, of the Politburo in 1943, and of the Central Committee in 1945.

Unwilling to cooperate after World War II, Mao and Chiang ended their united front and resumed the civil war from 1946 to 1949. After reorganizing his five million troops into the People's Liberation Army, Mao shifted his military strategy from a predominantly guerrilla war to a conventional mass offensive campaign in 1948. Soon he defeated Chiang's army, founded the People's Republic of China, and became the first president of the new Communist republic in 1949. Chiang moved the seat of the Nationalist government of the Republic of China from the mainland to Taiwan. Mao declared the "lean-to-one-side" policy, which stated that the new China would favor the Soviet Union and join the socialist and Communist camp in the Soviet-U.S. Cold War.

Mao's decision to enter the Korean War (1950-1953) and send three million Chinese troops to fight the United Nations (U.N.) Forces (mostly U.S. forces) led the People's Republic of China and the United States into their most hostile period in history. As an opportunity to stop a perceived U.S. invasion of China, Mao decided in early October, 1950, to organize and dispatch the Chinese People's Volunteer forces to Korea when Joseph Stalin asked him to rescue the North Korean regime after the U.N. forces crossed the thirty-eighth parallel and pressed northward. Mao mobilized the year-old republic to fight the "War to Resist America and Aid Korea" and appointed Marshal Peng Dehuai as chief commander of the Chinese forces. Though the Chinese forces successfully pushed those of the United Nations south of the thirty-eighth parallel, U.S. air and naval superiority caused the Chinese forces to suffer very heavy losses—nearly one million casualties—including Mao's son, who was killed in an air raid while working as a Russian translator at the Chinese People's Volunteer forces' headquarters. Noting that the U.N. forces could not be driven out of Korea by force, Mao began negotiations with the United States and South Korea in 1951 and concluded the truce agreement in 1953. His decisions and operations in the Indochina War of 1945-1954, the Taiwan Straits crises in 1954-1958, the Sino-Indian Border War in 1962, the Vietnam Conflict in 1961-1975, and in the first part of the Sino-Soviet border conflicts in 1969-1981 also reflected his unique strategic thinking and military tactics.

RESOURCES

Breslin, Shaun. *Mao: Profiles in Power*. New York: Longman, 1998.

Li, Xiaobing, and Hongshan Li. *China and the United States; A New Cold War History*. New York: University Press of America, 1998.

Liu, Jikun. *Mao Zedong's Art of War*. China: Hai Feng, 1993.

Spence, Jonathan. *Mao Zedong*. New York: Penguin Putnam, 1999.

Zhang, Shuguang. *Mao's Military Romanticism*. Lawrence: University Press of Kansas, 1995.

SEE ALSO: Chiang Kai-shek; Chinese Civil War; Indochina War; Korean War; Lin Biao; Sino-Soviet border disputes; Tibet, Chinese occupation of; Zhu De.

Xiaobing Li

Maps and Cartography

Maps are graphical representations in any medium of a given geographical space. Cartography comprises the techniques used in making maps. Accurate maps are critical in military navigation, in the planning and conduct of operations, and in targeting. Cartography has improved dramatically over time, greatly facilitating the conduct of war.

Early History: To 500 C.E.

There is only indirect evidence of the military use of maps in the West before the fifth century. The Assyrians and Egyptians, in the first millennium B.C.E., put maplike representations of battles and campaigns on their palaces and monuments. The ancient Greeks developed systems of projection, that is, means of transferring representations of the earth's spherical surface to a flat map, as well as the concept of lines of latitude and longitude. However, there is little proof that their maps were used in warfare.

The Romans were great surveyors, but the earliest mention of specifically military maps in the Roman world appears only in the fifth century of the common era, when Flavius Vegetius Renatus encouraged military commanders to use "painted itineraries" or road maps. No such maps survive, but it is unlikely that they were drawn to scale, and they probably were not based on any system of projection.

In contrast, there is clear evidence that the ancient Chinese made use of maps in war. For example, the *Book of Master Guan* (third century B.C.E.) includes an entire chapter on military maps. The Western Jin Dynasty's ability to reunite China in the third century of the common era was credited in part to the advantage it gained from having better maps than its enemies. Unlike the Romans, the Chinese clearly understood the use of scale, even as early as the second century B.C.E. Early Chinese maps sometimes employed a grid of evenly placed lines; however, the grid did not correspond to a system of longitude or latitude.

Middle Ages: 500-1450

Although the Arabs made Roman-style road maps for military purposes as early as the eighth century, there is little explicit evidence of European use of maps in warfare before the fifteenth century. However, European sea charts, widely employed in the Mediterranean by the fourteenth century, clearly had military uses. These charts were the first Western maps known to regularly display scale. By the early fifteenth century, writers on military affairs and others, such as the poet Christine de Pizan, recommended that military commanders use maps.

Early Modern Period: 1450-1800

The military use of maps in Europe increased greatly in the second half of the fifteenth century and continued to increase in the sixteenth century. This increase was due in large part to the introduction of the printing press, which made the reproduction of maps easier. Further, the rediscovery and improvement of ancient Greek systems of projection, together with refined surveying techniques, such as the plane table, increased the accuracy of maps.

Italy, the home of the Renaissance, initially led the way in map production and use, but by the end of the fifteenth century, northern powers also appreciated the value of maps for war. For example, before his invasion of Italy in the 1490's, Charles VIII of France commissioned a map of the Alpine passes he would probably use. Later, Henry VIII of England became a demanding consumer of maps, especially for planning coastal fortifications. Indeed, the rise of bastioned fortifications in the sixteenth century, which was necessary to resist artillery fire, would have been inconceivable without accurate maps. Better maps also facilitated the great European voyages of discovery and conquest of the fifteenth and sixteenth centuries.

By the mid-sixteenth century, the military use of maps had become routine; the French marshal François de Scepeaux, lord of Vieilleville, wrote that it would be foolhardy for a commander to march without maps. By the seventeenth century, accurate maps were considered a force multiplier, something that increases strength without requiring an increase in size. Thus, the Spanish blamed their defeats in Portugal in the 1640's in part on the superior maps of their opponents, which offset their smaller numbers.

Yet there was still considerable room for improvement in map accuracy in this period. Technical developments of the seventeenth century allowed for more accurate mapping based on an elaborate system of triangulated surveys of entire countries. The French led the way in these techniques, but other countries caught up by the end of the eighteenth century.

THE AGE OF NATIONALISM: 1800-1914

Military cartography became even more important in the national wars of the nineteenth century. Napoleon I relied heavily on accurate maps in his campaigns. The Prussian (later German) General Staff emphasized cartography. Indeed, a majority of the pre-World War I chiefs of the German General Staff, including Helmuth von Moltke, had worked as military surveyors. On the other hand, the French suffered badly from the lack of adequate maps in the Franco-Prussian War.

Accurate maps were also of crucial importance in the American Civil War. Jed Hotchkiss's superb maps helped make possible Stonewall Jackson's brilliant Shenandoah Valley campaign in 1862, while improved Union mapmaking facilitated William T. Sherman's march to Atlanta in 1864 by enabling him to use hitherto uncharted mountain passes.

Military cartography in the nineteenth century benefitted from the introduction of lithographic printing. However, one major difficulty remained: the ability to precisely depict elevations. The now-familiar contour lines rarely appeared on maps before 1900. Instead, cartographers relied on hachures, a pictorially attractive method of showing the steepness of slopes through the use of closely spaced lines. However, unlike contours, these lines did not indicate precise elevations. Improved surveying techniques made contour mapping possible just in time for World War I.

THE ERA OF THE WORLD WARS: 1914-1945

World Wars I and II saw a tremendous increase in the quantity and quality of military maps. The British alone produced some 35 million maps during World War I, including a series of contour maps of their sector of the western front. These maps were provided with numbered grids to allow for the more accurate and responsive use of artillery. In turn, this improvement in gunnery helped break the deadlock of trench warfare in 1918. World War I also saw the development of aerial photography, which is extremely important for the production of maps, especially of enemy territory; and new stereographic techniques permitted the creation of contour maps from aerial photographs.

Use of these new cartographic techniques continued during World War II. The German invasion of Russia in 1941 was preceded by an extensive aerial photographic mapping campaign, as were Allied operations, such as the invasion of Normandy. The U.S. Army Map Service alone created more than 500 million maps for use during the war. On the other hand, the U.S. Navy's farflung operations in the Pacific were hampered in some cases by a lack of adequate charts of the coastal waters of strategically important islands. Military maps were produced not only for ground and naval operations but also for air operations, including special radar lattice charts, which indicated navigational beams, critical for night flying.

THE MODERN AGE: 1945-2000

Military cartography became even more important during the Cold War, as the demand for more precise targeting of all classes of weapons necessitated more precise maps. Military mapmaking agencies continued to expand. For example, by the 1970's, the U.S. Defense Mapping Agency (DMA), which became part of the National Imaging and Mapping Agency in 1996, employed some 9,000 soldiers and civilians. In the same period, the DMA also developed techniques for more accurate mapping, such as inertial positioning, in order to provide the precise terrain maps required by the cruise missile. By the 1980's, the DMA was increasingly producing digital maps. These digital maps permit the storage and display of so much more data than traditional paper maps that they are referred to as Geographic Information Systems (GIS's).

RESOURCES

Black, Jeremy. *Maps and Politics*. Chicago: University of Chicago Press, 1997.

Bucholz, Arden. *Moltke, Schlieffen, and Prussian War Planning*. Providence, R.I.: Berg Publishers, 1991.

Buisseret, David, ed. *Monarchs, Ministers and Maps: The Emergence of Cartography as a Tool of Government in Early Modern Europe.* Chicago: University of Chicago Press, 1992.

Chasseaud, Peter. "British Artillery and Trench Maps on the Western Front." *Map Collector* 51 (1990): 24-32.

Elting, John R. *Swords Around a Throne: Napoleon's Grande Armée.* New York: Free Press, 1988.

Harley, J. B., and David Woodward, eds. *The History of Cartography.* Chicago: University of Chicago Press, 1987.

Morris, R. O. *Charts and Surveys in Peace and War: A History of the Royal Navy's Hydrographic Service, 1919-1970.* London: HMSO, 1995.

Nelson, Christopher. *Mapping the Civil War: Featuring Rare Maps from the Library of Congress.* Washington, D.C: Starwood, 1992.

Owen, Tim, and Elaine Pilbeam. *Ordnance Survey: Map Makers to Britain Since 1791.* London: HMSO, 1992.

Pizan, Christine de. *The Book of Deeds of Arms and of Chivalry.* University Park: Pennsylvania State University Press, 1999.

Vegetius, Flavius Renatus. *Epitome of Military Science.* Translated by N. P. Milner. Liverpool, England: Liverpool University Press, 1993.

SEE ALSO: American Civil War; Ancient warfare; Coastal defense; Cruise missile; Engineering, military; Medieval warfare; Moltke, Helmuth von (1848-1916); Napoleon I; World War I; World War II.

Mark S. Lacy

MARĀṬHĀ-MOGUL WARS

AT ISSUE: Possession of the Deccan
DATE: c. 1646-1707
LOCATION: Deccan, India
COMBATANTS: Marāṭhās vs. Moguls
PRINCIPAL COMMANDERS: *Marāṭhā*, Shahji, Shivājī (1627/1630-1680), Shambhaji; *Mogul*, Aurangzeb (1618-1707), Shayista Khan (d. 1694), Jai Singh
PRINCIPAL BATTLES: Parenda, Surat, Bijāpur, Golconda
RESULT: Marāṭhā kingdom established

BACKGROUND

The Marāṭhās, Hindu agriculturalists in the northwestern Deccan, served in the armies of the Muslim sultans of Ahmadnagar and Bijāpur. Hardy soldiers, they were masters of the sudden ambush and of harrying the enemy on the line of march. The arid Deccan plateau was ideal for guerrilla warfare, and the mobility and agility of the Marāṭhās gave them the advantage over less mobile forces, overburdened with baggage and camp followers. So long as the Deccani sultanates survived, the Marāṭhās had an assured place within a social structure that divided resources between the city-based Muslim elites and Marāṭhā leadership in the countryside, but this modus operandi could not survive the coming of the Moguls.

ACTION

Under Jahāngīr, the Moguls began, and under Shāh Jahān, they completed the conquest of the sultanate of Ahmadnagar. This presented the Marāṭhās with a dilemma: The Moguls were bound to confiscate conquered territory from its previous owners and redistribute it among their own followers, although Ahmadnagar nobles willing to change sides might retain their former lands and perhaps receive some in addition. By comparison, Marāṭhā landholders were at the bottom of the pecking order. For them, far more than for the Deccani Muslims, the Mogul conquest, destructive enough in itself, spelt ruin.

Some tried to survive by opportunism and effrontery in playing one side against the other. Such a one was Shahji Bhonsle, who, beginning as a trooper (*bargir*) in the army of the sultan of Ahmadnagar, rose to become a kingmaker in the last days of the sultanate. Following the Moguls' victory at **Parenda** (1634), he entered the service of Bijāpur, dying in 1664, a respected fighter, but also the embodiment of the mercenary without fixed loyalties.

From 1646, his son Shivājī was acquiring forts in Bijāpur, and in response to this aggression, the sultan sent a large army against him in 1659. During negotiations, Shivājī assassinated the Bijāpuri commander and then defeated the latter's demoralized forces. Meanwhile, the Moguls were advancing deeper into the Deccan. In 1663, Shivājī ambushed their commander, Shayista Khan, un-

Marāthās in the Mid-Eighteenth Century

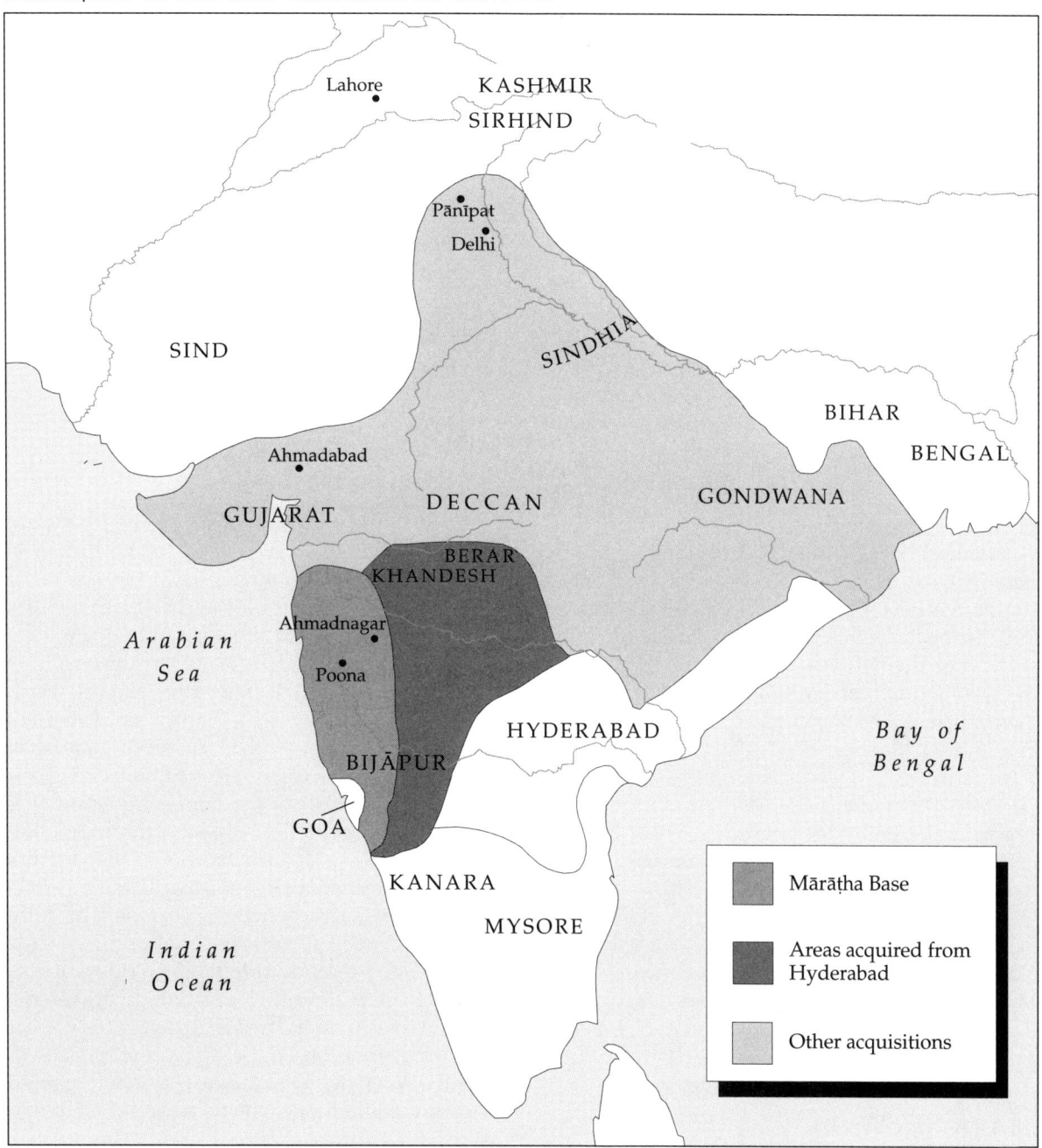

cle of Aurangzeb, and in 1664 sacked **Surat**, the principal port on the west coast of India. A new Mogul commander, Jai Singh, now took the initiative and forced Shivājī to come to terms (1665). Shivājī even attended the imperial court in Āgra (1666), but his reception was cool and, suspecting treachery, he fled back to the Deccan. In 1670, he again sacked Surat, and following a series of military successes, he had himself crowned as ruler of Maharahtra (1674). Shivājī was a superb leader of irregular troops, and because of the rivalry between Moguls and Bijāpuris, he was able to lay the foundations of future Marāṭhā ascendancy throughout central and south India.

Shivājī died in 1680 and his son, Shambhaji, was captured and executed by the Moguls in 1688; another son, Shahu, was taken to Delhi and raised as a Mogul protegé. Meanwhile, the struggle continued under Shambhaji's brother, Rajaram, from his base at Jinji in the Carnatic. Rajaram died in 1700 but his indomitable widow, Tarabai, continued fighting. The situation changed completely when, following Aurangzeb's death in 1707, his son Bahādur Shāh I sent Shahu south to claim his heritage. Of an unwarlike disposition but enjoying widespread support, Shahu brought the ruinous conflict to a close.

AFTERMATH

In the struggle with the Moguls, the Marāṭhās enjoyed only partial success, for they could not prevent the Moguls annexing **Bijāpur** (1686) and **Golconda** (1687). During Shahu's long reign (he died in 1749), power shifted from the king to his Brahmin minister (or peshwa), Balaji Vishvanath, and during the eighteenth century, the latter's descendants, the Peshwas of Poona, presided over the rise (and fall) of a Marāṭhā empire extending over much of the subcontinent.

RESOURCES

Gordon, S. *The Marāṭhās, 1600-1818*. Cambridge, England: Cambridge University Press, 1993.
Sen, S. N. *The Military System of the Marāṭhās*. Bombay, India: Orient Longmans, 1958.

SEE ALSO: Aurangzeb; Mogul Civil Wars; Mogul Conquest of the Deccan; Mogul-Persian Wars; Mogul-Sikh Wars; Rājput Rebellion.

Gavin R. G. Hambly

MARĀṬHĀ WARS

AT ISSUE: Hegemony in Central India
DATE: 1775-1818
LOCATION: Central India
COMBATANTS: Marāṭhā Confederacy vs. East India Company
PRINCIPAL COMMANDERS: *Marāṭhā*, Mahadji Shinde, Bājī Rāo II (r. 1796-1818); *British*, Lord Gerard Lake (1744-1808), Richard Wellesley (1760-1842), Arthur Wellesley, later duke of Wellington (1769-1852)
PRINCIPAL BATTLES: Wadgaon, Gwalior, Aligarh, Delhi, Laswari, Assaye, Argaon
RESULT: East India Company victorious; Marāṭhās reduced to mediated status

BACKGROUND

In the early eighteenth century, the Marāṭhās of the northwestern Deccan under their peshwas seemed about to replace the Mogul Empire with their own. However, in 1761, they were decisively beaten by an invading Afghan army at the Third Battle of Pānīpat. Thereafter, Marāṭhā territorial ambitions and those of the British East India Company proved incompatible, resulting in three Marāṭhā Wars (1775-1783, 1803-1805, and 1817-1818).

ACTION

In 1773, the peshwa was murdered by his uncle, Raghunath Rāo, who fled to the British in Bombay and offered territorial inducements for them to make him peshwa in the Treaty of Surat (1775), which marked the beginning of the First Marāṭhā War. A British force, advancing on Poona (the peshwa's capital), was ambushed at **Wadgaon** (1779) and forced to capitulate. Although the East India Company's governor-general in Calcutta, Warren Hastings, had originally disowned the conduct of the Bombay government, he felt that the company's prestige throughout India was at stake. He sent forces to march from Bengal to Ahmadabad, and then Bassein (1780), as other forces achieved the feat of taking the hitherto impregnable fortress of **Gwalior** by escalade (1780). Subsequently, Mahadji Shinde's forces were defeated at Sipri (1781). Shinde brokered a general peace (the Treaty of Salbai, 1783), in which the status quo before the war was restored. In this way, the East India Company gained twenty years of peace with its most formidable rivals in the subcontinent.

In 1794, Shinde died and was succeeded by his nephew, Daulat Rāo Shinde, and in 1796, Bājī Rāo II became peshwa. Both leaders lacked experience and judgment. Meanwhile, an aggressive new governor general, Richard Wellesley, fearing a revival of French influence, determined to crush the Marāṭhās. Bājī Rāo provided the opportunity. Both Shinde and Jaswant Rāo Holkar sought to control the peshwa, but before either could, Bājī Rāo seized Jaswant Rāo's brother and had him trampled by an elephant in the streets of Poona. An enraged Jaswant Rāo captured Poona (1801), and Bājī Rāo fled to the British in Bombay and signed, in return for his restoration, the Treaty of Bassein (1802), which made him a British puppet. Once back in Poona (1803), he repented of this agreement and allied with Shinde and Raghuji II Bhonsle I of Nagpur against the East India Company, resulting in the Second Marāṭhā War. To deal with Shinde, Wellesley dispatched an army from Calcutta under the command of Lord Gerard Lake, which won a series of victories at **Aligarh**, **Delhi**, and **Laswari** (all 1803). Meanwhile, in the Deccan, Arthur Wellesley, the governor general's brother and future duke of Wellington, defeated the combined forces of Shinde and Raghuji Bhonsle at **Assaye** and **Argaon** (both 1803). By the Treaty of Surji Argaon (1803), Shinde was reduced to being a mediated prince and the peshwa was returned to Poona. However, a colonel's disastrous retreat in 1804 and Lake's reverse below the walls of Bharatpur (in 1805) led to the governor-general's recall.

The reversal of Wellesley's "forward policy" left the Marāṭhās weakened, but the East India Company's campaigns against the freebooting Pindaris (1817-1818) tempted them to renew hostilities. The Third Marāṭhā War began in 1817, when Bājī Rāo attacked the British Residency in Poona. Defeated at Kirkee, he fled south and eventually surrendered to Sir John Malcolm in 1818. Meanwhile, Jaswant Rāo Holkar had been defeated at Mahidpur (1817), as was Appa Sahib, the new Bhonsle ruler, at Sitabaldi (1817).

Aftermath

Bājī Rāo's surrender marked the end of the wars between the Marāṭhās and the East India Company. Bājī Rāo was granted a generous pension and honorable retirement at Bithur on the Ganges, where he died in 1853. The East India Company made substantial territorial acquisitions. The Bhonsle state survived until 1854, the other Marāṭhā states until 1947.

Resources

Bennell, Anthony S. *The Making of Arthur Wellesley*. Hyderabad, India: Orient Longman, 1997.

Malcolm, John. *The Political History of India from 1784 to 1823*. 2 vols. London: John Murray, 1826.

Thompson, E. *The Making of the Indian Princes*. Oxford: Oxford University Press, 1943.

See also: Assaye; British India; Carnatic Wars; Laswari; Mysore Wars; Wellington, duke of.

Gavin R. G. Hambly

Marathon

Type of action: Ground battle in the Greco-Persian Wars
Date: September, 490 B.C.E.
Location: Twenty-two miles to the north of Attica on the Greek mainland next to the narrow straits and south of the southern tip of the Island of Euboea
Combatants: 10,000 Athenian and Plataean troops vs. 15,000 Persians
Principal commanders: *Persian*, Datis (fl. fifth century B.C.E.); *Greek*, Miltiades (c. 550-489 B.C.E.), Callimachus (d. 490 B.C.E.)
Result: Successful defense of Athens by Greek forces

This battle took place between the Athenians and their allies, the Plataeans, and elements of the Persian army on a narrow, undulating plain. The Athenian generals debated strategy because they feared the possibility of a seaborne attack as well as an overland invasion against their city. Miltiades argued for an immediate march against the Persians, and the polemarch, or war archon, Callimachus, agreed.

The Athenian and Plataean army of about 10,000 to 11,000 marched to Marathon to confront the soldiers of the Persian king Darius I the Great, who was not present. Darius had sent an expeditionary force against Athens and its allies in retaliation for aiding rebel Ionian Greek city-states. The Persians destroyed the city of Eretria on Euboea, an ally of Athens, and threatened free access to the Black Sea, from whence came grain supplies vital to Athens.

The Greeks were able to use the terrain very effectively. The mountains come almost to the sea, and both to the north and south of the battle site were marshes and streams that protected the flanks of the phalanx. The Persians had failed to seize the passes that led from the Bay of Marathon to Athens, perhaps reluctant to venture too far from their ships.

The Persian force consisted of Medes, arrayed in the center, and conscript levies stationed on the flanks. With their army were archers, but the Persian cavalry was not present. The Greeks, with only infantry arrayed in a phalanx, charged the Persians at the run, perhaps to avoid prolonged exposure to archers. According to historian Herodotus, they ran almost a mile. Callimachus, the polemarch, commanded the right wing, and the left was held by the Plataeans. To extend their battle line the necessary half-mile, the Greeks took troops from the center. It has been suggested that this was deliberate in order to achieve a victory rather like that at Cannae. The Medes and Sacae, the best of the Persian force, stationed in the center of their line, were able to break through the Greeks, but the extremes of the phalanx, anchored against small rivers and deeper in rank, held. Deliberate or not, the Greek flanks did not retreat and were able to envelope the Persian force and defeat it in detail by turning west. Herodotus, who provides the best description of the battle, indicates that the Greeks ceased pursuit of the Persians retreating toward their ships, turned, formed ranks, and moved west to trap the advancing Medes between two Greek forces. After inflicting defeat on this portion of the Persian army, the Greeks again moved east and north to complete the destruction of the Persians, finally reaching their ships, and taking some captives. It was at the moment of triumph that Callimachus fell. Some members of the Persian army, including Datis, were able to embark and sail away. Immediately, the Greeks had to force-march to Athens to protect it in case of invasion from the sea by the remainder of the Persian army. The Persians approached Attica but did not attempt landing when they realized that the Athenian army had returned.

Herodotus puts the Persian dead at 6,400 and the Athenian at 192. The Athenians chose to bury their fallen at the site of the battle, and the tumuli containing the Athenian dead still remain near the center of present-day Marathon. After the battle, a runner was dispatched to Athens to announce the victory and reportedly died of exhaustion after relating the news. The footrace known as a marathon gets its name and length (slightly more than twenty-six miles) from this messenger's run. Spartan soldiers, delayed by religious proscriptions, arrived at the scene only when the battle was concluded. They saluted the singular victory of the Athenians and Plataeans.

SIGNIFICANCE

The significance of Marathon was that it saved Athens from destruction at the hands of Persian forces and gave Greeks confidence in the phalanx as a supreme military formation. It was the first major Greek triumph over Persia on land. This, and the victory at Salamis a decade later, extended leadership to Athens and allowed it to form the Delian League.

RESOURCES

Balcer, J. M. "The Persian Wars Against Greece: A Reassessment." *Historia* 38 (1989): 117-143.

Green, P. *The Greco-Persian Wars*. Berkeley: University of California Press, 1996.

Hammond, N. G. L. "The Campaign and Battle of Marathon." *Journal of Hellenistic Studies* 88 (1968): 13-57.

Heredotus. *History of the Greek and the Persian War*. New York: Washington Square Press, 1963.

Lazenby, J. F. *The Defense of Greece: 490-479 B.C.* Warminster, England: Aris & Phillips, 1993.

SEE ALSO: Athenian Empire; Greco-Persian Wars; Persian Empire; Salamis.

Graham Haslam

MARCELLUS, MARCUS CLAUDIUS

BORN: c. 268 B.C.E.; place unknown
DIED: 208 B.C.E.; near Venusia, southern Italy
PRINCIPAL WARS: Gallic War, Second Punic War
PRINCIPAL BATTLES: Clastidium (222 B.C.E.), Nola (216 B.C.E.), Syracuse (212 B.C.E.)
MILITARY SIGNIFICANCE: Early in the Second Punic War, Marcellus was the only Roman commander to enjoy success against Hannibal and later was responsible for ending resistance in Sicily.

As consul in 222 B.C.E., Marcus Claudius Marcellus met a Gallic advance into Italy and near Clastidium routed an Insubrian army after killing its king in hand-to-hand combat. Then joining forces with his colleague, he forced the surrender of the remaining Gauls. For this success, Marcellus celebrated a triumph.

In 216 B.C.E. in the south of Italy, Marcellus commanded troops facing Hannibal's forces at Nola and handed Hannibal his first setback in Italy. As consul in 214 B.C.E., he directed operations against Rome's enemies in Sicily, remaining there until the fall of Syracuse in 212 B.C.E. A second triumph was thwarted by his political enemies. As consul in 210 B.C.E., Marcellus again faced Hannibal but was recalled to Rome in 209 B.C.E. on charges instigated by his political enemies. He was found innocent and reelected consul in 208 B.C.E. Rejoining his troops, he was drawn into an ambush while reconnoitering a hill overlooking Hannibal's camp and was killed.

Marcellus, though a cautious commander, came to be known as the "Sword of Rome" for his willingness to meet his enemy. The Romans' confidence in his abilities is demonstrated by his frequent consulships and proconsulships.

RESOURCES
Broughton, T. R. *The Magistrates of the Roman Republic*. Vol. 1. Reprint. Atlanta: Scholars Press, 1986.
Caven, Brian. *The Punic Wars*. New York: St. Martin's Press, 1980.
Lazenby, J. F. *Hannibal's War: A Military History of the Second Punic War*. Warminster, England: Aris & Phillips, 1978.
Peddie, John. *Hannibal's War*. Gloucestershire, England: Sutton Press, 1997.

SEE ALSO: Cannae; Hannibal; Punic Wars.
Donald M. Poduska

MARCUS AURELIUS

FULL NAME: Marcus Aurelius Antoninus
BORN: April 26, 121; Rome
DIED: March 17, 180; Sirmium or Vindobona (later Vienna)
PRINCIPAL WARS: Parthian War, Marcomannic Wars
MILITARY SIGNIFICANCE: Marcus Aurelius successfully defended the Roman Empire despite ongoing attacks on all fronts. Although he did little to change the organization of the Roman army, he exemplified Roman generalship.

Marcus Aurelius, born Marcus Aurelius Verus, is considered one of the great soldier-emperors of Rome and the last great stoic writer in antiquity. Emperor of Rome from 161 to 180, his strategy was to clear the enemy from the provinces behind the empire's frontiers, stabilize the frontiers, then press into barbarian lands. He demonstrated the usefulness of a mobile force when he assembled the best troops from around the empire to help defend depleted frontier garrisons.

The Parthian War (162-165) began when Vologases III of Parthia invaded Syria. Marcus Aurelius stayed in Antioch while Avidius Cassius defeated the Parthians and occupied Armenia and Mesopotamia. Roman troops returned from the campaign with the plague, which ravaged the empire from 166 to 167.

In 166-180, a series of wars, including the Marcomannic Wars (166-173, 173-180), were fought on the Danube frontier. The Marcomanni, Langobardi, and Quadi tribes crossed the Danube into what became modern Austria, and Teutons crossed the Alps into Italy and reached Verona. Marcus Aurelius subdued the Marcomanni by 171 and allowed many members of the group to settle lands depopulated by the plague. The Quadi and other tribes were defeated by 174.

In approximately 174, the Sarmatians crossed the lower Danube into Moesia, and further unrest broke out along the Danube in Germany. Marcus Aurelius marched on Germany and sent subordinates to deal with Moesia. He then marched on Syria to defeat the revolt of legate Avidius Cassius in 175. In 179, he returned to successfully defend the Danube frontier with his son Lucius Aelius Aurelius Commodus. He died the following year.

RESOURCES
Birley, Anthony Richard. *Marcus Aurelius*. New Haven, Conn.: Yale University Press, 1999.
Rutherford, R. B. *The Mediations of Marcus Aurelius: A Study*. Oxford Classical Monographs. Oxford: Clarendon Press, 1991.

SEE ALSO: Parthian Empire; Roman Empire; Roman Empire, Wars of the.
Thomas J. Roach

Marengo

Type of action: Ground battle in War of the Second Coalition
Date: June 14, 1800
Location: A plain near the Bormida River in Piedmont, Italy
Combatants: 33,800 Austrian forces vs. 28,500 French forces
Principal commanders: *Austrian*, General Michael Friedrich von Melas (1730-1806); *French*, First Consul and General Napoleon Bonaparte (1769-1821), General Louis Charles Desaix (1768-1800)
Result: French victory in the second of two battles on the same day leads to the withdrawal of Austrian troops from Lombardy

On June 14, 1800, at 8:00 in the morning, General Michael Friedrich von Melas attacked the French army under Napoleon Bonaparte. The French forces, who had been disrupting Melas's supply lines, were deployed on a flat stretch of land east of the farmstead Villa di Marengo. Napoleon, who had not anticipated the attack and had foolishly split his army—one division of 5,300 men under General Louis Charles Desaix had been sent south—now faced the Austrians with less than 22,000 troops. The Austrians pushed the French back with heavy losses. At 3:00 in the afternoon, Melas handed over field command to a subordinate and returned to Alessandria to write his victory dispatch. However about two hours later, Desaix fortuitously arrived on the field with his men and assumed direction of the battle. With Desaix in front, the French infantry slammed into the surprised Austrians, who broke off their pursuit and withdrew from the field. Desaix had saved the day for the French. Bonaparte hailed him as a hero but took credit himself for winning the battle. Desaix was not around to protest; he had been fatally wounded while leading the attack.

Significance

At Marengo, Bonaparte was fighting for the first time as head of state as well as field commander: A defeat at this point would probably have finished his career. However, he made the most of the victory, using it to further his godlike persona and confirm his authority as first consul. The war against Austria did not end with Marengo but with the Battle of Hohenlinden, won by General Jean Victor Moreau six months later. The subsequent Treaty of Lunéville of February 9, 1801, reconfirmed French possession of Belgium, the Left Bank of the Rhine, and northern Italy. The Second Coalition was now in ruins.

Louis Charles Desaix dies after being fatally wounded during the Battle of Marengo. (Library of Congress)

Resources

Connelly, Owen. *Blundering to Glory: Napoleon's Military Campaigns*. Wilmington, Del.: Scholarly Resources, 1990.

Esposito, Vincent J., and John Robert Elting. *A Military Atlas of the Napoleonic Wars*. New York: Praeger, 1964.

Forrest, Alan. *The Soldiers of the French Revolution*. Durham, N.C.: Duke University Press, 1990.

Schom, Alan. *Bonaparte*. New York: HarperCollins, 1997.

See also: French Revolutionary Wars; Napoleon I; Napoleonic Wars.

Wm. Laird Kleine-Ahlbrandt

Marignano

Type of action: Ground battle in Italian Wars
Date: September 13-14, 1515
Location: Near Marignano, Italy (later Melegnano, ten miles southeast of Milan)
Combatants: 33,000 French vs. 25,000 Swiss
Principal commanders: *French*, Francis I (1494-1547); *Swiss*, Matthäus Schinner (c. 1465-1522)
Result: Total French victory, recovery of Milan, favorable peace with all adversaries

With the aim of French hegemony in Italy, Francis I allied with Venice in opposition to the pope, the Holy Roman emperor, the Spanish, Florentines, Milanese, and Swiss. Effectively bypassing Swiss positions guarding the normal routes to Milan, Francis appeared south of the city. Swiss bishop-general Matthäus Schinner of Sion decided to strike before the French could join their Venetian allies. On September 13, 1515, Schinner attacked the French on marshy ground ten miles southeast of Milan at Marignano. His 25,000 troops were stalemated by the French force of 33,000 during the first day of combat. The French, using infantry and artillery to good effect, forced the Swiss to cease combat at nightfall. For eight hours on September 14, the battle resumed, with 10,000 French and 13,000 Swiss casualties. Assisted by Venetian cavalry, the French forced the Swiss to retreat.

Significance

A relatively swift and decisive battle, Marignano led to French recovery of Milan, peace with the Swiss (at Geneva on November 7, 1515), and gave Francis the ability to frustrate Habsburg, Spanish, and papal ambitions in Italy.

Resources

Durant, Will. *The Renaissance: A History of Civilization in Italy from 1304-1576*. New York: MJF Books, 1992.

Hays, Denys, and John Law. *Italy in the Age of the Renaissance, 1380-1530*. New York: Longmans, 1989.

Mattingly, Garrett. *Renaissance Diplomacy*. Boston: Houghton Mifflin, 1955.

Francis I is knighted after his victory at Marignano. (Library of Congress)

Thürer, Georg. *Free and Swiss: The Story of Switzerland*. Coral Gables, Fla.: University of Miami Press, 1971.

SEE ALSO: Italian Wars; Valois-Habsburg Wars.

C. George Fry

MARINES

Literally and originally, "soldiers of the sea." Marines first served in combat in the ancient Greek and Roman navies, hurling rocks, flaming projectiles, spears and arrows at enemy galleys while sailors or slaves guided the ship. During the seventeenth and eighteenth centuries, many European nations stocked their warships with soldiers who could discharge musketry and hurl grenades during close-quarters fighting with other vessels as well as serve as an integral part of landing parties. By the twentieth century, marines were especially associated with the latter duty. Marines played a significant role in amphibious operations in all theaters of World War II (1939-1945).

In the post-war period, marine forces displayed varying developmental patterns. Marines in the Netherlands, France, and Great Britain, for instance, fell into the relatively limited role of "commandos" or naval raiders (though the British and Dutch marines also specialize in arctic warfare). The United States Marine Corps is one of the most versatile. While maintaining their traditional role in amphibious warfare, U.S. marine units are well-prepared for land and aerial combat. The U.S. Marine Corps maintains one of the ten largest air forces in the world.

Jeremiah Taylor

MARINES, U.S.

The U.S. Marine Corps is an autonomous armed service commanded by a general, the commandant of the Marine Corps, who is a member of the Joint Chiefs of Staff. Its mission is to provide quick-response expeditionary forces for ground and air combat in company with the U.S. Navy during wartime or international disturbances short of war. It also detaches a small number of marines as security forces on Navy ships and bases and as guards at U.S. embassies. To meet these missions, 174,000 men and women marines, about one in nine of whom are officers, constitute operating forces and support forces, most of them stationed at sixteen major bases in the United States and Japan. The operating (combat) forces are organized into three Marine Expeditionary Forces, each of which consists of an infantry division, an aircraft wing, and a logistics support group. Enlisted Marines train at recruit depots at Parris Island, South Carolina, or San Diego, California. Midshipmen at the United States Naval Academy can choose to be commissioned as marine officers; however, most of the officer corps is trained at Officers Candidate School in Quantico, Virginia.

THE EARLY MARINE CORPS

The first contingent of marines formed on November 10, 1775—the official Marine Corps' birthday. These Continental Marines primarily served as guards on warships, although in 1776, a small battalion fought at the Battle of Princeton under General George Washington and another unit staged the Marines' first amphibious landing at New Providence Island in the Bahamas.

The Continental Marines disbanded in 1783, to be reformed in 1798 as the U.S. Marine Corps. As during the American Revolution (1775-1783), shipboard duty continued to be the Marines' main role. The Marines' performance during the American Civil War (1861-1865) was distinguished but limited because the U.S. Army had little use for marines and the Navy conducted few landings.

FINDING A DISTINCTIVE ROLE

The Marines began to realize its modern status during the Spanish-American War (1898), when a battle in Cuba brought it public acclaim. Combat during the Boxer Rebellion (1900-1901), Philippine Insurrection (1898-1902), and at Veracruz, Mexico (1914), Haiti (1915-1934), and Santo Domingo (1916-1924) added luster to the Marines' reputation and swelled its ranks with recruits. However, World War I (1914-1918) turned the Marines into a major fighting force. The commandant succeeded in sending a *brigade* (reinforced

U.S. Marines on Active Duty, 1805-1995

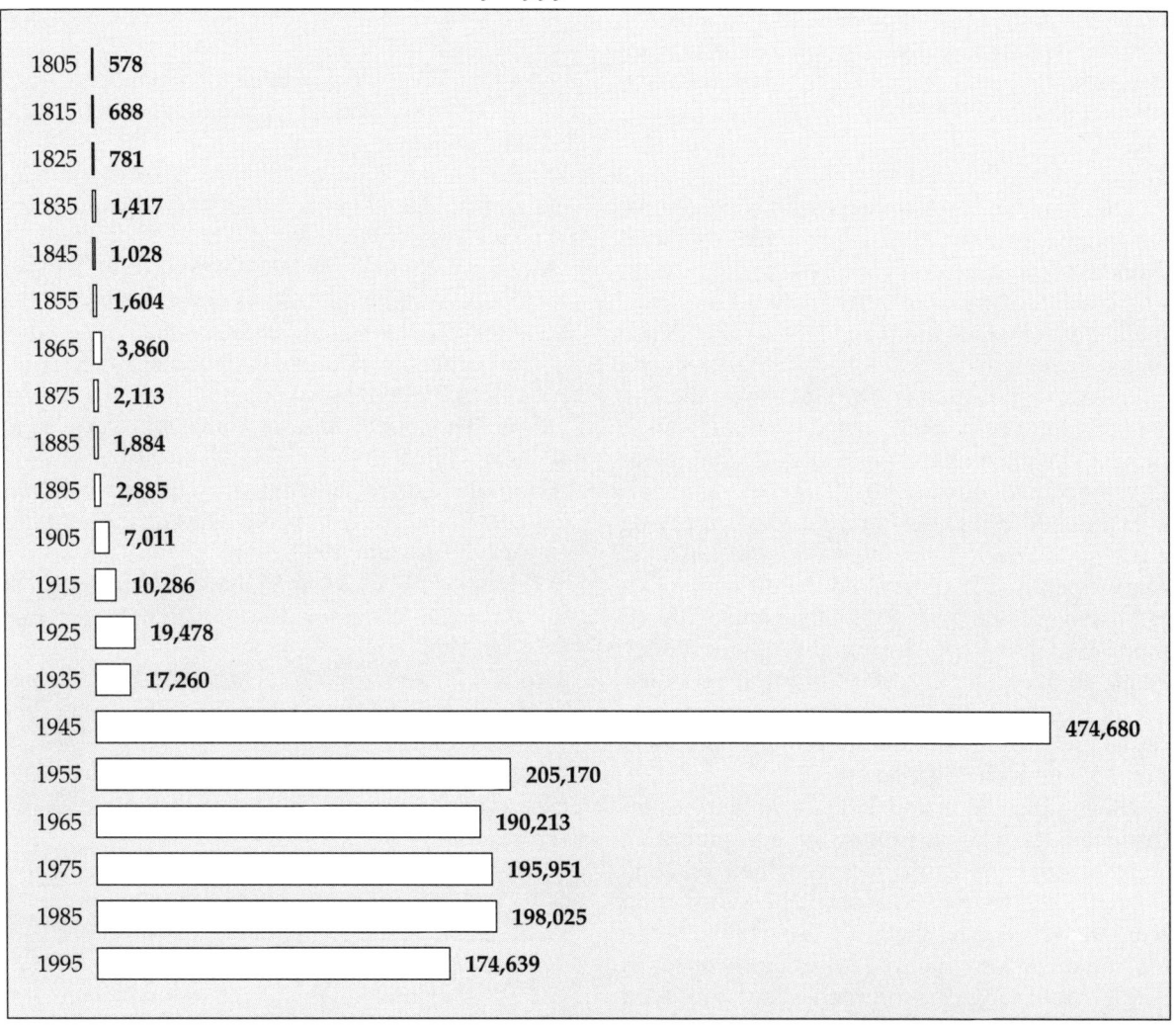

Year	Count
1805	578
1815	688
1825	781
1835	1,417
1845	1,028
1855	1,604
1865	3,860
1875	2,113
1885	1,884
1895	2,885
1905	7,011
1915	10,286
1925	19,478
1935	17,260
1945	474,680
1955	205,170
1965	190,213
1975	195,951
1985	198,025
1995	174,639

Sources: The data used in this graphic element are based on information found in *Historical Statistics of the United States: Colonial Times to 1970* (2 vols., Washington, D.C.: Government Printing Office, 1975) and *The Time Almanac 2000*, edited by Borgna Brunner (Boston: Information Please, 1999).

regiment) to France in 1917 even though the U.S. Army command did not want marines. Successful battles, often against overwhelming opposition, earned the Marines extensive newspaper coverage.

The Army resented the attention lavished on the Marines. Army generals argued that the nation did not need a second army, and the Marines should be integrated into its divisions. To save itself from Army control and preserve a share of shrinking military budgets during the 1920's and 1930's, the Marines developed a sophisticated amphibious landing capability as its distinctive combat mission. The Marines' general staff correctly assumed that the Pacific would soon be a major war theater and that the Marines would be the service best suited to spearhead U.S. campaigns by seizing beachheads with amphibious assaults, supported by Navy transportation, logistics, and gunfire. World War II (1939-1945) proved the Marines right. Amphibious landings on such South Pacific islands as Guadalcanal and Tarawa helped blunt the Japanese offensive in 1942 and 1943, and the battles for Iwo Jima and

Okinawa in 1945 gave the Allies bases for air raids on Japan itself. Despite opposition by the Army, the corps finally received statutory status as an independent armed force under the National Security Act of 1947.

The Cold War and After

The Marines staged successful amphibious landings during the Korean War (1950-1953) and pioneered the use of helicopters to deploy troops in combat, but the war turned into a long stalemate, during which the Marines were used much in the same way as army troops. Marines later were sent to Lebanon (1958, 1981-1984), the Dominican Republic (1965), and Grenada (1983) to protect U.S. citizens and political allies, but it was the Vietnam Conflict (1961-1975) that characterized the Cold War (1945-1991) era. First supplying advisers to South Vietnamese forces in 1962, the Marines gradually committed the majority of its land and air strength to combat and suffered more casualties than during any other conflict. While in Vietnam, the Marines improved their use of helicopters in "vertical envelopment" assaults and coordination with fighter-bombers to provide supporting firepower.

During the 1980's and 1990's, the Marines introduced the prepositioning of equipment in ships around the world to speed their reaction time in responding to crises. The innovation worked well during the Gulf War (1991), when Marine units were the first to set up defenses in Saudi Arabia. Marine divisions later provided large-scale diversionary attacks to distract Iraqi forces from the main thrust by the Army.

The Marines' goal for the twenty-first century is to use tilt-rotor aircraft and advanced amphibious vehicles, such as *hovercraft*, to carry marines ashore more quickly from farther out at sea and with heavier armaments.

Resources

Alexander, Joseph H. *A Fellowship of Honor: The Battle History of the United States Marines.* New York: HarperCollins, 1997.

Clancy, Tom. *Marine: A Guided Tour of a Marine Expeditionary Force.* New York: Berkley Books, 1996.

Clark, George B. *Devil Dogs: Fighting Marines of World War I.* Novato, Calif.: Presidio, 1999.

Lorelli, John A. *To Foreign Shores: U.S. Amphibious Operations in World War II.* Annapolis, Md.: Naval Institute, 1995.

Mersky, Peter B. *U.S. Marine Corps Aviation, 1912 to the Present.* 3d ed. Baltimore, Md.: Nautical and Aviation, 1997.

Millett, Allan R. *Semper Fidelis: The History of the United States Marine Corps.* Rev. ed. New York: Free Press, 1991.

Moskin, J. Robert. *The U.S. Marine Corps Story.* 3d ed. Boston, Mass.: Little, Brown, 1992.

Quilter, Charles J. *U.S. Marines in the Persian Gulf.* Washington, D.C.: Headquarters, Marine Corps, 1993.

Ricks, Thomas E. *Making the Corps.* New York: Scribner, 1997.

Simmons, Edwin Howard. *The United States Marine Corps: A History.* 3d ed. Annapolis, Md.: Naval Institute, 1997.

Whipple, A. B. C. *To the Shores of Tripoli: The Birth of the U.S. Navy and Marines.* New York: Morrow, 1991.

Woulfe, James B. *Into the Crucible: Making Marines for the Twenty-first Century.* Novato, Calif.: Presidio, 1998.

See also: Air Force, U.S.; Army, U.S.; Military organization, U.S.; Navy, U.S.

Roger Smith

Marion, Francis

Also known as: Swamp Fox
Born: 1732; Winyah Bay, near Georgetown, South Carolina
Died: February 27, 1795; Pond Bluff, South Carolina
Principal war: American Revolution
Principal battles: Charleston (1776), Eutaw Springs (1781)
Military significance: In 1780, he formed Marion's Brigade, a band of volunteers whose guerrilla activities served to frustrate British attempts to control the south after the fall of Charleston.

Francis Marion was a captain in the South Carolina Second Regiment at the outbreak of the American Revolution (1775-1783). In 1776, at

Charleston, he fired the last shot at the retreating British fleet. He was promoted to lieutenant colonel in the Continental Establishment, a rank he held when he avoided being taken prisoner after Charleston fell to the British in 1780.

Marion's attempt to attach a small band of rebels to the Southern Army was tepidly received by General Horatio Gates, and Marion served as a military scout in the South Carolina lowlands, where he organized Marion's Brigade in 1780. Engaging in skirmishes using military intelligence gained from his scouts and a network of informers, Marion craftily attacked the British forces, emerging from and disappearing into the swamps in such a fashion that he was called the "Swamp Fox." On September 8, 1781, he played an important role in the battle at Eutaw Springs, South Carolina. His attacks played an important role in keeping the British from dominating the south.

After the revolution, Marion served in the state militia, held several political offices, and concentrated on rebuilding his plantation. Marion's legend, enhanced by his comrades after his death, has remained intact for more than two centuries.

RESOURCES
Bass, Robert Duncan. *Swamp Fox: The Life and Campaigns of General Francis Marion.* New York: Holt, 1959.
Bodie, Idella. *The Revolutionary Swamp Fox.* Orangeburg, S.C.: Sandlapper Store, 1999.
Holbrook, Steward Hall. *The Swamp Fox of the Revolution.* New York: Random House, 1959.
Rankin, Hugh F. *Francis Marion: The Swamp Fox.* New York: Crowell, 1973.

SEE ALSO: American Revolution; Charleston, Siege of; Gates, Horatio.

Robert L. Patterson

MARIUS, GAIUS

BORN: 157 B.C.E.; Cereatoe
DIED: January 13, 86 B.C.E.; Rome
PRINCIPAL WARS: Jugurthine War, Celtic Wars, Roman Civil Wars of 88-30 B.C.E.
PRINCIPAL BATTLES: Aquae Sextiae (102 B.C.E.), Vercellae (101 B.C.E.)

MILITARY SIGNIFICANCE: Elected to the consulship an unprecedented seven times, Marius created a professional army and prepared the way for its use in Roman politics.

Gaius Marius was the first in his family to attain high office in Rome. He began enlisting citizens without property into the Roman army in 107 B.C.E. With these new recruits, Marius triumphed over the Numidian king Jugurtha in 104 B.C.E. in the Jugurthine War (112-106 B.C.E.). While serving as consul for five consecutive years (104-100 B.C.E.), Marius met the threat of invading Celtic tribes, killing or capturing 100,000 Teutones at Aquae Sextiae and defeating the Cimbri at Vercellae. After a democratic uprising supported by Marius was defeated by Sulla, Marius fled to Africa. He returned to support the democrats under Lucius Cornelius Cinna. In the Roman Civil Wars of 88-30 B.C.E., he and Cinna captured Rome in 87 B.C.E., then killed their political foes. He was elected consul before dying the following year.

During his career, Marius reorganized Roman legions by cohorts, groups of approximately 480 men consisting of six centuries. He introduced a new military pilum (spear) with a breakaway shaft and established the aquila (eagle) as the legion's chief standard, a focal point for loyalty and affection. He made soldiers more efficient and self-reliant. Because they were required to carry their own supplies and equipment, his soldiers earned the nick-name "Marius's Mules."

RESOURCES
Carney, Thomas F. *A Biography of Gaius Marius.* Chicago: Argonaut, 1970.
Evans, Richard J. *Gaius Marius: A Political Biography.* Pretoria: University of South Africa Press, 1994.
Keppie, Lawrence. *The Making of the Roman Army.* Norman: University of Oklahoma Press, 1998.

SEE ALSO: Roman Civil Wars of 88-30 B.C.E.; Roman Republic, Wars of the; Sulla.

Darryl A. Phillips

MARLBOROUGH, FIRST DUKE OF

FULL NAME: John Churchill, first duke of Marlborough

Born: May 26, 1650; Devonshire, England
Died: June 16, 1722; Windsor Lodge, Windsor, England
Principal wars: War of the Grand Alliance, War of the Spanish Succession
Principal battles: Sedgemoor (1685), Blenheim (1704), Ramillies (1706), Oudenarde (1708), Malplaquet (1709)
Military significance: The duke of Marlborough helped create and maintain the coalition against France during the War of the Spanish Succession.

Because of his good looks, courtly demeanor, and connections, John Churchill advanced quickly from his first positions under James, duke of York, the future James II of England. During the Anglo-Dutch Wars (1652-1678), Churchill saw action in the navy and in an English regiment under the French. His marriage to Sarah Jennings, a confidante of Princess Anne, the future queen, helped further his career. He became a brigadier general and helped defeat a rebellion led by James Scott, duke of Monmouth, at the Battle of Sedgemoor on July 6, 1685. Although James II continued to advance Churchill, he began correspondence with the leader of the Netherlands, William of Orange, the future William III of England, because of his concerns about James II's policies, which threatened the Protestant Church of England. When William of Orange invaded England in November, 1688, Churchill deserted James II for William even after James II had promoted him to lieutenant general. In 1689, William III rewarded Churchill with the earldom of Marlborough.

Marlborough participated in the War of the Grand Alliance (1688-1697) by organizing English coastal defenses and capturing several Irish ports in September-October, 1690, as part of William III's campaign to subdue Ireland. False accusations of treason caused Marlborough to be stripped of his offices in January, 1692, and he was briefly imprisoned in the Tower of London in May, 1692. In 1698, he began to return to favor. On July 1, 1701, William III appointed him commander of English troops in the Netherlands shortly before the outbreak of the War of the Spanish Succession (1701-1714).

Under Queen Anne, Marlborough became captain general of English forces and took command of Dutch troops in May, 1702. He helped arrange another grand alliance against France and was elevated to the dukedom of Marlborough. During the War of the Spanish Succession, he was frustrated at the hesitation of the Dutch and constantly urged that greater initiatives be undertaken against the French. In 1704, the French and Bavarians posed a serious threat to the southern German states and Austria, the territory of Holy Roman Emperor Leopold I. On August 13, 1704, Marlborough, with Imperial general Prince Eugene of Savoy, led 52,000 troops to a decisive victory over a combined French-Bavarian force of 60,000 at Blenheim, which relieved pressure on Vienna. He received the title of prince of Mindelheim from Leopold I, and England's parliament gave him funds to build Blenheim Palace as a reward.

Although victorious over the French at Ramillies (1706), Oudenarde (1708), and Malplaquet (1709), Marlborough was unable to break them. His exploits did, however, prevent French conquest of the Netherlands and force the French to engage in peace negotiations. His advocacy of continuing the war ran counter to the attempts of the English ministry to arrange a secret negotiated settlement with France. In December, 1711, Marlborough was dismissed from his positions. Although he was reinstated as captain general under George I, he never again played an active role militarily.

Military historians credit Marlborough with introducing the forced march and the massed cavalry charge that won the day at Blenheim. Leading from the front lines, he successfully executed bold strategy. By combining military actions and diplomacy, he was able to forge a European coalition against France that threatened the balance of power. Such policy inspired his descendant, British prime minister Winston Churchill, in his efforts to defeat Nazi Germany in World War II.

Resources

Chandler, David. *The Art of Warfare in the Age of Marlborough*. New York: Hippocrene Books, 1976.

_____. *Marlborough as Military Commander*. New York: Charles Scribner's, 1973.

Churchill, Winston S. *Marlborough: His Life and Times*. 6 vols. New York: Charles Scribner's, 1933-1938.

Jones, J. R. *Marlborough*. New York: Cambridge University Press, 1993.

Webb, Stephen Saunders. *Lord Churchill's Coup*. New York: Alfred A. Knopf, 1995.

SEE ALSO: Blenheim; Eugene of Savoy; Grand Alliance, War of the; Louis XIV; Malplaquet; Oudenarde; Ramillies; Sedgemoor; Spanish Succession, War of the.

Mark C. Herman

MARNE

TYPE OF ACTION: Ground battle in World War I
DATE: September 5-9, 1914
LOCATION: A line thirty miles east of Paris, from Meaux on the Marne River to the Marshes of St. Gond on the Petit Morin
COMBATANTS: French and British vs. Germans
PRINCIPAL COMMANDERS: *French*, General Joseph-Jacques-Césaire Joffre (1852-1931); *German*, General Helmuth von Moltke (1848-1916)
RESULT: The Allies repelled the German advance into France

By the evening of September 4, 1914, the exhausted German First and Second Armies had reached a line thirty miles east of Paris. General Joseph-Jacques-Césaire Joffre issued an order for an Anglo-French counteroffensive to begin on September 6, but the battle began a day early when troops dispatched from the Paris garrison by taxi ran into the right flank of the westernmost German army (the First). As the commander of the First Army pulled his troops west to meet this assault, a gap opened between his forces and those of the Second Army to his left. It was into this gap that Joffre sent the French Fifth Army and the British Expeditionary Force. Disconcerted by the developing situation, General Helmuth von Moltke sent a staff officer to survey the situation. Concerned that the First Army would be cut off and annihilated, the staff officer ordered the German forces to retreat to the Aisne River. This brought an end to the German advance into France and signaled an end to its hopes of the quick victory envisioned by the Schlieffen Plan.

French soldiers don German helmets and pose behind the equipment captured from the Germans after the Battle of the Marne. (Archive Photos/Hulton Getty Collection)

SIGNIFICANCE

The Battle of the Marne blunted the German advance into France. After September 9, a race by the competing armies to turn each other's flank resulted in a line of entrenchments that extended from the North Sea to Switzerland and inaugurated four years of trench warfare.

RESOURCES

The Battle of the Marne. Documentary. Films for the Humanities and Sciences, 1991.

Holmes, Richard. *Riding the Retreat: Mons to the Marne, 1914 Revisited.* London: J. Cape, 1995.

Keegan, John. *The First World War.* New York: Alfred A. Knopf, 1999.

SEE ALSO: Joffre, Joseph-Jacques-Césaire; Moltke, Helmuth von (1848-1916); Schlieffen, Count Alfred von; World War I.

George S. Vascik

MARSHALL, GEORGE C.

FULL NAME: George Catlett Marshall, Jr.
BORN: December 31, 1880; Uniontown, Pennsylvania
DIED: October 16, 1959; Washington, D.C.
PRINCIPAL WARS: World War I, World War II, Korean War
MILITARY SIGNIFICANCE: As chief of staff of the U.S. Army from September, 1939, to November, 1945, Marshall provided overall direction to the Army from his post in Washington, D.C., during World War II.

George C. Marshall graduated from Virginia Military Institute in 1901 and began his army career as a second lieutenant in 1902. He served two tours in the Philippines along with some stateside duty, graduated from the School of the Line in Leavenworth, Kansas, and taught there. He first earned distinction during World War I as a staff officer in France working on training and planning. His fine work won him a postwar job as chief aide to General John J. Pershing from 1919 to 1924, after which he spent three years in Tientsin, China, and later took charge of instruction at Fort Benning, Georgia, where he influenced a number of men who would become World War II gener-

George C. Marshall. (Library of Congress)

als. He made brigadier general in 1936, became chief of the War Plans Division in 1938, then deputy chief of staff, and, in September, 1939, he was named chief of staff.

In that position, he reorganized and mobilized the military during World War II, playing a key role in getting Congress to institute the draft in 1940 and to extend it in 1941. He planned the nation's rearmament, coordinated training, and saw that materials from the United States reached Great Britain while that nation stood alone against Nazi Germany. When the United States entered the war, Marshall directed much of the war effort. He convinced Congress to change the law so that promotions went to the most able officers, not the most senior. He attended all the major wartime conferences, including Casablanca in 1943, Teheran and Cairo in 1943, Yalta in 1945, and Potsdam in 1945. He argued against the 1942 North African invasion, a position that failed, and opposed British prime minister Winston Churchill's Mediterranean strategy, maintaining that an invasion across the English Channel would be more effective. He won that argument. President

Franklin D. Roosevelt had originally intended that Marshall become supreme commander of the invasion force but decided, to Marshall's disappointment, that his chief of staff was too valuable in Washington, so the nod went to Marshall's protégé, General Dwight D. Eisenhower. In December, 1944, Marshall got his fifth star, becoming general of the Army, outranking every other uniformed figure except Admiral William Leahy. Two months after the Allies won the war, Marshall resigned as chief of staff, permitting him to pursue the diplomacy that had been a big part of his wartime duties.

President Harry S. Truman sent him to China to negotiate an ill-fated truce between the warring Nationalist Chiang Kai-shek and Communist Mao Zedong during 1946. Then, in January 1947, Truman named him secretary of state, a critical military/diplomatic slot in the formative years of the Cold War (1945-1991). In 1947, Marshall provided Truman Doctrine-mandated assistance to Greece and Turkey, then announced the Marshall Plan to rebuild war-torn Europe. That hugely successful foreign aid program helped revive Europe, paved the way for the partnership of the North Atlantic Treaty Organization (NATO) in 1949, and won Marshall the Nobel Peace Prize for 1953. Marshall resigned because of ill health in January, 1949, but when the Korean War broke out, Truman called him out of retirement to serve from September, 1950, to September, 1951, as secretary of defense. In that position, he supported the president in his controversial decision to remove General Douglas MacArthur from command.

Resources

America's Five-Star Heroes: Gods of War. Documentary. A&E Home Video, 1998.
Cray, Ed. *General of the Army: George C. Marshall, Soldier and Statesman*. New York: W. W. Norton: 1990.
Pogue, Forrest C. *George C. Marshall: Education of a General, 1889-1939*. New York: Viking, 1963.
_____. *George C. Marshall: Ordeal and Hope, 1939-1943*. New York: Viking, 1966.
_____. *George C. Marshall: Organizer of Victory, 1943-1945*. New York: Viking, 1973.
_____. *George C. Marshall: Statesman, 1945-1959*. New York: Viking, 1987.

SEE ALSO: Chinese Civil War; Churchill, Winston; Eisenhower, Dwight D.; Korean War; MacArthur, Douglas; Roosevelt, Franklin D.; World War I; World War II.

John R. M. Wilson

Marston Moor

TYPE OF ACTION: Ground battle in the English Civil War of 1642-1651
DATE: July 2, 1644
LOCATION: Marston Moor, near Long Marston (six miles due west of York, England)
COMBATANTS: Approximately 18,000 Royalists vs. 25,000 Parliamentary and Scottish allies
PRINCIPAL COMMANDERS: *Royalist*, Prince Rupert (1619-1682), William Cavendish, earl of Newcastle (1592-1676); *Parliamentarian and Scottish*, Ferdinando Fairfax, second baron of Cameron (1584-1648), Alexander Leslie, earl of Leven (c. 1580-1661)
RESULT: Royalist defeat leads to capitulation of York

On June 14, 1644, King Charles I ordered Prince Rupert to relieve the besieged city of York. Rupert raised the siege on July 1 and forced Parliamentary forces to retreat southward, where his attacks on their rear guard forced them to give battle. On July 2, Royalist forces assumed an advantageous defensive position to the north of the Tockwith-Long Marston Road. A ditch blocked the Parliamentary advance, but after three hours, at five in the afternoon, Parliamentary forces charged through a rainstorm, and battle was joined. With the field thinned by casualties and desertions, the cavalry of Oliver Cromwell and Alexander Leslie, earl of Leven, broke Rupert's right, commanded by Sir John Byron. On the Royalist left, Lord George Goring's horse harassed Ferdinando Fairfax, second baron of Cameron, overwhelming the Scots but disordering themselves. William Cavendish, earl of Newcastle's infantry, the "Whitecoats" in the Royalist center, were pinned against a hedgerow, exhausted their ammunition, and were slaughtered in their ranks. About 6,000 were killed or mortally wounded on both sides. York surrendered to Parliamentary forces on July 16.

SIGNIFICANCE

Parliamentary failure to follow up destruction of the king's army in the north of England prolonged the first phase of the English civil war until 1646.

RESOURCES

Bennett, Martyn. *The Civil Wars in Britain and Ireland, 1638-1651*. London: Blackwell, 1997.
The English Civil War. Documentary. Films for the Humanities and Sciences, 1999.
Newman, Peter. *The Battle of Marston Moor, 1644*. Chichester, England: Anthony Bird, 1981.
Young, Peter, and Richard Holmes. *The English Civil War*. London: Eyre Methuen, 1974.

SEE ALSO: Cromwell, Oliver; Dunbar; Edgehill; English Civil War of 1642-1651; Naseby; Preston; Rupert, Prince; Worcester.

Myron C. Noonkester

MARTIAL LAW

The maintenance of civil order by the military when civilian courts and other normal mechanisms of governance are unable to operate. It is often imposed upon a territory by an invading army. In such an instance, it is usually a de facto dictatorship by the commander of the invasion force. It has also been exercised by militaries on their own soil—especially during times of insurrection and invasion. While European martial law is largely limited to an existing "state of siege" and well-defined military powers, its U.S. counterpart remains more flexible and ambiguous. Once martial law is proclaimed by the executive branch, military authorities are invested with the power to establish order by any reasonable means. Such power, however, has its limits. Upon restoration of civilian government, commanders can be called upon to justify acts taken while martial law was in effect. In one famous example, General Andrew Jackson was fined for contempt of court during proceedings concerning his unnecessary maintenance of martial law in New Orleans after he defeated the British there on January 8, 1815.

Jeremiah Taylor

MARTINET, JEAN

BORN: Probably before 1620; place unknown
DIED: June 21, 1672; fortress of Duisburg, Brandenburg (later Germany)
PRINCIPAL WAR: Dutch War
PRINCIPAL BATTLE: Siege of Duisburg (1672)
MILITARY SIGNIFICANCE: Martinet was instrumental in implementing a regular system of drill and discipline in the army of Louis XIV, in the great period of military transition following the Thirty Years' War.

Jean Martinet was born a commoner of obscure origins. He rose through the ranks in the 1660's when Marshals Henri de la Tour d'Auvergne, viscount of Turenne, and François-Michel Le Tellier, marquis de Louvois, were enacting a fundamental reorganization of the French army. Martinet was made lieutenant colonel of the regiment Du Roi (the king's foot guards), and diligently imposed a regular system of drill, discipline, and maneuvers. The regiment Du Roi was an oversized regiment (having fifty-four companies as opposed to the standard ten to sixteen) specifically created as a model to train other infantry units. Martinet was promoted to inspector general of infantry and established his assiduous methods throughout the army. He introduced elite regiments of grenadiers to the army and, by 1670, established the rule of one company of grenadiers to each infantry regiment. He also invented copper pontoon boats, which were widely used by 1672. He also attempted (unsuccessfully at the time) to introduce the plug bayonet to replace the pike.

Other individuals later spread Martinet's model of regular drill, discipline, and organization to other branches of the army. He was killed leading an assault at the Siege of Duisburg (1672) during the Dutch War (1672-1678). The word "martinet" has entered the English language to mean a strict disciplinarian.

RESOURCES

Lynn, John A. *Giant of the Grande Siècle: The French Army, 1610-1715*. Cambridge, England: Cambridge University Press, 1997.
_____. *The Wars of Louis XIV, 1667-1714*. New York: Addison Wesley Longman, 1999.
Parker, Geoffrey. *The Military Revolution: Military*

Innovation and the Rise of the West, 1500-1800. 2d ed. New York: Cambridge University Press, 1996.

SEE ALSO: Armies: Organization and tactics; Condé, the Great; Drill; Grenadier; Louis XIV; Louvois, François-Michel Le Tellier, marquis de; Turenne.

Nathan J. Latta

MASADA, SIEGE OF

TYPE OF ACTION: Siege in the First Jewish Revolt
DATE: February/March-April 15, 73 C.E.
LOCATION: Fortress on a desert plateau, west of the Dead Sea (ancient Judaea, modern Israel)
COMBATANTS: About 8,000 Romans vs. 500 Sicarii
PRINCIPAL COMMANDER: *Roman*, Flavius Silva
RESULT: Romans captured the fortress, ending the First Jewish Revolt

In the spring of 73 C.E., Flavius Silva, Judaea's Roman governor, marched on Masada, the last vestige of Jewish resistance, with the Tenth Legion and five or six auxiliary units, about 8,000 soldiers. There were 967 Sicarii (one of several Jewish rebel factions) in Masada, of whom no more than 500 were combatants. The Romans built roads to haul supplies and constructed siege camps and a circumvallation to cut off the fortress. Silva split his legion into two camps on either side of Masada, forcing the Sicarii to spread out their defense. The legionaries raised a siege ramp from the west, over a natural slope rising almost to the summit. From a stone tower on the ramp, the Romans employed suppressing fire from torsion artillery and placed a battering-ram, which smashed down Masada's walls. Entering the fortress on April 15, they found almost all the defenders had committed suicide. The siege probably lasted six to eight weeks.

SIGNIFICANCE

The capture of Masada ended the First Jewish Revolt (66-73 C.E.), but otherwise had no strategic or political importance.

RESOURCES

Netzer, Ehud. "The Last Days and Hours at Masada." *Biblical Archaeological Review* (November/December, 1991): 26-31.

Roth, Jonathan P. "The Length of the Siege of Masada." *Scripta Classica Israelica* 14 (1995): 87-110.

Shatzman, Israel. "The Roman Siege of Masada." In *The Story of Masada: Discoveries from the Excavations*, edited by Gila Hurvitz. Provo, Utah: Brigham Young University, 1997.

SEE ALSO: Jewish Revolts; Religion and war; Roman Empire; Roman Empire, Wars of the.

Jonathan P. Roth

MASSÉNA, ANDRÉ

FULL NAME: Masséna, André, duke of Rivoli and prince of Essling
BORN: May 6, 1758; Nice, France
DIED: April 4, 1817; Paris, France
PRINCIPAL WARS: Napoleonic Wars

André Masséna. (Library of Congress)

PRINCIPAL BATTLES: Rivoli (1797), Genoa (1800), Bussaco (1811), Fuentes de Onoro (1811)
MILITARY SIGNIFICANCE: Masséna demonstrated leadership skills both as a division leader and an army commander before 1800, but failed, largely for reasons of health, after that point.

As a youth, André Masséna joined the French army and rose to the rank of sergeant major before becoming a member of the revolutionary army. In this force, he rose quickly to command of first a regiment, then a brigade, and finally a division. As a corps commander in 1796, Masséna was both energetic and aggressive and was a major contributor to a score of battles. At Rivoli (1797), in particular, his divisions marched through the night and arrived just in time to save the battle and to guarantee a decisive victory.

Masséna's abilities resulted in independent commands in 1798 and 1800. In 1798, he managed more than 100,000 men and was responsible for the successful defense of eastern France. In 1800, he defended Genoa and distracted the enemy until Napoleon could defeat them in northern Italy.

His efforts were rewarded with success and promotion. In 1802, he was named a marshal of France, and six years later a duke. In 1805, he led corps at Ulm and Essling.

From 1810 to 1811, the duke of Rivoli commanded the Army of Portugal, but performed poorly. Declining health, his inability to control his subordinates or himself, and his failure to act decisively led to defeats by the duke of Wellington at Bussaco (1811) and Fuentes de Onoro (1811). The latter reverse resulted in his removal from command and active service.

RESOURCES
Chandler, David, ed. *Napoleon's Marshals*. New York: Macmillan, 1987.
Glover, Michael. *The Peninsular War, 1807-1814*. London: Archon, 1974.
Horward, Donald D. *Napoleon and Iberia: The Twin Sieges of Ciudad Rodrigo and Almeida, 1810*. Mechanicsburg, Pa.: Stackpole, 1994.
Marshall-Cornwall, James. *Masséna*. Oxford: Oxford University Press, 1965.
Sharpe's Company. Fiction feature. BFS Video, 1995.
Sharpe's Eagles. Fiction feature. BFS Video, 1995.

SEE ALSO: Napoleon I; Napoleonic Wars; Rivoli; Wellington, duke of.

Louis P. Towles

MASURIAN LAKES

TYPE OF ACTION: Ground battle in World War I
DATE: September 9-14, 1914
LOCATION: East Prussia (later Mazury region, Poland)
COMBATANTS: 145,000 Germans vs. 200,000 Russians
PRINCIPAL COMMANDERS: *German*, General Paul von Hindenburg (1847-1934), General Erich Ludendorff (1865-1937); *Russian*, General Pavel Rennenkampf (1854-1918)
RESULT: Russian withdrawal ending invasion of East Prussia

Following its stunning defeat of the Russian Second Army at the Battle of Tannenberg in the end of August, 1914, the German Eighth Army, commanded by Generals Paul von Hindenburg and Erich Ludendorff, advanced northeast against the Russian First Army, which had remained inactive during Tannenberg. The German plan was to turn the Russian left flank and, sweeping around behind the Russians, trap them against the Baltic coast and annihilate them.

German general Hermann von Franois's First Corps began to attack General Pavel Rennenkampf's southern positions on September 7. Following fierce fighting and fearing encirclement, Rennenkampf began withdrawing on September 9. By September 14, East Prussia had been cleared of Russian troops.

SIGNIFICANCE
While failing to trap the Russian First Army, the Germans were ultimately successful in repelling the Russian invasion of East Prussia. In only one week, the German Eighth Army killed, wounded, or captured 125,000 men in Rennenkampf's First Army and captured 150 of his guns and most of his transports, while losing a relatively light 15,000 men. Overall in the one-month campaign in East Prussia, the Russian First and Second Armies lost 227,000 soldiers, the majority of them captured (Russian casualty figures at

Tannenberg are unrecorded), along with 650 guns captured by the Germans. The German Eighth Army suffered only around 30,000 casualties.

RESOURCES

Clark, Alan. *Suicide of the Empires: The Battles on the Eastern Front, 1914-1918*. New York: American Heritage Press, 1971.

Stone, Norman. *The Eastern Front, 1914-1917*. Reprint. London: Penguin, 1998.

SEE ALSO: Hindenburg, Paul von; Ludendorff, Erich; Tannenberg; World War I.

Michael C. Paul

MATTHIAS I CORVINUS

ALSO KNOWN AS: Mátyás Hunyadi; Mátyás Corvin
BORN: February 24, 1443; Kolozsvár, Transylvania (later Cluj, Romania)
DIED: April 6, 1490; Vienna
PRINCIPAL WARS: Hungarian-Turkish Wars
MILITARY SIGNIFICANCE: King of Hungary who established a line of defense against the Ottoman forces in the south of Hungary. His wars against western enemies, however, deprived his successors of resources to counter later Ottoman incursions.

The first years of Matthias I Corvinus's reign (1458-1490) were characterized by a series of administrative reforms meant to both centralize and consolidate royal power. The king contended with a number of rebellions (1467 and 1471), putting them down with a mix of political reforms and military actions. His reign was strongly influenced by the looming presence of the expansionist Ottoman Empire. To counter the threat, Matthias strengthened a line of fortresses in the southern perimeter of the kingdom. This line proved effective for more than half a century, although during Matthias's reign, it was not seriously challenged.

Notwithstanding the Ottoman danger, Matthias became deeply involved in dynastic struggles over both the Czech lands and Austria. By 1479, he conquered Moravia and Silesia and became an elector of the Holy Roman Empire. This worsened Matthias's relations with Emperor Frederick III, who also had claims for the Hungarian throne. Matthias supported a number of rebellions against the emperor, though none of them were successful. His involvement in imperial affairs consumed considerable resources, to the detriment of his anti-Ottoman policies. To counter dangers of an Ottoman attack, Matthias signed a five-year truce with Sultan Bayezid II in 1483, renewed in 1888.

RESOURCES

Medgyes, Zsuzsa, ed. *Mathias Corvinus and His Age: Hungary, 1458-1490*. Hungary: Publishing and Promotion Company for Tourism, 1990.

Rázsó, Gyula. "The Mercenary Army of King Matthias Corvinus." In *From Hunyadi to Rákóczi: War and Society in Late Medieval and Early Modern Hungary*. New York: Columbia University Press, 1982.

SEE ALSO: Habsburg Dynastic War; Hungarian-Turkish Wars; Hungarian War with the Holy Roman Empire; Hunyadi, János.

Pongrácz Sennyey

MAU MAU REBELLION

AT ISSUE: Self-governance and economic control in Kenya
DATE: 1952-1956
LOCATION: Kenya
COMBATANTS: British colonists, the British government vs. Gikuyu tribesmen who had taken the Mau Mau oath
PRINCIPAL COMMANDERS: *British*, Governor Evelyn Baring; *Kikuyu*, Jomo Kenyatta (c. 1894-1978)
PRINCIPAL BATTLES: Lari Massacre, Marige Massacre
RESULT: The British government effectively crushed the Mau Mau Rebellion in 1956, but the rebellion laid the groundwork for Kenyan independence in 1963

BACKGROUND

Before the colonization of Kenya, the native peoples' economy was based on ownership of land and livestock. The British came to Kenya and attempted to "civilize" the local peoples and their

The British authorities hold prisoner in Kenya members of the Kikuyu tribe on suspicion that they are involved in the Mau Mau Rebellion. (Archive Photos/Hulton Getty Collection)

economic system. The British colonial government seized control of land that had been privately owned and quickly drove much of the native population into poverty and economic servitude.

The largest of Kenya's tribes, the Gikuyu, were hardest hit by this "land hunger" and fostered the bulk of anticolonial activities. The first such movement was the East African Association (EAA) led by Harry Thuku in 1922. The EAA's gathering in Nairobi was repressed by military force, and Thuku was arrested and exiled for seven years. Jomo Kenyatta joined the EAA in 1922 until it was reformed as the Kikuyu Central Association (KCA), with Kenyatta as its general secretary.

In 1931, the Carter Land Commission was convened to adjudicate questions of property rights in Kenya. Kenyatta presented evidence supporting the KCA's position, but the commission's decisions proved even more detrimental to the native Africans by creating permanent barriers between the white-owned lands and the African land units (reserves). Meanwhile the local chiefs and colonial landowners tightened their grip on the local economy by continuing to buy up available lands. As a result, the gap between the rich and the poor continued to grow.

World War II increased African discontent as many Africans fought alongside the colonial overlords yet were treated as second-class citizens when they returned to Kenya.

ACTION

By 1950, as anticolonial sentiments grew, many Kikuyu swore oaths to secret societies whose goal was to break British rule. The oaths bound members to wage war against Europeans and Africans who were collaborating with the British colonists. From these oaths, the Kikuyu-dominated Mau Mau organization was formed.

In 1952, sporadic outbreaks of violence led the new colonial governor, Evelyn Baring, to declare a state of emergency and request British troops be flown in to maintain the peace. On October 20, 1952, Kenyatta was arrested and charged with being the leader of the rebellion. This arrest triggered two critical events. The first occurred the next day when Mau Mau rebels, protesting the arrest, are said to have killed 97 procolonial Africans, in an event now called the **Lari Massacre**. Some rebels have denied responsibility for the massacre, calling it a colonial plot. Kenyatta was subsequently found guilty and sentenced to seven years of hard labor.

The second event occurred as a result of the arrest of Kenyatta; Kikuyu flocked to oath-taking ceremonies, swelling the ranks with new members and renewed hope. To counter this, the British had anthropologist L. S. B. Leakey and some of the wealthy tribal landowners compose a "cleansing oath" to reverse the Mau Mau oath. Suspects were screened and forced to swear their allegiance to the British. In retribution, on April 5, 1953, a number of rebels attacked a number of those who had taken the cleansing oath. The resulting slaughter was called the **Marige Massacre** and, in many ways, marked the beginning of the end of the rebellion. After the initial battles, the fighting developed into typical guerrilla warfare. The British launched Operation Anvil in April of 1954, placing 30,000 Kikuyus in detention camps and sealing Kikuyu lands from the rest of Kenya. Anvil ended the primary Mau Mau threat, and by the end of 1956 the rebellion was effectively crushed, but it was not until 1959 that the state of emergency was lifted.

In many respects, the fighting took the form of a Kenyan civil war as it became a battle between economic classes. In total, some 13,000 people died between 1952 and 1956, of which only about 100 were Europeans. Eighty thousand Kikuyu tribesman were held in detention camps.

Aftermath

The rebellion may have been a military failure, but it was a political success. In 1961, Kenyatta negotiated the constitutional terms leading to Kenya's independence in 1963.

Resource

Kershaw, Greet. *Mau Mau from Below*. Athens: Ohio University Press, 1997.

See also: British Colonial Wars.

B. Keith Murphy

Maurice

Full name: Flavius Tiberius Mauricius
Born: c. 539; Cappadocia
Died: November 27, 602; Constantinople
Principal wars: Byzantine-Persian Wars, Avar War
Principal battles: Dara (591), Lake Urmiah (591), Druzpara (597)
Military significance: A gifted Byzantine military leader and writer, Emperor Maurice won a two-front war in Asia and the Balkans.

As commander of the Byzantine army of the east from 572 to 581, Maurice distinguished himself campaigning in Persian Mesopotamia and Armenia. These victories, however, were virtually nullified by Byzantine defeats in southeastern Europe against the tribal armies of the Avars and their Slav vassals. Maurice's skills—and Byzantium's military peril—persuaded the dying Emperor Tiberius to designate him as his successor in 582.

Confronting Persians and Avars simultaneously, Emperor Maurice balanced demands on both fronts with holding actions, penetration raids, and bribery. In 590, Persia erupted in civil war, and Maurice threw his armies behind Shah Khasraw II. At Dara (590) and Lake Urmiah (591), Byzantine forces and Khasraw's troops crushed the usurpers, and Maurice thereby won a peace guarantee and extensive land concessions from the grateful shah. The Byzantines then shifted to the Balkans, gradually reclaiming lost territory. Hard-pressed, the Avar khan launched a massive invasion in 597, marching south and taking Druzpara. Maurice spent a year assembling his forces and then drove the Avars back across the Danube in 599. His military governate system (the Exarchates) and astute diplomacy enabled him to retain Byzantine holdings in Italy, Tunisia, and southern Spain. Despite his successes, Emperor Maurice was unpopular with his troops, and he was overthrown and killed in 602 by his successor, Phocas. However, his work on military strategy, *Strategikon* (fifth century; *Maurice's Strategikon: Handbook of Byzantine Military Strategy*, 1984), written before he became emperor, continued to influence the Byzantine military for centuries.

RESOURCES

Maurice. *Maurice's Strategikon: Handbook of Byzantine Military Strategy*. Philadelphia: University of Pennsylvania Press, 1984.

Treadgold, Warren. *A History of the Byzantine State and Society*. Stanford, Calif.: Stanford University Press, 1997.

Whitby, L. Micheal. *The Emperor Maurice and His Historian: Theophylact Simocatta on Persian and Balkan Warfare*. Oxford: Clarendon Press, 1988.

SEE ALSO: Byzantine Empire; Byzantine-Persian Wars.

Weston F. Cook, Jr.

MAURICE OF NASSAU, PRINCE

FULL NAME: Maurits, earl of Nassau, Vianden, Buren, Leerdam and Meurs (and since February 20, 1618) prince of Oranje (or Orange)
BORN: November 13, 1567; Dillenburg, Nassau
DIED: April 23, 1625; The Hague, Holland
PRINCIPAL WARS: Dutch Wars of Independence
PRINCIPAL BATTLES: Siege of Breda (1589), Siege of Nijmegen (1591), Siege of Geertruidenberg (1593), Siege of Groningen (1594), Nieuport (1600)
MILITARY SIGNIFICANCE: During his career, Prince Maurice of Nassau successfully besieged one hundred cities and Spanish strongholds and defeated the Spanish army at Nieuport. His actions prevented the repression of the Dutch religious rebellion and ultimately would ensure the independence of the Dutch Republic.

Raised by his uncle, Jan VI of Nassau-Dillenburg, Maurice of Nassau received early exposure to marksmanship, horsemanship, and combat. Maurice put this experience, together with the knowledge of mathematics and ancient warfare he acquired at the Universities of Heidelberg and Leiden, to good use when, in 1585, he succeeded his murdered father William of Orange (also known as William the Silent) as kapitein-admiraal-generaal (supreme commander) of Holland and Zeeland and stadholder of Holland, Zeeland, Utrecht, Gelderland, and Overijssel. The Dutch states, engaged since 1568 in a battle for religious freedom and independence from Spain, found in Maurice a skilled and determined military leader. In 1587, Maurice was appointed kapitein-admiraal-generaal over all Dutch states. He would command a force of up to 22,000 strong.

Maurice's first big success, the Siege of Breda in 1589, won him international acclaim. Although the plan to enter the fortification by smuggling into the city seventy soldiers hidden in a peat ship was not his own, Maurice's skillful execution of the plan took the Italian garrison completely by surprise. What made Maurice famous and feared in subsequent sieges, however, was the fact that he employed siege tactics that ensured a rapid defeat of the city, rather than relying on the traditional starvation method. After giving the defenders two opportunities to surrender, he would use a combination of redoubts to repel outside relief, and minings, bombardments, and siege towers to breach the walls. Often within a week, the defenders would experience Maurice's wrath for their refusal to open the gates. In all, Maurice successfully besieged forty-five cities and fifty-five strongholds. Most notable are the sieges of Nijmegen (1591) and Groningen (1594), because of the size of the cities, and Geertruidenberg (1593), because of the difficult geological conditions.

In 1590-1591, Maurice revolutionized combat by reorganizing his troops into smaller, and more easily maneuvered groups of ten rows deep. Iron discipline, endless drill, and prompt wage payments were used to control morale. In addition, Maurice introduced the marching step and designed a maneuver in which gunners, after firing a salvo, could offset their vulnerability by retreating to the rear to reload. Ironically, Maurice's only test of field warfare, the Battle of Nieuport, on February 2, 1600, remains a dubious victory. After a chaotic advance toward Dunkirk, Maurice's troops were surprised by the forces of Albrecht VII, archduke of Austria. Maurice fought an all-or-nothing battle on the beach and in the dunes, in which the Dutch naval guns, rather than his battle skills, had the deciding vote. Although the victory added little or nothing to the outcome of the war, and the objectives of the campaign, to siege Dunkirk and relieve Ostend, were never realized, Maurice nevertheless reached his pinnacle of success.

After 1600, Maurice's fame rapidly declined. Matched in skill and resources by his new opponent, Ambrosio de Spinola, marqués de los Balbases, and derailed by a twelve-year truce signed with Spain on April 9, 1609, Maurice's influence waned. Although credited with setting up the first military school in 1619, his intervention in internal religious quarrels, which led to the arrest, on August 29, 1618, and execution, on May 13, 1619, of Raadpensionaris Johan van Oldenbarnevelt, was ill-advised. After the war with Spain resumed in 1621, Maurice, old and sick, was no longer able to repel Spinola, culminating in the fall of Breda in 1625. Having survived assassination attempts in April, 1620, and January, 1623, Maurice died on April 23, 1625.

RESOURCES

Crompton, Samuel W. *One Hundred Military Leaders Who Shaped World History.* San Mateo, Calif.: Bluewood Books, 1999.

Tex, Jan den. *Oldenbarnevelt.* Cambridge, England: Cambridge University Press, 1973.

SEE ALSO: Dutch Wars of Independence; Nieuport; Ostend, Siege of.

Oscar E. Lansen

MAURYAN EMPIRE

DATE: 324-233 B.C.E.
LOCATION: India
PRINCIPAL MILITARY ACTION: Maurya-Greek War
MILITARY SIGNIFICANCE: The Mauryas unified India, creating a vast empire that extended over most of the subcontinent, and left a legacy of political and legal systems, including a belief in nonviolence.

The invasion of India and consequent wars waged by Alexander the Great in 326 B.C.E. seriously disrupted the existing political order and destroyed a number of political states. Political instability and socioeconomic upheaval caused by the presence of foreign invaders set the scene for the rise of a new aggressive and powerful Indian dynasty under the Mauryas. The Mauryas founded the first centralized and unified Indian Empire, which extended over most of the subcontinent and areas in the north that are no longer part of modern-day India. Its rulers had extensive diplomatic contacts with the outside world and traded with numerous countries. They made India one of the world's richest countries and created a complex administrative and legal system to govern their vast empire as well as a vast armed force to defend it. They left a legacy in law, administrative systems, ecological awareness, and political thought, including a belief in the importance of nonviolence. Emperor Asóka's dedication to nonviolence provided the inspiration for modern India's struggle for freedom from British rule.

The founder of the Mauryan dynasty, Chandragupta Maurya (ruled c. 324-301 B.C.E.), arose from obscure origins to conquer a vast empire from a variety of Indian and Greek rulers. His political career is said to have been guided by the Brahmin political writer Kauṭilya (also known as Viṣṇugupta or Cāṇakya), who wrote India's ancient treatise on politics, the *Artha-śāstra* (*Arthashastra*, 1992). Significantly, Kauṭilya suggested in his book that rulers should always prefer peace to war because of the immense problems generated by the latter. However, in practice, the earlier Mauryas were known primarily as great conquerors and unifiers.

In approximately 305 B.C.E., Chandragupta repulsed an invasion of Northern India by the Greek Seleucus I Nicator, who had gained control of part of the vast holdings of Alexander the Great. In the process of this war, Chandragupta is said to have acquired Kabul, Kandahar, Gandhara and Punjab. The conclusion of peace between Seleucus and Chandragupta resulted in the marriage of Chandragupta to the daughter of Seleucus and the exchange of diplomatic missions. Megasthenes, who served as ambassador to the Mauryan court, left a vivid account, *Indika* (now found only in fragmentary quotations in the works of other authors), of the Indian Empire, describing Pataliputra, its capital city, as being larger than Rome.

By about 304 B.C.E. the Mauryas commanded and militarily protected a vast empire extending from modern-day Afghanistan in the north to Mysore in South India and from Saurashtra in the west to Bengal in the east.

The army was an important element of Mauryan society. Kauṭilya had proposed an army with ranks based on heredity. The war office of the Mauryas consisted of six departments: cavalry, chariots, infantry, elephants, coordination between the army and navy, and transportation and provisioning. Mauryan wounded were treated by battlefield physicians who tended to their patients at aid stations positioned near the military lines. Ambulance corps helped carry the wounded to safety. Mauryan weapons included javelins, scimitars, shields and bows. The training of war elephants formed a significant part of the preparations for war. Each elephant carried three archers and a mahout (rider) into battle.

The Mauryan fascination with details of every facet of government extended to items such as the specific designs of the seven types of chariots used in battle, the types of chariot formations on the battlefield, and the precise number of riders in and followers outside each war chariot.

Greek sources mention a naval department in the Mauryan government that insisted that shipbuilding be a government monopoly. The navy protected both the rivers and the coastline of this huge empire.

The armed force of the Mauryan Empire has been estimated at about one million men, most of which were in the infantry. Megasthenes pointed to the high repute of the army and the generous salaries and benefits provided to the troops by the emperor. It appears that there was both a standing army and soldiers on temporary hire as well as some mercenaries. Additionally, allies were persuaded to provide soldiers when required.

Chandragupta's son Bindusāra (ruled c. 293 to 268 B.C.E.), continued the imperial traditions established by his father, accepted the presence of diplomatic missions from various foreign governments, maintained the extensive empire, and may have extended its boundaries by war and conquest in the south.

Given the size and significance of his great inheritance, Aśoka (ruled 268-233 B.C.E.) mainly concerned himself with protecting and extending his realm. One such campaign pitted him against Kalinga (later Orissa) in eastern India, where he faced ferocious resistance from people who cherished their freedom. Aśoka conquered Kalinga in about 261-260 B.C.E. The cost in human life and suffering was vast for ancient times; more than 100,000 were killed on the battlefield. The shock of this carnage traumatized the emperor, who after some serious soul searching, converted to Buddhism, adopted a policy of nonviolence, and dedicated his career to the rule of law and the peaceful betterment of his subjects. It proved to be a turning point in Indian history. Instead of carrying that vast military force to foreign conquest, Aśoka turned India to the philosophical conquest of the self and gave that nation a moral focus that became an ideal to be followed throughout its long history. Although many Indian kings failed to live up to the standards Aśoka established, the ideal has always remained an inspiration for the one billion people of that country. Aśoka is revered both in India and in Southeast Asia as one of the greatest emperors in world history.

RESOURCES
Kulke, Hermann, and Dietmar Rothermund. *A History of India*. London: Routledge, 1990.
Mookerji, Radha Kumud. *Chandragupta Maurya and His Times*. Madras, India: Madras University Press, 1988.
Nehru, Jawaharlal. *Discovery of India*. Garden City, N.Y.: Doubleday, 1960.
Thapar, Romila. *A New History of India*. Vol. 1. London: Penguin, 1990.
Wolpert, Stanley. *A New History of India*. New York: Oxford University Press, 1997.

SEE ALSO: Alexander the Great; Alexander's Wars of Conquest; Chandragupta Maurya.

R. K. L. Panjabi

Maximilian I

ALSO KNOWN AS: Maximilian von Habsburg
BORN: March 22, 1459; Wiener Neustadt, Austria
DIED: January 12, 1519; Wels, Austria
PRINCIPAL WARS: Franco-Austrian War, Italian Wars, Austro-Swiss War
PRINCIPAL BATTLE: Guinegate (1479)
MILITARY SIGNIFICANCE: Maximilian's campaigns and marriage alliances established the Habsburgs as a European power.

Maximilian's first war, the Franco-Austrian War, began in 1477 against the French, over the inheritance of his bride Mary of Burgundy, daughter of Duke Charles the Bold. On August 7, 1479, he defeated the French at Guinegate but could not exploit the victory. Intermittent fighting around the Netherlands and Franche-Comté ended in 1493, with Maximilian gaining most of the disputed territories despite armed revolts in the Low Countries. Between campaigns against France, Maximilian drove the Hungarian army out of Austria and invaded Hungary (1490-1491) in an unsuccessful bid for its crown.

In 1495, emperor-elect Maximilian joined the coalition against French intervention in Italy in the Italian Wars, but poverty and diplomatic reversals hindered his efforts. Rapprochement with France and a grand alliance against Venice in 1508 gained him little. The empire withheld support and the League of Cambrai dissolved. Maximilian's Italian adventures ended in 1516 with a peace sponsored by his grandson Charles I of Spain (later Holy Roman Emperor Charles V).

A by-product of the Italian Wars, Maximilian's campaign against the Swiss in 1499 ended with de facto recognition of Swiss independence. Maximilian's intervention in the Bayern-Landshut succession conflict in 1504, however, brought significant gains to the Habsburg patrimony, and his campaign in Hungary in 1506 helped secure a mutual succession pact with László VI of Hungary (Ladislas II of Bohemia).

Maximilian was the first major patron, if not the actual founder, of the Swiss-style German infantry known as Landsknechts.

RESOURCES
Benecke, Gerhard. *Maximilian I (1459-1519): An Analytical Biography*. London: Routledge & Kegan Paul, 1982.
Brady, Thomas A. "Imperial Identities: A New Biography of the Emperor Maximilian I." *Journal of Modern History* 62, no. 2 (June, 1990): 298-314.
Wheatcroft, Andrew. *The Habsburgs Embodying Empire*. New York: Viking, 1995.

SEE ALSO: Austro-Swiss Wars; Charles the Bold; Franco-Austrian War; Hungarian War with the Holy Roman Empire; Infantry; Italian Wars; Matthias I Corvinus.

Ken MacLennan

MAYAN EMPIRE

DATE: 250-900
LOCATION: Southern and eastern Mexico and northern Central America
PRINCIPAL MILITARY ACTIONS: Engagements between city-states
MILITARY SIGNIFICANCE: Military engagements and economic power made the larger city-states into centers of political, cultural, and economic dominance.

The Mayan territory extended from southeast Mexico, including the Yucatán Peninsula, through northern Central America. It is a geographically diverse area, varying in natural resources, rainfall, fertility, and forest density. The Maya inhabited the area as early as 2000 B.C.E. Although the Maya shared a common language family and some cultural traits, they varied from place to place and time to time.

During the Preclassic Period, extending to 250 C.E., the Maya built a civilization that included extensive trade and highly developed art and political organization. The city of Tikal in Guatemala's northern highlands emerged as the most advanced city and dominated the region during the classic period, 250-900. Art and architecture flourished in the city, and two calendars based on accurate astronomical observations and a system of writing were developed. The city's success was due to a strategic location, abundant natural resources, a controlling elite with marriage ties to the elite of neighboring cities, and trade ties with Teotihuacan, the dominant city in central Mexico.

Tikal also used military might to achieve and maintain its power. Ditches and artificial ridges or parapets were constructed both north and south of Tikal. The northern ditches and parapets protecting the city from its large neighboring city of Uaxactun ran for more than five miles. Defensive fortifications have been found at other sites, and some show evidence of considerable fighting.

Numerous carved monuments and painted murals in the Mayan cities depict military action between cities and warriors with captives. Captives are shown cowering at the feet of their captors, without clothes and with ropes around their necks or wrists. In some cases, beheaded captives are shown. Some of the best examples of murals showing captives and warriors are those at Bonampak in the northern highlands.

In the classic period, warfare seemed to be limited to raids, probably with one-on-one fighting. The object of war was to capture, not to kill. Captives could be executed, enslaved, or used as sacrificial victims. Slaves usually performed the manual labor required in agriculture. In some cases, slaves worked until needed as sacrificial victims.

Some Mayan cities were captured and their rulers executed by leaders of other Mayan cities, but there is little evidence of successful invasions from Mexico or Central America. However, there is evidence of cultural influence from Mexico, with which some Mayan cities maintained an active trading relationship. Teotihuacan influence can be seen in weapons of war, dress, and ceramics, especially in the southern lowlands. Tikal is a good example.

Mayan cities grew in size and power by two means, marriage and warfare. The all-powerful elite extended their power into the elite of neighboring cities by marriage, and in some cases the foreign elite took control. In other cases, power was extended by force. The city with a more defensible location could expand and attract a larger population. With more manpower, larger cities were able to raid neighboring cities and gain control. Wealth and weapons made available by trading ties with Teotihuacan gave Tikal an added advantage. Not only cities but also individuals could achieve advancement through military success. Toward the end of the classic period, warfare became more prevalent and more intense. Battles became larger and no longer consisted of individuals against individuals. There are examples of revolts of the lower class against the elite.

The southern lowland cities that were not destroyed by warfare began to decline. Reasons for the decline included drought, ecological degradation, famine, and insupportable population increases. Competition for food and land led to an increase in wars and further decline, and the center of the Mayan civilization moved to the Yucatán Peninsula.

RESOURCES

Culbert, T. Patrick. *The Classic Maya Collapse*. Albuquerque: University of New Mexico Press, 1973.

Henderson, John S. *The World of the Ancient Maya*. Ithaca, N.Y.: Cornell University Press, 1997.

Morley, Sylvanus G., George W. Brainerd, and Robert J. Sharer. *The Ancient Maya*. Stanford, Calif.: Stanford University Press, 1983.

Sabloff, Jeremy A. *The New Archaeology and the Ancient Maya*. New York: Scientific American Library, 1990.

SEE ALSO: Aztec Empire; Inca Empire.

Robert D. Talbott

MEADE, GEORGE G.

FULL NAME: George Gordon Meade
BORN: December 31, 1815; Cádiz, Spain
DIED: November 6, 1872; Philadelphia, Pennsylvania
PRINCIPAL WARS: Mexican-American War, American Civil War

George G. Meade. (Library of Congress)

PRINCIPAL BATTLES: Chancellorsville (1863), Gettysburg (1863)

MILITARY SIGNIFICANCE: Meade, named commander of the Army of the Potomac just days before the decisive Battle of Gettysburg in July, 1863, has been criticized for not taking advantage of General Robert E. Lee's retreat to counterattack and perhaps hasten the end of the Civil War.

George G. Meade, an 1835 graduate of the U.S. Military Academy at West Point, first saw combat as an army engineer during the Mexican-American War (1846-1848). He began the American Civil War (1861-1865) as a brigadier general in charge of a Pennsylvania brigade of volunteers. Meade's courage and aggressive leadership in several early battles marked him as a valuable commander. In May, 1863, as a newly appointed major general, he again distinguished himself in the Battle of Chancellorsville. As a result, on June 28, he was appointed commander of the Army of the Potomac, the primary Union force.

Because Robert E. Lee's Confederate army was moving north, Meade quickly concentrated his forces to protect Baltimore and Washington but did not attack. On June 30, 1863, scouting parties for both armies accidently met near the small Pennsylvania town of Gettysburg. The next day, the armies attacked. The three-day battle that followed was a turning point in the war. The Northern army emerged victorious, halting the Southern invasion. Meade, however, was later criticized for his failure to reinforce his flanks and hold out fresh reserves, and most importantly, for his failure to pursue Lee's army when it retreated. Critics argued that if Meade had done so, he could have ended the war. Instead, Meade was joined by Major General Ulysses S. Grant, who in effect assumed command of Meade's army until the surrender of the confederacy at Appomatox in 1865.

RESOURCES

Freeman, Cleaves. *Meade of Gettysburg*. Norman: University of Oklahoma Press, 1960.

Lyman, Theodore. *With Grant and Meade from the Wilderness to Appomattox*. Lincoln: University of Nebraska Press, 1994.

Meade, George. *Life and Letters of General George Gordon Meade*. Baltimore, Md.: Butternut & Blue, 1996.

SEE ALSO: American Civil War; Chancellorsville; Gettysburg; Grant, Ulysses S.; Lee, Robert E.

Jane Marie Smith

MEDICI, GIOVANNI DE' (1475-1521)

BORN: December 11, 1475; Florence, Italy
DIED: December 1, 1521; Rome, Italy
PRINCIPAL WARS: Italian Wars
PRINCIPAL BATTLE: Ravenna (1512)
MILITARY SIGNIFICANCE: Although the Battle of Ravenna was a victory for the invading French, it proved so costly they were forced temporarily to evacuate Italy.

Overweight and with poor eyesight, Giovanni de' Medici was unfit for the military but because of his superior intelligence, suited for an ecclesiastical career. In 1489, through family influence and venality, at the age of fourteen, he was given the rank of cardinal.

As cardinal and later as Pope Leo X (1513-1521), Giovanni pursued three main goals: to promote the interests of his family, to rid Italy of invading foreigners, and to establish a strong Italian state. In 1512, Pope Julius II organized a Holy League to drive the invading French from Italy. Cardinal de' Medici took part in the Battle of Ravenna as papal representative. Taken prisoner, he escaped. He then used the Holy League forces to march on Florence to force the Florentines to reinstate the exiled Medicis as their rulers. Influenced by the brutal sack of the nearby town of Prado, the Florentines complied—installing Giuliano, Cardinal Giovanni's younger brother, as ruler.

After becoming pope, Giovanni took military action against the duke of Urbino in 1516, seeking to replace him with the pope's nephew Lorenzo as ruler of a unified Italian state. Although successful, the campaign nearly bankrupted the papal treasury.

RESOURCES

Guicciardini, Francesco. *The History of Italy*. Princeton, N.J.: Princeton University Press, 1984.

Hibbert, Christopher. *The House of Medici.* New York: William Morrow, 1999.
Machiavelli, Niccolò. *The Prince.* Indianapolis, Ind.: Hackett, 1995.
Vaughan, Herbert M. *The Medici Popes, Leo X and Clement VII.* New York: Methuen, 1988.

SEE ALSO: Italian Wars; Machiavelli, Niccolò; Marignano; Ravenna.

Nis Petersen

to Which Is Added the Life of His Son, Cosimo I, Grand Duke of Tuscany: A Study of Heredity. New York: Charles Scribner's Sons, 1910.
Hibbert, Christopher. *The House of Medici: Its Rise and Fall.* New York: William Morrow, 1982.

SEE ALSO: Holy Roman Empire; Italian Wars; Machiavelli, Niccolò; Religion and war.

Cynthia Northrup

MEDICI, GIOVANNI DE' (1498-1526)

ALSO KNOWN AS: Giovanni delle Bande Nere (Giovanni of the Black Band)
BORN: April 6, 1498; Forli, the Papal States
DIED: November 30, 1526; Mantua
PRINCIPAL WARS: Italian Wars
PRINCIPAL BATTLE: Pavia (1525)
MILITARY SIGNIFICANCE: Throughout his military career, Medici displayed superior tactical ability and leadership capability.

Giovanni de' Medici was the great-grandson of Lorenzo de' Medici and a relative of Pope Leo X and father of the grand duke of Tuscany, Cosimo I. He trained from an early age for military service. In 1516, he received his first command and quickly demonstrated personal courage and skill while fighting for the pope and the emperor, Charles V, during the Italian Wars against the French king Francis I. He fought again in 1521-1522, in northern Italy, and during this campaign earned the nickname of Giovanni delle Bande Nere after he added a black band to his banner following the death of Leo X. By 1525, Medici, no longer restricted by family allegiances, switched sides and fought with Francis I against the forces of Charles V at the Battle of Pavia in 1525, where he received a severe wound. The next year, Medici joined forces again with Francis I and the League of Cognac and, during the ensuing battle at Mantua, died. The remarkable leadership of Medici deeply affected his troops, who remained together as a fighting unit for years after his death.

RESOURCES
Andrews, Marian. *The Romance of a Medici Warrior, Being the True Story of Giovanni delle Bande Nere,*

MEDICINE, MILITARY

Warfare has always been both a curse and a blessing to the medical profession. It is a curse because battlefield doctors are often frustrated at being unable to prevent death, relieve suffering, or mend wounds. It is a blessing because it provides wonderful opportunities to expand medical knowledge. Surgery, especially, has advanced tremendously in times of war.

THE ANCIENT AND MEDIEVAL ERAS

The detailed descriptions of wounds in the *Iliad* (c. 800 B.C.E.; English translation, 1616) show that the Greeks had an excellent basic knowledge of human anatomy. Ancient Chinese and Indian texts reveal similar levels of understanding. Such knowledge is a prerequisite for effective trauma surgery. This is not to say that ancient trauma surgery was effective—it usually was not. There was little a surgeon could do except pull out the arrow or spear, bandage the wound, splint or amputate the shattered limb, get the patient drunk, and hope for the best. Yet there were occasional successes, even miracles, and there is strong evidence in Greek and Roman literature that army surgeons were revered. The bravest soldiers and highest ranking officers were attended by the most skillful surgeons. Thanks to his doctors, Alexander the Great survived dozens of grim wounds before dying of fever at thirty-three. Even though ancient military surgeons frequently failed, it is obvious that they took their practical science seriously.

Medieval military surgery, like medieval medicine in general, regressed from the progress made in ancient cultures. Except for the contributions of Paul of Aegina, the Chinese, the Arabs, the School of Salerno, Lanfranc, and Guy de Chauliac, few advances in surgery occurred between the fall of Rome and about 1500. Medieval medical students learned anatomy from the works of Galen, not by direct experience. Before the laboratory dissection of cadavers began to become acceptable in the sixteenth century, studying battlefield casualties was about the only way that surgeons could gain first-hand knowledge of human anatomy.

The Dawn of Modern Military Surgery

Ambroise Paré is known as the father of military surgery. His fame was based on his reaction to a relatively new phenomenon in warfare, gunshot wounds. Earlier surgeons, such as Heinrich von Pfolspeundt, Hieronymus Brunschwig, Giovanni de Vigo, and Paracelsus, had written about gunshot wounds, but Paré was the first to discover how to treat them effectively. For two centuries after Paré, the French dominated surgery in general and military surgery in particular.

The Thirty Years' War, the early colonial conflicts between England and France, and other seventeenth and eighteenth century European wars led to significant increases in medical and surgical knowledge. John Woodall wrote the first textbook of naval surgery, *Surgions Mate: Or, Military and Domestique Surgury* (1617). Johann Schultes (Johannes Scultetus) wrote the standard text of surgical instruments and procedures. Richard Wiseman added much to the knowledge of gunshot wounds. Lorenz Heister developed the use of tourniquets. François-Michel Disdier, in his *Traité des bandages* (1776; treatise on bandages), helped to lay the groundwork for what eventually resulted in the superior first-aid bandaging techniques of Johann Friedrich August von Esmarch. In his posthumously published *Treatise on the Blood, Inflammation, and Gun-Shot Wounds* (1794), John Hunter drew on insights he had gained while serving in the Seven Years' War.

Perhaps the greatest military surgeon of all time was Dominique-Jean Larrey. A fervent Bonapartist, he accompanied Napoleon I from Egypt to Waterloo and took part in all major engagements of the Napoleonic Wars. In 1792, he invented the "flying ambulance," by which wounded soldiers could be quickly and safely evacuated. He emphasized first aid and im-

U.S. Navy corpsmen carry a wounded soldier to a Korean field hospital. The Korean conflict saw the first large-scale use of helicopters for evacuating the wounded from the battlefield. (U.S. Naval Historical Center)

proved the mobile battlefield hospital. The men adored him, and Napoleon himself called him "the most virtuous man I have ever known."

The War Against Disease

Military medicine is not only surgery. Disease is sometimes a greater threat than the human enemy. In the eighteenth century, the British began to succeed against some of the diseases that had plagued soldiers and sailors since ancient times. *Observations on the Diseases of the Army* (1752) by Sir John Pringle was a breakthrough text. James Lind and Sir Gilbert Blane conquered scurvy in the British navy.

Florence Nightingale founded the modern profession of military nursing during the Crimean War. Before her time, military nurses were typically camp followers, prostitutes, or girlfriends.

Major Walter Reed discovered the control for yellow fever in 1900 while stationed with the American occupation force in Cuba. Captain Edward B. Vedder, stationed in the Philippines in 1911, developed a cure for amoebic dysentery.

In eras when it was common for people to spend their entire lives within a few miles of their birthplaces, simple homesickness (then called "nostalgia") could sap a young soldier's or sailor's will to live and result in his debility or even his death. In the twentieth century, this problem was eliminated by initiatives such as the United Service Organizations (USO), as well as by the fact that teens and young adults had become more accustomed to travel far from home.

The American Civil War

The American Civil War established the Americans as world leaders in military medicine. *A Manual of Military Surgery* (1861) by Samuel D. Gross was the standard text. The surgical potential of anesthesia, introduced in the 1840's, was just beginning to be exploited. Throughout the war, infection and disease were more deadly than battles. Doctors began to notice that sanitation and hygiene were important to military health. New knowledge appeared in several classic works, including *Outlines of the Chief Camp Diseases of the United States Armies as Observed During the Present War* (1863) by Joseph Janvier Woodward and *A Treatise on Military Surgery and Hygiene* (1865) by Frank Hastings Hamilton.

Clara Barton attended the Union wounded as an independent nurse during the American Civil War, served with the International Red Cross in the Franco-Prussian War, and founded the American Red Cross in 1881.

The World Wars

Antisepsis, anesthesia, and hemorrhage control, the three prerequisites for complex surgical procedures, were all firm medical facts by the beginning of the twentieth century. World War I introduced the motorized ambulance and improved the field hospital. Gas warfare, artillery wounds, disease, and shell shock were the main concerns of doctors.

The American Medical Association published *War Medicine* in eight volumes from 1941 to 1945. This was the basic medical and surgical manual for World War II. American medical schools cooperated with the Department of War to found permanent or semi-permanent general hospitals in both the European and Pacific Theaters. Americans continued to lead the world in surgical innovations. Nazi intelligence routinely monitored Allied medical correspondence so that German military surgeons could be as up-to-date as the Americans.

Developments in the Late Twentieth Century

In the Korean War, helicopter evacuations of wounded from battlefields to mobile army surgical hospital (MASH) units became standard. This enabled the speedy application of more sophisticated care than medics could provide on the battlefield.

Challenges to military medicine at the end of the twentieth century included the chronic health problems of soldiers who were exposed to the defoliant Agent Orange in Vietnam; Gulf War syndrome (GWS), the mysterious biological ailment of veterans of that 1991 conflict; and post-traumatic stress disorder (PTSD, formerly known as "shell shock" or "battle fatigue"), psychologically damaging flashbacks to combat situations.

Resources

Apel, Otto F. *MASH: An Army Surgeon in Korea*. Lexington: University Press of Kentucky, 1998.

Binneveld, J. M. W. *From Shell Shock to Combat Stress: A Comparative History of Military Psychia-

try. Amsterdam: Amsterdam University Press, 1997.
Cooter, Roger, Mark Harrison, and Steve Sturdy, eds. *Medicine and Modern Warfare*. Atlanta, Ga.: Rodopi, 1999.
Cowdrey, Albert E. *Fighting for Life: American Military Medicine in World War II*. New York: Free Press, 1994.
Curtin, Philip D. *Disease and Empire: The Health of European Troops in the Conquest of Africa*. Cambridge, England: Cambridge University Press, 1998.
Cushing, Harvey. *From a Surgeon's Journal: 1915-1918*. Boston: Little, Brown, 1936.
Denney, Robert E. *Civil War Medicine: Care and Comfort of the Wounded*. New York: Sterling, 1995.
Garrison, Fielding H. *Notes on the History of Military Medicine*. Washington, D.C.: Association of Military Surgeons, 1922.
Ginn, Richard V. N. *The History of the U.S. Army Medical Service Corps*. Washington, D.C.: Office of the Surgeon General and Center of Military History, 1997.
Hartwick, Ann M. Ritchie. *The Army Medical Specialist Corps: The Forty-fifth Anniversary*. Washington, D.C.: Center of Military History, 1995.
Herman, Jan K., and Harold M. Koenig. *Battle Station Sick Bay: Navy Medicine in World War II*. Annapolis, Md.: U.S. Naval Institute, 1997.
Naythons, Matthew. *The Face of Mercy: A Photographic History of Medicine at War*. New York: Random House, 1993.

SEE ALSO: American Civil War; Ancient warfare; Chemical and biological warfare; Collateral damage; Ethics of warfare; Gulf War; Korean War; Laws of war; Medieval warfare; Mustard gas; Napoleonic Wars; Prisoners of war; Shell shock; Shrapnel; Thirty Years' War; Vietnam Conflict; War crimes; World War I, World War II.

Eric v. d. Luft

MEDIEVAL WARFARE

The term "medieval" (from Latin for "Middle Ages") really applies only to Western European history, from the fall of Rome around 500 C.E. to the beginning of European voyages of exploration and conquest around 1500 C.E. For most parts of the world, military practices continued through these centuries much as they had since ancient times. One military resource, however, seems to dominate the medieval period everywhere except the Americas: the horse. Hordes of horse-riding armies regularly swept out of Asia to create and destroy empires. Meanwhile, the rider became the *knight* in Europe and the *samurai* in Japan, not only creating new methods of warfare but also transforming their societies. Although infantry remained a vital part of many military forces, the preeminence of the horse warrior ended only as new weapons created modern warfare.

HORSE PEOPLES

Since ancient times, the horse-domesticating peoples of the steppes of central Asia used their nomadic mobility to plague neighboring civilizations. Their typical battle plan was for masses of horsemen to ride into shooting range, unleash huge volleys of arrows from their powerful *composite bows*, then swiftly retreat. After several waves of attacks, enemy formations would be broken and the horsemen would ride in with *swords* for the final slaughter.

For much of the medieval period, various horse peoples invaded Europe, the Middle East and East Asia. The brief Avar Empire on the plain of Hungary, destroyed by Charlemagne around 800 C.E., was soon followed by the Magyars. They plundered Germany, France, and Italy until stopped by Otto the Great at Lechfeld (955). After Bulgars threatened Byzantium, the Seljuk Turks successfully penetrated into Asia Minor and provoked the Crusades. In the thirteenth century, Genghis Khan reorganized the Mongols and stormed out of central Asia. The Mongols eventually conquered the Russians, the Turks, and China.

The failed attempts by Mongols to invade Japan sparked the development of the *samurai* warriors, who imitated the Mongol horse archery. By the fourteenth century, the samurai became a dominant class of armored swordsmen who fought under powerful competing lords. In Egypt, the *mamlūks*, warriors who combined skills of archers, heavy infantry, and heavy cavalry, also managed to resist the Mongols. After the Mongol Empire dissipated, the Ottoman Turks

Ten Military Innovations During the Middle Ages

Year	Innovation	Military Application
650	Greek fire	The Byzantines used this combustible liquid to attack ships and defend fortifications.
700's	Viking longboat	These boats allowed Norse raiders to strike anywhere on the European coastline.
900's	castles	From the simple motte and bailey to later concentric stone fortresses, these combinations of homes and fortifications defended Europeans and created social and political centers.
900's	couched-lance charge	A mass of charging mounted knights, secure in their saddles with stirrups and holding their lances tight under their arms, could deliver a decisive blow against opponents.
1050	crossbow	This easy-to-use missile weapon could puncture most armor.
1300	halberd	With this polearm combining axe, spear, and hook, infantry could defeat armored knights.
1320's	gunpowder weapons	Handguns and cannon eventually destroyed the effectiveness of cavalry and castles and allowed the development of large infantry armies.
1325	plate armor	This elaborate suit of articulated metal pieces protected a warrior from most weapons.
1330's	English longbow	By using concentrated volleys from archers, the dismounted English armies regularly defeated both the Scots and the French.
1420	*Wagenburg*/wagon-fortress	This mobile, armored gun-platform allowed the Hussites to defeat crusading armies.

seized the initiative, combining horse archers with heavy cavalry and infantry. In 1453, the Ottomans successfully crushed the Byzantine Empire and became a dominant power in the Balkans and the Middle East.

Islam

Part of the Turkish success derived from the religious fervor of Islam, to which the Turks had been converted in the tenth century. Founded in Arabia in the seventh century, Islam included the idea of *jihad*, or holy war. Inspired to conquer in the name of Allah, the heretofore militarily insignificant Arabs banded together and swept out of the Arabian Peninsula. Within a century, Arab armies had subjugated peoples in the Iberian Peninsula, across north Africa, throughout Mesopotamia, and deep across Asia into India. The Muslim armies almost destroyed the Byzantine Empire, which managed to defend itself only by reorganizing its own armies and employing *Greek fire*, an incendiary weapon. Although political divisions soon shattered the Arab empire, Islam later provided the motivation for many non-Arab conquerors to establish Muslim empires in places such as sub-Saharan Africa and India.

Early Medieval Europe: 500-900 c.e.

In the new kingdoms of Christian Europe, in which the bureaucracy of the Roman Empire collapsed after invasions by the Goths and Germans, societies became organized around war groups. A king as war-leader united the people as a whole, while alongside and under him served powerful lords supported by warriors in their households or retinues. Endemic petty warfare from feuds and the desire for power and plunder ravaged Europe for centuries. The aggressive campaigns of Charlemagne briefly succeeded in unifying much of Western Europe by 800. However, the quarrels of Charlemagne's successors and the raiding attacks of Vikings, Magyars, and Saracens shattered the empire and even broke down the central leadership of the king.

HIGH MEDIEVAL EUROPE: 900-1300

Europeans survived by building fortifications and by forming bands of heavy cavalry, soon called knights. On the defensive, the communal *burhs* (fortresses) were soon outmoded by residential forts, the *castles*. Castles allowed nobles to protect the local populace and thus establish dominion over a region. On the offensive, groups of mounted warriors, protected by *chain-mail armor* and often using the *couched-lance charge*, cleared Europe of foreign invaders.

The expense of building castles, raising horses, maintaining armor and weapons, and training for battle meant that the wealthy elites dominated warfare. In much of Europe, they reshaped government using their bonds of loyalty and military service with one another. Even though historians have exaggerated the pervasiveness of the so-called *feudal system*, knights did mold politics and society in their image. Their ideology was called *chivalry*, drawn from the French word for horse warrior. The aristocracy and nobility took up arms according to a code of honor immortalized by minstrels in courtly halls.

The realities of medieval warfare were more cruel than the romantic stories. Many medieval commanders, saddled with small, unreliable forces, avoided the risks of pitched battle. Because many military campaigns were waged over property, most military actions involved the raid or *chevauchée*: ravaging the enemy's undefended material and agricultural resources. Therefore, helpless populations repeatedly suffered plundering, arson, rape, slaughter, and famine. The logistic difficulty of marshaling large armies did prevent any one king from establishing an empire within Western Europe. Yet by 1050, the Europeans were strong enough to take the offensive against their non-Christian neighbors, especially using the religious calling of Crusades.

Although the knights dominated government and culture, other military forces, namely the artillery and infantry, never disappeared from the battlefield. Unlike samurai, western knights disdained the bow. Nonetheless, the value of long-range missile shot compelled many commanders to include archers among their troops. The *crossbow*, a specialty of *mercenaries*, became valued for its ability to pierce armor. The frequent *sieges* of castles and towns, the most common form of medieval military confrontation, also required specialized technicians for breaking castles and infantry to man the blockade or assault the walls.

LATE MEDIEVAL EUROPE: 1300-1500

The Hundred Years' War (1337-1457) saw both the culmination of medieval warfare and the beginning of its end. Notwithstanding the increasingly sophisticated *plate armor* that temporarily secured the superiority of the knight, foot soldiers and artillery ultimately triumphed. First, the *English longbow* archers, supported by dismounted knights, won key battles for the English. Then, *gunpowder weapons*, handguns, and cannons punctured armor and shattered castles. Finally, the Swiss perfected fighting with soldiers marching in formation carrying *pikes*, reminiscent of the Greek *phalanx* but now supported by swordsmen, archers, and increasingly, guns. The use of large armies of cheap infantry trained in pike and gun gradually ended the effectiveness of the mounted warrior everywhere.

RESOURCES

Bradbury, Jim. *The Medieval Siege*. Woodbridge, England: Boydell Press, 1992.
Castle. Documentary. PBS Home Video, 1983.
Contamine, Philippe. *War in the Middle Ages*. Oxford: Basil Blackwell, 1984.
Delbrück, Hans. *Medieval Warfare*. Lincoln: University of Nebraska Press, 1982.
DeVries, Kelly. *Medieval Military Technology*. Peterborough, Canada: Broadview Press, 1992.
Europe in the Middle Ages: The Feudal System. Documentary. Films for the Humanities & Sciences, 1989.
France, John. *Western Warfare in the Age of the Crusaders: 1000-1300*. Ithaca, N.Y.: Cornell University Press, 1999.
Holmes, Richard, ed. *The World Atlas of Warfare: Military Innovations That Changed the Course of History*. New York: Viking Studio Books, 1988.
Hooper, Nicholas, and Matthew Bennett. *Cam-

bridge Illustrated Atlas: Warfare: The Middle Ages: 768-1487. Cambridge, England: Cambridge University Press, 1996.

Hyland, Ann. *Warhorse, 1250-1600.* Stroud, England: Sutton, 1998.

Keen, Maurice, ed. *Medieval Warfare: A History.* New York: Oxford University Press, 1999.

Knights & Armor. Documentary. A&E Network, 1995.

Koch, H. W. *Medieval Warfare.* New York: Crescent Books, 1978.

The Middle Ages: Rise of Feudalism. Documentary. Britannica Films, 1966.

Oman, Sir Charles. *A History of the Art of War in the Middle Ages.* 2 vols. London: Greenhill Books, 1991.

Robards, Brooks. *The Medieval Knight at War.* London: Tiger Books International, 1997.

Verbruggen, J. F. *The Art of Warfare in Western Europe During the Middle Ages: From the Eighth Century to 1340.* Woodbridge, England: Boydell & Brewer, 1998.

The War Lord. Fiction feature. Universal Studios Home Video, 1965.

SEE ALSO: Ancient warfare; Byzantine Empire; Carolingian Empire; Crusades; Firearms; Hundred Years' War; Knights and chivalry; Mamlūks; Mongol Empire; Muslim Conquests; Ottoman Empire; Samurai; Sieges and siege weapons; Vikings.

Brian A. Pavlac

MEGIDDO, 1469 B.C.E.

TYPE OF ACTION: Ground battle in Thutmose III's first Asiatic campaign

DATE: April-October, 1469 B.C.E.

LOCATION: Megiddo, ancient Canaanite city in northern Palestine by the Kishon River on the southern edge of the Plain of Esdraelon (fifteen miles south of Haifa, Israel)

COMBATANTS: Egyptian expeditionary army vs. Syrian forces

PRINCIPAL COMMANDER: *Egyptian,* Thutmose III (d. 1450 B.C.E.)

RESULT: The Egyptians took Megiddo, setting the stage for Egypt's consolidation of the Syrian port cities

Tel Megiddo, the Old Testament's field of Armageddon (Har-Megiddo: The Mountain of Megiddo), was a critical defensive point for a confederation of Syrian nations that were trying to rebel against Egypt. The city of Megiddo was located at the end of the Aruna Pass between Mount Carmel and Har-Megiddo. The Aruna Pass was so narrow that the Egyptian forces would have to move through in single file before regrouping outside the city's gates. Any invasion of Syria would have to pass through either the Aruna Pass, a heavily guarded road that wound southward around Mount Carmel, or a wider northward pass that was also well guarded. Despite his lieutenants' fear of being easily trapped, Thutmose III chose to brave the Aruna Pass. This move caught the Syrians by surprise, dividing the defenders and allowing the Egyptians to re-form their lines around Megiddo. When the battle began the next morning, Thutmose quickly broke the Syrian lines and began a seven-month siege that starved Megiddo into surrender. From Megiddo, Thutmose's forces marched to the Lebanon Mountains, where the remaining Syrian resistors submitted to Egypt.

SIGNIFICANCE

This was the first recorded battle at the site historians believe has seen more battles than anywhere else on earth. Thutmose's records of the battle were inscribed on the walls of the Temple of Karnak, providing the first record of a military leader's role as a strategist. The victory over the Syrians also provided the Egyptians with a secure naval base for years.

RESOURCES

Breasted, James Henry. *Ancient Records of Egypt: Historical Documents from the Earliest Times to the Persian Conquest Collected, Edited, and Translated with Commentary.* London: Histories & Mysteries of Man, 1988.

Gabriel, Richard A. *Egypt, Megiddo: 1479* B.C. Carlisle Barracks, Pa.: Department of National Security and Strategy, U.S. Army War College, 1992.

SEE ALSO: Ancient warfare; Assyrian Empire; Egyptian Empire.

B. Keith Murphy

MEGIDDO, 1918

TYPE OF ACTION: Ground battle in World War I
DATE: September 20, 1918
LOCATION: Megiddo, fifteen miles south of Haifa, Israel
COMBATANTS: British vs. Turks and Germans
PRINCIPAL COMMANDERS: *British*, Lord Allenby (1861-1936); *German-Turkish*, Otto Liman von Sanders (1855-1929)
RESULT: Allenby's forces crushed the overwhelmed Turks and began the thirty-eight-day push to Aleppo, which resulted in the Armistice of Mudros

In 1918, the Turkish front stretched from Jordan westward to Jaffa. The original battle plan had called for Lord Allenby's Egyptian Expeditionary Force to cross the Jordan Valley, destroy the Turks' only supply line in the area, the Hejaz Railway, and follow the Mediterranean coastline to Beirut. Thanks, in part, to T. E. Lawrence's Arab forces' successful guerrilla raids on the railway, German Otto Liman von Sanders became convinced that the British assault would take place east of the Jordan river, and he placed the bulk of his Turkish defenses to the east of Allenby's forces.

Allenby instead attacked through Megiddo. On the morning of September 20, with a numerical superiority of nearly ten to one, Allenby's forces struck Megiddo, beginning with an infantry assault that cleared the way for a cavalry charge up the coastline. By the next morning, the entire Fourth Cavalry had reached the plains of Esdraelon. In the only significant skirmish, the Allied Second Lancers quickly routed the small Turkish advance guard; 46 Turks were killed and 470 captured compared with 1 Allied wounded.

Within thirty-six hours of launching the campaign, Allenby's forces had achieved their goal, routing the Turkish armies and seizing control of Palestine.

SIGNIFICANCE
In Allenby's own words, the battle resulted in the destruction of the enemy's army, the liberation of Palestine. It was the turning point in the war in the Middle East.

RESOURCES
Hughes, Matthew. *Allenby and British Strategy in the Middle East, 1917-1919*. London: F. Cass, 1999.
Savage, Raymond. *Allenby of Armageddon*. Indianapolis: Bobbs-Merrill, 1926.

SEE ALSO: Allenby, Lord; Lawrence, T. E.; World War I.

B. Keith Murphy

MEHMED II

ALSO KNOWN AS: Mehmet II, Mehmed Fatih, Muhammad II

Ottoman Turk Mehmed II stands in the shallow waters outside the besieged city of Constantinople. (Library of Congress)

Menelik II

BORN: March 30, 1432; Adrianople, Ottoman Empire (later Edirne, Turkey)
DIED: May 3, 1481; Hunkârçayiri, near Gebze, Ottoman Empire (later Turkey)
PRINCIPAL WARS: Byzantine-Ottoman Wars, Venetian War
PRINCIPAL BATTLES: Constantinople (1453), Belgrade (1456), Trebizond (1461), Bashkent (1473)
MILITARY SIGNIFICANCE: Ottoman ruler from 1451 to 1481, Mehmed conquered the historic city of Constantinople and built an Islamic empire encompassing Anatolia, the Crimea, and most of southeastern Europe.

When Mehmed II became Ottoman sultan in 1451, he resolved to become "a new Alexander, a new Caesar, a new Shah Cyrus." He began by capturing Constantinople (1453) in an epic firepower siege that finally extinguished the Byzantine Empire. Making Constantinople his new capital, Mehmed spent his life warring with his neighbors. Failing to wrest Belgrade (1456) from Hungary, he nonetheless occupied Athens, Serbia, Greece, and the Black Sea coast of Anatolia, including Trebizond (1461). In 1463, a grand alliance of Venice, Hungary, Albania, the Papacy, and Sultan Uzan Khan of Persia began sixteen years of war to contain Mehmed. However, the sultan won the Venetian War (1463-1479) and the Ottoman Empire took over Albania, Bosnia, Dalmatia, southern Romania, and the Crimean peninsula. In 1473, Mehmed defeated Sultan Uzan Khan at the Battle of Bashkent, thereby securing central Anatolia. A year before Mehmed's death in 1481, Ottoman forces landed on the heel of Italy and occupied Otranto, but the sultan died before he could march on Rome. Acknowledging his military achievements, Mehmed's contemporaries called him Fatih (conqueror).

Resources

Babinger, Franz. *Mehmed the Conqueror and His Time*. Princeton, N.J.: Princeton University Press, 1978.
Shaw, Stanford J. *History of the Ottoman Empire and Modern Turkey*. Vol. 1. Cambridge, England: Cambridge University Press, 1976.

SEE ALSO: Byzantine-Ottoman Wars; Constantinople, Siege of.

Weston F. Cook, Jr.

Menelik II

ALSO KNOWN AS: Sahle Mariam
BORN: August 17, 1844; Ankober, Shoa
DIED: December 12, 1913; Addis Ababa, Ethiopia
PRINCIPAL WAR: Italian-Ethiopian War
PRINCIPAL BATTLES: Amba Alagi (1895), Adowa (1896)
MILITARY SIGNIFICANCE: In 1896, Menelik defeated an Italian force of more than 20,000 at the Battle of Adowa. This victory effectively ended European colonial ambition in Ethiopia.

Menelik II rose to the center stage of Ethiopian politics in the 1870's. On the death of Emperor Yohannes IV in 1889, he assumed the Ethiopian throne. Menelik's attempts to foster Italian friendship culminated in the Treaty of Wichale (1889). Menelik sought Italian support to strengthen his hold over Ethiopia, while the Italians hoped to use Menelik to further their colonial ambitions in northeast Africa. Conflicting interests soon led to contradictory interpretations of the provisions of the treaty. The Italians claimed that Menelik had agreed to conduct his foreign relations through the agency of Italy, implying that Ethiopia had virtually become an Italian protectorate. Menelik fiercely opposed this interpretation and abrogated the entire treaty in 1893. He conducted a vigorous diplomatic campaign among European powers to show Ethiopia's determination to defend its sovereignty. Menelik's astute diplomacy won over Russia and kept France on Ethiopia's side long enough to allow him to import considerable arms.

Menelik rallied the nation behind him as no Ethiopian emperor had done in a long time. When Italy finally started its invasion in the fall of 1895, Menelik was able to march an army of 100,000 men to meet the Italian challenge. He first broke the southern defensive line of the Italians at Amba Alagi (1895). Then, on March 1, 1896, Menelik's army destroyed the Italian forces at the Battle of Adowa, thereby ensuring the survival of Ethiopian independence in the midst of the European powers' scramble for African territory. Having witnessed the humiliation of Italy, various European powers hastened to conclude treaties with Menelik recognizing the sovereignty of Ethiopia. After his victory over the Italians, Menelik focused on the expansion and centralization of the Ethiopian state.

RESOURCES
Caulk, Richard A. "Menelik II and the Diplomacy of Commerce: Prelude to an Imperial Foreign Policy." *Journal of Ethiopian Studies* 17 (1984).
Marcus, Harold G. *The Life and Times of Menelik II: Ethiopia, 1844-1944*. Oxford: Clarendon Press, 1975.
Rubenson, Sven. *The Survival of Ethiopian Independence*. London: Heinemann, 1976.

SEE ALSO: Adowa.

Shumet Sishagne

MERCENARIES

Soldiers "for hire" who are not part of a society's regular forces or even a member of that society for which they fight. Mercenaries have, in many respects, proved more effective than regular troops, for not only do they possess the advanced skills of a professional soldier, but they are also rarely moved by political sentiment. Without mercenaries, ancient Carthage could never have challenged Rome, nor could King Stephen of England (1135-1154) have warded off the Plantagenets for twenty years without his army of Flemish mercenaries. The era of true mercenaries had passed by the dawn of the nineteenth century, but they were briefly revived in 1960's, when many new African states employed them in the absence of native military organizations. Because the modern notion of national sovereignty precludes nonstate military activity, today's mercenaries are largely dependent on civilian security companies and drug cartels for their income.

Jeremiah Taylor

MEROË, KINGDOM OF

DATE: 750 B.C.E.-325 C.E.
LOCATION: Upper Nile, Sudan, Africa
PRINCIPAL MILITARY ACTIONS: Kushite-Egyptian Wars

MILITARY SIGNIFICANCE: Rise of the Kushite state and the conquest of Egypt.

Early Egyptian interactions with Nubia, or Kush (the Egyptian name for Nubia), involved trade. Nubia had established a flourishing trade with Egypt and the Horn of Africa. Egyptians, who had grown dependent on the gold, ivory, electrum, copper, ebony, leopard skins, and manpower made available by Kushite traders, knew the region of Kush as Ta-Seti, or the Land of the Bow. However, Egyptian unification (c. 3050 B.C.E.) brought raids and incursions into Nubia. Nubian middlemen were eventually eliminated as trading partners, and Egyptians constructed a series of massive forts along the Nubian portion of the Nile River.

Despite periodic alliances, Egyptians and Kushites often found themselves in conflict. In the Fourth Dynasty (2575-2465 B.C.E.), the Egyptian king Snefru led a successful campaign to crush the "rebels" of Nubia. During the reigns of Merenre and Pepi II in the Sixth Dynasty (2325-2155 B.C.E.), the Nubian chiefdoms of Irtjet, Zatju, and Wawat united under a single leader to resist the Egyptian colonization of Nubia. This fueled the consolidation of the first Kushite state at Kerma.

Many early sources, including the Bible, speak of the Kushites in terms of their military prowess, extensive trade contacts on the Red Sea, and role in serving the armies and pharaohs of Egypt. The Kushites fought or were called on to serve the armies of the Egyptians, Hyksos, Greeks, and Romans throughout the millennium before the common era and shortly thereafter. The superior skills of Kushite archers and the ferocity of Kushite warriors filled a critical need for kingdoms seeking mercenaries or allies. During the Sixth Dynasty of the Old Kingdom, the Egyptian pharaoh Pepi I advanced on Canaan in the company of a great army composed of both Egyptian soldiers and Kushite mercenaries drawn from among five different Nubian peoples.

In 732 B.C.E., Thebes sought the intervention of the Kushite king Piye or Piankhi (c. 753-713 B.C.E.) when threatened by the advance of the chiefdom of Saïs. Because of a period of political instability, Thebes became a protectorate of Piye, who established a military garrison in the area. During the

Travelers pass by partially ruined pyramids, remnants of the Kingdom of Meroë. (Library of Congress)

Saite advance, the Kushite king ordered his army to lift the Siege of Heracleopolis. A second force stopped the Saite advance in Middle Egypt, and Piye besieged the Saite coalition at Memphis. After a bloody battle, Piye emerged victorious and was crowned king of Upper and Lower Egypt. He unified Egypt and Nubia under Kushite rule, with the center of the new state at Napata. Political and cultural unification was sustained by Piye's Kushite successors, Shabako (713-698 B.C.E.), Shebitku (698-690 B.C.E.), Taharqa (690-664 B.C.E.), and Tanwetamani (664-663 B.C.E.), creating an unprecedented succession of sub-Saharan or black African kings as pharaohs of Egypt.

The Assyrian invasions of 663 B.C.E. forced the Kushites to withdraw from Egypt. By 200 B.C.E., the Kushites had moved their capital to Meroë, and their civilization endured at that site until 325 C.E. Egyptian influence on Kush and the Kingdom of Meroë survived in the form of palaces, pyramid-tombs, weapons, war chariots, obelisks, hieroglyphs, and temples dedicated to both Egyptian and Nubian gods. The Kingdom of Meroë developed its own writing system and pantheon of gods. The Kushites pioneered the use of elephants in warfare, an innovation that Hannibal later adopted for Roman warfare.

Resources

Africa: A History Denied. Documentary. Time-Life's Lost Civilizations, 1995.

Connah, G. *African Civilizations: Precolonial Cities and States in Tropical Africa.* Cambridge, England: Cambridge University Press, 1987.

O'Connor, D. *Nubia: Egypt's Rival in Africa.* Philadelphia, Pa.: University Museum Press, 1993.

Phillipson, D. *African Archaeology.* Cambridge, England: Cambridge University Press, 1992.

Vogel, J., ed. *Encyclopedia of Precolonial Africa: Archaeology, History, Languages, Cultures, and Environments.* Walnut Creek, Calif.: Altamira Press, 1997.

SEE ALSO: Egyptian Empire.

Ruben G. Mendoza

Messenian Wars

AT ISSUE: Spartan control of the southern Peloponnese
DATE: c. 736-455 B.C.E.
LOCATION: Southern Peloponnese (Greece)
COMBATANTS: Spartans vs. Messenians
PRINCIPAL BATTLES: Great Trench, Ithome
RESULT: Spartan victory; reduction of Messenians

to state slaves (helots) of Sparta and partition of Messenia into plots of land assigned to individual Spartan citizens

Background

The Messenian Wars were the result of Spartan expansion in the southern Peloponnese. Both the Messenians and Spartans were Dorians, a tribe of Greeks who supposedly settled in the Peloponnese during the Dorian Invasion of the eleventh and tenth centuries B.C.E. One group of Dorians settled at Sparta in Laconia, a fertile district in the central and eastern parts of the southern Peloponnese. Another occupied Messenia, the region immediately to the west of Laconia and separated from it by Mount Taygetus.

In the course of the ninth century B.C.E., the inhabitants of Sparta conquered all Laconia. They made some of the local population helots, state slaves who worked the land for the Spartans. Others became perioeci. Perioeci were free, lived in their own communities, and had some local autonomy. However, they were politically subject to Sparta and were required to serve in the Spartan army.

Action

The Messenian Wars began when Sparta turned its attention from Laconia to the fertile plains of Messenia. The details and dates of the early wars are shrouded in myth and legend, but later Spartan tradition told of two wars fought in the eighth and seventh centuries B.C.E. The First Messenian War broke out around 736 B.C.E. and lasted for twenty years. The Spartans invaded Messenia and took control of its central plain. Some Messenians sought refuge on Mount Ithome, a mountain in the center of Messenia, but after a long siege, they were forced to capitulate. A few Messenians escaped and settled in Sicily and southern Italy, but most were reduced to helot status. The Spartans divided the conquered portions of Messenia into plots of land that were assigned to individual Spartans. Helots farmed these plots and surrendered as much as half of their produce to their Spartan masters.

The Messenians revolted against the Spartans in the middle of the seventh century B.C.E. in the Second Messenian War. Its dates are uncertain, but the revolt may have been precipitated by a defeat of the Spartans by the Argives at Hysiae (669 B.C.E.). The Second Messenian War was among the first in which hoplite tactics were used, and the Spartans fared poorly at first, as the Messenians received assistance from the Arcadians and Argives, both longstanding enemies of Sparta. However, the Spartans rallied and at the Battle of the **Great Trench** (date and location unknown), they defeated the Messenians. The Messenians fled to Mount Ira in the northern part of Messenia but were again besieged and overcome. By 600 B.C.E., all Messenia was under Spartan control. The inhabitants of a few Messenian communities enjoyed status as perioeci, but the vast majority lived as helots.

Although the details of the first two Messenian Wars are unclear, the conquest of Messenia had a profound impact on Spartan life. Control of Messenia made Sparta a wealthy state, and it freed the Spartans from having to work their land themselves. However, the Messenian helots were numerically superior to the Spartans, and the Spartans lived in constant fear of a helot revolt. Spartan life became even more militaristic to meet this threat. Spartan men began military training at age seven, and they served on active duty from the age of twenty to sixty. Each year, the Spartans declared war on the helots, and young Spartan men served in the Krypteia, a secret police force that traveled through the countryside and murdered potentially dangerous helots. Thus, the Spartans lived in a state of constant military readiness designed to suppress the helots. This lifestyle had the additional effect of turning the Spartans into the best and most feared warriors of the Greek world.

The philosopher Plato mentions a Messenian revolt that occurred about 490 B.C.E., but nothing more is known of it. More significant was the Third Messenian War. Around 465 B.C.E., a great earthquake struck Sparta and inflicted heavy casualties. The Messenian helots seized the opportunity to revolt and again took refuge on Mount **Ithome**. Because the Spartans were not adept at siege warfare, they summoned their allies to assist them. These included the Athenians, who under the general Cimon came to Sparta's aid with a force of 4,000 hoplites (462 B.C.E.). However, the Spartans grew suspicious of the Athenians and sent them back home. This insult caused a break in relations between Athens and Sparta and contributed to the outbreak of the First Peloponnesian War (460-446 B.C.E.). The Messenians on Mount Ithome finally came to terms with the Spartans around 455 B.C.E. They were given safe passage out of Messenia and were settled by the Athenians at Naupactus on the north coast of the Corinthian gulf.

AFTERMATH

Although unrest among the Messenian helots continued throughout the fifth and fourth centuries B.C.E., Messenia remained securely in Spartan hands until the middle of the fourth century B.C.E. After defeating the Spartans at Leuctra (371 B.C.E.), the Theban general Epaminondas led an army into Messenia, freed the helots, and founded a new state with a capital at Messene (369 B.C.E.). Although the Spartans never recognized Messenian independence, they were never able to reconquer the lost territory. Without the support of the Messenian helots, Sparta quickly sank to the level of a second-rate military power in the Greek world.

RESOURCES

Cartledge, Paul. *Sparta and Laconia: A Regional History.* London: Routledge, 1979.

Forrest, W. G. *A History of Sparta, 950-192 B.C.* 2d ed. London: Duckworth, 1980.

Parker, Victor. "The Dates of the Messenian Wars." *Chiron* 21 (1991): 25-47.

SEE ALSO: Cimon; Dorian Invasion of Greece; Leuctra; Peloponnesian Wars; Spartan Empire.

James P. Sickinger

METZ, SIEGE OF, 1552-1553

TYPE OF ACTION: Siege in the Valois-Habsburg War
DATE: October 14, 1552-January 1, 1553
LOCATION: Metz in northern Lorraine (northeastern France)
COMBATANTS: 45,000 Imperialists (Habsburgs) vs. 6,000 French (Valois)
PRINCIPAL COMMANDERS: *Imperialist*, Charles V (1500-1558); *French*, Duke Francis of Guise (1519-1563)
RESULT: French held Metz

On October 14, 1552, the first units of Charles V's army reached Metz and began to establish siege lines. The French had captured Metz the previous April, and Henry II, expecting an imperial counterattack, had placed Duke Francis of Guise in command. Guise had energetically rebuilt the fortifications and strengthened the garrison, making Metz a formidable stronghold. Full-scale battering of the walls began only after Charles arrived on November 20. The attack concentrated on the south side of the city because the other three sides were well protected by rivers. On November 28, after being hammered by forty great guns, part of the wall collapsed, but the imperial assault was stopped by an eight-foot-high earthen wall, referred to as a double Pisan rampart, erected behind the curtain wall. The same device prevented a second breach from being exploited. Aided by the coldest and wettest weather in memory, the French held out until Charles admitted defeat and retreated from Metz on January 1. He lost as many as 20,000 men to the fighting and disease. The French lost about 500.

SIGNIFICANCE

With their successful defense of Metz, the French had irrevocable control of the three bishoprics of Lorraine, giving them a foothold in the duchy that they would exploit to its complete takeover in the early eighteenth century.

RESOURCES

Baumgartner, Frederic. *Henry II King of France.* 1988. Reprint. Durham, N.C.: Duke University Press, 1996.

Duffy, Christopher. *Siege Warfare: The Fortress in the Early Modern World 1494-1660.* New York: Routledge, 1979.

Knecht, R. J. *French Renaissance Monarchy: Francis I and Henry II.* New York: Longman, 1996.

SEE ALSO: Cerisolles; Charles V; Gravelines; Italian Wars; Pavia; Saint-Quentin; Sieges and siege weapons; Valois-Habsburg War.

Frederic J. Baumgartner

METZ, SIEGE OF, 1870

TYPE OF ACTION: Siege in Franco-Prussian War
DATE: August 18-October 29, 1870
LOCATION: Metz, France

COMBATANTS: French vs. Prussians
PRINCIPAL COMMANDERS: *French*, Achille-François Bazaine (1811-1888); *Prussian*, Prince Friedrich Karl (1828-1885)
RESULT: The surrender of the French Army of the Rhine at Metz marked the end of the frontline armies that France could field against Prussia during the war

Metz was a major fortress in Lorraine, northeastern France, about 175 miles east of Paris. It guarded the approaches from southern Germany. After severe fighting, General Achille-François Bazaine fell back on Metz and, on August 18, pulled his army, numbering about 154,000 men, back into the fortress.

The Prussians, under Prince Friedrich Karl, besieged Metz on August 19 with approximately 168,000 men. One of France's two frontline armies was now bottled up and consequently no longer capable of mobile operations. The second army, the Army of Châlons, would soon suffer defeat at Sedan. Bazaine, whose lack of decisiveness proved to be a major handicap for the French, ordered and subsequently cancelled a breakout on August 26. On August 31, French troops made a half-hearted attempt to sortie from the fortress to join the rest of the French army, but the Prussians easily drove them back. On October 7, a raid for supplies, which Bazaine had originally conceived as another breakout attempt, failed to achieve its objective. The fortress, running out of food supplies, surrendered on October 29.

SIGNIFICANCE
The French Army of the Rhine was captured.

RESOURCES
Hogg, Ian V. *Battles: A Concise Dictionary*. New York: Harcourt Brace, 1995.
Horne, Alistair. *The Fall of Paris: The Siege and the Commune 1870-1871*. New York: Doubleday, 1965.
Howard, Michael. *The Franco-Prussian War*. New York: Dorset Press, 1961.

SEE ALSO: German Wars of Unification; Sieges and siege weapons.

Oliver Griffin

MEUSE-ARGONNE

TYPE OF ACTION: Ground battle in World War I
DATE: September 26-November 11, 1918
LOCATION: Northeastern France in the Argonne Forest west of Meuse River
COMBATANTS: Americans vs. Germans
PRINCIPAL COMMANDERS: *American*, General John J. Pershing (1860-1948); *German*, Max von Gallwitz (1852-1932), Crown Prince Wilhelm (1882-1951)
RESULT: Argonne Forest essentially cleared of German military forces

The 1918 Meuse-Argonne offensive was part of a large Allied counteroffensive to break the German defenses and bring the war to a close. The American First Army under General John J. Pershing was to spearhead the offensive west of the Meuse River through the heavily fortified Argonne Forest. The relatively inexperienced U.S. troops began the offensive on September 26 but after two days of fighting were unable to reach the main German defenses. Undaunted, Pershing called for reserves and ordered additional attacks through October.

The Germans, under Max von Gallwitz and Crown Prince Wilhelm, stubbornly defended their positions, and the battle evolved into the same sort of trench warfare that had marked the war since 1914. During the battle, the First Battalion of the Seventy-seventh Division, under the command of Lieutenant Colonel Charles Whittlesey, was trapped for five days several miles beyond the German lines, earning itself the title of the "Lost Battalion." By the time relief troops broke through to free the battalion, its casualties had mounted to 406 of its original 600 troops. Also during the battle, Sergeant Alvin York, a Tennessee sharpshooter, picked off fifteen German soldiers and with his patrol took a total of 132 prisoners, making him a lasting hero in U.S. military history. By October 10, the Argonne Forest was cleared of Germans, though some held out on fortified hills between the forest and the west bank of the Meuse until November 6, when the Americans reached the Meuse. Americans marched on Sedan, which was taken by the French, and hostilities continued through November 10.

SIGNIFICANCE

The Meuse-Argonne illustrated graphically to both the Allied and the German leaders that the fresh U.S. troops arriving in France by the hundreds of thousands were willing and capable of holding their own and more in World War I and that their numbers would ultimately enable the Allies to win the war.

RESOURCES

Braim, Paul F. *The Test of Battle: The American Expeditionary Forces in the Meuse-Argonne Campaign.* 2d ed. Shippensburg, Pa.: White Mane Books, 1998.

Matloff, Maurice, ed. *American Military History.* Washington, D.C.: Center of Military History, United States Army, 1985.

Millett, Allan R., and Peter Maslowski. *For the Common Defense.* New York: Free Press, 1984.

Triplet, William S. *A Youth in the Meuse-Argonne: A Memoir of World War I, 1917-1918.* Columbia: University of Missouri Press, 2000.

SEE ALSO: Pershing, John J.; World War I.

Wilton Eckley

MEXICAN-AMERICAN WAR

AT ISSUE: The establishment of a permanent border between Mexico and the United States
DATE: May 6, 1846-February 2, 1848
LOCATION: Mexico, Texas, New Mexico, California
COMBATANTS: Americans vs. Mexicans
PRINCIPAL COMMANDERS: *American*, Zachary Taylor (1784-1850), Winfield Scott (1786-1866), Stephen W. Kearny (1794-1848); *Mexican*, Antonio López de Santa Anna (1794-1876), Mariano Arista (1802-1855), Pedro de Ampudia
PRINCIPAL BATTLES: Palo Alto, Monterrey, Buena Vista, Cerro Gordo, Chapultepec
RESULT: Treaty of Guadalupe Hidalgo established the permanent border between the United States and Mexico

BACKGROUND

The United States, by the middle of the nineteenth century, had expanded its western frontier to the Mississippi River through purchases of territory from France and Spain. Many Americans, however, felt that the country had a manifest destiny to expand its horizons across the continent to the Pacific Ocean. Standing in the way of such an expansion was the even younger republic, the United Mexican States, which had achieved its independence from Spain in 1823.

At the invitation of the Mexican government, a substantial number of U.S. citizens had moved into Texas, setting up towns and ranches, often accompanied by their African slaves. In 1836, these Texan immigrants rebelled against their Mexican overlords. After defeats at the Alamo and Goliad, the Americans, under General Sam Houston, defeated the Mexican army of Antonio López de Santa Anna at San Jacinto, captured the Mexican leader following the battle, and forced him to acquiesce to their independence. However, they failed to establish a clear line of demarcation between Mexico and the new Texas Republic.

The U.S. government acceded to the wishes of the Texans and annexed their republic in 1845. The U.S. Congress declared Texas the twenty-eighth state in the Union on December 22, 1845. The Mexican government and people reacted negatively. Because General Santa Anna's actions had been forced by the Texans, the Mexican government never officially recognized Texas as independent. The Mexicans were even more reluctant to accept Texas's incorporation into the United States.

President James K. Polk sought to solve the border problem and the acquisition of Texas by seeking to buy all the lands claimed by Mexico between the United States and the Pacific Ocean. He sent an emissary, John Slidell, to Mexico to negotiate with the government. The Mexican state had been politically chaotic since achieving its independence from Spain. General Mariano Paredes y Arrillaga, a fervent nationalist, refused to even receive the U.S. envoy. Thus the stage was set for a confrontation between the two countries.

ACTION

President Polk struck first. He ordered General Zachary Taylor to lead an army into the disputed territory and take a stand at the Rio Grande, the southernmost point in the land claimed by the Americans. Mexican General Mariano Arista,

Battle Sites in the Mexican-American War

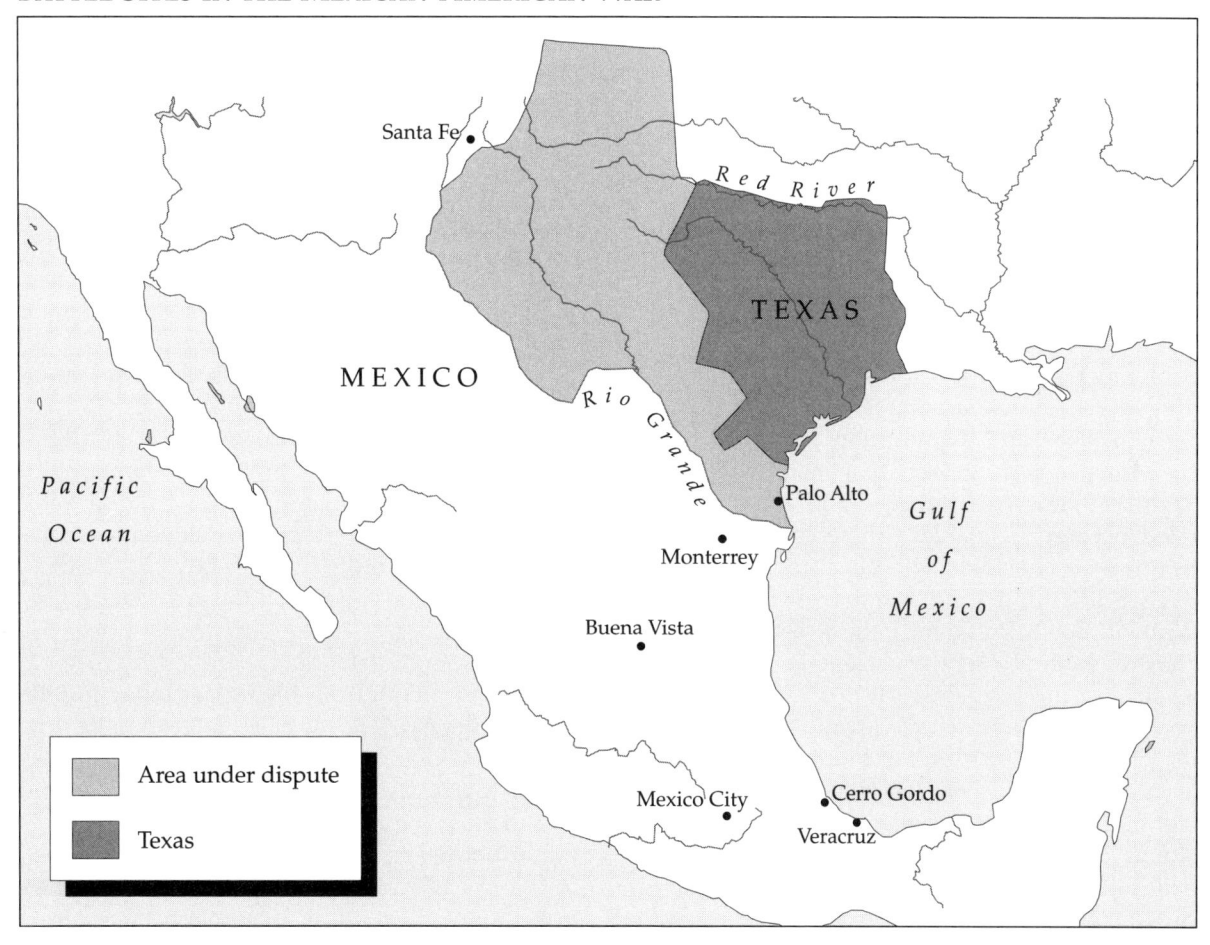

Map showing battle sites including Santa Fe, Palo Alto, Monterrey, Buena Vista, Mexico City, Cerro Gordo, and Veracruz. Legend: Area under dispute; Texas.

commander of the Mexican troops at Matamoros, received his orders from Mexico City to attack the U.S. Army. On paper, the odds favored the Mexicans, who outnumbered the Americans, 3,700 men to 2,290. However, the Mexicans lacked modern artillery and were using ordinance that still shot cannonballs. The Americans, who had cannons of a much greater range, could fire explosive shells into the ranks of the Mexican infantry at little risk to themselves. This difference in weaponry, together with the fact that the Mexican army consisted of ill-equipped, ill-fed and poorly led draftees, led to convincing victories for the Americans under Taylor at **Palo Alto** (May 8, 1846) and the battles in Texas and northern Mexico that followed. In the Palo Alto battle, Taylor sustained only 9 killed, 44 wounded, and 2 missing. The Mexican forces at Palo Alto, and at the Resaca de la Palma battle (May 9) that followed shortly thereafter, lost more than 1,000 men, hundreds of prisoners, and huge quantities of war equipment and supplies.

Mexican General Pedro de Ampudia had a force of approximately 10,000 troops to defend the major Mexican stronghold of **Monterrey** (September 20-24, 1846). The defenders manned a stone fortress known as the Black Fort, containing 400 defenders and a dozen guns, some of them eighteen pounders. They awaited Taylor's attack on September 21, 1846. Taylor saw the city's western defenses as the Mexican weak spot and sent 2,000 men under General William Worth on a detour around those points. When the Mexican cavalry rushed to attack the Americans, the U.S. artillery opened up, sending the Mexican horsemen back in disorder. Worth then cut off any supplies to the beleaguered city from the south. However, Mexican defenses within the city itself proved to be formidable. They poured heavy fire on the Americans from the windows of the city's buildings. Taylor lost more than 400 men during a direct frontal assault on the city's eastern positions. The next day, Worth, continuing his attack on the western sector, had more success. He took the major strongpoints there, turned captured guns on the retreating Mexicans, and took the pressure off Taylor's troops in the east. The Americans advanced into the city, taking it street by street. On September 25, the Mexicans surrendered the city and marched out, leaving behind virtually all their artillery and ammunition as agreed to in the terms signed by Mexican general Ampudia. Taylor's total casualties, dead and wounded, totaled 453 men. Casualties suffered by Ampudia's troops were considerably higher.

In addition to the armies of Taylor and Winfield Scott, President Polk directed those of General John E. Wool and General Stephen W. Kearny to move against Mexico. General Wool and his army had orders to invade Mexico's center and join Taylor's force at **Buena Vista** (February 22-23, 1847), where the two combined to defeat the self-styled "Napoleon of the West," Santa Anna. The Mexican general had returned from exile following his loss of Texas some eleven years previously. Although the Mexican army acquitted itself well in this critical confrontation and appeared to be winning the battle, Santa Anna chose to retreat toward the capital rather than continue his engagement with Taylor.

Polk ordered General Kearny to lead a force into New Mexico and ultimately to California to secure these Mexican outposts. Polk also expected Commodore John D. Sloat to support Kearny's army by seizing California ports with Sloat's Naval Pacific Squadron. First General Kearny marched nearly nine hundred miles from Fort Leavenworth, Kansas, and occupied Santa Fe without firing a shot. Once the U.S. flag flew over New Mexico, Kearny prepared to move farther west to the Pacific Coast. At the same time, Brevet Captain John C. Frémont marched into Northern California, at Sacramento. This invasion proved premature, for when Frémont discovered that Mexican general José Castro proposed to block his entry into California's settled coastal area, he broke camp and retreated to Oregon.

Meanwhile, Kearney had entered Southern California, and after some difficult negotiations and with the aid of the naval forces, he managed to secure control of the state through a treaty with the resident Californios, who did not identify with the government in Mexico City. Despite some sporadic skirmishing with the locals in the takeover, Kearney managed to secure California for the United States with little loss to the men under him. Frémont agreed to accept Kearny's authority as well, thus ending his independent effort.

While the Mexicans had attempted to defend themselves from Taylor's army in the north, other U.S. forces under General Scott landed at Veracruz (1847). The Americans experienced only minor opposition before the port city surrendered. Scott then began the march toward Mexico City itself.

The Mexican defenders were led by General Santa Anna, fresh from his retreat following the battle at Buena Vista. He had a force of more than 20,000 men, double that of Scott's. The two armies met at **Cerro Gordo** on April 18, 1847. Captain Robert E. Lee found a path around Santa Anna's flank that led to a quick defeat of the Mexican forces. The Mexican general left the battlefield so precipitously that all his personal possessions—his silverware, official papers, money, even his dinner—fell into the hands of the Americans. Puebla, at that time Mexico's second city, surrendered without a fight on May 15. The U.S. forces were only one hundred miles from the capital.

Santa Anna fell back to prepared positions around Mexico City itself. Again he failed to anticipate the moves of his opposition, and one of his commanders allowed himself to be surrounded. At the Battle of Contreras on August 20, American forces, led by Scott, inflicted a crushing defeat on the Mexican army. The Americans suffered only a few casualties, and the Mexicans lost 700 men and their best cannons. Also on August 20, at almost the same time, American forces attacked Churubusco. Scott's forces also attacked at Molino del Rey (September 8). Scott's desire to keep the pressure on a disorganized enemy cost him many casualties. At Churubusco alone, the Americans lost 137 killed, 879 wounded, and 40 missing in action. This list contained the worst casualties sustained by the invaders up to that time. Mexican losses were estimated at more than 2,000.

During the Churubusco battle, the Americans captured a group of Irish deserters from the U.S. Army who had switched allegiance to the Mexicans. Called the St. Patrick's Battalion, the captured Irish received harsh treatment at the hands of the Americans. Most were later executed by the U.S. Army while the U.S. flag was raised over Chapultepec Castle.

The culminating battle of the Mexico City campaign centered on the storming of **Chapultepec** Castle on September 13, 1847. Among the defenders was a group of Mexican cadets, many of them little more than children, who tried to fight off the Americans. Several threw themselves off the battlements wrapped in Mexican flags rather than surrender to the invaders. They are known in Mexico as "los niños héroes"—the child heros. Shortly after the castle fell, Mexican resistance in the capital for all intents and purposes ceased. Scott's troops occupied Mexico City on September 14, 1847. The United States had won the war.

Aftermath

Faced with U.S. occupation of its capital city as well as a number of states along its northern border, the Mexican government was forced to sue for peace. In the treaty, signed at the Villa de Guadalupe in the small village of Guadalupe Hidalgo on February 2, 1848, the Mexican government ceded Texas, New Mexico, Arizona, and California to the United States in exchange for $15 million. The Rio Grande became the boundary between the two countries. The border line extended to the Pacific Ocean, ending approximately fifteen miles below the city of San Diego.

General Santa Anna died impoverished in his native state of Veracruz. General Taylor won election to the presidency of the United States in 1848, only to die in 1850 a few months after taking office. General Scott ran for president in 1852 but was defeated by another Mexican-American War hero, General Franklin Pierce.

Resources

Bauer, Karl Jack. *The Mexican War, 1846-1848*. New York: Macmillan, 1974.

Dufour, Charles L. *The Mexican War: A Compact History, 1846-1848*. New York: Hawthorne Books, 1968.

Eisenhower, John S. D. *So Far from God: The U.S. War with Mexico 1846-1848*. New York: Random House, 1989.

Griswold Del Castillo, Richard. *The Treaty of Guadalupe Hidalgo: A Legacy of Conflict*. Norman: University of Oklahoma Press, 1990.

Miller, Robert Ryal. *Shamrock and Sword, The Saint Patrick's Battalion in the U.S.-Mexican War*. Norman: University of Oklahoma Press, 1989.

See also: Buena Vista; Chapultepec; Kearney, Stephen W.; Monterrey; Perry, Matthew C.; Santa Anna, Antonio López de; Scott, Winfield; Taylor, Zachary.

Carl Henry Marcoux

Mexican Civil Wars

At issue: Preservation of liberal rule and Mexican sovereignty
Date: 1854-1876
Location: Mexico
Combatants: Liberals vs. conservatives and the French; liberals vs. liberals
Principal commanders: *Liberal generals*, Ignacio Comonfort (1812-1863), Ignacio Zaragoza, Porfirio Díaz (1830-1915); *Conservative generals*, Félix Zuloaga (1814-1876), Miguel Miramón (1832-1867), Tomás Mejía; *French generals*, Charles Ferdinand Latrille, comte de Lorencez, Élie-Frédéric Forey (1804-1872), Achille-François Bazaine (1811-1888)
Principal battles: Coquillo, Peregrino, Salamanca, Guadalajara, San Luis Potosí, Veracruz, Estancia de las Vacas, Silao, Siege of Guadalajara, Calpulalpan, Puebla, Querétaro, Tecoac
Result: Beginning of Mexico's thirty-five-year rule by Díaz, a period of peace, progress, and repression known as the Porfiriato (1876-1911)

Background

After losing their northern provinces to the United States in the Mexican-American War (1846-1848), Mexicans were demoralized. Some wanted annexation to the United States; others wanted a monarch. What they got was Antonio López de Santa Anna, recalled from exile as the only man who could unite Mexico. Assuming the title Most Serene Highness, Santa Anna imposed a dictatorship, exiling Benito Juárez and other liberal leaders. To support his extravagant regime, he raised taxes, sold Mayan prisoners into slavery in Cuba, and transferred territory to the United States for ten million dollars (Gadsden Purchase).

ACTION

On March 1, 1854, Juan Álvarez and protegé Ignacio Comonfort issued the Plan de Ayutla, calling for Santa Anna's removal and a constitutional congress. The Ayutla movement spread quickly, but military operations were confined to Álvarez's southern base, where his peasant army lost at **Coquillo** (1854) and **Peregrino** (1854) and elsewhere. When Santa Anna resigned in August, 1855, it was because he could not pay his troops. Elected president at the Cuernavaca Convention, Álvarez assembled a cabinet of talented liberals with Juárez as minister of justice and Miguel Lerdo de Tejada at treasury. He then retired. Comonfort, the new president, ruled by decree, promulgating the "Ley Juárez" abolishing military and ecclesiastical *fueros* (special privileges), "Ley Lerdo" mandating privatization of corporate church and village lands, and "Ley Iglesias" regulating church fees.

The 1857 constitution abolished slavery; guaranteed freedom of expression, assembly, and the press; and ratified the earlier anticlerical laws. When conservatives raised the old banners of *religión y fueros*, Comonfort resigned in favor of General Félix Zuloaga, the conservative commander of Mexico City's garrison. Zuloaga dismissed congress, abolished the constitution, and tried to arrest Juárez, who, as chief justice, should have succeeded to the presidency. Juárez fled and settled his liberal government at Veracruz, with its access to port customs revenues and arms shipments. Conservatives consolidated their hold on central Mexico with victories by Miguel Miramón and Tomás Mejía at **Salamanca** (March 10, 1858) and by Miramón and Luis Osollo at **Guadalajara** (March 23) and **San Luis Potosí** (April 17). Cities traded hands. Miramón took Zacatecas on April 10, and seventeen days later, the liberals recovered it. Tampico fell on May 14 to the conservative Indian general Mejía, then to the liberals three months later. However, liberal control of the coasts could not be broken. Miramón's siege of **Veracruz** (February-March, 1860) failed when U.S. naval vessels prevented the conservatives' blockade of the port with warships purchased from Cuba. After Miramón became president, the conservative cause hit its peak, ending with his defeat of Santos Degollado's peasant army at **Estancia de las Vacas** (November 13, 1860). In 1861, liberals regained the near northern cities with Ignacio Zaragoza's victory over Miramón at **Silao** (August 10, 1861) and their successful **Siege of Guadalajara** (September 26-November 3). Liberal armies routed Miramón at **Calpulalpan** (December 22) near Mexico City and took the capital.

The goal of Emperor Napoleon III's invasion of Mexico was to install Austrian Hapsburg archduke Maximilian as a barrier to incipient Anglo hemispheric hegemony. His excuse was Juárez's suspension of debt payments to France, Spain, and Great Britain. In January, 1862, Mexico's creditors dispatched a combined war fleet to Veracruz to collect, but Spain and Britain withdrew when the French commander, Charles Ferdinand Latrille, comte de Lorencez, deployed Zouave troops inland. Lorencez moved on Puebla, which was defended by Zaragoza's army. After a heavy bombardment, the Zouaves were turned back, retreating in a blinding rainstorm before the cavalry of Porfirio Díaz. It was the Fifth of May, 1862—Cinco de Mayo. Lorencez requested more troops, and Napoleon sent thirty thousand reinforcements under general Élie-Frédéric Forey, who took command of the French forces. In March, 1863, Forey lay siege to **Puebla**, which fell after sixty-two days. On June 10, the French took Mexico City, and again Juárez presided over a liberal government on the run. However, by the time Maximilian arrived in April of 1864, French forces, then commanded by Achille-François Bazaine, were stretched thin. With the end of the American Civil War, the United States put diplomatic and military pressure on Napoleon. Knowing the war had to be concluded quickly, frustrated by guerrilla war in the north, and harassed by Díaz's Army of the East in the south, Bazaine pressured Maximilian into signing a decree allowing the execution of any Mexican taken under arms. In the spring of 1866, a republican offensive gave them control in the north, while Díaz secured Oaxaca in the south. In March, 1867, Napoleon withdrew his last troops, and Díaz took Puebla and Mexico City. Maximilian was captured at **Querétaro** after a three-month siege, then was tried and shot with Miramón and Mejía on the Hill of Bells (June 19).

AFTERMATH

Permitted a technically unconstitutional third term by a grateful nation, Juárez began a liberal state-building project characterized by close cooperation with the United States. In 1871, Juárez ran again, and Díaz initiated his Noría Rebellion, invoking the constitutional principle of no reelection. When Juárez died of a heart attack, Díaz accepted amnesty from Chief Justice Sebastián Lerdo (brother of the author of Ley Lerdo), who served out the presidential term. When Lerdo announced for president again, Díaz launched his Tuxtepec Rebellion, which, after an uncertain start, triumphed at **Tecoac** (November 16, 1876). Except for the interregnum of Manuel González (1880-1884), Díaz would rule until 1911.

RESOURCES

Fehrenbach, T. R. *Fire and Blood: A History of Mexico*. New York: Da Capo Press, 1995.

Werner, Michael S., ed. *Encyclopedia of Mexico: History Society and Culture*. Chicago: Fitzroy Dearborn, 1997.

SEE ALSO: Latin American Wars of Independence; Mexican-American War; Mexican Revolution; Mexican Wars of Independence; Santa Anna, Antonio López de; South American Wars of Independence.

William Schell, Jr.

MEXICAN REVOLUTION

AT ISSUE: Control of the Mexican state
DATE: 1910-1920
LOCATION: Mexico and U.S.-Mexican borderlands
COMBATANTS: Mexican government vs. various rebels
PRINCIPAL COMMANDERS: *Mexican government*, Porfirio Díaz (1830-1915); *Mexican rebels*, Francisco Madero (1873-1913), Emiliano Zapata (1879-1919), Pascual Orozco, Victoriano Huerta (1854-1916), Venustiano Carranza (1859-1920), Pancho Villa (1878-1923), Álvervo Obregón (1880-1928); *United States*, General John J. Pershing (1860-1948)
PRINCIPAL BATTLES: Ciudad Juárez, La Decena Trágica, Veracruz, Torreón, Zacatecas, Guadalajara, Querétaro, Celaya, León, Agua Prieta, Columbus, Carrizal
RESULT: The creation of a stable, flexible, one-party state

BACKGROUND

The Mexican Revolution resulted primarily from the inability of President Porfirio Díaz to transfer power smoothly to a successor. The period known as the Porfiriato (1876-1911) began with such transfers. Díaz, who himself had revolted under the constitutional banner of no reelection, surrendered office to his elected successor and friend, Manuel González (1880-1884), who returned it to him by election. The constitution was then changed to permit reelection, and Díaz ruled as a republican monarch. He used North American capital to make Mexico an economic miracle of the late nineteenth century and used the opportunities it created to conciliate diverse regional strongmen (*caciques*) and their factions (*camarillas*). Díaz was advised by technocrats known as the *científicos*, who, in the regime's last years, favored European capital over American, particularly in the petroleum industry. In 1904, *científicos* led by Finance Minister José Limantour forced the aging Díaz to allow the creation of a vice presidency to clarify the succession. Social unrest by peasants deprived of land by modernization grew, as did political unrest by radical liberals upset both by Díaz's reconciliation with the Catholic Church and by his perpetuation in office. In 1908, pressured by the U.S. government and his own advisers, Díaz stated that he would not be president again and encouraged formation of an "opposition party"—by which he meant a Catholic party. Economic recession that year worried advisers, who convinced Díaz to remain in office; however, in the brief democratic flurry, Francisco Madero, scion of one of Mexico's wealthiest families, declared for the 1910 election, taking Díaz's old slogan of "no reelection." When

Madero's crowds grew large, Díaz imprisoned him until the election was over. Released on bail, Madero slipped across the border into Texas and began his revolution.

ACTION

In Texas, backed financially by Standard Oil and tacitly by the United States, Madero issued his Plan de San Luis Potosí, calling for an uprising against Díaz and political reform. However, many, including Pascual Orozco in Chihuahua and Emiliano Zapata in Morelos, joined to redress social and economic injustices inflicted by local *caciques*. In fact, Madero's movement was united only in its opposition to Díaz. The insurgents made no military progress, but the Mexican army could not put down their revolt. It was obvious, however, that Díaz had to go, so Limantour opened secret talks with Madero's representatives in New York. The unauthorized attack by Orozco's forces on **Ciudad Juárez** (May 8-10, 1911) forced the issue, and Díaz resigned on May 25. Madero, elected president in October, was unwilling to satisfy demands for reform or rewards, so Zapata declared against him in November, followed by Orozco in March, 1912. As the situation deteriorated, a military plot coalesced.

On February 9, 1913, army generals marched on the National Palace, where loyal troops opened fire, forcing the generals' withdrawal to the Ciudadela arsenal. This began a period of fighting in Mexico City known as **La Decena Trágica** (Ten Tragic Days). Without the United States government's knowledge, ambassador Henry Lane Wilson brought the plotters together in the Pact of the Embassy, convincing Madero's general Victoriano Huerta to change sides by promising him the presidency. Madero was arrested and executed, and Venustiano Carranza and Pancho Villa declared against Huerta, as did Zapata. Incoming U.S. president Woodrow Wilson also refused to recognize Huerta. He allowed arms to cross the border to the Constitutionalists and used a trivial incident as an excuse to occupy **Veracruz** (April 21-November 22, 1914) to deprive Huerta of arms and divert them to the Constitutionalists. Carranza, the main beneficiary, nonetheless protested U.S. violation of Mexican sovereignty. Victories by Villa at **Torreón** and **Zacatecas** in April and May of 1914 and by Álvervo Obregón at **Guadalajara** and **Querétaro** in the same months forced Huerta's resignation, opening Mexico City to the Constitutionalists (August 15, 1914). The revolutionaries gathered at the Aguascalientes Convention (October 10-November 12), where Zapatistas and Villistas proposed radical reforms unacceptable to the conservative Constitutionalists. Thus, civil war erupted.

While Zapata defended his stronghold in the states of Morelos, Guerrero, and Puebla, Villa prepared to attack the Constitutionalist center. Obregón fortified Celaya and León using methods then being employed in Europe's Great War. Villa's first attack on **Celaya** in early April, 1915, was repulsed by barbed wire, machine guns, and artillery using interlocking fields of fire. In his second offensive, cavalry charges produced 9,000 dead or wounded. It was the same at **León** (May-June, 1915). Villa withdrew to Chihuahua, rebuilt, and attacked the Constitutionalists at **Agua Prieta** (November 1-4, 1915). The siege failed. The U.S. government had recognized Carranza's government in October and allowed him to reinforce his army through the United States. Enraged, and influenced by a German agent who wanted war

Francisco Madero, with the financial backing of Standard Oil, started the Mexican Revolution in 1910. (Library of Congress)

between Mexico and the United States to keep the Americans out of World War I, Villa raided **Columbus** (March 9, 1916). Washington sent a punitive expedition under General John J. Pershing (March 15, 1916-February, 1917). Even with reconnaissance aircraft, it never found Villa, although it skirmished with Villista guerrillas at Parral (April 12) and again at **Carrizal** (June 30), leaving fifty Americans dead.

AFTERMATH

In February, 1917, Carranza promulgated a new constitution and scheduled elections, which he won. Obregón retired to private life, a clear signal that he intended to run for president after Carranza. Meanwhile, Carranza eliminated Zapata, who was betrayed and assassinated (April 10, 1919), though Villa remained at large. In 1920, Carranza tried to hold power by appointing his successor. Obregón, supported by the army, declared against Carranza, who was killed trying to flee with bags of gold pesos from the treasury. Obregón then became president, bought off Villa with a hacienda, and set about healing Mexico's wounds by bringing all factions into a single "revolutionary family."

RESOURCES

Hart, John M. *Revolutionary Mexico: The Coming and Process of the Mexican Revolution.* Berkeley: University of California Press, 1997.

Katz, Friedrich. *The Secret War in Mexico.* Chicago: University of Chicago Press, 1981.

Knight, Alan. *The Mexican Revolution.* 2 vols. New York: Cambridge University Press, 1986.

SEE ALSO: Latin American Wars of Independence; Mexican Wars of Independence; Mexico, U.S. Invasion of; Villa, Pancho; Zapata, Emiliano.

William Schell, Jr.

MEXICAN WARS OF INDEPENDENCE

AT ISSUE: Mexico's independence from the Spanish crown
DATE: 1810-1823
LOCATION: Mexico
COMBATANTS: Mexican revolutionaries vs. Spanish armed forces

PRINCIPAL COMMANDERS: *Mexican*, Miguel Hidalgo y Costilla (1753-1811), Ignacio Allende (d. 1811), José María Morelos y Pavón (1765-1815), Agustín de Iturbide (1783-1824); *Spanish*, Félix María Calleja del Rey (1755?-1828)

PRINCIPAL BATTLES: Guanajuato, Calderón, Valladolid

RESULT: The campaigns waged by Hidalgo, Allende, and Morelos led eventually to the establishment of Mexico as an independent republic. Iturbide successfully appealed to the major elements of Mexican society to accept his leadership in a declaration of independence from the Spanish crown.

BACKGROUND

In 1808, Napoleon Bonaparte invaded Spain, deposed its ruler, the Bourbon king Ferdinand VII, and installed his brother Joseph as king. The centuries-old domination of Spanish Latin America by the Spanish crown ended with Ferdinand's exile from the mother country.

The Spanish liberals refused to accept Joseph as Spain's ruler and organized a resistance movement against the French. They formed the Cortes of Seville in 1812 in opposition to the invaders. The liberals invited representatives of the Spanish colonies in the Americas to join them and to participate in the movement.

The Spaniards of the mother country refused, however, to provide equal representation by the colonists in the interim government. This denial led to the development of separate wars of independence throughout Spanish America. Mexico, the mother country's richest colony, began such a battle in 1810.

ACTION

Miguel Hidalgo y Costilla, the curate of Dolores, a small village in Mexico's state of Guanajuato, joined a plot with a number of other creoles (Spaniards born in America) to spread discontent with Spanish rule and to overthrow Spain's viceroy in Mexico City. When the Spanish authorities discovered the plot, Hidalgo felt that he had no other choice but to call for an outright rebellion against the government.

On September 16, 1810, he rang the bell of the Dolores church to summon the general population. From the steps of the church, Hidalgo appealed to the masses—the Indians, the mestizos, the mulattos, the deprived and impoverished who made up more than 70 percent of the colony's population. He led this ill-equipped and untrained mob against the city of **Guanajuato**, the center of Mexico's silver mining and one of the richest communities in New Spain, as Mexico was called at that time. After capturing the city, the invaders slaughtered all the Spanish residents as well as some of the creoles who had taken shelter in the city's granary with them.

The ferocity of the attack and the resulting deaths of the city's most prominent residents terrified the colony's white population, those from Spain as well as the Americans. A royalist army, under the command of General Félix María Calleja del Rey, formed to combat Hidalgo's horde. On January 11, 1811, the two armies met at **Calderón**, near the city of Guadalajara. Calleja and his troops routed the revolutionaries. Hidalgo, Ignacio Allende (his second in command), and their subordinates were captured while retreating in northern Mexico; from there they were taken to Chihuahua and, after a brief trial, executed.

After the death of Hidalgo, the mantle of leadership of the independent movement fell to another priest, José María Morelos y Pavón. A much more capable military leader than his predecessor, he fought the Spanish armies successfully for almost five years. Morelos established a formal revolutionary government and also sought the support of the creole group, pointing out to them that they, too, had been exploited by the peninsular Spaniards. At the same time, he promised equality for all the Indians, mestizos, mulattos, and other minorities that made up his army.

The indefatigable Calleja, now named viceroy by the restored Spanish king Ferdinand, pursued a campaign of all-out war against Morelos. In December of 1813, Calleja caught up with the rebel leader and defeated him in a pitched battle at **Valladolid**. Both Morelos and the nascent Mexican congress formed to rule the revolutionary government took to the road. Royalist forces captured Morelos and executed him at Mexico City on December 22, 1815.

With the death of Morelos, the revolutionary movement lost its central direction and became a series of local conflicts between Spanish military commanders and guerrilla rebels. It appeared that the movement had been defeated. In the mother country, after Napoleon's defeat, the restored King Ferdinand VII sought to reestablish absolutist rule throughout the Spanish empire. Sent to wipe out a group of recalcitrant guerrillas, a royalist colonel, Agustín de Iturbide, bargained with the rebels instead. He released and published a proclamation, called the Plan de Iguala, containing three guarantees—of union, of religion, and of independence. While vague in nature, the plan attracted the support of the majority of Mexicans, rich and poor alike.

On September 28, 1821, a junta composed of the country's most prominent citizens signed Mexico's declaration of independence. Iturbide pressed his luck, however. He contrived to have himself named Mexico's emperor, and this undemocratic move resulted in his ultimate downfall. He found it expedient to leave the country. On July 1, 1823, Iturbide attempted to return from exile. After he landed in Tamaulipas, local authorities captured him. He was tried and executed.

AFTERMATH

Following Iturbide's deposition, Mexico's political leaders adopted a governmental structure very much like that of its neighbor to the north, the United States. They established a constitutional government providing for a popularly elected president, a senate, and a chamber of deputies. President Vicente Guerrero suppressed slavery on September 15, 1829. The provision of an equal social, political, and economic status for the country's large Indian population proved to be a much more difficult task.

RESOURCES

Fuentes, Carlos. *The Buried Mirror: Reflections on Spain and the New World*. Boston: Houghton Mifflin, 1992.

Lynch, John. *The Spanish American Revolutions 1808-1826*. 2d ed. New York: W. W. Norton, 1986.

Robertson, William Spence. *Rise of the Spanish American Republics*. New York: Free Press, 1946.

SEE ALSO: Latin American Wars of Independence; Mexican Civil Wars; Mexican Revolution; Napoleon I; South American Wars of Independence.

Carl Henry Marcoux

Mexico, U.S. Invasion of

AT ISSUE: United States involvement in Mexican politics
DATE: March 15, 1916-February 5, 1917
LOCATION: Northern Mexico
COMBATANTS: U.S. Army vs. revolutionary soldiers of Pancho Villa and sometimes Mexican regulars
PRINCIPAL COMMANDERS: *United States*, General John J. Pershing; *Mexican*, Pancho Villa
PRINCIPAL BATTLE: Carrizal (1916)
RESULT: Villa eludes capture and the United States further alienates Mexican citizens and politicians

Background

Upon assuming the presidency of the United States in 1912, Woodrow Wilson began to actively support liberal movements throughout Latin America. When Mexican general Victoriano Huerta ousted the liberal reformer Francisco Madero from the presidency in 1913, Wilson refused to recognize Huerta and directed U.S. naval units to halt arms shipments to his regime. Wilson's policy led to a brief invasion of the Mexican city of Veracruz in 1914, further straining relations between the two neighbors.

Huerta was forced to resign in July, 1914, setting off a power struggle for the Mexican presidency. Pancho Villa had early U.S. support, but his battlefield losses led Wilson in October, 1915, to recognize the government of Venustiano Carranza, a former associate of Madero. Many Mexicans, including Villa, believed that recognition was part of a corrupt bargain that would make Mexico subservient to the United States. Villa revolted against Carranza early in 1916, pursuing a deliberate policy of provocation in order to show his contempt for the United States and to embroil Carranza in a war with Mexico's northern neighbor. In January, Villa murdered eighteen Americans at Santa Isabel, and on March 9, he sacked and burned Columbus, New Mexico, killing some two dozen Americans.

Action

The Columbus raid led Wilson to station 158,000 U.S. regular and National Guard troops along the Mexican border and to authorize a punitive expedition under the command of Brigadier General John J. Pershing, who entered Mexico on March 15 with 4,800 troops, though the number eventually rose to 10,000. Carranza reluctantly permitted the invasion, hoping for U.S. dollars and support.

In late March, Pershing established his headquarters 125 miles south of Chihuahua. Employing cavalry, tanks, and airplanes, he fruitlessly scoured northern Mexico for Villa. In early April, acting on a tip, Pershing ordered the Thirteenth Cavalry to Parral. Four hundred ten miles into the interior, American troops clashed with local civilians, as well as Mexican regulars, leading Carranza to demand U.S. withdrawal, which Wilson refused. On June 21, Pershing routed a force of Mexican regulars at Carrizal, eighty-five miles south of Ciudad Juárez (across the border from El Paso, Texas); twenty-three Americans were taken prisoner.

An ultimatum was sent to Carranza, demanding release of prisoners and threatening a full-scale war. Although Carranza submitted, Villa was still on the loose and continued to attack and capture Mexican towns held by the Carranzistas. By January, 1917, however, Villa's troop losses had lessened his threat to the Carranza government. Wilson used this as a pretext for withdrawal.

Aftermath

Although Pershing failed to capture Villa, the Mexican general never again threatened the United States border. The punitive expedition also provided an early field test for American tanks and airplanes. The invasion did alienate Carranza, however, and the Mexican president was sympathetic toward Germany throughout World War I, inviting German intrigue into the Western Hemisphere. In the most famous incident, German foreign minister Arthur Zimmermann proposed to the German minister in Mexico a defensive alliance between the two countries, with the proviso that Mexico reconquer "lost territory in New Mexico, Texas, and Arizona." The Zimmermann telegram was intercepted and decoded by British intelligence, passed on to the United States, and published on March 1, 1917. Its publication did much to convince Americans that war was inevitable.

Resources

Clendenen, C. C. *The United States and Pancho Villa*. Ithaca, N.Y.: Cornell University Press, 1961.

Cumberland, Charles Curtis. *Mexican Revolution: The Constitutionalist Years*. Austin: University of Texas Press, 1972.

Gardner, Lloyd. *Wilson and Revolutions: 1913-1921*. Philadelphia, Pa.: Lippincott, 1976.

Gilderhus, Mark T. *Diplomacy and Revolution: U.S.-Mexican Relations Under Wilson and Carranza*. Tucson: University of Arizona Press, 1977.

Katz, Friedrich. *The Life and Times of Pancho Villa*. Stanford, Calif.: Stanford University Press, 1998.

_____. *The Secret War in Mexico: Europe, the United States, and the Mexican Revolution*. Chicago: University of Chicago Press, 1981.

Stout, Joseph Allen. *Border Conflict: Villistas, Carrancistas, and the Punitive Expedition, 1915-1920*. Fort Worth: Texas Christian University Press, 1999.

SEE ALSO: Mexican Revolution; Pershing, John J.; Villa, Pancho.

John Powell

Miani

TYPE OF ACTION: Ground battle in the Sind Campaign
DATE: February 17, 1843
LOCATION: Miani and surrounding area of British residency of Hyderabad, India
COMBATANTS: 2,800 British and Indian troops vs. 20,000 Beluchis
PRINCIPAL COMMANDERS: *British*, General Sir Charles Napier (1782-1853); *Beluchi*, Emir of the Sind
RESULT: British victory over Beluchis

On February 15, 1843, 8,000 Beluchis, who resented the humiliating terms demanded by the British governor general George Eden, earl of Auckland, attacked the British residency at Hyderabad, defended by British officer James Outram. General Sir Charles James Napier, with 2,800 Indian and British troops, was dispatched to bring the conflict to an end. He encountered about 20,000 Beluchi troops under the emir of the Sind at Miani on February 17.

General Napier, at the age of sixty-one, fought with musket in hand as he personally led his troops into the fray. In savage hand-to-hand combat, the British were nearly overwhelmed by the greater number of Beluchis, but the tide was turned with the charge of the Ninth Bengal cavalry. The Beluchis were routed with a loss of 5,000 men and several stores of weapons. The British lost only 256 killed and wounded.

Significance

This decisive victory raised the spirits of the British after the demoralizing war in Afghanistan (1838-1842).

Resources

Bhatia, H. S., ed. *Military History of British India, 1607-1947*. New Delhi: Deep and Deep, 1977.

Lambrick, H. T. *Sir Charles Napier and Sind*. Oxford: Clarendon Press, 1952.

Subrahmanyam, T. G. *Famous Battles in Indian History*. Dehra Da: Palit and Dutt, 1969.

SEE ALSO: British Colonial Wars; British India.

Jason Ridler

Midway

TYPE OF ACTION: Sea and air battle in World War II
DATE: June 4, 1942
LOCATION: Cental Pacific
COMBATANTS: Four Japanese carriers vs. three American carriers and defenders
PRINCIPAL COMMANDERS: *Japan*, Admiral Chuichi Nagumo (1886-1944); *United States*, Admiral Raymond A. Spruance (1886-1969)
RESULT: The Americans won, sinking all four Japanese carriers and losing one of their own

The Doolittle bombing raid in April, 1942, prompted the Japanese military to take Midway Island in the central Pacific. They could not allow an attack on their home islands to happen again—their duty was to protect the emperor. They believed they could take Midway and fatally lure the U.S. carriers into battle. However, the Americans were aware of their plans because they had

Ships Sunk at Midway, June 4, 1942

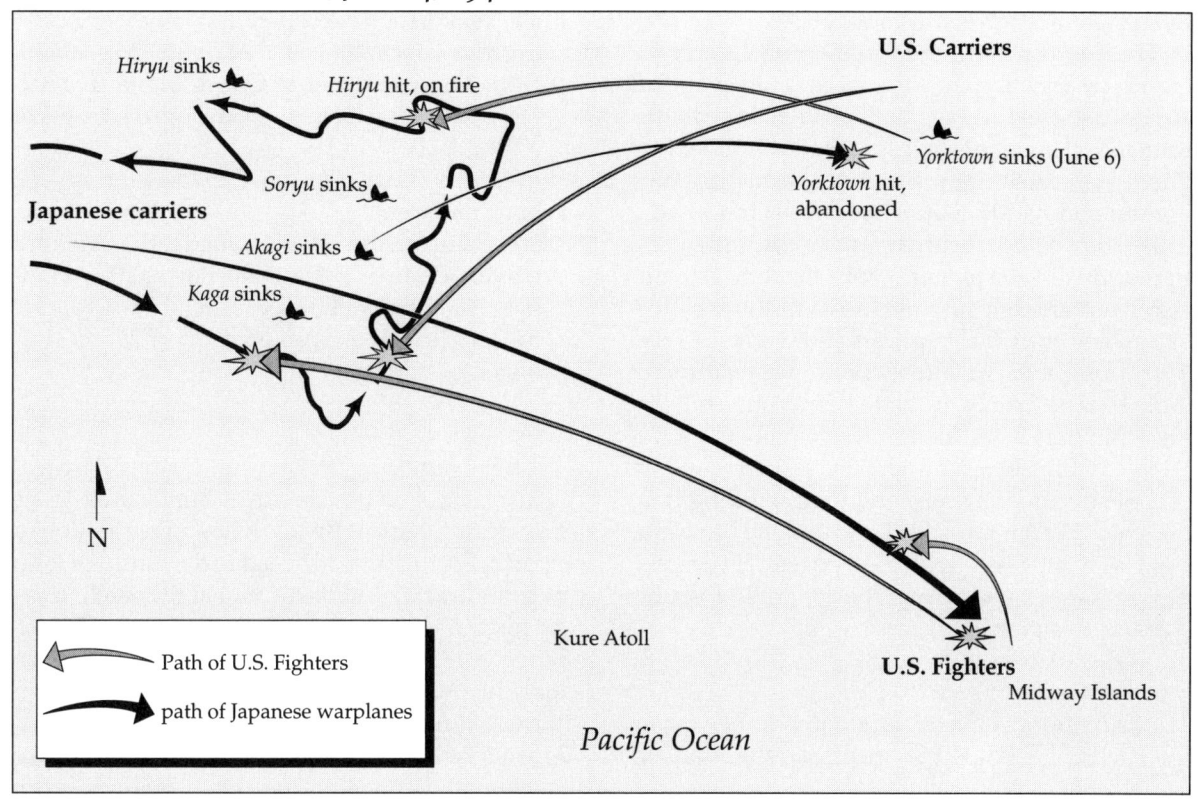

broken the Japanese code and planned an ambush of their own.

Early on the morning of June 4, 1942, the first wave of planes from the four Japanese carriers took off for Midway. U.S. scout planes sighted and followed the Japanese, and radar on Midway detected the incoming aircraft. All serviceable planes left the atoll. The fighters headed for the incoming planes. The bombers and torpedo planes made an ineffective, uncoordinated attack on the Japanese carriers. The Japanese shot up all U.S. planes and bombed and strafed Midway.

Chuichi Nagumo decided the first strike had not been sufficient and ordered a second wave to attack Midway. However, suddenly, the first-wave planes returned. Deck crews took the second strike force below in order to retrieve and refuel the first wave as well as the Zeros defending the fleet. Then a search plane reported a U.S. carrier within striking distance. Nagumo ordered his planes rearmed for an attack against the carrier instead of Midway. The deck crews had to replace regular bombs with torpedoes and armor-piercing bombs. There was not enough time to observe safety procedures.

Admiral Raymond A. Spruance had been waiting for this moment; he launched his planes toward the enemy's location. However, Nagumo was not there; he had turned toward the Americans. The U.S. pilots spread out in a search mode. The torpedo planes from the *Hornet* found the Japanese and attacked immediately. The combat air patrol dove down and engaged them. Only one man out of thirty total survived.

During this attack, Japanese destroyers had laid down smoke screens that attracted the pilots from the *Enterprise*'s torpedo squadron. The U.S. planes carried the torpedoes externally, which meant they could fly at only 100 to 120 mph and were sitting ducks. Ten out of twenty-eight men—five pilots and five gunners—from this squadron survived. The torpedo planes from the *Yorktown* arrived next on the scene. Again the defending Zeros attacked, often braving their own antiaircraft fire. Only three Americans out of twenty-four survived this assault.

The Japanese carriers were now ready to launch and swung into the wind. However, the American dive bombers had arrived at the battle undetected and more or less at the same time. The Zeros were down low, finishing off the torpedo planes, and had no opportunity to climb to altitude. The dive bombers came streaking down unopposed. The two to four bombs that hit each carrier were enough to sink them because of the armed and fully fueled planes and because of the munitions and gasoline containers scattered around. The planes from the *Enterprise* hit the *Kaga* and the *Akagi*. The *Yorktown* bombers hit the *Soryu*. Within five minutes, these three carriers became blazing infernos, and the exploding munitions made it impossible to control the fires. The fighting continued, and the carriers *Hiryu* and *Yorktown* were also sunk. The Japanese lost the battle at this point.

SIGNIFICANCE

The battle was the turning point of the war in the Pacific. The United States gained the strategic initiative and never lost it.

RESOURCES

Cressman, Robert J., et al. *A Glorious Page in Our History*. Missoula, Mont.: Pictorial Histories, 1990.

Fuchida, Mitsuo, and Masatake Okumiya. *Midway*. Annapolis, Md.: Naval Institutes Press, 1955.

Midway. Fiction feature. Universal, 1976.

Prange, Gordon W. *Miracle at Midway*. New York: McGraw Hill, 1982.

SEE ALSO: Coral Sea; Guadalcanal; Guam; Iwo Jima; Nagumo, Chuichi; Saipan; Spruance, Raymond A.; World War II.

Emerson Thomas McMullen

MIGUELITE WARS

AT ISSUE: The formation of a representative national assembly (Cortes) in Portugal
DATE: 1828-1834
LOCATION: Portugal

COMBATANTS: Portuguese monarchical absolutists vs. Portuguese constitutionalists
PRINCIPAL COMMANDERS: *Absolutists (Miguelites)*, Dom Miguel, regent to Queen Maria II (1802-1866); *Constitutionalists*, Dom Pedro I, emperor of Brazil (1798-1834)
PRINCIPAL BATTLES: Oporto, Cape St. Vincent, Lisbon, Santarém
RESULT: Formation of the Quadruple Alliance (Britain, France, Spain, and Portugal) to combat absolutism in Europe; exile of Dom Miguel to Germany and establishment of Maria II as queen of Portugal

BACKGROUND

After Napoleon Bonaparte invaded Portugal in 1807, the Portuguese royal family fled to its American colony of Brazil. A liberal revolution in Oporto, Portugal, in 1820, led to the return of John VI from Brazil as a constitutional monarch, leaving his son Dom Pedro as prince regent of Brazil. Between 1820 and 1828, civil war flared between absolute monarchists and constitutionalists in Portugal, in part leading to the creation of an independent and liberal Brazil in 1822, with Pedro as emperor. Pedro's brother, Dom Miguel, led an absolutist insurrection in 1823, and the following year was sent into exile in Austria.

Dom Pedro, who had nominally succeeded to the throne of Portugal upon the death of his father in 1826, refused to leave Brazil, instead appointing his young daughter Maria II queen, with Dom Miguel as regent. Pedro, acting as King Peter IV of Portugal, tried to effect a compromise between liberals and absolutists in Portugal. He first issued a constitutional charter, which provided for a parliamentary regime authorized by the monarchy rather than by the people. He then conditionally abdicated the Portuguese throne in favor of Maria on two conditions: that she marry her uncle Dom Miguel and that he accept the parliamentary charter.

ACTION

Hoping that Pedro would renounce all rights to the Portuguese throne, the Council of Regency refused to publish the charter until General João Carlos de Saldanha Oliveira e Daun forced the issue, supported by a British expeditionary force of 5,000 men. Dom Miguel took the oath in October,

1827, returning as regent to Lisbon in February, 1828, with the British withdrawing in April. Almost immediately, Miguel's supporters began persecuting the liberals. Miguel seized the throne in July, with the Miguelites seizing all of Portugal except the island of Terceira, in the Azores, which then became the base of operations for Portuguese liberals.

Though virtually all of the mainland was in absolutist hands, the Miguelite fleet was turned back at Praia Bay, on August 12, 1828. The liberals purchased a small squadron of ships with a British loan and courted France, whose people had been persecuted in Portugal. In 1831, Dom Pedro abdicated the Brazilian throne, traveling to Europe to raise money and diplomatic support for the reconquest of Portugal. In July, 1831, France seized the Miguelite fleet in the Tagus River.

In July, 1832, an expedition of 6,500 volunteers from Brazil, England, France, and Portugal sailed from the Azores and seized **Oporto**. The city then suffered a year-long siege by 80,000 absolutist troops. Gradually, support for Miguel waned. On July 5, 1833, the liberal squadron under Captain Charles James Napier defeated a Miguelite flotilla off **Cape St. Vincent**. Napier and Antonio José de Sousa Manuel, duke of Terceira, then landed in the Algarve. Terceira captured **Lisbon** on July 24, 1833.

Spain then attacked the absolutist base at Coimbra in an attempt to capture Don Carlos, pretender to the Spanish throne, who had been given shelter by Dom Miguel. This led to the formation of the Quadruple Alliance in April between liberal forces in Britain, France, Spain, and Portugal, which supported Spanish aid to the constitutionalists, who quickly captured Viseu, Coimbra, and Tomar. Liberal forces combined with Saldanha Oliveira e Daun to defeat Miguel at the decisive Battle of **Santarém**, on May 16, 1834.

Aftermath

Miguel surrendered on May 26 at Évora-Monte, renounced his claim to the throne, and was allowed to go into exile in Germany. Pedro reinstated the liberal constitution of 1826 but died in September, paving the way for Maria II to become queen at age fifteen.

Resources

Costa, Sergio Correa da. *Every Inch a King: A Biography of Dom Pedro I, First Emperor of Brazil*. Translated by Samuel Putnam. London: Hale, 1972.

Livermore, H. V. *Portugal: A Short History*. 2d ed. New York: Cambridge University Press, 1976.

Macaulay, Neill. *Dom Pedro: The Struggle for Liberty in Brazil and Portugal, 1798-1834*. Durham, N.C.: Duke University Press, 1986.

See also: Carlist Wars; South American Wars of Independence.

John Powell

Miles, Nelson A.

Full name: Nelson Appleton Miles
Born: August 8, 1839; Westminster, Massachusetts
Died: May 15, 1925; Washington, D.C.
Principal wars: American Civil War, Sioux Wars, Spanish-American War
Principal battles: Antietam (1862), Fredericksburg (1862), Chancellorsville (1863), Spotsylvania Court House (1864), Petersburg (1864-1865)
Military significance: Miles was a brave and competent army officer during the American Civil War, numerous campaigns against Native Americans in the West, and the Spanish-American War.

During the American Civil War (1861-1865), Nelson A. Miles was appointed first lieutenant in a Union army volunteer company. He served in multiple engagements, including at Antietam (1862), Fredericksburg (1862), Chancellorsville (1863), Spotsylvania Court House (1864), and Petersburg (1864-1865). He was wounded four times, emerging a brevet major general. As commander at Fort Monroe, Virginia, he ordered Jefferson Davis, a prisoner there, to be briefly shackled in 1865.

Miles obtained a transfer in 1869 to a Kansas infantry regiment. There, he served in the Sioux Wars (1862-1891), attacking Sitting Bull in 1876, Crazy Horse in 1877, and the Nez Perce in 1877. He headed the Department (later Division) of the Missouri in 1885. He campaigned against Geron-

Nelson A. Miles (right) speaks to his men during the Spanish-American War. (Library of Congress)

imo and accepted his surrender in 1886. Miles suffered humiliation when a subordinate colonel caused the Wounded Knee slaughter in 1890.

Appointed commanding general of the U.S. Army in 1895, Miles supervised the conquest of Puerto Rico during the Spanish-American War in 1898. After retiring from military service in 1903, Miles entertained ill-conceived ambitions to become president in 1904.

RESOURCES

Greene, Jerome A. *Yellowstone Command: Colonel Nelson A. Miles and the Great Sioux War, 1876-1877.* Lincoln: University of Nebraska Press, 1991.

Miles, Nelson A. *Personal Recollections and Observations of General Nelson A. Miles.* Chicago: Werner, 1896. Reprint. 2 vols. Lincoln: University of Nebraska Press, 1992.

Pohanka, Brian C. *Nelson A. Miles: A Documentary Biography of His Military Career, 1861-1903.* Glendale, Calif.: Arthur H. Clark, 1985.

Wooster, Robert. *Nelson A. Miles and the Twilight of the Frontier Army.* Lincoln: University of Nebraska Press, 1993.

SEE ALSO: American Civil War; Antietam; Chancellorsville; Crazy Horse; Geronimo; Petersburg; Sioux Wars; Sitting Bull; Spanish-American War; Spotsylvania Court House.

Robert L. Gale

MILITARISM

A vigorous martial spirit or a tendency to elevate military matters over other concerns of the state. The term militarism originated in the 1860's and has been used in various, sometimes ambiguous, contexts. The foremost question among scholars, however, is whether militarism—dominance of military thought and action—is a product of the past (for example, the theory that twentieth century German militarism is a scion of Prussian culture) or a modern phenomenon, a direct result of industrialism. While such arguments may be applied to a complex, militaristic state such as Germany in 1930's and 1940's, "warlordism"—the brand of chaotic, divisive militarism that, for instance, distinguished civil war-torn Chinese society during the 1910's and 1920's—is widely accepted as having a simple explanation: A complete failure of civil government creates a political vacuum that can only be filled by military strength.

Jeremiah Taylor

MILITARY ACADEMY

A national academy or private school that concentrates upon training young men and women to be officers. Cadets in institutions such as the United States Military Academy (also known as West Point) in Orange County, New York, are subjected to a rigorous curriculum that combines mathematics, engineering and basic sciences, arts and humanities, military science, and physical education. Strict military discipline is maintained at all times, and cadets are groomed to be career officers. National academies like West Point present graduates with a lieutenant's commission, as well as a baccalaureate degree.

Jeremiah Taylor

Military organization, U.S.

Organization is what differentiates the military from an armed mob. The many levels within the military enable its millions of members to perform complex and often dangerous duties at the command of the president of the United States. Organization allows each member of the military to know his or her duties.

Civilian Leadership

The U.S. Constitution places the president of the United States as *commander in chief* of the military. General George Washington began the tradition of unquestioning obedience to civilian authority within the military during the American Revolution (1775-1783). The president appoints a civilian *secretary of defense* as the cabinet member charged with overseeing the military. Assisting the secretary are the *joint chiefs of staff*, made up of the military leaders of each service branch, with a *chairman*. The chairman may come from any branch and serves as the president's top military adviser.

The military establishment of the United States is divided into three departments, *Army*, *Navy*, and *Air Force*, each with a civilian secretary as its head. The Navy department includes the Navy and the *Marine Corps*. The *Coast Guard*, part of the *Department of Transportation*, falls under the Navy during wartime.

Reserves

The military is further divided between the *active components*, consisting of that portion of the military on full-time service, and the *reserve components*. Each branch has its corresponding reserve. The reserves are divided into three classifications. The *Retired Reserve* consists of retired military members liable for mobilization in the event of war or national emergency. The *Individual Ready Reserve* consists of former military members with a liability for recall as individuals in the event of war or national emergency. The *Ready Reserve* consists of units that train part-time and are liable for mobilization as units during war or emergency.

The Army and Air Force also have *National Guard* units as part of their reserve structure. Units in the National Guard have as their primary mission fighting wars as part of the federal military, but have an additional obligation to serve their state governments in the event of a local emergency. In general, National Guard units tend to be more combat-oriented and Army Reserve and Air Force Reserve units tend to fill support functions.

Composition of Units

The U.S. Army is divided into *field commands*, which are responsible for the major functions of the army, such as training or health services. At the same level are the *unified commands*, responsible for operations in a specific area of the world. Large operations are usually conducted by a *numbered field army*, containing two or more *corps* and a headquarters.

A corps consists of between two and five *divisions* and is commanded by a lieutenant general. A division contains two or more *brigades* and is normally commanded by a major general. Modern divisions usually have between twelve thousand and eighteen thousand soldiers organized in three brigades. Divisions in the U.S. Army are one of five types: *infantry, mechanized infantry, armored, airborne,* or *air assault*.

A brigade is made up of two or more *battalions*, usually five, and is commanded by a colonel. A battalion contains two or more *companies*, usually four, and is headed by a lieutenant colonel. A company consists of two or more *platoons*, usually three, and is commanded by a captain. A platoon consists of two or more *squads*, usually three, and is commanded by a second lieutenant. A squad contains two or more *teams* and is led by a sergeant. A team contains at least three soldiers and is led by a corporal.

Armor, Cavalry, and Artillery

At the lower levels, this structure is modified for specific types of units. An armored platoon, which is a platoon with tanks, normally has four tanks. The platoon is further divided into two *sections*. Each tank has four crew members—loader, driver, gunner, and *tank commander*. The platoon leader, a second lieutenant, is one of the tank commanders. The platoon sergeant, a sergeant first class, is another tank commander. Staff sergeants command the remaining two tanks, for a total of sixteen men in an armored platoon.

In cavalry and aviation, a battalion-sized unit is called a *squadron*, while a company-sized unit is called a *troop*. In artillery, a company-sized unit is called a *battery*, and a squad is called a *section*. In addition, the Army often uses *task forces*, which are units temporarily assembled for a specific missions.

The Marine Corps and Air Force

The Marines generally follow Army organization, although a large portion of the Marine Corps is committed to the *Fleet Marine Force*, which serves with the Navy. During prolonged ground operations, Marine brigades are often attached to Army divisions. The Air Force has a structure similar to the Army's with different names. From largest unit to smallest they are designated *major command*, *numbered air force*, *air division*, *wing*, *group*, *squadron*, *flight*, and *squad*. However, except for in a few specialized units, the Air Force does not normally have lieutenants in charge of units. Most Air Force lieutenants in combat units serve as pilots, navigators, or missile launch crew members.

Organization Before World War I

From the colonial period through the early twentieth century, land forces of the United States were normally organized around the *regiment*. A regiment usually consisted of ten companies, each designated by a letter, plus a headquarters unit. A colonel commanded the regiment. A typical regiment at full strength contained between five hundred and one thousand men. Divisions and corps existed only during wartime. Traditionally the United States maintained a small standing army. During war, the Army expanded through state-based regiments of volunteers. Companies were raised at the community level, organized into regiments by the states, and offered to the federal government for limited periods of service. Under the regimental system, all officers except for general officers belonged to a regiment. In practice, this meant that all officers on staff assignments or at headquarters units had to be on detached duty from their regiment, and almost no regiment ever had its full complement of officers.

Regiments remain part of unit lineages but not normally as tactical units. Therefore, most battalions are numbered as either the first or second battalion of a particular regiment, but no regimental headquarters exists. The exceptions are a few armored cavalry regiments that exist to perform traditional cavalry functions for division commanders.

The Twentieth Century

When the United States entered World War I (1914-1918), the *War Department*, the federal agency that ran the army, developed a new divisional system. U.S. divisions of World War I were larger than those of European armies, averaging around 25,000 men. The division was meant to be a fully contained combat unit that could sustain combat operations on its own. After the war, the divisional system was retained, although most of the divisions were relegated to the National Guard or *Organized Reserves*. The Organized Reserves would later be named the *Army Reserve*, but the basic divisional structure would exist into the twenty-first century.

World War II (1939-1945) saw little change in the basic structure of the Army, although the size of the division was shrunk to make it more mobile. Divisions with more emphasis on tanks or airborne soldiers were created, but the basic structure remained. In 1942, the Army reorganized into three major branches; *Ground Forces*, *Air Forces*, and *Service Forces*. This new organization reflected the importance of air power in war fighting.

Reorganization After World War II

The secretary of the Navy and the secretary of war were cabinet members until 1947, when Congress reorganized the military establishment. The War Department was divided into the Department of the Army and the Department of the Air Force. These and the Department of the Navy were relocated to the subcabinet level, and the newly created Department of Defense, headed by the secretary of defense, had responsibility for coordinating missions and budgets between the services.

END OF SEGREGATION

President Harry S. Truman abolished racial segregation within the armed forces in 1948, ending the practice of maintaining separate regiments and divisions for African Americans. In the 1970's, the services ended sexual segregation, although women remained forbidden by law from serving in most combat roles.

RESOURCES

Carp, E. Wayne. *To Starve the Army at Pleasure: The Continental Army Administration and American Political Culture*. Chapel Hill: University of North Carolina Press, 1990.

Coffman, Edward M. *The Old Army: A Portrait of the American Army in Peacetime, 1784-1898*. New York: Oxford University Press, 1986.

Fukuyama, Francis, and Abram N. Shulsky. *The "Virtual Corporation" and Army Organization*. Santa Monica, Calif.: RAND, 1997.

MacGregor, Morris J., Jr. *Integration of the Armed Forces, 1940-1965*. Washington, D.C.: Center of Military History, 1989.

Organization of the American Expeditionary Forces. Vol 1. in *United States Army in the World War, 1917-1919*. Washington, D.C.: Government Printing Office, 1989.

Sorter, Ronald E. *Army Active/Reserve Mix: Force Planning for Major Regional Contingencies*. Santa Monica, Calif.: RAND, 1995.

Weigley, Russell F. *History of the United States Army*. New York: Macmillan, 1967.

SEE ALSO: Air Force, U.S.; Army, U.S.; Coast Guard, U.S.; Marines, U.S.; Navy, U.S.; Rank in the military.

Barry M. Stentiford

MILITARY THEORY

Throughout the course of world history, states have attempted to achieve political and economic advantages through warfare. Military and political leaders have traditionally debated over when it is advisable to initiate hostilities and what tactics should be employed in military theaters of operation. While military history surrounds itself with the general causes and conduct of specific wars, military theory pertains to the overall ideas surrounding the decision making involved with the how, when, and why a nation forsakes peaceful diplomacy for aggressive warfare. Simply put, it is an attempt to develop a systematic approach toward warfare that will enhance the opportunity for victory while minimizing the overall destructive costs of war. With the advent of sophisticated weaponry and technology, states are consistently formulating new plans, which eliminate the need for vast armies and rely on unmanned missile systems, air power, and naval fleets. Superpowers claim that these new destructive arsenals serve as a deterrence and will ultimately eliminate warfare altogether, but as recent wars in the Persian Gulf, the Balkans, and Africa indicate, military leaders still depend on some of the basic ideas first introduced over two thousand years ago.

THE ART OF WAR

Sunzi's *Bingfa* (c. 510 B.C.E.; *The Art of War*, 1910) represents one of the most frequently read and definitive guides on military theory in history. Written more than twenty-four hundred years ago, during the "warring states" era in China, it serves as one of the first systematic attempts to apply scientific rules and principles to warfare. His ideas on military preparedness, command structures, espionage, battlefield tactics, and the importance of psychology and troop morale have influenced countless military leaders. He emphasized the importance of developing an aggressive and assertive offensive spirit, but he also stressed that military power could be employed as a strategic deterrence. Sunzi also maintained that states should enter into warfare only if they were certain that a military victory would produce long-term strategic and political advantages.

Before a leader declares war and orders mobilization, he or she must first acquire the necessary resources. Defeat can often be attributed to insufficient resources, and Sunzi declared that if the state lacks an overwhelming material advantage, victory will be difficult. He underscored the need for taxes and conscription and advised leaders to avoid costly supply lines by securing provisions and foodstuffs from captured enemies. According to his theory, states must also recognize how

Ten Landmark Works in Military Theory

Title in English (original)	Author	Pub. Date (original/trans.)	Significance
The Art of War (Bingfa)	Sunzi Bingfa	c. 510 B.C.E./1910	Represented one of the earliest attempts to establish a set of principles and ideas to increase a state's chances for victory and survival
The History of the Peloponnesian War (Historia tou Peloponnesiacou polemou)	Thucydides	431-404 B.C.E./1550	Underscored how fear of the unknown can lead to war
The Prince (Il principe)	Niccolò Machiavelli	1513/1994	Outlined the essential characteristics for successful leadership
On War (Vom Kriege)	Carl von Clausewitz	1832-1834/1873	Highlighted the relationship between war and political aims
The Influence of Sea Power upon History, 1660-1783	Alfred Thayer Mahan	1890	Stressed the need to build large warships to attack an enemy's fleet rather than focusing on raiding commerce
Imperialism: The Highest Stage of Capitalism (Imperializm, kak noveyshy etap kapitalizma)	Vladimir Lenin	1917/1933	Claimed that war is an inherent component of a capitalist system
Winged Defense	William Mitchell	1925	Pioneered the importance of air power
"On Protracted War"	Mao Zedong	1938	Provided a blueprint for guerrilla warfare in order to eliminate foreign occupation
Nuclear Weapons and Foreign Policy	Henry Kissinger	1957	Stressed the importance of tactical nuclear weapons as a means of defense
Guerrilla Warfare (La guerra de guerillas)	Che Guevara	1961	Served as a tactical how-to guide for Guevara, who waged a national war of liberation

war will affect the home front by producing material shortages, high prices, and property losses and be willing to accept sacrifices to ensure victory.

Because long conflicts can ultimately devastate a state's infrastructure, leaders should mobilize for total war and seek out a quick and decisive victory. Thus certain types of warfare should be avoided. For example, if an army organized a siege of a city's fortifications, it would slowly drain the military of its capability to fight. This strategy forces the army to build costly defensive bulwarks and stockpile months of supplies, and it destroys the army's aggressiveness. If the siege, moreover, failed to produce capitulation, the army would inevitably suffer catastrophic losses because it would be forced to attack entrenched defensive positions and scale the city's walls.

An army must also depend upon mobility and troop maneuvers in order to gain a strategic advantage. Sunzi warned that leaders must learn how to use the terrain. When confronting an enemy in the mountains, troops should never fight uphill into the teeth of their defenses. An army should always avoid battles in rivers and swamps and never march into areas that contain natural barriers such as cliffs and ravines. When fighting on the open plains, an army should concentrate its forces in the center, but it should also rely on flanking maneuvers in order to strike its opponents from all sides. Most important, goes his advice, do not initiate an attack unless you possess numerical superiority.

Sunzi was one of the first theorists to understand the importance of psychology and troop morale. He outlined various characteristics that all military leaders should forsake. If a commander seeks glory and has a death wish, he will lead his forces to disaster. If he is temperamental, he can be baited and trapped. While a leader should care for his troops, he must avoid personal attachments and accept the likelihood that many will die. Finally, if he is too concerned for his own life, he will be likely to capitulate.

Similar ideas were later introduced by the Italian philosopher Niccolò Machiavelli and the Prussian military leader Carl von Clausewitz. Machiavelli maintained that leaders must be feared rather than loved. Because warfare requires a disregard for one's own life and the acceptance of potentially tragic personal sacrifices, he argued that leaders must be able to instill a sense of discipline and organization among his troops. Like Sunzi, Machiavelli maintained that if a leader fails to commit the majority of his resources and energy to military affairs, he will likely be scorned and defeated.

Clausewitz, on the other hand, stated that war possessed a dual nature and differentiated between total and limited wars. He also declared that war simply is the pursuit of political ends through military means. In order to be successful, a state must clarify its objectives, destroy its adversary's ability to prosecute a war, occupy and conquer territory, and decimate the will of the people. Because war is intended to satisfy political rather than military ambitions, its conduct must always remain in the hands of political leaders. Yet he also contended that ethical considerations should remain outside any theory of war, and that states must use their military resources for the sole purpose of achieving victory.

Early Western Theory

Thucydides, the Greek historian, was one of the first writers to address the importance of fear and deterrence in military theory. Covering the history of the Peloponnesian Wars from 431 to 404 B.C.E., he concluded that states often initiate preemptive strikes before the enemy can obtain a strategic advantage. He declared that although neither party desired the outbreak of the Peloponnesian Wars, Sparta attacked Athens because it feared Athenian ambitions. With the growth of its navy, Athens could easily defend its shores and conduct sieges. If its power remained unchecked, it would eventually eliminate both Sparta's and Corinth's ability to conduct trade in the Greek islands. He contended that naval power was critical for military success because it could be used as either an offensive weapon to spearhead an invasion or as a defensive shield to defend native shores. Thucydides stressed the need to build coastal fortifications and walls to protect major cities, and he insisted that a state should finance and encourage rebellion in its enemy's colonies in order to force its adversary to fight a two-front war.

The Greeks, followed by the Romans, also perfected the use of infantry and introduced tactics designed to secure victory in large-scale, pitched battles. Soldiers were equipped with spears, swords, and shields, and no effort was made toward securing the element of surprise. Cavalry was assembled on the flanks with infantry massed in the center. Battles erupted following an artillery barrage from the archers. Infantry charged the center as each army, with the cavalry attacking from the flank, attempted to smash through the opposing forces. Because horses played a minor role in combat until the creation of a suitable riding harness in the tenth century, mobility and speed played a secondary role to the use of overwhelming concentrations of heavily armored foot soldiers.

Medieval Combat

Before the invention and application of gunpowder and naval technology, military theorists focused their energies on the construction of massive siege weaponry, primitive artillery pieces, and eventually the use of cavalry. Most combat took place in fixed pitched battles. Mounted knights were quite effective until the Middle Ages, when advances in metallurgy significantly limited their effectiveness. By the fourteenth century, defenders used long pikes to erect barriers that hindered the knights' maneuverability, and with the creation of the metal crossbow, knights were forced to resort to heavier armor. This limited movement and overworked the horses. With the emergence of the English longbow in 1337, moreover, trained marksmen were able to attack from a range of more than two hundred yards. This weapon left soldiers dangerously exposed in the open field, and the English used it to unleash deadly artillery barrages on charging troops. During the Hundred Years' War at the Battle of Crécy in 1346, English troops, despite being outnumbered by a two-to-one ratio, were able to defeat the French by remaining outside their attackers' range. Yet despite the longbow's usefulness, it would quickly become outmoded during the onset of the gunpowder revolution. Because this style of combat generated a high casualty rate, leaders often resorted to fear, violent reprisals, and the use of mercenaries in order to field an army.

Siege Warfare

Until the end of the Middle Ages, most conflicts revolved around a state's ability to conduct siege warfare and build defensive fortifications. All major cities and towns were surrounded by walls, forts, and castles, which blocked an army's advance. Nineveh, the ancient capital city of Assyria, was protected by stone walls that were over one hundred feet high and approximately thirty feet thick. The Great Wall of China, first constructed around 200 B.C.E., protected more than fourteen hundred miles of the Chinese frontier. These barriers allowed the defenders to mount artillery barrages and create special fire positions for armed marksmen. Catapults and large crossbows provided additional artillery support. For example, the famous mathematician Archimedes built a catapult that could hurl a 1,800-pound stone at advancing troops. These bastions also provided security over large stretches of territory.

Offensive theorists, however, formulated tactics and ideas to offset the defender's advantages. Because siege warfare was costly, was expensive, and resulted in protracted wars, supplies and resources were critical for success. Troops would encircle the area and blockade all traffic outside the area, and if a city lacked sufficient stockpiles, it would be forced to surrender. After a nine-month siege, Spain captured Breda in the Low Countries in 1625 without firing a shot against an almost impregnable network of forts, batteries, and a double line of fortifications. Conflict unfolded slowly and siege trains were required to carry enough equipment to supply the army while it prepared to scale the fortifications. Few strongholds were taken by surprise and most sieges took months. During this time, the attackers dug an elaborate network of trenches and tunnels in order to move troops, artillery, and platforms into position for an assault. Armies also manufactured large fighting towers complete with battering rams, which enabled them to breech a city's defenses. These efforts required months of painstaking labor, but a besieging army was difficult to dislodge and a considerable amount of defenses proved worthless as many cities were starved into surrender.

Siege warfare continued to serve a prominent role in military theory throughout the twentieth century. During World War II, the Germans unsuccessfully attempted to conquer the Soviet Union by conducting sieges of such major cities as Leningrad (1941-1944) and Stalingrad (1942-1943). The North Vietnamese stymied American troops by besieging fortresses and fire bases such as Khe Sanh in 1968. Finally, the American air assault against Iran in 1991 can also be viewed as an attempt to starve Baghdad into surrender. Although states continue to perfect more sophisticated means of siege warfare, sieges remain a viable alternative for leaders interested in procuring capitulation without attacking their enemy's entrenched positions.

Naval Power

The ability to sail the open seas has proven to be one of the principal determinants of power throughout military history, yet prior to the twentieth century, navies devoted all their attention to disrupting their opponent's trade. The British blockade and the policing of Atlantic sea lanes contributed to the causes of both the Napoleonic Wars and the War of 1812. With the publication of Alfred Thayer Mahan's seminal work, *The Influence of Sea Power upon History 1660-1805*, in 1890, coupled with the creation of steam propulsion and steel hulls, all the major powers began to adopt the British idea of constructing large fleets of destroyers. This tactic became so prevalent in Germany that it subsequently sparked a naval arms race that contributed to the outbreak of World War I. Destroyers, moreover, served a vital role in amphibious landings. When the Allied forces stormed the beaches of Normandy in 1944, naval guns ensured their success by softening German coastal defenses with artillery barrages. With the advances in technology over the course of the twentieth century, destroyers would continue to play a prominent role in combat as these ships were ultimately equipped to fire unmanned missiles and laser-guided bombs.

If states lacked supremacy in surface ships, however, they resorted to the use of submarines. Pioneered during the American Civil War, submarines could be deployed to disrupt supply lines. These vessels, however, proved to be extremely vulnerable because they were slow, contained insufficient deck guns, and could be easily destroyed by depth charges. The invention of nuclear power submarines considerably altered their role in combat. Being able to attain unprecedented speeds and armed with nuclear weapons, submarines evolved into an effective means of monitoring and controlling the oceans' sea lanes.

Air Power

With the advent of powered flight, military theorists turned their attention toward the use of air power in combat. During World War I, airplanes provided reconnaissance for artillery, harassed enemy ground troops, and deployed some rudimentary bombing techniques, but they failed to play a decisive role in combat. World War II, however, elevated air power to a primary role among military strategists. German Blitzkrieg tactics used air power to destroy ground defenses and allowed infantry and motorized battalions to advance at unprecedented speeds. By strafing enemy positions, attacking key transportation hubs, and destroying vital supply depots, Germany was able to conquer Poland in less than a month. Other powers quickly followed suit. Both the United States and Great Britain relied on strategic bombing campaigns to eliminate German wartime industries, and Japan's successful raid on Pearl Harbor was the direct result of a new strategy that emphasized the importance of aircraft carriers and long-range naval bombing campaigns. The United States also relied on air power to release its atomic bombs over Hiroshima and Nagasaki.

Following World War II, all the major powers recognized that their defenses would be extremely vulnerable without sufficient air power. Theorists developed plans to implement long-range bombing strategies capable of attacking civilian, government, and industrial centers. Control of the open skies became increasingly important during the Cold War (1945-1991), as both the United States and the Soviet Union employed aircraft to conduct surveillance and espionage. Aircraft were also used as military and equipment transports. Because strategists began to rely on the use of longer-range aircraft, refueling tankers were constructed as well. Eventually, helicopters were used to ferry ground troops from one combat zone to another. Air power ultimately evolved into a dominant role among strategists and led to the construction of stealth fighters capable of avoiding radar detection. During the war in Afghanistan (1979-1989), the Soviet Union was forced to withdraw after losing air superiority, and in the Gulf War (1991), American air power ensured a quick and rapid victory over Iraq. By the end of the twentieth century, air power had emerged as a primary weapon that allowed nations to minimize the use of ground troops and consequently avoid high casualty rates.

Nuclear Deterrence

Nuclear weapons drastically altered the theory of warfare. These weapons of destruction eliminated the use of ground troops and increased the emphasis on delivery systems, aircraft, and navies. Theorists adopted policies of massive retaliation and Mutual Assured Destruction (MAD) and argued that nuclear arsenals served as an effective means of deterrence because nuclear powers realized that any offensive strike would result in a counterattack that could destroy all of its key military and population centers. Theorists continue to debate whether the proliferation of nuclear weapons enhances the potential for peaceful conflict resolution, but as nuclear technology becomes easier to obtain in the twenty-first century, many strategists fear an attack from either a rogue nation or a terrorist group.

Guerrilla Warfare

Evidence of guerrilla warfare stretches back to the beginning of recorded history. Small bands of guerrillas have traditionally employed ambush tactics and small-scale skirmishes to overthrow oppressive governments or eliminate colonial occupation. Guerrilla warfare was also prevalent during the Roman Empire. Guerrilla bandits operated freely in northern China during the end of the Ming Dynasty (1628-1644). After Napoleon I defeated Spain's army, guerrilla units harassed French forces and forced him to devote a disproportionate amount of time and resources to a campaign to pacify the countryside from 1808 to 1813. The importance of guerrilla warfare, however, escalated following the rise of capitalism and imperialism in the world system as countless nationalist movements struggled to eliminate colonialism and foreign influences in their states.

Countless writers, including Clausewitz, contributed to the wealth of material on the theory of guerrilla warfare, but Mao Zedong and Che Guevara were primarily responsible for inspiring and shaping the numerous wars of liberation throughout the second half of the twentieth century. Operating against two opponents, the Japanese Army and the Chinese Nationalists, Mao developed an overall theoretical approach to guerrilla warfare that helped defeat Japan in World War II and Chiang Kai-shek by 1949. Mao maintained that the guerrilla must always be careful to solicit the aid of the people, and that all guerrilla activity should strive toward obtaining greater support for the revolution. Guerrillas also need the countryside for shelter, food, and defensive bases. Civilian casualties and atrocities must be avoided at all cost. Mao warned that guerrillas must prepare for a protracted war because it was extremely unlikely that small skirmishes and ambushes would produce a decisive victory. Yet Mao predicted that consistent harassment of enemy troops would take a psychological toll on government or foreign troops, and ultimately, peasant guerrilla armies would prevail.

Guevara served as one of Fidel Castro's commanders during the Cuban Revolution (1956-1959). After Castro solidified his power throughout the island, Guevara unsuccessfully tried to implement his ideas on guerrilla warfare in Africa and South America. Although he died fighting in Bolivia in 1967, his writings on guerrilla warfare remained extremely popular among twentieth century revolutionaries. Guevara agreed with Mao's emphasis on protracted wars in the countryside and supported his ideas on offensive initiatives. He also highlighted the importance of night operations. Because guerrillas enjoyed the advantage of selecting both the time and place for an ambush or skirmish, they could inflict a high rate of casualties in a brief period of time and escape into their defensive bases in the countryside. Guevara stressed the importance of land mines and sabotage of government facilities, but he advised against terrorist acts because any civilian casualties would have adverse effects upon the rebels' support in the countryside. According to Guevara, the guerrilla should be between twenty-five and thirty-five years old, physically fit, mobile, and able to carry heavy packs on long marches. Finally, Guevara believed in gender equality and underscored the vital contributions of female guerrillas both in combat and on the home front.

Resources

Cowley, Robert, ed. *What If? The World's Foremost Military Historians Imagine What Might Have Been*. New York: G. P. Putnam's Sons, 1998.

George, Alexander, and Richard Smoke. *Deterrence in American Foreign Policy*. New York: Columbia University Press, 1974.

Hagan, Kenneth J. *This People's Navy: The Making of American Sea Power*. New York: Free Press, 1991.

Katzenstein, Peter J., ed. *The Culture of National Security: Norms and Identity in World Politics*. New York: Columbia University Press, 1996.

Kennedy, Paul, ed. *Grand Strategies in War and Peace*. New Haven, Conn: Yale University Press, 1991.

Laquer, Walter. *Guerilla: A Historical and Critical Study*. Boston: Little, Brown, 1976.

Lebow, Richard Ned. *Nuclear Crisis Management*. Ithaca, N.Y.: Cornell University Press, 1987.

Paret, Peter. *Makers of Modern Strategy: From Machiavelli to the Nuclear Age*. Princeton, N.J.: Princeton University Press, 1986.

Parker, Geoffrey. *The Military Revolution: Military Innovation and the Rise of the West, 1500-1800*. Cambridge, England: Cambridge University Press, 1996.

Rood, Tim. *Thucydides: Narrative and Explanation*. Oxford: Clarendon Press, 1998.

Waltz, Kenneth, and Scott Sagan. *The Spread of Nuclear Weapons: A Debate*. New York: W. W. Norton, 1995.

Walzer, Michael. *Just and Unjust Wars*. New York: Basic Books, 1977.

SEE ALSO: Guerrilla warfare; Guevara, Che; Machiavelli, Niccolò; Mao Zedong; Sunzi.

Robert D. Ubriaco, Jr.

MILITIA

An armed force raised from a civilian population. The first militiamen were the hoplites of the ancient Greek city-states, citizen-soldiers who served in politics as well as in battle. During the Middle Ages, it was not uncommon to muster civilians into service during times of emergency. The same practice was followed in many parts of the world, including China and Japan before 1603. Although militia performed well in the Seven Years' War (1756-1763), particularly in its American phase; the French and Indian War (1754-1763); and the American Revolution (1775-1783), it was becoming increasingly apparent that their lack of formal military training made them a liability. In the nineteenth century, Britain and the United States instituted militia forces whose members agreed to regular training on their own time. These ultimately became the U.S. National Guard and the British Territorial Force/Army. At the turn of the twenty-first century, no nation, save Switzerland, fully depended on militia for its security.

Jeremiah Taylor

MILVIAN BRIDGE

TYPE OF ACTION: Ground battle in the Roman Civil Wars of 235-394
DATE: October 28, 312
LOCATION: Plain north of Tiber (1.5 miles north of Rome)
COMBATANTS: About 40,000 Eastern Roman soldiers vs. 100,000 Western Roman soldiers
PRINCIPAL COMMANDERS: *Eastern Roman*, Constantine the Great (c. 272/285-337); *Western Roman*, Marcus Aurelius Valerius Maxentius (d. 312)
RESULT: Annexation of Italy and north Africa by Constantine

In the early spring of 312, Constantine the Great declared war on Marcus Aurelius Valerius Maxentius and invaded Italy. In three hard-won victories, at Segusio, Turin, and Verona, he defeated Maxentius's main forces. Thereafter, Constantine marched on Rome and placed the capital under siege.

On the day before the battle, Constantine reportedly saw a sign in the sky which he and his entourage interpreted as representing the god of the Christians. That same evening, he had a dream in which this sign reappeared to him, with a voice saying, "In this sign you will conquer." Later known as the *labarum*, this sign was scratched upon the shields of his troops.

Civil unrest within Rome forced Maxentius to issue forth from the city and join in combat with Constantine in the plain to the north of the Tiber and near the Milvian Bridge. The decisive element of the encounter was the cavalry charge on Constantine's side. In the ensuing rout, Maxentius and many of his soldiers drowned in the Tiber.

SIGNIFICANCE
Through victory at the Battle of the Milvian Bridge, Constantine became the sole emperor to rule in the western half of the Roman Empire and was consequently recognized by the Senate as the senior Augustus. Moreover, the visionary experience that accompanied this victory made him into Rome's first Christian emperor.

RESOURCES
Barnes, Timothy D. *Constantine and Eusebius*. Cambridge, Mass.: Harvard University Press, 1981.

Cameron, Averil, and Stuart G. Hall. *Eusebius: Life of Constantine*. Oxford: Clarendon Press, 1999.

Ridley, Ronald T., ed. and trans. *Zosimus: New History*. Canberra: Australian Association for Byzantine Studies, 1982.

SEE ALSO: Constantine the Great; Roman Civil Wars of 235-394.

Richard Westall

MINAMOTO YOSHITSUNE

ALSO KNOWN AS: Ushiwaka
BORN: 1159; Japan
DIED: June 15, 1189; Fort Koromogawa, Hiraizumi, Japan
PRINCIPAL WAR: Gempei War
PRINCIPAL BATTLES: Uji (1184), Ichinotani (1184), Yashima (1185), Dannoura (1185)
MILITARY SIGNIFICANCE: Yoshitsune destroyed the rival Taira clan, helping establish the shogunate, which imposed warrior rule on Japan for seven centuries.

Minamoto Yoshitsune and his older half-brother Minamoto Yoritomo were sons of Minamoto Yoshitomo, who helped Taira Kiyomori gain power but later died attempting a coup. A second Minamoto rebellion started the Gempei War (1180-1185). Clan leader Yoritomo's cousin Minamoto Yoshinaka captured Kyoto but proved untrustworthy and was crushed in 1184 at Uji (March 5) and Ōmi by Yoshitsune and another half-brother, Minamoto Noriyori. The Minamoto then attacked the Taira base at Ichinotani (March 20). Yoshitsune's surprise descent down a steep ravine with a small band brought confusion and defeat to the Taira, who fled by sea to Yashima. The following year, Yoshitsune crossed in a violent storm to Shikoku and marched overnight to attack Yashima (March 2, 1185) at dawn from the landward side, frightening the Taira to their ships before they grasped his modest numbers. A month later, he engaged them at Dannoura (April 25) in the straits between Kyushu and Honshu. Closing only when treacherous tides turned favorable, he used archers to decimate their seamen, then boarded and annihilated his foe.

Yoritomo gave Yoshitsune scant reward for these brilliant victories that established Minamoto hegemony. Perhaps jealous or threatened by Yoshitsune's military genius and friendship with the imperial court, Yoritomo outlawed his brother, hounding him to death at age thirty. This tragic fate evoked enduring sympathy. Yoshitsune, along with his companion, the loyal fighting monk Benkei, lives in legend as one of Japan's most beloved warrior heroes.

RESOURCES

McCullough, Helen. *Yoshitsune*. Stanford, Calif.: Stanford University Press, 1971.

Morris, Ivan. *Nobility of Failure*. New York: Noonday Press, 1988.

Sansom, George. *A History of Japan to 1334*. Stanford, Calif.: Stanford University Press, 1958.

Sugawara Makoto. "Bushido." *The East* 17-18 (1981-1982).

SEE ALSO: Bakufu; Gempei War; Japanese Wars of Unification.

R. Craig Philips

MINDEN

TYPE OF ACTION: Ground battle in the Seven Years' War
DATE: August 1, 1759
LOCATION: Minden, on the Weser River (thirty-five miles southwest of Hanover, Germany)
COMBATANTS: 42,500 British and Prussians vs. 54,000 French
PRINCIPAL COMMANDERS: *British/Prussian*, Duke Ferdinand of Brunswick (1721-1792); *French*, Marshal Marquis Louis de Contades (1704-1795)
RESULT: The British and German victory forced the French to retreat from Hanover

As a powerful French army, under Marshal Marquis Louis de Contades, advanced on Hanover in the spring of 1759, Duke Ferdinand of Brunswick assembled a force of British, Prussian, and Hanoverian troops to meet the threat. The two forces met on August 1 and deployed for battle.

Obeying a misunderstood order, nine infantry battalions of the British-Prussian army advanced against the French cavalry, a movement against all contemporary military thought. However, the British-Prussian troops defeated the French cavalry, then smashed the French infantry massed in the center. As the French began to break, Brunswick three times ordered a cavalry charge, but Lord George Sackville, the cavalry commander, refused each order. Sackville was later court-martialed and dismissed from the service, but the French army made its escape.

SIGNIFICANCE

The French defeat at Minden saved Hanover from capture. The battle also demonstrated that disciplined troops could successfully execute unorthodox maneuvers. The six British units involved in the attack became some of the most famous in the British army, and their feat is remembered in the annual celebration of Minden Day.

RESOURCES

Chandler, David, ed. *The Oxford Illustrated History of the British Army*. Oxford: Oxford University Press, 1994.

Cowley, Robert, and Geoffrey Parker, eds. *Readers Companion to Military History*. Boston: Houghton Mifflin, 1996.

Duffy, Christopher. *The Military Experience in the Age of Reason*. New York: Atheneum, 1988.

Parker, Geoffrey, ed. *Cambridge Illustrated History of Warfare*. Cambridge, England: Cambridge University Press, 1995.

Regan, Geoffrey. *Famous British Battles*. London: Michael O'Mara Books, 1997.

SEE ALSO: Hochkirch; Leuthen; Minden; Plassey; Quiberon Bay; Rossbach; Seven Years' War; Torgau.

Michael Witkoski

MITCHELL, BILLY

FULL NAME: William Lendrum Mitchell
BORN: December 29, 1879; Nice, France
DIED: February 19, 1936; New York, New York
PRINCIPAL WAR: World War I
PRINCIPAL BATTLE: St. Mihiel (1918)
MILITARY SIGNIFICANCE: Mitchell, who advocated quick victory through strategic bombing, es-

Billy Mitchell. (Library of Congress)

tablished a reputation as an excellent air power theorist.

Billy Mitchell initially served in the U.S. Army's Signal Corps. He helped lay a telegraph line across Alaska and, in 1912, became the youngest officer ever to serve on the general staff.

During World War I, Mitchell turned to aviation. He rapidly advanced from major to brigadier general while commanding the Air Service of the First Corps, then of the First Army, and finally of the First Army Group. In September, 1918, at St. Mihiel, he organized the largest Allied air effort of the conflict, involving 1,481 planes, more than half of which were French. At war's end, he was planning paratrooper operations and large-scale strikes against Germany.

During the subsequent demobilization, Mitchell, seeking independent status for military aviation, claimed that bombers could replace battleships in defense of U.S. coasts. Given the existing aircraft technology, Mitchell's arguments were questionable, but in highly publicized trials, his planes sank several anchored, obsolete warships. Increasingly intemperate, Mitchell forced his own court-martial by making reckless charges against the country's military leadership. Convicted of unbecoming conduct, he received a light sentence and resigned his commission in 1926.

Handsome and magnetic, Mitchell is still revered in the U.S. Air Force for his vision of quick victory through strategic bombing; skeptics argue that this fixation hobbled the U.S. Army during World War II. Congress awarded him a special Medal of Honor posthumously (1946).

RESOURCES

Futrell, Robert Frank. *Ideas, Concepts, Doctrine: Basic Thinking in the United States Air Force, 1907-1960*. Maxwell Air Force Base: Air University Press, 1989.

Hurley, Alfred H. *Billy Mitchell: Crusader for Air Power*. Bloomington: Indiana University Press, 1975.

Meilinger, Phillip S. *The Paths of Heaven: The Evolution of Airpower Theory*. Maxwell Air Force Base: Air University Press, 1997.

SEE ALSO: Air Force, U.S.; Aircraft, military; St. Mihiel; World War I.

Malcolm Muir, Jr.

MITHRIDATIC WARS

AT ISSUE: Control of Asia Minor
DATE: 88-65 B.C.E.
LOCATION: Asia Minor and Greece
COMBATANTS: Pontic forces vs. Romans
PRINCIPAL COMMANDERS: *Pontic*, Mithridates VI Eupator, king of Pontus (c. 132-63 B.C.E.); *Roman*, Sulla (138-78 B.C.E.), Lucius Licinius Lucullus (fl. first century B.C.E.), Pompey the Great (106-48 B.C.E.)
PRINCIPAL BATTLES: Athens, Chaeronea, Orchomenus, Cyzicus, Tigranocerta
RESULT: Roman victory; acquisition of new Roman provinces in Asia Minor

BACKGROUND

The death of King Attalus III in 133 B.C.E. left the kingdom of Pergamum to the Roman people. This territory, organized as the province of Asia, became a rich source of revenue for Rome. The neighboring regions of Bithynia, Galatia, Cappadocia, and Pontus remained nominally independent allies of the Roman people but often were subject to Roman intervention. Mithridates VI Eupator, king of Pontus, expanded his kingdom from its ancestral region in northern Asia Minor to the Crimea. Capitalizing on provincial resentment of Roman rule and the Social War (91-88 B.C.E.) raging in Italy, Mithridates aimed at overthrowing the Romans and establishing his own empire in the eastern Mediterranean. His first step was the annexation of Cappadocia and Bithynia, states bordering Roman territory.

ACTION

Rome was the aggressor in the First Mithridatic War (88-85 B.C.E.) as Roman and allied troops moved against Pontic forces in Bithynia and Cappadocia. Mithridates turned back the Romans and pursued them through the province of Asia, where secret arrangements were made for the massacre of some 80,000 resident Italians and Romans (88 B.C.E.). With this action, the people of Asia proclaimed their independence. The revolt against Roman rule spread to Greece, where the Athenians welcomed the Pontic general Archelaus as their liberator. Herod Archelaus quickly secured central Greece for Mithridates. In 87 B.C.E., the Romans launched a counterattack. Sulla arrived from Italy with five legions and besieged and captured **Athens** (March 1, 86 B.C.E.). Archelaus withdrew to northern Greece, where he met up with reinforcements. After two costly defeats at **Chaeronea** and **Orchomenus** (86 B.C.E.), Archelaus began negotiations for peace. Meanwhile, Roman troops commanded by Sulla's rival Lucius Valerius Flaccus invaded Asia Minor. Soon, Mithridates accepted the terms of peace (August, 85 B.C.E.) and withdrew his forces to Pontus.

A series of Roman raids against the Pontic kingdom followed (the Second Mithridatic War, 83-81 B.C.E.). Advancing north from Cappadocia, Lucius Licinius Murena overran some four hundred villages, before withdrawing and reinstating the status quo of the peace treaty.

The bequest to the Roman people of the kingdom of Bithynia precipitated the Third Mithridatic War (74-65 B.C.E.). Mithridates, allied with the Sertorian rebels in Spain, invaded Bithynia to prevent Rome's expansion. His army was cut off by the Roman commander Lucius Licinius

Milestones in the Mithridatic Wars

Date	Event
First Mithridatic War	
88 B.C.E.	Mithridates VI of Pontus invades Bithynia and Cappadocia, then Greece.
87-86	Roman Sulla drives the Mithridatic-Greek armies into Athens and the Piraeus; a Roman fleet defeats a Mithridatic fleet off Tenedos.
86	Using field fortifications, Sulla soundly defeats Mithridatic commander Archelaus at Chaeronea.
85	Sulla again defeats Archelaus, despite being outnumbered, at Orchomenus and prepares to invade Asia.
85	Sulla refuses to acknowledge the authority of a Roman army sent to replace him. The army's commander, Lucius Valerius Flaccus, is murdered by Gaius Flavius Fimbria, who supports Sulla against Mithridates.
84	Mithridates makes peace. After Sulla convinces Fimbria's army to join his forces, Fimbria commits suicide.
Second Mithridatic War	
83-81	Mithridates clashes with Lucius Licinius Murena, Roman governor of Asia, then establishes peace.
Third Mithridatic War	
75-74	After Nicomedes III of Bithynia bequeaths his kingdom to Rome, Mithridates declares war, invading Cappadocia, Bithynia, and Paphlagonia.
73	Roman Lucius Licinius Lucullus defeats Mithridates' lieutenant at Cyzicus.
72-70	Lucullus defeats Mithridates at the Battle of Cabira and takes over the kingdom; Mithridates flees to Armenia.
69-67	Lucullus invades Armenia, defeating Armenian ruler Tigranes at the Battle of Tigranocerta and winning a battle at Artaxata.
66	Roman Pompey ambushes and defeats Mithridates in the Battle of the Lycus; Mithridates escapes to the Crimea.
65	Tigranes is captured and gives up his conquests; Mithridates commits suicide a year later.

Lucullus and failed to capture the strategic city of **Cyzicus** (73 B.C.E.). Lucullus then took the offensive, capturing all of Pontus by 70 B.C.E. Mithridates fled to the court of his son-in-law, Tigranes the Great of Armenia. Lucullus followed, winning a pitched battle against Tigranes and capturing the capital **Tigranocerta** (69 B.C.E.). Though recognized as the victor over Mithridates, Lucullus was stripped of much of his power by political opponents in Rome. Mithridates rallied his forces and returned to Pontus in 68, only to be driven out by Pompey the Great, who assumed the command of the Roman forces in 66. Tigranes capitulated to the Romans, and the war ended the following year, when Mithridates abandoned Pontus for his Crimean kingdom.

Aftermath

After a series of costly wars, Rome's most dangerous threat in the east was eliminated. Rome acquired new provinces in Asia Minor, expanding the empire across the eastern Mediterranean.

RESOURCES

Crook, J. A., Andrew Lintott, and Elizabeth Rawson, eds. *The Cambridge Ancient History.* 2d ed. London: Cambridge University Press, 1994.

McGing, Brian C. *The Foreign Policy of Mithridates VI Eupator, King of Pontus.* Leiden: E. J. Brill, 1986.

Magie, David. *Roman Rule in Asia Minor.* 2 vols. Princeton, N.J.: Princeton University Press, 1950.

Rubinsohn, Zeev W. "Mithradates VI Eupator Dionysos and Rome's Conquest of the Hellenistic East." *Mediterranean Historical Review* 8, no.1 (1993): 5-54.

SEE ALSO: Chaeronea, 86 B.C.E.; Pompey the Great; Roman Civil Wars of 88-30 B.C.E.; Roman Republic, Wars of the; Sulla; Tigranes the Great.

Darryl A. Phillips

MOBILIZATION

The procedure of preparing an armed force for war. Mobilization was sometimes as simple as hiring mercenaries or assembling militia, but in the twentieth century, it became much more complex. The essence of mobilization originated in nineteenth century Prussia, where draft laws required limited terms of peacetime service in the army and in the reserves. At the onset of the Franco-Prussian War (1870), Prussia was able to draw upon these trained reserves to quickly raise more than 850,000 men. Such methods were emulated by many European nations—not always successfully. The widespread belief that modern wars would be short and decisive led to a fatal neglect of economic mobilization. As a result, the massive troop mobilizations of World War I (1914-1918) could not overcome the inefficiency of ill-prepared economic and industrial infrastructures. Except in such nations as Switzerland—where militia is the basis of the armed forces—traditional mobilization is an anachronism. Warfare of the twenty-first century is largely dependent on standing professional forces, the organization and readiness of which preclude large-scale mobilization.

Jeremiah Taylor

MOBUTU SESE SEKO

FULL NAME: Mobutu Sese Seko Koko Ngbendu wa Za Banga
ALSO KNOWN AS: Joseph Désiré Mobutu
BORN: October 14, 1930; Lisala, Belgian Congo
DIED: September 7, 1997; Rabat, Morocco
PRINCIPAL WARS: Congolese Civil War, Shaba rebellions
MILITARY SIGNIFICANCE: Mobutu was one of the United States' most loyal clients during the Cold War and served as a bulwark against communism in central Africa.

After Belgium granted the Congo independence in 1960, political stability within the country rapidly deteriorated as several factions vied for power in a violent civil war. Mobutu Sese Seko emerged as the leader of a pro-American faction and benefitted from the support of the Central Intelligence Agency. Fearful that other Marxist leaders would allow the Congo to become part of

Mobutu Sese Seko. (Library of Congress)

the Soviet satellite system, the United States supplied Mobutu's military regime with the essential arms and resources to establish a dictatorship. President Lyndon B. Johnson sent C-130 aircraft to the region to transport troops into battle, and Mobutu used his position to eliminate opposition within the mineral-rich Katanga province. This, in turn, provided the United States with valuable resources such as cobalt and copper. Mobutu also helped eliminate guerrilla campaigns in neighboring states, and his ability to pacify the region allowed the United States to abandon its paramilitary activity in central Africa.

Mobutu's success depended upon Western arms. When the rebels in Shaba attempted to form an independent state in Katanga in 1977 and 1978, American, Belgian, and French troops aided Mobutu's army. Mobutu also demonstrated his allegiance during the Angolan War of Independence by allowing anticommunist troops sanctuary in Zaire. His relationship with the United States guaranteed the West a profitable mining trade and a friendly ally in Africa. Unfortunately for his Western backers, Mobutu instituted a system of brutality and torture in Zaire. His actions impoverished the nation and left it with an insurmountable international debt. He was forced to abdicate in 1997, after he proved incapable of defeating a popular revolt.

RESOURCES

Ayittey, George B. *Africa Betrayed*. New York: St. Martin's Press, 1992.

Kwitny, Jonathan. *Endless Enemies: The Making of an Unfriendly World*. New York: Penguin Books, 1986.

Schrader, Peter J. *United States Foreign Policy Toward Africa*. New York: Cambridge University Press, 1994.

SEE ALSO: Angolan Civil War; Angolan War of Independence; Congolese Civil War.

Robert D. Ubriaco, Jr.

MOGUL CONQUEST OF THE DECCAN

AT ISSUE: Possession of the Deccan
DATE: 1591-1687
LOCATION: Deccan, India

COMBATANTS: Moguls vs. sultans of Khandesh, Ahmadnagar, Bijāpur, Golconda
PRINCIPAL COMMANDERS: *Mogul*, Akbar (1542-1605), Abdur Rahim Khan, Shāh Jahān (1592-1666), Aurangzeb (1618-1707); *Deccani*, Chand Bibi, Malik ʿAmbar (d. 1626), Fath Khan
PRINCIPAL BATTLES: Sieges of Ahmadnagar, Asirgarh, Daulatabad, Bijāpur, Golconda
RESULT: Mogul domination established

BACKGROUND

In about 1600, the Mogul Empire consisted of northern India as far south as the Narmada river, traditional frontier of the Deccan. At that time, the Deccan consisted of several Muslim sultanates that were the epigones of the vanished Bahmanid sultanate (1347-1527). Between the Narmada and the Tapti was the sultanate of Khāndesh (1370-1601). Due south lay the sultanate of Ahmadnagar (1491-1633), spanning the northwestern Deccan. Farther southwest was the sultanate of Bijāpur (1490-1686), with that of Golconda to the southeast.

ACTION

In 1591, the Mogul padshah, Akbar, sent missions to the Deccani courts, demanding their submission. In 1593, Akbar despatched his friend, Abdur Rahim Khan, to the Deccan. By 1595, the Moguls were besieging **Ahmadnagar** city, which was heroically defended by Chand Bibi, daughter of a former sultan. However, because of her limited resources, she prudently ceded Berar to the Moguls in 1596, and the reigning sultan acknowledged Mogul overlordship. In 1599, Akbar invaded Khāndesh and in 1601 captured the fortress of **Asirgarh**, hitherto regarded as impregnable. Khāndesh was annexed to the empire. Before his death, Akbar had gained a considerable foothold in the Deccan.

During the reign of Akbar's son, Jahāngīr (ruled 1605-1627), the Moguls proceeded with the conquest of the Ahmadnagar sultanate, hindered by their field commanders' rivalries, a forbidding terrain, and the skill of the sultanate's de facto master, Malik ʿAmbar, an Ethiopian slave who had risen to supreme command over the armies of the sultanate and who kept the Moguls at bay until his death in 1626. Only then were the Moguls able to annex the region, gaining by trickery the great fortress of **Daulatabad** (as they had done with Asirgarh). They finally completed the conquest in 1633 during the reign of Jahāngīr's son, Shāh Jahān (r. 1627-1658), assisted by the treachery of Malik ʿAmbar's son, Fath Khan, who thereafter entered the Mogul imperial service.

In the course of these campaigns, however, the Moguls aroused the apprehensions of the Marāṭhās, splendid Hindu fighters of the northwestern Deccan, who thereafter would become implacable foes of the Mogul advance southward. In 1636, the sultan of Bijāpur, feeling threatened by Shāh Jahān's ambitions, agreed to pay an annual tribute to the Moguls, but this was a diversionary tactic, and sporadic fighting continued between Bijāpuris and Moguls, made more complicated by the new factor of Marāṭhā intransigence and skill at guerrilla warfare.

During Shāh Jahān's reign (r. 1636-1644), his third son, Aurangzeb (r. 1653-1658), as viceroy of the Mogul Deccan, vigorously executed his father's expansionist policies, his own ambitions being whetted both by his long-term plans to seize his father's throne and his personal animosity toward the sultans of Bijāpur and Golconda, who were Shiites. Once on the throne, Aurangzeb relentlessly continued the struggle, although progress was slow and the cost in manpower and resources immense. Finally, he conquered **Bijāpur** city in 1686 and **Golconda** city in 1687, annexing both former sultanates to the Mogul empire, although the ongoing struggle with the Marāṭhās, indubitable masters of much of the Deccan, continued down to and beyond Aurangzeb's death in 1707.

Aftermath

The result of more than a century's campaigning in the Deccan was that Aurangzeb ruled more of the Indian subcontinent than any other ruler before the establishment of the British Raj. However, the value of the prize was much reduced by decades of ruinous warfare, which left an impoverished and famine-stricken countryside and numerous villages abandoned by their cultivators. The Mogul Deccani wars were perhaps the major factor in Mogul imperial decline.

Resources

Richards, J. F. *The Mughal Empire*. Cambridge, England: Cambridge University Press, 1993.

Sarkar, J. N. *History of Aurangzib*. 5 vols. Bombay, India: Orient Longman, 1973.

Shyam, R. *Life and Times of Malik ʿAmbar*. Delhi, India: Munshiram Manoharlal, 1968.

See also: Akbar; Aurangzeb; Marāṭhā-Mogul Wars; Mogul-Persian War; Mogul Wars of Succession.

Gavin R. G. Hambly

Mogul-Persian War

At issue: Possession of Kandahar
Date: 1622-1653
Location: Kandahar, Afghanistan
Combatants: Safavids (Persians) vs. Moguls
Principal commanders: *Safavid*, ʿAbbās I (1571-1629), ʿAbbās II (1632-1667); *Mogul*, Aurangzeb (1618-1707)
Result: Safavids retained Kandahar region but Mogul attempts to acquire it contributed to the Mogul Empire's fiscal exhaustion

Background

The Safavid Dynasty in Iran (1501-1732) coincided with the Mogul Dynasty in India (1526-1858). The Safavid shahs were Ithna-Ashariyya ("Twelver") Shīʿites, while the Mogul padshahs (or emperors) were Sunni Muslims. These religious differences were significant, although over more than two centuries, their relationship was highly symbiotic, involving diplomatic, commercial, and cultural exchanges. Military conflict between Safavids and Moguls was sporadic, centering on the Kandahar region in what later became Afghanistan. On the road to India, Kandahar was of great strategic importance and a bone of contention between Safavids and Moguls.

In 1522, Kandahar was occupied by Bābur, who became the first Mogul padshah in 1526. Bābur's second son, Kamran Mirza, ruled Kandahar until 1545, when he was expelled by the troops of the Safavid shah, Ṭahmāsp i, who were helping to restore Bābur's eldest son, Humāyūn. Humāyūn had agreed, on gaining possession of Kandahar, to hand it over to the Safavids, but he treacherously declined to do so. It thus remained in Mogul hands until 1558, when Shah Ṭahmāsp occupied it. In 1595, before a new shah, ʿAbbās the

Great, had consolidated his position in Iran, his own governor of Kandahar handed it over to the Mogul padshah, Akbar.

ACTION

Shah ʿAbbās bided his time until he had established himself as one of Iran's powerful rulers. Then, in 1622, observing the feckless rule of Akbar's successor, Jahāngīr, he launched a determined assault on Kandahar. Although a place of great natural strength, Kandahar's defenses had been neglected during the previous decade when Jahāngīr's administration had been distracted by familial rivalries. After a siege of forty-five days, Shah ʿAbbās recaptured the city.

The Safavids ruled Kandahar from 1622 until 1638, when, history repeating itself, its governor, Ali Mardan Khan, who had aroused the suspicions of his paranoiac master, Shah Safi, handed the city over to Shāh Jahān. Kandahar remained a province of the Mogul empire for the next ten years. Then, following the failure in 1646-1647 of the Moguls to conquer Balkh in northern Afghanistan, a new shah, ʿAbbās II, judged the time opportune to take back Kandahar, and after a two-month siege, Kandahar capitulated.

Humiliated by the loss of Kandahar, Shāh Jahān determined to regain it, launching three costly and ineffective expeditions into that remote and unfriendly region. The first, in 1649, was commanded by his vizier, Sadullah Khan, and his third (and ablest) son, Aurangzeb, with approximately fifty thousand men. The army reached Kandahar but could make no impression upon its defenses and was forced to withdraw before the onset of winter. Aurangzeb tried again in 1652 and failed again, underscoring the superiority of Safavid to Mogul artillery and also the logistical difficulties of maintaining an army in the field so far from its base. A third expedition in 1653, commanded by the padshah's favorite son, Dara, also proved disastrous. In 1656, Shāh Jahān planned another attempt but was dissuaded by his advisers.

AFTERMATH

Thereafter, Kandahar remained in Safavid hands until the Ghilzais occupied it between 1709 and 1738, when Nādir Shāh reintegrated it into his short-lived Iranian empire. With his death in 1747, it became the capital of the newly established Durrāni kingdom, the precursor of modern Afghanistan. The years of Mogul occupation left no permanent trace, but Shāh Jahān's costly attempts to regain it contributed to the empire's ensuing fiscal crisis.

RESOURCES

Begley, W. E., and Z. A. Desai. *The Shāh Jahān Nama*. Delhi: Oxford University Press, 1990.
Lockhart, L. *The Fall of the Safavi Dynasty and the Afghan Occupation of Persia*. Cambridge, England: Cambridge University Press, 1958.
Richards, J. F. *The Mughal Empire*. Cambridge, England: Cambridge University Press, 1993.
Savory, R. *Iran Under the Safavids*. Cambridge, England: Cambridge University Press, 1980.

SEE ALSO: ʿAbbās the Great; Akbar; Aurangzeb; Bābur; Bābur, conquests of; Marāthā-Mogul Wars; Mogul Conquest of the Deccan; Rājput Rebellion.

Gavin R. G. Hambly

MOGUL-SIKH WARS

AT ISSUE: Preservation of the Sikh religion and culture
DATE: 1675-1716
LOCATION: Punjab, northwest India
COMBATANTS: Moguls vs. Sikhs
PRINCIPAL COMMANDERS: *Mogul*, Emperor Jahāngīr (1569-1627), Shāh Jahān (1592-1658), Aurangzeb (1618-1707), Farrukh Siyar (d. 1719); *Sikh*, Arjun (1563-1606), Hargobind (1596-1644), Bandā Bahādur (d. 1716)
PRINCIPAL BATTLES: Amritsar, Lahira, Khidrana, Mukhlisgarh, Siege of Gurdespur
RESULT: Sikhs established their religion and culture and helped destroy the Mogul empire

BACKGROUND

The Sikh religion originated with Nānak (1469-1539) in the Punjab. Because of its saintly tradition, its egalitarian ideas, and especially its highly popular economic policies whereby land was distributed to the poor, the Sikh religion attracted large numbers of followers.

Jahāngīr, the Mogul emperor, resented the growing popularity of Arjun and the assistance he had given his son, Khusrau, in his rebellion against Jahāngīr. Arjun was arrested and tortured, and on May 20, 1606, he died. His successor, Hargobind, began the Sikh martial tradition by welcoming offerings of arms and horses instead of money. He trained an army and built fortresses. Arrested, he spent about a year in prison.

ACTION

With the accession of Shāh Jahān, the Sikhs' problems really began. In **Amritsar**, in 1628, Hargobind was ordered arrested. After a clash, he fled, and in 1630, the Moguls were badly mauled at **Lahira**. In 1634, realizing he could not face the Moguls on the plains, Hargobind moved to Kiratpur in the Himalayan foothills. The succeeding Gurus (Har Rai and Hari Kishen) led peaceful lives, but Mogul Aurangzeb ordered Teg Bahadur arrested and murdered.

The guru's successor, Gobind Singh, the last of the ten gurus, introduced the concept of *dharma yudh* (battle for the sake of righteousness), which made it a duty to resist an avowed enemy with all the means at one's disposal. He also welcomed volunteers for the Khalsa, the army he created in 1699. Hindu regional rulers resented his growing power and asked Aurangzeb to destroy the Khalsa. Gobind was besieged at Nirmoh, Basali, and Anandpur before breaking out to Chamkaur, where he lost his two elder sons. He was smuggled out, but his two remaining sons, aged nine and seven, were murdered. Thousands of people joined him because of their deaths, and Gobind defeated the Moguls at **Khidrana** (1708). Gobind was stabbed by an assassin and died a few days later on October 7, 1708, but the Khalsa now composed a hard core of nearly 100,000 men with an even larger number of supporters.

With the new Mogul emperor, Bahādur Shāh I, fighting in the south, Gobind's successor, Bandā Bahādur, commander of the army, attempted to destroy Mogul power in the north using the famous Sikh tactic of hit, run, turn back, and hit again. By 1710, only Lahore and Kasur in the Punjab remained under Mogul control. Bahādur Shāh hurried back to the north and called for a general mobilization and a jihad (holy war) against the Sikhs. In 1712, his successor, Jahandar Shāh, besieged Bandā at **Mukhlisgarh**. Under Farrukh Siyar, Bandā was besieged at **Gurdespur** for eight months (1715-1716) and captured; hundreds were massacred. Bandā was taken to Delhi along with carts filled with several hundred prisoners, and in March, 1716, the prisoners were killed. On June 19, 1716, Bandā, his four-year-old son, and a final batch of Sikhs were executed.

AFTERMATH

The Sikh rebellions helped destroy the Mogul Empire. The Mogul policy of repression toward the Sikhs had the effect of strengthening the Sikh religion and community as the Sikhs developed a martial tradition to defend their way of life. As the Sikhs became militarily powerful, they were able to acquire great tracts of land in the Punjab which, in turn, attracted more followers. The Sikh success encouraged the Rohillas, the Rājputs, the Jats, and others to rebel.

RESOURCES

Hintze, Andrea. *The Mughal Empire and Its Decline*. Brookfield, Vt.: Ashgate, 1997.

Richards, John F. *The Mughal Empire*. Cambridge, England: Cambridge University Press, 1993.

Singh, Khushwant. *A History of the Sikhs: 1469-1839*. Princeton, N.J.: Princeton University Press, 1963.

SEE ALSO: Akbar; Aurangzeb; Marāṭhā-Mogul Wars; Marāṭhā Wars; Mogul Civil Wars; Mogul Conquest of the Deccan; Rājput Rebellion.

Roger D. Long

MOGUL WARS OF SUCCESSION

AT ISSUE: Mogul succession
DATE: 1657-1720
LOCATION: India
COMBATANTS: Mogul princes
PRINCIPAL COMMANDERS: *Mogul princes*, Akbar (1542-1605), Jahāngīr (1569-1627), Shāh Jahān (1592-1666), Aurangzeb (1618-1707), Bahādur Shāh (1643-1712)
PRINCIPAL BATTLES: Benares, Dharmatpur, Samugarh, Ajmer, Jajau
RESULT: Skillful commanders won the throne

BACKGROUND

The Mogul Dynasty in India (1526-1858) experienced recurring succession struggles as younger sons competed with elder sons for their inheritance. Humāyūn spent most of his reign dealing with rebellions by his brothers. His son Akbar had to deal with the revolt of his heir, Jahāngīr, who was fearful of being superseded by his eldest son, Khusrau. During Jahāngīr's reign, his sons engaged in rivalry from which the third, Khurram (the future Shāh Jahān), emerged successful, having killed two brothers, two nephews, and two cousins.

Action

By 1657, Shāh Jahān, sick and senile, wanted his eldest son, Dara, whom he kept with him in Delhi, to succeed him. Dara's brothers, Shuja, Aurangzeb, and Murad, governors respectively of Bengal, the Deccan, and Gujarat, aspired to displace him. On the news of Shāh Jahān's illness, Shuja proclaimed himself padshah (emperor), but Dara's forces defeated him near **Benares** (February, 1658). In the meantime, Murad had proclaimed himself padshah in December, 1657, and Aurangzeb agreed to support him.

In February, 1658, Aurangzeb marched north to join Murad. At **Dharmatpur** (near Ujjain) and then at **Samugarh**, near Āgra (both May, 1658), Aurangzeb and Murad defeated Dara's supporters, and Dara fled toward Lahore. The victors entered Āgra, imprisoned their father in the fort (where he remained a captive until his death in 1666), and seized the imperial treasury. However, tensions surfaced between the two brothers, and Aurangzeb treacherously arrested Murad and sent him to the state prison at Gwalior (June, 1658), crowning himself padshah in Delhi (July, 1658), before dealing with a renewed threat from Shuja in Bengal (December, 1658). Defeated again, Shuja eventually fled to Arakan, where he was murdered.

Meanwhile, Dara had raised a fresh army, only to be defeated near **Ajmer** (March, 1659), after which Aurangzeb staged a second coronation (June, 1659). Dara, captured in flight, was sent to Delhi and executed, together with his second son. Murad was executed in Gwalior in 1661. Dara's eldest son was captured and executed in 1662.

Thereafter, Aurangzeb ruled until 1707, although, mindful of his father's and his own fratricides, he remained obsessively suspicious of his five sons: Muhammad Sultan, whom he kept prisoner in Gwalior until his death in about 1676; Muazzam, who succeeded him as Bahādur Shāh I (ruled 1707-1712); Muhammad Azam; Akbar, who rebelled against his father and fled to Iran, dying between 1704 and 1706; and Kam Bakhsh. At Aurangzeb's death, Muazzam, Muhammad Azam, and Kam Bakhsh, governors respectively of Kabul, Gujarat, and Bijāpur, embarked on a fratricidal struggle for the succession. Muazzam swiftly occupied Delhi and assumed the title of Bahādur Shāh. Muhammad Azam marched north to fight him, but at **Jajau** (June, 1707), he was killed in battle with his two sons. Bahādur Shāh then marched on the Deccan and near Hyderabad eliminated Kam Bakhsh and two of his sons (January, 1709).

Following Bahādur Shāh's death in 1712, four of his sons battled for the throne. The eldest, Jahandar, won but proved a poltroon and was murdered by his nephew, Farrukh Siyar, the puppet of the Sayyid brothers, court kingmakers. When Farrukh Siyar showed signs of independence, the Sayyid brothers murdered him, then successively proclaimed two grandsons of Bahādur Shāh, whom they immediately eliminated in favor of a third and then a fourth, Muḥammad Shāh. Proclaimed padshah in 1719, Muḥammad Shāh was determined to escape the thralldom of the kingmakers. They attempted unsuccessfully to replace him with a cousin in 1720, but the plot miscarried, and by 1722, both were dead.

Aftermath

Of the five successors of Muhammad Shah, one was murdered and two were blinded, but not in intrafamily rivalries. The wars of succession had led to the emergence of two strong rulers, Shāh Jahān in 1627 and Aurangzeb in 1658. In contrast, those who acquired the throne between 1707 and 1719 were mere puppets of the Mogul nobility.

Resources

Bernier, F. *Travels in the Mogul Empire*. Westminster, England: Archibald Constable, 1891.

Irvine, W. *Later Mughals*. Delhi, India: Manoharlal, 1971.

Richard, J. F. *The Mughal Empire*. Cambridge, England: Cambridge University Press, 1993.

See also: Akbar; Aurangzeb; Mogul Conquest of the Deccan.

Gavin R. G. Hambly

Mohács

Type of action: Ground battle in the Hungarian-Turkish Wars
Date: August 29-30, 1526
Location: High plain of Mohács, to the west of Buda, Hungary
Combatants: 100,000 Turks vs. 25,000 Hungarians
Principal commanders: *Ottoman*, Süleyman I (1494/1495-1566); *Hungarian*, King Louis II (1506-1526)
Result: Decisive military battle that crushed Hungarian resistance and established Ottoman domination over central Europe

Süleyman I led 100,000 soldiers on a second campaign into Hungary on April 23, 1526, having captured Belgrade on a previous expedition into the country. Hampered by torrential rains and hailstorms, Ottoman forces finally crossed the River Sava, a tributary of the Danube, on a bridge built by advance troops. Most of the Hungarian forces had retreated but a few remained in the fortress of Peterwardein. Süleyman's grand vizier, İbrahim Paşa, captured the city, beheading five hundred Hungarian soldiers and selling the inhabitants into slavery.

Crossing the Drava River on a pontoon bridge, Süleyman expected to engage the Hungarians but found no resistance because of internal rivalries and their inability to coordinate supplies. Süleyman advanced his troops to the plain of Mohács, where they encountered the Hungarian king Louis II and four thousand of his troops. By the time of the battle, approximately 25,000 reinforcements had arrived from various groups, including the Poles, Germans, and Bohemians. Most of the Hungarian commanders urged a retreat to Buda, allowing time for additional troops to join the main force and lengthening the Ottoman lines of communication and supply in the process. A group of Magyar nobles demanded that the king take the offensive immediately. Their strategy was to engage in battle on the plain of Mohács, allowing the Hungarian cavalry room to maneuver, a decision that gave the advantage to the Ottomans, who had a much larger cavalry.

Hungarian tactics during the battle proved even more disastrous. The Hungarians, led by Louis, initiated the battle with a head-on charge of their cavalry into the center of the Ottoman line. The Hungarians, believing that the tactic had been successful, initiated a general charge of all of their forces. Süleyman, who had placed the main line of the Ottoman forces farther back, ordered them forward, and as the Hungarian forces advanced, they encountered the main Janissary troops. Heavy hand-to-hand fighting occurred, but in the end, the Turkish artillery proved superior. The Ottomans managed to encircle the Hungarian troops, slaughtering them by the thousands and scattering the rest. Within an hour and a half, the battle was over. During the battle, Süleyman narrowly escaped injury, but the Hungarian king received a head wound and later died. That day, twenty-four thousand Hungarians died on the plain of Mohács.

Süleyman entered Buda on September 10, slaughtering the peasants and burning the city. After resting a few weeks, the sultan and his troops marched back to Istanbul.

Significance

The complete destruction of the Hungarian forces guaranteed Ottoman control over the heart of Europe for several centuries. The death of the Hungarian king Louis, who did not leave an heir, resulted in a civil war between Archduke Ferdinand of Habsburg (later Ferdinand I), the brother-in-law of the dead king, and John Zápolya, the prince of Transylvania. Süleyman recognized Zápolya in exchange for tribute and initiated the Austro-Turkish Wars in his support.

Resources

Cook, M. A., ed. *A History of the Ottoman Empire to 1730*. New York: Cambridge University Press, 1976.

Fodor, Pál, and Géza Dávid, eds. *Ottomans, Hungarians, and Habsburgs in Central Europe: The Military Confines in the Era of Ottoman Conquest*. Boston: Brill, 2000.

Junt, Metin, and Christine Woodhead, eds. *Suleyman the Magnificent and His Age: The Otto-*

man Empire in the Early Modern World. New York: Longman, 1995.

SEE ALSO: Austro-Turkish Wars; Hungarian Civil Wars; Janissaries; Ottoman Empire; Süleyman I.

Cynthia Northrup

MOLTKE, HELMUTH VON (1800-1891)

FULL NAME: Helmuth Karl Bernhard von Moltke
BORN: October 26, 1800; Parchim, Mecklenberg
DIED: April 24, 1891; Kreisau, Germany
PRINCIPAL WARS: Austro-Prussian War, Franco-Prussian War
PRINCIPAL BATTLES: Könnigrätz (1866), Siege of Metz (1870), Sedan (1870)
MILITARY SIGNIFICANCE: Moltke was the father of the modern general staff and the architect of Germany's rise to military dominance. Under his aegis, Germany rose from a collection of small states to the leading power in Europe.

Helmuth von Moltke initially served with the Danish military, but in 1821, he joined the vaunted Prussian army. He attended the War College, 1823-1826, graduated with distinction, and subsequently displayed a flair for writing. In 1833, he was dispatched to Turkey as adviser to Sultan Mahmud during the war with Muhammed Ali of Egypt. On June 24, 1839, Moltke commanded the Turkish artillery during the disgraceful defeat at Nezib but managed to bring off his guns. He later wrote about his experiences, which brought him to the attention of the Prussian royal family. Moltke gained appointment as an aide-de-camp to Prince Frederick (later Frederick III) in 1854, and the following year, he joined the Prussian general staff.

As a staff officer, Moltke brought his considerable military genius to bear and instituted reforms that made his general staff the envy of Europe. He was impressed by the military potential of railroads and telegraphs, and incorporated their usage into army maneuvers. Furthermore, he labored strenuously to devise a mobilization scheme that permitted large numbers of trained reserves to expand the regular army promptly and efficiently, thereby multiplying its effectiveness. He also introduced the concept of long-range strategic thinking for armies that had grown so large that effective planning was essential to victory. In 1864, he successfully tested his theories during the brief conflict with Denmark. Two years later, Prussia deemed itself sufficiently strong to challenge the Austrian empire for dominance in Germany in the Austro-Prussian War. Moltke's clever use of railways and troop concentrations brought the Austrian army to bear at Könnigrätz on July 3, 1866, soundly defeating it. The war was successfully concluded in only six weeks and left Prussia undisputed leader of the German confederation.

Over the next four years, Moltke worked hard at correcting operational and tactical mistakes that

Helmuth von Moltke. (Library of Congress)

had surfaced during the Austrian war, and the Prussian army reached new heights of efficiency. Chancellor Otto von Bismarck then cleverly orchestrated a showdown with Prussia's final adversary, France, whose army was widely regarded as the best in Europe. When the Franco-Prussian War erupted in 1870, Moltke again displayed strategic genius by quickly mobilizing the army, overwhelming the French in the field, and using converging lines of march to trap the bulk of enemy forces at Metz under Marshal Achille-François Bazaine. When a relief force was raised under Marshal Marie E. P. M. de MacMahon, Moltke's men quickly outflanked and captured it at Sedan. By mid-1870, Prussian forces were closely besieging Paris and waging a relentless antipartisan war in the countryside. When the French at Metz finally surrendered, the Prussians proclaimed a unified German empire. For his role in this spectacular victory, Moltke was elevated to field marshal and restored to his role as head of the general staff.

For the rest of his life, Moltke continually refined the general staff, military strategy, and the vaunted Germany army. However, after Germany's primacy was secure, he strongly opposed military adventurism and sought to convince the new kaiser, William II, that peace was the country's best guarantee for survival. The staff concepts he introduced have become standard military procedure in armies around the world.

RESOURCES

Addington, Larry H. *The Blitzkrieg Era and the German General Staff*. New Brunswick, N.J.: Rutgers University Press, 1971.

Bucholz, Arden. *Moltke, Schlieffen, and Prussian War Planning*. New York: Berg, 1991.

Craig, Gordon A. *The Politics of the Prussian Army, 1640-1945*. New York: Oxford University Press, 1956.

Dupuy, Trevor N. *A Genius for War: The German Army and General Staff*. Englewood Cliffs, N.J.: Prentice-Hall, 1977.

Friedrich, Otto. *Blood and Iron: From Bismark to Hitler: The von Moltke Family's Impact on German History*. New York: HarperCollins, 1995.

SEE ALSO: Bismarck, Otto von; Könnigrätz; Metz, Siege of; Sedan.

John C. Fredriksen

MOLTKE, HELMUTH VON (1848-1916)

FULL NAME: Helmuth Johannes Ludwig von Moltke
BORN: May 25, 1848; Gersdorff, Mecklenburg (later in Germany)
DIED: June 18, 1916; Berlin, Germany
PRINCIPAL WAR: World War I
PRINCIPAL BATTLE: Marne (1914)
MILITARY SIGNIFICANCE: The failure of the German offensive on the western front was to a considerable extent caused by Moltke's modifications of the Schlieffen Plan.

The military career of Colonel General Helmuth von Moltke was marked by unusually rapid advancement. By 1882, he served as adjutant to his uncle, the chief of the general staff, Field Marshal Helmuth von Moltke. In 1903, the younger Moltke advanced to the position of quartermaster general and, in 1906, succeeded General Alfred von Schlieffen as chief of the general staff, a position he accepted with considerable reluctance.

Moltke's revisions of the Schlieffen Plan involved a weakening of the German right wing of attack and a strengthening of the left wing, which was designed to protect Alsace-Lorraine. When the Germans unexpectedly found themselves on the defensive in the Battle of the Marne in 1914, Moltke was unable to act decisively and left crucial decisions to a subordinate. In view of the worsening strategic situation, William II decided to replace Moltke with General Erich von Falkenhayn.

RESOURCES

Asprey, Robert B. *The First Battle of the Marne*. London: Weidenfeld & Nicolson, 1962.

Barnett, Correlli. "The Tragic Delusion." In *The Sword Bearers*. London: Eyre & Spottiswoode, 1963.

Friedrich, Otto. "The Nervous Nephew." In *Blood and Iron, From Bismarck to Hitler: The von Moltke Family's Impact on German History*. New York: HarperCollins, 1995.

Goerlitz, Walter. "War Without Generals." In *History of the German General Staff, 1657-1945*. New York: Praeger, 1953.

Monck, George

FULL NAME: George Monck, first duke of Albemarle
BORN: December 6, 1608; Potheridge, Devonshire, England
DIED: January 3, 1670; London, England
PRINCIPAL WARS: Bishops' Wars, English Civil War of 1642-1651, Anglo-Dutch Wars
PRINCIPAL BATTLE: Dunbar (1650)
MILITARY SIGNIFICANCE: Monck helped usher in peace after the divisive English Civil War and enabled the restoration of Charles II and the British monarchy.

George Monck began his military training in the expedition to Cádiz (1625) and enhanced his military skills as captain in the Dutch service (1629). He served in the Bishops' Wars against Scotland (1639-1640) and commanded his own regiment in the Great Irish Rebellion (1641-1652). Captured four years later and charged with high treason, he was imprisoned in the Tower of London, where he wrote a military science manual, *Observations upon Military and Political Affairs* (1671).

After he was released from prison and cleared of charges, Monck returned to the war in Ireland as an adjutant general and became the civil administrator of Ulster (1647), where he negotiated a tentative peace. He led a Parliamentary regiment into Scotland and was one of the chief commanders at Oliver Cromwell's victory at Dunbar (1650).

In 1659, the council of state appointed Monck the commander in chief of all forces in England and Scotland to assist the peaceable reestablishment of the monarchy. The following year, he helped King Charles II draft the Declaration of Breda (1660). He became the first lord of the treasury (1667-1668) and assisted the British navy during the Second Anglo-Dutch War.

RESOURCES
Ashley, M. *General Monck*. Totowa, N.J.: Rowman & Littlefield, 1977.
Jamison, Ted R., Jr. *George Monck and the Restoration: Victor Without Bloodshed*. Fort Worth: Texas Christian University Press, 1975.
Stoyle, Mark. "The Honour of General Monck." *History Today* 43 (August, 1993): 43-48.

SEE ALSO: Anglo-Dutch Wars; Cromwell, Oliver; Dunbar; English Civil War of 1642-1651.

Susanna Calkins

Mongol Empire

DATE: c. 1200-1759
LOCATION: Mongolia
PRINCIPAL MILITARY ACTIONS: Conquest of Asia, Russia, Eastern and Central Europe, the Middle East, and Africa
MILITARY SIGNIFICANCE: Under the strategic leadership of Genghis Khan, the Mongol Empire became a great military state.

In the early thirteenth century, the Mongols were pastoral nomads living in eastern Mongolia. Their way of life made them skilled horsemen and archers, talents that made them a potentially formidable fighting power; however, their small tribes lacked strength. Genghis Khan bound the nomadic Mongol tribes together by promulgating a societal code, the Yassa, which required loyalty, religious belief, strict obedience, and respect for cultural tradition. He also built a general staff from trusted family members and close friends and trained them to conduct combined arms operations over large territorial areas, employing mobility, shock power, and strategic surprise. The Mongol army was organized into units of ten thousand (*tuman*) and subunits of a thousand (*guran*) and divided into ten companies and ten platoons. Its heavy cavalry was armed with lances, heavy swords, axes, and full armor protection, and its light cavalry was equipped with heavy and light bows, javelins, heavy and light swords, and partial body armor.

Under Genghis Khan, in 1209, the Mongols launched an invasion of the Western Xia state in preparation for war against the Jin Empire. In late 1211, 70,000 Mongols invaded Jin. In 1215, the Mongols overran Beijing, a Jin stronghold, in an orgy of wanton destruction. In late 1218, the

The Mongol Empire in 1260

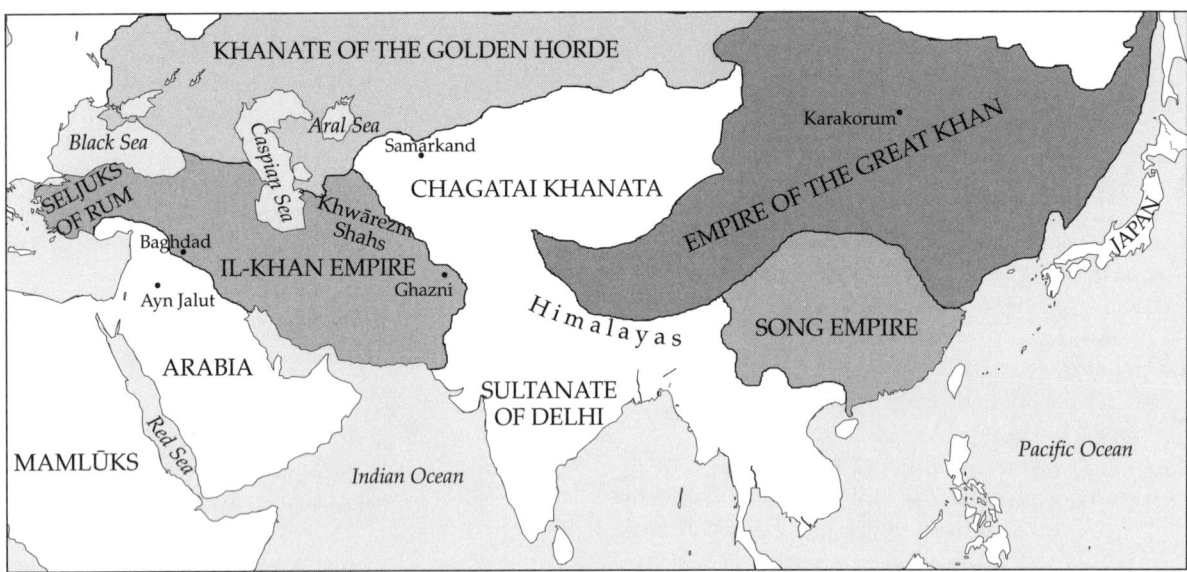

Mongols sent a trade caravan to meet with the Shah Muhammad in Khwārezm, on the western edge of the empire, but its members were beheaded. In 1219, a Mongol army of 200,000 men moved into the Khwārezm state. By the end of 1220, the Khwārezm state was shattered and the fleeing shah dead from pneumonia. Meanwhile, a strong Mongol force, led by generals Subatai and Jebe, raced through the southern Caucasus, Iraq-Ajemi, Azerbaijan, and the kingdom of Georgia, invading Russia in 1222. In 1226, Genghis Khan attacked the Western Xia state for its belligerent policies toward him and its ties with the Jin. In August, 1227, during his campaign against the Western Xia state, Genghis Khan died, and his son, Ogatai, was named great khan.

The Mongol expansion continued with the reconquest of Persia, the Caucasus, and Korea. In 1235, Ogatai gave command of 120,000 troops to Batu and Subatai with orders to conquer Russia and Eastern Europe (Poland, Silesia, Bohemia, Hungary, Bosnia, Slovenia, Croatia). The conquest of Russia was completed in 1240. Meanwhile, in 1230, Ogatai had renewed the Mongol assault against the Jin, receiving help from the Song. In 1234, the state of Jin collapsed. The alliance between the Mongols and the Song ended in 1235, and the Mongols invaded and conquered the Song in 1258.

In 1241, Batu and Subatai defeated the Teutonic Knights in Poland and Hungarian troops led by King Béla IV. The Mongols proceeded to ravage Eastern Europe, approaching Vienna, but were called back after the death of Ogatai in late 1241. Succession disputes fragmented the Mongol Empire. Batu returned to the steppes of Eurasia and established the Golden Horde. The Chagatai Khanate controlled Central Asia, and the Empire of the Great Khan controlled the Mongol homeland.

In 1246, Güyük was chosen as the third great khan. In 1248, Mangu was elected as the fourth great khan, and he invaded Africa, Poland, the Song Empire, and the Middle East, where he conquered Baghdad and Persia and established the Il-Khan Empire. In 1259, Mangu died, and Kublai Khan was elected the fifth great khan. In 1260, a Mongol force at ʿAyn Jāhlūt in Syria suffered a crushing defeat at the hands of the Mamlūks in Egypt, shattering the Mongol myth of invincibility. Kublai Khan's expeditions against Japan (1274 and 1281), Southeast Asian (1280's), and Java (1292-1293) were expensive failures. The Mongol Empire began to lose strength, and began a dissolution that was largely complete by the middle of the fourteenth century.

In the 1400's and 1600's, Mongol leaders attempted to revive the empire; however, in 1759,

Manchu emperor Qianlong seized and annexed Mongolia.

RESOURCES

Allsen, Thomas T. *Mongol Imperialism: The Policies of the Grand Qan Mongke in China, Russia, and the Islamic Lands, 1251-1259*. Los Angeles: University of California Press, 1987.
Genghis Khan. Documentary. Time-Life Video, 1996.
Genghis Khan: Terror and Conquest. A&E Home Video, 1995.
Marshall, Robert. *Storm from the East: From Genghis Khan to Khubilai Khan*. London: BBC Books, 1993.
Nicolle, David. *The Mongol Warlords: Genghis Khan, Kublai Khan, Hulegu, Tamerlane*. London: Brookhampton Press, 1998.
Saunders, J. J. *History of the Mongol Conquests*. London: Routledge & K. Paul, 1971.
Storm from the East. Documentary. 4 parts. NHK/BBC/Lionheart Television/Dubs Incorporated, 1993.

SEE ALSO: Genghis Khan; Kublai Khan; Mongol Empire; Ogatai.

Michael J. Siler

MONITOR VS. VIRGINIA

TYPE OF ACTION: Naval battle in the American Civil War
DATE: March 9, 1862
LOCATION: Hampton Roads, Virginia, a harbor at the confluence of the James, Nansemond, and Elizabeth Rivers into Chesapeake Bay
COMBATANTS: USS *Monitor*'s 58-man crew vs. CSS *Virginia*'s 150-man crew
PRINCIPAL COMMANDERS: *Union*, Lieutenant John Worden (1818-1887), Lieutenant Samuel Dana Greene (1840-1884); *Confederate*, Captain Franklin Buchanan (1800-1874), Lieutenant Catesby ap Roger Jones (1790-1858)
RESULT: The battle was basically a draw, though the *Monitor* succeeded in its mission to protect the USS *Minnesota*

On March 8, 1862, the Northern steam frigate *Merrimack*, salvaged, armored, armed, and rechristened the CSS *Virginia* by the Southerners, destroyed the wooden warships USS *Cumberland* and USS *Congress*. During the action against the *Congress*, the *Virginia*'s captain, Franklin Buchanan, was wounded, and command passed to Lieutenant Catesby ap Roger Jones. He hoped, on

The Merrimack, *the first ironclad built in the United States, would later see service as the CSS* Virginia. *(Corbis)*

the following day, to complete the destruction of every Union warship in lower Chesapeake Bay, especially the frigate *Minnesota*, which the *Virginia* had run aground.

After sunset, the USS *Monitor* steamed into Hampton Roads and anchored near the *Minnesota*. The *Monitor*, like the *Virginia*, was an ironclad but had a revolving turret carrying two eleven-inch guns. Soon after dawn on March 9, 1862, the battle between the Confederate ironclad, dubbed a "half-submerged barn," and the Union ironclad, called a "can on a shingle," began. First at long range, then at very close quarters, the two ships fired shots and shells at each other, with neither gaining supremacy. Midway in the fight the nimbly maneuverable *Monitor* withdrew to shallow water to resupply its powder and shot. Following the respite, the *Monitor* repulsed the *Virginia*'s attempts to board her. When a Confederate shell exploded near one of the *Monitor*'s sighting slits, iron flecks blinded Lieutenant John Worden and Lieutenant Samuel Greene took over. Around noon, the sounds of shots slamming into and ricocheting off ironplate ceased, and the *Virginia*, low on ammunition and leaking at the bow, withdrew to its navy yard. The *Monitor* did not pursue, Greene deciding to remain near the *Minnesota*.

Significance

On March 8, 1862, the Confederate ironclad *Virginia*, with its ten guns, easily sank the Union warships *Cumberland* and *Congress*, with their total of seventy-four guns, proving that wood was no match for iron. On March 9, 1862, when it was iron versus iron, the *Monitor* fought the *Virginia* to a standstill. The battle between the *Monitor* and the *Virginia*, which made wooden warships obsolete, started a new era in naval warfare.

Resources

Baxter, James Phinney. *The Introduction of the Ironclad Warship*. Cambridge, Mass.: Harvard University Press, 1933.

Davis, William C. *Duel Between the First Ironclads*. New York: Doubleday, 1975.

Hearts in Bondage. Fiction feature. Republic, 1936.

Mokin, Arthur. *Ironclad: The Monitor and the Merrimack*. Novato, Calif.: Presidio, 1991.

The Monitor and the Merrimack. Documentary. Frith Films, 1972.

See also: American Civil War; Navies: Organization and tactics; Warships.

Robert J. Paradowski

Monmouth

Type of action: Ground battle in the American Revolution
Date: June 28, 1778
Location: Monmouth Courthouse, New Jersey
Combatants: 10,000 Americans vs. 10,000 British
Principal commanders: *American*, General George Washington (1732-1799); *British*, General Sir Henry Clinton (1738-1795)
Result: The Americans and British fought to a draw in the last major battle of the American Revolution in the north

On June 18, 1778, General Sir Henry Clinton evacuated Philadelphia after an eight-month occupation and marched toward New York City. George Washington pursued with an army that had been extensively trained by Baron Friedrich Wilhelm von Steuben during the preceding winter at Valley Forge. On June 28, the Americans caught the British rearguard near Monmouth Courthouse and attacked at 10:00 A.M. General Charles Lee directed the assault but issued no firm orders, and the Americans were soon in full retreat. Washington rallied his army and organized a new line. The two armies then fought in the sweltering heat until dark, as the Americans repulsed a series of disjointed British attacks. Clinton then withdrew and resumed his march to New York. The British had at least 147 killed, many from sunstroke, 170 wounded, and 64 missing. Washington lost 106 dead, 161 wounded, and 95 missing.

Significance

Monmouth demonstrated the growing professionalism in the American army. For the remainder of the war, the army would be able to stand up to the British in open combat. The battle was also the last major engagement in the north. Washington would station his army near New York City, awaiting an opportunity to attack, until the Yorktown campaign in 1781.

RESOURCES

Kwasny, Mark V. *Washington's Partisan War, 1775-1783*. Kent, Ohio: Kent State University Press, 1996.

Middlekauff, Robert. *The Glorious Cause: The American Revolution, 1763-1789*. New York: Oxford University Press, 1982.

Thayer, Theodore. *The Making of a Scapegoat: Washington and Lee at Monmouth*. Port Washington, N.Y.: Kennikat, 1976.

SEE ALSO: American Revolution; Steuben, Baron Friedrich Wilhelm von; Washington, George; Yorktown and Virginia Capes.

Michael P. Gabriel

Monongahela

TYPE OF ACTION: Ground battle in the French and Indian War
DATE: July 9, 1755
LOCATION: Monongahela River, nine miles southwest of Fort Duquesne (Pittsburgh)
COMBATANTS: 1,400 British and Americans vs. 855 French, Canadians, and Native Americans
PRINCIPAL COMMANDERS: *British*, Major General Edward Braddock (1695-1755); *French*, Captain Daniel-Hyacinthe-Marie Liénard de Beaujeu (1711-1755)
RESULT: French crush a British army, stopping an offensive against Fort Duquesne

On July 9, 1755, Major General Edward Braddock's 1,400-man army neared Fort Duquesne after a month-long march from Fort Cumberland, Maryland, through the wilderness. Captain Claude-Pierre Contrecoeur, Duquesne's commander, sent Captain Daniel-Hyacinthe-Marie Liénard Beaujeu and more than 600 Native Americans to slow the British advance. The two forces met in early afternoon. Beaujeu was killed immediately, but his men drove the British vanguard into the main body and quickly encircled it. Then, unseen by the British, they rained fire on them from the forest. Braddock's regulars, tightly packed in their linear formations, blindly returned the fire and were slaughtered. His provincial troops tried to fight from cover but to no avail. After several hours, the British army broke and ran. George Washington, one of the general's aides, helped conduct the retreat. The French inflicted 977 casualties, including 73 percent of the officers, and mortally wounded Braddock, while losing only 23 dead and 16 wounded. They also captured large amounts of military equipment.

SIGNIFICANCE

The first major battle of the French and Indian War, the defeat at the Monongahela greatly shook Anglo-American morale. Furthermore, it left the frontier vulnerable to Indian raids as the French retained Fort Duquesne.

RESOURCES

Kopperman, Paul E. *Braddock at the Monongahela*. Pittsburgh, Pa.: University of Pittsburgh Press, 1977.

O'Meara, Walter. *Guns at the Forks*. Englewood Cliffs, N.J.: Prentice-Hall, 1965.

Williams, Noel St. John. *Redcoats Along the Hudson: The Struggle for North America, 1754-1763*. London: Brassey's, 1997.

SEE ALSO: Braddock, Edward; Fort Duquesne; French and Indian War; Washington, George.

Michael P. Gabriel

Mons Graupius

TYPE OF ACTION: Ground battle in the Roman conquest of Britain
DATE: 84 C.E.
LOCATION: Perthshire in northern Scotland, in the Grampian mountains
COMBATANTS: Roman forces versus Caledonian League
PRINCIPAL COMMANDERS: *Roman*, Gnaeus Julius Agricola (40-93 C.E.); *Caledonian*, Calgacus (Galgacus)
RESULT: Romans routed and killed 10,000 Caledonians with only 360 Roman casualties

The Roman legions led by Gnaeus Julius Agricola pursued the Caledonians and their leader Calgacus into a region now known as the Grampian Mountains in northern Scotland. The exact location of the climactic battle is not known with certainty. About 30,000 Caledonians gathered on the side of a hill known as Mons Graupius. They vastly outnumbered the Romans, who faced them at the base of the hill. The Caledonians were tall, often red-haired people who fought with great individual strength and bravery, using their long swords and small circular shields. Their charioteers darted back and forth, stopping to discharge spears and other missiles. The Romans prevailed by covering themselves with their long heavy shields, advancing relentlessly, and stabbing with short, thick swords. The rout was completed by a flank attack of the Roman cavalry.

Significance

Agricola had sought to subdue the whole of Scotland and add it to the Roman Empire, but he was recalled in 84 C.E. by the Emperor Domitian before the conquest was complete. However, a series of forts and a road system were built. During the century after Mons Graupius, the Romans abandoned their offensive strategy in favor of a defensive one.

Resources

Hanson, W. S. *Agricola and the Conquest of the North*. London: Batsford, 1991.

Maxwell, Gordon S. *A Battle Lost: Romans and Caledonians at Mons Graupius*. Edinburgh, Scotland: Edinburgh University, 1990.

Salway, Peter. *The Oxford Illustrated History of Roman Britain*. Oxford: Oxford University Press, 1993.

See also: Agricola, Gnaeus Julius; Celts; Roman Empire, Wars of the.

John R. Phillips

Montcalm, Louis-Joseph de

Full name: Louis-Joseph de Montcalm-Gozon
Also known as: marquis de Montcalm
Born: February 28, 1712; Candiac, France
Died: September 14, 1759; Quebec City
Principal wars: War of the Polish Succession, War of the Austrian Succession, French and Indian War
Principal battles: Prague (1741), Piacenza (1746), Oswego (1756), Fort William Henry (1757), Fort Ticonderoga (1758), Quebec (1759)

Military significance: Popular with his troops, Montcalm demonstrated that he was a worthy match for any British general in the New World, but his temper, combined with the noncooperation of Quebec's civil governor, led to the loss of the French colonies.

A commissioned ensign at age twelve and an active soldier at age fifteen, Louis-Joseph de Montcalm first saw action against the Austrians at the outset of the War of Polish Succession (1733-1738). An aristocrat by birth, he nevertheless risked his life repeatedly, entering the War of Austrian Succession (1740-1748), getting wounded during the defense of Prague in 1741, and suffering five saber wounds at the Battle of Piacenza in 1746.

As commander of French forces in North America, he arrived in Quebec to find that he had no real authority except that permitted him by the marquis de Vaudreuil, who frequently quarreled with him. Montcalm captured Oswego in 1756, establishing French control of Lake Ontario, and also captured the strongly garrisoned Fort William Henry. With the help of only 3,800 men, he repulsed Sir James Abercrombie's army of 15,000 at Fort Ticonderoga in 1758. However, he was frustrated in his battles against the British general James Wolfe by Vaudreuil's lack of support. Defeated by Wolfe on the Plains of Abraham in 1759, Montcalm suffered a fatal wound; Wolfe was killed in action. Quebec surrendered five days later.

Resources

LaPierre, Laurier. *1759: The Battle for Canada*. Toronto: McClelland and Stewart, 1990.

Parkman, Francis. *Montcalm and Wolfe*. New York: Viking, 1984.

Stacey, C. P. *Quebec (1759): The Siege and the Battle*. Toronto: Macmillan, 1959.

See also: Austrian Succession, War of the; French and Indian War; Quebec, Siege of; Wolfe, James.

Keith Garebian

Monte Cassino

Type of action: Ground battle in World War II
Date: November, 1943-June, 1944

Only the walls of the Monte Cassino Monastery remain standing after the Allied bombing. (Archive Photos/Hulton Getty Collection)

LOCATION: Italy

COMBATANTS: Germans vs. British, Americans, and Polish

PRINCIPAL COMMANDERS: *German*, Albert Kesselring (1885-1960); *British*, Harold Alexander (1891-1969); *American*, Mark Clark (1896-1985); *Polish*, Władysław Anders (1892-1970)

RESULT: Allied victory, fall of the Gustav Line

The Allies landed in southern Italy in early September, 1943, but made slow progress due to a skillful defense by German Albert Kesselring. By year's end, a powerful German position, the Gustav Line, barred further progress to the Fifteenth Army Group under Harold Alexander, which was composed of British Eighth (under Oliver Leese) and American Fifth Armies (under Mark Clark). Frustrated, the Allies launched Operation Shingle on January 22, 1944, an amphibious landing at Anzio, behind the German front, to combine with an assault on the Gustav Line. The key to the German position (under Heinrich von Vietinghoff) was Monte Cassino, topped by a venerable Benedictine monastery.

The first efforts, late in 1943 alternately by the Fifth and Eighth Armies, made little progress. The attack by the U.S. Thirty-sixth Division to coordinate with Shingle failed with heavy losses on January 17-19, 1944. The Americans, meanwhile, were pinned to the beaches at Anzio. A major U.S. assault on Cassino was repulsed on February 12, as was a New Zealand attack a few days later. The aerial bombardment in conjunction with these attacks destroyed the monastery but was ineffective. On May 17-18, Polish troops under Władysław Anders, serving with the British Eighth Army, took Cassino after ferocious combat. It was the most famous Polish action on the western front.

SIGNIFICANCE

The fall of the Gustav Line led rapidly to a breakout at Anzio and the fall of Rome (June 4); however, Kesselring was able to form a new position south of Bologna.

Resources

Anders, Władysław. *An Army in Exile*. London: Macmillan, 1949.
Evans, Bradford A. *The Bombing of Monte Cassino*. Monte Cassino: Pubblicazioni Cassinesi, 1988.
Hapgood, David, and David Richardson. *Monte Cassino*. New York: Berkeley Books, 1986.
Piekalkiewicz, Janusz. *Battle for Cassino*. Indianapolis, Ind.: Bobbs-Merrill, 1980.
The War in Europe. The War Chronicles: World War II series. Documentary. A&E Home Video, 1983.

See also: Anzio; Clark, Mark; World War II.

M. B. B. Biskupski

Montenegrin Wars of Independence

At issue: Independence of Montenegro
Date: 1852-1878
Location: Western Balkans
Combatants: Montenegrins vs. Turks
Principal commanders: *Montenegrin*, Omar Latas Pasha, general (1806-1871), Mukhtar Pasha, general (1839-1919); *Monarchist/Turkish*, Mirko Petrovic, general (1820-1867), King Nicholas I (1841-1921)
Principal battles: Grahovo, Vucji Do, Zeta River, Bjelopavica Valley
Result: Montenegrin independence

Background

Montenegro, a remote part of the Ottoman Empire, enjoyed a long-standing autonomy. Its Slavic Orthodox population were really of Serbian nationality. Since the seventeenth century, the country was ruled by its prince bishop of the Njegos Dynasty. In 1852, Danilo I came to the throne, married, and secularized the crown.

Action

Border clashes between Montenegro and Turkey occurred frequently during the Ottoman period. Furthermore, the Turks regarded Montenegro a vassal state while the Montenegrins asserted their independence. On several occasions, Istanbul succeeded in forcing the Montenegrins to recognize their suzerainty, but the Montenegrins would just as quickly ignore the treaties. In 1853, the Turkish commander in the region, Omar Latas Pasha, began a long war hoping to put Montenegro under direct Ottoman control. Danilo sought to increase his territory at the expense of the Turks and strengthen his ties to the Serbs of Herzegovina, who also were battling the Turkish guard posts. In 1858, the Montenegrin army increased to 5,800. Led by the prince's brother Mirko Petrovic, the army defeated the Ottomans at the major Battle of **Grahovo** (January 5, 1858). Danilo looked for support to the great powers, which sent a commission to fix a border for the small state. Traditionally Montenegro relied on Russia, which it regarded as the only other independent Slavic Orthodox country. However, because of St. Petersburg's lack of interest in pushing his claims, Danilo turned to France. Although this irritated Russia, Austria, and even Serbia, after Grahovo, Danilo persuaded the powers to pressure Turkey to recognize Montenegrin independence and fix its borders. However, Danilo's political rivals assassinated him in 1860.

Danilo's nephew Nicholas, son of General Petrovic, returned from his studies in France and assumed the crown. The Turks renewed their attacks on Montenegro (May 22, 1862). Initially the Montenegrins held the Turkish forces off at Novo Selo, but Omar was able to counter in strength and approach the Montenegrin capital. Only intervention by the great powers prevented the complete destruction of the state. The war brought large casualties on both sides—3,500 for the Montenegrins and more than 8,000 for the Turks. Nicholas accepted the Turkish offers for peace, which included recognition of Ottoman suzerainty. However, Nicholas did not honor this treaty and began almost immediately to prepare for a new battle. Skirmishes between the two states continued but neither side won a decisive victory until the general Balkan uprising of 1875.

Throughout the 1860's and early 1870's, Turkey was beset with revolts from all of its Christian provinces and could not devote much attention to the Montenegrins. In 1875, a major uprising occurred among the Serbs in Bosnia-Herzegovina. The troubles spread to Serbia, Bulgaria, and Montenegro. In June, 1876, Serbia and Montenegro, linked by a mutual defense treaty, declared war on Turkey. The Serbs lost, but led by King Nicholas himself, the Montenegrin army defeated the Turks at Fundina, Trijebaca, Medun, Spuz, and more than two dozen smaller skirmishes (1876). The army also won two decisive victories at **Vucji Do** (July 18, 1876), on the **Zeta River** (1876), and at the **Bjelopavica Valley** (1876). At Vucji Do, where Mukhtar Pasha commanded the Ottomans, the Turkish casualties mounted to more than 38,000, including two pashas, while the Montenegrins suffered less than 2,000 casualties. Podgorica (the modern capital), Nicksic, Ulcinj, Bar, and other towns and villages were added to Montenegro's borders and the size of the country doubled.

Aftermath

The great powers resolved the Balkan problem in the Treaty of Berlin (1878), which granted Montenegro—along with Serbia and Romania—complete independence from Turkey.

Resources

McDowell, Ian. *The "Montenegrin" Revolver*. Melbourne: Chadstone Computing, 1991.

Pavlovich, Paul. *The Serbians: The Story of a People*. Toronto: Serbian Heritage Books, 1988.

Petrovich, Michael Boro. *A History of Modern Serbia, 1804-1918*. New York: Harcourt Brace Jovanovich, 1976.

See also: Ottoman Empire; Serbo-Ottoman Conflict; Slavs; Turks.

Frederick B. Chary

Monterrey

Type of action: Ground battle in the Mexican-American War
Date: September 21-24, 1846
Location: Monterrey, Mexico (state capital of Nuevo León, Mexico)
Combatants: 6,220 Americans vs. 7,303 Mexicans
Principal commanders: *American*, Major General Zachary Taylor (1784-1850); *Mexican*, Major General Pedro de Ampudia
Result: Successful U.S. takeover of Monterrey

In the mid-afternoon on Sunday, September 20, 1846, General Zachary Taylor issued orders for 6,220 U.S. troops to begin their two-pronged attack on the city of Monterrey. Guarded by 7,303 Mexican soldiers, Monterrey lay nestled between forts, earthworks, natural cliffs, and the Santa Catarina River.

Taylor planned to cut off the city from its supply line and only escape route while at the same time taking the heights above the city. Then, despite any defensive action by the army of General Pedro de Ampudia, the city would fall quickly. Though the campaign was poorly executed and hampered by driving rain, U.S. forces were successful after two days of fierce fighting. On September 23, U.S. soldiers entered the city after finding the Mexicans' outer defenses abandoned.

Near dawn the next day, following bloody street warfare, Ampudia asked for an armistice. In the melee, 367 Mexicans had been killed or wounded defending the city. Americans dead numbered 120, with nearly 370 wounded.

Significance

Monterrey was a key locale on the approach to Saltillo, which, when occupied, would isolate Mexico City from northern Mexico.

Resources

Bauer, K. Jack. *The Mexican War, 1846-1848*. New York: Macmillan, 1974.

McCaffrey, James M. *Army of Manifest Destiny: The American Soldier in the War with Mexico*. New York: New York University Press, 1992.

Winders, Richard Bruce. *Mr. Polk's Army: The American Military Experience in the Mexican War*. College Station: Texas A&M Press, 1997.

See also: Buena Vista; Cerro Gordo; Mexican-American War; Taylor, Zachary.

John C. Pinheiro

Montgomery, Bernard Law

Also known as: Viscount Montgomery of Alamein
Born: November 17, 1887; London, England
Died: March 24, 1976; Alton, Hampshire, England
Principal wars: World War I, World War II
Principal battles: El Alamein (1942), Normandy Invasion (1944), Arnhem (1944)

MILITARY SIGNIFICANCE: Montgomery handed the German army its first significant defeat of World War II at the Battle of El Alamein in 1942 and commanded the invasion of Normandy, which opened the way for Allied victory in the war.

Bernard Law Montgomery graduated from the Royal Military Academy, Sandhurst, in 1908, serving in India until the outbreak of World War I. During the war, he saw action at the first Battle of Ypres, the Somme, Arras, and Passchendaele. After the war, he studied and taught at the Camberley Staff College as well as commanded a number of campaigns in the Middle East.

At the outbreak of World War II, he successfully evacuated his division from Dunkirk (1940). After several home commands, he was appointed commander of the embattled Eighth Army in North Africa in the summer of 1942. By a combination of strategy and careful planning that was to mark his style, he defeated the Axis forces at El Alamein (1942) and pushed them out of Africa. Under General Dwight D. Eisenhower, he led the Eighth Army through Sicily into Italy in 1943.

In 1944, still under Eisenhower, he was frontline general in charge of the Normandy Invasion forces. Promoted to field marshal, he took command of British and Canadian armies. Despite a setback at Arnhem in 1944, he accepted the German surrender in northwest Germany in 1945.

After the war, he was made chief of the Imperial General Staff, then Eisenhower's deputy in the newly founded North Atlantic Treaty Organization (NATO). He held that position until retirement in 1958.

RESOURCES
Gelb, Norman. *Ike and Monty: Generals at War*. New York: William Morrow, 1994.
Hamilton, Nigel. *Monty*. 3 vols. London: H. Hamilton, 1981-1986.
Home, Alistair, and David Montgomery. *The Lonely Leader: Monty, 1944-1945*. London: Macmillan, 1994.
Montgomery, Field Marshal. *The Memoirs*. London: Collins, 1958.

SEE ALSO: Arnhem; El Alamein; Normandy Invasion; World War II.

David Barratt

Bernard Law Montgomery. (National Archives)

MONTMORENCY, ANNE, DUKE OF

BORN: 1493; Chantilly, France
DIED: November 12, 1567; Saint-Denis, France
PRINCIPAL WARS: Valois-Habsburg Wars, Anglo-French Wars, French Wars of Religion
PRINCIPAL BATTLES: Marignano (1515), Pavia (1525), Saint-Quentin (1557), Dreux (1562)
MILITARY SIGNIFICANCE: Montmorency was the principal French commander in the many wars involving France, until his death in 1567.

Born into ancient nobility, Anne, duke of Montmorency, was a childhood companion of Francis I. When Francis became king in 1515, Montmorency was raised to a cavalry command. He fought at Marignano (September 13-14, 1515) and Pavia (February 24, 1525), being captured at the latter battle. Once ransomed, he served the monarchy in a series of offices until he became constable in 1540. He fell out of favor and stayed away from court until Henry II became king in 1547. He

Anne, duke of Montmorency. (Library of Congress)

became that king's closest adviser. As a commander, his strength lay in skillful defensive work. His mishandled attempt to relieve Saint-Quentin (August 10, 1557) resulted in his capture by Philip II's forces. The need to ransom him hastened the Treaty of Cateau-Cambrésis (1559). After Henry II died in 1559, Montmorency withdrew from the court but returned to action as part of the Catholic triumvirate in the first of the French Wars of Religion. As Catholic/royalist commander, he was captured by the Huguenots at the Battle of Dreux (December 19, 1562), while his counterpart was captured by the Catholics, an unique happenstance in history. He stayed active in the religious wars until his death on November 12, 1567, two days after the Battle of Saint-Denis.

RESOURCES
Baumgartner, Frederic. *Henry II King of France.* 1988. Reprint. Durham, N.C.: Duke University Press, 1996.

Oman, Charles. *A History of the Art of War in the Sixteenth Century.* 1937. Reprint. Mechanicsburg, Pa.: Stackpole Books, 1999.

SEE ALSO: Anglo-French Wars; French Wars of Religion; Marignano; Pavia; Saint-Quentin; Valois-Habsburg Wars.

Frederic J. Baumgartner

MONTROSE, JAMES GRAHAM, MARQUESS OF

BORN: 1612; Scotland
DIED: May 21, 1650; Edinburgh, Scotland
PRINCIPAL WAR: English Civil War of 1642-1651
PRINCIPAL BATTLE: Philiphaugh (1645)
MILITARY SIGNIFICANCE: Montrose was the greatest Royalist general from Scotland in the English Civil Wars.

The early years of James Graham, marquess of Montrose, were uneventful. After university and a tour of Europe, he became interested in politics. In February, 1638, he signed a covenant that protested against the imposition of Anglican beliefs in Scotland. In August, 1640, Montrose helped lead the Covenanters in a counterattack against the English army, which was on the Scottish border.

The covenant Montrose had signed supported King Charles I of England, not the Anglican religion; when the Covenanters began to turn against the king, Montrose left them and joined Charles I. In February, 1644, Charles I made Montrose lieutenant governor and captain general in Scotland. In August, 1644, Montrose assembled an army of Irish and Highland men, who won six battles in 1644-1645. Montrose was finally defeated by a Covenanter army at Philiphaugh on September 12-13, 1645.

After Charles I ordered Montrose to disband in 1646, Montrose went to the Continent, where he became a field marshal for France and a field marshal under Ferdinand III, with permission to recruit soldiers for Charles I's cause. In 1649, Montrose warned Charles II against accepting the crown from the Scottish Covenanters. In April, 1650, Montrose returned to Scotland to try to win the crown for Charles II, but he was defeated at Invercarron, captured, and executed at Edinburgh.

Resources

Reid, Stuart. *The Campaigns of Montrose*. Edinburgh, Scotland: Mercat Press, 1990.
Stevenson, David. *Alasdair MacColla and the Highland Problem in the Seventeenth Century*. Edinburgh: John Donald, 1980.
Wedgwood, C. V. *Montrose*. New York: St. Martin's Press, 1995.

See also: Civil war; English Civil War of 1642-1651; Irish Rebellion, Great.

Allison Angell

Morat

Type of action: Ground battle in the Franco-Burgundian Wars
Date: June 22, 1476
Location: Morat, Fribourg Canton, Switzerland
Combatants: 25,000 Swiss vs. 12,000 Burgundians
Principal commanders: *Swiss*, Wilhelm Herter; *Burgundian*, Duke Charles the Bold (1433-1477)
Result: Swiss defeated Burgundians

On June 9, 1476, Duke Charles the Bold, who had energetically rebuilt his army after Granson (March 2, 1476), established siege lines around the town of Morat. He created a powerful line of circumvallation against the expected Swiss relief force, choosing as its site a field deemed highly favorable for the use of artillery and cavalry. The Swiss attack was delayed by the decision to wait for a large contingent from Zurich. Scouts kept Charles informed of the massing of the Swiss four miles away, but on June 22, he concluded that no attack would occur that day. Once the Zurichers arrived, however, the Swiss, as was their style, moved immediately to attack, marching though a dense woods until they were close to the Burgundian lines. Catching the Burgundians by surprise, the Swiss, under Wilhelm Herter, charged through artillery and arrow fire to overwhelm the palisade and smash into Charles's camp. Few Burgundian units could form up in effective battle lines before the Swiss reached them. In short order, the Burgundians were in full flight. The Swiss pursued vigorously, and the presence of a lake to the east of the battlefield made escape difficult. Charles lost more than one-third of his army; the Swiss, perhaps 3,000 men.

Significance

Like the earlier Battle of Granson, Charles's defeat had few immediate consequences. The Swiss did not follow up on their victory, and Charles still had enough resources to form his army against and attack Nancy (1477) at the end of 1476.

Resources

Bonjour, Edgar, et al. *A Short History of Switzerland*. 1955. Reprint. Westport, Conn.: Greenwood Press, 1985.
Fahrni, Dieter. *An Outline History of Switzerland: From the Origins to the Present Day*. Zurich: Pro Helvetia, 1994.
Vaughan, Richard. *Charles the Bold: The Last Valois Duke of Burgundy*. London: Longman, 1973.

See also: Charles the Bold; Franco-Burgundian Wars; Granson.

Frederic J. Baumgartner

Moscow

Type of action: Ground battles in World War II
Date: 1941-1942
Location: Near the city of Moscow in the Soviet Union
Combatants: Nearly 1 million Germans vs. 1.5 million Russians
Principal commanders: *German*, Field Marshal Fedor von Bock (1880-1945); *Soviet*, General Georgy Zhukov (1896-1974)
Result: Successful Soviet defense of Moscow; German retreat from the outskirts of the city

After the successful destruction of the Soviet armies around Vyazma, the German army under Field Marshal Fedor von Bock pushed toward Moscow at the beginning of October, 1941. Arrayed from north to south against the Soviet defenders were the Ninth Army, the Third and Fourth Panzer Groups, the Fourth Army, and the Second Panzer Group. The initial drive to Moscow was slowed by the autumn rains. The unpaved roads became little more than mudholes, preventing any movement of men or equipment.

The advance sped up as the ground froze, and by the start of November, the Ninth Army and Third Panzer group swept into the cities of Klin and Kalinin, crossing the Volga River north of Moscow. This formed the spearhead that was to envelop Moscow from the north, then sweep eastward beyond the capital.

The southern arm of force consisted of the Second Panzer Group, commanded by General Heinz Guderian. Weakened by several months of continuous fighting, the panzer group was checked by the Soviets at the city of Tula, a hundred miles south of Moscow. Directly to the west of the capital, the Fourth Army and Fourth Panzer group drove steadily eastward, capturing the cities of Mohaisk and Maloyaroslavets. As the Germans came within sight of the city itself, resistance stiffened as Soviet troops from Siberia came to the defense of the capital.

The Germans never reached Moscow. Two factors contributed to their failure. The spreading of their forces across several hundred miles of front prevented the Germans from concentrating troops at vulnerable sections of the Soviet line. The sudden onset of the worst Russian winter in several decades, with below-zero temperatures and several feet of snow, halted the German advance in its tracks. The Germans lacked the clothing and equipment for winter fighting. With German troops scattered widely around Moscow, the Russians were presented with a counteroffensive opportunity.

Under the command of General Georgy Zhukov, the Soviet army crashed through the overextended Germans on December 7, 1941. The Ninth and Fourth Armies suffered from the brunt of the attack. The twin attacks to the north and south of the main German armies threatened to surround and destroy them. To hasten this goal, the Soviets dropped forces behind the German lines in an effort to disrupt any retreat. Instead, the Soviets were surrounded and eventually destroyed in 1942.

As the German soldiers retreated, the high command also suffered losses with the dismissal of most of the army commanders participating in the attack and the retirement of the army's commander in chief, Field Marshal Walther von Brauchitsch. The winter weather took a heavy toll on the Germans as frostbite casualties exceeded deaths. In addition, much of their equipment froze. As the Soviet forces advanced, German resistance stiffened. The Russians recovered several hundred miles of territory including such cities as Kalinin, Kaluga, and Velikiye Luki. However, they were unable to destroy the German armies in front of Moscow.

The retreat from the capital cost the Germans more than 300,000 casualties and destroyed their sense of invulnerability. The start of the spring thaw halted the Soviet advance and left a series of salients two hundred miles from Moscow that would be evacuated by the Germans in the spring of 1943. The German army would never again get as close to Moscow as they were in 1941.

SIGNIFICANCE

The Russian defense of Moscow protected the main communications artery of the Soviet Union. The larger German losses limited the army's capabilities and eventually led to its defeat.

RESOURCES

Seaton, Albert. *The Battle for Moscow*. New York: Sarpedon, 1997.

_____. *The Russo-German War*. New York: Presidio Press, 1993.

The War in Europe. The War Chronicles: World War II series. Documentary. A&E Home Video, 1983.

Ziemke, Earl, and Magna Bauer. *Moscow to Stalingrad*. New York: Military Heritage Press, 1985.

SEE ALSO: Guderian, Heinz; World War II; Zhukov, Georgy.

Douglas Clouatre

Moscow, Retreat from

TYPE OF ACTION: Guerrilla fighting in the Napoleonic Wars
DATE: October-November, 1812
LOCATION: Moscow to Vilno
COMBATANTS: Russians vs. multinational army of Napoleon I
PRINCIPAL COMMANDERS: *French*, Joachim Murat (1767-1815), Michel Ney (1769-1815), Louis Davout (1770-1823); *Russian*, Mikhail Illarionovich Kutuzov (1745-1813), Prince Ludwig

Adolf Wittgenstein (1769-1843), Mikhail A. Miloradovich (1771-1825)

RESULT: A crushing defeat for the Grand Armée of Napoleon I

After Napoleon I occupied Moscow on September 2, 1812, he waited six weeks in the Kremlin for Czar Alexander I to surrender. On October 5, fearing the onset of winter and anxious to settle problems at home, Napoleon decided to bring his 110,000 soldiers home. Russian general Mikhail Illarionovich Kutuzov, realizing the enemy's need for food, hastened Napoleon's withdrawal by suddenly striking at French general Joachim Murat's army near Tarutino on October 6.

Kutuzov harassed the French by launching a many-sided guerrilla war. Napoleon strove to reach Kaluga for supplies, but Kutuzov barred the path and defeated the French at Maloiaroslavets on October 12. Napoleon was forced to travel by the Smolensk road as Kutuzov followed a parallel path. From the north, Russian prince Ludwig Adolf Wittgenstein took Polotsk from the French occupiers, and Kutuzov coordinated the partisans who relentlessly pursued the French forces. At Viazma and Krasnyi, Russian general Mikhail A. Miloradovich defeated French rear guards led by Louis Davout and Michel Ney, respectively. Only 21,000 men crossed the border of the Russian Empire when winter finally arrived, and on November 3, Czar Alexander I thanked the Russian people for delivering the enemy from the fatherland.

SIGNIFICANCE

Napoleon's defeat during the retreat from Moscow exalted the reputations of both Kutuzov and Alexander. Tactics, not weather conditions, were responsible for the outcome.

RESOURCES

Esposito, Vincent J. *A Military History and Atlas of the Napoleonic Wars*. Rev. ed. London: Greenhill, 1999.

Rothenberg, Gunther E. *The Napoleonic Wars*. London: Cassell, 1999.

Seward, Desmond. *Napoleon and Hitler: A Comparative Approach*. New York: Viking, 1989.

SEE ALSO: Alexander I; Davout, Louis; Kutuzov, Mikhail Illarionovich; Murat, Joachim, king of Naples, duke of Cleve and Berg; Napoleon I; Napoleonic Wars; Ney, Michel.

John D. Windhausen

MOUNT BADON

TYPE OF ACTION: Ground battle in defense of Britain
DATE: between 495 and 516
LOCATION: probably Bath, England
COMBATANTS: Celts vs. Saxons
PRINCIPAL COMMANDERS: *Celtic*, Arthur (c. 475-c. 537); *Saxon*, Aelle (fl. 500)
RESULT: Significant defeat of the Saxons

Although the historical evidence for the Battle of Mount Badon is thin, there is little reason to doubt it. It is referred to by Gildas in his *De Excidio Britanniæ* (*The Ruin of Britain*), written sometime in the late 540's. He dates it to the year of his birth, forty-three years earlier. This would place the battle around 503. However the *Annales Cambriæ* (*Welsh Annals*) date it at 516, and a later date has much in its favor. It was the last of twelve battles by Arthur, the Celtic king. These ran the length and breadth of Britain against Saxons and other aggressors, including the Picts and Irish. The likeliest location for Badon is in southwest Britain, probably Bath, although many other sites have been suggested as far afield as Wales, Scotland, and Northern Ireland. The battle lasted for three days. A possible scenario is that Arthur drew his cavalry onto a hilltop, probably Soulsbury Hill outside Bath, and was there besieged by Saxon infantry, under Aelle of the southern Saxons, who was the Saxon *bretwalda*. Arthur led a charge against the Saxons where he killed almost one thousand.

SIGNIFICANCE

The battle was so decisive that it halted the Saxon advance and ushered in a period of relative calm, lasting for about forty years, an Arthurian Golden Age. It probably destroyed the southern Saxons, as they disappeared from the *Chronicles* for more than 150 years.

RESOURCES

Arthur: Myth and Reality Documentary. Castle Communications, 1994.

Dumville, D. N. "Sub-Roman Britain: History and Legend." *History* 62 (1977).
Holmes, Michael. *King Arthur: A Military History*. London: Blandford, 1998.
Lapidge, Michael, and David Dumville. *Gildas: New Approaches*. Woodbridge: Boydell Press, 1984.

SEE ALSO: Angles, Saxons, and Jutes; Celts; Saxon Raids.

Mike Ashley

MOUNTBATTEN, LOUIS

FULL NAME: Louis Francis Albert Victor Nicholas
ALSO KNOWN AS: Prince Louis of Battenberg; Louis, First Earl Mountbatten of Burma
BORN: June 25, 1900; Frogmore House, Windsor, England
DIED: August 27, 1979; off Mullaghmore, on Donegal Bay, Ireland
PRINCIPAL WARS: World War I, World War II
PRINCIPAL BATTLES: Crete (1941), Raid on Dieppe (1942), Burma (1942-1945)
MILITARY SIGNIFICANCE: Mountbatten was largely responsible for the decision that led to the disaster at Dieppe, but he also helped make the 1944 invasion of Normandy a success and contributed to victories in Burma.

Louis Mountbatten was a member of the British royal family, great-grandson of Queen Victoria and son of Prince Louis of Battenberg. In 1917, the family changed its name from Battenberg to Mountbatten because of anti-German sentiment. Mountbatten entered the Royal Navy in 1913. He served on battle cruisers during World War I and as commander of destroyers, including HMS *Kelly*, early in World War II. He was appointed chief of combined operations, responsible for planning the disastrous Raid on Dieppe of 1942, and then supreme commander of the China-Burma-India theater. He accepted the Japanese surrender in Burma and reestablished colonial rule. In 1946-1947, he served as the last viceroy of India, overseeing independence. After returning to the navy, he became first sea lord of the Admiralty and Chief of Defense Staff, effectively, the professional head of the armed forces, retiring in

British vice admiral Lord Louis Mountbatten (right) talks with U.S. major general George S. Patton in French Morocco in January, 1943. (Library of Congress)

1965. His assassination by Irish terrorists was a shocking, sensational episode. In 1979, Mountbatten was killed while yachting with his grandson and a local boy when his vessel was blown up by Irish Revolutionary Army (IRA) terrorists.

RESOURCES
In Which We Serve. Fiction feature. United Artists, 1942.
The Life and Times of Lord Mountbatten. Documentary. Twentieth-Century Leaders Series. Imperial War Museum, 1966-1967.
Poolman, Kenneth. *The Kelly: HMS Kelly, the Story of Mountbatten's Warship*. New York: W. W. Norton, 1980.
Rasor, Eugene L. *Earl Mountbatten of Burma, 1900-1979: Historiography and Annotated Bibliography*. Westport, Conn.: Greenwood Press, 1998.

Ziegler, Philip. *Mountbatten: The Official Biography*. London: Collins, 1985.

SEE ALSO: Dieppe, Raid on; India, Partition of; Indian Civil War; World War II.

Eugene L. Rasor

MOZAMBICAN CIVIL WAR

AT ISSUE: Political control of Mozambique
DATE: 1974-1992
LOCATION: Mozambique
COMBATANTS: Mozambique Liberation Front (FRELIMO) vs. Mozambique National Resistance (RENAMO)
PRINCIPAL COMMANDERS: Samora Machel (1933-1986), Alfonso Dhlakamu (1953-   )
RESULT: A 1992 cease-fire led to elections in 1994, which gave FRELIMO a slight majority; use of land mines by both sides added to worldwide discussions about the use of land mines

BACKGROUND

From 1964 to 1974, the Mozambique Liberation Front (FRELIMO) a Marxist liberation movement, fought to end Portuguese colonial rule in Mozambique. The leaders of FRELIMO were mostly intellectuals from southern and central Mozambique, but most of the fighting occurred in rural northern Mozambique, resulting in regional tension. Independence came suddenly, when a coup in 1974 produced a left-wing regime in Portugal that quickly set the African colonies loose.

White settlers planned a coup in the summer of 1971 to preempt black majority rule, but when South Africa stated it would not intervene, the plan failed. Once in power, FRELIMO announced it would support liberation struggles in South Africa as well as the Rhodesians who had organized a group called Mozambique National Resistance (RENAMO), designed to destabilize Mozambique. RENAMO unleashed one of the most brutal wars in the country's history.

ACTION

In the 1970's, RENAMO drew its soldiers from the group of FRELIMO defectors and speakers of the Ndau language group in central Mozambique. The RENAMO campaign featured a novel approach. Because RENAMO knew it was too weak to defeat the FRELIMO forces, it focused exclusively on civilian targets in an effort to strike a blow against the infrastructure and promote widespread terror.

Another distinctive feature of the war in Mozambique was the lack of interest in the outcome displayed by the Cold War superpowers. Compared to Angola, Rhodesia, or the Horn of Africa, Mozambique had very little strategic value. Although the superpowers did not provide much support to FRELIMO or RENAMO, the destructive impact of the fighting nevertheless crippled the economy of Mozambique. Years after the final cease-fire, Mozambique remains one of the poorest nations in the world, with scant resources to rebuild the war-ravaged infrastructure, education system, and health network. Because the superpowers had so very little at stake in Mozambique, successful cease-fire negotiations had to wait until 1992.

FRELIMO strategy most likely contributed to the length of the war. Although FRELIMO guerrilla tactics had defeated the Portuguese, Samora Machel decided to equip and train a conventional army and use conventional tactics to deal with the RENAMO threat. Also, Machel, in his speeches, set a very Manichaean view of the struggle, even going so far as to portray lukewarm FRELIMO supporters as individuals who contributed to the success of RENAMO. Often Machel seemed more concerned with internal dissent than with the RENAMO military threat to FRELIMO control.

Although largely ignored outside Africa, the brutal tactics of RENAMO gradually became known. The cynicism of its attempt to destroy the health and educational systems of the country were only part of the story. RENAMO also gained worldwide notoriety by engaging frequently in murder, rape, looting, arson, involuntary servitude, and forced recruiting. In one village, RENAMO officers ordered a young local man to kill his family members in order to prove his loyalty to the organization. Unlike other anticommunist groups that placed a priority on public relations, RENAMO proved unable or unwilling to polish its tarnished image.

The fall of the white minority government in Rhodesia in 1980 did not bring the RENAMO campaign to a halt. The leaders of the white minority regime in South Africa resented the fact that Mozambique allowed the African National Congress (ANC), a black Marxist liberation organization, to operate in Mozambique and use that country as a base for raids into South Africa. South Africa was eager to welcome RENAMO when that group was forced to leave Rhodesia. The South Africans hoped to gain two goals by assisting RENAMO. One was to force FRELIMO to renounce their support for the ANC. The other was to justify white minority rule by contrasting it with the chaos in Mozambique.

By 1984, FRELIMO and RENAMO were finally willing to begin negotiations to end the civil war. The Nkomati Accord that resulted obligated FRELIMO to end its support of the ANC and South Africa to cease assistance for RENAMO. Almost immediately, FRELIMO and RENAMO hurled charges that the other group had violated the treaty. International observers concluded that FRELIMO honored the treaty but RENAMO soldiers did not. Then, in September, 1985, documents captured by FRELIMO revealed that the South African army had ignored orders to end assistance to RENAMO.

It was at this time that Mozambique surfaced briefly in American policy debates. The administration of U.S. president Ronald Reagan, despite its staunch anticommunist agenda, sponsored a bill authorizing humanitarian aid to FRELIMO. Angry conservatives in America, at the urging of Pat Buchanan and William Casey, sponsored a bill to send assistance to RENAMO. Both bills failed, and Mozambique quickly sank back into obscurity.

In 1986, Machel met with South African leaders to try to revive the cease-fire. His plane crashed in South African territory on the way back, killing Machel. South African authorities denied any role in the crash at the time, but after the fall of apartheid in 1993, it became known that South African officials had successfully plotted to kill Machel.

The war dragged on until 1992 before a new set of negotiations began. The new negotiations were facilitated by Portuguese and Italians, along with concerned Vatican officials sensitive to the suffering of Catholics in Mozambique. After meeting in Rome, FRELIMO officials agreed to national elections in 1994, while RENAMO would disarm. The elections in 1994 resulted in a slim FRELIMO majority.

Aftermath

Very little of a positive nature resulted from the war that led to the death of one million Mozambiquans. FRELIMO eventually modified its doctrinaire Marxist policies in order to remain in power, but the burden of repaying a $6 billion foreign debt while rebuilding the health, education, and transportation system was likely to cripple Mozambique for a long time.

Resources

Ciment, James. *Angola and Mozambique: Postcolonial Wars*. New York: Facts on File, 1997.

Cline, Sibyl. *RENAMO*. Washington, D.C.: United States Global Strategy Council, 1989.

Landmines in Mozambique. New York: Human Rights Watch, 1994.

Munslow, Barry, ed. *Samora Machel: Selected Speeches and Writings*. London: Zed Books, 1985.

See also: Civil war; Mozambican War of Independence.

Michael John Polley

Mozambican War of Independence

At issue: Mozambique's determination to achieve independence from Portugal
Date: September 25, 1964-September 25, 1975
Location: Mozambique (southeast Africa)
Combatants: Mozambican nationalists vs. Portuguese
Principal commanders: *Mozambican*, Filipe Magaia, Samora Machel (1933-1986); *Portuguese*, General Kaúlza de Arriaga (1915-   ), General Tomas Basto Machado
Result: Mozambican nationalist victory

Background

Located in southeast Africa, Mozambique was one of the oldest European colonies in Africa. Vasco da Gama set foot on Mozambican soil in 1498. He and his successors claimed it and much of the East African coast as Portuguese territory.

Because it was an area in which Arabs and Europeans were fiercely attempting to get a foothold, the Portuguese crown ordered the construction of forts and factories. This important activity was entrusted to intrepid captains and governors to ensure Portuguese monopoly over such trading commodities as gold, silver, wax, cloves, and, later, African slaves. Missionaries, mainly Jesuits and Dominicans, were sent to the coast and the interior of the colony to convert both the people and the authorities.

However, Arab and Dutch competition, the adverse climate, the long distance from the metropolis, corruption among the clergy, and the hostile attitude toward the church in Portugal during the eighteenth and nineteenth centuries caused a sharp decline in interest in the colony of Mozambique. During this period, Mozambique, just like Angola, simply became a source of slaves for Brazil, for the landholding institution called *prazo* in the Zambezi Valley, and for the French islands located along Africa's eastern coast.

Portugal's renewed interest in its east African territory occurred only during the 1880's, in the wake of the European scramble for Africa and the Berlin Conference (1884-1885). Portugal was fearful that Great Britain, France, or Germany might deprive it of its old possessions on the continent. Having been, by and large, quite successful in preserving its empire, Portugal attempted to benefit economically from Mozambique by dispensing monopolistic rights on mineral, forestry, and agricultural resources to concessionaire companies. These companies were invariably owned by foreign entrepreneurs, even though the figurehead might be a Portuguese citizen. The system of concessionaires was abolished by Portuguese premier Antonio Salazar after 1932 and replaced by a system of partnership between the colonial government and private Portuguese companies. Under this policy, nonassimilated Africans were subject to forced labor on behalf of the government, Portuguese settlers' companies, individual Portuguese, and assimilated Africans. Although the nonassimilated Africans had to pay taxes, their property could be expropriated without compensation by the colonial authorities and the settlers. Even though, for centuries, assimilation of Africans had remained the Portuguese official policy—bestowing on the colonized the rights of Portuguese citizenship—only a handful of Africans (indeed, less than 1 percent of the population) ever achieved that status in Mozambique. Political repression and oppression, economic exploitation, and cultural subjugation were the norm in the colony, especially during the 1950's and 1960's when the nationalist movement spread over Africa.

As elsewhere in Africa, Mozambicans attempted to form parties and demanded to have the right to dissent, petition, march in protest, and vote, but to no avail. Africans invited the Portuguese colonial authorities to sit down with them and negotiate a peaceful transition to self-government, as was happening in other parts of Africa. Claiming that Mozambique was a province of Portugal, the Portuguese not only refused to listen but also heightened their oppression. They arrested, imprisoned, and killed many Mozambicans. Using informers and their Policia Internacional para a Defesa do Estado (PIDE), a secret police force, the Portuguese created a true police state designed to maintain colonial law and order.

Action

In 1964, the first organized guerrilla activity was carried out by about 250 men in Cabo Delgado, in northern Mozambique, under the banner of the Mozambique Liberation Front (FRELIMO), an amalgam of three nationalist movements: the National Democratic Union of Mozambique (UDENAMO), established in southern Rhodesia in 1960; the Mozambique African National Union (MANU), created in Kenya in 1961; and the African National Union of Independent Mozambique (UNAMI), created by exiles in Malawi in 1961. These liberation movements met in Dar es Salaam at the request of presidents Julius Nyerere of Tanzania and Kwame Nkrumah of Ghana in 1962. There were other nationalist fronts, such as the Comite Revolucionario de Mocambique (COREMO), founded in Kenya in 1965, but they had virtually no impact on the war against the Portuguese government in the colony. Tanzania offered bases to FRELIMO to wage its war of liberation.

For its president, FRELIMO chose Eduardo Mondlane, a Syracuse professor who had received a doctorate in anthropology from Northwestern University. However, in February, 1969,

Mondlane was assassinated. After much bickering and acrimony within FRELIMO's Central Committee, a former auxiliary nurse, Samora Machel, emerged as the successor to Mondlane as well as the new commander of the guerrilla war (the first commander, Filipe Magaia, had also been murdered under suspicious circumstances). The Soviet Union, China, and their allies provided massive financial, technical, training, and military assistance to the rebels, forcing the Portuguese to station some 60,000 troops in the colony. The more FRELIMO advanced and galvanized the minds of the Mozambicans, the more brutal the Portuguese reaction became, including massacres of innocent civilians (as happened in Wiriyamu, Tete), the accelerated use of the napalm bomb, the creation of hamlets to protect and control the population, the burning of homes and farms, and mutilations of suspects. Aided by its allies in the North Atlantic Treaty Organization (NATO), including the United States, Portugal vowed during the mid-1960's and early 1970's never to give up its "province" of Mozambique.

By 1970, FRELIMO forces had reached the Tete and Manica e Sofala districts, forcing the Portuguese to constantly reexamine their tactics and strategies. In an effort to wipe out the guerrilla offensive, the Portuguese government entrusted total control of the colonial army to Brigadier General Kaúlza de Arriaga during 1970-1973. Arriaga named his counterinsurgency plan Operation Gordian Knot. His strategy was to win the war on the battlefield by reinforcing the bombing of the enemy's strategic areas and at the same time attempting to win the hearts of the Mozambicans. Treating the wounded with compassion, in the same hospitals as the Portuguese military, was one such approach. Protecting the civilians by creating "human walls" made of concrete houses and building schools, post offices, markets, technical colleges, and paved roads was another. Arriaga visited General William Westmoreland in Washington, D.C., in the hope of learning the lessons of the Vietnam War. As part of his overall strategy, Arriaga also attempted to block river routes and prevent infiltration of guerrillas, especially from Tanzania.

The operation was put in motion with such fanfare that the nationalists in Mozambique and Angola grew apprehensive. However, hampered by factors such as heavy rains, lack of resources, vast distances, low morale among the Portuguese troops, and FRELIMO's determination to fight on, Operation Gordian Knot turned out to be such a failure that Kaúlza was replaced by General Tomas Basto Machado in August, 1973. Meanwhile, the war continued to rage.

Unexpectedly, on April 25, 1974, young officers of the armed forces, calling themselves the Movimento das Forcas Armadas, overthrew the government of Premier Marcello Caetano in Lisbon. In September, 1974, the new rulers signed an agreement in Lusaka that would hand over power in Mozambique to FRELIMO on September 25, 1975.

Aftermath

On September 25, 1975, Mozambique became the independent People's Republic of Mozambique, with Machel, returning triumphantly from Dar es Salaam, as the first nonelected president. The new government proclaimed itself Marxist-Leninist and, by 1977, had nationalized virtually every institution and resource in the country. FRELIMO also introduced a policy of eliminating all elements it called the "reactionary bourgeoisie." Unfortunately, FRELIMO's lack of experience, misplaced "revolutionary" zeal against the governments of South Africa and Rhodesia, mismanagement of the economy, repression, dogmatism, utter contempt for the Catholic Church, and the institution of forced collective villages resulted in widespread discontent in the country. The white-controlled regimes of Rhodesia and South Africa struck back with aerial bombardments of parts of Mozambique, targeted at guerrillas. These factors led to the emergence of the Mozambique National Resistance (RENAMO) in 1977 and the bloody internal conflict that ended only in 1992. By then, most of the country's infrastructure had been almost completely destroyed.

Resources

Azevedo, Mario. *Historical Dictionary of Mozambique*. Metuchen, N.J.: Scarecrow Press, 1991.

Finnegan, William. *A Complicated War: The Harrowing of Mozambique*. Berkeley: University of California Press, 1992.

Minter, William. *Apartheid's Contras*. London: Zed Books, 1994.

Newitt, Malyn. *A History of Mozambique*. Bloomington: University of Indiana Press, 1995.

See also: Angolan War of Independence; Guerrilla warfare; Machel, Samora; Mozambican Civil War; Portuguese Colonial Wars.

Mario J. Azevedo

Mubārak, Hosnī

Full name: Muḥammad Hosnī Said Mubārak
Born: May 4, 1928; Al-Minūfiyah governate, Egypt
Principal war: Israeli-Arab October War
Military significance: A key air force officer, Mubārak became president of Egypt in 1981.

After graduating from the Egyptian Military Academy in 1947, Hosnī Mubārak entered the air force. From 1952 to 1968, he held various training commands and attended the Soviet's Frunze General Staff Academy. Promoted to air vice marshal and air force chief of staff in 1969, Mubarak pushed hard to train pilots and replace the heavy losses suffered during the Six-Day War (1967).

Mubārak worked closely with General Muhammad Ali Fahmi, commander of Air Defense Forces, to create a strategy for attacking the Israeli-occupied Sinai. This included an "impenetrable wall" of antiaircraft missile batteries, plus a surprise strike by Egyptian aircraft.

Their plan did well during the initial phases of the Israeli-Arab October War (1973). Although Israeli forces struck back hard, when the fighting ended, Egypt's air force remained operational and could claim to have traded blow-for-blow with the best aviators in the Middle East.

As with many Egyptian military officers, Mubārak's career also had a political side. Appointed deputy minister of war in 1972, he was promoted to vice president by Anwar el-Sadat in 1975. Significant civil and diplomatic missions marked Mubārak as an important member of Sadat's inner circle, and the government maintained close ties with Egypt's armed forces.

After Sadat's assassination in 1981, Mubārak became president. In military affairs, he directed an internal war against Islamic fundamentalists, while maintaining a foreign policy of "positive neutrality." In 1991, Mubārak supported a United Nations action against Iraq, sending 38,000 Egyptian soldiers to participate in the Gulf War (1991). On a smaller scale, Egyptian forces also supported United Nations peacekeeping forces in Somalia, Rwanda, and Bosnia.

Resources
Solecki, John. *Hosnī Mubārak*. New York: Chelsea House, 1991.
Tripp, Charles, and Roger Owen. *Egypt Under Mubārak*. London: Routledge, 1990.

See also: Gulf War; Israeli-Arab October War; Israeli-Arab Wars; Israeli Military; Sadat, Anwar el-; Suez War.

John P. Dunn

Hosnī Mubārak. (Archive Photos/Hulton Getty Collection)

Muḥammad Ahmad

Full name: Muḥammad Ahmad ibn As-Sayyid ʿAbd-Allāh
Also known as: al-Mahdī ("messiah"); Mohammed Ahmed of Dongola

BORN: August 12, 1844; Dongola, Sudan
DIED: June 22, 1885; Omdurman, Sudan
PRINCIPAL WAR: Mahdist Uprising
PRINCIPAL BATTLE: Siege of Khartoum (1884-1885)
MILITARY SIGNIFICANCE: Defeated British and Egyptian forces under General Charles George Gordon and blunted British imperialist expansion.

Muḥammed Ahmad was a charismatic religious leader and founder of his own Dervish order. He gathered his followers on an island in the Nile, where he acquired a reputation for holiness and mystical powers. He became convinced that he was the Mahdi, the divinely chosen messiah foretold by Islamic tradition, the one who would come to free the people and purify the faith. Egypt had long suppressed the Sudan and conducted a series of campaigns there, which led, in 1876, to the bankruptcy of the khedive's government. A strong nationalist, the Mahdi began a jihad (holy war) in 1881 against Egyptian overlordship. The year, 1300 in the Islamic calendar, was popularly believed to be the date that Mahdi would inaugurate a kingdom of justice. When the British took control of Egypt in 1882 in the wake of the economic collapse, the Mahdist revolt spread throughout the Upper Nile basin. Egyptian forces were swept before the Mahdists, confirming Allah's blessing on the movement as well as providing modern captured arms.

Within a year, the Mahdi had captured El Obeid and Darfur and defeated the Anglo-Egyptian forces under General William Hicks Pasha. The Mahdists then marched on to Khartoum (1884-1885), which they took after a long but futile defense by General Charles George Gordon. Gordon confronted Mahdist soldiers on the steps of his command center and was cut down by their spears and then beheaded. In victory, the Mahdi crossed the Nile and began building a military headquarters city, Omdurman, which became the new capital. Within six months, Muḥammad Ahmad was dead of typhus, but the Mahdist state continued on for thirteen years, and his religious brotherhood still exists.

RESOURCES
Farwell, Byron. *Prisoners of the Mahdi*. New York: W. W. Norton, 1989.

Featherstone, Donald F. *Khartoum 1885: General Gordon's Last Stand*. London: Osprey, 1998.

SEE ALSO: Abu Klea; British Colonial Wars; Gordon, Charles George; Khartoum, Siege of; Religion and war.

Norbert Brockman

MUḤAMMAD ʿALĪ PASHA

ALSO KNOWN AS: Mehmet Ali
BORN: 1769; Kavalla, Macedonia
DIED: August 2, 1849; Alexandria, Egypt
PRINCIPAL WARS: Napoleonic Wars, Greek War of Independence, Egypto-Turkish Wars
PRINCIPAL BATTLES: Aboukir (1799), Konia (1832)
MILITARY SIGNIFICANCE: First fighting and then joining the French during the Napoleonic Wars, Muḥammad ʿAlī created the modern Egyptian state by defeating his enemies. Although he failed to replace the sultan in his war against Turkey in the 1830's, he did confirm his dynasty.

Muḥammad ʿAlī, an Albanian police official and tobacco merchant from Kavalla, led his city's

Muḥammad ʿAlī Pasha. (Library of Congress)

company against the French in Egypt (1798). His action at the Battle of Aboukir (1799) distinguished him as an outstanding leader and a courageous warrior. He later became the khedive (viceroy) of Egypt (1805) and joined with the French in the War of the Third Coalition. Over the next decade, Muḥammad ʿAlī successfully battled the remnants of the Mamlūk warlords and the British, gaining complete control of Egypt. He sent Egyptian troops under his son Ibrāhīm Pasha to put down the Greek revolt (1824). He modernized his country, creating a powerful Near Eastern empire of his own. He took over Syria and Palestine (1831), and Ibrahim defeated the Turks at Konia (1832) in the Egypto-Turkish Wars. After a tentative peace, Muḥammad ʿAlī began his assault again in 1839. The great powers prevented him from bringing down the Ottoman Empire, but he was made hereditary ruler of Egypt and reigned until July, 1848.

RESOURCES
Bowring, John. *Report on Egypt 1823-1838: Under the Reign of Muhammad Ali*. London: Triade, 1998
Fahmy, Khaled. *All the Pasha's Men: Mehemed Ali, His Army, and the Making of Modern Egypt*. New York: Cambridge University Press, 1997.
Lawson, Fred Haley. *The Social Origins of Egyptian Expansionism during the Muhammad Ali Period*. New York: Columbia University Press, 1992.
Raymond, Andre. "Muhammad Ali and Palmerston." In *Studies in Arab History: The Antonius Lectures, 1978-1987*. New York: St. Martin's Press, 1990.

SEE ALSO: Aboukir; Alexandria; Egypto-Turkish Wars; French Revolutionary Wars; Greek War of Independence; Mamlūks; Napoleonic Wars; Ottoman Empire; Pyramids.

Frederick B. Chary

MUHAMMAD OF GHOR

FULL NAME: Muʿizz-ud-Dīn Muḥammad ibn Sām
ALSO KNOWN AS: Muhammad Ghūrī, Shihāb-ud-dīn Muḥammad Ghūrī
BORN: date and place unknown
DIED: March 15, 1206; Damyak, India

PRINCIPAL BATTLES: Tarain (1192, 1193)
MILITARY SIGNIFICANCE: Through his conquests and those of his subordinates, Muhammad of Ghor founded Muslim rule in India.

Muhammad of Ghor was the younger brother of Sultan Ghiyas-ud-dīn of Ghor, south of Herat in Afghanistan, who appointed him in 1173 to be the sultan of the Ghaznavid territories in eastern Afghanistan. By his death, he ruled over a kingdom that stretched from eastern Persia and central Asia to India. Muhammad of Ghor led his first expedition into India to Multan in 1176. In 1179, he captured Peshāwar. In 1181, he captured Lahore and established the fortress at Sialkot. He returned to the Punjab in 1186 and began leading a series of raids and sending his viceroys across north India, capturing all the lands as far as Bengal. In 1192, Muhammad of Ghor was wounded and defeated by Prithviraj, raja of Delhi and Ajmer, at Tarain, and the following year, also at Tarain, Muhammad of Ghor scored a decisive victory against Prithviraj, capturing and killing him. Delhi was captured by one of his viceroys, Qutbuddin Aibak, in 1193 and became the capital of Muslim India for the next seven hundred years. In 1203, on the death of his brother, Muhammad of Ghor became the sole ruler of the kingdom. On the banks of the Indus river, on March 15, 1206, Muhammad of Ghor was assassinated by Shias, followers of a heterodox Muslim sect, whom he had attacked in 1199. His body was taken to Ghazni for burial.

RESOURCES
Chattopadhyaya, Brajadulal. *The Making of Early Medieval India*. New York: Oxford University Press, 1994.
Habib, Muhammad. *Politics and Society During the Early Medieval Period*. Aligarh, India: Peoples Publishing House, 1981.
Lal, K. S. *Early Muslims in India*. New Delhi: Books and Books, 1984.
Pandey, A. B. *Early Medieval India*. Allahabad, India: Central Book Depot, 1965.
Singh, Meera. *Medieval History of India*. New Delhi: Vikas, 1978.

SEE ALSO: Delhi Sultanate, Wars of the; Muhammad of Ghor, conquests of

Roger D. Long

Muhammad of Ghor, Conquests of

At issue: Control of north India, Muslim dominance over Hindus
Date: 1175-1206
Location: Punjab, Delhi, Gujerat, Bihar, Bengal
Combatants: Ghaznavids from Afghanistan vs. Hindu rulers of north India
Principal commanders: *Ghaznavid*, Qutbuddin Aibak, or Qutb-ud-din Aybak (d. 1210), Muhammad Khaljī, or Ikhtiyar-ud-din Muhammad (d. 1206); *Hindu*, Prithviraj, or Prithvirah Chouhan, or Rai Pithora (d. 1193), Jai Chand, raja of Kanauj (d. 1194)
Principal battle: Tarain
Result: Muslim rule was established in India for seven centuries

Muhammad of Ghor founded Muslim rule in India. In his conquests, he made raids into India to capture booty and slaves, typically returning to Ghanzi, Afghanistan, and leaving behind viceroys to govern his territories. Muhammad of Ghor's first expedition into India was to Multan in 1176. He captured Peshāwar in 1179 and he seized Lahore and established a fortress at Sialkot in 1181. In 1186, he returned to the Punjab and led a series of raids, also sending his viceroys across north India. He intended to rule India as well as to plunder it. In 1191, he captured Bhatinda in Prithviraj's kingdom of Delhi. Prithviraj, raja of Delhi and Ajmer, attacked at **Tarain** in 1192. A javelin pierced the arm of Muhammad of Ghor, and his army was defeated. In 1193, with an army of some 10,000 mounted archers, he again met Prithviraj at **Tarain**, and defeated and killed him. This victory gave Muhammad of Ghor all the lands from Afghanistan up to Delhi. Several fortresses also fell to him, and he marched on to Ajmer, which he captured and plundered.

Muhammad of Ghor left these newly conquered areas under the command of one of his most able and loyal soldiers, Qutbuddin Aibak, who founded the Delhi sultanate in 1206. Qutbuddin Aibak was free to administer Muhammad of Ghor's territories and to extend them. The Jats attacked in 1192, and Qutbuddin Aibak marched out to defeat them and then seized the fortress of Meerut. Delhi was captured by the beginning of 1193, and Qutbuddin Aibak made it his headquarters. For the next seven hundred years, it was to be the capital of Muslim India. In the meantime, one of Qutbuddin Aibak's officers, Muhammad Khaljī, raided Bihar, where he sacked the Buddhist monastery at Nalanda, murdering the monks. He returned to Qutbuddin Aibak in the summer of 1193 with an enormous amount of plunder, including the monastery's library. As a reward, he was appointed governor of Bihar.

Qutbuddin Aibak then attacked territories to the east of Delhi before joining Muhammad of Ghor, who had returned to India, in capturing and plundering Benares in 1194 and attacking Jai Chand, raja of Kanauj. Muhammad of Ghor returned to Ghazni with the booty. An 1194 rebellion in Ajmer led Qutbuddin Aibak to take control over the city, and the following year, he devised a plan to exact revenge on the Rājputs in Gujerat for defeating Muhammad of Ghor in 1178. He was highly successful, and Muhammad of Ghor was so pleased with his victory and the booty he seized that he named Qutbuddin Aibak his viceroy for the Muslim territories in India. In 1197, Qutbuddin Aibak put down another rebellion in Gujerat. For the next five years, Muhammad of Ghor was involved in disputes in Central Asia and did not return to India, although Muhammad Khaljī captured Bengal in 1202. Qutbuddin Aibak also led forays against various Hindu rajas and in 1205 was called on to deal with a rebellion in the Punjab, where he was joined by Muhammad of Ghor, who had suffered a reverse the previous year in Central Asia. After their victory, they exacted terrible revenge on the rebels and enslaved a very large number of them. On his way home to Ghazni, on March 15, 1206, Muhammad of Ghor was assassinated by Shias, followers of a sect he had previously attacked.

Significance

The capture of north India established Muslim rule in India and began the process of conversion, which would leave India with a very large Muslim population.

Resources

Habib, Muhammad. *Politics and Society During the Early Medieval Period*. Aligarh, India: Peoples Publishing House, 1981.

Lal, K. S. *Early Muslims in India*. New Delhi: Books and Books, 1984.
Pandey, A. B. *Early Medieval India*. Allahabad, India: Central Book Depot, 1965.
Sarma, Sripala. *History of Medieval India*. New Delhi: Mohit Publications, 1999.
Singh, Meera. *Medieval History of India*. New Delhi: Vikas, 1978.

SEE ALSO: Delhi Sultanate, Wars of the; Muhammad of Ghor.

Roger D. Long

MUHAMMAD I ASKIA

FULL NAME: Muḥammad Ibn Abī Bakr Ture
ALSO KNOWN AS: Muḥammad Ture
BORN: Date and place unknown
DIED: March 2, 1538; Gao, Songhai Empire
PRINCIPAL WARS: Against the Tuaregs of Aïr, Taghanza, Mossi of Yatenga, the Dogon, the Hausa
MILITARY SIGNIFICANCE: Muḥammad I Askia usurped the throne of the Songhai Empire and, in a series of conquests, greatly expanded and strengthened the empire. Between 1498 and 1502, he was victorious over the Mossi of Yatenga and the Tuaregs of Aïr.

Although seventeenth century Tombouctou writers excoriated Sonni ʿAlī as a tyrant, they showered praise on Muḥammad I Askia, founder of the Askia Dynasty. Muḥammad Askia strengthened the administration of the empire, consolidated Sonni ʿAlī's conquests, and promoted Islam. He maximized Songhai's benefit from the trans-Saharan trade by extending the empire into the desert, driving back the Tuareg of Aïr, then capturing Aïr and the salt-producing center of Taghanza in the north. He sent an army as far west as Takrur and fought off the Middle Niger raiders—the Mossi of Yatenga and the Dogon. Eastward, his armies overran the Hausa states of Gobir, Katsina, and eventually Kano. These acquisitions expanded the trading network of Songhai.

Muḥammad Askia divided the empire into four vice-royalties under viceroys, each under a governor—usually from the royal family or a trusted servant. In terms of central administration, Muḥammad Askia established a council of ministers composed of the *balama* (commander in chief), *fari-mundya* (chief tax collector), *hi-koy* (navy chief), *korey-farma* (minister responsible for foreigners), *warrey-farma* (minister in charge of property), and the *hari-farma* (minister in charge of fisheries). He raised revenue for administration from tribute from vassals, proceeds from royal farms, taxes on peasants, contributions from his generals, and duties on trade. He used Islam to reinforce his authority and unite his empire, and went on a pilgrimage to Mecca soon after his accession. In Cairo, he persuaded the Egyptian caliph to recognize him as "caliph" of the Sudan. On his return from Mecca in 1496, Muḥammad Askia revived Tombouctou as a great center of Islamic learning and made Islam a state religion. He was deposed in 1528.

RESOURCES
Boahen, A. Adu. *Topics in West African History*. London: Longman, 1986.
Davidson, Basil. *Africa in History*. New York & London: Touchstone, 1995.
Shillington, Kevin. *History of Africa*. New York: St. Martin's Press, 1995.

SEE ALSO: Egyptian Empire; Songhai Empire.

Edmund Abaka

MÜHLBERG

TYPE OF ACTION: Ground battle in Schmalkaldic War
DATE: April 24, 1547
LOCATION: Mühlberg, Germany (thirty-five miles east of Leipzig)
COMBATANTS: 13,000 Imperial and Papal groups vs. combined armies of Saxony and Hesse
PRINCIPAL COMMANDERS: *Imperial*, Charles V (1500-1558), Fernando Álvarez de Toledo, duke of Alva (1507-1582); *Schmalkaldic League*, John Frederick, elector of Saxony-Wittenberg (1503-1554)
RESULT: Rout of the Schmalkaldic army, capture of John Frederick, triumph of Charles V in Germany

On April 24, 1547, the forces of the Schmalkaldic League, led by Saxon Elector John Frederick, were totally routed by an imperial army under Emperor Charles V and Fernando Álvarez de Toledo, duke of Alva. Formed in 1531, the League allied nine German Protestant states under Philip of Hesse. Charles was forced to give it de facto recognition in 1544. Though the league's forces initially outnumbered Charles's five to one, the emperor, helped by Pope Paul III, fielded a force of 13,000. The duke of Alva, at the onset of war in 1546, wisely allowed Protestant money, morale, and military power to dissipate. Then moving through the Rhine and Main valleys, Alva crossed the Elbe at Mühlberg, halfway between Dresden and Wittenberg, taking John Frederick by surprise. The elector's incompetence and Alva's tactical superiority led to a rout. Charles said, "I came, I saw, God conquered." John Frederick was imprisoned, Philip (not present) surrendered, and the emperor prevailed (temporarily) in Germany.

SIGNIFICANCE

Mühlberg, like Marignano (1515), was a swiftly decided battle occurring at the apex of Charles's power in Germany. The battle's political impact was nullified by persistent Protestantism, princely particularism, and the opposition of Germany's neighbors to a united Empire.

RESOURCES

Brandi, Karl. *The Emperor Charles V: The Growth and Destiny of a Man and a World Empire*. London: Jonathan Cape, 1968.

Fernandes Alvarez, Manuel. *Charles V, Elected Emperor and Hereditary Ruler*. London: Thames & Hudson, 1975.

Heer, Friedrich. *The Holy Roman Empire*. New York: Frederick A. Praeger, 1968.

Hughes, Michael. *Early Modern Germany, 1477-1806*. Philadelphia: University of Pennsylvania Press, 1992.

SEE ALSO: Alva, duke of; Charles V; Schmalkaldic War.

C. George Fry

MUKDEN

TYPE OF ACTION: Ground battle in the Russo-Japanese War

DATE: February 21-March 10, 1905
LOCATION: City in southeastern Manchuria
COMBATANTS: 310,000 Russians vs. 310,000 Japanese
PRINCIPAL COMMANDERS: *Russian*, General Aleksei Kuropatkin (1848-1925); *Japanese*, General Iwao Oyama (1842-1916)
RESULT: After heavy losses on both sides, Russian forces retreated, leaving Mukden in Japanese hands

In February, 1905, General Iwao Oyama attempted to encircle Aleksei Kuropatkin's Russian army at Mukden, an important rail center. With fighting erupting across a forty-seven-mile front, Japanese general Maresuke Nogi's Third Army pushed back Russian general Nikolai Kauban's troops on the right, but Kuropatkin's timely use of reserves stymied the Japanese advance. Oyama reinforced Nogi's army and again attacked Kauban. From March 6-8, savage fighting resulted in heavy pressure on the Russian right, and Japanese troops entered Mukden.

Kuropatkin realized his right had been pushed back so far that his line of communications was in jeopardy. Rather than risk complete encirclement, he disengaged from the battle and retreated to Tieling and Harbin. The Russians lost some 100,000 men killed, wounded, or captured, and Japanese casualties were near 70,000 killed and wounded.

SIGNIFICANCE

With Mukden lost, demoralized Russian forces stopped fighting land battles as the action shifted to naval combat. The string of Russian defeats, coupled with revolution in European Russia, pushed the government to end the war. Japan, though victorious, had also realized heavy casualties in Manchuria and likewise sought an end to the conflict.

RESOURCES

Martin, Christopher. *The Russo-Japanese War*. New York: Abelard-Schuman, 1967.

Walder, David. *The Short Victorious War: The Russo-Japanese Conflict 1904-1905*. New York: Harper & Row, 1973.

Warner, Denis, and Peggy Warner. *The Tide at Sunrise: A History of the Russo-Japanese War, 1904-1905*. New York: Charterhouse, 1974.

Westwood, J. N. *Russia Against Japan 1904-1905: A New Look at the Russo-Japanese War.* London: Macmillan, 1986.

Yung, Louise. *Japan's Total Empire: Manchuria and the Culture of Wartime Imperialism.* Berkeley: University of California Press, 1998.

SEE ALSO: Nogi, Maresuke; Port Arthur, Siege of; Russo-Japanese War; Tōgō, Heihachirō; Tsushima; Yalu River.

Kenneth P. Czech

MULHOUSE

TYPE OF ACTION: Land battle in the Gallic Wars
DATE: 58 B.C.E.
LOCATION: The plains of Upper Alsace between Mülhausen and Thonn
COMBATANTS: Four Roman legions and Gallic cavalry vs. approximately 6,000 German light infantry and 6,000 cavalry
PRINCIPAL COMMANDERS: *Roman*, Julius Caesar, Roman governor of Gaul (100-44 B.C.E.); *German*, Ariovistus, king of the German Suevi (fl. 71?-58 B.C.E.)
RESULT: Nearly two-thirds of the German force perished

In the first year of Julius Caesar's governorship, Ariovistus was consolidating his hold over the Gallic tribes in Alsace. Claiming that he was acting to stem a dangerous German advance, Caesar moved against the Germans at the Battle of Mulhouse. At first contact, Ariovistus tried to use his superior mobility against Caesar's line of supply, but Caesar built a second fortified camp to guard his flank. To lessen the fear among his soldiers, Caesar employed inspiring rhetoric and daily forays to draw the Germans into battle. Their long-delayed attack came suddenly and with great force in seven closely formed columns that closed quickly with the Romans. Caesar personally led the Roman right, but it was the legate Publius Licinius Crassus who ordered in the reserves to hold the startled left and rout the Germans.

SIGNIFICANCE

The battle broke up the alliance of the Suevi and initiated a long period of security for the Gauls along the Rhine. It demonstrated the boldness, speed, and energy that characterized all of Caesar's Gallic campaigns. The initiative shown by Publius Crassus demonstrated the wisdom of having legates in direct control of battle units.

RESOURCES
Bernard, Charlotte. *Caesar and Rome.* New York: Henry Holt, 1996.
Dodge, Theodore A. *Caesar.* New York: Da Capo Press, 1997.
Meier, Christian. *Caesar.* New York: Basic Books, 1982.

SEE ALSO: Alesia, Siege of; Gallic Wars; Vercingetorix.

Ronald J. Weber

MUNDA

TYPE OF ACTION: Ground battle in Roman Civil Wars of 88-30 B.C.E.
DATE: March 17, 45 B.C.E.
LOCATION: Southeast of Ecija in Spain, near Osuna or Montilla.
COMBATANTS: Caesar's eight veteran but understrength legions (32,000? men) vs. eleven understrength largely non-Italian legions (45,000? men)
PRINCIPAL COMMANDERS: *Roman*, Julius Caesar (100-44 B.C.E.); *Rebel*, Gnaeus Pompeius (d. 45 B.C.E.), Sextus Pompeius (d. 35 B.C.E.), Titus Labienus (d. 45 B.C.E.)
RESULT: Caesar killed three-quarters of the opposing army

Julius Caesar had already defeated Republican armies at Pharsalus in Greece and Thapsus in Africa, and his most prominent political enemies were dead. Domitius Ahenobarbus and Pompey the Great had died in 48 B.C.E., Metellus Scipio and Cato Uticensis in 46 B.C.E. Diehards refusing to accept battlefield verdicts or Caesar's pardon assembled in Spain. After the Thapsus campaign and quadruple triumph in Rome (October, 46 B.C.E.), Caesar left for Spain, picking up troops along the way. Ancient accounts of the campaign are unclear; evidently a tough fight near Munda became a rout. Titus Labienus was killed in the battle and Gnaeus Pompeius in flight in 45 B.C.E. Sextus Pompeius fought Caesarians until his death in 35 B.C.E.

SIGNIFICANCE

Munda was the last effort of the Republicans and Pompeians to beat Caesar militarily. When it fell, so did Spain. Having gained control of Rome, Caesar pushed reforms, received honors, and displayed clemency. However, Republican leaders remained opposed to Caesar, forming the Liberator Party, and he was compelled to rely on his associates and take more power into his own hands. In February, 44 B.C.E., he was made dictator for life; on March 15, he was killed. Many of his assassins were Republicans who had previously received pardons from Caesar.

RESOURCES

Brunt, P. A. *Italian Manpower 225 B.C.-A.D. 14*. Oxford: Clarendon Press, 1971.
Gelzer, Matthias. *Caesar: A Politician and Statesman*. Oxford: Blackwell, 1968.
Grant, Michael. *Julius Caesar*. New York: M. Evans, 1992.
Keppie, Lawrence. *The Making of the Roman Army*. Norman: University of Oklahoma Press, 1998.

SEE ALSO: Caesar, Julius; Pharsalus; Pompey the Great; Roman Civil Wars of 88-30 B.C.E.

Thomas H. Watkins

MURAD I

BORN: 1326?; place unknown
DIED: June 20/28 or August 28, 1389; Kosovo Pole, Serbia
PRINCIPAL WARS: Turkish Wars of European Expansion
PRINCIPAL BATTLES: Adrianople (1365), Kosovo (1389)
MILITARY SIGNIFICANCE: Murad expanded the Turks' European bridgehead into a major holding and established a standing army, giving future leaders a significant edge over the less effective feudal levies of their Balkan rivals.

Murad I ascended the throne in 1359/1360. His first major victory was the capture of Adrianople (Edirne) in 1365. He declared it his new capital, marking a new Ottoman interest in Balkan affairs. Another change was Murad's formation of a body of regular infantry called *yeni ceri*, or Janissaries. The nucleus of a standing army, these disciplined troops added significant muscle to an already powerful military machine.

The new soldiers quickly entered battle, as Murad sent his lieutenants deeper into the Balkans. At Marica (1365), Samakov (1371), and Second Marica (1371), they secured great victories over Serbs, Bulgars, Hungarians, and other regional Christians. A final showdown took place at Kosovo Pole on June 20, 1389, where Murad faced an allied force of Serbs, Bosnians, and Albanians. During the short but hotly contested action, Murad commanded the center. During a lull, a Serbian knight, Miloš Obilić, pretended to desert in order to meet Murad. Once in his presence, Obilić fatally wounded Murad.

RESOURCES

Inalcik, Halil. *The Ottoman Empire: The Classical Age 1300-1600*. Reprint. London: Phoenix, 1994.
Shaw, Stanford. *History of the Ottoman Empire and Modern Turkey*. Vol. 1. New York: Cambridge University Press, 1976-1977.

SEE ALSO: Byzantine-Ottoman Wars; Janissaries; Kosovo; Ottoman Empire; Turkish Wars of European Expansion.

John P. Dunn

MURAT, JOACHIM

ALSO KNOWN AS: Marshal of France; grand duke of Berg and Cleves; king of Naples
BORN: March 25, 1767; La Bastide-Fortunière (later Labastide-Murat), Gascony, France
DIED: October 13, 1815; Pizzo, Calabria, Italy
PRINCIPAL WARS: Napoleonic Wars
PRINCIPAL BATTLES: Pyramids (1798), Marengo (1800), Austerlitz (1805), Jena (1806), Eylau (1807), Borodino (1812), Leipzig (1813), Tolentino (1815)
MILITARY SIGNIFICANCE: Murat, who also excelled at reconnaissance, was Napoleon Bonaparte's gifted and daring leader of the cavalry,

an essential component in Napoleon's military success.

Born the son of an innkeeper, Joachim Murat abandoned theological studies for the military. After the outbreak of the French Revolution in 1789, he joined the revolutionary army and was attracted to the young Corsican officer, Napoleon Bonaparte. He secured the necessary cannons so that Napoleon could put down the threat to the revolutionary government in 1795.

He served as a cavalry officer in Egypt at the Battle of the Pyramids (1798) and at Aboukir (1799). After returning to France in 1799, Murat led the bayonet charge against the deputies who opposed Napoleon becoming dictator. Murat married Napoleon's sister Caroline in 1800. He participated in all of Napoleon's military campaigns except the last at Waterloo. He commanded the calvary at the battles of Marengo (1800), Austerlitz (1805), and Jena (1806). His charge against the Russian center at Eylau (1807) is regarded as one of the best cavalry charges in military history. He fought at Borodino (1812) during the Russian campaign.

After the defeat at Leipzig (1813), Murat tried to save his own kingdom by dealing with the allies. Murat reached an agreement with the allies, but after Napoleon's escape from Elba in 1815, he found the allies did not trust him. He tried to gain favor with Napoleon by winning Italy's independence from Austria but was defeated at Tolentino (1815). His treachery helped convince the allies there was no dealing with Napoleon and that he must be destroyed. Murat, who had fled to Corsica, was captured when he attempted to enter his former kingdom and summarily executed.

RESOURCES
Cole, Hubert. *The Betrayers: Joachim and Caroline Murat*. London: Eyre Methuen, 1972.
Macdonell, A. G. *Napoleon and His Marshals*. London: Prion, 1999.
Seward, Desmond. *Napoleon's Family*. New York: Viking Press, 1986.

SEE ALSO: French Revolution; French Revolutionary Wars; Jena and Auerstädt; Moscow, retreat from; Napoleon I; Napoleonic Wars; Pyramids.
Nis Petersen

MŪSĀ IBN NUṢAYR

ALSO KNOWN AS: Mūsāb Nusair
BORN: 640; Syria
DIED: 716-717; Damascus, Syria
PRINCIPAL WARS: Muslim Conquests of North Africa and Spain
MILITARY SIGNIFICANCE: From 700 to 714, Mūsā ibn Nuṣayr oversaw the Muslim conquest of North Africa and Spain, allowing the Islamic High Caliphate to establish a tricontinental foothold within a century of its founding.

Mūsā ibn Nuṣayr began his career in government service as a revenue official in the administration of Caliph ʿAbd al-Malik. Falling under suspicion of embezzlement and fleeing to Egypt, ibn Nuṣayr's career was saved only through the intercession of Caliph al-Walid.

Adopting Mūsā ibn Nuṣayr as his protégé, al-Walid appointed him governor of the province of Ifrikiya in northwest Africa sometime around the year 700. As governor, Mūsā ibn Nuṣayr extended Muslim power and the Islamic faith across North Africa to Tangier at the expense of the religious and political autonomy of the native Berber peoples.

Soon Mūsā ibn Nuṣayr and his Berber lieutenant Ṭāriq ibn-Ziyād were plotting an invasion of Spain. In 711, Ṭāriq crossed into Europe, and on July 19 crushed the Visigothic forces of the Spanish king Roderick. Mūsā ibn Nuṣayr, jealous of Ṭāriq's success and wishing to press the Muslim advantage, entered Spain the following year at the head of an army of eighteen thousand, wiping out lingering Spanish resistance in a band of cities stretching from Seville to Saragossa.

Muslim lore records Mūsā ibn Nuṣayr's triumphant return to Damascus in 714, loaded with plunder and captives. However, the Caliph Sulaymān harbored a political grudge against Mūsā ibn Nuṣayr, and he died estranged from the government he had served.

RESOURCES
Kennedy, Hugh. *The Prophet and the Age of the Caliphates*. London: Longman Group, 1986.
Saunders, J. J. *A History of Medieval Islam*. Reprint. London: Routledge, 1999.
Watt, W. Montgomery, and Pierre Cachia. *A His-*

tory of Islamic Spain. Edinburgh: Edinburgh University Press, 1965.

See also: Muslim Conquests; Reconquest of Spain; Ṭāriq ibn-Ziyād.

Timothy L. Wood

Music, martial

While most contemporary militaries have relegated music to a largely ceremonial role, historically it has proven to be an integral part of war making. In addition to inspiring soldiers in combat, music has served a vital communications function in variety of military activities—from drilling soldiers and organizing the daily ritual of military life to coordinating movements in battle.

Ancient Period: To 500 c.e.

The oldest form of martial music is most likely the war song, chanted by warriors as a prelude to battle. The war song served to ritualize and formalize conflict, often performing a specifically religious function. For instance, Sioux warriors performing the Sun Dance chanted songs or blew tunes into eagle bones in order to win the protection in battle from ancestors or animal spirits. This treatment of music as a form of magic is also evident in the biblical account of the Israelites' Siege of Jericho (c. 1400 b.c.e.) in which the sonic assault of their ram's horns reputedly caused the city walls to tumble down. A less fanciful example of music's importance in archaic battle can be found in the bas-relief of the Battle of Kadesh (1283 b.c.e.), located in the temple of Abu Simbel, which features trumpeters prominently in the battle lines and, significantly for Egyptian iconography, depicts them in the same size as their fellow warriors.

Like the other martial civilizations of the ancient Near East, the Israelites and Egyptians used music in battle for primarily psychological purposes—to incite their own troops to bravery and to intimidate the enemy. Yet the tactical use of music in battle is generally credited to the Greco-Roman culture of the first millennium b.c.e. Although ancient civilizations such as the Parthians and the Chinese are credited with introducing drums to direct battles, the Greeks relied instead on horns—and a wide vocabulary of military calls—to direct the sophisticated troop movements required of the *phalanx*. Unlike their military predecessors, the Greeks, and in turn the Romans, took a largely rationalistic approach to the use of music in battle. Thus Greco-Roman military historian Polybius argued against the use of archaic battle horns to startle the enemy in favor of lighter instruments such as the *cornu*, which a musician could easily mount over his shoulder and carry within the tight battle formations. The cornu's precision allowed its player to perform a wide variety of musical calls to dictate actions in combat (advances, retreats) or camp (assembly, mess, hours of the watch, warnings of surprise attacks). The Roman army's sophisticated use of musical calls gave them a tactical advantage over their Celtic enemies, who carried into battle the threatening but unwieldy *carnyx* (a rudimentary horn terminating in the shape of an animal head).

Medieval Period: 500 c.e. to 1500 c.e.

For a time in the early medieval period, successful militaries such as the Byzantines and the Arabs opted for relative silence on the battlefield. Such practice seemed in part to conform to a prevailing cultural austerity that upheld the ideal of a "holy warrior," fighting for God rather than material gain or personal vainglory. Indeed, the banishment of music among the armies of Muhammad and his successors may have been a deliberate attempt to distance themselves from pre-Islamic Arabs whose women would sing and dance suggestively during battle in order to spur their men to battle. The banishment of military music from the field also resulted from the practical realization that too heavy a reliance on auditory signals only added to the noise and confusion of battle. Moreover, in the rapid warfare of the horse-dominated Arab armies, military music was considered a luxury that only impeded military objectives and sapped precious resources.

Martial music made something of a comeback during the Crusades. In this slower, siege-dominated warfare, music resumed its twin psychological functions of morale-boosting and intimidation. At first Crusaders used music sparingly on the battlefield—martial orders such as the Knights Templars and Hospitalers sang psalms in preparation for battle. However, the Crusaders quickly adopted the large military bands of their Muslim opponents. Such bands, which included large sections of winds, brass, and percussion, not only roused men to battle but also advertised an army's wealth and power. During the late Middle Ages in Europe, as the code of chivalry affected the ideal if not the reality of warfare, the military band expanded to include court minstrels, ready to inspire the troops to bravery and to record their royal patrons' courage in battle.

Modern Period: 1500-2000

As the division of labor in combat increased—as well as the size and complexity of Renaissance warfare—music in battle became socially stratified. In general, fife-and-drum corps became associated with infantry troops, and trumpets and other horns ranging from bugles to clarinets became tied to cavalry. In his *Dell' arte della guerra* (1521; *The Art of War*, 1560), Niccolò Machiavelli insisted on this division for pragmatic reasons, arguing that different types of instruments were needed to direct different tactical maneuvers and, in general, to avoid confusion in battle. His dictates were successfully put into effect in the Battles of Marignano (1515) and Pavia (1525). Yet at the same time that music on the battlefield was becoming more specialized and utilitarian, the military band as a whole was evolving from a hodgepodge of sackbutts and small pipes into a strictly regulated number of horns, winds, and drums. The development of the military band mirrored the development of professional armies in seventeenth century Europe, with training centered increasingly around drill and close-order marching coordinated by musicians. At the same time, music became an integral part of naval life, with instruments such as pipes and horns used to coordinate the multitudinous activities on a warship.

The military band reached its apogee in the eighteenth century, as it took on a central function in the highly formalized warfare of the period. Music dictated the tempo for marching soldiers to battle and, once they were there, it coordinated their every movement. On ship, pipers directed seamen to trim sail or to fire cannon shot. Yet for

Ten Major Musical Compositions

Title	Year	Composer	Action
Lilli Burlero	1687	Thomas Wharton/ Henry Purcell	British Rebellion of 1688
Rule, Brittania	1740	James Thomson/ Thomas Arne	British Jacobite Rebellion of 1745
Yankee Doodle	c. 1755	Anonymous	American Revolution
La Marseillaise	1792	Clause Joseph Rouget de Lisle	French Revolution
Dixie	1859	Dan Emmett	American Civil War
Battle Hymn of the Republic	1861	Julia Ward Howe (lyrics)	American Civil War
Watch on the Rhine	1870	Max Schneckenburger	Franco-Prussian War of 1870
L'Internationale	1871	Eugene Pottier/ Pierre Degeyter	Paris Commune Rebellion
A Soldier's Song	1907	Peadar Kearney/ Patrick Heeney	Irish Easter Uprising of 1916
The March of the Volunteers	1935	Tian Han/Nie Er	Chinese Civil War

all its innovative force, music also humanized warfare that was becoming increasingly dominated by military technology (for example, repeating rifles and long-range artillery) that lessened the role of individual bravery and initiative in battle. As armies and navies ventured increasing distances from their homeland, military musicians adapted traditional airs to inspire the troops and remind them of why they were fighting. Foot soldiers and common sailors added doggerel verses to martial tunes to make them into "signature" songs. For instance, in the American Revolution (1775-1783), American troops adapted "Yankee Doodle" from a popular British marching tune. In the American Civil War (1861-1865), battle songs ranging from "The Battle Hymn of the Republic" to "Dixie" played a crucial function in reminding troops of the larger issues for which they were fighting. Indeed, Robert E. Lee, who positioned military bands in the woods to play during George E. Pickett's charge at Gettysburg, is reported to have said that without music there would have been no armies.

Despite its psychological importance, martial music was already on the wane by the American Civil War. In new era of highly technical, far more lethal warfare, music in battle became little more than a comforting anachronism. For instance, the sentimentalization of the "little drummer boy" on the American Civil War battlefield masked the fact that children were often exploited in such positions because they were most expendable personnel; indeed, they were often explicitly targeted by enemy sharpshooters to disrupt the opponent's battle line. In the twentieth century, further increases in communications and transportation technologies helped to relegate the bugle, fife, and drum to their present ceremonial function. Just as the two-way radio did away with the need for musical calls in battle, so the use of rail, tank, and automobile lessened the need for the infantry march guided by musical instruments. Moreover, the widespread adoption of guerrilla tactics has further rendered the military band superfluous. Sound recordings and radio technology have obviated the final and perhaps most human function of military music—providing entertainment and solace to soldier and sailor. Perhaps the real future of martial music lies in the psychological use of recorded music as the information media merge the battle and home fronts. For instance, during the Gulf War (1991), pop singer Lee Greenwood's "God Bless the USA" became a patriotic rallying cry for the United States' military action both at home and on the battlefield.

RESOURCES

Blom, Eric, ed. *Grove's Dictionary of Music and Musicians*. New York: St. Martin's Press, 1961.

Camus, Raoul F. *Military Music of the American Revolution*. Chapel Hill: University of North Carolina Press, 1976.

Connolly, Peter. *Greece and Rome at War*. London: Greenhill Books, 1998.

Lloyd, Alan B., ed. *Battle in Antiquity*. London: Duckworth, 1996.

Nicolle, David. *Medieval Warfare Source Book*. London: Arms & Armour, 1995.

Olson, Kenneth. *Music and Musket: Bands and Bandsmen of the American Civil War*. Westport, Conn.: Greenwood Press, 1981.

The Victory Collection: The Smithsonian Remembers When America Went to War. Audio recording. BMG Music, 1995.

White, William Carter. *A History of Military Music in America*. Reprint. Westport, Conn.: Greenwood Press, 1975.

SEE ALSO: American Civil War; Communications; Crusades; Drill; Jericho; Kadesh; Machiavelli, Niccolò; Marignano; Muslim Conquests; Pavia; Phalanx; Roman Empire.

Luke A. Powers

MUSKET

A smoothbore muzzle-loading firearm that was first developed in seventeenth century Spain. It replaced the *arquebus* (also spelled *harquebus* or called a hackbut), a matchlock gun that, in the mid-fifteenth century, became the world's first shoulder firearm. Early muskets were large, unwieldy weapons (commonly five and one-half feet long and weighing around twenty pounds), which were often handled by two men and fired from a portable gun rest. Such weapons propelled a two-ounce ball about 175 yards, but were notoriously inaccurate. By the early seventeenth century, the advent of flintlock ignition systems and general improvements in firearm technology had made the musket smaller and more reliable. Ranging in caliber from about 0.69 inch to greater than 0.75 inch, the musket remained the basic infantry weapon of militaries until the mid-nineteenth century, when it was gradually replaced by breech-loading rifles.

Jeremiah Taylor

Muslim Civil War of 657-661

AT ISSUE: Control of Muslim world
DATE: 657-661
LOCATION: Syria and Iraq
COMBATANTS: Supporters of ʿAlī as caliph vs. supporters of Muʿāwiyah as caliph
PRINCIPAL COMMANDERS: ʿAlī ibn Abī Ṭālib (c. 600-661), Ḥasan (624-680), and Ḥusayn (626-680); Muʿāwiyah (c. 602-680), ʿAbd Allāh ibn az-Zubayr (624-692), and Yazīd (c. 645-683)
PRINCIPAL BATTLES: Ṣiffīn (657)
RESULT: The first Muslim Civil War temporarily delayed the Arab conquests, laid the foundations for the rise of Umayyad Dynasty (661-750), and created the perpetual rift between Sunni and Shiite Muslims.

Background

As the cousin, adopted son, and son-in-law of Muḥammad, ʿAlī ibn Abī Ṭālib was the closest male relative of the Prophet, and thus a major contender for the office of caliph—successor to Muḥammad and ruler of the Muslims. Deemed too young to take the reins of power at the time of the Prophet's death (632), ʿAlī was eventually elected caliph after the murder of the third caliph ʿUthmān in 656. His election was disputed by a number of opposition groups, leading to civil war.

Action

The first threat came from ʿAbd Allāh ibn az-Zubayr, a prominent early companion of Muḥammad who was viewed by many as a preferable candidate. Enlisting the support of the Prophet's beloved widow ʿĀʾishah, al-Zubayr assembled a small army of supporters in Arabia and marched to southern Iraq, hoping the Arabs would rally around the Prophet's widow. However, the army in Iraq remained loyal to ʿAlī, who defeated the rebels in the Battle of the Camel (December, 656). Al-Zubayr was killed and ʿĀʾishah exiled.

ʿAlī's problems did not end with this victory. Muʿāwiyah I, governor of Syria and commander of a strong Arab army, refused to swear an oath of allegiance to ʿAlī. The third caliph, ʿUthmān, Muʿāwiyah's kinsman, had been assassinated, and as leader of the Umayyad clan Muʿāwiyah had a tribal responsibility to avenge the murder. Although ʿAlī was not directly implicated in the crime, some of his supporters were. Muʿāwiyah demanded that ʿAlī execute those involved in the plot before he would swear allegiance. Because punishing the assassins would undermine ʿAlī's power base, ʿAlī refused.

With negotiations deadlocked, both sides mobilized their armies, meeting at **Ṣiffīn** in Syria. However, neither side was willing to initiate hostilities against other Muslims. The armies therefore remained encamped opposite each other for three months. Battle was finally joined (August, 657), with ʿAlī's army initially gaining the upper hand. However, Muʿāwiyah's soldiers rode into battle with pages from the Qurʾan tied to their lances, calling for arbitration rather than the shedding of Muslim blood; a truce was thus declared.

ʿAlī agreed to arbitration, which continued for several years without any resolution. In the meantime, ʿAlī's position was undermined by the defection of Egypt and by increasing disillusionment among many of his adherents. This devout faction opposed arbitration with Muʿāwiyah, proclaiming that God was the only true arbitrator, and His decision would manifest itself through trial by combat. ʿAlī's willingness to compromise was seen as a sign of weakness and lack of faith. Those who withdrew their support became known as the Khawārij ("those who go out"); they remained a significant faction in Islam for centuries. In 661, a Khārijite murdered ʿAlī in the mosque at Kūfah.

Aftermath

ʿAlī's eldest son Ḥasan abandoned his claim to the caliphate in return for a large pension, leaving Muʿāwiyah free to ascend the throne and establish the Umayyad Dynasty at Damascus (661-

750), which would lead Arab armies in a glorious period of conquests in North Africa, Spain, Iran, Anatolia, and parts of Central Asia. However, ʿAlī's second son, al-Ḥusayn, continued the struggle for the rights of the Prophet's family to rule the empire. Upon the death of Muʿāwiyah in 680, Ḥusayn led a small band in rebellion against Muʿāwiyah's son and successor Yazīd. The grandson of the Prophet and his followers were massacred at the Battle of Karbalāʾ (October 10, 680), scandalizing the Muslim world.

The first Muslim Civil War thus laid the basis for increasing fragmentation of the Islamic world along religious and political lines. Thereafter religious animosity and occasional warfare between Sunni and Shīʿite Muslims has remained a constant factor in Near Eastern military history.

Resources
Hinds, G. "The Banners and Battle Cries of the Arabs at Siffin (657 A.D.)." *Al-Abhath* 24 (1971): 3-42.
_____. "Kufan Political Alignments and Their Background in the Mid-Seventh Century A.D." *International Journal of Middle East Studies* 2 (1971): 346-367.
Jafri, S. *The Origins and Early Development of Shi'a Islam*. New York: Longman, 1979.
Petersen, E. *Ali and Muʿāwiya in Early Arabic Tradition*. Copenhagen: Munksgaard, 1964.
Tabari. *The History of al-Tabari*. 39 vols. Albany: State University of New York Press, 1965-1999.
Wellhausen, J. *The Religio-Political Factions in Early Islam*. Amsterdam: North-Holland, 1975.

See also: Muslim Conquests.

William J. Hamblin

Muslim Civil War of 861-870

At issue: Stability and control of the caliph of Baghdad in the ʿAbbāsid Dynasty
Date: 861-870
Location: Caliphate of Baghdad
Combatants: Various caliphs vs. their successors or relatives, both sides aided by Muslim/Turkish military leaders
Principal commanders: *Caliph*, al-Mutawakkil (822-861), al-Muntaṣir (d. 862), al-Mustaʿīn (d. 866), al-Muʿtazz (d. 869), al-Muhtadī (d. 870), al-Muʿtamid (d. 892); *Military leaders*, Salih ibn Wasif, Utāmish (d. 863), Ahmad ibn al-Khaṣīb, Musa ibn Mugha
Result: After a decade of instability, a Muslim Golden Age occurred

Background
When al-Mutawakkil became caliph of Baghdad in 847, he restored Islamic orthodoxy and persecuted all nonorthodox or non-Muslim groups. He faced both internal and external enemies, with rebellions and wars in outside provinces constantly plaguing his rule. He would be killed, however, by Turkish mercenaries directed by his eldest son, al-Muntaṣir, who feared the loss of his succession. Although al-Mutawakkil was widely disliked, his death sparked a decade of unprecedented instability and civil war.

Action
Al-Muntaṣir worked quickly to ensure his sole, unopposed rule. He reconstituted all previous laws and mandates set up by his father and deposed two brothers from the line of succession in favor of his own child. The rival Turkish *shakiriyya* army and a prominent military leader, Salih ibn Wasif, were deployed on the Byzantine front to get rid of any other rivals. Two men surfaced as aides to al-Muntaṣir and his rule: Utāmish, one of the leaders of the Sāmarrā army (a force suppressed under al-Mutawakkil), and Ahmad ibn al-Khaṣīb, a member of the Iraqi landowning families. Al-Muntaṣir's attempts to solidify an unopposed rule, however, would prove to be fruitless, as he died of a heart attack only six months later, in 862.

A hastily assembled council decided to forgo any further members of the al-Mutawakkil family line, instead selecting an eighteen-year-old grandson of al-Muʿtasim, the caliph who preceded al-Mutawakkil. Given his young age, al-Mustaʿīn was probably chosen out of necessity rather than because he was a strong and capable ruler. The council then elevated Utāmish to the position of *wazir* (chief minister) and Ahmad ibn al-Khaṣīb to that of *katib* (administrative assistant). Within this arrangement, the council hoped to recognize the separation of military and financial affairs.

Utāmish, however, wanted to consolidate titles and power in order to further his career and ideas. Ahmad ibn al-Khaṣīb was quickly dismissed and exiled to Crete after only one month in office. Utāmish appointed a new *katib*, securing power through the selection of one of his followers. Utāmish, who possessed a strong sense of military power, reorganized the Sāmarrā army as well as civil laws pertaining to it. Although Utāmish's changes showed professionalism and foresight, they caused rumblings within the army, and in 863, Utāmish was murdered, and all his changes were declared invalid.

This allowed the two other leaders of the Sāmarrā army, Wasif and Musa ibn Mugha, who lacked the desire for supreme control, to take charge of the situation. They quickly appointed a well-trained bureaucrat to assume control of the administrative tasks. When a military leader was murdered by Wasif and Mugha over the granting of estates, however, a civil war once again erupted. The Sāmarrā army turned against Wasif and Mugha, who were supported by the *shakiriyya*, and an open conflict ensued. Al-Mustaʿīn attempted to calm the rising emotions of the Sāmarrā forces but to no avail. Realizing their position, Wasif and Mugha sought support from the al-Mustaʿīn and the Tahirid forces in Baghdad. The conflict became one between Sāmarrā and Baghdad.

Sima al-Sharabi, having emerged as the leader of the Sāmarrā forces, planned for the inevitable fight against Baghdad. One of al-Mutawakkil's sons, al-Muʿtazz, was brought out of prison and proclaimed the rival ruler. His brother, Abu Ahmad, was put in charge of the expected military operations. With their operations and administration in order, Abu Ahmad and the entire army approached Baghdad. The siege began, and the city was soon suffering from food shortages. When fighting broke out, neither side could gain an advantage over the other. With a stalemate evident, Abu Ahmad called for negotiations. After much opposition, terms were agreed upon. Al-Muʿtazz was accepted as ruler, and al-Mustaʿīn was deposed and exiled (866). Wasif and Mugha were appointed governors in Sāmarrā but were later murdered for fear that they would attempt to regain their lost power.

However, fighting quickly broke out in Baghdad, as forces sent to aid in the fight against the Sāmarrā went unpaid. Resources were taken from the *shakiriyya* to appease the forces from the east, only to begin the fighting, which would later see the Tahirid forces prevail and the *shakiriyya* dispersed.

With his new position as ruler, al-Muʿtazz seems to have wanted complete power through the control of the army. This desire led him to arrest his brother, Abu Ahmad, who had just won him a victory, to depose his other brother, and to murder al-Mustaʿīn, who was already in exile. A few months later, he banished both of his brothers, who took refuge with the Tahirids in Baghdad. To gain control of the army, al-Muʿtazz attempted to win the favor of the most powerful generals by granting them provincial governorships. The attempt to satisfy every general was not an easy task, however, and he quickly fell out of favor with Wasif. At this point, an open struggle began between al-Muʿtazz and the generals. A power struggle began involving bureaucrats divided between al-Muʿtazz and the generals. Eventually the military won, and Wasif took control, deposing al-Muʿtazz and replacing him with his nephew, al-Muhtadī.

Conflicts, however, would continue. When Mugha, who was on a minor policing operation, heard of the developments in the capital, he was concerned and decided to return. Upon his arrival, Wasif went into hiding, and the power struggle began anew. However, the men of the army were growing tired of the struggle among generals. They unified and pledged support for al-Muhtadī in an effort to end the constant fighting. Their support was conditional and focused mainly on their own fiscal concerns. Although he wanted the army's support, al-Muhtadī was not able to meet all these demands, and once again fighting broke out. In the struggle, several generals saw their chance to depose him. However, al-Muhtadī called on those who sought to support him, and some of the generals were arrested. In this attempt to gain control, al-Muhtadī was wounded and died in 870, only eleven months into his reign. Once again a son of al-Mutawakkil, al-Muʿtamid, was released from prison and proclaimed successor.

Aftermath

After all the conflict that had plagued his father and brothers, al-Muʿtamid enacted a compromise to end the fighting and laid the foundations for military peace and economic prosperity throughout the region. For the first time in a decade, the Islamic empire would see an era of prosperity and progress. In industry and commerce as well as the arts and sciences, al-Muʿtamid would begin an era that would later be called the Golden Age of Islam.

Resources

Hitti, Philip. *History of the Arabs*. New York: St. Martin's Press, 1970.

Hourani, Albert. *A History of the Arab Peoples*. New York: Warner Books, 1991.

Shaban, M. A. *Islamic History*, A.D. 600-750: *A New Interpretation*. Vol 2. Cambridge, England: Cambridge University Press, 1976.

See also: Byzantine-Muslim Wars.

Andrew Bielakowski

Muslim Conquests

At issue: The spread of Islam in Africa, the Mediterranean, and Central Asia
Date: 622-750
Location: Near East, North Africa, Spain, Mediterranean, and Central Asia
Combatants: Muslims vs. Byzantines, Sāsānids, Libyans, Tunisians, Berbers, Indians, Turks, Chinese, Spanish, French
Principal commanders: *Muslim*, Muḥammad (c. 570-632), Khālid ibn-al-Walīd (d. 642), ʿAmr ibn al-ʿĀṣ (585-664), ʿUqbah ibn Nāfir (d. 683), Muʿāwiyah I (c. 602-680)
Principal battles: Badr, Trench, Yarmūk, Ctesiphon, Nahāvand, Heliopolis, Babylon, Alexandria, Masts, Karbalāʾ, Marj Rahit, Multan, Talas River, Guadalete, Constantinople
Result: The Muslim Conquests created an empire stretching from the Indus River to the Atlantic Ocean and laid the foundation for Islamic religion and civilization

Background

Like Moses and Joshua, Muḥammad, the founder of Islam, was both prophet and military commander. Although persecuted in his hometown of Mecca, he was accepted as prophet in Medina (622), where he organized a small city-state. In the following decade, the ensuing war between Muḥammad and the Meccans generally favored Muḥammad, with notable Muslim victories against great odds at **Badr** (624) and the Battle of the **Trench** (627). Through a combination of military conquest, deft diplomacy, marriage alliances, and religious conversion, many of the nomad tribesmen of Arabia flocked to Muḥammad's banner. The Meccans, being practical merchants, finally submitted and converted to Islam (630). By his death, Muḥammad had united all the Arab tribes into a new theocratic state.

Action

With the Prophet dead, many of the tribesmen of Arabia—who viewed their alliance as a personal bond of loyalty to Muḥammad—refused submission to the new caliph Abū Bakr. In a series of lightning campaigns known as the Ridda Wars (632-634), Khālid ibn-al-Walīd and other Muslim generals defeated these "apostates" and reunified the tribes of Arabia.

This new Arabian tribal confederation bordered two great empires to the north. The Byzantines and Persian Sāsānids were just recovering from an exhausting twenty-five-year war. In a remarkable military achievement, the Arabs simultaneously defeated both empires, destroying the Sāsānids and bringing the Byzantines to their knees.

Using their control of desert trails to mask rapid movement, the Arabs were able to pick the time and place of attack. Raids into Palestine and Syria brought the mobilization of a large Byzantine army at **Yarmūk** (August, 636), which was disastrously defeated. The destruction of the Byzantine field army allowed the Arabs to attack at will. Many inland cities surrendered, accepting the generous terms of the Arabs: Jerusalem, Damascus, and Antioch all fell within the next two years. The coastal cities, receiving support from the Byzantine navy, were able to hold out longer against weak Arab siege capacity: Caesarea fell in 640 and Tripoli in 645.

The Arab invasion of Sāsānid Mesopotamia broadly followed the same pattern. It began with intermittent raids from the desert on the western river basin of the Euphrates. The Sāsānid Dynasty responded by mobilizing a massive army at Qadisiya under their general Rustem. The Arabs, gathering together their scattered raiders, defeated the Persians after a fierce three-day battle, and swept on to capture the Persian capital at **Ctesiphon** (637). With Mesopotamia subdued, the Arabs established large military camps at Kufa and Basra to serve as bases for further operations in Iran. Collecting their reserves from the east, the Sāsānids bravely opposed Arab advances into Iran, but after a crushing defeat at **Nahāvand** (641-642), organized Persian resistance collapsed. In the following decade, the Arabs consolidated their hold on central Persia. Eastern Persia proved more difficult, with local warlords offering strong guerrilla resistance. Nonetheless, Arab armies reached the Indus River by 663 and captured Samarkand in 676, bringing them into contact with the Turkish nomads of Central Asia.

Whereas the conquest of Iran required a fairly straightforward strategy of a steady drive eastward, the Arabs faced a strategic dilemma against the Byzantines. Their conquest of Syria had created three military fronts: northwest in Anatolia, southwest against Egypt, and the eastern Mediterranean. Egypt was the natural first choice, both because of the rich booty it offered and because it could be used as a Byzantine base to retake Palestine and cut communications with Mecca. Egypt was invaded in 639 under the brilliant ʿAmr ibn al-ʿĀṣ with only 12,000 men. Following a victory over the Byzantine army at **Heliopolis** (June, 640), the Arabs captured **Babylon** (Old Cairo) after a seven-month siege in April, 641. Once again, the capture of coastal Alexandria proved more difficult; the city did not surrender until 642. With

Muslim Empire in 760

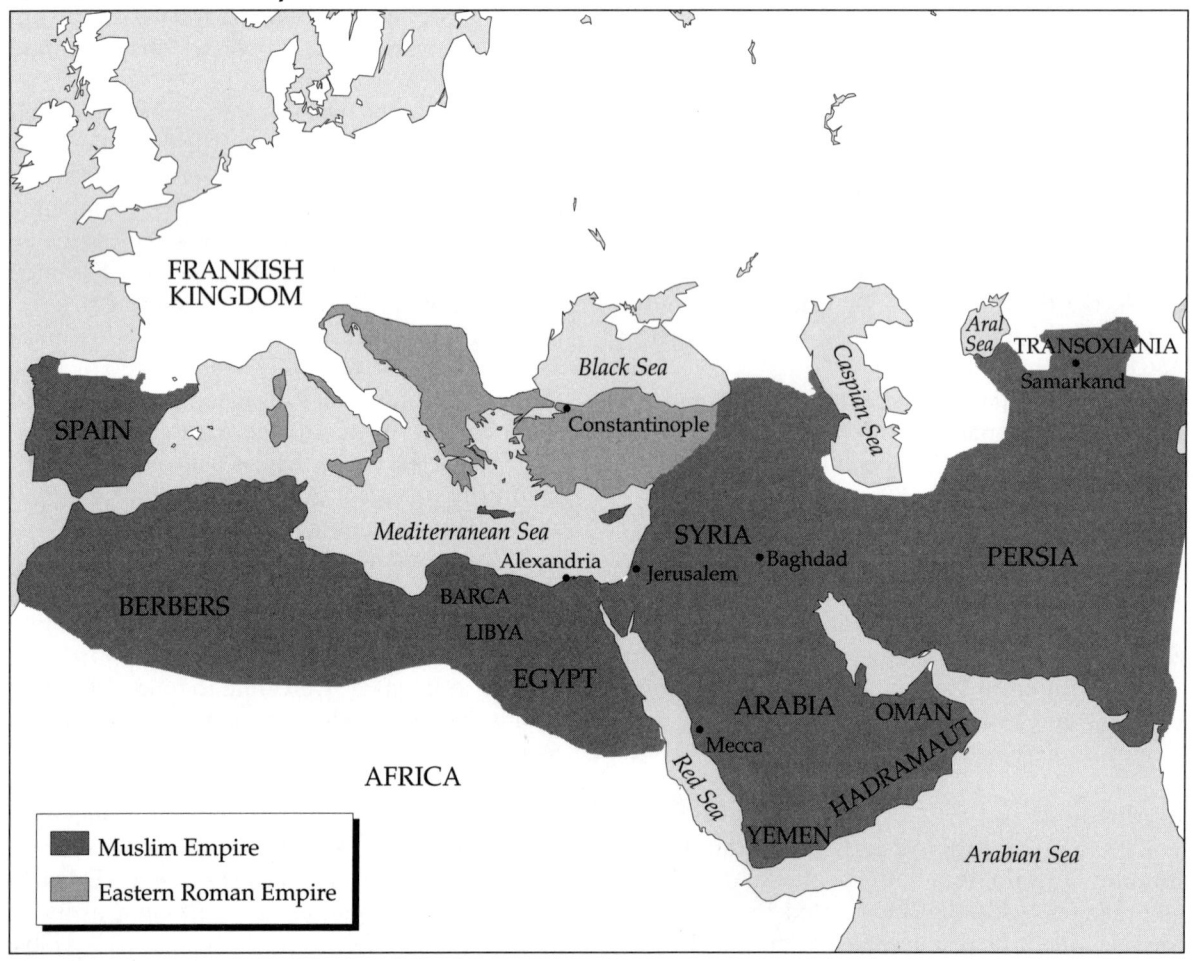

control of the sea, however, the Byzantines launched a naval operation that retook **Alexandria** in 645. While marching, the Byzantines were bested by an Arab army and quickly decided to evacuate the country.

The Byzantine use of naval power to defend their coastal cities and briefly reconquer of Alexandria demonstrated to the Arabs the importance of naval power. Using conscripted maritime workers and sailors of their newly captured ports of Caesarea and Acre, and the plunder of their conquests for financing, the Arabs rapidly created a naval power to rival the Byzantines. The Arabs were not all nomads. Many from the coasts of Arabia had a long-standing naval experience in the Indian Ocean. Assisted by the sailors of the conquered population, the Arabs were able to build and launch a significant fleet, placing the Byzantines on the defensive. The Arabs captured Cyprus (649) and Rhodes (654), bringing the naval conflict into the Aegean. The Byzantines responded by mobilizing most of their navy to retake the initiative. This fleet was destroyed at the Battle of the **Masts** (655), giving the Arabs naval supremacy and laying the foundation for an assault on Constantinople itself.

Using newly conquered Egypt as a base, Arab armies also expanded into North Africa, capturing Libya (643) and plundering Tunisia (647-649). In the following years, Arab attention was distracted by a civil war and other campaigns. By 665, however, raids against Tunisia were resumed, and in 670 the Arabs established a permanent military camp at Qayrawan. Although the capital at Carthage held out, the countryside of Tunisia was overrun, and some of the Berber (Moorish) tribes converted to Islam, adding their numbers to the Arab armies. Overextending himself, the Arab commander ʿUqbah ibn Nāfir marched across North Africa, defeating or allying with Berber chiefs, and reaching the Atlantic Ocean (681-683). He was defeated and killed (683), however, leading to a revolt among the Berbers and a temporary withdrawal of the Arabs from Tunisia. They returned in force with an army of forty thousand men, capturing Carthage (698) and defeating Kahina, a Berber prophetess who attempted to unite her tribes against the Arabs. The following decade was spent defeating or converting the Berber tribes of Algeria and Morocco.

By 710, the Arabs had conquered all of North Africa.

In the Middle East, the succession of ʿAlī ibn Abī Ṭālib to the caliphate precipitated the Muslim Civil War of 657-661, temporarily delaying the Arab conquests. Muʿāwiyah I emerged as caliph in 661, founding the Umayyad Dynasty. He then focused his attention on the capture of the Byzantine capital at Constantinople. Whereas the Persian capital at Ctesiphon had been vulnerable to Arab attacks from the nearby desert, Constantinople was the strongest fortified city in the world and lay across the Sea of Marmara. After Muʿāwiyah had obtained naval supremacy at the Battle of the Masts in 655, an attack on Constantinople had at last become a possibility. Muʿāwiyah sent almost annual raids into Anatolia in the 660's, plundering as far as Chalcedon on the straits opposite Constantinople. A rebellion in Sicily culminated in the murder of emperor Constans (668). Seizing the opportunity, Muʿāwiyah sent an army to attack Tunisia (665) and a fleet against Sicily (669). A significant portion of Byzantine power was deflected to the west because of an internal attack, permitting Muʿāwiyah to make his master stroke against Constantinople. In 670, he established a strong base at Cyzicus, near Constantinople, from which his fleet terrorized the Byzantine coasts and harried the capital for a number of years. The Byzantines, using a newly invented liquid incendiary known as Greek fire, decisively defeated the Arab navy (677). Surviving ships of the Arab fleet were sunk in a storm, while the retreating army was harassed. Muʿāwiyah was forced to pay tribute and agree to a truce.

Although the failure of the Siege of Constantinople was the first major defeat of the Arabs, they still were the dominant military power in the world. Further Arab conquests were temporarily halted by the Muslim Civil War of 680-684 after the death of Muʿāwiyah in 680. The rebellion of Ḥusayn, Muhammad's grandson, was easily crushed by Muʿāwiyah's son Yazīd at the Battle of **Karbalāʾ** (680). The revolt of ʿAbd Allāh ibn az-Zubayr in 682 was much more dangerous; he was able to gain control of Arabia, Iraq, and Egypt. Although the rebels' advance on Damascus was defeated at the bloody Battle of **Marj Rahit** (684), it still took the Umayyads eight more years to reunite their empire (684-692).

By 700, the Umayyads were in undisputed control of an empire stretching from the Atlantic Ocean to the Indus River. The next fifty years witnessed further conquests on four fronts. First, from 708 to 712, the Arabs conquered the province of Sind in the Indus Valley, culminating in the Siege of **Multan** in 712. Strong resistance by the Hindu Rājput kings of northwest India prevented further Arab advances at that time, but the planting of Islam in the Indus Valley laid the foundation for the eventual conquest of India in the eleventh century.

At the same time, Arab armies based in Iran invaded Turkestan and Transoxiana (708-713). In the ensuing decades, the Arabs fought numerous guerrilla-style wars against Turkish nomads and city-states, slowly gaining the upper hand and the support of some Turkish tribes. The Arab conquests in the east reached their farthest advance in 751 at the Battle of **Talas River**, when an allied Arab-Turkish army defeated a Tang Chinese force. Although the Arabs did not move farther east, their victory brought a collapse of Chinese influence among the Turks in Central Asia, who would eventually convert to Islam. At roughly the same time other Arab armies crossed the Caucasus and raided the Turkish Khazars (727-737).

The third major front of Arab expansion was in Spain and France. In 711, an Arab-Berber army under Ṭāriq crossed the straits of Gibraltar. The Visigoths of Spain were embroiled in a succession dispute, and Roderick's factious army was unable to contain the invasion. Defeated at the Battle of **Guadalete** (711), the Visigothic kingdom disintegrated; its capital, Toledo, was captured in 712. Further resistance by local Visigothic warlords could not withstand the Arab and Berber troops that swept through Spain and into southern France. Narbonne and several other cities in southern France were captured (718-732), with Arab raiders plundering northward. Charles Martel, the Merovingian warlord, mobilized an army to oppose the Arabs at Tours (732). There, he won a significant victory, with the Arabs retreating following the death of their commander ʿAbd ar-Raḥmān. However, Tours was not decisive; Arab raids continued in southern France until 751 and ended because rebellion and civil war sapped the military resources.

The most important military front was Anatolia, with the overriding objective of Constantinople. Invasions of Anatolia were renewed, and parts of the southeast were conquered (710-714). The main thrust of attack was again by sea, with an Arab fleet blockading **Constantinople** from 717 to 718. The Byzantines, weakened by a series of coups and revolts during the past two decades, were fortunate that the brilliant general Leo III seized the throne as the Arabs approached Constantinople with a reported 120,000 men and 1,800 ships under their finest general, Maslamah ibn ʿAbd al-Malik. The Arabs completely invested the city by land, but the Byzantines, with their superior Greek fire technology, prevented a secure naval blockade. In the spring of 718, the Arabs sent a strong fleet to resupply their army. Many of the sailors were conscripted Egyptian and North African Christians—former subjects of the Byzantines. Many of them deserted with their boats, bringing their cargo of supplies to Constantinople. The supplies of the Arab besiegers were thus cut. Combined with pestilence and attacks from the Bulgars, who had allied with the Byzantines, the Arab position became untenable. The besiegers withdrew only to face further disasters from storms at sea and Byzantine harassment during their retreat. Although Arab raids into Anatolia continued for another few decades, Constantinople would not be seriously threatened by a Muslim army for another seven centuries.

Aftermath

The end of the great Arab conquests was not caused so much by the military prowess of the Merovingians and Byzantines as civil war among the Arabs and the subsequent fragmentation of the Arab Empire. Various revolts against the Umayyads plagued the empire from 741 to 747, when the ʿAbbāsid clan in northeastern Iran successfully launched a army west toward Damascus. The Umayyads won decisively at the Battle of the Zab River (750), and the rival ʿAbbāsid caliphs seized to the throne. Although military operations continued under the ʿAbbāsids, they made no major new conquests. The age of the great Arab conquests had ended.

Resources

Blankinship, K. *The End of the Jihad State*. Albany: State University of New York Press, 1994.

Brooks, E. W. "The Arabs in Asia Minor (641-750), from Arabic Sources." *Journal of Hellenic Studies* 18 (1898): 182-208.

Butler, A. J. *The Arab Conquests of Egypt*. 2d ed. Brooklyn, N.Y.: A&B Publishing, 1998.

Collins, Roger. *The Arab Conquest of Spain, 710-797*. Oxford: Blackwell, 1989.

Dixon, A. A. *The Umayyad Caliphate, 65-86/684-705*. London: Luzac, 1971.

Donner, F. *The Early Islamic Conquests*. Princeton, N.J.: Princeton University Press, 1981.

Haldon, J. F. *Byzantium in the Seventh Century*. Cambridge, England: Cambridge University Press, 1990.

Jandora, John. *The March from Medina*. Clifton, N.J.: Kingston Press, 1990.

Kaegi, Walter. *Byzantium and the Early Islamic Conquests*. Cambridge, England: Cambridge University Press, 1992.

Kennedy, Hugh. *The Prophet and the Age of the Caliphates*. London: Longman, 1986.

Nichephorus. *Short History*. Washington, D.C.: Dumbarton Oaks, Research Library and Collection, 1990.

Savage, Elizabeth. *A Gateway to Hell, a Gateway to Paradise: The North African Response to the Arab Conquest*. Princeton, N.J.: Darwin Press, 1997.

Sharon, M. *Black Banners from the East*. Jerusalem: Max Schloessinger Memorial Fund, Hebrew University, 1990.

Shoufani, E. *Al-Riddah and the Muslim Conquest of Arabia*. Toronto: University of Toronto Press, 1973.

Stratos, A. N. *Byzantium in the Seventh Century*. 5 vols. Amsterdam: Adolf M. Hakkert, 1968-1980.

Tabari. *The History of al-Tabari*. 39 vols. Albany: State University of New York Press, 1985-1999.

Theophanes. *The Chronicle of Theophanes the Confessor*. Oxford: Clarendon Press, 1997.

Wink, Andre. *Al-Hind: The Making of the Indo-Islamic World*. Leiden: Brill, 1990.

SEE ALSO: ʿAbbāsid Revolution; ʿAmr ibn al-ʿĀṣ; Byzantine-Muslim Wars; Constantinople, Siege of, 717-718; Frankish-Moorish Wars; Khālid ibn al-Walīd; Leo III; Mūsā ibn Nuṣayr; Muslim Civil War of 657-661; Navāvand; Talas River; Ṭāriq ibn Ziyād; Tours; Yarmūk.

William J. Hamblin

MUSLIM UNREST IN CHINA

AT ISSUE: Ethnic rivalries between Hui Muslims and Han Chinese
DATE: 1862-1873
LOCATION: Shaanxi and Gansu provinces, part of Ningxia Hui autonomous region
COMBATANTS: Han Chinese (Qing government) vs. Muslim rebels
PRINCIPAL COMMANDERS: *Qing*, Zuo Zongtang (1812-1885); *Muslim rebels*, Ma Hualong (d. 1868), Ma Guiyuan, Ma Wenlu
RESULT: Delayed the reunification of Qing China following the Taiping, Panthay, and Nian Rebellions; exacerbated tensions between Han Chinese and the Muslims in northwest China; depopulated regions of China's northwest for a generation

BACKGROUND

As Western nations impinged on China in the nineteenth century, the Qing state was suffering from serious internal problems. The army, based on the traditional banners (military and administrative units), had deteriorated to the point of uselessness. The Taiping Rebellion (1850-1864) disrupted China south of the Chang Jiang for a decade and a half. In the Nian Rebellion (1853-1868), bandits terrorized the area south of Beijing. The Panthay Rebellion (1855-1873), involving Muslims, broke out in Yunnan, and south China suffered from the activities of the Triads. Adding to these problems, corrupt and venal officials deprived the state of revenue and competent administration.

Before the mid-1800's, violence involving the Hui (Sinophone Muslims) had occurred in the northwest. However, most of the conflicts, including Ma Mingxin's Rebellion in the 1780's, were primarily conflicts within the Hui community; however, they did create a Hui reputation for ferocity.

ACTION

In the mid-1800's, civil society in northwest China broke down for a number of reasons: Troops had been removed to suppress rebellions in other provinces, taxes had been increased to pay for these military activities as well as foreign indemnities; and officials had become corrupt and inept. Banditry and crime increased. To protect themselves, people in Shaanxi began to construct local fortifications and create local militias. Some of these groups, including the Han Chinese, were antagonistic toward their Muslim fellow citizens. Farther west, in Gansu, the various Sufi brotherhoods harbored long-standing animosities toward one another. All these local tensions were increased by occasional forays into the area by Taiping and Nian rebels.

In 1862, a squabble in a marketplace between a Han and a Muslim led to a riot. Violence quickly escalated as local militia joined the conflict. The rumor that the Han intended to "wash away the Hui" led to Muslim reprisals. Eventually, Muslim forces laid siege to Xi'an but lacked equipment to breach the walls. The Qing government declared that a Muslim uprising was in progress and appointed Zuo Zongtang pacification commander. After a delay of a couple of years while rebels farther east were eradicated, Zuo began operations.

Despite constant government pleas for quicker action, Zuo believed military operations required careful planning. He took time to organize his troops and ensure sufficient supplies, and he planted crops to guarantee food for his army. Showing some leniency, by 1868, he had cleared Shaanxi of Muslim rebels; a number of refugees fled west into Gansu.

There, swelled by the refugees, Muslims formed four main concentrations. Because of previous disputes within Muslim communities, they were unable to unite against the Qing army. The strongest, at Jinjipu in northeastern Gansu, was led by Ma Hualong. Zuo turned his forces against them in 1868. After four months, Ma's forces were defeated. He and all of his family were executed.

Despite his earlier, more humane, warfare in Shaanxi, Zuo massacred large numbers of Muslims. Slowly moving farther west, he attacked the remaining Muslim forces one by one. After some early successes, the Muslims around Hezhou (Linxia) joined the Qing side. Zuo defeated the Muslims under Ma Guiyuan in the Xunhua area (Qinghai province), again massacring noncombatants because many of these were of the Salar nationality and thought to be more violent than the Hui. Finally, the army of Ma Wenlu in the western Gansu corridor was crushed in late 1873.

Aftermath

With these victories, Zuo reestablished Qing authority within China proper. During this period, the Hui received no help from the Turkic-speaking Muslims of Xinjiang who viewed the Hui as Chinese. The rebellion confirmed the Chinese myth that the Hui were a violent people and not easily assimilable. It took some years to rebuild the population of China's northwest. With the collapse of the Qing Dynasty in 1911, this area was controlled by warlords (most of them Muslim) until finally reunified into China by the People's Liberation Army and administrators from the Chinese Communist Party. At the beginning of the twenty-first century, Han-Hui tensions still existed in this part of China.

Resources

Chu, Wên-chang. *The Moslem Rebellion in Northwest China*. The Hague: Mouton, 1966.

Israeli, Raphael. *Muslims in China*. London: Curzon Press, 1980.

Leslie, Donald. *Islam in Traditional China*. Belconnen, A.C.T., Australia: Canberra College of Advanced Education, 1986.

Lipman, Jonathan. *Familiar Strangers*. Seattle: University of Washington Press, 1997.

See also: Chinese Revolution; Taiping Rebellion; Zuo Zongtang.

Art Barbeau

Mussolini, Benito

Full name: Benito Amilcare Andrea Mussolini
Also known as: Il Duce (the leader); Capo Del Governo (head of government)
Born: July 29, 1883; Predappio, Italy
Died: April 28, 1945; Giulino de Mezzegra, near Dongo, Italy
Principal wars: Spanish Civil War, World War II
Military significance: Mussolini glorified war and as dictator of Italy was determined to increase its power and influence through war. Between 1935 and 1945, the country fought a succession of conflicts in Africa and in Europe.

Benito Mussolini's direct knowledge of strategy and tactics was scant, as his military experience

Benito Mussolini. (National Archives)

was restricted to a two-year service in the Italian army during World War I. He was discharged early, in September 1917, for wounds received during grenade practice. Nonetheless, he returned to civilian life boasting of his life under fire. After the war, he determined to re-create the power of the old Roman Empire and mark his age "like a lion with its claws." He created a paramilitary fascist government in 1919-1921 and became dictator of Italy in 1922.

He quickly became involved in a succession of exhaustive wars: Libyan War (1922-1932), Somalian War (1923-1927), Ethiopian War (1935-1936), Spanish Civil War (1936-1939), and the conquest of Albania (1939). In 1933, Mussolini became the virtual commander in chief of Italy's armed forces when he assumed control of the ministries of war, navy, and air.

Mussolini constantly fostered the impression he was a forceful, accomplished warrior, but in practice, his leadership was weak and erratic. He established no effective liaison between the military services to handle joint operations; he oftentimes urged offensives despite lack of adequate reserves and against the opposition of his commanders in the field. He frequently promoted men based on their "fascist merit" rather than real ability. Unwilling to admit an absence of adequate supplies, he fantasized about miracle weapons that would win the war. Mussolini usually ascribed reverses to the failure of his subordinates to show proper courage.

Mussolini's Pact of Steel with German leader Adolf Hitler on May 22, 1939, brought Italy into World War II in September, 1939, a conflict for which it was ill-prepared militarily and psychologically. For a time, Mussolini tried to carry on a parallel war by concentrating his military actions in the Balkans and the Mediterranean. However, the Germans had to rescue his offensives in both Greece and Libya in 1940. Henceforth, Hitler took charge of future Italian operations. In 1941, Hitler saved Mussolini from a military coup. In July, 1943, Hitler rescued Mussolini from another attempt to overthrow him and installed him as puppet dictator over northern Italy. Mussolini was captured and shot by Italian partisans in 1945. Mussolini's desire to create a nation of warriors led to a loss of Italian independence and to eventual defeat, humiliation, and impoverishment.

RESOURCES

Adams, Henry Hitch. *Italy at War*. Alexandria, Va.: Time-Life Books, 1982.

Blinkhorn, Martin. *Mussolini and Fascist Italy*. London: Routledge, 1994.

Knox, MacGregor. *Mussolini Unleashed, 1939-1940: Politics and Strategy in Fascist Italy's Last War*. New York: Cambridge University Press, 1982.

Ridley, Jasper Godwin. *Mussolini*. New York: St. Martin's Press, 1998.

Smith, Denis Mack. *Mussolini*. New York: Alfred A. Knopf, 1982.

SEE ALSO: Hitler; Adolf; Spanish Civil War; World War II.

Wm. Laird Kleine-Ahlbrandt

Mustard gas

A type of poison gas first used in warfare during World War I (1914-1918). Mustard gas is a vesicant, or blistering agent, which is compounded from carbon, sulfur, hydrogen, and chlorine. It was introduced by Germany in 1917 and, in 1918, was extensively used by both sides. Thanks to gas masks and other protective gear, it inflicted relatively few fatalities. Although vesicants like mustard gas and lewisite, irritants like CS, and, beginning in the 1940's, nerve agents have been stockpiled by many nations, chemical warfare has rarely been resorted to in the decades following World War I. Where such weapons have been used, it has usually been against poorly equipped forces that lack gas masks—as in Ethiopia (1935-1936) and the Iran-Iraq War (1980-1988).

Jeremiah Taylor

Muster and review

The formal assemblage and subsequent inspection by officers of troops or a ship's crew. An ancient practice, muster and review serves both practical and ceremonial purposes. While fostering the psychological readiness and heightened morale that comes with martial pomp, muster and review also presents an excellent opportunity to take roll call. Moreover, like drilling, it is a coordinated activity that helps create a strong *esprit de corps* among troops who fall into muster together. In warfare, coordination and cooperation are indispensable—indeed, often the difference between death and life, defeat and victory. Thus, exercises of discipline like muster and review have long been an important part of military life.

Jeremiah Taylor

Mutiny

Mass military insubordination. Mutiny, an occurrence of great antiquity, usually has its origin in the common soldier or sailor's concern about poor living and working conditions. For instance, when sailors of the British Royal Navy mutinied at *Invergordon* in 1931, it was because of general discontent with large pay cuts. Despite popular conceptions created by such films as *Mutiny on the Bounty* (Metro-Golwyn-Mayer, 1935), mutinies are not always bloody affairs; they sometimes amount to a mere laying down of arms. Nevertheless, the legacy of violent mutiny is real, as is the instability and embarrassment mutinies lend to any organization that experiences one. As a result, militaries have traditionally acted to put them out quickly and to severely punish participants. Before the twentieth century, mutiny was often punishable by death. Among the Romans and other ancient societies, punishment was meted out by "decimation," the execution of every tenth man. The impracticality and inhumanity of such penalties led to more lenient treatments of mutineers in the twentieth century.

Jeremiah Taylor

My Lai Massacre

Type of action: Massacre in the Vietnam Conflict
Date: March 16, 1968
Location: Village of My Lai, in the Quang Ngai province in Vietnam
Combatants: Platoon of thirty men from Charlie Company, First Battalion, Twentieth Infantry, U.S. Army vs. 200-500 unarmed Vietnamese civilians
Principal commanders: *United States*, Lieutenant William Calley
Result: Massacre of civilians created a major military scandal

Acting on reports that a small guerrilla army was based in My Lai, Captain Ernest Medina, the commanding officer of Charlie Company, sent Lieutenant William Calley and his platoon of some thirty men into the village to eliminate them. Encountering no opposing fire, Calley's platoon of some thirty men advanced on the village, shooting and throwing grenades into the dwellings. The advance rapidly degenerated into a sadistic killing spree against the unarmed villagers. U.S. soldiers burned the village to the ground, shot families as they fled their huts, raped and murdered women, shot the livestock, and drove the rest of the village's old men, women, and children into a ditch where they were killed with machine-gun fire. Although there were attempts to suppress knowledge of the massacre, thirteen officers and enlisted men were charged with war crimes, and twelve more were charged with a coverup. Only Calley was court-martialed, found guilty, and sentenced to life imprisonment. He was paroled a few years later with a dishonorable discharge.

Significance

The massacre led to questions about U.S. military conduct in Vietnam, particularly with regard to failures in leadership and to a moral climate that fostered an illegal operation that violated military codes and human rights.

Resources

Andersen, David L. *Facing My Lai: Moving Beyond the Massacre*. Lawrence: University Press of Kansas, 1995.

Hersh, Seymour M. *My Lai Four: A Report on the Massacre and Its Aftermath*. New York: Random House, 1970.

Olson, James. *My Lai: A Brief History with Documents*. Boston: Bedford Books, 1998.

See also: Ethics of warfare; Vietnam Conflict; War crimes.

Margaret Boe Birns

Mysore Wars

At issue: Future of Mysore
Date: 1767-1799
Location: Mysore, India
Combatants: Sultans of Mysore vs. East India Company
Principal commanders: *Mysore*, Haydar Ali (1722-1782), Tipu (1749/1753-1799); *British*, Eyre Coote (1728-1783), Lord Charles Cornwallis (1738-1805), Richard Wellesley (1760-1842), George Harris (1746-1829)
Principal battles: Porto Novo, Siege of Mangalore, Bangalore
Result: East India Company victorious; extinction of Muslim state and restoration of Hindu dynasty

Background

Haydar Ali (also Hyder Ali), a Muslim soldier of fortune, overthrew the Hindu dynasty of Mysore and reigned as sultan from 1761 until 1782. His ambitions and those of his son, Tipu (r. 1782-1799), threatened the interests of the East India Company, which had recently fought three wars for control of southeastern India, the First, Second, and Third Carnatic Wars (1746-1748, 1751-1754, and 1756-1763).

Action

The Mysore sultans and the East India Company fought four wars, in 1767-1769, 1780-1784, 1790-1792, and 1799. By 1767, the beginning of the First Mysore War, Haydar Ali had aroused the combined hostility of the Marāṭhā peshwa in Poona, the niẓām of Hyderabad, and the East India Company. He spread terror and devastation as he swept down onto the plains of the Carnatic, reaching the outskirts of Madras by March, 1768. In April, 1769, he dictated a peace that restored the state existing before the war. Mysore and the East India Company signed a defensive alliance.

In 1771, the peshwa's forces invaded Mysore, but the East India Company failed to come to Haydar Ali's assistance. In 1780, the Second Mysore War began when Haydar Ali launched a fresh attack on the Carnatic, occupying Arcot, the capital, and laying waste the countryside around Madras. Haydar Ali retained the initiative until Sir Eyre Coote defeated him at **Porto Novo** (July 1, 1781), but Haydar Ali found new allies in France and Holland.

Coote moved north and won two more engagements. Meanwhile, at sea, Admiral Sir Edward Hughes captured Negapatam from the Dutch and, a year later, Trincomalee. However, a powerful French fleet arrived in the Bay of Bengal, commanded by Bailli de Suffren, who landed French reinforcements. When Haydar Ali died unexpectedly in December, 1782, his son, Tipu, proceeded to besiege **Mangalore** (May 16, 1783-January 30, 1784). Expecting no further help from his European allies, Tipu signed the Peace of Mangalore on the basis of the status quo (March 7, 1784).

A new British governor-general, Lord Charles Cornwallis, entered into an engagement with the niẓām of Hyderabad. Tipu regarded this as a

Milestones in the Mysore Wars

Date	Event
First Mysore War	
1766-1769	Mysore ruler Haydar Ali battles British troops to a stalemate, then signs agreement forming alliance with the East India Company.
Second Mysore War	
1780	Haydar Ali declares war on British, joins French, and attacks British forces at Perambakam.
July, 1781	British forces defeat Haydar Ali at the Battle of Porto Novo.
August-September, 1781	British defeat Haydar Ali at Pollilur and Sholingarh.
1782	French capture port of Trincomalee, retaining control of the Indian Ocean; Haydar Ali dies.
1784	French sign peace treaty with England and withdraw aid to Mysore; Haydar Ali's son, Tipu Sahib ends war.
Third Mysore War	
1789-1792	Tipu attacks Travancore; British, led by Lord Cornwallis, invade Mysore, storming its capital and besieging Tipu in Seringapatam.
March, 1792	Tipu signs peace agreement giving half his lands to the British.
Fourth Mysore War	
1799	British forces, led by Governor General Richard Wellesley, attempt to rid India of French influence; Tipu refuses to cooperate, and Wellesley sends armies into Mysore, driving Tipu into Seringapatam, where he is killed after the British breach the wall.

breach of the Mangalore treaty and ravaged the state of Travancore (December, 1789). Cornwallis regarded this as grounds for war and initiated a triple alliance with the Marāṭhās and the niẓām of Hyderabad that resulted in the Third Mysore War. Late in 1790, three British columns advanced on Mysore, but Tipu's generalship prevented them from achieving anything. In December, 1790, Cornwallis took the field in person and captured **Bangalore** (March 21, 1791), but was forced to fall back from Tipu's capital, Seringapatam. In 1791, Cornwallis again reached Seringapatam, and Tipu opened negotiations. In the Treaty of Seringapatam (March 1, 1792), Tipu lost half his state, which was divided between the allies, agreed to pay an indemnity, and surrendered his sons as hostages.

The Fourth Mysore War began in 1798, when an aggressive new governor general, Richard Wellesley, demanded that Tipu accept a subsidiary treaty with the East India Company, which would have reduced his status. Wellesley treated Tipu's refusal as a cause for war and ordered three British columns (one led by the governor general's brother, Arthur Wellesley, future duke of Wellington) to besiege Seringapatam. In a general assault led by General George Harris on May 4, 1799, Tipu fell, sword in hand, mortally wounded.

Aftermath

Haydar Ali and Tipu were two of the most remarkable Indian military leaders of the eighteenth century. With Tipu's death, the East India

Company decided against annexation of Mysore, perhaps to avoid sharing the spoils with its allies, and instead restored the former Hindu dynasty. Mysore survived as a princely state until 1947.

RESOURCES

Bowring, Lewin B. *Haidar Ali and Tipu Sultan*. Oxford: Oxford University Press, 1998.

Shephard, E. W. *Coote Bahadur: A Life of Lieutenant-General Sir Eyre Coote*. London: W. Laurie, 1956.

Wilks, Mark. *Historical Sketches of the South of Indian History: From the Earliest Times to the Last Muhammadan Dynasty*. Vol. 21 in *Indian Historical Researches*. Reprint. New Delhi: Cosmo Publications, 1990.

Wilson, W. J. *History of the Madras Army*. 5 vols. Madras, India: Government Press, 1882.

SEE ALSO: British India; Carnatic Wars; Cornwallis, First Marquess; Marāṭhā Wars; Wellington, duke of.

Gavin R. G. Hambly

N

Nādir Shāh

Also known as: Ṭahmāsp Qolī Khān; Nādr Qolī Beg
Born: October 22, 1688; Kobhān, Safavid Iran
Died: June, 1747; Fatḥābād, Safavid Iran
Principal wars: Persian-Afghan Wars, Persian Civil Wars, Turko-Persian Wars
Principal battles: Hamadān (1730), Baghavand (1735), Karnal (1739), Kars (1745)
Military significance: Nādir Shāh defeated the Ottoman Turks, the Mogul Empire, and various bordering khanates, briefly reestablishing the glory of Persian empires of the past.

Nādir Shāh came from a Turcoman tribe long established in northeastern Iran. He matured fighting frontier bandits and came to serve the Persian Safavid Dynasty as a military commander and governor. When the Afghans invaded the northeast in 1722, Russia and Turkey invaded the northwest simultaneously, dividing up western Persia. Nādir crushed the Afghans and then defeated the Turks in the west at Hamadān in 1730 in the Persian-Afghan Wars. Nādir usurped the incompetent Shah Ṭahmāsp II as regent, regained the northwest provinces from Russia, and again defeated the Turks at Baghavand in 1735. Nādir crowned himself shah in 1736. From 1737 to 1741, he invaded Afghanistan and northwestern India, defeating the Moguls at Karnal in 1739. He defeated and incorporated numerous khanates in the north and again defeated the Turks at Kars in 1745. Nādir failed as an administrator, however, and was hated by his subjects for his severe taxation and cruelty, which led to his assassination. Iran lapsed into a half-century of anarchy upon his death.

Resources
Avery, Peter, ed. *The Cambridge History of Iran.* Vol. 7. Cambridge, England: Cambridge University Press, 1991.
Hewson, Robert H. "Nadir Shah." In *Historic World Leaders.* Vol. 1. Edited by Anne Commire. Detroit, Mich.: Gale Research, 1994.
Lockhart, Laurence. *Nadir Shah: A Critical Study Based Mainly Upon Contemporary Sources.* London: Luzac, 1938.

See also: Afghan Expansion, Wars of; Ottoman Empire; Persian-Afghan Wars; Persian Civil Wars.

Nathan J. Latta

Nagashino

Type of action: Ground battle in the Japanese Wars of Unification
Date: June 29, 1575
Location: Nagashino Castle, Mikawa province (forty miles east-southeast of Nagoya, Aichi prefecture, Japan)
Combatants: 15,000 Takeda clan members vs. 38,000 allied army forces
Principal commanders: *Takeda,* Takeda Katsuyori (1546-1582); *Allied,* Oda Nobunaga (1534-1582)
Result: The allied army successfully raised the Siege of Nagashino Castle

When Takeda Katsuyori's initial plan against his enemy, Tokugawa Ieyasu, collapsed, he decided to attack Tokugawa's lightly garrisoned Nagashino Castle instead. However, Takeda let the Siege of Nagashino Castle, which began on June 16, 1575, with little success, become an obsession. To lift the siege, Oda Nobunaga led an allied army containing samurai who were subject to Ieyasu and Toyotomi Hideyoshi. As the allied army approached, Takeda ignored the advice of his generals to withdraw or make an all-out attempt to take the castle and fight from within it.

At 5 A.M. on June 29, 1575, Takeda's cavalry charged 3,000 musketeers positioned behind palisades. The key to Nobunaga's victory was his confidence in his musketeers. After two unsuc-

1078

cessful cavalry charges, Takeda eventually ordered a full-scale attack that accomplished nothing. After Takeda's last charge, Nobunaga advanced his samurai through the palisades to end the battle. In the end, the allied army lost 6,000 soldiers and Takeda 10,000.

SIGNIFICANCE

The battle devastated the Takeda clan, but they held onto power for seven more years until the death of Katsuyori. The battle's large-scale use of firearms marked a change from medieval to a more modern form of warfare. The destruction of the Takeda clan removed Nobunaga's greatest obstacle and allowed him to nearly unify Japan.

RESOURCES

Turnbull, Stephen. *Battles of the Samurai*. New York: Arms & Armour, 1987.

_____. *Samurai: A Military History*. London: Osprey, 1977.

_____. *Samurai Warfare*. London: Arms & Armour, 1996.

SEE ALSO: Japanese Wars of Unification; Oda Nobunaga; Samurai; Tokugawa Ieyasu; Toyotomi Hideyoshi.

C. E. Wood

NAGUIB, MUḤAMMAD

ALSO KNOWN AS: Mohammed Neguib
BORN: February 20, 1901; Khartoum, Anglo-Egyptian Sudan
DIED: August 28, 1984; Cairo, Egypt
PRINCIPAL WAR: First Israeli-Arab War
PRINCIPAL BATTLE: Faluja Pocket (1949)
MILITARY SIGNIFICANCE: Played an important role in the 1952 coup that radically altered modern Egypt.

After graduating from the Egyptian Military Academy in 1921, Muḥammad Naguib joined the army. He entered the general staff in 1940 and was promoted to colonel in 1947. Much of his combat experience took place in the First Israeli-Arab War (1948-1949). Although surrounded in the Faluja Pocket (1949), Naguib directed a skillful defense lasting until the armistice.

Promoted to general in 1950, Naguib was one of the few high-ranking officers still popular with the public. He then served as a prop for the corrupt government of King Farouk. The Free Officers, a group of junior and mid-ranking military men, also recognized Naguib's political value. Although not directly linked with this cabal, the general agreed to help test their power in 1951, when they proposed Naguib run for president of Cairo's Officers' Club. This placed him in direct opposition to the candidate endorsed by Farouk. Naguib's victory confirmed Free Officer support throughout the armed forces.

On July 22, 1952, the Free Officers staged a coup that quickly gained control of Egypt. Viewed as a well-known and respected public figure, Naguib became prime minister and minister of war. Less than a year later, on the abolition of the monarchy, he became president of the Arab Republic of Egypt.

Despite increased popularity and international recognition, Naguib soon lost a power struggle with Gamal Abdel Nasser, the Free Officers' leader. The latter viewed Naguib as a temporary figurehead and, by November, 1954, forced Naguib to resign.

RESOURCES

Naguib, Mohammed. *Egypt's Destiny: A Personal Statement*. Westport, Conn.: Greenwood Press, 1984.

Vatikiotis, P. J. *The Egyptian Army in Politics: Pattern for New Nations?* Westport, Conn.: Greenwood Press, 1961.

_____. *Nasser and His Generation*. New York: St. Martin's Press, 1978.

SEE ALSO: Egyptian Insurrection; Israeli-Arab Wars; Nasser, Gamal Abdel; Sādāt, Anwar el-.

John P. Dunn

NAGUMO, CHUICHI

BORN: March 25, 1887; Yamagato Prefecture, Japan
DIED: July 8-13, 1944; Saipan
PRINCIPAL WAR: World War II
PRINCIPAL BATTLES: Pearl Harbor attack (1941), Midway (1942)

MILITARY SIGNIFICANCE: Nagumo led the fleet that attacked U.S. forces based at Pearl Harbor, Hawaii, on December 7, 1941.

Admiral Chuichi Nagumo is best known for having led the Japanese fleet that attacked Pearl Harbor on what is known as the Day of Infamy, December 7, 1941. His naval career began without any hint of connection to air power. He did service aboard battleships, cruisers, and destroyers as well as staff duty ashore. After being promoted to captain, he briefly commanded the light cruiser *Naka* before spending two years with the naval general staff. In 1934, Nagumo took command of the battleship *Yashiro*, and a year later, he was promoted to rear admiral.

At the beginning of World War II, Nagumo was placed in command of the First Air Fleet, which attacked Pearl Harbor. Although the first two waves of the attack were a stunning success, he held back against his pilots' clamor for a third wave. After Pearl Harbor, he was involved in a number of major actions, including the Battle of Midway (1942). Finally, unable to wrest even a semblance of victory from defeat, he committed seppuku (ritual suicide) on the island of Saipan.

RESOURCES
Prange, Gordon W. *At Dawn We Slept: The Untold Story of Pearl Harbor.* New York: Penguin, 1981.
Stinnett, Robert B. *Day of Deceit: The Truth About FDR and Pearl Harbor.* New York: Free Press, 1999.
Toland, John. *Infamy: Pearl Harbor and Its Aftermath.* New York: Berkley, 1991.
Tora! Tora! Tora! Documentary. CBS Fox Video, 1970.

SEE ALSO: Kimmel, Husband Edward; Pearl Harbor attack; Short, Walter C.; World War II.

Leigh Husband Kimmel

NAHĀVAND

TYPE OF ACTION: Siege of city in Muslim invasion of Persian Highlands
DATE: 641-642
LOCATION: City of Nahāvand, south of Hamadān in a plain of the Zagros Mountains
COMBATANTS: 30,000 Arab Muslims vs. more than 30,000 Sāsānids
PRINCIPAL COMMANDERS: *Muslim*, Naaman ibn Muqarrin; *Sāsānid*, Shah Yazdigird III (d. 651)
RESULT: Sāsānid Shah Yazdigird III was defeated by Arab Muslim forces, leading to an effective end to Sāsānid rule; additionally, Iraq and Iran were captured by Muslims

Having been defeated in 636 at the Battle of al-Qadisiyya, Shah Yazdigird III raised another army that was concentrated in a fortified position outside the city of Nahāvand in 641-642. The Sāsānid army had scattered the ground in front of its defense works with small iron spikes capable of crippling the horses of the Arab cavalry. The Arabs, under Naaman ibn Muqarrin, attacked, then feigned a disorganized retreat in order to lure the Sāsānid army out of its defensive positions. Once out in the clear, the Sāsānid army was set upon by the entire Arab army, which had remained concealed from sight. After intense close-quarter fighting and heavy casualties, the Sāsānid army broke ranks, trying to retreat back through its own minefield. The Sāsānid army was destroyed and the general killed, although Yazdigird III managed to escape. He was, however, unable to raise another army and no longer held any effective power in the remnants of the Sāsānid Empire.

SIGNIFICANCE
The city of Nahāvand surrendered shortly after the battle, and organized resistance in Persia ended.

RESOURCES
Cameron, Averil, ed. *States, Resources, and Armies.* Vol. 3 in *The Byzantine and Early Islamic Near East.* Princeton, N.J.: Darwin Press, 1995.
Juynboll, G. H. A., trans. *The Conquest of Iraq, Southwestern Persia, and Egypt.* Vol. 13 in *The History of al-Tabari.* Albany: State University of New York Press, 1989.
Yarshater, Ehsan, ed. *The Seleucid, Parthian, and Sasanian Periods.* Vol. 3 in *The Cambridge History of Iran.* Cambridge, England: Cambridge University Press, 1983.

SEE ALSO: Muslim Conquests; Sāsānid Empire.

Victoria Erhart

Namibian War of Independence

At issue: Majority black rule in South Africa, independence for Namibia
Date: 1960-1990
Location: South Africa, Namibia
Combatants: Minority white government of South Africa forces vs. forces of African National Congress and Umkhonto we Sizwe, Pan-Africanist Congress, and Southwest African People's Organization
Principal commander: *African National Congress*, Nelson Mandela (1918-   )
Principal battle: Sharpeville (1960)
Result: Minority white rule ended in both South Africa and Namibia; Namibia gained independence from South Africa

Background

White settlers throughout southern Africa had a long history of practicing racial discrimination, beginning during the period of Dutch settlement at Cape Town in the early seventeenth century. Discriminatory policies were continued after reconciliation between British and Boer factions, after the Boer War led to creation of the Union of South Africa in 1910. During World War I, South Africa seized neighboring German South West Africa (later known as Namibia), extending white rule. In 1919, South Africa was granted control of the former German protectorate as part of a mandate to be administered under the auspices of the League of Nations. The Mandates Commission of the League frequently cited South African abuses of the system, including exploitation of black labor and an absence of social programs. When South Africa sought formal recognition of the incorporation of South West Africa from the United Nations, the request was refused. Defying international law, the South African government administered South West Africa as a fifth province of the state, extending discriminatory legislation there.

In 1948, the National Party came to power and immediately began to formalize the economic and social segregation that had existed since the foundation of the republic. The key measures of apartheid (separateness) included the Population Registration Act (1950), which classified all people according to race; the Group Areas Act (1950), which determined where each race could live; and the Native Labour Act (1953), which prohibited strikes and discouraged unionization. These measures, along with numerous other measures and decrees, forced black Africans to remain in low-paying jobs and to live in the most inhospitable areas of the country and, at the same time, cut off all peaceful means of resisting such discrimination.

This systematically racist legislation led to widespread resistance. In 1952, the African National Congress (ANC) organized a Defiance Campaign, which led to thousands of arrests. In 1955, the ANC and other racial and tribal groups proposed a nonracist, socialist blueprint for a new South African government. The white ministry played upon Cold War fears, suggesting that such reforms were being directed by the Soviet Union. Harsher laws were enacted in order to quash political opposition. By 1960, when most countries in sub-Saharan African had either become independent or were on the verge of becoming independent of European colonial powers, black Africans in South Africa and South West Africa were more tightly controlled than ever before.

Action

The era of relatively peaceful protest ended in 1960. In South Africa, police brutally suppressed a demonstration at **Sharpeville**, south of Johannesburg, killing 69 and wounding 180 unarmed demonstrators. Riots in the aftermath of Sharpeville were handled with similar brutality, while the ANC and Pan-Africanist Congress (PAC) were banned, and thousands of their members arrested. This led to a growing international condemnation of the system of apartheid and withdrawal of South Africa from the British Commonwealth, in 1961. The ANC reluctantly adopted a plan of armed resistance, forming the Umkhonto we Sizwe (MK, "Spear of the Nation"), which became closely associated with the South African Communist Party. A series of sabotage attacks in 1963 led to the arrest of their high command, including Nelson Mandela, who was sentenced to life imprisonment.

In 1960, the Southwest African People's Organization (SWAPO) was founded for the purpose of gaining independence, with a military wing known as the People's Liberation Army of Namibia (PLAN). Early insurgency was ineffective, and young rebels were sent to China, Algeria,

Tanzania, and North Korea for training. By the early 1970's, PLAN's use of Soviet mines was becoming more effective, and in 1974, the South African government had to shift South West African operations from the police to the military.

When Angola and Mozambique gained their independence from Portugal in 1974, South Africa had to be concerned with both the spread of revolutionary ideas along the northern frontier and the creation of safe havens for SWAPO rebels in Angola. The South African military launched several armed invasions of Angola between 1975 and 1988, striking SWAPO bases and supporting Jonas Savimbi's União Nacional para a Independência Total de Angola (UNITA), which in turn was resisting the Movimento Popular de Libertação de Angola (MPLA) and its Cuban allies. The United States discreetly supported both UNITA and South Africa as a part of its ongoing Cold War struggle with the Soviet Union.

In South Africa itself, the antiapartheid struggle escalated in the wake of the Soweto uprising in 1976, in which more than 400 people were killed in three weeks of fighting between rioters and police. The South African Defense Force raided ANC headquarters in Maputo, Mozambique, in 1981, and Maseru, Lesotho, in 1982. The following year saw the beginning of a car-bomb campaign by the MK. When a new apartheid constitution was being considered in 1983, the grassroots United Democratic Front (UDF) was created to coordinate the activities of more than 600 antiapartheid organizations. In 1984, Bishop Desmond Tutu won the Nobel Peace Prize, fixing the world's attention on the antiapartheid struggle and finally forcing the South African government to begin negotiations for a settlement.

As some of the harshest elements of apartheid were relaxed after 1984, continuing opposition violence made it clear that no half measures were likely to be successful. With the growing inability to maintain order in black townships, security forces were given extraordinary powers, which led to U.S. economic sanctions. When F. W. de Klerk succeeded P. W. Botha as president and leader of the Nationalist Party in 1989, he recognized the futility of further resistance, and during the next two years repealed apartheid legislation, legalized the ANC and other opposition parties, and released Mandela from prison. South African Defense Forces countered Cuban involvement in Angola but found it increasingly difficult to defend the border. In December, 1988, a peace agreement was signed between Angola, South Africa, and Cuba, leading to withdrawal of Cuban troops in 1989 and to independence for Namibia in 1990.

Aftermath

Once black opposition parties were legalized, it was just a matter of time and negotiation until majority rule would prevail. It was also a bloody period, as every faction, black and white, vied for position in the new governing structure. The most extensive conflict was between the UDF and the Inkatha Freedom Party (IFP) of Mangosuthu Gatsha Buthelezi, which sought to protect Zulu ethnic rights in the new South African state. The Inkatha War began in 1986 but remained localized until it became clear that a majority government was on the horizon. Between February, 1990, and July, 1992, more than 7,000 were killed in township violence. Violence declined in the wake of South Africa's first all-race elections, in April of 1994, but continued to flare, particularly in KwaZulu province, through the end of the century.

Resources

Clayton Anthony. *Frontiersmen: Warfare in Africa Since 1950*. London: UCL Press, 1999.

Cowell, Alan. *Killing the Wizards: Wars of Power and Freedom from Zaire to South Africa*. New York: Simon & Schuster, 1992.

Katjavivi, Peter. *A History of Resistance in Namibia*. London: J. Curry, 1988.

Leys, Colin T., and John S. Saul. *Namibia's Liberation Struggle: The Two-Edged Sword*. London: J. Curry, 1994.

Lodge, Tom. *Black Politics in South Africa Since 1945*. London: Longmans, 1983.

Steenkamp, Willem. *South Africa's Border War*. Gibraltar: Ashanti Publications, 1989.

Thompson, Leonard. *A History of South Africa*. Rev. ed. New Haven, Conn.: Yale University Press, 2001.

Worden, Nigel. *The Making of Modern South Africa*. 2d ed. Cambridge, Mass.: Blackwell, 1995.

See also: Angolan Civil War; Angolan War of Independence; Cold War.

John Powell

Nanjing, Rape of

TYPE OF ACTION: Battle in Second Sino-Japanese War
DATE: December 13, 1937-January, 1938
LOCATION: Nanjing, China
COMBATANTS: Japan's Central China Expeditionary Forces vs. Chinese soldiers and civilians
PRINCIPAL COMMANDERS: *Japanese*, Prince Yasuhiko Asaka, General Kesago Nakajima, Lieutenant General Heisuke Yanagawa
RESULT: The Japanese seized Nanjing, slaughtering thousands of Chinese soldiers and civilians and committing rapes and other atrocities

On December 13, 1937, the city of Nanjing, China, capital of the Chinese government under Chiang Kai-shek, fell to the Japanese. The Japanese soldiers began the occupation, which was marked by the brutal slaughter of the Chinese soldiers who were unable to escape after the city's fall and many of its civilians. Estimates of those killed range from the Japanese government's conservative 40,000 to the Chinese government's more than 300,000. Japanese soldiers raped an estimated 20,000 Chinese women of all ages, mutilating and torturing some of them. Although some of these women were eventually killed by the Japanese, others committed suicide. Wounded soldiers, elderly men and women, and children fell victim to Japanese gunfire. The Japanese rounded up thousands of young men, many of whom were machine gunned, soaked with gasoline, and burned alive, or used for bayonet practice. A group of Westerners in the international safety zone provided protection for thousands of Chinese citizens. John Rabe, a German Nazi, was one of those who protected the Chinese.

Significance

The Japanese, led by Prince Yasuhiko Asaka, General Kesago Nakajima, and Lieutenant General Heisuke Yanagawa, perpetrated a brutal, six-week-long assault on the Chinese in Nanjing, yet the incident has never prompted a high level of public condemnation or gained much public recognition. Although eyewitness accounts and photographs of many of the atrocities exist, members of the Japanese government and others have denied that the massacre occurred or downplayed the level of violence.

Resources

Chang, Iris. *The Rape of Nanking: The Forgotten Holocaust of World War II*. New York: Penguin Books, 1997.

Katsuichi, Honda. *The Nanking Massacre: A Japanese Journalist Confronts Japan's National Shame*. Armonk, N.Y.: M. E. Sharpe, 1999.

Wickert, Erwin., ed. *The Good Man of Nanking: The Diaries of David Rabe*. New York: Alfred A. Knopf, 1998.

SEE ALSO: Japanese Colonial Wars; War crimes; World War II.

Mary Kathryn Barbier

Napier, Charles James

BORN: August 10, 1782; London, England
DIED: August 29, 1853; Portsmouth, Hampshire, England
PRINCIPAL WARS: Napoleonic Wars
PRINCIPAL BATTLES: Miani (1843), Hyderabad (1843)
MILITARY SIGNIFICANCE: Napier added the region of the Sind to the British Empire in India and paved the way for control of all northern India by his campaign of 1843.

As the son of the famous Lady Sarah Lennox and the grandson of a duke, Charles James Napier received political preference—especially after his cousin, Charles James Fox, became prime minister. Of course, his bravery, ability, and personal charm played an even greater role in his success. In the Napoleonic Wars (1803-1815), he was wounded six times and captured. After serving in Greece in the 1820's and as commander of the military forces in Northern England, he took command of the forces in the Upper and Lower Sind in India. There he discovered that local emirs were forming an offensive alliance, and he decided to annex the Sind to British India. With 2,800 British and native troops, he defeated an estimated 22,000 local forces at the Battle of Miani (February 17, 1843). He then marched in 110-degree heat to Hyderabad to attack the most im-

Charles James Napier. (Library of Congress)

portant of the emirs, the "Lion of Mirpur." After receiving reinforcements, he defeated the Lion's army of 26,000 men and fifteen cannon with 5,000 men on March 24, 1843. He remained as governor of the Sind until 1847. In addition to his military accomplishments, he was a prolific author. He wrote many works on military and administrative subjects in addition to historical novels.

RESOURCES
Butler, William F. *Sir Charles Napier.* London: Macmillan, 1905.
Lambrick, H. T. *Sir Charles Napier and Sind.* Oxford: Clarendon Press, 1952.
Napier, Priscilla Hayter. *Black Charlie: A Life of Admiral Sir Charles Napier RCB, 1787-1860.* Wilby, England: Michael Russell, 1995.

SEE ALSO: British India; Napoleonic Wars.
Philip Dwight Jones

NAPIER, ROBERT

FULL NAME: Robert Cornelis Napier, first baron Napier of Magdala
BORN: December 6, 1810; Colombo, Ceylon
DIED: January 14, 1890; London, England
PRINCIPAL WARS: Sikh Wars, Indian Mutiny
PRINCIPAL BATTLE: Arogee (1868)
MILITARY SIGNIFICANCE: Napier led a well organized expeditionary force that defeated Ethiopian troops at the Battle of Arogee and secured the release of British citizens detained by the Ethiopian ruler.

After completing his military training at the royal engineer establishment at Chatham, Robert Napier sailed to India as a first lieutenant in 1828. He distinguished himself during the Sikh Wars and the Indian Mutiny. He was promoted brigadier general in 1858.

In 1867, Napier was instructed to organize and command a military expedition to Ethiopia to resolve a dispute with the Ethiopian ruler, who had detained the British consul and several other Europeans. Napier equipped a force that consisted of some 13,000 fighting men and several thousand auxiliaries, who landed on the Red Sea coast and marched 420 miles over an elevation of more than 7,000 feet before reaching the fortress of Magdala, where the Battle of Arogee took place. There they defeated Tewodros II's troops on April 10, 1868, and secured the release of the prisoners. Napier withdrew his troops from Ethiopia in June, 1868.

Napier displayed great talent in logistical organization and political acumen in assuring the local powers that he had no ambition over Ethiopia other than the release of British citizens. Back in England, Napier was received with great pomp and ceremony. Parliament voted him thanks, and the queen made him a peer with the title of baron Napier of Magdala. In January, 1870, he was appointed commander in chief in India. In 1876, he was appointed governor of Gibraltar, and in 1883, he was made a field marshal.

RESOURCES
Arnold, Percy. *Prelude to Magdala: Emperor Theodore of Ethiopia and British Diplomacy.* London: Bellew, 1991.
Farwell, Byron. *Queen Victoria's Little Wars.* New York: Harper & Row, 1972.

SEE ALSO: Arogee; British Colonial Wars; Indian Mutiny.
Shumet Sishagne

Napier, William

Full name: Sir William Francis Patrick Napier
Born: December 17, 1785; Celbridge, County Kildare, Ireland
Died: February 10, 1860; Clapham Park, Surrey, England
Principal wars: Napoleonic Wars
Principal battles: Madrid (1808), Siege of Saragossa (1808-1809), Talavera (1809), Vitoria (1813)
Military significance: Napier's popular history of the Peninsular War remained the standard work on the conflict until the early 1900's.

William Napier and three of his brothers, Charles, George, and Henry, all rose to prominence in the military. William Napier fought in the Napoleonic Wars, particularly in the Peninsular War in Spain and Portugal. Participating in battles at Madrid, Saragossa, Talavera, Fuentes de Onoro (1811), Salamanca, and Vitoria, he was wounded several times. At the close of the Peninsular campaign in 1819, Napier retired from the army.

In 1828, Napier began writing his account of the *History of the War in the Peninsula and in the South of France* (1832-1840), completing the sixth volume in 1840. Napier based his writings on his own combat experiences, as well as those of two commanders in the Peninsular conflicts, Arthur Wellesley, the duke of Wellington, and French marshal Nicolas Jean de Dieu Soult. Because of its vigorous battle scenes and powerful style, Napier's book was the standard work on the Peninsular War until the early 1900's, when Sir Charles Oman published *History of the Peninsular War* (1902-1930). Napier was knighted in 1848.

Resources
Davies, David W. *Sir John Moore's Peninsular Campaign*. The Hague, Netherlands: Martinus Nijhoff, 1974.
Hall, Christopher D. *British Strategy in the Napoleonic War*. New York: Manchester University Press, 1992.
Muir, Rory. *Britain and the Defeat of Napoleon*. New Haven, Conn.: Yale University Press, 1996.
Napier, Priscilla. *Revolution and the Napier Brothers*. London: Michael Joseph, 1973.

See also: Napier, Charles James; Napoleonic Wars; Saragossa, Siege of; Soult, Nicolas Jean de Dieu; Talavera; Vitoria; Wellington, duke of.

Alvin K. Benson

Napoleon I

Full name: Napoleon Bonaparte
Also known as: The Little Corporal, First Consul
Born: August 15, 1769; Ajaccio, Corsica
Died: May 5, 1821; St. Helena Island
Principal wars: Napoleonic Wars, Peninsular War, War of 1812-1814
Principal battles: Lodi (1796), Rivoli (1797), Pyramids (1798), Aboukir (1799), Marengo (1800), Austerlitz (1805), Jena and Auerstädt (1806), Friedland (1807), Wagram (1809), Borodino (1812), Dresden (1813), Leipzig (1813), Waterloo (1815)
Military significance: Napoleon fought, conquered, and dominated much of Continental Europe and established the French Empire. His brilliant victories over Austria, Prussia, Russia,

Napoleon I. (Library of Congress)

and their allies brought him fame and glory and recognition as a great military genius.

Napoleon Bonaparte graduated from the French military school and was appointed an artillery officer in the army in 1785. When the French Revolution (1789-1792) came, he welcomed it and made a name for himself early in 1793, when he delivered the city of Toulon from British control. Two years later, he saved the government of the convention from a royalist insurrection. In 1796, he was appointed commander of the French army in northern Italy, where he defeated the Austrians at Lodi and at Rivoli the following year.

In 1798, Napoleon planned to crush the British by invading Egypt and reaching India. However, the Egyptian Campaign was a failure, despite an early victory at the Pyramids (1798). Admiral Horatio Nelson destroyed the entire French naval force at Aboukir Bay in 1799. Napoleon returned to France in 1799, overthrew the directory, established the consulate, and was named first consul. A victory against the Second Coalition at Marengo in 1800 added to his reputation. On December 2, 1804, he officially proclaimed the French Empire and crowned himself emperor of the French.

The European powers were concerned by Napoleon's overweening ambitions. In 1805, they formed a new anti-French coalition. Napoleon, however, met and defeated the combined armies of Austria, Prussia, and Russia in a series of brilliant victories, including those at Austerlitz, Jena, Auerstädt, Friedland, and Wagram.

Napoleon's military successes against the coalition powers demonstrated his ability to conduct modern warfare based on rapid assaults against defensive and offensive positions. He used massive infantry troops to fight in line formation, attacking the center, left and right flanks of the enemy, and cavalry regiments to deliver the charge in closed order, thereby spreading panic and confusion in its ranks. Moreover, he personally led his troops in the battlefield, inspired his soldiers with confidence, and shared with them his triumphs, excitement, and patriotic enthusiasm. In the course of the battle, everything depended upon his final decision, usually made on the spur of the moment.

By 1807, Napoleon had become the master of Europe. Only one great enemy remained—Britain. Again he tried to destroy the country by imposing an economic blockade, known as the continental system. This was the first attempt in history to win a war by economic means. However, the French naval disaster at Trafalgar (1805) ended his plans to invade Britain.

The turning point in Napoleon's military career came in 1812, when he invaded Russia, winning an early but costly victory at Borodino, then occupying Moscow. However, the Russian campaign turned into a disaster and marked the beginning of Napoleon's end. In 1813, Napoleon won a battle against combined Russian, Prussian, and Austrian forces at Dresden, then lost at Leipzig. The allied army pursued him and entered Paris in March, 1814. He abdicated and was exiled to the island of Elba. When he escaped from Elba and returned to France, the allies raised a new army, which defeated him at Waterloo on June 18, 1815, ending Napoleon's military career.

Besides his military successes, Napoleon preserved and institutionalized many achievements of the French Revolution. He introduced the Code Napoleon, a legal code that became the model for other European countries. He promoted the spread of liberalism and nationalism to the countries he conquered. Although he did not give France a true representative government and political liberties, a majority of the French regard him as the "Man of Destiny."

RESOURCES
Connelly, Owen. *Blundering to Glory: Napoleon's Military Campaigns*. Wilmington, Del.: Scholarly Resources, 1990.
Napoleon Bonaparte. Documentary. Films for the Humanities & Science, 1996.
Nosworthy, Brent. *With Musket, Cannon, and Sword: Battle Tactics of Napoleon and His Enemies*. New York: Sarpedon, 1996.
Riehn, Richard, K. *Napoleon's Russian Campaign*. New York: McGraw-Hill, 1990.

SEE ALSO: Aboukir; Alexander I; Austerlitz; Borodino; Dresden; Friedland; Jena and Auerstädt; Leipzig; Lodi; Marengo; Moscow, retreat from; Napoleonic Wars; Nelson, Horatio; Pyramids; Rivoli; Toulon, Siege of; Wagram; Waterloo.

James J. Farsolas

Napoleonic Wars

At issue: Struggle for the Napoleonic empire
Date: 1803-1815
Location: Europe and Egypt
Combatants: French vs. Germans, Russians, Spanish, and English
Principal commanders: *French*, Napoleon (1869-1821), Pierre-Charles de Villeneuve (1763-1806), Joachim Murat (1767-1815), Michel Ney (1769-1815), Auguste Marmont (1774-1852), Nicolas Jean de Dieu Soult (1769-1851), Louis Davout (1770-1823); *Prussian*, Gebhard Leberecht von Blücher (1742-1819); *Austrian*, Baron Karl Mack von Leiberich (1752-1828), Karl Philipp Schwarzenberg (1771-1820); *Russian*, Mikhail Illarionovich Kutuzov (1745-1813); *English*, Horatio Nelson (1758-1805), Arthur Wellesley, duke of Wellington (1769-1852)
Principal battles: Hanover, Ulm, Trafalgar, Austerlitz, Jena and Auerstädt, Eylau, Friedland, Bailén, Essling and Wagram, Ciudad Rodrigo, Siege of Badajoz, Salamanca, Vitoria, Borodino, Lützen, Bautzen, Leipzig, Waterloo
Result: Though Napoleon's European empire was dismantled after his defeat, the military struggle between France and the European countries resulted in the spread of nationalism

Background

Revolutionary France had been embroiled since April, 1792, in a struggle for survival against foreign threats. The French defense was strengthened by Lazare Carnot, who as the head of the military section of the Committee of Public Safety introduced mass conscription (*levée en masse*). Consequently France was able not only to repulse continental threats but also from the late 1790's to begin to expand its "natural frontiers" (the Pyrenees, the Alps, and the Rhine) by annexing Belgium and Luxemburg (September, 1795), the left bank of the Rhine (January, 1798), and Geneva (April, 1798). In the wake of military expansion, several satellite republics had been formed in the lands around France.

Action

However, France's reverses in foreign wars following the formation of the Second Coalition in Europe (Britain, Austria, Russia, Naples, and Turkey) in 1798 and the subsequent fall of the Directory in 1799 brought about a decisive change in France's military objectives and goals. After the Treaties of Lunéville (with Austria in 1801) and Amiens (with Britain in 1802), Napoleon Bonaparte began imperialistic wars culminating in the annexation of Piedmont, Elba, and a part of Switzerland to France; the transformation of the Cisalpine Republic into Italian Republic; and a fantastic but futile colonial program with the purchase of Louisiana in America. Meanwhile Napoleon's blockade of British trade with Europe as well as his unwillingness to evacuate Holland, his interference in the Helvetic Confederation in 1803 coupled with the British refusal to evacuate Malta, ruptured the Treaty of Amiens, and Britain declared war on France on May 16, 1803. Napoleon retaliated by moving troops into Germany to occupy **Hanover**, a family possession of King George III, and by building his most effective striking force, the *Grande Armée*, or Grand Army, at Boulogne (1805).

The Grand Army's order of battle consisted of some 194,000 men with 396 guns, divided among seven corps, the Imperial Guard (the *corps d'elite* numbering 7,000 men), a cavalry reserve of six heavy mounted divisions containing around 23,000 horsemen, and the artillery reserve, in which almost a quarter of all available guns was concentrated. Napoleon practiced a personal, highly centralized command. Imperial headquarters (Napoleon had been crowned emperor on November 6, 1804) consisted of three major divisions: the emperor's personal staff (the *Maison*), the general staff of the Grand Army, and the staff of the commissary general.

On August 22, 1805, the emperor ordered Admiral Pierre-Charles de Villeneuve to enter the English Channel for the invasion. Meanwhile, aware of the recently formed coalition against him by England, Austria, Russia, and Sweden (Third Coalition, August 9, 1805), Napoleon ordered the Grand Army to march for Germany. In Germany, Napoleon faced an army of 70,000 under General Karl Mack von Leiberich, who also received reinforcements and backups from Austria and Russia.

The Austrians were surprised at their rear by the French, who were advancing from the Rhine to the Danube, and were bottled up at **Ulm** where they surrendered on October 20, 1805. The French success in Germany was helped by Prince André Masséna, commander of the French army in north Italy, who contained the 90,000-strong Austrian army under Archduke Charles. Unfortunately, Napoleon suffered a setback on the next day. On October 21, 1805, the French fleet led by Admiral Villeneuve was routed by the English navy commanded by Admiral Horatio Nelson at **Trafalgar**. Villeneuve's mission was to lure Nelson's fleet from the English Channel to the West Indies, lose him, and slink back to the channel and, in combination with French fleets from Brest and Rochefort, mount the projected invasion of England. The strategy worked up to a point, but Villeneuve's ship, on its journey back to Europe, was detected by the British and failed to rendezvous with the anticipated reinforcements. It was damaged by the British fleet commanded by Sir Robert Calder and sailed to Cádiz. Villeneuve sailed from Cádiz to meet Nelson at Trafalgar, where he was overwhelmed by the British.

Meanwhile, Napoleon's army in Central Europe confronted the advancing Russians, and on December 2, 1805, the French defeated an Austro-Russian force led by Czar Alexander I at **Austerlitz**. Napoleon's success was due to his effective command system and integration of different arms, including forces led by Michel Ney, Auguste Marmont, Louis Davout, and Nicolas Jean de Dieu Soult. Following this defeat, Austria withdrew from the coalition, and in July, 1806, Napo-

Selected Battle Sites in the Napoleonic Wars

leon dismantled the Holy Roman Empire, thus completing a process begun in 1803.

After Prussia joined the Third Coalition, the French force with its massed artillery and skirmishers commanded by Marshal Davout inflicted a crushing defeat on the Prussians at **Jena and Auerstädt** on October 13-14, 1806. On October 25, Napoleon arrived at Berlin and, on November 21, issued the Berlin Decree, instituting the continental system—an economic blockade designed to destroy the British continental trade. At the end of 1806, he created the duchy of Warsaw, ostensibly to liberate the Poles from Prussian control and named Frederick Augustus (later Augustus II, king of Poland) (who had deserted Prussia and allied with France) king of Saxony as well as ruler of the duchy of Warsaw.

By December, 1806, the Russian army had met the French in Poland and almost defeated the latter at **Eylau** on February 8, 1807. Though the fight actually resulted in a draw, the French had 25,000 killed and wounded. However, the Russians were beaten at **Friedland** on June 13-14 and forced to sue for peace (Treaty of Tilsit, July 7-9, 1807). Alexander agreed to the partition of Prussia and to recognize the new grand duchy of Warsaw and boycott British goods and ships, while Napoleon let the czar occupy certain Turkish territories and take Finland from Sweden. Denmark and Sweden eventually participated in the continental system and chose Napoleon's Marshal Jean-Baptiste-Jules Bernadotte as the crown prince.

After the collapse of the Third Coalition and the extension of the continental system to the Baltic, a leak developed through Portugal, a British ally since 1703. A joint Franco-Spanish army (Spain had been France's ally since 1795) captured Lisbon. However, when in the spring of 1808, Napoleon forced the Spanish king Charles IV and the Crown Prince Ferdinand to renounce their throne in favor of his brother Joseph Bonaparte, a national revolt erupted in Spain. The beleaguered French corps surrendered to the Spanish nationalist rebels at **Bailén** (July 21), and an advancing French army was intercepted by the British force under Sir Arthur Wellesley, the future duke of Wellington, at Vimeiro (August 21). Napoleon personally intervened, defeated the poorly trained and commanded Spanish forces, and entered Madrid on December 4.

The Peninsular War stirred national unrest in Germany, and the Austrian government began to arm for a general uprising. Napoleon conferred with Alexander at Erfurt and got him to restrain Austria. The French emperor had by now become quite unpopular in Europe, and the Austrians mounted a heavy and successful resistance at **Essling** (May 21-22, 1809) against a surprise French attack. However, they failed to sustain their *élan* against a French counterattack at **Wagram** on July 5-6. Though the Austrians were not routed as in Austerlitz, they failed to match Napoleon's superior command as well as the operation of the French corps.

Yet the French were unable to dislodge the British from Portugal or suppress the guerrilla resistance in Spain. The British supplied many regular troops and its command of the sea stimulated the Spanish resistance. By 1810, Napoleon had moved 370,000 men into Spain, and Masséna, the ablest French marshal, was given 130,000 of them to conquer Portugal, which was defended by a joint Anglo-Portuguese force of 50,000 men. The French army met with Wellington's force on a steep range of hills near Bussaco but fared poorly against the British and the Portuguese. On November 10, the French began to retreat and on March 11, 1811, Masséna left Portugal. In 1812, Wellington took the offensive, storming **Ciudad Rodrigo** (January 19) and **Badajoz** (April 19). He defeated the French at **Salamanca** (July 22, 1812), then a year later won a decisive victory at **Vitoria** (June 21, 1813) that led to the allied success in the Peninsular War.

Napoleon's continental system also triggered the Russian war. The czar broke with the system on December 31, 1810, when he issued a *ukase*, which imposed high tariffs on French imports and opened his ports to neutral shipping. Napoleon invaded Russia on June 24-25, 1812, with more than half a million men, including Austrians led by Karl Philipp Schwarzenberg and various German, Polish, and Italian troops. The Russians fell back, thus denying Napoleon the decisive battle that he had anticipated, and the Russians' scorched earth strategy and guerrilla activity led to the French loss of manpower through hunger, disease, and fatigue. On September 7, in the Battle of **Borodino**, the Russians, led by Mikhail Illarionovich Kutuzov, tried unsuc-

The allies opposed to Napoleon march into Paris in March, 1814. (Library of Congress)

cessfully to resist French advance to Moscow, though they harassed the invaders with guerrilla resistance. It was a pyrrhic victory for the French, who found both the Russian army and the Russian winter too stubborn and severe to control. They had to turn back, but their retreat, beginning December 9, turned into a nightmare. The French lost nearly 570,000 personnel, 200,000 cavalry and draught horses, and 1,050 cannons. Another 100,000 French were captured by the enemy.

In early 1813, Napoleon's military reputation was shattered and his diplomatic position collapsed. Prussia declared war on France in March. Though Napoleon rebuilt his army to a force of more than 400,000 plus his artillery, the new recruits had little field experience. More unfortunately for Napoleon, he had failed to replace the fine cavalry he lost in the Russian campaign. Admittedly, he defeated the Prussians and the Russians in the Battles of **Lützen** (May 2, 1813) and **Bautzen** (May 20-21), but these engagements were far from decisive as he could not sustain pressure on the enemy because of a lack of cavalry and hence agreed to an armistice. After he rejected the peace terms in the summer, Napoleon confronted in fall, 1813, a joint Austro-Russian-Prussian-Swedish force of more than 600,000 men, while his army totaled 370,000. The allies adopted the so-called Trachenburg Plan—the battle strategy decided upon by the commanders of Austria, Prussia, and Russia at Trachenburg in southwest Poland in July—according to which they were to avoid battle with Napoleon and try to isolate and destroy his subordinates. The Prussians defeated detached French forces at Grossbeeren (August 23), on the Katzbach River (August 26), and at Dennewitz (September 6). The Austrians won the Battle of Kulm (August 30).

Napoleon's policy of centralized command had deprived his marshals of training and experience in independent command.

Though Napoleon defeated the Prussians at Dresden (August 27), he failed to achieve an envelopment of the enemy. Instead he was outnumbered and outmaneuvered by the converging allied forces at **Leipzig** (October 16-19, 1813). After this battle of the nations, Napoleon retreated as his former allies deserted him. In the early months of 1814, he recovered his position somewhat and attacked the Austro-Prussian forces that had invaded eastern France, but his 70,000-strong army could not match the enemy's 200,000 men. Napoleon's victors marched on Paris. After the city surrendered, a provisional French government deposed the emperor, who was exiled to the island of Elba on April 20, 1814. He was restored to power on March 19, 1815, following his escape from the island on February 26. On June 15, 1815, Napoleon began his last campaign with 120,000 men and attacked the nearest allied concentration in Belgium. Three days later, a 68,000-strong Anglo-Dutch-Prussian army under the duke of Wellington was attacked by Napoleon's 72,000-strong force on a ridge at Mont-Saint-Jean. In the Battle of **Waterloo** (June 18, 1815), Napoleon failed to crush the opponents' defensive firepower and was finally overwhelmed by the arrival of the Prussian forces on the French right. His military career was over. He abdicated four days later and was exiled, finally, to St. Helena in the South Atlantic in early August.

AFTERMATH

Napoleon profited from eighteenth century military thought and also from the social and economic progress brought about by the Industrial Revolution. Several commanders before him had appreciated the usefulness of rapid and secure movement, ease of maneuver, and efficient supply for forcing the enemy into a major battle followed by vigorous pursuit, but they lacked the physical means to translate their theories into practice. As an absolute ruler of state and commander in chief, making superb use of the army corps, Napoleon was able to realize these theories in his short, relentless and decisive land warfare, notably in the Ulm-Austerlitz and Jena-Auerstädt campaigns. Unfortunately, combining all aspects of government and war under a single authority led to overcentralization and neglect of detail. Additionally, Napoleon's neglect of technological innovation and his army's unwieldy size and excessive dependence on charismatic leadership rendered it ineffectual in altered circumstances, as in the Peninsular and the Russian Wars as well as at Waterloo.

RESOURCES

Black, Jeremy, ed. *European Warfare*. New York: St. Martin's Press, 1999.

Chandler, David G. *The Campaigns of Napoleon*. New York: Macmillan, 1966.

Connelly, Owen. *Blundering to Glory: Napoleon's Military Campaigns*. Wilmington, Del.: Scholarly Resources, 1990.

Gates, David. *The Napoleonic Wars 1803-1815*. London: Arnold, 1997.

Napoleon Bonaparte. Documentary. Films for the Humanities & Science, 1996.

The Napoleonic Wars. Documentary. Films for the Humanities and Sciences, 2000.

SEE ALSO: Alexander I; Austerlitz; Badajoz, Siege of; Berthier, Louis Alexandre; Blücher, Gebhard Leberecht von; Borodino; Brunswick, Charles William Ferdinand, duke of; Clausewitz, Carl von; Davout, Louis; French Revolution; French Revolutionary Wars; Friedland; Jena and Auerstädt; Kutuzov, Mikhail Illarionovich; Lannes, Jean; Leipzig; Lützen; Masséna, André; Moscow, retreat from; Murat, Joachim; Napoleon I; Nelson, Horatio; Ney, Michel; Oudinot, Nicolas Charles; Pyramids; Quatre Bras; Salamanca; Trafalgar; Wagram; Waterloo; Wellington, duke of.

Narasingha P. Sil

NARSES

BORN: c. 478; Persian-ruled Armenia
DIED: c. 573; probably Rome or Constantinople
PRINCIPAL WAR: Gothic War
PRINCIPAL BATTLES: Taginae (552), Mons Lactarius (552), Casilinum (554)
MILITARY SIGNIFICANCE: As commander of the Byzantine army in Italy from 551 to 567, Narses ended eighty years of Gothic rule in Italy, returning it to the Byzantine Empire.

Narses, a foreign-born eunuch, rose in the Byzantine bureaucracy, as did many eunuchs in his time, and became grand chamberlain by 530. He acquired some experience subverting or fighting rioters in Constantinople (532) and Alexandria (535). Then, he went to Italy with 7,000 troops in 538 to reinforce Belisarius against the Goths, where he gave good advice but was insubordinate. He was recalled in 539.

In 551, after the recall of Belisarius and the reconquests of the new Gothic king Totila, Narses was appointed supreme commander in Italy and marched there overland with 20,000 men. He met Totila's army in the Apennines near Taginae (552), routed it, and killed Totila. Narses then took Rome by storm against an inadequate Gothic defending force and, at the end of 552, defeated the Goths at Mons Lactarius in south Italy. He let the surviving Goths leave Italy, defeated an invasion of Franks at Casilinum in north Italy in 554, and ruled it until dismissed by Justin II in 567. His military success was partly due to the fact that he insisted on adequate numbers of troops, supplies, and money. In addition, because he was a eunuch and thus unable to become emperor, Justinian I trusted him with the troops and supplies in contrast to his parsimonious policy toward Belisarius.

Resources

Fauber, Lawrence. *Narses, Hammer of the Goths: The Life and Times of Narses the Eunuch.* New York: St. Martin's Press, 1990.

Hodgkin, Thomas. *The Imperial Restoration.* Vol. 4 in *Italy and Her Invaders, 535-553.* 1885. Reprint. New York: Clarendon Press, 1967.

Procopius of Caesarea. *The Gothic Wars.* Vols. 5-8 in *History of the Wars.* Loeb Classical Library series. Cambridge, Mass.: Harvard University Press, 1919-1928.

See also: Belisarius; Byzantine Empire; Gothic War; Goths; Justinian I; Taginae.

Jane Bishop

Narva

Type of action: Ground battle in the Great Northern War

Date: November 30, 1700
Location: Estonia
Combatants: Swedes vs. Russians
Principal commanders: *Swedish*, Charles XII of Sweden (1697-1718); *Russian*, Peter the Great (1672-1725)
Result: Peter used the lessons from this Russian defeat to prepare for later battles with King Charles

The Great Northern War brought two young kings into combat. One sought to expand Swedish power on the European continent, the other to gain his country's access to the Baltic Sea. Poland, Denmark, and Russia saw an opportunity to profit from the inexperience of a new and youthful king of Sweden and took the initiative to seize his lands. Charles XII first subdued Denmark in August, 1700, at Zealand, then defeated Czar Peter the Great at Narva in November. Peter laid siege to the Swedish port at Narva in September. His army was already weary and short on supplies. In November, Charles arrived with 9,000 well-trained soldiers—reputed to be the best in Europe—to face 40,000 Russian soldiers. In a snowstorm, he took advantage of the thin lines of Peter's troops to divide his army into smaller segments. Russians were so ill-trained that a great many fled; thousands were taken captive, and about 9,000 were killed.

Significance

Victory at Narva boosted the confidence of the Swedish king, encouraging him to seek greater martial glory to the West. In the end, Charles failed by neglecting to consider the limited resources of his sparsely populated kingdom. Peter, on the other hand, would later achieve his "window to the West," Russia's first permanent warm-water port. The Battle of Narva gave Peter the experience to reshape his army for the long war.

Resources

Aberg, Alf. "The Swedish Army from Lutzen to Narva." In *Sweden's Age of Greatness: 1632-1718*, edited by Michael Roberts. New York: St. Martin's Press, 1973.

Anderson, Matthew S. *Peter the Great.* 2d ed. London: Longman, 1995.

Hughes, Lindsey. *Russia in the Age of Peter the*

Great. New Haven, Conn.: Yale University Press, 1998.

See also: Charles XII; Great Northern War; Peter the Great; Poltava.

John D. Windhausen

Naseby

Type of action: Ground battle in the English Civil War of 1642-1651
Date: June 14, 1645
Location: Naseby, Northamptonshire (twenty miles south of Leicester)
Combatants: 11,000 Royalists vs. 17,000 Parliamentarians
Principal commanders: *Royalist*, Charles I (1600-1649), Prince Rupert (1619-1682), Jacob, Lord Astley (1579-1652); *Parliamentarian*, Thomas Fairfax, third baron of Cameron (1612-1671), Oliver Cromwell (1599-1658)
Result: Decisive Parliamentary victory and the turning point in the first phase of the English Civil War

The Royalist war council was divided about engaging the Parliamentarians' New Model Army in Northamptonshire in early June, 1645. Though flushed with victory after storming Leicester on May 31, some counseled relieving Oxford; others urged a march north to aid forces at Pontefract and Scarborough and to win new recruits. Still others cautioned against action until reinforcements arrived; however, those favoring immediate confrontation with the New Model Army carried the day, and the army moved into position near Naseby. Underestimating the strength of the Parliamentary army, the Royalists abandoned an advantageous line to search out their enemy. They located them entrenched on high ground to the north of the village on June 14. Although outnumbered, the Royalists remained confident of victory and initiated the action.

Oliver Cromwell's Roundheads held their ground as the Royalists advanced across Broad Moor to the base of Mill Hill. They were equally convinced of success. Prince Rupert pressed his cavalry forward, following the pattern set at Edgehill in 1642. Rupert and the cavalry sliced through the Parliamentary horsemen of Henry Ireton, pursuing them until they reached the army's main baggage train near Naseby. Rupert's precipitous action drew his forces far from the battleground. When the cavalry advance finally met musket resistance, he returned to the main arena; however, it was too late. Initially, the Royalist infantry under Jacob, Lord Astley, also advanced successfully and seemed to be winning the day.

To halt the infantry advance, Cromwell's cavalry attacked the right wing of the Royalist cavalry and the flank of their infantry as they crossed wet ground and sought to progress uphill. In a fierce, bloody struggle, this assault routed the Royalist horsemen under Sir Marmaduke Langdale and exposed the main body of Astley's infantry. Thomas Fairfax, third baron of Cameron's regiment, supported by Cromwell and powered by its numerical advantage, moved forward, hammered the enemy left and crushed them. By the end of the battle, Fairfax's veteran New Model Army had seized the original Royalist position and Charles I was in full retreat. Most of his cavalry escaped; however, the Royalists abandoned their artillery and lost the bulk of their veteran foot soldiers. Among those killed or captured were the last soldiers who had followed Charles faithfully since 1642. The backbone of the royal army had been broken.

Although the loss was catastrophic for the Royalists, their casualties at Naseby were remarkably small. They suffered approximately 600 dead; however, about 5,000 prisoners were taken, including 500 officers. Therefore, even if the king could muster new recruits, his experienced officer corps was fatally depleted. He could never again match Parliament's growing military advantage. Compounding these seemingly insurmountable military difficulties, a packet of the king's letters to his wife, Henrietta Maria, fell into Parliamentary hands. They illuminated Charles's desperation and had enormous propaganda value in England. In the letters, the king expressed willingness to grant religious concessions to Roman Catholics in exchange for their military support and even proposed to import French mercenaries.

By the end of June, the Royalists surrendered five garrisons. Ten more, including Pontefract and Scarborough, were taken in July, and more than twenty additional garrisons were in Parliamentary hands by January. The Parliamentary armies understood the blow struck at Naseby and vigorously followed up their advantage to end the war.

Significance

Parliament's overwhelming victory turned the tide against the royalists in the first phase of the English Civil War. After Naseby, the New Model Army pursued the king and his armies. Charles moved from garrison to garrison and sought to negotiate with Parliament for better terms. Failing, he finally surrendered to the Scots in May, 1646.

Resources

Ashley, Maurice. *The Battle of Naseby and the Fall of King Charles I*. Stroud, Gloucestershire, England: Alan Sutton and St. Martin's Press, 1992.

Carlton, Charles. *Going to the Wars: The Experience of the British Civil Wars, 1638-1651*. London: Routledge, 1992.

Gentles, Ian. *The New Model Army in England, Ireland, and Scotland, 1645-1653*. Oxford: Blackwell, 1992.

Kishlansky, Mark A. *The Rise of the New Model Army*. Cambridge, England: Cambridge University Press, 1979.

Young, Peter. *Naseby, 1645: The Campaign and the Battle*. London: Century, 1985.

See also: Cromwell, Oliver; Dunbar; Edgehill; English Civil War of 1642-1651; Marston Moor; Preston; Rupert, Prince; Worcester.

Michael J. Galgano

Nashville

Type of action: Ground battle in the American Civil War
Date: December 15-16, 1864
Location: Nashville and Franklin, Tennessee
Combatants: 65,000 Union vs. 40,000 Confederate forces
Principal commanders: *Union*, General George H. Thomas (1816-1870), Major General John Schofield (1831-1906); *Confederate*, General John Bell Hood (1831-1879)
Result: Hood's Army of Tennessee was left in shambles

Confederate general John Bell Hood planned to move into middle Tennessee to cut off Union general William T. Sherman's advance into the lower south. However, Hood's operation was doomed from the start because he did not begin until mid-November and lacked troops to execute such a campaign. He failed to strike a serious blow to retreating Union forces commanded by General John Schofield. This allowed Schofield time to set up a defensive perimeter outside of Franklin, twenty-five miles south of Nashville. Unfortunately, Hood ordered a frontal assault against Union positions and suffered huge casualties including a number of generals. Hood's offensive was shattered, but Union general George H. Thomas delayed in delivering a counterstrike because of bad weather. On December 15, Thomas finally attacked Hood's flank. The next day, Union troops launched an all-out offensive and soundly defeated the rebel forces.

Significance

Hood's army was in complete ruins, and he resigned from command. With Hood no longer a threat, Sherman completed his March to the Sea Campaign, and Union troops captured Savannah, Georgia, later that month.

Resources

The Civil War: 1864—War Is All Hell. Documentary. PBS Video, 1989.

Cox, Jacob D. *The March to the Sea: Franklin and Nashville*. New York: J. Brussel, 1959.

Huddleston, Edwin. *The Civil War in Middle Tennessee*. Nashville, Tenn.: Nashville Banner, 1965.

Maslowski, Peter. *Treason Must Be Odious: Military Occupation and Wartime Reconstruction in Nashville, Tennessee, 1862-1865*. New York: KTO Press, 1978.

Sword, Wiley. *Embrace an Angry Wind: The Confederacy's Last Hurrah: Spring Hill, Franklin, and Nashville*. New York: HarperCollins, 1992.

See also: American Civil War; Atlanta; Hood, John Bell; Savannah; Sherman, William T.

Gayla Koerting

Nasser, Gamal Abdel

Also known as: Jamal ʿAbd an-Nāṣer
Born: January 15, 1918; Alexandria, Egypt
Died: September 28, 1970; Cairo, Egypt
Principal wars: Palestine War, Suez War, Six-Day War, War of Attrition
Principal battles: Falluja (1952)
Military significance: Nasser managed to convert the Suez War from a military loss into a major political and personal triumph.

Born to Abdel Nasser Hussein, a postal clerk, and Fahima Hammad, young Gamal Abdel Nasser became familiar with both the privileged class on their large landed estates and the peasantry. As a student, Nasser was caught up in the political fervor of Egypt for the Egyptians and opposed British control of the country.

After a short stint in law school, Nasser enrolled in Cairo's Military Academy, motivated by his patriotism, economic need, and status improvement possibilities. Thanks to the accelerated program there, Nasser was commissioned in seventeen months in 1938 rather than the traditional three years.

Second Lieutenant Nasser's initial assignment was to Mankabad, Upper Egypt. One of his close companions there was Anwar el-Sadat, who succeeded Nasser to the presidency in 1970. On Nasser's transfer to the Anglo-Egyptian Sudan, he joined another friend from the Military Academy, Abdel Hakim Amer, later the discredited Egyptian commander in chief.

Early in 1943, Captain Nasser became an instructor at the Cairo Military Academy, where he met other young men who were angered by Egypt's subservient role to its British occupiers and by the social and economic injustices in the essentially feudal society.

Lieutenant Colonel Nasser's defining moment militarily occurred during the first Palestinian War of 1948-1949. As commander of the Sixth Battalion, he was ordered to move to the Falluja enclave near Gaza. The pocket was soon surrounded and isolated by the advancing Israelis. Nasser, though wounded in the chest and with an acute shortage of supplies, refused to surrender until relieved by the Egyptian-Israeli armistice of February, 1949.

At Falluja, Nasser, observing the sad state of Egyptian arms (which he attributed to inefficiency and corruption in high places), decided that the real battleground was not in Palestine but in fact at home. This widely shared feeling among the younger officers led to their Free Officers' military coup of July 23, 1952, ousting the corrupt and effete King Farouk and later establishing a republic.

At first, a respected older general, Muḥammad Naguib, was the Free Officers' choice as front man. Nasser, the effective leader, was content with being minister of the interior in 1953, becoming prime minister in 1954. Naguib opposed the younger officers' plans for more radical change and was eased out. Nasser was elected president of Egypt in 1956.

The tripartite Anglo-French-Israeli attack of October-November, 1956, in the Suez War led to the defeat of the Egyptian armed forces. Nasser, with the political backing of much of the world, managed to transform it into a stunning political

Gamal Abdel Nasser. (National Archives)

and personal victory. Accordingly, by early 1957, the three invading forces had withdrawn, the Suez Canal blocked by Nasser's orders was cleared, and its tolls thenceforth collected by the Egyptian Suez Canal Authority. Nasser became the unchallenged hero of the Arab world.

The Six-Day War of June, 1967, was an even greater military disaster for Egypt. The Israelis occupied the entire Sinai Peninsula as well as the Egyptian-administered Gaza Strip. The action had been triggered by Nasser's termination of the United Nations Emergency Force and subsequent precluding of Israel from access to its only Red Sea port, Eilat. Nasser's abdication because of the "setback" was rejected by the legislature and especially by unprecedented mass demonstrations of popular support.

The artillery and air war across the Suez Canal—the War of Attrition—began in 1969 and was inconclusive when Nasser died from a heart attack in 1970. His civilian achievements had in fact transformed a military *coup d'état* into a full-blown political, social, and economic revolution, and he had initiated a short-lived but impressive Arab unity movement. His defiance of the West and participation as a founding member in the nonaligned movement also left a lasting legacy.

Resources
Gordon, Joel. *Nasser's Blessed Movement: Egypt's Free Officers and the July Revolution*. New York: Oxford University Press, 1992.
Vatikiotis, Panayotis J. *Nasser and His Generation*. New York: St. Martin's, 1978.
Woodward, Peter. *Nasser*. London: Longman, 1992.

See also: Egyptian Insurrection; Israeli-Arab Wars; Sadat, Anwar el-; Sinai; Six-Day War; Suez War.

Peter B. Heller

National Guard

In the United States, federally supported militia. After the American Civil War (1861-1865), many state-supported military organizations developed throughout the United States. Composed of those who could supply their own arms and uniforms, they largely served a social purpose. By the 1870's and 1880's, these militia units—which came to be called the National Guard—were being called upon by state governments to break strikes. The National Guard, having been granted in the same period federal funds for acquiring weapons, soon became the United States' only trained reserve force. Although other reserve forces were created in the twentieth century, the National Guardsmen maintained an important role, sometimes serving as relief, police, and work forces during state- or nation-wide emergencies, and, at other times, being called into military service by the general government. Indeed, the National Guard played an important combat role during World War I (1914-1918) and World War II (1939-1945).

Jeremiah Taylor

Naval weapons

Warfare at sea has been a part of international relations since ancient times. As populations grew and technologies improved, the seas became highways for trade and political conquest. Peoples living near coastal areas learned that controlling access to their territory was necessary for survival in a world where pirates, kings, and conquerors were bent on plunder or the extension of political power. Possession of superior naval weaponry was often the key to political or cultural survival.

Ancient Period: To 500 c.e.

For most of history, ships were used for war without being designed specifically for war. Around 1400 b.c.e., "sea peoples" living along the coast of the Mediterranean Sea began to refine the use of ships as weapons of war as they systematically raided coastal regions. Around 700 b.c.e., the Phoenicians built the first ships specifically designed for fighting. *Galleys* were longer and narrower than traditional sailing ships, strengthened at the bow with bronze sheeting. They were eventually fitted with a projecting ram or metal beak extending from the bow. Because they were powered by both sails and oars, galleys were more reliable in battle and thus became the deci-

Galleys powered by sails and oars were used in the Peloponnesian Wars. (Library of Congress)

sive instrument in naval warfare for more than two thousand years.

Many variations of the galley were tried across the centuries, most of which employed several hundred oarsmen ranged in two (*bireme*), three (*trireme*), or five (*quinquireme*) banks (levels) along both sides of the ship. To maintain control of the Mediterranean Sea, the imperial Roman navy relied on fast *liburnians* fitted with weapons that maximized skills developed in land battle. The *corvus*, a hinged bridge fitted with grappling hooks, and the *harpax*, a pole fitted with a grappling hook that could be shot from a catapult, enabled Roman soldiers to board enemy vessels for hand-to-hand combat.

The Middle Ages: 500-1500

For a thousand years following the fall of the Roman Empire (476), the principal conflicts at sea were between the Byzantine Empire and various Muslim states. The galley remained the principal warship, with the Byzantines adopting a compromise between maneuverability and sturdiness in their *dromon*.

Various barbarian tribes, notably the Vikings, were effective long-range marauders, but their *longboats* were principally for transport of fighting men and probably could not have matched the navies of ancient Greece or Rome in pitched battle.

In an age of relatively few changes in naval weaponry, the Byzantines developed an early flamethrower around 670, which provided the basis for their naval dominance throughout much of the Middle Ages. The exact recipe for *Greek fire* has been lost, but it probably included sulfur, naphtha, and quicklime. When forced out of wooden tubes by a jet of pressurized water, the mixture burst into flames, igniting enemy ships.

With the advent of firearms in the fourteenth century, galleys were adapted to accommodate this new offensive weapon, but the results were disappointing. The *galliot* was a smaller, faster ship mounting a few guns; the *galleass* was a seaworthy, double-sized galley able to mount up to seventy guns. Most early cannons, however, were for killing men rather than for destroying ships.

Early Modern Period: 1500-1650

Until 1500, most warships were essentially fighting platforms. The introduction of the *port* (a side opening) dramatically altered both the design of ships and the nature of warfare at sea, allowing heavy cannons to be used below the center of gravity. Gradually the armed galleys and makeshift cargo designs gave way to *ships of the line*. These represented a combination of the graceful English *galleon* ship design and modern naval armament in the form of muzzle-loading bronze or cast-iron cannons. Firing through ports on two or three decks on each side, ships of the line provided the first long-range naval capability, establishing naval operations as an important independent military operation.

A number of innovations in weaponry were developed in East Asia during this period. Small rockets and fused mines were used in Asian waters, though their effectiveness was limited by lack of effective means of guidance. More important was the ironclad warship designed by Admiral Yi Sun-shin of the Korean state of Chola. Starting with the basic galley design, Yi wrapped his ships in iron and ringed them with spikes to repel enemy boarding. These *tortoise ships*, using two or more cannons fired through gun ports and archers using fiery arrows, successfully repelled Japanese invasions in 1592 and 1598.

The Age of Sail: 1650-1850

By the beginning of the nineteenth century, a first-rate ship of the line carried one hundred or more cannons on three decks. In theory, naval operations were conducted according to the same principles that had been used in the early modern period, relying upon wooden hulled ships under sail power. However, the gradual implementation of improved cannon carriages for ease of reloading, red-hot shot for setting enemy ships on fire, and flintlock gunnery for more efficient firing collectively marked an enormous advance in fighting effectiveness. These refinements also made it possible to diversify fleets. Fast-sailing frigates, for instance, could now carry operationally significant armament, thus making war at sea more complex.

The use of sailing ships as weapons was perfected during the Napoleonic Wars (1803-1815). Although experiments with steam power and explosive shells were carried out early in the nineteenth century, most naval leaders resisted the trend toward modernization for another forty years.

Industrial Age: 1850-1945

The Industrial Revolution ensured that naval change would be rapid after the mid-nineteenth century. Russian success with explosive shell projectiles during the Crimean War (1853-1856) convinced planners that wooden ships under sail were vulnerable. The introduction of breech-loading, rifled gun barrels, and improved cylindrical projectiles during the last half of the nineteenth century increased the range and accuracy of naval shelling.

Soon after the Crimean War, France and Britain produced early versions of armor-plated steamships, though their first actual test in war was the battle between the CSS *Virginia* (the resurrected remains of the *Merrimack*) and the *Monitor* during the American Civil War (1861-1865). The *Monitor* also introduced the first effective revolving battery. From this beginning, *battleships* steadily grew in size and firepower until Britain introduced the world's first all-big-gun battleship, HMS *Dreadnought*, in 1906. Faster *battle cruisers*, which nearly matched battleships in firepower but lacked the same degree of protective armor, became effective in both scouting and sinking light cruisers and battleships.

While the battleship was revolutionizing war at sea, a radically new and important countermeasure was being developed for use under water. The first submarine was used in the Civil War, but it was not an effective combat weapon until development of the self-propelled *torpedo* (1860's) and more advanced forms of propulsion. By World War I (1914-1918), German submarines (U-boats) had become remarkably effective in blockade and counterblockade activities. By World War II (1939-1945), improvements in armor and propulsion enhanced the striking capability of the submarine, as was demonstrated by Germany's sinking of 2,117 ships in the first forty months of the war. In response, Allied leaders further diversified their surface fleets, deploying fast but fragile *torpedo boats* and larger torpedo-boat *destroyers*.

World War II saw the acceleration of a number of trends in naval weaponry, but none was more revolutionary than refinement of carrier-based aircraft. As the war progressed, it became clear that battleships were incapable of resisting attack from the air. As battleships and heavy cruisers were increasingly marginalized, the *aircraft carrier* became the primary striking weapon of surface naval forces.

Modern Age: 1945-2000

The development of nuclear power after World War II increased the importance of naval warhead delivery systems, and at the same time freed ships and submarines from dependence on land bases. The United States launched the first nuclear-powered submarine, the USS *Nautilus*, in 1954, and during the 1960's began to deploy some nuclear-powered surface ships as well.

At the end of the twentieth century, the aircraft carrier was the top ship in a complex naval ranking order, with the submarine also playing a leading role. The largest submarines, which could remain submerged almost indefinitely, were designed to launch missiles carrying nuclear warheads. Attack submarines, operating at speeds of more than forty knots and equipped with a variety of torpedoes and missiles, were built to destroy enemy ships.

By the beginning of the twenty-first century, naval warfare operated as an integral part of a complex combination of air, land, and sea strategies linked by new developments in guided missiles, electronic sensors, satellite communication and surveillance systems, underwater sound technology, and propulsion systems. This required the most sophisticated navies to maintain extensive battle fleets, with each ship providing specific offensive or defensive roles in the projection of power.

Resources

American Defense. Documentary. New Line Home Video, 1995.

The Athenian Trireme. Documentary. Films for the Humanities and Sciences, 1993.

Bruce, A. P. C., Tony Bruce, and William B. Cogar. *An Encyclopedia of Naval History*. New York: Facts on File, 1998.

Friedman, Norman. *Naval Institute Guide to World Naval Weapons Systems*. 2d ed. Annapolis, Md.: Naval Institute Press, 1992.

Gardiner, Robert, and Arne Emil Christensen, eds. *The Earliest Ships: The Evolution of Boats into Ships*. Annapolis, Md.: Naval Institute Press, 1996.

Great Ships. Documentary. A&E Entertainment, 1998.

Greene, Jack, and Allessandro Massignani. *Ironclads at War: The Origin and Development of the Armored Warship, 1854-1891*. Pennsylvania: Combined Publishing, 1998.

Hamer, David J. *Bombers Versus Battleships: The Struggle Between Ships and Aircraft for the Control of the Surface of the Sea*. Annapolis, Md.: Naval Institute Press, 1998.

Ireland, Bernard, Eric Grove, and Ian Drury. *Jane's War at Sea: 1897-1997*. New York: HarperCollins, 1997.

Jane, Fred T. *The British Battle Fleet: Its Inception and Growth Throughout the Centuries*. London: Conway Maritime Press, 1997.

Koburger, Charles W., Jr. *Sea Power in the Twenty-first Century: Projecting a Naval Revolution*. Westport, Conn.: Greenwood Press, 1997.

Layman, R. D. *Naval Aviation in the First World War: Its Impact and Influence*. Annapolis, Md.: Naval Institute Press, 1996.

Lenton, H. T. *British and Empire Warships of the Second World War*. Annapolis, Md.: Naval Institute Press, 1998.

Massie, Robert Kinloch. *Dreadnought*. New York: Ballantine, 1992.

The Military Prepares. Documentary. New Line Home Video, 1995.

National Research Council Staff. *Technology for the United States Navy and Marine Corps, 2000-2035: Becoming a Twenty-first-Century Force*. New York: National Academy Press, 1997.

Pemsel, Helmut. *A History of War at Sea: An Atlas and Chronolgy of Conflict at Sea from Earliest Times to the Present*. Translated by G. D. G. Smith. Annapolis, Md.: Naval Institute Press, 1977.

Poolman, Kenneth. *The Winning Edge: Naval Technology in Action, 1939-1945*. Annapolis, Md.: Naval Institute Press, 1997.

Sea Power: A Destiny upon the Waters. Documentary. U.S. Department of the Navy, 1968.

Todd, Daniel, and Michael Lindberg. *Navies and Shipbuilding Industries: The Strained Symbiosis*. Westport, Conn.: Praeger, 1996.

Whitley, M. J. *Battleships of World War Two: An International Encyclopedia*. Annapolis, Md.: Naval Institute Press, 1998.

See also: Coast Guard, U.S.; Coastal defense; Chola kingdom; Constantinople, Siege of, 717-

718; Dreadnought; Leyte Gulf; Marines, U.S.; Midway; Napoleonic Wars; Navies: Organization and tactics; Navy, U.S.; North Atlantic; Piracy; Punic Wars; Salamis; Submarine; Warships; Yi Sun-shin.

John Powell

Navarro, Pedro

FULL NAME: Pedro Navarro de Roncal, count of Oliveto
BORN: c. 1460; Garde, Spain
DIED: 1528; Naples
PRINCIPAL WARS: Italian Wars, War of the Holy League, Valois-Habsburg Wars
PRINCIPAL BATTLES: Naples (1503), Gaeta (1503-1504), Oran (1509), Bugia (1510), Tripolis (1510), Ravenna (1512), Genoa (1522), Naples (1528)
MILITARY SIGNIFICANCE: Navarro pioneered the use of gunpowder in mines against fortifications.

Pedro Navarro was born in the autonomous Pyrenee kingdom of Navarre on the Gulf of Biscay. In 1487, he mined Sarzana in the Florentine-Genoese War. After corsairing in the Mediterranean, he mined St. George in Gonzalo Fernández de Córdoba's attack on Turkish Cephalonia. Captain of infantry under Fernández, he participated in the expulsion of the French from Naples in 1503 during the Italian Wars (1494-1559). He took the Tower of St. Vincent and mined the Castelnuovo and the Castello dell'Ovo. He took the Torre d'Orlando above Gaeta in 1503, resulting in French surrender in 1504.

King Ferdinand II appointed Navarro as count of Oliveto and captain general of infantry and charged him with expanding Aragonese Mediterranean Africa. In the North African Campaign, Navarro took Oran (May 18, 1509), Bugia (January 6, 1510), and Tripolis (July 25, 1510). Ordered to join Viceroy Raymond of Cardona's Holy League army in Italy, he extricated his infantry from Cardona's defeat at Ravenna (April 11, 1512). Wounded, he was taken prisoner by the French. Not ransomed, Navarro was freed by King Francis I to fight for France in the Valois-Habsburg Wars (1521-1559). Taken prisoner twice more, at Genoa and Naples, and terminally ill, he died in the Castelnuovo.

RESOURCES
Fernandez-Armesto, Felipe. *Ferdinand and Isabella*. London: Weidenfeld, 1975.
Knecht, R. J. *Renaissance Warrior and Patron: The Reign of Francis I*. Cambridge, England: Cambridge University Press, 1994.
Living Islam. Documentary. Ambrose, 1993.
Purcell, Mary. *The Great Captain*. Garden City, N.Y.: Doubleday, 1962.

SEE ALSO: Fernández de Córdoba, Gonzalo; Italian Wars; Ravenna.

Reinhold Schumann

Navies: Organization and Tactics

A navy is a nation's maritime military force, organized and equipped to use weapons directly against shipping or targets ashore, support land combat operations, blockade an enemy, deliver an amphibious assault, protect lines of communication and commerce, and act as a visible symbol of the nation's strength. A navy includes not only ships and their crews but also aircraft and missile forces, commandos, shore installations for repair and resupply, and communication centers. As navies grew larger and more technologically complex, the proportion of shore personnel and matériel to sailors and ships grew ever larger. Advances in technology also led to changes in fleet organization and tactics and the way forces are maneuvered in combat.

The Origin of Warfare at Sea

The first warships probably appeared about 4,000 years ago, launched by the Minoan civilization of Crete in the eastern Mediterranean Sea. Used to protect shipping along coastal trade routes, the Minoan galley, which relied on oarpower, set the pattern of warships for centuries afterward. Historians believe that either Greek or Phoenician shipwrights developed the first true open-sea warship in the sixth or seven century B.C.E., and a century later Athens in Greece became the first state to maintain a permanent fleet.

From classical times through the Middle Ages, both in Europe and Asia, naval warfare was basically an extension of land warfare. Ships served as floating platforms from which marines could shoot arrows or throw spears until enemy ships came alongside each other. Then fierce hand-to-hand combat ensued as each crew tried to board and capture the enemy ship. However, galleys also carried a distinctively naval weapon, the metal-sheathed ram, which protruded forward from the bow just below the waterline so that with sufficient speed and skillful maneuvering, a ship could gouge a hole in an enemy's hull.

ANCIENT TACTICS

The generals who led seaborne armies arranged their forces for battle with *ramming* in mind. Enemies faced each other side by side in long ranks, much like cavalry, and charged to work up ramming speed while angling just to one side of a target. At the last moment, the captain turned bow-on toward the enemy's side and guided home the ram. The maneuver often failed, but meanwhile marines fired into the enemy in preparation for the secondary tactical goal, boarding and capture. Fleet commanders exerted little control after the initial attack, which turned into a general melee as ships sought enemies to grapple with. Made of wood and therefore buoyant, the ships seldom sank, even when rammed, so the tactical goal was primarily to kill enemy warriors or render them unable to fight by disabling their galley. Nonetheless, from the outset naval warfare entailed dangers that did not affect ground combat in the same way. Fire aboard ship was often disastrous and was practically the only way a ship could be made to sink quickly. Storms threatened to wreck the fleets of victors and vanquished alike, and the ever-present threat of drowning confined fighters to their ships.

In the fourth century B.C.E., stone-throwing catapults were taken aboard large galleys for bombarding the enemy at distances of several hundred yards, and the seventh century warships of the Byzantine Empire introduced *Greek fire*, a much-feared secret weapon. Projected from a tube, it was a flammable compound that clung to wood and sailcloth and could not be extinguished. Still, ramming and boarding remained the standard tactics, because neither catapults nor Greek fire could destroy the agile galleys fast enough in a fleet engagement. In the Scandinavian north, the longship, the principle war vessel during the Middle Ages, also served as an infantry platform. It lacked a ram.

FIREPOWER AND MANEUVERABILITY: 1250-1700

In the thirteenth century, the introduction of the stern rudder and multiple masts on ships made long sea voyages possible. During war, merchantships, called *galleons*, could be converted to warships by building a castle on the stern, from which archers shot down into enemy ships. Cannons were mounted in the bow on fixed carriages. Small and difficult to aim, these early guns were used only in support of boarders.

During the fifteenth century, larger muzzle-loaded cannons were developed and deployed on rolling carriages in rows down both sides of the ship. The muzzle could be elevated and moved side-to-side in a narrow arc, thus improving the range and aim. By the end of the century, such cannons supplied the main fighting power on ocean-going ships that were direct descendants of the galleon. The size and number of cannons varied with the size of the ship: from small cannons shooting a ball weighing as little as three pounds to massive sixty-pounders. Such firepower influenced tactics, as commanders relied more on cannons. At Lepanto in 1571, for instance, six large cannon-carrying ships formed the van of the fleet of the Holy League (Venice, Spain, and the Papal States), leading galleys into battle. Their heavy guns confused the Turkish fleet, and although the damage they inflicted on the Turks was slight, the gun ships helped the Holy League to victory.

Hand-to-hand combat dominated tactics until July 31, 1588. On that day, the Armada of Spain was on its way to invade England when an English fleet met it. The large Spanish galleons formed a crescent, intending to grapple the English ships and send their marines aboard. The English fleet comprised a motley assortment of galleons and smaller craft, all more maneuverable than the Spanish ships and armed with guns of longer range. The English attacked in four squadrons, taking advantage of their position upwind of the Spanish, a tactic called the *weather gauge*, to swoop down upon them, fire broadsides of cannons, then sail away before the Spanish ships could come near. Over the next few days, thanks to their superior gunnery, the English destroyed twenty Spanish ships, damaged many more, and foiled the invasion. It was the first fleet engagement fought solely with cannons, and although boarding remained an important tactic afterward, gunnery became paramount.

The Golden Age of Sail: 1775-1815

During the American Revolution (1775-1783) and Napoleonic Wars (1803-1815), England, France, and Spain brought sailing ships to their highest efficiency and deadliness in fleet actions. The largest of the warships, called *men-of-war*, carried from 74 to more than 120 cannons. They were known as *ships of the line* from the battle formation that had been developed to bring to bear the maximum firepower from them. Admirals formed their fleets in lines—sometimes miles long for a large fleet—so they followed single file and fired broadsides as they came within range of the enemy, also in single file. The ships of the line bore the brunt of the battle, but because they were awkward to maneuver and the battle produced immense clouds of gunsmoke, admirals, positioned in the center of the line, often could not see ships in the van or the rear. To support the men-of-war, smaller, faster ships were added to the fleet as messengers and scouts. These were frigates, sloops, corvettes, and brigs, and they ranged forward and beside the line of battle.

The size of fleets made command and control difficult for admirals. They communicated with ship captains by systems of signals with flags, cannon firing, or both. The systems were limited and cumbersome. Moreover, captains often could not see the flagship from which the admiral commanded. Therefore, signaling had to be repeated by intermediary ships, magnifying delays and the possibility of error. For such reasons, admirals seldom departed from the strict line of battle formation, even though it was unwieldy and dangerous to ships near shore, where most battles took place, and it almost never produced a decisive battle. However, the times produced a tactical genius in Vice Admiral Horatio Nelson (1758-1805). In two battles against the French, Aboukir in 1799 and Trafalgar in 1805, he abandoned the line of battle and triumphed. In both cases, he maneuvered his ships so that they doubled up on enemy men-of-war, destroying them one by one before unengaged French ships could come to the rescue.

Weaponry and Armament: 1805-1918

Trafalgar ended the dominance of the line of battle in naval fleet action. It was also the last great battle for sailing ships because during the nineteenth century, four basic innovations made them obsolete: steam power, armor, torpedoes, and long-range guns. In 1843, the U.S.S. *Princeton* became the first warship driven by a screw propeller mounted beneath the rudder. The piston engine and propeller improved handling, speed, and survivability of warships; gradually, these inventions replaced sails as the main propulsion system. At the same time, fleet deployment altered. Sailing ships could stay at sea almost indefinitely and were ideal for blockading. Steamships and the oil-powered vessels that succeeded them had to refuel periodically, limiting their range and time on patrol and requiring overseas supply bases.

Major navies also began to use breech-loaded, rifled guns, which could be operated faster and shoot farther and truer than the old cannons. Exploding shells multiplied their destructive power. In defense, hulls of wooden ships were draped with plate iron. During the American Civil War (1861-1865), these *ironclads* proved a new era in naval technology had begun. In 1862, to cite the most famous battle, the Confederate *Virginia* (formerly *Merrimac*) destroyed several Union wooden frigates in Chesapeake Bay. It was unscathed until the *Monitor*, an armored barge with a single turret and large gun, challenged it. The battle ended in a draw, with both vessels battered but still operational. The trend for naval armor was firmly established, and soon some nations, starting with England, constructed all-iron ships.

Further reason for armor arose with the invention of *underwater mines* (originally called torpedoes). Minefields, deadly even to large well-armored ships, became a means of protecting harbors and sea lanes. In 1866, a British inventor built the first automotive torpedo, designed to strike a ship below the water line. The invention revolutionized small-boat tactics. *Torpedo boats,* swift and nimble, could dart out from a harbor and launch torpedoes at larger ships, then run to safety—a type of fleet small nations could afford to build and operate. To defend large ships from them, the torpedo-boat destroyer was designed, ancestor of the modern destroyer. Capable of up to thirty knots, it carried small-caliber, quick-firing guns and its own torpedoes. Admirals deployed them ahead of fleets to act as screens against enemy destroyers. Intermediate-size ships called cruisers were sent in squadrons to scout out the enemy. Battleships, however, were still considered the prime weapons of the fleet; their huge guns, some with twelve-inch bores, could accurately hurl shells at targets more than ten thousand yards away. To exploit such firepower effectively, admirals maneuvered to "cross the T"—that is, to sail their battleships across the line of oncoming enemy ships so that all big guns could concentrate their fire while only the forward enemy guns could be used.

In 1890, Alfred Thayer Mahan, an American naval captain, published *The Influence of Sea Power upon History 1660-1805*, a book that profoundly influenced subsequent naval organization. In it he argued that only powerful ocean-going fleets could protect the commercial shipping of a nation and assure its prosperity. He concluded that conflicts between strong navies would be settled in large decisive battles. German, England, the United States, and Japan rushed to build ever-larger, faster battleships and cruisers. This arms race ended in the Battle of Jutland (1916) during World War I (1914-1918), in which the British Grand Fleet drove the German High Seas Fleet back to port after an engagement on the scale that Mahan had predicted, but only after appalling losses to the English. After World War I, treaties limited the size and number of battleships and cruisers.

Aircraft Carriers and Submarines

The three-century-long development of the warship as an artillery platform culminated in the *battleship*, which became easier for admirals to deploy after radio communications was introduced, but even as the battleship reached its greatest destructive potential, two inventions were already rendering it obsolescent: the submarine and the airplane. During World War I, the Royal Navy converted two ships to *carriers*, launching biplanes against shore targets and German U-boats. Following the war, tactics called for carriers to provide air cover for battleships.

By the end of World War II (1939-1945), the roles of the two types of warship had reversed. The fleet carrier proved to be the key to early Japanese success, especially the attack on Pearl Harbor in 1941, and to final victory at sea by Allied forces. The U.S.S. *Midway*, for example, could sail at thirty-three knots and hold 145 dive-bombers and torpedo planes, whose range far exceeded that of the largest guns. Because of such aircraft-delivered firepower, major battles occurred while fleets were hundreds of miles apart. To protect themselves from enemy aircraft, fleets evolved into carrier-centered battle groups in which battleships and cruisers acted as antiaircraft screens. The big guns of battleships saw most of their action when firing in support of amphibious landings.

Submarines date from as early as 1778 and saw limited service in the American Civil War (1861-1865) but did not become significant weapons until the torpedo was perfected. German U-boats decimated merchant shipping during World Wars I and II, sometimes attacking individually and sometimes in groups, popularly known as *wolf packs*. Naval commanders scrambled to invent tactics to stop them. An array of inventions helped, including the depth charge and underwater sensors, particularly the sonar. Carrier- and shore-based aircraft also proved effective. Nevertheless, the Battle of the North Atlantic (1939-1945) during World War II turned into one of the costliest and most protracted battles in the history of naval warfare. Only by innovative use of destroyers and by grouping ships into large rectangular convoys could admirals move merchant ships to Europe to supply the land war.

Twentieth Century

After World War II, the aircraft carrier remained the center of U.S. and British battle groups that ranged the oceans, dominating hundreds of miles of the sea and land around them with their aircraft. Jet planes, some capable of delivering nuclear weapons, made carriers the most powerful surface vessels in history. Arrayed around to protect them and scout for enemy ships are guided missile cruisers, destroyers, and frigates. Their radar and uplinks to reconnaissance satellites reveal any approaching objects, and their surface-to-air missiles (SAMs), ship-to-ship missiles (SSMs), and antisubmarine torpedoes and depth charges provide the defensive firepower. To keep up with the fast pace of battle, computers help manage the complex battle systems. Admirals control fleets from special command ships, which are primarily communications centers.

The U.S. Third Fleet is a typical example of modern naval organization. It guards the eastern and northern Pacific approaches to the United States under the command of a vice admiral who reports to the full admiral in charge of the Pacific Fleet. Trained to respond to a crisis within ninety-six hours, the Third Fleet consists of at least one carrier battle group. The carrier holds seventy-five to eighty combat aircraft and is escorted by four to six combat ships with helicopters, missiles, air defense systems, and anti-submarine systems. Two nuclear attack submarines patrol underwater. As the need arises, the fleet may add such specialty vessels as mine sweepers or troop ships in "amphibious ready groups" carrying marine expeditionary units.

However, few nations can afford such large, technologically sophisticated formations as the carrier battle group. Smaller nations rely on destroyer-size craft to patrol their coasts and submarines to extend their influence into the ocean. Among them was the Soviet Union. The Soviet navy based its strategy on long-range submarines, not aircraft carriers, although it also had a sizeable fleet of guided missile cruisers. Navies deploy submarines of two basic types. Nuclear-powered ballistic missile submarines (also known as "boomers"), possessed by only a few nations, carry long-range missiles with nuclear warheads, making them strategic weapons of devastating power. They are stalked by attack submarines, which may be powered either by nuclear reactors or conventional diesel engines. The introduction of nuclear power in the 1950's greatly enhanced the range and cruising time for submarines and surface ships. Ballistic missile submarines cruise for months beneath the surface, controlled by the naval high command, rather than a local fleet commander. Difficult to detect underwater, they are also difficult to communicate with when submerged, so ship captains act under a heavy weight of responsibility.

Long-range missiles, satellite communications and reconnaissance, global positioning systems, and sophisticated electronic warfare defenses have fundamentally changed naval warfare in two respects. During World War II, high-speed maneuvering of the fleet was essential to tactical success, but soon afterward the speed of ships became far less important than the speed of their weapons—missiles and jet aircraft. Likewise, maneuverability itself provides little protection from radar-guided missiles; accordingly, scouting for the enemy and missile countermeasures grew in importance. Old-fashioned weapons still influence battle tactics, however, as became dramatically apparent during the Gulf War (1991) when an Iraqi mine nearly sank a U.S. cruiser.

RESOURCES

Coletta, Paolo E. *The American Naval Heritage*. 4th ed. Lanham, Md.: University Press of America, 1997.

Gleto, Jan. *Warfare at Sea, 1500-1650: Maritime Conflicts and the Transformation of Europe*. New York: Routledge, 2000.

Gray, Colin S., and Roger W. Barnett, eds. *Seapower and Strategy*. Annapolis, Md.: Naval Institute Press, 1989.

Hartmann, Frederick H. *Naval Renaissance: The U.S. Navy in the 1980's*. Annapolis, Md.: Naval Institute Press, 1990.

Hughes, Wayne P. *Fleet Tactics*. Annapolis, Md.: Naval Institute Press, 1986.

Keegan, John. *The Price of Admiralty: The Evolution of Naval Warfare*. New York: Penguin Books, 1988.

Lambert, Nicholas A. *Sir John Fisher's Naval Revolution*. Columbia: University of South Carolina Press, 1999.

Massie, Robert K. *Dreadnought: Britain, Germany, and the Coming of the Great War*. New York: Ballantine Books, 1991.

Miller, Nathan. *The U.S. Navy*. 3d ed. Annapolis, Md.: Naval Institute Press, 1997.

Reynolds, Clark G. *Navies in History*. Annapolis, Md.: Naval Institute Press, 1998

Roskill, S. W. *The Strategy of Sea Power*. London, England: Collins, 1962.

Sea Power: A Destiny Upon the Waters. Documentary. U.S. Department of the Navy, 1968.

Secrets of War. Television documentary series. The History Channel, 1999-2000.

Sokolsky, Joel J. *Seapower in the Nuclear Age: The United States Navy and NATO 1949-80*. Annapolis, Md.: Naval Institute Press, 1991.

Southworth, John van Duyn. *The Ancient Fleets*. New York: Twayne, 1968-1972.

Sundt, Wilburn A. *Naval Science*. 3d ed. Annapolis, Md.: Naval Institute Press, 1991.

Tunstall, Brian. *Naval Warfare in the Age of Sail: The Evolution of Fighting Tactics*. Annapolis, Md.: Naval Institute Press, 1990.

Watts, Anthony J. *The Royal Navy*. Annapolis, Md.: Naval Institute Press, 1994.

SEE ALSO: Aboukir; Armada, Spanish; Camperdown; Coast Guard, U.S.; Dreadnought; Falkland Islands War; Lepanto; Leyte Gulf; Mahan, Alfred Thayer; Marines, U.S.; Midway; Napoleonic Wars; Naval weapons; Navy, U.S.; Nelson, Horatio; Piracy; Salamis; Submarine; Trafalgar; Warships; World War II.

Roger Smith

NAVY

A military organization whose primary function is fighting at sea. Navies are composed of warships, auxiliary vessels, maintenance facilities on the shore, and, beginning in the twentieth century, ship-based airplanes. The earliest known specialized navies appeared in Greece in the fifth century B.C.E. For the following 2,000 years, technical restrictions kept naval operations close to shorelines. By the fifteenth century, however, the compass, gunpowder artillery, and improved sailing vessels had broadened the scope of naval warfare. The sixteenth century witnessed the advent of large, heavily armed men-of-war—the defenders of mercantilistic traffic. By the eighteenth century, European warships had shaken off the navigational safety of the coasts and were battling each other around the globe. Steam power and iron-clad warships came into their own during the last half of the nineteenth century. The basic form of the modern battleship was developed in the late nineteenth century: heavily armored, swiftly moving vessel armed with large, powerful, extremely accurate long-range guns.

Jeremiah Taylor

NAVY, U.S.

The United States Navy has a historical tradition dating back to the American Revolution (1775-1783). Warships played important roles in all of the country's wars, although in peacetime, the Navy tended to dwindle in numbers and significance, particularly in the nineteenth century. The U.S. Navy also enjoys a tradition of technical innovation, resulting in naval forces at the cutting edge of naval technology. In terms of personnel, the U.S. Navy included (as of April, 2000) 367,522 on active duty, 183,321 ready reserve, and 186,008 civilians. Operational aircraft numbered 4,108, and there were 315 ships and 41 bases.

EARLY NATIONAL PERIOD: 1776-1848

The first American Navy, the Continental Navy, was a small force of approximately fifty ships that played a limited role during the American Revolution. Heavily outnumbered by the British Royal Navy, the Continental Navy could do little more than harass the British before the Continental Congress disbanded the squadron in 1783. The U.S. Navy did not appear until 1798, when foreign policy concerns dragged the United States into the Quasi-War (1798-1800) with France, a series of skirmishes with the Barbary Pirates, and the War of 1812 (1812-1815) with Great Britain. Although small by European standards, the American Navy, using a small fleet of powerful frigates, often defeated its European rivals in ship-to-ship duels.

Especially important during these conflicts were the U.S. Marines. Established as a branch of the Navy in 1798, the Marines served as expeditionary troops and imposed discipline on the ship's crew. A landing by Marines backed by Navy ships offshore became the hallmark of many subsequent U.S. military operations. The long peace after the War of 1812 caused a decline in the number of U.S. Navy ships, but the service was sufficient to defeat the small Mexican Navy during the Mexican-American War (1846-1848).

U.S. Navy Personnel on Active Duty, 1805-1995

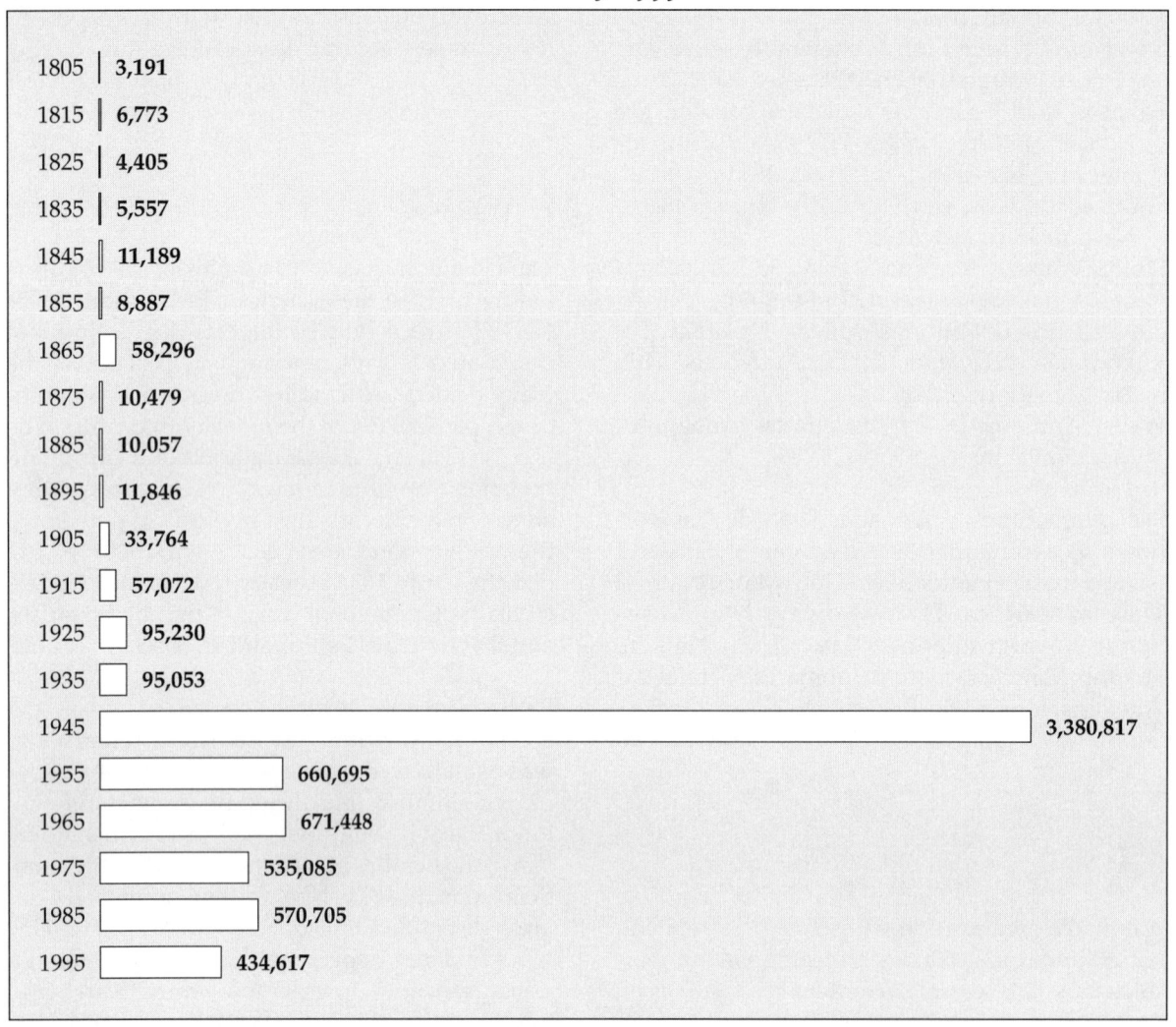

Year	Personnel
1805	3,191
1815	6,773
1825	4,405
1835	5,557
1845	11,189
1855	8,887
1865	58,296
1875	10,479
1885	10,057
1895	11,846
1905	33,764
1915	57,072
1925	95,230
1935	95,053
1945	3,380,817
1955	660,695
1965	671,448
1975	535,085
1985	570,705
1995	434,617

Note: Data for years through 1945 include U.S. Army personnel assigned to the Air Force Command.

Sources: The data used in this graphic element are based on information found in *Historical Statistics of the United States: Colonial Times to 1970* (2 vols., Washington, D.C.: Government Printing Office, 1975) and *The Time Almanac 2000*, edited by Borgna Brunner (Boston: Information Please, 1999).

Vital to overcoming the shortage of ships was the quality of U.S. officers. Opened at Annapolis, Maryland, in 1845, the Naval Academy (first called the Naval School) began a rigorous curriculum to provide qualified officers for U.S. naval service. In 1851, the school reorganized to offer a four-year course leading to a bachelor of science.

Late Nineteenth Century: 1848-1898

Although a small force after the Mexican-American War, the U.S. Navy swelled in size during the American Civil War (1861-1865). At its peak strength, the Union Navy manned more than six hundred ships of various sizes carrying more than 50,000 officers and crew. The Civil War generated a wide range of technical innovations that the Navy successfully integrated into its operations: ironclad warships, amphibious landings, combined arms operations with the Union Army, and specialized riverine warships. The Union Navy performed the diverse tasks of seizing southern rivers, blockading southern ports, and hunting Confederate commerce raiders. After the Civil War, however, the Navy lost its national importance as U.S. economic development turned toward the American West. The Navy languished in obscurity until the international revival of interest in naval power triggered by Alfred Thayer Mahan's book *The Influence of Sea Power upon History 1660-1805* (1890) reintroduced updated technologies to the U.S. Navy. Modern warships introduced in the 1890's allowed the United States to decisively defeat the Spanish Navy during the Spanish-American War (1898) and secure an overseas empire. Crushing victories at Manila Bay and Santiago demonstrated the United States' new naval strength and position as a world power.

Two World Wars: 1898-1945

The U.S. Navy entered World War I (1914-1918) a powerful naval force ill-equipped to deal with its German adversary. Instead of large fleet actions, the Navy found itself hastily constructing small craft to hunt German submarines preying on merchant ships. Although it did not have a significant impact on the war, the U.S. Navy emerged from World War I as a primary tool of U.S. foreign policy. The United States' determination to build a "Navy second to none" brought other naval powers to the negotiating table. The Washington Naval Treaty (1922) restricted the size of the world's navies and placed the U.S. Navy on an equal status with the Royal Navy. Restricted by the treaty from building battleships, the U.S. Navy experimented with aircraft carriers, a process that served the Navy well after the Japanese attack on Pearl Harbor (1941).

Thrust into World War II in 1941, the U.S. Navy had to fight two very different adversaries at the same time. In the Atlantic, the Navy hunted German U-boats, transported American troops to the European battlefields, and provided logistics for U.S. Army operations. The Pacific campaign, however, was the Navy's primary domain. Large numbers of mass-produced warships protected a highly specialized fleet of amphibious warfare ships carrying Marines to seize Japanese-held islands. The aircraft carriers emerged as the most vital warships, replacing the battleships as the Navy's primary capital ships. Aircraft had greater range, equal destructive power, and more flexibility than the battleship's big guns. Driving the Japanese back toward their homeland in a series of "island-hopping" campaigns, the Navy and Marines prepared to invade Japan itself before the atomic bombings ended the war.

The Post-War Era

After World War II, the Navy found itself with no one to fight. Great Britain, the only other major naval power, was a staunch ally, and all other naval rivals lay in ruins. The Korean War (1950-1953) and Vietnam War (1961-1975) were land wars, with the Navy contributing mostly air support from its aircraft carriers. The Cold War (1947-1991) brought a naval threat from the Soviet Union in the form of a huge submarine fleet, but the Soviets could not challenge U.S. dominance of the sea. The biggest naval challenge became integrating rapidly changing technologies into the naval service: jet aircraft, antiship missiles, electronic warfare, and submarine-fired ballistic missiles. With the decline of the Soviet Union in the 1990's, the U.S. Navy turned its attention from large-scale battles with the Soviets to coastal operations in support of expeditionary or peacekeeping forces.

Resources

Beach, Edward L. *The United States Navy: Two Hundred Years*. New York: Holt, 1986.

Dictionary of American History. New York: Charles Scribner's Sons, 1976.

Hagan, Kenneth J. *This People's Navy: The Making of American Sea Power*. New York: Free Press, 1991.

Howarth, Stephen. *To Shining Sea: A History of the United States Navy, 1775-1991*. New York: Random House, 1991.

Millett, Allan R. *Semper Fidelis: The History of the United States Marine Corps*. New York: Free Press, 1991.

Moskin, J. Robert. *The U.S. Marine Corps Story*. Boston: Little, Brown, 1992.

O'Connor, Raymond G. *Origins of the American Navy: Sea Power in the Colonies and the New Nation*. Lanham, Md.: University Press of America, 1994.

See also: American Civil War; Coast Guard, U.S.; Leyte Gulf; Manila Bay; Marines, U.S.; Midway; Navies: Organization and tactics; Pearl Harbor attack; Santiago; Spanish-American War; Warships.

Steven J. Ramold

Nelson, Horatio

Full name: Viscount Horatio Nelson
Born: September 29, 1758; Burnham Thorpe, Norfolk, England
Died: October 21, 1805; at sea off Cape Trafalgar, Spain
Principal wars: Napoleonic Wars
Principal battles: Aboukir (1799), Copenhagen (1801), Trafalgar (1805)
Military significance: Nelson pioneered new naval tactics by departing from the traditional single line of battle and concentrating his ships against a few enemy vessels.

Horatio Nelson became interested in the sea through the exploits of his mother's older brother, Captain Maurice Suckling. Nelson's mother died in 1767, and in March of 1771, Horatio signed aboard his uncle's ship as a midshipman. Because his ship was assigned to a mundane duty, Suckling arranged for young Horatio to join the crew of a commercial vessel headed for the West Indies. Horatio returned to naval service a year later and received his commission as a lieutenant in April, 1777.

Napoleon Bonaparte, meanwhile, had just conquered much of Europe and had resolved to invade Egypt. Rear Admiral Nelson was sent to keep an eye on the French fleet at Toulon on the Mediterranean coast. The French fleet sailed undetected in mid-May, 1799, its destination unknown to the British. Nelson searched the Mediterranean for the French. Finally in late July, he located Napoleon's fleet at anchor in Aboukir Bay at the mouth of the Nile River.

The line of French ships was anchored parallel to the shore with the head of the line near the beginning of shallow water. The French assumed the British fleet would attack only on the seaward side, but Nelson sent some of his ships through the narrow space between the first French ship and the shallows. These ships attacked the French from their landward side as the rest of Nelson's ships attacked from seaward. Nelson concentrated on the forward third of the French line and pounded them from both sides. As these ships surrendered or sank, the British moved down the French line. At the close of the battle, ten French ships were captured or sunk, one exploded, and two escaped. Napoleon and his army were trapped ashore in Egypt. The British fear that Napoleon would invade other Mediterranean ports and move on to India was permanently laid to rest, and Nelson became a national hero.

Promoted to vice admiral in 1801, Nelson sailed for Copenhagen in a squadron commanded by Admiral Hyde Parker. Czar Paul of Russia had formed an alliance with Denmark and Sweden to keep the British out of the Baltic Sea. Parker and Nelson were instructed to put a stop to that. Arriving off Copenhagen, the British found the Danish fleet anchored close to shore under the guns of a powerful fortress. The Danes had placed their strongest ships at the north end of the line because they expected the British attack to come from that direction. On April 2, 1801, Nelson's ships executed some tricky maneuvering around a shoal and attacked from the south where the weaker Danish ships lay. After four hours, the southern half of the Danish line was devastated. Although the British fleet had also taken heavy losses, Nelson and Parker persuaded the Danes to surrender. Ironically, the battle was unnecessary because the czar had been assassinated on March 24, but the news did not reach Copenhagen until April 9.

Nelson's last and most famous battle took place off Cape Trafalgar at the southwest corner of Spain. On October 19, 1805, a combined French and Spanish fleet sailed from Cádiz, Spain, to do battle with the British. The French-Spanish fleet was sailing northward in single line. Nelson's fleet approached from the west in two parallel columns, a dangerous and unusual tactic. The lead ships of the British columns took heavy fire from many enemy ships as they approached their battle line. However, once the British ships cut through the line, the French and Spanish fleet fell into great disarray, and the British beat them badly. Nelson was mortally wounded by a musket ball fired by a soldier in the rigging of a French ship.

Resources

Bradford, Ernle. *Nelson: The Essential Hero.* New York: Harcourt Brace Jovanovich, 1977.
Pocock, Tom. *Horatio Nelson.* New York: Alfred A. Knopf, 1988.
Southey, Robert. *Life of Nelson.* Annapolis, Md.: U.S. Naval Institute, 1990.

See also: Napoleon I; Napoleonic Wars; Trafalgar.

Edwin G. Wiggins

Německý Brod

Type of action: Ground battle in Hussite Wars
Date: January 8-10, 1422
Location: Havlíčkuv Brod, Czech Republic (forty miles Southeast of Kolín)
Combatants: 16,000 Hussites vs. 23,000 Germans and Hungarians
Principal commanders: *Hussite*, Jan Žižka (1376-1424); *German-Hungarian*, Zawisza of Garbów (c. 1376-1422)
Result: Czechs destroy rearguard to German-Hungarian retreat from Bohemia with a short siege

On January 6, 1422, Hussite forces under Jan Žižka routed a German-Hungarian army at Nebovidy. As King Sigismund's mercenaries failed to stem the Hussite tide at Kutná Hora and Habry over the next two days, the king abandoned his Bohemian campaign and fled across the Sázava River into Moravia, ordering a rearguard at Německý Brod. Zawisza of Garbów valiantly defended the town, enabling his king to escape. Žižka spent January 9 pounding the walls with cannons, but to no avail, and began negotiations the next morning, before one of his soldiers found a way in. Soon whole platoons of Hussites ran through the town wreaking havoc and killing Germans and Hungarians. Most of the men were killed, although women and children were spared, and the Hussites took the Polish noblemen to Prague as prisoners of war.

Significance

Německý Brod represents the height of Hussite power, dealing a mortal blow to German-Hungarian forces from which they would not recover until Bohemia's reconciliation into Catholic Europe in 1437. Sigismund would not return to Bohemia until 1426.

Resources

Barbs, F. M. *The Hussite Revolution, 1424-1437.* Columbia, N.Y.: Columbia University Press, 1966.
Heymann, Frederick. *John Žižka and the Hussite Revolution.* Princeton, N.J.: Princeton University Press, 1955.
Kaminsky, Howard. *A History of the Hussite Revolution.* Berkeley: University of California Press, 1967.
Kejr, Jiri. *The Hussite Revolution.* Prague: Orbis Press Agency, 1988.

See also: Hussite Wars; Žižka, Jan.

Matt Schumann

Nero, Gaius Claudius

Born: date and place unknown
Died: c. 200 B.C.E.; place unknown
Principal war: Second Punic War
Principal battle: Metaurus River (207 B.C.E.)
Military significance: After an unspectacular early military career, Nero, as consul in 207 B.C.E., led a brilliant, unexpected forced march to join forces with his fellow consul and defeat a relief force under Hasdrubal at the Metaurus River, thus preventing reinforcements from reaching Hannibal.

Gaius Claudius Nero first appears in Roman history in 216 B.C.E. as a cavalry officer serving under Marcus Claudius Marcellus at Nola, where he failed to carry out his assignment and was censured. As praetor in 212 B.C.E., he was sent to Capua to participate in its siege and remained there as propraetor until the city's fall in 211. Reassigned to a command in Spain, he entrapped forces of the Carthaginian commander Hasdrubal, but was tricked into allowing the enemy to escape.

Elected consul for 207 B.C.E., he was given command of forces facing Hannibal in southern Italy, where he received intercepted letters from Hasdrubal to his brother Hannibal detailing an attempt to reman Hannibal's forces. Keeping Hannibal in the dark about his whereabouts, Nero rushed his troops to the north to join with his fellow consul and meet the forces of Hasdrubal at the Metaurus River. The battle resulted in a complete Roman victory, and Nero returned south before Hannibal realized that he had been absent.

Resources
Broughton, T. R. *The Magistrates of the Roman Republic*. Vol. 1. Reprint. Atlanta: Scholars Press, 1986.
Caven, Brian. *The Punic Wars*. New York: St. Martin's Press, 1980.
Lazenby, J. F. *Hannibal's War: A Military History of the Second Punic War*. Warminster, England: Aris & Phillips, 1978.
Peddie, John. *Hannibal's War*. Gloucestershire, England: Sutton Press, 1997.

See also: Hannibal; Marcellus, Marcus Claudius; Punic Wars.

Donald M. Poduska

Neutrality

Neutrality is a state's abstention from participation in hostilities between other states. Although the concept of neutral rights dates to antiquity, its maintenance has usually been grounded in military strength. The daunting defenses of Switzerland allowed that nation to remain neutral during World War I (1914-1918) and World War II (1939-1945), for no one was willing to risk such a difficult invasion. Small and ill-prepared nations have often found it difficult to defend their neutrality. As the Athenians told the inhabitants of Melos in 416 B.C.E., "The strong do as they will and the weak suffer what they must."

Nevertheless, there have been international attempts to codify the laws of neutrality—most significantly, the Declaration of Paris of 1856 and the Hague Convention of 1907. According to the resultant rules, nations wishing to remain impartial to all warring parties should issue a declaration of neutrality. Such a declaration is not, however, required by international law. Moreover, a neutral state may repeal or modify its position of neutrality during hostilities—provided no bias is shown to either belligerent.

Jeremiah Taylor

Neville's Cross

Type of action: Ground battle in the Hundred Years' War
Date: October 17, 1346
Location: Neville's Cross, Durham, England
Combatants: Scottish vs. English armies
Principal commanders: *British*, Queen Phillipa of Hainaut (c. 1314-1369); *Scottish*, King David II (1324-1371)
Result: Successful British defeat of the Scots

The Scots, led by King David II, invaded England in 1346. In October, the Scots advanced on Durham, partly with the aim of helping the French by diverting English king Edward III from the Siege of Calais. They met the English, led by Edward's wife, Queen Phillipa of Hainaut, at Neville's Cross, just outside of Durham, on October 17. Several chroniclers described the battle, although many of the details have been disputed. When the Scots hesitated, not wanting to attack because of the terrain, English archers were sent in to goad them into action. David chose not to disperse the archers with a cavalry charge. Instead, he ordered an advance that brought his first two divisions into awkward positions. The first division fell back on the second, which was commanded by David. His third division fled. David was wounded and eventually captured.

Significance
The battle at Neville's Cross marked an important stage in the long conflict between the English and the Scots. The capture of David effectively ended the Scottish raids on northern England.

Resources
Cantor, Norman F. *The Civilization of the Middle Ages*. New York: HarperCollins, 1993.
Dickenson, J. W. *The Battle of Neville's Cross*. Durham, N.C.: Ian Copinger, 1991.
Fines, John. *Who's Who in the Middle Ages*. New York: Stein and Day, 1970.

Holmes, George. *The Oxford Illustrated History of Medieval Europe.* New York: Oxford University Press, 1988.

SEE ALSO: Anglo-Scottish Wars of 1290-1388; Hundred Years' War.

Maryanne Barsotti

NEW ORLEANS

TYPE OF ACTION: Ground battle in the War of 1812
DATE: January 8, 1815
LOCATION: Chalmette, Louisiana
COMBATANTS: 3,000 Americans v. 6,000 British troops
PRINCIPAL COMMANDERS: *American*, General Andrew Jackson (1767-1845); *British*, Major General Sir Edward Pakenham (1778-1815)
RESULT: Stunning British defeat

Preliminary skirmishes of this battle began on December 23, 1814, when General Andrew Jackson directed a night attack on the British camp south of New Orleans. An artillery duel followed on January 1, 1815. The British, led by Major General Sir Edward Pakenham, began their attack at daybreak on January 8. Jackson had directed his men to construct breastworks at Chalmette, six miles south of New Orleans. When the British neared their line, the Americans opened a deadly fire from Kentucky and Tennessee riflemen, local militiamen, and cannons provided by the pirate Jean Laffite. The British were soon defeated, but the artillery kept firing until 2:30 P.M. British casualties reached almost 2,000, and U.S. casualties numbered 71, including 7 killed.

SIGNIFICANCE

If they prevailed in this battle, the British intended to reopen negotiations of a peace treaty with the Americans and demand possession of the Mississippi Valley. Although the ambassadors completed the treaty on December 24, 1814, before the battle occurred, the outcome was significant because it prevented the British from revoking the agreement. After the U.S. victory, both countries dutifully ratified the treaty.

General Andrew Jackson led the Americans to victory over the British at New Orleans. (Library of Congress)

RESOURCES

Albright, Harry. *New Orleans: Battle of the Bayous*. New York: Hippocrene Books, 1990.

The Buccaneer. Fiction feature. Kartes Video Communications, 1958.

DeGrummond, Jane Lucas. *The Baratarians and the Battle of New Orleans*. Baton Rouge, La.: Legacy, 1979.

Reilly, Robin. *The British at the Gates: The New Orleans Campaign in the War of 1812*. New York: Putnam, 1974.

Remini, Robert. *The Battle of New Orleans*. New York: Viking, 1999.

SEE ALSO: 1812, War of; Jackson, Andrew.

Jerry P. Sanson

NEY, MICHEL

FULL NAME: Michel Ney
ALSO KNOWN AS: Bravest of the Brave
BORN: January 10, 1769; Saarlouis, France
DIED: December 7, 1815; Paris, France
PRINCIPAL WARS: Wars of the First to Seventh Coalitions
PRINCIPAL BATTLES: Hohenlinden (1800), Elchingen (1805), Jena (1806), Eylau (1807), Friedland (1807), Borodino (1812), Retreat from Moscow (1812), Waterloo (1815)
MILITARY SIGNIFICANCE: Noted for courage, thorough training of his men, and a hot temper, Ney was an outstanding battle commander, although he suffered weaknesses at higher army command levels.

Enlisting in the French forces in 1787, Michel Ney earned a commission in October, 1792. Combat in the Rhine and German theaters brought promotion to brigadier general in August, 1796, and to division general in March, 1799. He distinguished himself in the Battle of Hohenlinden in 1800. Napoleon sent Ney as military and political emissary to Switzerland in 1802 and in 1803 gave him command of the Sixth Corps, which Ney trained to high proficiency. His attack on Elchingen (October 14, 1805) led to the surrender of Ulm. Ney served in Germany and Russia (1805-1807), playing significant roles in the battles at Jena (1806), Eylau (1807), and Friedland (1807), and in Spain (1808-1811). His service at Borodino (1812) earned him the title Prince of the Moscow River. His daring command of the rear guard on the retreat from Moscow (1812) saved thousands of French soldiers, for which Napoleon nicknamed him "Bravest of the Brave." Ney fought in Germany in 1813 and in France in 1814.

In 1814, he led other marshals in forcing Napoleon's abdication. However, he rallied to Napoleon in the Hundred Days and commanded unsuccessfully at Waterloo in 1815. The Bourbons convicted him of treason and executed him.

RESOURCES

Chandler, David G. *The Campaigns of Napoleon*. New York: Macmillan, 1966.

Duffy, Christopher. *Borodino and the War of 1812*. London: Seeley, Service, 1972.

Foster, John T. *Napoleon's Marshal: The Life of Michel Ney*. Fairfield, N.J.: Morrow, 1968.

Horricks, Raymond. *Marshal Ney: The Romance and the Real*. New York: Hippocrene, 1982.

Muir, Rory. *Tactics and the Experience of Battle in the Age of Napoleon*. New Haven, Conn.: Yale University Press, 1998.

Napoleon Invades Russia. Documentary. Ambrose Video, 1997.

The Napoleonic Wars. Documentary. Films for the Humanities and Sciences, 2000.

SEE ALSO: Borodino; French Revolutionary Wars; Friedland; Hohenlinden; Jena and Auerstädt; Moscow, retreat from; Napoleon I; Napoleonic Wars; Quatre Bras; Waterloo.

James K. Kieswetter

NEZ PERCE WAR

AT ISSUE: Whether several bands of Nez Perce should be forcibly relocated to reservations
DATE: June 15-October 5, 1877
LOCATION: Eastern Oregon, Idaho, Wyoming, Montana
COMBATANTS: U.S. troops vs. Nez Perce
PRINCIPAL COMMANDERS: *United States*, Colonel Nelson A. Miles (1839-1925), General Oliver O. Howard (1830-1909); *Nez Perce*, Chief Joseph (c. 1840-1904), Chief Looking Glass (c. 1823-1877)

PRINCIPAL BATTLES: White Bird Canyon, Clearwater, Big Hole, Bear Paws
RESULT: U.S. victory; Nez Perce removed to Fort Leavenworth, Kansas

BACKGROUND

The first treaty between the United States and the Nez Perce was signed in 1855. The Nez Perce were assured that their homelands would be protected, but white settlement nevertheless increased. In addition, in 1860, gold was discovered on their reservation. An 1863 treaty reduced reservation lands, but half of the autonomous Nez Perce bands refused to accept the new provisions—including the Looking Glass band that already lived within the new boundaries. These groups became known as nontreaty Indians.

In 1877, only a year after General George A. Custer's defeat at Little Bighorn, a rumor circulated that the Wallowa Nez Perce were planning a massacre. General Oliver O. Howard demanded that all nontreaty Nez Perce move to the reservation. Committed to peace, tribal leaders reluctantly agreed, planning to arrive by the deadline of June 14, 1877. While the group camped and rested two miles from the reservation, renegade tribesmen conducted two raids against nearby settlers, precipitating war.

ACTION

In the Nez Perce War, U.S. troops led by General Howard pursued five bands of autonomous but allied Nez Perce Indians for more than 1,300 miles. The fleeing bands believed they would be safe if they outdistanced Howard, but throughout the journey, they were attacked by other troops.

The first battle at **White Bird Canyon** (June 17, 1877) involved bands led by Chief Joseph, Toolhoolhoolzote, and others against an advance party of 100 men led by Captain David Perry. The Americans shot at Nez Perce carrying a truce flag, and fighting ensued. More than 30 of the troops died, but no Nez Perce were killed. Howard, fearing a general Indian uprising, waited at Lapwai, Idaho, for reinforcements. Then, with around 400 soldiers, he began pursuit. The Nez Perce led him on chases through difficult terrain, a tactic they continued throughout the war. Howard sent a small force to attack a nontreaty band already on the reservation. Their shocked leader, Looking Glass, then united his people with Joseph and the others.

The Nez Perce were now at their strongest, with 180 to 190 warriors. All decided to head for Montana, but while they were still on the **Clearwater** River (July 11-12), Howard attacked. After a twenty-four-hour battle in which only 13 soldiers and 4 warriors died, the Indians retreated. The Nez Perce traveled up the Lolo Trail to Montana, looping south to **Big Hole** (August 9-10), where they were surprised by an attack led by Colonel John Gibbon, who ordered the slaughter of women and children. The Nez Perce losses exceeded 90, while U.S. Army losses were near 30. Nevertheless, the tribe escaped, traveling south and east through Yellowstone Park and then north, hoping to join Sitting Bull in Canada. Forty miles from the Canadian border, troops led by Captain Nelson A. Miles attacked at **Bear Paws** (September 30-October 5). During this battle, General Howard arrived with his troops. Outnumbered, with Toolhoolhoolzote and Looking Glass dead, Chief Joseph surrendered, uttering his now famous words, "I will fight no more forever." During the night, White Bird led nearly 200 Nez Perce in an escape to Canada.

AFTERMATH

In all nearly 400 people died in a war that cost the United States more than $1 million. Chief Joseph and about 400 Nez Perce were sent to Kansas and later Oklahoma, where many died of disease.

RESOURCES

Beal, Merrill D. *"I Will Fight No More Forever": Chief Joseph and the Nez Perce War.* Seattle: University of Washington Press, 1966.

A Clash of Cultures; "I Will Fight No More Forever." Documentary. Discovery Channel, 1993.

Haines, Francis. *The Nez Perces: Tribesmen of the Columbia Plateau.* Norman: University of Oklahoma Press, 1963.

Josephy, Alvin M., Jr. *The Nez Perce Indians and the Opening of the Northwest.* New York: Houghton Mifflin, 1997.

Lavender, David. *Let Me Be Free: The Nez Perce Tragedy.* Norman: University of Oklahoma Press, 1999.

Sacred Journey of the Nez Perce. Documentary. Idaho Public Television, 1996.

See also: American Indian wars; Joseph, Chief; Miles, Nelson A.

Margaret A. Dodson

Nicaragua, Walker's invasion of

At issue: Independence of Nicaragua
Date: 1855-1857
Location: Nicaragua
Combatants: William Walker vs. Nicaraguan conservatives
Principal commanders: William Walker (1824-1860); *Nicaraguan*, Ponciano Corral (d. 1855)
Principal battles: Virgin Bay, Granada
Result: Nicaraguan victory preserved its independence

Background

Since its independence, Nicaragua had been subject to civil wars between liberals in León and conservatives in Granada. After the U.S. annexation of California in 1848 and the gold rush the following year, the United States became more interested in Nicaragua because it provided a relatively safe transit route. Commodore William K. Vanderbilt organized a profitable transportation system through Nicaragua for passengers going from the eastern United States to California. The idea of manifest destiny was still popular among many U.S. citizens, and people in the South thought of Central America and Cuba as areas of expansion for slavery.

Action

After an unsuccessful attempt in 1853-1854 to invade Mexico, William Walker decided to invade Nicaragua. Walker received a land grant from Francisco Castellon, the liberal claimant to the presidency of Nicaragua. Recruits were enlisted as colonists to circumvent the U.S. neutrality laws. Walker was able to recruit only 58 men, who sailed to Nicaragua on May 4, 1855. They landed unopposed at Realejo (later Corinto), on the Pacific Coast, and marched to León. Walker decided to capture Rivas, which controlled the western end of the transit route, where Walker could receive men and supplies from the United States. The Americans faced 500 defenders and were forced to retreat to León. After recruiting 125 Nicaraguans, Walker marched to **Virgin Bay** (1855) and won a battle that impressed everyone, especially Nicaraguans.

Reinforced from the United States, Walker took the offensive and mounted a surprise attack on **Granada** (1855). His victory made Walker master of Nicaragua and a hero to many Americans. Walker adopted a conciliatory policy. He did not

Milestones in Walker's Invasion of Nicaragua

Date	Event
May 4, 1855	U.S. soldier of fortune William Walker, along with fifty-eight others, heads for Nicaragua, invited by a local faction.
May, 1855-April, 1856	Walker takes control of Granada and becomes president of Nicaragua.
May, 1856	U.S. president Franklin Pierce recognizes Walker's regime, but Walker's actions are opposed by Cornelius Vanderbilt, who seeks monopoly control over travel across Nicaragua.
May 1, 1857	Walker surrenders to the U.S. naval authorities and is taken to San Francisco.
November 25, 1857	Walker returns to Nicaragua but is soon deported.
August, 1860	Walker enters Honduras but is arrested by British naval control and turned over to the Honduran government.
September 12, 1860	After a trial, Walker is executed by firing squad.

execute the defeated or confiscate their property. Walker made himself commander in chief of the Nicaraguan army, but he also carefully kept command of the American army, the decisive military element in the country.

Walker made a major mistake at the end of 1855 when he seized the property of the Accessory Transit Company. Vanderbilt, the major stockholder of the company, sent all passengers to Panama, ending revenue for Nicaragua, and persuaded the British to blockade Greytown, Nicaragua's major Caribbean port. Great Britain also sent rifles and ammunition to Costa Rica for an invasion of Nicaragua.

Costa Rica invaded Nicaragua without a declaration of war, won a decisive victory, and occupied Rivas and Virgin Bay, thus controlling the transit route. Walker counterattacked successfully. The Costa Ricans returned home, and Walker was more popular than ever.

In June, 1856, Walker won the presidential election and issued two unpopular decrees. One made English the second language, and the other confiscated the property of supporters of the Costa Rican invasion. Most of the confiscated property was purchased by Americans, disappointing the poor, who had thought they would benefit.

In September, 1856, Walker nullified part of the constitution. He was accused of attempting to reintroduce slavery, and not only the poor in Nicaragua but also the antislavery North in the United States objected.

Honduras, El Salvador, Guatemala, Costa Rica, and dissident Nicaraguans joined in an invasion from the north and the south. Vanderbilt and the British aided with supplies and money. When Costa Rica seized the transit route, Walker was no longer able to get supplies and men from the United States. Walker, isolated in the country's interior, surrendered in late April, 1857, to the commander of the U.S. squadron that had been sent to Nicaragua. He and his men were evacuated to the United States.

Walker tried to invade Nicaragua twice more. In the second attempt, he surrendered to the commander of a British naval squadron, who turned him over to Nicaraguan authorities. He was tried, convicted, and executed at Trujillo on September 12, 1860.

Aftermath

Nicaragua did not become a dependency of the United States. The invasion confirmed the Central American nations' distrust of the United States. Great Britain extended its control of the Caribbean coast of Central America at the expense of the United States.

Resources

Bruns, Roger, and Bryan Kennedy. "El Presidente Gringo." *American History Illustrated* 23 (February, 1989): 14.

Gerson, Noel B. *Sad Swashbuckler: The Life of William Walker.* New York: Thomas Nelson, 1976.

Rosengarten, Frederic, Jr. *Freebooters Must Die: The Life and Death of William Walker, the Most Illustrious Filibuster of the Nineteenth Century.* Wayne, Pa.: Haverford House, 1976.

Walker, William. *War in Nicaragua.* Detroit, Mich.: Blaine Etheridge Books, 1971.

See also: Latin American Wars of Independence; Nicaraguan Civil War of 1925-1933; Walker, William.

Robert D. Talbott

Nicaraguan Civil War of 1925-1933

At issue: Political control of Nicaragua; U.S. involvement in Nicaraguan internal affairs
Date: 1925-1933
Location: Nicaragua
Combatants: U.S. Marines and Conservative faction vs. Liberal faction
Principal commanders: *Liberal*, José María Moncada (1912-1958), Augusto César Sandino (1895-1934); *Nicaraguan National Guard*, Anastasio Somoza García (1896-1956)
Result: Sandino laid down his arms after the withdrawal of the U.S. Marines in 1933; within months, Somoza had Sandino killed and initiated a dictatorship that lasted until 1980

Background

The origins of the Nicaraguan Civil War date back to 1909, when Liberal president José Santos Zelaya resigned because of American diplomatic

U.S. Marines pose with a captured flag of Augusto César Sandino, the rebel leader. (National Archives)

pressure and strong political opposition from the Conservative faction. The United States disliked Zelaya because he had agreed to let Germany build a canal across Nicaragua that would compete with the canal being built by the United States across Panama. In 1909, U.S. Marines arrived in Nicaragua with the excuse of protecting American lives and property, which hastened Zelaya's departure. Under the watchful eye of the United States, the Liberals and Conservatives agreed to alternate occupation of the presidency and created a coalition government. Despite the agreement, in 1912 the United States refused to recognize the right of a Liberal politician to become president, prompting a Liberal rebellion against the Conservative government of Adolfo Díaz. Díaz quickly requested military assistance and 2,700 U.S. Marines landed in Nicaragua. Although the number of soldiers fluctuated, a Marine presence remained to keep Conservatives in power until mounting opposition in the United States led to their removal in 1925.

ACTION

Soon after the Marines' departure, new Conservative-Liberal hostilities erupted, which forced U.S. officials once again to send the Marines to restore peace. Although the primary Liberal leader, General José María Moncada, focused attention on fighting Conservative opponents, another Liberal leader, Augusto César Sandino, sought to rid Nicaragua of both U.S.-trained Nicaraguan forces and U.S. Marines. Sandino, a strong nationalist, envisioned a Nicaragua without constant U.S. interference, and acting without Moncada's aid or support, he led a guerrilla war against the Marines. Mounting U.S. losses prompted American politicians to push for an end to the fighting. In 1927, American negotiators created a deal that settled the differences between the Conservatives and Liberals, but Sandino refused to accept the terms and continued his guerrilla war. Under U.S. supervision, an election was held in 1928, and Moncada became president. Despite the Liberals' seizure of power, Sandino continued to fight with the support of a Nicaraguan peasant population that was also tired of U.S. interference. A countrywide network of peasant rebels continued to inflict losses on both the Marines and U.S.-owned mines, despite vigorous pursuit by the Marines.

Meanwhile, U.S. military advisers trained an American-funded Nicaraguan National Guard. The advisers intended for the National Guard to be an apolitical peacekeeping force that would take over the Marines' role of stopping Conservative-Liberal warfare. In 1933, isolationist beliefs in the United States, coupled with the change in foreign policy under President Franklin D. Roosevelt, led to the Marines' withdrawal from Nicaragua. Having fulfilled his primary goal of ridding Nicaragua of the United States, Sandino agreed to lay down his weapons in exchange for a promise that he and his soldiers would be left alone. Although the government granted his soldiers land and freedom from persecution, Sandino refused to surrender because he felt that the National Guard was unconstitutional and distrusted its ambitious leader, Anastasio Somoza. In February, 1934, Nicaragua's president invited Sandino to Managua, where they agreed that the guard's power would be diminished and planned to remove Somoza from its command. Afraid of the threat to his power, Somoza arranged for National Guardsmen to kidnap and kill Sandino while he was returning from dinner with the president. Sandino's death ended the civil war.

Aftermath

Within a month, guardsmen killed the majority of Sandino's followers. Nicaragua's president opposed the actions, but Somoza ignored his demands to stop. Once in command of the country's only military group and without a strong political opponent, Somoza appointed himself president in 1937 and began a dictatorial dynasty that ruled Nicaragua until 1980.

Resources

Bermann, Karl. *Under the Big Stick: Nicaragua and the United States Since 1848*. Boston: South End Press, 1986.

Diederich, Bernard. *Somoza and the Legacy of U.S. Involvement in Central America*. New York: Dutton, 1981.

Ramírez, Sergio. *Sandino, the Testimony of a Nicaraguan Patriot: 1921-1934*. Princeton, N.J.: Princeton University Press, 1990.

See also: Sandino, Augusto César.

William Bridges

Nicaraguan Civil War of 1977-1989

At issue: U.S.-backed overthrow of the leftist Nicaraguan government, a regime backed by the Soviet Union and Cuba

Date: January, 1977-May, 1989

Location: Rural eastern Nicaragua

Combatants: U.S.-backed counterrevolutionaries vs. the Soviet Union- and Cuba-backed Nicaraguan army

Result: The Contra campaign caused so much damage to the Nicaraguan economy that the president, Daniel Ortega, agreed to open elections in exchange for rebel disarmament

Background

On July 19, 1979, Nicaragua's president, Anastasio Somoza II, left the country for exile abroad. The Somoza family had controlled Nicaragua for forty-three years. Somoza's father, the first Anastasio Somoza, had seized control of the country after the departure of an American occupying force. He ruled until 1956, when he was assassinated. His other son, Luis Anastasio Somoza Debayle, took over the helm until his death of natural causes in 1967. Luis's younger brother, Anastasio II, then the commander of the national guard, succeeded him.

The Somoza family ruled with an iron fist. It controlled the country both politically and economically. Any attempt on the part of citizens to seek a democratic revision of the political system failed until, finally, a group of rebels calling themselves the Sandinistas (after a hero of the resistance to the U.S. occupation of the 1920's, Augusto César Sandino) managed to wrest control away from the Somozas. Part of their success could be attributed to the decision by the United States to stop supporting the Somoza family.

Initially the new Sandinista government received support from both the United States and other Latin American countries, such as Costa Rica, Panama, Venezuela, and Mexico. Very soon after the Sandinistas' accession to power, they formed strong alliances with both Cuba and the Soviet Union. Under the leadership of the newly formed Sandinista Directorate, Nicaragua was reorganized along Marxist/Leninist lines.

The Directorate set up a new structure for the army under close party supervision, established a government-controlled economy, and began the takeover of much of the private sector. The Sandinistas excluded non-Marxist opposition leaders from participation in the government. They arrested and imprisoned those they felt had Somocista leanings. The new regime invited hundreds of Cuban doctors, teachers, and military and security advisers to help them rule the country.

Soon an exodus of economically powerful private citizens began. The United States government also looked on the increasingly Soviet-oriented Sandinista government with some concern. It saw another leftist regime like the one that controlled Cuba beginning to take shape.

Action

Opposition developed quickly to the Sandinista regime. Among the immediate targets of the Sandinistas were the former members of Somoza's National Guard. Some were sought out and killed immediately by vengeful supporters of the new government. Others suffered arrest and imprisonment for serving in the National Guard. Many escaped the country. They then sought to regroup to begin a military campaign against the Sandinista state.

Many noncommunist allies of the new regime, before it took over the government, became disillusioned quickly when they observed the Marxist path chosen by the Sandinistas. They had allied themselves with the leftists, thinking that democracy would be restored to the country following years under the yoke of the Somoza dictatorship. The Sandinista alliance with the Cubans and the Soviets alienated this liberal segment of Nicaraguan society. Business owners also learned that their activities would now be closely controlled by the government. Many lost their business enterprises as a result of the authoritarian approach adopted by the Sandinistas in dealing with the country's economy.

Nicaragua's neighbors also became worried by the actions of the government. The Sandinistas publicly supported the leftist rebels in neighboring El Salvador and sent arms across the border to the Salvadoran opposition trying to overthrow the government there. Costa Rica and Honduras, alarmed at the aggressive stance taken by the Sandinistas, began to ignore the military buildup of the Nicaraguan dissidents on their respective borders.

Soon both former National Guard soldiers and disaffected former Sandinistas began a series of raids into Nicaragua's eastern rural provinces. The U.S. Central Intelligence Agency began to furnish both training and arms to what came to be called the Contras. At the same time, the Soviet Union poured a half a billion dollars' worth of sophisticated military equipment into a massive buildup of the Sandinista Nicaraguan army.

The major successes achieved by the Contras came through the raids of their troops operating out of Honduran bases north of the Nicaraguan border. The American-backed invaders received a great deal of support from the peasants living in the rural areas. The native population living along the Atlantic coast also refused to support the Sandinistas. Despite its heavy weaponry and air superiority, the Sandinista army could not defeat the elusive Contra raiders. Soon the Nicaraguan economy began to crumble, a victim of both the Contras and governmental ineptitude.

Aftermath

Finally, under the auspices of the other Central American governments, the Sandinistas signed a peace treaty with the Contras. In 1989, they agreed to schedule presidential elections monitored by outside independent observers. In February, 1990, in the elections that followed, the Sandinista president, Ortega, suffered a crushing defeat at the hands of Violeta Chamorro, the candidate of the Unified Nicaraguan Opposition. Although the Sandinistas still represented a powerful political faction in Nicaraguan life, their rule of the country ended with the election of Chamorro.

Resources

Christian, Shirley. *Nicaragua: Revolution in the Family.* New York: Vintage Books, 1985.

Garvin, Glenn. *Everybody Had His Own Gringo: The CIA and the Contras*. Washington, D.C.: Brassey's, 1992.

SEE ALSO: Nicaraguan Civil War of 1925-1933.

Carl Henry Marcoux

NICEPHORUS II PHOCAS

BORN: c. 912; Cappadocia
DIED: December 10/11, 969; Constantinople
PRINCIPAL WAR: Ḥamdānid War
PRINCIPAL BATTLES: Tarsus (965), Cyprus (965), Antioch (969), Aleppo (969)
MILITARY SIGNIFICANCE: From 963 to 969, Byzantine emperor Nicephorus II annexed Cyprus and most of northern Syria, revived Byzantine heavy armored cavalry, and provoked a Russian attack on his overbearing neighbor, Bulgaria.

A Byzantine nobleman, Nicephorus II Phocas rose to become a senior army commander fighting in Crete and northern Syria. In 963, he seized the Byzantine throne when the emperor, Romanus II, died unexpectedly. Nicephorus began a systematic campaign against the Ḥamdānid Amirs of Syria. After breaking through the Cicilian range with 40,000 troops, he laid siege to the fortress town of Tarsus. Tarsus fell in 965, and that same year, the imperial fleet captured the island of Cyprus. The emperor besieged Antioch in 966, occupying the city in 969. That same year, Aleppo capitulated and became a Byzantine vassal. Victories in the Middle East, however, were partly offset by the Russian conquest of Bulgaria. Nicephorus had encouraged the pagan Rus to punish the Bulgarians for demanding tribute from Byzantium, but Russian occupation would present Constantinople with a greater menace in the next decade. Niceophorus was assassinated in 969 by John I Zimisces.

Nicephorus II presided over the adoption of heavy cavalry lancers in the Byzantine army. His military tactics emphasized offensive deployment by heavy cavalry to shatter enemy formations and strike at the commanders while using infantry to anchor the defense. At the time, his tactics proved decisive against the light cavalry forces of the Syrians and Bulgars.

RESOURCES
Haldon, John. *Warfare, State, and Society in the Byzantine World, 565-1204*. London: University College London Press, 1999.
McGeer, E. *Sowing the Dragon's Teeth: Byzantine Warfare in the Tenth Century*. Washington D.C.: Dumbarton Oaks, 1995.
Nicephorus II Phocas. *On Skirmishing. Three Byzantine Military Treatises*. Washington D.C.: Dumbarton Oaks, 1985.

SEE ALSO: Bulgarian-Byzantine Wars; Byzantine Empire; Byzantine-Muslim Wars; Cavalry; John I Zimisces.

Weston F. Cook, Jr.

NICHOLAS, GRAND DUKE

FULL NAME: Nikolai Nikolaevich Romanov
BORN: November 18, 1856; St. Petersburg, Russia
DIED: January 5, 1929; Cap d'Antibes, France
PRINCIPAL WAR: World War I
PRINCIPAL BATTLES: Łódź (1914), Masurian Lakes (1914), Gorlice-Tarnow (1915)
MILITARY SIGNIFICANCE: Grand Duke Nicholas's lack of military experience and Russian inadequacies led to Russia's disastrous losses to Germany in World War I, causing the end of a dynasty.

The reactionary Grand Duke Nicholas had great influence on his cousin, Czar Nicholas II. In 1914, the czar unexpectedly appointed him commander in chief of Russian troops in World War I. His imposing figure (six feet, six inches tall) and stern demeanor earned him the respect and popularity of the troops, but his unfamiliarity with the Russian military conditions at the beginning of the war helped lead to its disastrous outcome. The Russians advanced easily against the Austrians. However, Nicholas's army could not stand up to the Germans, who won an easy victory at Tannenberg. During the winter of 1914-1915, the Germans occupied Poland. Nicholas participated in the victory at Łódź and the Russian defeats at Masurian Lakes and Gorlice-Tarnow. Historians disagree on how much blame for the loss should be attributed to Nicholas, but the court made him the scapegoat. In September, 1915, against the advice of his advisers, the czar personally replaced him, a disastrous move, which helped lead to the Bolshevik Revolution (1917-1921). In 1919, Nicholas escaped Russia on a British ship with other Romanovs. Even after his exile, many recognized Grand Duke Nicholas as head of the imperial family.

RESOURCES

Bezobrazov, Vladimir Mikhailovich. *Diary of the Commander of the Russian Imperial Guard, 1914-1917.* Boynton Beach, Fla.: Dramco, 1994.

Effect of World War I on Russia and Germany. Documentary. Open University, 1973.

Russia in World War I. Ten Days That Shook the World series. Documentary. Granada Television, 1971.

Rutherford, Ward. *The Ally: The Russian Army in World War I.* London: Gordon and Cremonesi, 1977.

Washburn, Stanley. *On the Russian Front in World War I: Memoirs of an American War Correspondent.* New York: R. Speller and Sons, 1982.

SEE ALSO: Gorlice-Tarnow; Hindenburg, Paul von; Ludendorff, Erich; Masurian Lakes; Tannenberg, 1914; World War I.

Frederick B. Chary

NICOPOLIS

TYPE OF ACTION: Ground battle in Turkish Wars of European Expansion
DATE: September 25, 1396
LOCATION: Bulgaria
COMBATANTS: Hungarians, Crusaders, Turks
PRINCIPAL COMMANDERS: *Hungarian*, Sigismund (1367-1437); *Turkish*, Sultan Bayezid I (1347-1403)
RESULT: Roman Catholic Europe failed to drive back the Turks, leaving them in control of the Balkans for the next five hundred years

When the Turks crushed the Serbs at Kosovo (June 15, 1389), they made themselves the dominant power in the Balkans. Western Christians, led by the new king of Hungary, Sigismund of Luxembourg, made plans to rescue the Christians there and to relieve the Muslim pressure on Constantinople by calling on his brother, Holy Roman emperor Wenceslas of Bohemia, and the pope to raise crusaders.

At this meeting, Burgundy was represented by Jean II le Meingre, known as Boucicault, and Enguerrand de Coucy and France by Jean de Nevers. There was a large contingent from Wallachia and volunteers from Poland, Germany, and Bohemia. Without proper siege machines, however, they could not take the strong fortress of Nicopolis except by starvation. While the crusaders spent their time drinking and gambling, Bayezid I hurried north from Constantinople.

SIGNIFICANCE

Sigismund, too young and feckless to control his army, had to acquiesce in the French and Burgundian demand to lead the attack. The knights routed the first units they met, but when completely exhausted, they came upon the Turkish army waiting just beyond the skyline. Sigismund and a handful of noble companions escaped down the river to Constantinople; only a handful of French nobles were ransomed.

RESOURCES

Aziz, Atiya. "The Crusade in the Fourteenth Century." In *A History of the Crusades.* Madison: University of Wisconsin, 1975.

_____. *The Crusade in the Later Middle Ages.* London: Metheuen, 1938.

Froissart, John. *The Chronicles of England, France, and Spain.* New York: Dutton, 1961.

Urban, William. *Tannenberg and After.* Chicago: Lithuanian Research and Studies Center, 1999.

SEE ALSO: Crusades; Hungarian-Turkish Wars; Kosovo; Turkish Wars of European Expansion.

William L. Urban

NIEUPORT

TYPE OF ACTION: Ground battle in the Dutch Wars of Independence
DATE: July 2, 1600
LOCATION: Near Nieuport (Nieuwpoort in Flemish), Spanish Netherlands (later Belgium)

COMBATANTS: 11,000 Dutch vs. 12,000 Spanish
PRINCIPAL COMMANDERS: *Dutch*, Prince Maurice of Nassau (1567-1625); *Spanish*, Albrecht VII, archduke of Austria (1559-1621)
RESULT: Dutch victory over the Spanish

Years of reorganizing the Dutch army resulted in numerous successes for Prince Maurice of Nassau in the 1590's. Beginning with the capture of Breda, he took one enemy stronghold after another in systematically planned actions. However, farther south, he was less successful. With reluctance, Maurice was persuaded to try to rouse the Flemings to repel their Spanish conquerors and reunite the northern and southern Netherlands.

At the end of June, 1600, Maurice deployed his army among sand dunes, near the coastal town of Nieuport, ten miles southwest of Ostend. On July 2, a Spanish army under Archduke Albrecht VII, moving inland to avoid the tide and enemy warships, clashed with the Dutch on broken ground near the North Sea. Weary from a twelve-hour march, the Spanish initially gained the upper hand. However, the Dutch adapted to the terrain more easily and their greater mobility resulted in a break in Albert's line. The Spanish retired with losses exceeding 4,000, double that of the Dutch.

SIGNIFICANCE

Despite his victory, Maurice was compelled to withdraw. The Flemings refused to join the revolt. Later, Ostend, the last Dutch garrison in the south, would surrender after a siege of more than three years. The outcome took even Maurice by surprise. The defeat revealed one area of military reform he had overlooked: intelligence. A bitter Maurice reluctantly agreed first to an armistice (1607) and then a twelve-year truce with Spain (1609). The Netherlands remained divided.

RESOURCES
Parker, Geoffrey. *The Dutch Revolt*. London: Penguin, 1990.
Rady, Martyn. *From Revolt to Independence*. London: Hodder & Stoughton, 1990.

SEE ALSO: Dutch Wars of Independence; Maurice of Nassau, Prince; Ostend, Siege of.

Randall Fegley

NIGERIA-BIAFRA CIVIL WAR

AT ISSUE: Secession of the nation of Biafra from Nigeria
DATE: July, 1967-January, 1970
LOCATION: Southeast Nigeria
COMBATANTS: Nigerian federal army vs. Biafran army
PRINCIPAL COMMANDERS: *Nigerian*, Yakubu Gowon (1934-   ); *Biafran*, Chukuemeka Odunegwu Ojukwu (1933-   )
RESULT: Biafra surrendered on January 15, 1970

BACKGROUND

The war in Biafra, along with the Congolese Civil War, sent a message to Africa and the world that postcolonial Africa was a violent region caught in the crosscurrent of powerful destabilizing forces. The war lasted from July, 1967, to January, 1970, and left permanent scars that continue to influence politics in Nigeria.

ACTION

Independent Nigeria encompassed three major ethnic groups, the Hausa, Yoruba, and Ibo. The Ibo originated in southeastern Nigeria and dominated the skilled professions throughout the nation. This created smoldering tension with the Hausa people of northern Nigeria. In 1966, violence erupted, and 40,000 Ibo died at the hands of Hausa mobs. As a result, a massive internal migration of Ibo to their southeastern homeland took place. Then, in 1967, a plan to reorganize Nigeria from three regions to twelve threatened to strip the Ibo of their political power. The Ibo reacted by establishing the independent state of Biafra, with Chukuemeka Odunegwu Ojukwu as its president, in a 30,000-square-mile area including 14 million people.

Military experts the world over predicted a quick defeat for Biafra. The British Broadcasting Corporation (BBC) believed it was unnecessary to send any reporters to Biafra and predicted the war would last only ten days. These predictions soon proved to be wildly inaccurate.

Biafra achieved major early success in the war for two reasons. First, the majority of senior army commanders in the federal army were Ibos who defected to Biafra. Second, the majority of Nigeria's journalists were Ibo, and they used their

Milestones in the Nigeria-Biafra Civil War

Date	Event
May 30, 1967	Led by Army Lieutenant Colonel Chukuemeka Odunegwu Ojukwu, Biafra secedes from Nigeria.
June 7, 1967	Colonel Yakubu Gowon moves to subdue the rebels; Biafran forces capture the nation's capital, Benia.
September, 1967-May, 1968	Nigerian federal forces take nearly half of Biafra but fail to reach the capital of Umuahia.
September, 1968	Nigerian troops capture Aba and Owerri; Biafrans lose access to the sea but maintain an airlift.
February-March, 1969	Biafran forces move toward Aba in an attempt to gain a seaport; both sides enter into a stalemate marked by bombing of Biafran targets.
June-December, 1969	A massive, well-armed Nigerian army attacks and destroys the Biafran forces.
January 15, 1970	Biafra surrenders; Colonel Ojukwu flees to the Ivory Coast.

skills to generate worldwide sympathy for the Biafran cause.

Biafran forces were able to take the offensive in the first weeks of the war. At one point, Biafran units were only one hundred miles from the federal capital of Lagos, with minimal resistance ahead of them. However, the Biafran commander suddenly halted the advance and declared his intention to establish an independent Yoruba nation.

Biafra in the long run faced numerous strategic obstacles to victory. The federal army, led by Yakubu Gowon, had the active support of Great Britain and the Soviet Union. The United States' declaration of neutrality undoubtedly hurt the Biafrans. The only nations willing to support Biafra were France, Portugal, and South Africa. The federal blockade meant that all supplies had to be airlifted to Biafra, the airlift being carried out using old planes under very hazardous conditions. The Biafrans also had to deal with a catastrophic refugee situation. Ibo civilians always fled from the advancing federal troops. During the last months of the war, millions of Ibos crammed into 3,000 square miles of Biafran territory.

The federal blockade and the refugee situation contributed to the tragic malnutrition that became synonymous with Biafra the world over. Both parties deserve some blame for the human-made famine. The federal leaders clearly hoped famine in Biafra would lead to a quick end to the hostilities. The federal officials agreed to allow humanitarian aid to Biafra only if it was inspected first in federal territory. The Biafran leaders stubbornly refused, stating that the procedure would be a violation of Biafra's sovereignty. Relief groups grew indignant and resorted to media campaigns to break down the barriers to humanitarian aid. In particular, Irish priests from the Holy Ghost Fathers were relentless in their media campaign for Biafra. News competition from Vietnam and the Middle East made coverage of Biafra sporadic, while the media technology of the time discouraged more extensive coverage. The fact that the BBC, the preeminent media resource for West Africa, was compelled by British politicians to maintain a pro-federal stance, sealed the fate of the Biafran worldwide public relations campaign.

Aftermath

In the last month of fighting, Biafra was pounded into submission on the ground and from the air, where Soviet Ilyushin bombers with Egyptian crews took advantage of federal air superiority. The last Biafran airfield fell on January 11, and Biafra surrendered on January 15, 1970.

The war in Biafra solved none of the problems of Nigeria and left deep and ugly ethnic divisions. The pattern of the Nigeria-Biafra War set the standard for numerous postcolonial wars in Africa, which have broken out with alarming regularity.

RESOURCES

Forsyth, Frederick. *News Out of Africa*. London: Heinemann, 1986.

Schwab, Peter, ed. *Biafra*. New York: Facts on File, 1971.

Thompson, Joseph. *American Policy and the Politics of American Famine*. Westport, Conn.: Greenwood Press, 1994.

SEE ALSO: Civil war; Gowon, Yakubu.

Michael John Polley

NIMEIRI, GAAFER MUHAMMAD AL-

ALSO KNOWN AS: Jaʿfar Muḥammad an-Numayrī; also spelled Nimeiri, Nimeiry, Nemery, Numeyri, Numayri

BORN: January 1, 1930; Wad Nubawi, Omdurman, Sudan

PRINCIPAL WAR: Sudanese Civil War

MILITARY SIGNIFICANCE: Nimeiri seized control of Sudan, but after his regime was overthrown, the country was left in economic bankruptcy and in a state of civil war.

Gaafer Muhammad al-Nimeiri was a graduate of Sudan Military College. During General Ibrahim Abboud's military dictatorship, Nimeiri served in the south (1959-1963). At the time of Nimeiri's coup (May 25, 1969), he was commander of the Gebeit Training School (1967-1969). Nimeiri and his fellow army officers, who planned the coup, were members of the Sudanese Free Officers Movement. The movement, made up of young army officers, initially aimed at improving government efficiency. After a failed attempt to topple Abboud in 1959, the Free Officers sought a revolutionary transformation of the Sudanese economy, society, and politics.

From 1970 onward, Nimeiri attempted to do just that. He confiscated, sequestered, or nationalized privately owned businesses and banks, established more aggressive tax collection measures, instituted land reform, and attempted to phase out native administration. In foreign affairs, the regime's policy was nonalignment, though its early links with communist countries implied the contrary.

The abortive communist coup of 1971, however, produced a swing to the right both in economics and politics. Legislation was passed (1971, 1974, 1976, 1980) to attract and protect foreign investment. Economic policies consistent with International Monetary Fund (IMF) doctrines were adopted to give confidence to potential investors, and communists were removed from government. Furthermore, the civil war in the south was ended by granting southerners autonomy in 1972, and the country's first permanent constitution was passed in 1973.

In later years, Nimeiri surrounded himself with opportunistic politicians and tolerated corruption. Before long, his achievements were destroyed. In 1985, his regime was overthrown in a popular uprising, leaving a legacy of civil war and a bankrupt economy.

RESOURCES

Khalid, Mansour. *The Government They Deserve: The Role of the Elite in Sudan's Political Evolution*. London: Kegan Paul International, 1990.

_____. *Nimeiri and the Revolution of Dis-May*. London: Kegan Paul International, 1985.

Niblock, Tim. *Class and Power in Sudan: The Dynamics of Sudanese Politics, 1898-1985*. New York: State University of New York Press, 1987.

O'Ballance, Edgar. *Sudan: Civil War and Terrorism, 1956-99*. New York: St. Martin's Press, 2000.

SEE ALSO: Sudanese Civil War.

Kenneth Okeny

NIMITZ, CHESTER W.

FULL NAME: Chester William Nimitz

BORN: February 24, 1885; Fredericksburg, Texas

DIED: February 20, 1966; Yerba Buena Island, San Francisco, California

PRINCIPAL WAR: World War II

PRINCIPAL BATTLES: Coral Sea (1942), Midway (1942), Leyte Gulf (1944), Iwo Jima (1945), Okinawa (1945)

In November, 1945, Chester W. Nimitz, standing on the deck of a submarine in Pearl Harbor, speaks during the ceremonies marking his transfer of command of the Pacific Fleet to Admiral Raymond A. Spruance, who stands behind him. (AP/Wide World Photos)

MILITARY SIGNIFICANCE: Admiral Nimitz was the master strategist of the "island hopping" campaign that defeated the Japanese.

Although he had no combat experience, Admiral Chester W. Nimitz was dispatched from Washington, D.C., to assume command of the Pacific Fleet in the aftermath of the Pearl Harbor disaster. Arriving in Hawaii on Christmas morning, 1941, he found anger rather than defeatism among navy personnel. He quickly launched aircraft carrier raids against Japanese-held Marshall and Gilbert Islands as well as the Doolittle bombing raid on Tokyo.

Many of Nimitz's advisers suggested attacking Japanese-held islands one by one, but Nimitz conceived the "island hopping" strategy that struck at major strongholds while bypassing minor ones. This strategy was highly successful because the minor islands were easy to capture after the central ones fell.

In the Battle of Coral Sea (1942), U.S. forces under Nimitz's overall command suffered heavier losses than the Japanese, but the enemy advance was stalled. At Midway (1942), his strategy resulted in Japanese losses of ships, airplanes, and pilots from which Japan never really recovered. At Leyte Gulf (1944), the U.S. fleet dealt a crushing blow that rendered the Japanese fleet powerless for the remainder of the war. In addition, Nimitz directed the capture of Iwo Jima (1945) and Okinawa (1945).

Following the war, Nimitz became chief of naval operations, exercising command over the entire U.S. Navy.

RESOURCES

America's Five-Star Heroes: Gods of War. Documentary. A&E Home Video, 1998.
Brink, Randall. *Nimitz: The Man and His Wars*. New York: Penguin USA, 2000.
Potter, E. B. *Nimitz*. Annapolis, Md.: U.S. Naval Institute, 1976.
Warner, Oliver. *Command at Sea*. New York: St. Martin's Press, 1976.

SEE ALSO: Coral Sea; Iwo Jima; Japanese military; Leyte Gulf; Midway; Okinawa; World War II.

Edwin G. Wiggins

NIVELLE, ROBERT

FULL NAME: Robert Georges Nivelle
BORN: October 15, 1856; Tulle, France
DIED: March 23, 1924; Paris, France
PRINCIPAL WAR: World War I
PRINCIPAL BATTLES: Marne (1914), Verdun (1916), Vimy Ridge (1917)

MILITARY SIGNIFICANCE: Nivelle's 1917 offensive failed to overwhelm German defenses and resulted in disaster for French forces. It proved the limitations of heavy artillery barrages and the superiority of entrenched machine gun positions in open terrain.

At the outbreak of World War I, Robert Nivelle was a colonel with more than a quarter-century of experience as an artillery officer serving in Algeria, Indochina, and China. He played a timely role in helping stop the German advance in the Battle of the Marne (1914) and was promoted in October, 1914, to brigadier general.

In command of the Third Corps, Nivelle was instrumental in halting the German advance during the early stages of the Battle of Verdun (1916). By May, 1916, he replaced General Henri-Philippe Pétain as commander of the Second Army at Verdun. An artillery tactician, Nivelle used creeping barrages of heavy artillery fire to decimate German lines, coupled with strong frontal assaults that recaptured Fort Doaumont and other key forts at Verdun. He immediately became a national hero for his role at Verdun, and by December, 1916, he was catapulted into the position of commander in chief of the French armies, replacing General Joseph-Jacques-Césaire Joffre.

Nivelle's extroverted personality and perfect English put him in good standing with David Lloyd George, the British prime minister, who gave his full support to Nivelle's plan to win the war using the same tactics that had led to success at Verdun. However, the German general staff was also fully aware of his plans, and when the "great breakthrough" on the Aisne front was launched in April, 1917, German forces had already withdrawn to a strong secondary line of trenches, leaving only observers to man the front lines. The French were easy targets for German troops returning to strategically placed machine gun nests. Although he lacked the element of surprise, Nivelle continued with the attack, which ultimately resulted in 120,000 French casualties. The British attack on the Aisne was also costly, but limited gains were made. Vimy Ridge, one of the strongest German positions on the western front, was taken on April 12, largely because of the fierce determination of Canadian infantry.

For France, the Nivelle offensive was an unmitigated disaster. Nivelle was replaced by Pétain on May 15, and by December, Nivelle was assigned to North Africa.

RESOURCES

Buffetaut, Yves. *The 1917 Spring Offensives: Arras, Vimy, Le Chemin Des Dames*. Paris: Histoire & Collections, 1997.

McKee, Alexander. *The Battle of Vimy Ridge*. New York: Stein & Day, 1967.

Spears, Edward. *Prelude to Victory*. London: J. Cape, 1939.

Travers, Timothy. *The Killing Ground: The British Army, the Western Front, and the Emergence of Modern Warfare*. London: Routledge, 1987.

SEE ALSO: Pétain, Henri-Philippe; Verdun; Vimy Ridge; World War I.

Irwin Halfond

NOGI, MARESUKE

BORN: November 11, 1849; Yamaguchi, Japan
DIED: September 13, 1912; Tokyo, Japan
PRINCIPAL WARS: Sino-Japanese War, Russo-Japanese War
PRINCIPAL BATTLES: Port Arthur (capture, 1894; siege, 1904-1905), Mukden (1905)
MILITARY SIGNIFICANCE: In the Sino-Japanese War, Nogi captured Port Arthur in one day. Assigned the same task in the Russo-Japanese War, he led a successful but costly six-month siege.

A samurai, Maresuke Nogi fought against the Tokugawa shogunate to help "restore" the Meiji emperor to power in 1868. In 1871, he was commissioned as a major in the newly formed Japanese army and helped suppress the Hagi (1876) and Satsuma (1877) Rebellions. Rising quickly through the ranks, he was promoted to major general in 1885. Nogi traveled to Germany where he studied the army (1886-1888). He retired because of illness but returned to fight in the Sino-Japanese War (1894-1895), participating in the capture of Port Arthur (1894). Nogi was then appointed governor general of the colony of Formosa/Taiwan (1896-1898), which he helped pacify. Nogi again retired, was recalled, and promoted to full general at the outbreak of the Russo-

Japanese War (1904-1905), during which his two sons were killed. He besieged Port Arthur (1904-1905) and participated in the Battle of Mukden (1905). He served as a military councillor of state and, in 1907, became a count and head of the Peers' School, an educational institution for the nobility, where the emperor appointed Nogi to personally instruct his grandson, Hirohito, who would become the Showa emperor. In accordance with the traditional samurai-lord relationship, Nogi and his wife committed seppuku (ritual suicide) on the day of the Meiji emperor's funeral.

RESOURCES

Lone, Stewart. *Army, Empire, and Politics in Meiji Japan.* Basingstoke: Macmillan, 2000.

Peattie, M. R. "The Last Samurai: The Military Career of Nogi Maresuke." *Princeton Papers in East Asian Studies: Japan* 1 (1972).

Scherer, James A. B. *Three Meiji Leaders: Ito, Tōgō, Nogi.* Tokyo: Hokuseido Press, 1936.

SEE ALSO: Mukden; Port Arthur, Siege of; Russo-Japanese War; Samurai; Sino-Japanese War.

Gregory C. Ference

NONGOVERNMENTAL ORGANIZATIONS' ROLES IN WARFARE

Nongovernmental and extranational organizations play a unique role in the exercise of modern warfare and in the resolution of war and violent conflicts.

A nongovernmental or extranational organization is a group consisting of several states or of members of many nationalities that works to bring international resources to bear on situations involving one or more nation-states. Nongovernmental organizations have taken the form of humanitarian agencies such as the International Committee of the Red Cross, diplomatic associations such as the League of Nations and the United Nations, military associations such as the North Atlantic Treaty Organization (NATO) and the Warsaw Pact, and economic/political organizations such as the Association of Southeast Asian Nations.

Nongovernmental organizations work in areas in which nations, for political, military, and economic reasons, are prohibited from acting or where they cannot act alone. Although nongovernmental organizations may participate in direct action initiatives, they most frequently take the form of consensus-building organizations. Nongovernmental organizations operate to unite disparate interests extranationally in a way that domestic politics would never allow.

EARLY NONGOVERNMENTAL ORGANIZATIONS

Among the earliest nongovernmental organizations to play a role in modern warfare were humanitarian organizations. In 1864, the International Committee of the Red Cross sponsored and lobbied for the adoption of the first Geneva Convention, the first international rules of war. The Red Cross has remained active in promoting standards of conduct in all types of warfare throughout the twentieth century.

International diplomatic organizations have also played a significant role in the resolution of warfare and in the maintenance of peace. Among the earliest Western nongovernmental organizations formed to maintain peaceful relations in the west was the League of Nations. Following World War I (1914-1918), the Allied nations formed the league to foster greater cooperation within Europe and to oversee the terms of surrender of Germany and her allies. At the Paris Peace Conference in 1919, the league approved its covenant and distributed its offices and powers among the member states. The headquarters of the League of Nations was established in Geneva, Switzerland. The league was seriously weakened however, when the U.S. Congress failed to ratify the Treaty of Versailles, which included its covenant. In the 1930's, the league proved powerless to respond to instances of German and Japanese aggression. The onset of World War II (1939-1945) eclipsed the League of Nations, which was unable to impose sanctions on nonmember states. The league was disbanded and was replaced by the United Nations in 1946.

AFTER WORLD WAR II

Following World War II, the number of nongovernmental organizations increased exponentially. Some of these organizations, such as the

Important Nongovernmental Organizations (NGOs)

Organization	Areas of Activity as of 2000	Dates of Engagement	International Role
Association of Southeast Asian Nations	11 Southeast Asian states	Since 1970's	Economic assistance, conflict resolution
Commonwealth of Independent States	12 former Soviet states	Founded in 1991	Economic assistance, military exchange
International Committee of the Red Cross	More than 50 countries	Founded in 1863	Humanitarian relief, human rights monitoring
North Atlantic Treaty Organization	Peacekeeping in the Balkan states	Since 1949	Peacekeeping, international security
Organization of American States	More than 15 Latin American and Caribbean states	Founded in 1948	Conflict resolution, drug control, economic aid
United Nations	More than 150 countries worldwide	Founded in 1946	Conflict resolution, peacekeeping, humanitarian aid, economic assistance

Red Cross, had a history of extragovernmental work dating back to the nineteenth century; however, most of these organizations were new. They were framed by the political limitations of the Cold War (1945-1991). They became either truly multinational, as did the United Nations, or developed almost completely bilateral orientations, as did NATO and the Warsaw Pact.

After the war, Western Europe and the United States became deeply concerned with stopping the spread of communism. However, neither the European nations nor the United States had the military strength to defeat the Soviet Union and its satellite states in open conflict. To provide a common front in the face of Soviet communist expansion, the Western nations formed a variety of political/military alliances that took the form of multinational nongovernmental organizations. In Europe and the United States, this alliance took the form of NATO. In South America, the United States sponsored the Organization of American States (OAS). The OAS charter was signed on April 30, 1948. Member nations (nearly all Latin American states at the time) promised, among other economic and political affirmations, to promote peace and the defense of the Western Hemisphere from outside aggression. Similar organizations developed within the following two decades in Africa (Association of African Unity) and Asia (Association of Southeast Asian Nations) that, to a greater or lesser extent, united member states in political, military, and economic alliances to prevent the spread of communism.

After the Cold War

Following the momentous events in 1989—the fall of the Berlin wall, the restructuring of communist governments in Eastern Europe, and the dissolution of the Soviet Union—new nongovernmental organizations developed to respond to the new political, humanitarian, and military situation. Old extragovernmental organizations such as NATO were restructured to respond to new multilateral challenges.

Rather than disunite, nations associated through anti-Soviet alliances during the Cold War have extended membership opportunities to former Cold War enemies. NATO has accepted Poland, the Czech Republic and other former Warsaw Pact nations into its alliance. Similarly, the Association of Southeast Asian Nations has allowed former Soviet- and Chinese-supported regimes under its economic and political/military umbrella.

New challenges have arisen that make cooperation more important in the post-Cold War era. Nongovernmental organizations are still involved in humanitarian relief, conflict resolution, and other roles as in the past, but they also have begun participating in human rights monitoring, sustainable development programming, and other modern goals. The role of nongovernmental and extranational organizations has expanded immensely since the mid-nineteenth century, when the Red Cross lobbied simply for the humanitarian care of prisoners. With new missions and new challenges, the role of extranational organizations will probably only increase as multilateral alliances become both necessary and regular in twenty-first century warfare.

Resources

Aall, Pamela. *NGOs and Conflict Management*. Washington, D.C.: United States Institute of Peace, 1996.

Archer, Clive. *International Organizations*. Rev. ed. London: Routledge, 1992.

Boissier, Pierre. *From Solferino to Tsushima: History of the International Committee of the Red Cross*. Geneva, Switzerland: Henri Dunant Institute, 1985.

Boli, John, and George M. Thomas, eds. *Constructing World Culture: International Nongovernmental Organizations Since 1875*. Stanford, Calif.: Stanford University Press, 1999.

Clark, John. *Democratizing Development: The Role of Voluntary Organizations*. West Hartford, Conn.: Kumarian Press, 1991.

Czempiel, Ernst Otto, and James Roseneau, eds. *Governance Without Government: Order and Change in World Politics*. Cambridge, England: Cambridge University Press, 1992.

Murphy, Craig. *International Organization and Industrial Change: Global Governance Since 1850*. New York: Oxford University Press, 1994.

Northedge, Frederick. *The League of Nations: Its Life and Times*. Leicester, England: Leicester University Press, 1988.

Rotberg, Robert I. *Vigilance and Vengeance: NGOs Preventing Ethnic Conflict in Divided Societies*. Washington, D.C.: Brookings Institution Press, 1996.

Turner, Bryan S. "Outline of a Theory of Human Rights." In *Citizenship and Social Theory*, edited by Bryan S. Turner. London: Sage, 1993.

Weiss, Thomas George, et al. *NGOs, the UN, and Global Governance*. Boulder, Colo.: Lynn Reinner, 1996.

See also: Cold War; Geneva Conventions; North Atlantic Treaty Organization; United Nations and conflict resolution.

Cynthia Mahmood and Geoffrey Wingard

Nördlingen

Type of action: Ground battle in the Thirty Years' War
Date: September 6, 1634
Location: Nördlingen, near Donauwörth on the Danube River (south central Germany)
Combatants: 25,000 Swedes and Germans (Protestant) vs. 35,000 Imperialists and Spanish (Catholic)
Principal commanders: *Swedish-German*, Swedish general Gustav Horn (1592-1649), Bernard, duke of Saxe-Weimar (1604-1639); *Habsburg/Imperial*, King Ferdinand of Hungary (1608-1657); *Spanish/Imperial*, Cardinal Prince Ferdinand of Spain
Result: Swedish-German armies were almost annihilated by the Imperial-Spanish armies, leaving the Habsburgs as virtual masters of the Holy Roman Empire

At the Battle at Nördlingen on September 6, 1634, Swedish-German forces were completely overwhelmed by combined Imperial-Spanish forces. Although they were outnumbered, the tactical plan was for General Gustav Horn to attack the Imperial right while Bernard, duke of Saxe-Weimar, pinned the Imperial left and prevented the shifting of forces. Despite the bravery of the Swedish troops, the Imperial-Spanish army, led by Ferdinand II, king of Hungary and Holy Roman emperor, and Cardinal Prince Ferdinand of Spain, used a strong natural position to repulse the poorly conceived attack. When Horn attempted to withdraw from his untenable position, Habsburg forces maintained contact at the Swedish rear. Simultaneously, Habsburg attacks on Bernard's position routed the Swedish-German right. Those troops then wheeled into Horn's flank and virtually annihilated the Swedes, killing more than 6,000 Swedish infantry. Of the entire Swedish-German army, only 11,000 later rejoined their units at Frankfurt. Habsburg losses were light, with but 1,200 casualties of 36,000 engaged.

SIGNIFICANCE

The Swedish defeat destroyed the army created by Gustavus II Adolphus and brought France into the Thirty Years' War. The war that followed left many areas of the Holy Roman Empire devastated and depopulated.

RESOURCES

Friedrichs, Christopher R. *Urban Society in an Age of War: Nördlingen, 1580-1720*. Princeton, N.J.: Princeton University Press, 1979.

Parker, Geoffrey. *European Soldiers, 1550-1650*. New York: Cambridge University Press, 1977.

Wedgwood, C. V. *The Thirty Years War*. London: Folio Society, 1999.

SEE ALSO: Gustavus II Adolphus; Richelieu, cardinal de; Thirty Years' War.

William S. Brockington, Jr.

NORMAN-BYZANTINE WARS

AT ISSUE: Defense of Byzantine Empire against conquest by southern Italian Normans
DATE: May, 1081-autumn, 1085; autumn, 1107-September, 1108
LOCATION: Southwestern Byzantine Empire (Albania and Greece)
COMBATANTS: Normans vs. Byzantines and Venetians
PRINCIPAL COMMANDERS: *Norman*, Robert Guiscard, duke of Apulia (c. 1015-1085), Bohemund, prince of Antioch (c. 1050/1058-1111); *Byzantine*, Emperor Alexius I Comnenus (1048-1118)
PRINCIPAL BATTLES: First Siege of Dyrrachium, Siege of Larissa, Corfu, Second Siege of Dyrrachium
RESULT: Normans beaten in both wars; Byzantine autonomy preserved

BACKGROUND

Adventurers from Normandy began the conquest of southern Italy and Sicily in the first half of the eleventh century. Norman Robert Guiscard, also known as Robert de Hauteville, emerged as the leader on the mainland. Along with Arab and Lombard land, in 1071, the last Byzantine holding in Italy fell to the Normans. Byzantine emperor Michael VII courted Robert with honors and offices, and Robert sent his daughter to marry Michael's infant son and heir. When Michael fell from power in 1078, Helen wound up in a monastery. Robert used this insult as an excuse to extend his power over the Byzantine Empire itself. After the Battle of Manzikert in 1071, Byzantine power had weakened in both the east and west. Held up by rebellious vassals, Robert delayed attacking the Byzantines until early 1081. By then, Alexius I Comnenus had seized the throne and begun a tentative defense.

ACTION

Robert's son Bohemund, also known as Bohémond, led a vanguard across the Adriatic. Shortly thereafter, in May, 1081, Robert's main fleet and army of 1,300 knights and thousands of infantry, arrived at Valona (Vlon) in modern Albania. The fleet proceeded to seize Corfu to the south, and the army to the north took Dyrrachium, the main port of Byzantine Illyria. Alexius had bargained with the Venetians for use of a fleet, and Venetian Doge Domenico Selva led it against the Norman fleet off of Dyrrachium. The victorious Venetians took **Dyrrachium**, and the Normans besieged it. Alexius arrived with a weak army of primarily mercenaries—including Anglo-Saxon Varangian guardsmen who hated the Normans—and suffered defeat at the hands of Robert, his warrior-wife Sichelgaita, and Bohemund on October 18, 1081. Dyrrachium held out until betrayed by a treacherous Venetian resident in February, 1082. Dyrrachium was at the western end of the Roman Via Egnatia, which linked the Adriatic Sea with Constantinople, and the Normans followed this across Illyria and Thessaly.

Meanwhile, Alexius was raising trouble in Robert's rear by rousing Norman nobles to rebel and the German king Henry IV to pressure the pope and the Norman state. He also seized Orthodox Church plates and treasures and had them melted down to finance a new army, which proved ineffective at first but successfully raised the Norman Siege of **Larissa** in the summer of

1083. Robert had returned to Italy in April, and now Bohemund was forced to retreat to Kastoria with an unpaid, dispirited, homesick army. Alexius's offers of bounties to men who would desert helped the Norman army melt away. When Bohemund returned to Italy to raise needed funds, his followers surrendered. Venetians quickly retook Dyrrachium and Corfu.

Robert returned, however, with 150 ships, outfoxed a Venetian fleet, and landed on **Corfu** (autumn, 1084), where he wintered. Typhus broke out, killing and incapacitating many Normans. Robert tried to join his son Roger in an attack on Cephallonia but died en route. Further progress was halted by bickering over inheritance.

Bohemund, prince of Antioch after the First Crusade, resumed the attack on the Byzantine Empire in 1107, arranging support from both English Henry I and French Philip I. In autumn, the Normans landed at Valona and proceeded to **Dyrrachium**, which they besieged until September, 1108. Famine, malaria, a blockading Venetian fleet, and the appearance of Alexius with an army broke the siege, and Bohemund signed the Treaty of Devol (1108).

Aftermath

The treaty formally recognized Bohemund as Alexius's vassal for Antioch and other Near Eastern territories. The Byzantine hold on the Balkans was strengthened, and further Italian invasions put off for forty years.

Resources

Norwich, John Julian. *The Normans in Sicily.* London: Penguin, 1992.

Sewter, E. R. A. *The Alexiad of Anna Comnena.* New York: Penguin, 1969.

Treadgold, Warren. *The History of the Byzantine State and Society.* Stanford, Calif.: Stanford University Press, 1999.

SEE ALSO: Alexius I Comnenus; Antioch; Byzantine Empire; Manzikert; Robert Guiscard; Sicilian-Byzantine Wars.

Joseph P. Byrne

Norman Conquests

AT ISSUE: Rule of England
DATE: 1066-1071
LOCATION: Southern England
COMBATANTS: Norman French vs. Anglo-Saxons
PRINCIPAL COMMANDERS: *Norman*, William the

Norman Conquests

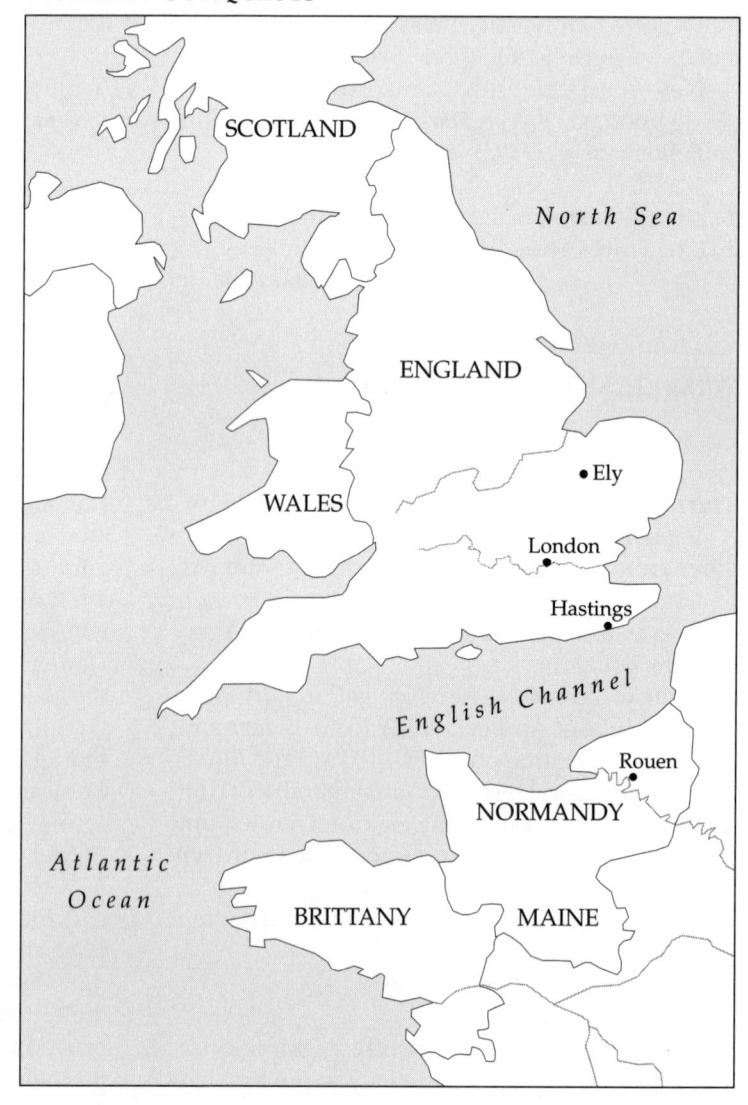

Conqueror (1028-1087); *Anglo-Saxon*, Harold II Godwinson, earl of Wessex and king of England (1022?-1066)

PRINCIPAL BATTLES: Hastings, Isle of Ely

RESULT: Norman victory; William crowned king of England

BACKGROUND

In 1051, Duke William (later William the Conqueror), a fierce warrior and harsh ruler of Normandy (France), visited his heirless cousin, Edward the Confessor, king of England, exacting a secret oral promise that William would become England's next king. This pledge was strengthened in 1064 when Harold II Godwinson, earl of Wessex, became an unwilling guest of William after shipwrecking on the Normandy coast. To secure release, Harold swore an oath to support William's claim to the English crown, even though Harold was Edward's principal adviser and de facto ruler of England.

Before Edward died in January, 1066, however, he acknowledged Harold as the next king. Harold was duly elected by the Anglo-Saxon witan (Great Council) and accepted the crown in Westminster Abbey on January 6. When William received the news, he denounced Harold as an illegally elected usurper and began to prepare for an invasion to claim the crown he believed was rightfully his.

ACTION

Although William's barons initially opposed his planned invasion, the promise of rich rewards convinced them to participate. William requested—and received—support from neighboring dukes and the king of France, as well as the blessing of Pope Alexander II.

During the summer, William began assembling troops near the coast of Normandy, where specially constructed boats for transporting both armored men and their horses across the English Channel waited. By August, the army of nearly 700 vessels and about 7,000 men waited only for a southern wind to convey them to the riches of England.

Harold, however, had learned of William's intentions and amassed an army on England's southern coast where the invasion was expected. The army waited all summer for William's arrival, but as harvest time approached and William had not appeared, Harold disbanded the army and returned to London.

Meanwhile, Tostig, Harold's revengeful half-brother, having been ousted from his earldom in northern England, convinced King Harold III Hardraade of Norway to attack northern England where defenses were weak. The Norwegians landed in September, within days of Harold's return to London. Harold then hastened northward, with as much of an army as he could muster on short notice, to challenge the invaders. After a week's march, Harold's army confronted the Norsemen and killed Harold III Hardraade and Tostig at Stamford Bridge (September, 1066), thus vanquishing the intruders. On Harold's return from this campaign, news reached him that on September 28 William had landed in the south and was ravaging the countryside.

Harold hastened to London to gather an army and marched toward Hastings where William waited. On the evening of October 13, 1066, Harold took up a position on a hill north of **Hastings** to compel the invaders to initiate an attack. The next day, William's troops advanced, and the decisive battle of the Norman invasion commenced. It was a long and hard battle, lasting all day. William's army consisted of about 5,000 knights and several thousand archers, while Harold had only foot soldiers wielding axes and spears. Initially the repeated cavalry charges of the knights were not able to break the shield wall of Harold's tightly packed men. The Norman knights had never encountered such stubborn resistance and suffered serious losses. Although shields provided some safety for the English, the showers of arrows gradually took a toll, and by late afternoon, the defensive line was breached. William directed the archers to shoot high into the air so arrows would fall behind the shield wall. One of these missiles pierced Harold's right eye, blinding him and knocking him to the ground. The battle was now decided; William and his bodyguards broke through the ranks and hacked Harold's body to pieces while the remaining English troops fled.

The southeastern section of England now lay open, but the greater part of England remained unconquered, and there was no guarantee that the English would acknowledge William as king.

When news of Harold's slaughter reached London, the witan immediately appointed Edgar the Ætheling as his successor.

Because England did not initially resist the invaders, William viciously ravaged villages and demanded submissions from local earls as he marched toward London. Following a circuitous route marked by considerable devastation, William thus frightened southern England into surrendering, but he lacked sufficient force to take London by storm. Arriving directly south of London, still unacknowledged as Edward's heir, William burned the city of Southwark as a warning before continuing his destructive march around the west and north of London.

The policy proved successful; despite the earlier proclamation of Edgar the Ætheling as king, the witan capitulated and acknowledged William's claim. William entered London and was crowned William I, king of England, on Christmas Day, 1066. However, William's oath promising to be the guardian of English law and protector of English people turned out to be a meaningless veneer, for he soon confiscated the estates of everyone who had acknowledged the usurper Harold.

William, now ostensibly king of England, would need another four years to subjugate England. Saxon nobles who still opposed William had to be conquered individually. The new monarchy and the new feudalism had to be rigorously enforced by William's new military system, until every shire was ruled by French-speaking knights beholden to the king.

By the end of 1068, William was the true lord of southern England, and the north at least acknowledged him as king, although the estates of this region had not yet been confiscated. In 1069, William crushed the last bulwark of English resistance in the northeast by so completely ravaging the land that it remained uninhabited for years. This foul deed served its purpose; the remaining independent earls realized that opposition was pointless. The military drama of the conquest ended when a group of English outlaws defended the **Isle of Ely** against William until late in the year 1071. Undertaken too late, this was the last, noblest, and most futile of the regional revolts. By 1072, the Norman conquest of England was complete. All rebellions had been squelched, all insurrections crushed, and all offenders punished. William ruled England sternly but fairly, although English nobles were not allowed to hold positions of authority. Under the newly imposed French system of strict territorial feudalism, England lost liberties previously enjoyed, but gained cohesiveness as its new masters hammered an aggregation of stubbornly independent regions into a nation.

Aftermath

Under William, England's independent earldoms were abolished and the land distributed to loyal Norman followers, thus eliminating the chief source of domestic strife and national weakness. The Normans had a genius for law and government, and they ruled England with great ability for the next three centuries, transforming all social, cultural, legal, political, and economic systems into a balanced feudal monarchy. William revised the judicial system, curtailed the power of the church, stimulated the growth of towns, and brought England into the mainstream of continental commerce. However, he did not enjoy unlimited despotic power nor did those who succeeded him; they remained bound to the ancient Saxon laws they had sworn to uphold. It was from the marriage of these ancient laws to the imported French customs that English liberties and laws eventually evolved.

Resources

Hollister, Warren, ed. *The Impact of the Norman Conquest*. Malabar, Fla.: Krieger, 1982.

Howarth, David. *1066: The Year of the Conquest*. New York: Barnes & Noble, 1993.

Whitelock, Dorothy. *The Norman Conquest: Its Setting and Impact*. London: Eyre & Spottiswoode, 1966.

See also: British Dynastic Wars; Hastings; Stamford Bridge; William the Conqueror.

George R. Plitnik

Normandy Invasion

Type of action: Ground campaign in World War II
Date: June 6-August 21, 1944
Location: Northwestern France

Normandy Invasion, 1944

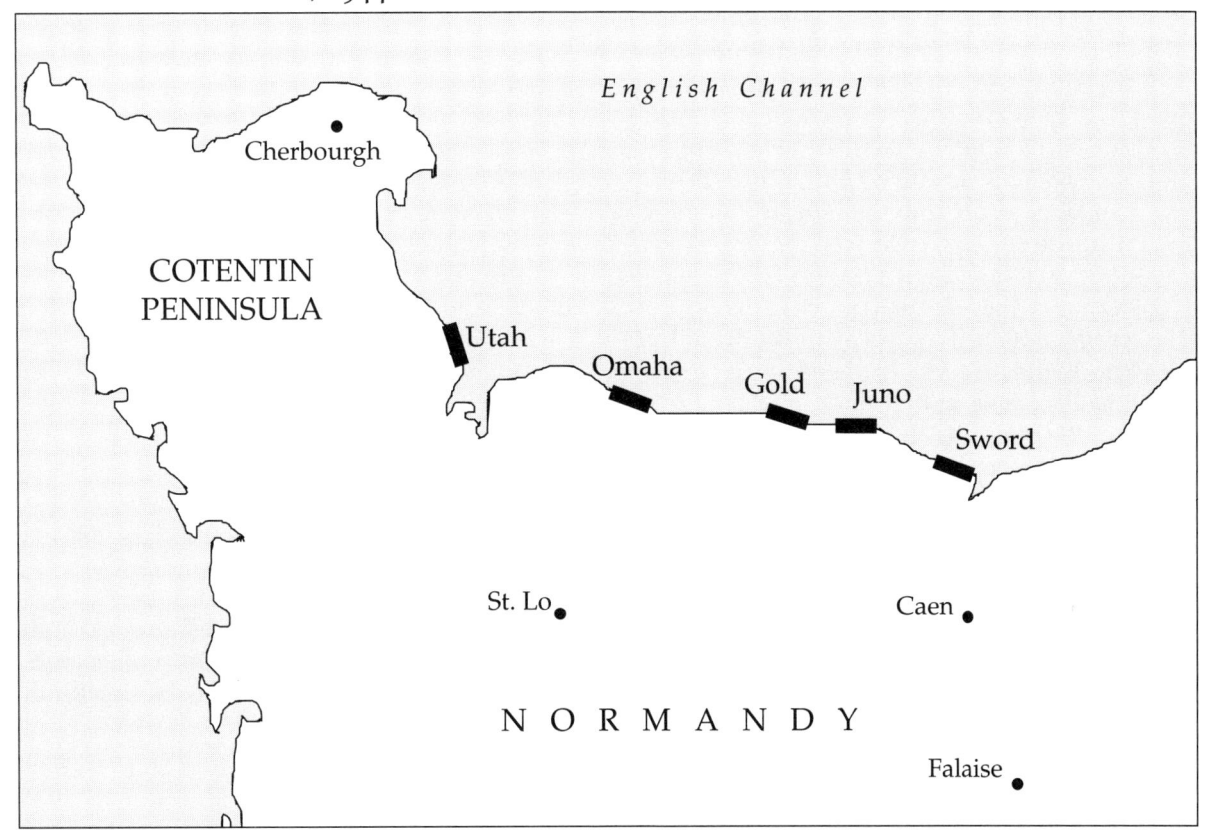

COMBATANTS: Allied (Americans, British, Canadians) vs. Germans
PRINCIPAL COMMANDERS: *Allied*, General Dwight D. Eisenhower (1890-1969); *German*, Field Marshal Erwin Rommel (1891-1944), Field Marshal Günther von Kluge (1882-1944)
RESULT: Allied defeat of German forces

In 1943, the Allies began preparations for Operation Overlord, a large-scale invasion of Northwestern Europe. Normandy was selected as the invasion site because it was within range of Allied aircraft based in Britain and possessed the port of Cherbourg, through which the Allies could bring in reinforcements and supplies. By May, 1944, General Dwight D. Eisenhower had 2,876,000 Allied soldiers, sailors, and airmen under his command. The Allies had about 11,000 aircraft and 7,000 naval and transport vessels. Field Marshal Erwin Rommel, commander of German forces in Northern France, Belgium, and the Netherlands, expected an invasion at Calais but, in early 1944, had his more than 500,000 troops work to strengthen coastal defenses along the entire English Channel.

Overlord began in the early hours of D day, June 6, 1944, when U.S. and British airborne troops landed in Normandy and secured the flanks of the invasion front. Following a massive naval bombardment, assault troops began landing on the beaches at about 6:30 A.M. At the westernmost beach (called Utah by the Allies), U.S. troops met only light resistance and quickly began to move inland, but at the key central beach (Omaha), Americans encountered strong defenses and suffered heavy casualties. However, due to the heroic leadership of individual officers and effective naval support fire, they began moving inland by late morning. Further east, British and Canadian troops secured Gold, Juno, and Sword Beaches. Although the Allies fell short of their first day's objectives, they had established a foothold and landed about 156,000 troops by the evening of June 6.

By June 13, Allied airborne and assault forces had linked up and established a single continuous front. However, the Allied advance inland was slowed by effective German defense of the Norman hedgerow country. During June, British and Canadian forces failed in repeated attempts to capture the key city of Caen on the Orne River. On July 7-9, following a massive Allied aerial bombardment, they captured much of the city but the Germans retained control of the south bank of the Orne. To the west, U.S. forces advanced up the Cotentin Peninsula and secured Cherbourg by June 27. By mid-July, the Allies and Germans were locked in a seemingly endless stalemate. However, by July 20, the Allies had landed almost 1.5 million men in Normandy, which gave them a considerable numerical advantage over the German forces. Meanwhile, Rommel was wounded on July 17 and replaced by Field Marshal Günther von Kluge.

In late July, Allied forces began a two-pronged offensive designed to achieve a breakout beyond hedgerow country. On July 18-20, the British and Canadians attacked to the east of Caen. They achieved only limited gains but forced the Germans to move reserve armored units to the eastern end of the invasion front. In the west, after massive aerial bombardment of German positions near St. Lo on July 25, U.S. forces broke through at Avranches and advanced rapidly to the south, west, and east.

In early August, German forces faced British and Canadians to the north and Americans to the west and south and were in danger of being trapped in a shrinking pocket south of Falaise. On August 16-21, about 100,000 Germans were subjected to massive aerial and artillery bombardment as Allied units fought to close the German escape route to the east. Although some German units did escape, about 10,000 Germans were killed and 50,000 captured in the Falaise pocket.

Significance

In the Normandy campaign, the Allies destroyed a substantial portion of the German forces in northwestern France. This led to the liberation of Paris (August 25) and the remainder of France, which put the Allies in position to advance into the Low Countries and ultimately Germany itself.

Resources

Ambrose, Stephen E. *D-Day, June 6, 1944: The Climactic Battle of World War II*. New York: Simon & Schuster, 1994.

The Beachhead at Anzio: D-Day, the Normandy Invasion. Vol. 2. The War Chronicles: World War II series. Documentary. A&E Home Video, 1995.

Blumenson, Martin. *The Battle of the Generals*. New York: William Morrow, 1993.

Chandler, David G., and James L. Collins, Jr. *The D-Day Encyclopedia*. New York: Simon & Schuster, 1994.

Hastings, Max. *Overlord: D-Day and the Battle for Normandy*. New York: Simon & Schuster, 1984.

Ryan, Cornelius. *The Longest Day*. New York: Simon & Schuster, 1959.

See also: Bradley, Omar N.; Eisenhower, Dwight D.; Montgomery, Bernard Law; Patton, George S.; Ridgway, Matthew B.; Rommel, Erwin; Rundstedt, Gerd von; World War II.

Thomas I. Crimando

North Atlantic

Type of action: Air and sea battle in World War II
Date: September 3, 1939-May 4, 1945
Location: North Atlantic ocean
Combatants: Primarily German submarines vs. Allied surface vessels and aircraft
Principal commanders: *German*, Admiral Karl Dönitz (1891-1980); *American*, Ernest King (1878-1956)
Result: Eventual decisive victory for Allied forces

The Battle of the North Atlantic began on September 3, 1939, with the sinking of the British liner *Athenia* by the German submarine U-30. At the time, neither side was prepared for what was to follow. Germany had only fifty-six operational submarines of which only twenty-two were suited for service in the Atlantic Ocean. The British did not attach a high priority to planning and equipment for antisubmarine warfare, thinking that they could improvise at the outbreak of hostilities.

At the outset of the war, the Germans sought to impose a submarine blockade of all British ports. This proved not to be the best strategy. The commander of U-boats, Admiral Karl Dönitz, was soon convinced that operating in coastal waters made the U-boats too vulnerable to land-based aircraft and that they should instead concentrate in the mid-Atlantic, which was out of reach for most aircraft at that time. In this first phase, U-boats operated singly rather than as a group. However, the Allies, including the U.S. Navy under Ernest King, soon organized a convoy system, and the Germans adapted by attacking in groups called wolfpacks.

Dönitz calculated that sinking a monthly average of 800,000 tons of shipping would cripple the British war effort and bring about its capitulation. Without merchant shipping, the British could neither eat, run their industries, or continue fighting. In the early years of the war, losses of merchant ships exceeded the rate of ship production by a 2-1 margin. It was not until August, 1942, that ship production balanced the losses.

By April, 1943, more than 400 U-boats were in service, and victory in the Atlantic was almost achieved by the Germans. Abruptly, however, the tide of battle turned. The Allies were able to close the gap and provide air cover the entire width of the Atlantic. Improved radar enabled the allies to pinpoint the location of German submarines after only a brief radio transmission. The United States was constructing merchant ships at a rate far exceeding losses. More than 2,500 of these wartime merchant vessels known as Liberty ships were built in American shipyards.

In May, 1943, the Germans lost thirty-five submarines with only 96,000 tons of shipping to show for it. It was now clear that it was pointless to send submarines into the North Atlantic to attack shipping as the losses would exceed any reasonable return. Dönitz temporarily withdrew U-boats from the North Atlantic and used them in other locations where they would not be so vulnerable. The U-boats were returned to the Atlantic, but their main function became to slow and harass Allied shipping and force the Allies to continue devoting resources to an antisubmarine campaign, thus preventing these resources from being used elsewhere. The end came on May 4, 1945, when Dönitz sent a radio signal to all U-boats to stop all hostile action against Allied shipping.

The battle was costly to both sides. During the course of the war, the Allies lost more than 2,600 ships. More than 30,000 merchant seaman and supporting naval personnel lost their lives. The Germans lost more than 750 U-boats, which amounted to more than 85 percent of all operational boats. Of the approximate 40,000 who served as U-boat crewmen, 27,491 died in action.

SIGNIFICANCE

Winning the Battle of the North Atlantic was essential for an Allied victory. Britain could not be sustained nor could offensive operations be undertaken on the European continent without control of the North Atlantic.

RESOURCES

Battlefield Series: The Battle of the Atlantic. Documentary. PolyGram Video International, 1996.
Buchheim, Lothar-Gunther. *U-boat War.* New York: Bonanza Books, 1986.
Gannon, Michael. *Operation Drumbeat.* New York: Harper & Row, 1990.
Kaplan, Philip, and Jack Currie. *Convoy, Merchant Sailors at War.* Annapolis, Md.: Naval Institute Press, 1998.
_____. *Wolfpack, U-boats at War, 1939-1945.* Annapolis, Md.: Naval Institute Press, 1997.

SEE ALSO: Convoy; Dönitz, Karl; King, Ernest; Submarine; World War II.

Gilbert T. Cave

NORTH ATLANTIC TREATY ORGANIZATION (NATO)

Organization founded for the implementation of the North Atlantic Treaty of 1949, which sought to establish an international counterweight against the Soviet presence in Eastern Europe. Its members include Belgium, Canada, Denmark, France, Germany, Greece, Iceland, Italy, Luxembourg, The Netherlands, Norway, Portugal, Spain, Turkey, the United Kingdom, the United States, and, as of 1999, Poland, the Czech Republic, and Hungary. At the treaty's—and, hence, NATO's—very heart, the signing nations agree that an attack on one NATO member is an attack on all, and all declare that the organization must work "to maintain the security of the North Atlantic Area." Although the Soviet Union collapsed in 1991, NATO has survived. Indeed, NATO's peacekeeping operations in Bosnia and Herzegovina in the mid-1990's reflected its new role as a regulator of international stability in Europe.

Jeremiah Taylor

NORTHERN IRELAND CIVIL WAR

AT ISSUE: The union between Great Britain and its province of Northern Ireland, and the nature of that province's government
DATE: Beginning August 14, 1969
LOCATION: Northern Ireland, with important actions in England and the Republic of Ireland
COMBATANTS: The British army, Special Air Service (SAS), and Royal Ulster Constabulary (RUC) vs. republican and loyalist paramilitary forces; those paramilitary forces vs. one another
PRINCIPAL COMMANDER: *Irish*, Sinn Féin president, Gerry Addams
PRINCIPAL BATTLES: Bogside (1969), Belfast (1969)
RESULT: Paramilitary cease-fires in the mid-1990's paved the way for intense peace negotiations leading to the establishment in late 1999 of a power-sharing Northern Ireland Assembly; many contentious issues remained unsolved

BACKGROUND

A civil rights movement, modeled on that in the United States, began in Northern Ireland in 1968 with demonstrations calling for equality in voting, jobs, and access to housing. A majority of the demonstrators, though certainly not all, were Catholics who had been discriminated against since the creation in 1920 of the British province of Northern Ireland. The province had been governed by one-party Unionist rule since its inception, and that party had boasted of creating "a Protestant state for a Protestant people," although Protestants constituted only about 60 percent of the population.

Most Catholics would have preferred to be part of a unified Ireland governed by the Republic of Ireland rather than live under the union that made them citizens of the United Kingdom.

Beginning in the 1920's, there had been frequent violent conflicts between Protestants and Catholics. The fact that both the political administration and the police, the RUC, were Protestant-controlled made the Catholics feel particularly vulnerable.

Civil rights marches from summer, 1968, through early 1969 often led to clashes with the RUC, which on some occasions reacted with excessive violence against the demonstrators. The conflicts escalated to large-scale rioting in August, 1969, in the two largest cities, Belfast and Derry.

The RUC was no longer capable of maintaining order, and on August 14, the British government sent in the army to quell the disturbances, but violence continued to escalate.

ACTION

The army entered Derry during the Battle of the **Bogside** (August 12-14, 1969) and **Belfast** soon after. There would be few pitched battles that earned a name in what became a decades-long irregular war that was a political as well as a military conflict. Its nature began to emerge when the Irish Republican Army (IRA), revitalized by the violence, barricaded Catholic areas of Belfast and Derry, establishing "no-go areas" that the police and army could not enter. It became clearer still when the IRA began a sustained bombing campaign aimed primarily at economic targets. It was the goal of the IRA to drive the British out of Northern Ireland and to create an all-Ireland socialist republic. In its overall aims, the IRA commanded little support, but as a force resisting the British and the Northern Irish system, they had the backing or at least the sympathy of many Catholics.

Demonstrations against the administration and the army continued. In Derry, British paratroopers fired into a crowd, killing 13 on what became known as Bloody Sunday (January 30, 1972). The paratroopers claimed they were fired on first, but serious doubts about that claim have been a political issue ever since. An IRA bombing assault that killed 9 in Belfast became known as Bloody Friday (July 21, 1972).

Loyalist paramilitaries from the Protestant

community, the Ulster Volunteer Force (UVF) and the Ulster Defense Association (UDA), engaged in violence in their determination to reestablish supremacy over Catholics, defeat the IRA, and block any change in Northern Ireland's links with Britain. In 1974, the UVF set off bombs (May 17) in various places in the Irish Republic, killing 30.

From the mid-1970's to the mid-1980's the conflict dragged on, a dispiriting round of assassinations, bombings, and ambushes that the security forces were unable to halt. The IRA was responsible for the larger number of casualties during this period and for the most dramatic events, such as the assassination of the queen's cousin, the distinguished Lord Louis Mountbatten (August 27, 1979), and the bombing of the Grand Hotel in England, where the Conservative Party was meeting (October 12, 1984). Prime Minister Margaret Thatcher barely escaped with her life.

Neither political experiments nor stepped-up security (for example, sending in the SAS in January, 1976) proved effective in halting the killing.

The IRA's actual strength went up and down, but it always remained prominent and defiant in public. It gained considerable public support following the death of 10 of its members who went on hunger strikes in prison. Most prominent was Bobby Sands, elected to the British parliament while on a hunger strike, who died May 5, 1981.

The IRA continued to kill and be killed. Their attacks widened, sometimes directed at those who merely provided services for the security forces. The SAS ambushed 8 who were preparing an attack at Lough Gall (May 8, 1987) and shot 3 others, who were allegedly planning a car bombing, killing them on the street in Gibraltar without the chance to surrender (March 6, 1988).

The loyalist paramilitaries stepped up their campaigns, sometimes assassinating Catholics at random. In the 1990's, these loyalists claimed more victims than the IRA. As the government opened up talks with the IRA through its political wing Sinn Féin and its president Gerry Addams, loyalists began for the first time to attack the RUC.

British soldiers guard houses in the central area of Belfast that have been ruined by bombs fired by the IRA. (Archive Photos/ Hulton Getty Collection)

Aftermath

In late 1994, both sides of the paramilitary forces announced cease-fires. Serious, often secret, talks went on at length. The cease-fires broke down from time to time, and few were optimistic about the chances for peace. However, the Republic of Ireland had been drawn into talks with the British that the administration of U.S. president Bill Clinton joined, pressing for a solution. Agreements were reached in 1998 regarding a power-sharing executive and assembly entity and cross-border links between Northern Ireland and the Irish Republic. Despite bitter disputes concerning the IRA's failure to decommission weapons, elements of the peace agreement became a reality in late 1999 and early 2000.

Resources

Bardon, Jonathon. *A History of Ulster.* Belfast: Blackstaff, 1992.

Bell, J. Bowyer. *The Irish Troubles: A Generation of Violence, 1967-1992.* New York: St. Martin's Press, 1993.

Coogan, Tim Pat. *The Troubles: Ireland's Ordeal 1966-1996 and the Search for Peace.* Boulder, Colo.: Roberts Rinehart, 1996.

Mirror, Mirror: Northern Ireland. Documentary. Films for the Humanities and Sciences, 1994.

O'Malley, Padraig. *The Uncivil Wars: Ireland Today.* 3d ed. Boston: Beacon, 1997.

The Road to Bloody Sunday: How the Troubles in Northern Ireland Began. Documentary. Public Broadcasting Service, 1998.

Smith, M. L. R. *Fighting for Ireland? The Military Strategy of the Irish Republican Movement.* New York: Routledge, 1995.

Understanding Northern Ireland. Documentary. Films for the Humanities and Sciences, 1993.

See also: Anglo-Irish War; Collins, Michael; Guerrilla warfare.

Richard Gruber

Northern War

At issue: Swedish supremacy in the Baltic
Date: July, 1655-June, 1660
Location: Baltic region of Europe
Combatants: Swedes vs. Polish-Lithuanians, Brandenburg forces, Danish, Austrians, Russians, English, and the Dutch
Principal commanders: *Swedish*, Charles X, king of Sweden (1622-1660); *Polish*, John II Casimir, king of Poland (1609-1672); *Brandenburg*, Frederick William, the Great Elector (1640-1688)
Principal battles: Sandomierz, Warsaw, Frederiksodde, Nyborg
Result: Swedish acquisition of southern Scandinavian peninsula from Denmark

Background

The Swedish Empire included Sweden, Finland, and several Baltic islands, as well as Ingria, Estonia, Karelia, and Livonia in northeast Europe. Much of this land had been acquired by military conquest against Denmark, Poland-Lithuania, and Russia. The Thirty Years' War and the Peace of Westphalia (1648) established Sweden as the leading power in the Baltic. Sweden acquired Verden, Bremen, Wismar, and West Pomerania in northern Germany. However, Sweden sought to acquire control of Scania from Denmark and the Baltic coastline and ports from Poland.

In 1648, the Ukrainian Cossacks rebelled against the rule of John II Casimir of Poland. The Cossacks allied with Czar Alexis I of Russia in 1654, resulting in a Russian invasion of Poland. Charles X Gustav of Sweden was encouraged to attack Poland based on the success of the Russian invasion and the belief that Poland was about to collapse.

Action

In July, 1655, Sweden launched a two-prong invasion of Poland. The Swedes captured Poznan, Warsaw, and then forced the main Polish army to surrender at Cracow in October, 1655. Charles X then invaded East Prussia and impelled Frederick William, the Great Elector, to ally with Sweden.

In 1656, the Poles rebelled against foreign occupation. The Polish army, under Stefan Czarniecki, trapped Charles X for a few weeks at **Sandomierz** (April, 1656), which allowed Casimir to clear southern Poland from Swedish occupation and regain Warsaw (June 30, 1656). However, Charles X and Frederick William defeated the Poles at **Warsaw** (July 28-30, 1656), and then reoccupied the city.

In May, 1656, Czar Alexis declared war against Sweden. The Swedes defeated Russian attempts to invade Ingria, Livonia, Estonia, and Karelia in 1656 to 1658. The czar was forced to agree to a three-year truce with Sweden in 1658.

In July, 1657, Frederick III of Denmark declared war against Sweden. The Danes invaded Bremen. Charles X left Poland and drove the Danes out of Bremen. The Swedes then invaded Jutland and defeated the Danes at **Frederiksodde** (October 24, 1657). From there, in January and February, 1658, Charles X led an army of 10,000 soldiers across the frozen sea using the islands of Fyn, Taasinge, Langeland, Lolland, and Falster as stepping stones to attack Copenhagen. This maneuver forced the Danes to accept the humiliating Treaty of Roskilde in February, 1658.

Charles X renewed the war with Denmark in August, 1658. The Swedes landed on the island of Zealand and besieged Copenhagen. Subsequently, Frederick William led a coalition army of 30,000 Brandenburgers, Austrians, and Poles against the Swedes, forcing them out of Schleswig and Holstein. In addition, Dutch and English naval action pressured the Swedes to end the Siege of Copenhagen. When Charles X refused to negotiate a peace settlement, the allies pursued an offensive against Swedish positions in Denmark and West Pomerania. Dano-Dutch forces defeated the Swedes at **Nyborg** (November, 1659) on the island of Fyn, and Frederick William invaded and captured most of West Pomerania in December, 1659.

Aftermath

The death of Charles X changed the diplomatic scene in February, 1660. In May, the Swedes ended the war with Poland, Brandenburg, and Austria in the Treaty of Oliva. Sweden and Denmark agreed to the Treaty of Copenhagen in June, 1660. The Russo-Swedish conflict ended with the Treaty of Kardis in June, 1661. As a result of these treaties, Sweden acquired the Danish territories of Scania, Blekinge, Boshuslän, Halland, and the island of Bornholm.

Resources

Kirby, David. *Northern Europe in the Early Modern Period: The Baltic World 1492-1772*. London: Longman, 1990.

Lisk, Jill. *The Struggle for Supremacy in the Baltic, 1600-1725*. New York: Funk & Wagnalls, 1967.

Oakley, Stewart P. *War and Peace in the Baltic, 1560-1790*. London: Routledge, 1992.

See also: Frederick William, the Great Elector; Thirty Years' War.

William A. Young

Northumberland, Duke of

Full name: John Dudley, viscount Lesle, earl of Warwick, lord high admiral and lord protector
Born: 1520; place unknown
Died: August 22, 1553; place unknown
Principal wars: Anglo-Scottish Wars of 1513-1560, Kett's Rebellion
Principal battle: Pinkie (1547)
Military significance: The duke of Northumberland fought in the Battle of Pinkie, which preceded the English occupation of Edinburgh.

The duke of Northumberland is primarily remembered for his faction fight with the Seymour family during the reign of Edward VI (1547-1553). Although minor English nobility, he managed to attain several titles that gave him political power and recognition. He was instrumental in the downfall and execution in 1552 of Protector Edward Seymour, first duke of Somerset, which left him virtual ruler of England, as the young King Edward VI became weaker through his final illness. A strong Protestant, Northumberland, in an attempt to prevent the succession of Edward's Catholic sister, Mary, plotted to replace her with Lady Jane Grey, to whom he married his son, Lord Guildford Dudley. Having persuaded the dying king to name Jane Grey his heir and set aside the succession, he held Jane (and her husband) as the legitimate Protestant heirs to the throne, but popular support for Mary ended the reign of Jane Grey in only nine days. Queen Mary I, later known as "Bloody Mary," executed all three as traitors.

Resources

Elizabeth R. Fiction feature. BBC, 1971.

Elton, Geoffrey. *England Under the Tudors*. New York: Routledge, 1991.

Erickson, Carolly. *Bloody Mary*. New York: Griffin Trade Paperback, 1998.
Guy, John. *Tudor England*. New York: Oxford University Press, 1990.
Lady Jane. Fiction feature. Paramount Pictures, 1986.
Prall, Stuart E., and David Harris Willson. *A History of England*. Vol. 1. Fort Worth, Texas: Holt, Rinehart, and Winston, 1991.

SEE ALSO: Anglo-Scottish Wars of 1513-1560; Kett's Rebellion; Pinkie; Somerset, Edward Seymour, first duke of.

Pamela M. Gross

NOVGOROD, MUSCOVITE CONQUEST OF

AT ISSUE: Control of Novgorod
DATE: 1471-1479
LOCATION: Novgorod, Russia
COMBATANTS: Principality of Novgorod vs. Duchy of Muscow
PRINCIPAL COMMANDERS: *Novgorodian*, Dmitrii Boretsky (d. 1471); *Russian*, Ivan the Great, grand prince of Russia (1440-1505)
PRINCIPAL BATTLES: Shelon River, Novgorod
RESULT: Moscow absorbed Novgorod, laying the way for the unification of all the Russian principalities

BACKGROUND

After the downfall of Kiev, Novgorod in the thirteen and fourteenth centuries was the queen of Russian principalities. A mercantile city, part of the Hanseatic League, it was ruled by its merchants as well as by its prince as a constitutional monarchy. By the fifteenth century, however, differences between the wealthy merchants and the poorer populace led to tensions. In addition, the city faced the rising power of Moscow, whose princes controlled the position of grand prince of the Russian appanages and "gathered them" in one by one to a growing Muscovite empire. Ivan the Great ascended the throne in Moscow (1462) and sought to acquire the last of the independent Russian appanages. Novgorod was the most important.

ACTION

Many Novgorodians preferred Ivan to their own leaders. Novgorod, furthermore, lacked the strength to face Russia's most powerful ruler, who had even assumed the title of czar and autocrat. After Ivan's father Basil II had forced Novgorod to accept an unfavorable treaty, the city's leaders, the Boretsky family, including the legendary Martha Boretska, the widow of one the *posadniki* (mayors), turned to Lithuania for help. However, the commoners disliked that country as much as their own leaders did. The troops showed little spirit in the war against the popular Ivan. Novgorod's army had little room to maneuver because Moscow controlled much of the surrounding territory. The city's archbishop refused to lead his troops against the czar. Ivan defeated the Novgorodians at the **Shelon River** (1471). Accusing the Novgorodians of apostasy because of their allegiance to the pope at the Council of Florence (1439), Ivan released the city of Pskov from its oath to Novgorod and enlisted its inhabitants in his forces. He sent his generals to burn the land surrounding **Novgorod**. Furthermore, the dry summer of that year allowed Ivan to use his cavalry without fear of the swamps that impeded past invaders. The Novgorodians tried to outflank Moscow's army by arriving on boats on Lake Ilmen but failed. The Chronicle of Novgorod records five hundred men from Novgorod were killed.

The city was at Ivan's mercy. He extracted their allegiance to him as well as to his heir, the future Basil III. He required a large indemnity and the surrender of territory. He executed the Novgorodian leader Dmitrii Boretsky, Martha's son. However, he left the institutions intact.

The war was not yet over. The Novgorodian leadership broke the treaty, reneged on recognizing the overlordship of Ivan, and once more asked Lithuania for help. Furious, Ivan led his second campaign against the recalcitrant city in 1478. Novgorod's Lithuanian allies did not come. The leaders split over tactics and surrendered their city without a fight. Ivan executed or exiled his opponents, deported many of the families, and abrogated the constitution. He even removed the town assembly bell to Moscow, a severe blow to the pride of the city. The democratic institutions of Novgorod ended in 1479 as Moscow absorbed the city and Ivan III became the absolute ruler. Martha was sent to a nunnery.

Aftermath
Novgorod was incorporated into the Moscovite duchy.

Resources
Birnbaum, Henrik. *Lord Novgorod the Great: Essays in the History and Culture of a Medieval City-state.* Columbus, Ohio: Slavica, 1981.
Levin, Eve. *The Role and Status of Women in Medieval Novgorod.* Ann Arbor, Mich.: University Microfilms International, 1985.
Martin, Janet. *Medieval Russia, 980-1584.* Cambridge, England: Cambridge University Press, 1995.
Novgorod Chronicles. Gulf Breeze, Fla: Academic International Press, 1981.
Novgorod Icons: Twelfth-Seventeenth Century. Leningrad: Aurora Art, 1983.

See also: Ivan the Great; Ivan the Terrible; Russian Civil War of 1425-1453.

Frederick B. Chary

Nuclear and atomic weapons

The most powerful man-made bombs or warheads are those based on manipulating the atom. Atomic weapons obtain their explosive force from splitting the atom's nucleus (fission). The explosive power of nuclear weapons comes either from splitting atoms or by joining them (fusion). In spite of their ominous use, the development of nuclear weapons is one of the great scientific and technological achievements of the twentieth century.

The Beginnings
The development of nuclear weapons began with efforts in the 1930's to make elements with a higher atomic number than uranium, which is 92. Teams of physicists were bombarding uranium with neutrons, but were actually splitting the uranium atom. In 1938, the team in Germany—Otto Hahn, Lise Meitner, and Fritz Strassmann—finally realized that the atom was fissioning and giving off a lot of energy. Word got out quickly within the scientific community. Other experimenters confirmed the discovery and also found an isotope of uranium, uranium-235, was the one undergoing fission. Furthermore, besides the energy, the reaction produced excess neutrons. Some of these neutrons could strike other uranium atoms and split them, making a chain reaction possible that would produce a powerful explosion—an atomic bomb.

European scientists in the United States such as Leo Szilard realized that Nazi Germany might be the first to develop an atomic weapon. A letter from Albert Einstein to President Franklin D. Roosevelt got the U.S. government behind what would become the Manhattan Project. The United States' entry into World War II (1939-1945) spurred on atomic research. Several methods for isolating the rare uranium-235 were pursued simultaneously. Teams of scientists were working on different bomb designs. Calculations were being made to determine the critical mass that would produce the explosion. Researchers were investigating another fissionable element, plutonium-239. Nuclear cross sections for fast neutrons had to be determined. The metallurgy of uranium and plutonium was studied. The work was going on across the country, from New York City to Berkeley, California, but it became increasingly concentrated at the former Los Alamos Ranch School, north of Albuquerque, New Mexico. The overall project head was U.S. Army Corps of Engineers General Leslie Groves.

Building the Atomic Bomb
In June, 1942, J. Robert Oppenheimer became director of the group designing the bomb. The emphasis in 1943 was on a "gun" method in which subcritical masses were fired into each other, producing a critical mass, the amount of uranium that would sustain a chain reaction. However, the gun method would work only for uranium-235; plutonium-239 would predetonate. The plutonium bomb design finally ended up as an implosion device in which many subcritical, wedge-shaped pieces were arranged spherically and driven together into a critical mass by shaped charges. The implosion happens so fast that the plutonium does not have time to predetonate.

Scientists were positive that the gun-type design would work. By the middle of 1945, the gaseous diffusion plant at Oak Ridge, Tennessee, had not produced enough highly refined uranium-235 for both a test and a bomb. The fifty kilograms of high-purity material was saved for the bomb, which was nicknamed "Little Boy." The first atomic device, "Fat Man," was filled with plutonium-239 from the Hanford Atomic Energy Works on the Columbia River near Richland, Washington. On July 16, 1945, in south central New Mexico, scientists detonated the implosion device at 5:29:45 A.M. Mountain Time. Code named "Trinity," the test yield was much higher than expected, equal to about 20,000 tons (20 KT) of TNT. The world had entered the atomic age.

Using the Atomic Bomb

At the time of the Trinity test, Germany had already surrendered and U.S. military personnel were in transit to the Pacific theater, if they were not already there. Fighting had been desperate at Iwo Jima and Okinawa. Planners expected up to one million U.S. casualties from the invasion of the home islands; Japanese casualties would be even higher. A high-level committee, which included Oppenheimer, reported to President Harry S. Truman that it could come up with no technical demonstration of the bomb that was likely to end the war. Against this backdrop, Truman approved the use of atomic bombs against Japan, which had rejected a veiled threat from the Potsdam Conference to surrender or else suffer annihilation.

On August 6, 1945, at 8:15 A.M., the *Enola Gay*, a specially prepared B-29, dropped a 20 KT gun-type uranium-235 bomb that air burst 2,000 feet over Hiroshima. About two-thirds of the city was destroyed, and 70,000 persons were killed. When Japan still did not surrender, another B-29, *Bock's Car*, passed up bombing Kokura because of clouds and dropped a duplicate of the Trinity bomb on Nagasaki. It destroyed about half of the city and killed about 40,000 persons. The United States was preparing a third bomb, but Emperor Hirohito intervened into the conduct of the war and ordered Japan's surrender.

In 1946, under the Baruch plan, the United States offered complete control of all aspects of its atomic monopoly to the United Nation (U.N.), but Andre Gromyko, the U.N. representative for the Soviet Union, vetoed it. The world found out why in 1949, when, against all expectations, the Soviet Union exploded *Joe 1*, its first atomic bomb. It was a copy of the Trinity device, and its plutonium was made in a copy of the Hanford 305 reactor. The reason the Soviet Union had advanced so quickly was because it had obtained information on the Manhattan Project via a machinist, David Greenglass, a physicist, Klaus Fuchs, and others. Fuchs had also passed to the Soviet Union Ed-

Major Nuclear Events in the Twentieth Century

Date	Location	Description
July 16, 1945	New Mexico, USA	United States tests first atomic device
August 6, 1945	Hiroshima, Japan	United States drops first atomic bomb
August 9, 1945	Nagasaki, Japan	United States drops second atomic bomb
1949	Soviet Union	Soviet Union tests its first atomic device
1952	Eniwetok atoll	United States tests first thermonuclear device
1953	Soviet Union	Soviet Union tests its first thermonuclear device
1962	Cuba	United States threatens nuclear war with Soviet Union over Soviet missiles in Cuba
1967	China	China tests its first thermonuclear device

ward Teller's idea of a *thermonuclear bomb*, where light elements are fused together instead of heavy ones split apart.

The Hydrogen Bomb

Work on the more powerful fusion bomb as well as other nuclear programs accelerated because of the Cold War rivalry between the United States and the Western democracies and the Soviet Union and its satellites. Other countries began to join the exclusive "nuclear club." In 1952, the United Kingdom exploded its first atomic bomb.

The United States selected a site in South Carolina on the Savannah River for production of the heavy water for the hydrogen bomb. The first full-scale thermonuclear explosion was the "Mike" event at Eniwetok atoll in the Pacific in 1952. The Soviet Union tested its first thermonuclear device in 1953, and the United States unveiled the *atomic cannon*, which fired a 280-millimeter projectile with a yield of 15 KT. The United States also developed a variety of other nuclear weapons including antisubmarine and air defense weapons.

In 1957, the United Kingdom tested its first thermonuclear device. In 1960, France tested its first atomic bomb. In 1961, the Russians cynically broke a test moratorium to explode the biggest bomb ever—57 megatons (MT). In 1962, a U.S. nuclear-powered submarine fired a nuclear-tipped *Polaris missile*, and in early 1963, the U.S. Air Force tested its nuclear-tipped *Minuteman missile*. All of this hardware nearly came to be used in late 1962 when the United States discovered that the Soviet Union was locating nuclear-tipped missiles in Cuba. After a tense confrontation, the Soviets removed the missiles.

Limiting Nuclear Weapons

On August 5, 1963, the United States, the United Kingdom, and the Soviet Union signed a treaty banning all nuclear weapons testing in the atmosphere, in outer space, or under water. Up to one hundred countries also became signatories. However, in 1964, China tested its atomic bomb in the atmosphere. In 1967, it tested a thermonuclear bomb, while France tested its in 1968. Following the lead of the United States, France, the United Kingdom, and the Soviet Union also developed nuclear-powered submarines capable of launching nuclear-tipped missiles.

In the 1970's, the United States upgraded its Polaris and Minuteman missiles with multiple independently targeted warheads. It also fielded the low-flying *cruise missile*, which could carry a nuclear warhead. In the 1980's, President Ronald Reagan started development of a defensive system against nuclear-tipped missiles.

Resources

Altshuler, B. L., et al., eds. *Andrei Sakharov: Facets of a Life*. France: Editions Frontieres, 1991.

Blumberg, Stanley A. and Gwinn Owens. *Energy and Conflict: The Life and Times of Edward Teller*. New York: G. P. Putnam's Sons, 1976.

Clearwater, John. *U.S. Nuclear Weapons in Canada*. Toronto: Dundurn Press, 1999.

Groves, Leslie R. *Now It Can Be Told: The Story of the Manhattan Project*. New York: Harper & Brothers, 1962.

Henshall, Philip. *Vengeance: Hitler's Nuclear Weapon, Fact or Fiction?* Stroud, Gloucestershire, England: Sutton, 1998.

Kunetka, James W. *Oppenheimer*. Englewood Cliffs, N.J.: Prentice-Hall, 1982.

Nuclear Weapons Test Films. U.S. film declassification project. Lockheed Martin Services, Video Production Center, 1999.

The Red Bomb. Documentary. Discovery Communications, 1994.

Rhodes, Richard. *Dark Sun, The Making of the Hydrogen Bomb*. New York: Simon & Schuster, 1995.

_____. *The Making of the Atomic Bomb*. New York: Simon & Schuster, 1986.

Serber, Robert. *The Los Alamos Primer*. Berkeley: University of California Press, 1992.

Sherrow, Victoria. *The Making of the Atom Bomb*. San Diego, Calif.: Lucent Books, 2000.

Trinity and Beyond: The Atomic Bomb Movie. Documentary. Visual Concept Entertainment, 1995.

Ulam, Stanislaw M. *Adventures of a Mathematician*. Berkeley: University of California Press, 1991.

Weisgall, Jonathan M. *Operation Crossroads*. Annapolis, Md.: Naval Institute Press, 1994.

Williams, David L. *Nuclear Myths and Social Discourse: The U.S. Decision to Pursue Nuclear Weapons*. Monterey, Calif.: Naval Postgraduate School, 1996.

Zaloga, Steven J. *Target America*. Novato, Calif.: Presidio, 1993.

SEE ALSO: Cold War; Cuban Missile Crisis; Disarmament; LeMay, Curtis; Rickover, Hyman G.; World War II.

Emerson Thomas McMullen

NUREMBERG TRIALS

A series of trials held in Nuremberg, Germany, in 1945-1946, in which Nazi leaders were tried for crimes against humanity and for committing aggression, a new concept in international law. Despite suggestions from Winston Churchill, Franklin Roosevelt, and others that leading German war criminals be punished without trial, arguments for due process prevailed; an international tribunal composed of French, American, Soviet, and British judges convened in Nuremberg in the fall of 1945. Of twenty-one original defendants, eleven were condemned to hang, seven received lighter sentences and three were acquitted. The most notorious of those sentenced to death, Reichsmarschall Hermann Göring, committed suicide by ingesting cyanide a little over an hour before his appointment with the hangman.

Jeremiah Taylor

NURHACI

ALSO KNOWN AS: Wu Huangdi (Wu Huang-ti); Qing Taizu (Ch'ing T'ai Tsu); Hurhachu;

Germans suspected of war crimes sit in rows at the Nuremberg Trials. Front row, left to right, Hermann Göring, Rudolph Hesse, Joachim von Rippentrop, and Wilhelm Keitel; back row, left to right, Karl Dönitz, Erich Raeder, Baldur von Schirach, and Fritz Sauckel. (Digital Stock)

Kundulun Khan; Geren Gurum Be Ujire Genggiyen
BORN: 1559; Manchuria
DIED: September 30, 1626; Manchuria
PRINCIPAL WAR: Manchurian Conquest of China
MILITARY SIGNIFICANCE: Under Nurhaci's leadership, Manchu rose and defeated China's Ming Dynasty and established the Qing Dynasty.

After his father's death, Nurhaci became the chief of his tribe at age twenty-four. Between 1583 and 1588, he defeated his rivals and unified his area of Jianzhou. Then he allied with other powerful clans and chiefdoms through marriage connections. After he unified Manchuria, he established the Late Jin state in 1616 and made himself the khan.

Nurhaci's most important contribution was to build up a permanent army by creating the eight banner system, in which every Manchu man was a soldier and served in the army his entire life. Soldiers would go to battle when war broke out and would work in the field during peacetime. The banner was a military and civilian unit, which contained not only the soldiers but also their families. The entire Manchu society was organized into eight banners, and every Manchu had to belong to a banner-unit, which was under a captain who was both a military commander and administrative officer. The formation of the banner system greatly strengthened the combat effectiveness of the Manchus. In 1616, Nurhaci died while fighting Chinese troops. His sons and grandsons continued his cause and finally defeated the Ming Dynasty and conquered China in 1644.

RESOURCES
Hsu, Immanuel. *The Rise of Modern China*. 6th ed. New York: Oxford University Press, 1999.
Spence, Jonathan, et al. *From Ming to Ch'ing: Conquest, Region, and Continuity in Seventeenth-Century China*. New Haven, Conn.: Yale University Press, 1979.
Wakeman, Frederic, Jr. *The Great Enterprise: The Manchu Reconstruction of Imperial Order in Seventeenth Century China*. Berkeley: University of California Press, 1985.

SEE ALSO: Chinese Imperial Wars; Manchu Expansion, Wars of.

Kan Liang

O

Oda Nobunaga

Born: June, 1534; Owari Province, Japan
Died: June 21, 1582; Kyoto, Japan
Principal wars: Japanese Wars of Unification
Principal battles: Okehazama (1560), Anegawa (1570), Nagashino (1575)
Military significance: Nobunaga began the process of unifying Japan and placing it under a military government.

Oda Nobunaga was born into a minor daimyo (feudal baron) family from Owari Province that claimed to be descendants of the Taira clan. He was a ruthless ruler who eventually fought his way to the top of his clan. He won many battles against neighboring daimyo though often outnumbered.

Nobunaga began to gain a reputation when his powerful neighbor, Imagawa Yoshimoto, sought to march on Kyoto and establish ties with the emperor and shogun, but the Oda clan stood in his path. In 1560, Nobunaga's 2,000 warriors defeated the 25,000 warriors of Yoshimoto at **Okehazama**. Yoshimoto did not take Nobunaga seriously because of his small force, but Nobunaga ambushed the Imagawa as they rested in a wooded gorge. Yoshimoto died in the attack, led by Nobunaga's vassal Toyotomi Hideyoshi. After the battle, Nobunaga began to solidify power around Nagoya.

To gain alliances and secure his holdings, Nobunaga made a series of political marriages to protect his northern and western flanks. He also gained an alliance with Matsudaira Takechiyo (later known as Tokugawa Ieyasu), a hostage of Yoshimoto, who was freed upon Yoshimoto's death and ended up ruling his territory.

In 1568, Nobunaga made his big move, entering Kyoto at the head of 30,000 men and installed the rightful shogun, Ashikaga Yoshiaki (later deposing him for conspiring with Nobunaga's enemy, Takeda Shingen). In addition, he provided the emperor with an income in exchange for titles and social prestige.

Nobunaga's attitude toward religion was always political. He hated the warrior monks of Buddhism but was open to Christianity and the firearms that the Roman Catholic Portuguese brought. In 1571, he began a controversial campaign. His enemies, the Asai and the Asakura, were still a threat after the Battle of **Anegawa** (1570) ended in a draw. He could not tolerate the presence of the hostile warrior monks of Mount Hiei, who were allies of an Oda enemy. Nobunaga could not allow them to sit astride his lines of communication from Kyoto to domains farther north. Nobunaga's men marched up Mount Hiei, killed everyone they found, and burned the temples to the ground. He took their land and gave it to his vassals. As a result of this campaign against the warrior monks, Takeda Shingen, a devout Buddhist, became Nobunaga's last major obstacle to the unification of Japan.

Nobunaga took control of Japan because of his skills as a warrior. He commanded a very large and well-organized army, but he was also an innovator. He was noted for his use of water to end sieges, causing either great thirst or a flood depending on the situation. Nobunaga was most famous for his large-scale use of firearms. In June, 1575, he used 3,000 musketeers to decimate the cavalry of his last major rival Takeda Katsuyori (Shingen's son) at the Battle of **Nagashino**.

On June 21, 1582, Nobunaga was at Nichiren Temple for a tea ceremony when he was attacked by one of his own vassals, Akechi Mitsuhide, a man Nobunaga had slighted and embarrassed. When escape became impossible, Nobunaga committed suicide rather than be taken. By the time of his death, Nobunaga controlled one-third of Japan.

In retaliation for Nobunaga's death, Hideyoshi killed Mitsuhide. Four of Nobunaga's major vassals became regents to Nobunaga's son. Hideyoshi was one of them, but he soon usurped all power.

Resources

Berry, Mary Elizabeth. *Hideyoshi*. Cambridge, Mass.: Harvard University Press, 1982.

Shogun: The Supreme Samurai. Documentary. A&E Home Video, 1997.

Turnbull, Stephen. *Battles of the Samurai*. New York: Arms & Armour, 1987.

_____. *Samurai: A Military History*. London: Osprey, 1977.

_____. *Samurai Warfare*. London: Arms & Armour, 1996.

See also: Japanese Wars of Unification; Samurai; Tokugawa Ieyasu; Toyotomi Hideyoshi.

C. E. Wood

Offa's Wars

At issue: The supremacy of Mercia and control of access to Europe
Date: 771-786
Location: England
Combatants: Mercia vs. surrounding kingdoms
Principal commanders: *Mercian*, Offa (d. 796); *Wessex*, Cynewulf (d. 786); *Kent*, Egbert II (d. 784)
Principal battles: Sussex, Otford, Welsh raids, Bensington, Kent
Result: Mercia became the supreme power in England to the extent that Offa was recognized as "king of the English"

Background

It took Offa several years to bring Mercia's internal affairs under his control following the murder of Æthelbald in 757 and the ensuing civil war. Evidence suggests Offa was a cautious man and an opportunist who used military strength when all else failed, but who nevertheless ruled like a despot once in command. At the start of his reign, with his efforts focused inward, the network of control developed by Æthelbald, which had subjugated most other kingdoms in England, had weakened. Wessex and Kent regained most of their autonomy, and even the Mercian subkingdoms of Hwicce and Lindsey gained some independence. The Welsh, especially in Powys, recognized Mercia's weakness and recovered territory lost to Æthelbald—there was early conflict at Hereford (760).

Once in control of his internal affairs, Offa's first external actions were generally peaceful, building alliances and working with his neighbors. Although Mercia was not landlocked, it was important to Offa to have control over routes to the Continent via the Thames and the southern and eastern ports. He already had the East Saxon and East Anglian kingdoms under his thumb. In 764, he took advantage of political unrest in Kent to invade and install puppet rulers. This was a "friendly" show of force with no overt military action.

In 771, unrest among the southern Saxons caused Offa to flex his muscles and saw the start of a series of military activities that would stretch over the next fifteen years.

Action

Offa invaded **Sussex** (771), ejected the incumbent kings (although he reinstalled one), and set up his own puppet kings. By the late 780's, he had had these kings demoted to "dukes" and treated himself as king of the southern Saxons. He extended this same authority over Kent, whose king, Egbert II (who had been installed by Offa), rebelled in 776, inflicting a defeat on the Mercians at **Otford**.

Offa was unable to deal with Kent at the time as he had more important campaigns. From 777 to 784, he undertook several forays deep into Welsh territory (the **Welsh raids**). Although he never conquered Wales (nor planned to do so), much of south and central Wales recognized his power. He ordered the construction of the massive earthen structure now called Offa's Dyke, to mark the boundary between Wales and England. At the same time, he took the offensive against Wessex, defeating its king, Cynewulf, at **Bensington** (779). When Cynewulf was killed in 786, Offa used his influence to gain Beorhtric the throne, thus making Wessex beholden to him. Beorhtric married Offa's daughter Eadburh. In 784, the Kentish king Egbert II died, and Offa used this moment to invade **Kent**. The rebellious successor, Ealhmund, was murdered, and Offa took over direct rule.

After 786, Offa's activities were directed more against the church than against his neighbors, but he continued to rule as a dictator. In 794, suspecting the East Anglian king Æthelbert of plotting against him, Offa had him murdered. The only

English kingdom over which Offa did not have control was Northumbria, although that kingdom was in such disarray that it offered no threat. Nevertheless he sought alliance in 792 through the marriage of another daughter to the Northumbrian king Æthelred I.

Aftermath

Offa was recognized not only as *bretwalda* but also as *rex Anglorum* (king of the English) and certainly had command over more of Britain than any previous king or any other until Æthelstan. He sought to emulate the empire of Charlemagne and even had his son crowned as king of the Mercians in 787 when Offa was granted his own archiepiscopal see by the pope. Unfortunately his "empire" did not long survive his death, and within a few years, Wessex, under King Egbert, was in the ascendance.

Resources

Kirby, D. P. *The Earliest English Kings*. London: Unwin Hyman, 1991.

Stenton, Frank M. "The Supremacy of the Mercian Kings." *English Historical Review* 33 (1970).

See also: Æthelbald; Æthelbald's Wars; Angles, Saxons, and Jutes.

Mike Ashley

Officer

A person holding a position of authority in a military organization. Among Homeric warriors, there were no true officers; those most successful in single combat earned the respect of their fellows and a limited authority that dissolved in the heat of individual battle. By the fifth century B.C.E., the Greeks had developed the phalanx, a military organization directed by a crude command system. The Romans, however, created the most efficient command system in antiquity: Units, called legions, were divided into cohorts and other smaller units, all directed by subordinate officers. These could be effectively commanded from the rear by a general. The collapse of the Roman Empire, however, heralded centuries of primitive military command. Such Dark Age armies were no better than the rulers and warlords who directed them. Europeans rediscovered the Roman command system during the Renaissance, though they altered it considerably—particularly during the French Revolutionary Wars (1792-1802) and Napoleonic Wars (1803-1815), when the division, corps, and other modern command structures were developed. By the mid-nineteenth century, the Prussians had made another important contribution to command: the introduction of highly trained staff officers who could distribute and collect information for a general and thus make increasingly large armies more manageable. During World War I (1914-1918), the German army first developed the "mission-oriented" tactics that gave subordinate officers more initiative and rendered twentieth century armies less "rigid" than their nineteenth century counterparts.

Jeremiah Taylor

Ogatai

Also known as: Ögödei; Ogadai; Ogdai; Ogotai
Born: c. 1185; Mongolia
Died: December 11, 1241; Karakorum, Mongolia
Principal wars: Mongol Wars in North China and Central Asia, Mongol invasion of Russia and Eastern Europe
Principal battle: Siege of Urgench (1219)
Military significance: Ogatai presided over the *quriltai* (council, public assembly) that planned the conquest of Russia and Eastern Europe by a Mongol army of 150,000 under the nominal command of his nephew, Batu, and the brilliant general Subatai.

The third son of Genghis Khan, Ogatai was sent with his quarrelsome brothers Jochi and Chagatai to fight the Khwārezm Empire in 1219. Genghis appointed Ogatai to oversee the Siege of Urgench (1219). The Mongols, lacking stones, made missiles from the trunks of mulberry trees soaked in water and captured the city after seven months.

Ogatai was chosen by his father before his death in 1227 to succeed him and was elected khan by a *quriltai* in 1229. He ruled during the final conquest of North China (1234) and founded the Mongol capital at Karakorum in Central Mongolia in 1235.

Crossing the Volga in winter, 1237, Mongol armies conquered Russia, defeating Grand Prince Yuri II of Vladimir's army at Sil River (March 4, 1238) and sacking Kiev (December 6, 1240). Over the next two years, the Mongols advanced to the Adriatic after destroying the armies of Bohemia and Hungary at Liegnitz (April 9, 1241) and Sajó River (April 11, 1241). Batu and other commanders returned to Mongolia to elect a new khan after Ogatai's death in 1241, and shortly afterward, in 1242, the Mongols abandoned their campaign in Europe. The commanders' return to Mongolia probably saved Europe from being conquered.

A U.S. Marine runs through Death Valley on Okinawa. (Digital Stock)

Resources

Juvaini, Ala-ad-Din Ata-Malik. *The History of the World Conqueror.* 2 vols. Cambridge, Mass.: Harvard University Press, 1958.

Onon, Urgunge, trans. *The Secret History of the Mongols.* Richmond, Va.: Curzon, 2000.

Vernadsky, George. *The Mongols and Russia.* New Haven, Conn.: Yale University Press, 1953.

See also: Genghis Khan; Mongol Empire; Sajó River.

Michael C. Paul

Okinawa

Type of action: Air, ground, and sea combat in World War II
Date: April 1-July 2, 1945
Location: Okinawa, 350 miles southwest of the Japanese main islands
Combatants: 208,750 Americans vs. 77,199 Japanese and 40,000 Okinawans
Principal commanders: *United States*, Admiral Chester W. Nimitz (1885-1966); *Japanese*, Lieutenant General Mitsuru Ushijima (1887-1945)
Result: The United States took Okinawa from the Japanese

On April 1, some 60,000 U.S. troops landed, largely unopposed, on Okinawa. Intense fighting began a few days later when the Americans reached the strong, inland Japanese fortifications. Grueling ground combat raged throughout the spring until the last line of significant Japanese defenses, led by Lieutenant General Mitsuru Ushijima, was overcome on June 22.

The naval portion of the war was similarly bloody and drawn out. The Japanese launched several thousand aircraft and one naval task force against the Americans, led by Admiral Chester W. Nimitz. The task force was intercepted and routed, and the largest battleship in the world, the *Yamato*, was sunk on April 7. However, nearly 2,000 missiles and kamikaze (suicide planes) helped cause the worst U.S. naval losses in history.

By the time the battle was officially declared over on July 2, the United States had suffered 12,281 dead, more than 50,000 wounded and other casualties, 763 planes lost, and 36 ships sunk and 368 damaged. Japanese losses included 110,071 killed, 7,401 captured, 7,830 planes lost, and 16 ships sunk and 4 damaged.

Significance

Okinawa was the bloodiest campaign of the Pacific war, and the high casualty rate was influential in the decision to drop the atomic bomb on Japan.

Resources

Leckie, Robert. *Okinawa: The Last Battle of World War II*. New York: Viking, 1995.

Our Century: Okinawa, The Final Battle. Documentary. The History Channel, 1995.

Sledge, Eugene B. *With the Old Breed at Peleliu and Okinawa*. Annapolis, Md.: Naval Institute Press, 1996.

Yahara, Hiromichi. *The Battle for Okinawa*. New York: John Wiley & Sons, 1997.

SEE ALSO: World War II; Yamamoto, Isoroku.

Paul John Chara, Jr.

Omani Conquest of Eastern Africa

AT ISSUE: Control of Indian Ocean and Red Sea trade
DATE: 1631-1730
LOCATION: Southern Arabian peninsula, east coast of Africa
COMBATANTS: Sultanate of Oman vs. Portuguese vs. members of Swahili principalities
PRINCIPAL COMMANDERS: *Omani*, Sultan ibn Seif al-Yaʿrubi; *Portuguese*, various captains of Mombasa; *Malind/Mombasai*, Sheikh Yūsuf bin Ḥasan
PRINCIPAL BATTLES: Mombasa, Siege of Fort Jesus
RESULT: Portugal was driven from eastern Africa, north of Mozambique; Islam became an important cultural force in East Africa

Background

The loosely organized trading principalities of the eastern African coastline—known to Arabs as the Land of Zenj—had been closely linked to Islamic Indian Ocean trade routes since the eighth century. African ivory was an especially prized international commodity, and the coastal cities also exported ambergris, mangrove poles, slaves, and gold. As the number of Muslim Arabs settling on islands or in port cities along the coast began to increase, intermarriage became common, producing a unique coastal society built upon trade and embracing both African and Islamic elements. Some forty Swahili city-states developed between Mogadishu and Sofala, including Pate, Lamu, Malindi, Mombasa, Pemba, Zanzibar, Mozambique, and Kilwa. After 1500, the political authority of these principalities was steadily undermined by both Portugal and a variety of inland Bantu peoples. The Portuguese first arrived on Vasco da Gama's voyage to India in 1498, and by the 1590's dominated trade south of Mogadishu, operating a loose system of alliances and tribute collections from the strategically important base at Fort Jesus (Mombasa). After 1580, the coastal city-states also suffered attacks by the Zimba, a Bantu-speaking people, who migrated from the region of Lake Malawi. The economy of the region suffered from Portuguese military administration, while Portugal's imperial presence in Africa and Asia was weakened in the late sixteenth and early seventeenth centuries by attacks from Spain, England, France, Holland, and the Ottoman Empire.

Action

In times of strength, Portugal was unassailable, given the level of technology and political cohesion among the Swahili cities. By the early seventeenth century, however, a number of factors were beginning to undermine Portugal's position. Tribal warfare in the hinterlands kept the region in a constant state of alarm. To the north, the Ottoman Empire was expanding its Red Sea presence, and Portugal's empire, from Africa to eastern Asia, was under frequent attack, especially by the Dutch, the English, and the Omanis, nominally loyal to the Ottoman Empire. Uprisings along the eastern African coast during the first half of the seventeenth century were unsuccessful, though a royal revolt of nominal ally Sheikh Yūsuf bin Ḥasan of Mombasa, in 1631, was cause for concern. Such disturbances became more ominous after Omani sultan ibn Seif al-Yaʿrubi drove the Portuguese from Muscat and the Arabian coast in 1650. Using the ships captured from the Portuguese fleet and employing Dutch and English navigators and gunners, Oman built the most formidable fleet in the western Indian Ocean. Encouraged by Omani success, a number of Swahili principalities rebelled. Pate, for instance, revolted in 1660, 1678, 1686, and 1687. Although Portugal was successful in quelling the rebellions, they were constantly short of men and money and found the task of holding the coastline increasingly difficult.

With Portugal in decline, the Omanis attacked Faza and **Mombasa** in 1661 and almost captured

Milestones in the Omani Conquest of Eastern Africa

Date	Event
1650	Omanis of Arabia expel the Portuguese from Muscat, then begin attacking Portuguese commercial ports.
1652	Omanis support rebellions at Pate and Zanzibar.
1661	Omanis attack Faza and Mombasa.
1670	Omanis fail to take Mozambique.
1678-1679	Portuguese forces launch largely ineffective counterattack.
1687	Portuguese suppress Pate rebellion.
1698	Omanis seize Fort Jesus.
1701	Omanis capture Zanzibar.
1727	Pate forms alliance with Portuguese to rid itself of Omani control.
1728-1729	Portuguese recapture Mombasa.
1730	Omanis drive Portuguese out of Mombasa.

Mozambique in 1670. In 1687, a former king of the island of Pate asked for Portuguese help in ridding his principality of the Omanis. The Portuguese fleet was driven off by a stronger Omani fleet, ushering in a more intense period of conflict. The turning point came when **Fort Jesus** fell to an army from Oman and Pate, in December, 1698, after a three-year siege. The Portuguese loss was more closely related to the effects of disease and low morale than to Omani strength, as the sultan had no siege artillery and few firearms. These were, however, common and largely unmet problems for Portugal for the duration of their Indian Ocean empire.

Zanzibar's fall in 1701 marked the effective end of Portuguese rule in the central coastal region. After an Omani mutiny in 1727, Pate again allied itself with Portugal, and Mafia, Malindi, Pemba, and Kilwa revolted. Portugal briefly reclaimed Mombasa in 1728-1729 and reestablished the slave trade there, but the Portuguese were soon at odds with local rulers and by 1730 had been driven out of the entire coastal region north of Mozambique.

Aftermath

The Portuguese continued their imperial decline and were forced to concentrate their eastern African holdings in Mozambique. The Omanis had been welcomed as liberators, but the Swahili principalities would not willingly submit to their political rule, a point demonstrated by their willingness to ally with Portugal again in 1727. Until the 1820's, Persian threats and civil discord preoccupied Oman. Although many Arabs remained in the coastal enclaves, the eastern African principalities remained substantially free of Omani control and developed the slave trade with France as an important part of their economy.

Resources

Boxer, C. R. *The Portuguese Seaborne Empire: 1600-1800*. London: Hutchinson, 1969.

Kirkman, J. *Fort Jesus: A Portuguese Fortress on the East African Coast*. London: Oxford University Press, 1974.

Russell Wood, A. J. R. *A World on the Move: The Portuguese in Africa, Asia, and America, 1415-1808*. New York: St. Martin's Press, 1992.

Strandes, Justus. *The Portuguese Period in East Africa*. Nairobi, Kenya: East African Literature Bureau, 1968.

See also: Portuguese Colonial Wars.

John Powell

Omdurman

TYPE OF ACTION: Ground battle in reconquest of Sudan
DATE: September 2, 1898
LOCATION: Near Khartoum, Sudan
COMBATANTS: 25,800 Anglo-Egyptians vs. 35,000-52,000 Sudanese
PRINCIPAL COMMANDERS: *Sudanese*, Khalifa ʿAbd Allāh (?-1899); *Anglo-Egyptian*, Lord Kitchener (1850-1916)
RESULT: Decisive Anglo-Egyptian victory

No battle from the age of imperialism better illustrates the tremendous advantage of "science versus pluck." At Omdurman, Sudanese defenders faced not only a well-led adversary but also one that employed armored gunboats, quick-fire artillery, and machine guns. Against this stood warriors with spears, swords, or delapidated single-shot rifles.

The only logical defense was to abandon Khartoum and conduct partisan warfare. Yet few dared suggest such tactics, for the Sudanese commander, ʿAbd Allāh, deemed his army ready to defeat the smaller force of Anglo-Egyptians. He even ruled out a night assault, thus condemning his troops to fight under conditions favorable to the invaders.

Despite tremendous bravery, Sudanese attacks could not penetrate the wall of fire surrounding Lord Kitchener's soldiers. Even Egyptians armed with obsolete Martini-Henry rifles pinned Sudanese attacks at five hundred yards. This was far beyond the effective range of ʿAbd Allāh's best-armed troops. Only a rash charge conducted by the Twenty-first Lancers put any Anglo-Egyptians in harm's way. In the end, ʿAbd Allāh's army was shattered, with 10,000 dead and countless wounded. Anglo-Egyptian casualties amounted to 48 dead and 434 wounded.

SIGNIFICANCE
Destruction of the Mahdist state followed the Battle of Omdurman and allowed for the establishment of an Anglo-Egyptian Sudan.

RESOURCES
Barthorp, Michael. *War on the Nile*. Poole, Dorset, England: Blanford Press, 1984.
Harrington, Peter, and Frederic A. Sharf. *Omdurman 1898: The Eye-Witnesses Speak*. London: Greenhill Books, 1998.
Zulfo, Ismat Hasan. *Karari*. London: F. Warne, 1980.

SEE ALSO: ʿAbdullāh et Taʿāʾisha; British Colonial Wars; Kitchener, Lord.

John P. Dunn

Ōnin War

AT ISSUE: Right of succession to shogunate in Ashikaga family
DATE: 1467-1477
LOCATION: Primarily in the region around the capital, Kyoto
COMBATANTS: Hosokawa Katsumoto and adherents vs. Yamana Mochitoyo and adherents
PRINCIPAL COMMANDERS: *Hosokawa*, Hosokawa Katsumoto (1430-1473), Ashikaga Yoshimasa (1436-1490); *Yamana*, Yamana Mochitoyo, later Yamana Sōzen (1404-1473)
PRINCIPAL BATTLE: Kyoto
RESULT: The senseless and destructive struggle marked the beginning of a century in which local warlords dominated and the shogunate lacked central authority

BACKGROUND
The Ōnin War reflected the breakdown of the authority of the shogunate, the country's warrior government, at a time when old relationships and institutions were disintegrating at every level of Japanese society. Fierce competition for power provoked succession disputes in leading warrior families throughout the country, and the most successful vied for influence in the capital.

Such rivalry between the two most powerful warriors in the country, Hosokawa Katsumoto and Yamana Mochitoyo, precipitated this war. Katsumoto, who was *kanrei* (shogun's deputy), initially allied with the volatile, ambitious Mochitoyo, marrying his eldest daughter and adopting his youngest son but later enraged Mochitoyo by making the boy a Buddhist priest after having a son of his own. The two men backed competing candidates for control of two powerful families, one of whom was to supply the next *kanrei*, as well as rival candidates to succeed the cultured but feckless Shogun Ashikaga Yoshimasa. Katsumoto favored Yoshimasa's younger brother Ashikaga Yoshimi; Mochitoyo preferred his infant son Ashikaga Yoshihisa.

ACTION

By early 1467, both Katsumoto and Mochitoyo had assembled armies of more than 80,000 in Kyoto. Yoshimasa sought to keep peace by threatening to declare the instigator of violence in the capital a rebel (legalizing attacks on him and seizure of his estates). Yet by late May, 1467, violence had spread from the outskirts of the city into **Kyoto**, which became the principal battleground of the war. By late June, thousands of acres of the city had been leveled by fire, and trenches and barricades were being built by both sides.

Katsumoto induced Yoshimasa to declare Mochitoyo a rebel, causing some desertions, and instigated disorder in his supporters' territories, inducing some to return home to protect their interests. But Mochitoyo gained reinforcements, most notably a 20,000-man contingent from western Japan that arrived in August. By then Katsumoto's force, the Eastern Army, was confined to the northeast corner of the city, including the imperial palace and the shogun's compound. Mochitoyo's Western Army eventually gained control of much of the capital, including six of its seven gates. By late September, Mochitoyo had seized the palace with 50,000 men, though Katsumoto had already removed the emperor to the shogun's compound. The most vulnerable of Katsumoto's remaining holdings, Shōkokuji, a great Zen monastery, was stormed and burned on November 1, a cataclysmic day of fighting that left the capital's streets littered with thousands of corpses.

However, both sides were exhausted, and the Western Army made no effort to take the adjacent shogunate's headquarters. During the coming months, there was little fighting as massive defensive works were erected, reportedly including a twenty-foot-wide, ten-foot-deep ditch separating the adversaries. The five months of horrific street fighting had devastated Kyoto, partly because of the use of *ashigaru* ("light-footed soldiers"). Rebellious farmers hired as mercenaries, the *ashigaru* were much given to arson and looting.

AFTERMATH

Throughout 1468, fighting was desultory, though many more monasteries, mansions, and houses were burned. After 1468, stalemate persisted in the capital, and the only significant military activity was in the provinces, where usurpers sought to replace absent leaders. Oddly, Yoshimi ended up a general on Mochitoyo's side, and Yoshimasa declared his four-year-old son his successor, making the conflict now between Yoshimasa and his brother Yoshimi. Mochitoyo's bizarre attempt in 1471 to gain advantage by putting forward a pretender from the long-defunct Southern Court as emperor came to naught, and when Mochitoyo and Katsumoto both died in 1473, the occupying armies diminished rapidly. Still some held on, and sporadic fighting and destruction continued until evacuation of the remnants of the Western Army in December, 1477, brought an end to an eleven-year war that epitomizes senseless, destructive futility. Sadly, the war initiated a century of lawlessness, the Sengoku (Warring States) period, and the evaporation of all central authority, as successive shogun would be mere puppets of rival warlords (daimyo).

RESOURCES

Henshall, Kenneth G. *A History of Japan: From Stone Age to Superpower*. Basingstoke, England: Macmillan, 1999.

Sansom, George. *A History of Japan, 1334-1615*. Stanford, Calif.: Stanford University Press, 1978.

Sugawara Makoto. "The Ōnin Disturbance." *The East* 22, no. 3 (June, 1986): 8-13.

Totman, Conrad D. *A History of Japan*. Malden, Mass.: Blackwell, 2000.

Varley, Paul. *The Ōnin War*. New York: Columbia University Press, 1967.

SEE ALSO: Japanese Civil Wars of 1331-1392; Japanese Civil Wars of 1450-1550.

R. Craig Philips

OPIUM WARS

AT ISSUE: Continued and increased trade between the Western powers and China, colonial domination of China

Opium Wars

DATE: 1839-1842, 1856-1860
LOCATION: China
COMBATANTS: Chinese vs. British and French
PRINCIPAL COMMANDERS: *Chinese*, Commissioner Lin Zexu (1785-1850), Prince Sengguolinqin (d. 1865); *British*, Captain Charles Elliot (1801-1875), Sir Henry Pottinger (1789-1856), Victor Alexander Bruce Elgin (1849-1917); *French*, Baron Gros (1793-1870), General Cousin de Montauban (1796-1878)
PRINCIPAL BATTLES: Chuenpi, Whompoa, Ningpo (Ninghsien), Guangzhou (Canton), Dagu (Taku) Forts
RESULT: The defeat and subjugation of China; forced acceptance of the opium trade; payment of indemnities; loss of territory

Background

The principal reason for the Opium Wars was the British desire for economic and imperialistic expansion. By the beginning of the nineteenth century, a mass market had developed in Britain for Chinese tea. Paying for the tea presented problems because the Chinese did not want British goods in trade and preferred silver, of which the British had only limited amounts. The British solved their problem by promoting a covert trade in opium grown in India and fostering an addiction to the drug among the Chinese. Drug addiction became so widespread and the outflow of silver to pay for the drug so acute that by 1838, the alarmed Chinese authorities took action. Lin Zexu was appointed commissioner to suppress the trade and to destroy the opium stock. In retaliation, the British took military action, resulting in the First Opium War.

Despite its huge size and population, China was unprepared for war. The equipment of its army and navy was antiquated, and its military personnel for the most part were incompetent and untrained for modern warfare. China also lacked a diplomatic system. Its traditional contacts with the outside world were based on foreign powers paying tribute to or submitting to the will of the emperor, a system that was rejected by the Western powers.

Action

The First Opium War (1839-1842) was primarily a series of naval engagements, the two most

Members of the French Foreign Legion attack on a bridge eight miles from Peking during the Second Opium War. (Archive Photos/Hulton Getty Collection)

important of which were **Chuenpi** (November 3, 1839) and **Whompoa** (May 21, 1841), both in Guangzhou Harbor. The British under Captain Charles Elliot and Sir Henry Pottinger virtually destroyed the Chinese navy. In order to force the Chinese government to negotiate, the British threatened the Dagu forts guarding the mouth of the Hai river leading to Tianjin and Beijing, the capital. They then made plans to sail up the Yangtze (Chang) River, intending to bombard the important city of Nanjing. The Chinese suffered heavy casualties attempting to repulse the British at **Ningpo** (March 4, 1842). The shaken imperial government agreed to negotiate, resulting in the Treaty of Nanjing (August, 1842).

The Treaty of Nanjing stipulated a payment to Britain of $21 million and the opening of five ports to trade and foreign residence. It ceded to Britain the island of Hong Kong and established a customs tariff, not to be changed without British consent. The treaty was followed a year later by a supplementary treaty that set the tariff at a low rate, gave Britons the right to be tried in British courts (extraterritoriality), and contained a most-favored-nation clause.

In the Second Opium War (1856-1860), using an alleged insult to the British flag as a pretext, the British under Victor Alexander Bruce Elgin renewed the war. They were joined by the French, eager for imperialist expansion. Both Russia and the United States joined as "interested neutrals," mainly to protect and to further their interests. **Guangzhou** was largely destroyed by bombardment in December of 1857. The Dagu Forts were again taken, and Tianjin and Beijing were threatened. The imperial government, weakened by internal rebellion and headed by the incompetent Emperor Xian Feng, agreed to the Treaty of Tianjin (June, 1858).

The Treaty of Tianjin opened eleven more Chinese ports to trade and stipulated payment of $8 million each to Britain and France. It gave foreigners the right to conduct missionary activity anywhere in China and to travel throughout China. Ambassadors were given right of residence in the capital. In addition, the expression "barbarian" was not to be used in reference to the Western powers.

Because the emperor failed to ratify the treaty, the allies prepared for a major land battle. In June of 1859, they again attacked the **Dagu Forts** but were this time repulsed by the Chinese under General Sengguolinqin. The allies regrouped and returned the following summer. They reduced the forts and proceeded toward Tianjin and Beijing. The emissaries sent by Elgin were taken prisoner, and some were mistreated. The emperor fled the capital. In retaliation for the mistreatment of the emissaries, Elgin ordered the two hundred buildings of the summer palace outside the city burned.

The Peking Treaty (October, 1860) increased the indemnities to $11 million, added Tianjin to the list of treaty ports, and ceded a part of Kaulun (Kowloon) to Britain. Later negotiation legalized the opium trade. China signed separate treaties or concessions with France, Russia, and the United States.

AFTERMATH

As a result of the wars and the treaties, China was humiliated, weakened, and impoverished. Humiliation led to a growing hatred of all foreigners, and weakness invited later attacks by the Japanese and further loss of territory. Impoverishment led to the infamous "coolie system" that in many ways replaced slavery. Public resentment led to the overthrow of the Manchus of the Qing Dynasty in 1911, the establishment of a republic, and the beginning of a new era for China.

RESOURCES

Beeching, Jack. *The Chinese Opium Wars*. New York: Harcourt Brace Jovanovich, 1975.

Chu, Henry. "Chinese Officials Ban Perfume Opium, Saying Name Could Prove Harmful to Society." *Los Angeles Times*, January 13, 2000.

Hsü. Immanuel C. Y. "The Opium Wars." In *The Rise of Modern China*. New York: Oxford University Press, 1995.

Newsinger, John. "Britain's Opium Wars." *Monthly Review* 44, no. 5 (October, 1997): 35.

Waley, Arthur. *The Opium Wars Through Chinese Eyes*. Stanford, Calif.: Stanford University Press, 1958.

SEE ALSO: Boxer Rebellion; Japanese Colonial Wars; Taiping Rebellion.

Nis Petersen

Orléans, Siege of

Type of action: Ground battle in the Hundred Years' War
Date: October, 1428-May, 1429
Location: Loire Valley, central France
Combatants: English vs. French
Principal commanders: *English*, William de la Pole, earl of Suffolk (1396-1450); *French*, Jean, comte de Dunois, known as the Bastard of Orléans (1403-1468), Joan of Arc (1412-1431)
Result: By lifting the Siege of Orléans, Joan of Arc ended the English reputation for military invincibility

The Siege of Orléans was undertaken by the English in the hope of forcing a quick end to the Hundred Years' War. Despite the victory at Agincourt in 1415 and the 1420 Treaty of Troyes as well as the presence in Paris of English John of Lancaster, duke of Bedford as regent for the French boy-king Henry VI, active resistance continued on behalf of the Dauphin. In 1428, the English Parliament voted funds to finance an expedition to capture the city of Orléans on the north bank of the Loire.

The earl of Salisbury began the operation by establishing a chain of forts northwest of Orléans, as well as upstream and downstream on the Loire. On October 22, 1428, the English capture of the Orléans bridge and its south-bank fortifications began the siege. However, Salisbury's 4,000 soldiers faced a defense garrison of 2,000 troops, 2,000 militia, and about 30,000 townspeople. The effectiveness of the new French artillery was demonstrated when a cannonball killed Salisbury himself. English command then passed to the unenterprising William de la Pole, earl of Suffolk, who had to do battle with Jean, comte de Dunois, a highly capable French commander.

Meanwhile, in France south of the Loire, the Dauphin, claiming to rule as Charles VII, was scraping together money to pay for a relief expedition to Orléans. A somewhat improbable volunteer, a seventeen-year-old peasant girl named Joan of Arc, appeared at the Dauphin's court, perfectly sincere and serious in her claim that heavenly voices had told her to lead the relief of Orléans and then have Charles crowned at Rheims. After prolonged examination, Joan was given a vague leadership title, equipped as a religious and quasi-military figure, and sent to join the French army of about 5,000 at Blois on the Loire. Setting out for Orléans on April 27, 1429, Joan and her entourage reached the city on April 29, and entered as part of a torchlight parade.

While the army leaders discussed plans, Joan mixed with the troops and citizens of Orléans. On May 4, the comte de Dunois attacked the English garrison in the church of St. Loup east of Orléans. Joan joined the fray and was so effective in rallying French troops that she was assigned a part in the next attack. On May 6, the French committed about 4,000 troops to assaulting English positions at the south end of the Orléans bridge. In a day of fighting, the French captured the fortified monastery of Augustine, although the English held out in the fortified towers on the bridge itself. Joan insisted on renewing the attack on May 7 and repeatedly rallied the French until a complex night attack (including a fireboat) overwhelmed the English. The recovery of the bridge made the rest of the siege nearly meaningless. The English army challenged the French to battle on May 8, then marched away after the French declined. The siege was over, and Orléans gave the credit to the peasant girl.

In the ensuing days, the French proceeded against the smaller English outposts on the Loire. Joan persuaded the French commanders to attack a 5,000-man English relief army on the march near Patay. The English army, surprised, was destroyed as an organized force. After the 1429 coronation of the Dauphin as Charles VII, Joan's later failures, capture, trial for heresy, and execution in 1431 naturally diminished her moral influence.

Significance

How far Joan of Arc inspired the generation that drove the English out of France cannot be measured. Her military success proved that the English could be driven out of the Loire Valley, even by a common peasant girl claiming heavenly approval.

Resources

Belloc, Hilaire. *Joan of Arc*. London: Cassell, 1929.
Burne, Alfred. *The Agincourt War*. London: Eyre and Spottiswode, 1956.

DeVries, Kelly. *Joan of Arc: A Military Leader.* Stroud, England: Sutton, 1999.
Gies, Frances. *Joan of Arc: The Legend and the Reality.* New York: Harper & Row, 1981.
Sackville-West, Vita. *Saint Joan of Arc.* New York: Doubleday Doran, 1936.

SEE ALSO: Agincourt; Hundred Years' War; Joan of Arc.

K. Fred Gillum

OSAKA CASTLE, SIEGE OF

TYPE OF ACTION: Siege in the Japanese Wars of Unification
DATE: 1614-1615
LOCATION: Osaka
COMBATANTS: Osaka daimyo (feudal barons) vs. eastern daimyo
PRINCIPAL COMMANDERS: *Osaka daimyo*, Toyotomi Hideyoshi (1537-1598); *Eastern daimyo*, Tokugawa Ieyasu (1543-1616)
RESULT: Ieyasu solidified his grip on a unified Japan by eliminating his most serious potential challenger, Toyotomi Hideyori

Osaka Castle was built by Toyotomi Hideyoshi in 1538 and served as his headquarters until his death in 1598. Hideyoshi's son, Hideyori, was only five years old at the time of his father's death, and for a while, Tokugawa Ieyasu, who had risen to power, ignored the potential threat posed by Hideyori. However, Hideyori's vassals and numerous masterless samurai (*ronin*) began to gather at the castle, and in 1614, Ieyasu denounced Hideyori for allegedly subversive behavior. He besieged Osaka Castle in December. Peace was arranged through a truce, but Ieyasu had the outer moats of the castle filled in. He resumed the siege in May, 1615, capturing the castle, but not destroying it, on June 3. Hideyori and his mother committed suicide the next day. Jesuit histories say that a hundred thousand soldiers perished in this conflict.

SIGNIFICANCE

With the death of Hideyori, his last potential challenger, Ieyasu became the supreme ruler of Japan. His family, the Tokugawa, would control Japan through the shogunate until 1867. However, for the next four decades, the discontent felt by masterless samurai, forced to find other employment during peacetime, would produce several uprisings.

RESOURCES

Berry, Mary Elizabeth. *Hideyoshi.* Harvard East Asian Monographs, 146. Cambridge, Mass.: Harvard University Press, 1989.
Kure, Mitsuo. *The Samurai.* Marlborough: Crowood, 2000.
Tarnstrom, Ronald L. *The Wars of Japan.* Lindborg, Kan.: Trogen Books, 1992.

SEE ALSO: Japanese Wars of Unification; Sekigahara; Tokugawa Ieyasu; Toyotomi Hideyoshi.

Ceferina Gayo Hess

OSTEND, SIEGE OF

TYPE OF ACTION: Siege in the Dutch Wars of Independence
DATE: 1601-1604
LOCATION: Ostend (Oostende in Flemish), Spanish Netherlands (later Belgium)
COMBATANTS: 60,000 Spanish vs. 30,000 Dutch
PRINCIPAL COMMANDERS: *Spanish*, Albrecht VII, archduke of Austria (1559-1621), Federico Spinola (d. 1601), Ambrosio Spinola (1569-1630); *Dutch*, Sir Francis Vere (1560-1609), Prince Maurice of Nassau (1567-1625), Daniel van Hertaing
RESULT: Spanish capture of Ostend, the last Dutch stronghold in the southern Netherlands

Originally a fishing village, Ostend was fortified in 1583 and became the last Dutch stronghold in what became Belgium. Defeated at Nieuport in 1600 and failing to convince Madrid to negotiate with the Dutch, Archduke Albrecht VII marched north and laid siege to Ostend on July 5, 1601. Genoese admiral Federico Spinola's attempt to cut Ostend off from the sea failed, resulting in his death. Prince Maurice of Nassau was unable to relieve the city. However, its garrison, led first by Sir Francis Vere and later by Daniel van Hertaing, held out stubbornly. Conducting the siege at his own expense, Federico Spinola's brother Ambrosio captured the city on September 14, 1604.

Significance

Both sides suffered heavy losses, and hardly a building in Ostend remained undamaged, but Spanish control of the southern Netherlands was reasserted. Spinola went on to win victories in Friesland (northern Holland). However, Philip III could not raise the funds needed to continue the campaign. The Spanish recognized Dutch independence, but the Dutch refused to withdraw from recent conquests in the Americas and the East Indies or to tolerate Catholicism. The two sides concluded an armistice in 1607 and then in 1609 a twelve-year truce. Rebuilt, Ostend later enjoyed a period of prosperity under Austrian rule.

Resources

Melegari, V. *The Great Military Sieges*. New York: Thomas Crowell, 1972.

Parker, Geoffrey. *The Dutch Revolt*. London: Penguin, 1990.

Rady, Martyn. *From Revolt to Independence*. London: Hodder & Stoughton, 1990.

See also: Dutch Wars of Independence; Maurice of Nassau, Prince; Nieuport.

Randall Fegley

Ostrogoths

Date: 470's-552
Location: The Balkans, Italy
Principal military action: Gothic War
Military significance: The Ostrogoths conquered Italy from the general Odoacer, who himself had overthrown the last Roman emperor in the west. After consolidating their own kingdom, the Ostrogoths fought hard against the resurgent Eastern Roman Empire before succumbing at the Battle of Mons Lactarius (553).

Though they spoke a Germanic language, the Ostrogoths were composed of many ethnic groups. Their main cohesion was supplied by the reigning Amal Dynasty as well as their identity as a military force. The Ostrogoths' military strength was their cavalry, which they used in swift surprise attacks. The Ostrogoths had been subject peoples of the Huns in Pannonia, then in the 470's emerged as a forceful power in the Balkans. Under the Amal king Theodoric, their foot soldiers and horsemen caused so much trouble that the Eastern Roman emperor Zeno convinced them to invade Italy and overthrow Odoacer. In Italy, Theodoric established a strong realm that allowed the Roman aristocracy some role in government. When Theodoric died, weak monarchs left the Ostrogoths open to a Roman reconquest. The Roman general Belisarius seemed about to conquer all when a new Ostrogoth leader, Totila, emerged. Under Totila's leadership, the Ostrogoths defeated the Romans at Faenza and reconquered Rome in 546. However, Totila lost to the Romans under Narses at Taginae in 552. After Totila's death, the last leader of the Ostrogoths, Teias, was weakened by the defection of his naval commander and subsequently lost to Narses at Mons Lactarius in 553.

Resources

Amory, Patrick. *People and Identity in Ostrogothic Italy, 489-554*. New York: Cambridge University Press, 1997.

Goffart, Walter. *The Narrators of Barbarian History*. Princeton, N.J.: Princeton University Press, 1988.

Heather, Peter. *The Goths*. Oxford: Blackwell, 1998.

Wolfram, Herwig. *History of the Goths*. Berkeley: University of California Press, 1988.

_____. *The Roman Empire and Its Germanic Peoples*. Berkeley: University of California Press, 1998.

See also: Belisarius; Gothic War; Goths; Huns; Justinian I; Narses; Taginae.

Nicholas Birns

Otto I

Also known as: Otto the Great
Born: October 23, 912; Saxony
Died: May 7, 973; Memleben, Thuringia
Principal wars: German Civil War of 939-941, Italian Campaigns, Magyar Invasions
Principal battle: Lechfeld (955)
Military significance: Otto I unified and expanded Germany, dominated northern Italy, ended the Magyar threat and revived the Holy Roman Empire.

Otto I. (Library of Congress)

In 936, the Saxon Dynasty placed Otto I on the German throne. He battled against his half-brother Thankmar from 938 to 939 for the crown. Then five princes refused to recognize his authority, and civil war erupted. By 941, Otto had quashed the rebellion, defeated Louis IV of France, who supported the rebels, and unified Germany.

In 951, Otto became involved in Italian affairs. When a debate arose regarding the line of succession, Otto invaded, defeated other contenders, and became king of Italy. In 961, Otto again intervened. Berengar, the marquis of Friuli, threatened papal lands and claimed the kingship of Italy. Otto invaded and by 965 had defeated Berengar's army, saved Pope John XII, and retained his authority in Italy. As a reward, he was crowned Holy Roman emperor by the pope, but good relations between the two soon ended. In 966, Otto demanded the right to approve future popes. When the pope refused, Otto invaded again, deposed John XII, and oversaw the election of a new pope, John XIII. This move won him few supporters, and he remained in Italy until 972 to consolidate his control.

In the meantime, Magyars, longtime enemies of the Saxons, invaded Bavaria and besieged the city of Augsburg. For nearly a year, Otto fought the Magyar forces, and in 955 at the Battle of Lechfeld (near Augsburg), he destroyed their armies, ended the Magyar threat, and revitalized the Holy Roman Empire.

Resources
Arnold, Benjamin. *Medieval Germany, 500-1300: A Political Interpretation*. Toronto: The University of Toronto Press, 1997.
Barraclough, Geoffrey. *The Origins of Modern Germany*. New York: W. W. Norton, 1984.
Gallagher, John. *Church and State in Germany Under Otto the Great*. Washington, D.C.: The Catholic University Press, 1938.

See also: Holy Roman Empire; Lechfeld; Magyars.

Gregory S. Taylor

Ottoman Civil Wars

At issue: Struggle for the throne
Date: May 3, 1481-April 5, 1513
Location: Anatolia (Turkey)
Combatants: Sultan Bayezid II vs. Prince (Sultan) Cem; Sultan Selim I vs. Prince (Sultan) Ahmed
Principal commanders: Bayezid II (1448-1512), Cem (1459-1495), Selim I (1470-1520), Ahmed (1465-1513)
Principal battles: First Yenişehir, Çukurçimen Yaylak, Ankara, Çorlu, Second Yenişehir
Result: Bayezid II and Selim I were victorious; both ascended to the throne

Background
With the death of Mehmed II on May 3, 1481, the law regarding the succession to the throne resulted in not only a quarrel between the brothers but also a civil war. The competition over the throne was also a continuation of a dispute between Grand Vizier Karamani Mehmed Pasha and the former vizier, Ishak Pasha. The Shiite propaganda must also have played a role.

The Janissaries, upon Mehmed's death, looted the houses of rich men and killed Grand Vizier Karamani Mehmed Pasha, Prince Cem's supporter. They secured the throne for Bayezid II, declaring his son Korkud as sultan until the arrival of Bayezid (May 20, 1481).

Action

With a force of 1,000 men, Cem, the governor of Karaman, marched on to Bursa, where he defeated a force of 2,000 Janissaries commanded by the third vizier, Ayas Pasha. Cem defeated Ayas Pasha and his forces in a battle that took place outside the city. Bayezid later defeated Cem and his Turkomen instigators at the **First Battle of Yenişehir** Plain (June 20, 1481). Cem escaped Konya and left for Egypt on June 28.

Kasim Bey, the former ruler of Karaman, and Mehmed Bey, the *sancakbey* of Ankara, sent letters to Cem urging him to come back. He did, but Bayezid's forces defeated him and his instigators first at **Çukurçimen Yaylak**, then at **Ankara** on June 8, 1482. Cem escaped again on July 20 and took refuge with the Knights of St. John (Hospitalers) at Rhodes, who took him to Europe.

Bayezid both ascended and descended the throne in dispute. There was discontent with him in Anatolia and Karaman because of his passive policy that had opened the way to bribery in acquiring government positions. Bayezid's love for Prince Ahmed and the latter's insistence on refusing the appointments of the other princes to positions close to the capital gave rise to dispute among the competitors for the throne and their supporters.

Selim I, discontent with his father's passive policy toward Kizilbashes and convinced of not being able to find supporters in Anatolia in case of a struggle over the throne, left for Rumelia via Kefe. This act, as well as the instigators in Istanbul, incited Bayezid against Selim. Bayezid's 40,000 troops confronted Selim's 30,000 and defeated them near **Çorlu** on August 3, 1511. Selim escaped to Kefe.

The rebellion that Şahkulu, leader of Kizilbashes, had started with 1,000 men on April 19, 1510, continued. The Grand Vizier Ali Pasha's forces defeated them at Gökçayi on July 2, 1511, but Ali Pasha was killed on the battlefield.

Ali Pasha's death meant a loss of an important supporter for Prince Ahmed when he was secretly called to Istanbul to succeed his aging, sick father. The Janissaries raided and looted the houses of those supporting Prince Ahmed, then assembled before the Porte demanding the dismissal of all high officials (September, 1511). They blocked the strait and did not allow Prince Ahmed, who had camped at Maltepe, to cross. Prince Ahmed marched on to Karaman and took over the governorship from Prince Mehmed's son Şehinşah. Meanwhile, Nur Ali Halife, the leader of Kizilbash Turkomen, took advantage of this dispute and rebelled. The rebels were only defeated after Selim ascended the throne.

Prince Ahmed's passivity against the Kizilbash uprising created a dislike for him in Istanbul. This facilitated the decision to call Selim to take over the throne (April 24, 1512). Bayezid left the capital for Dimetoka to retire, but he died on the way in Söğütlüdere near Edirne on May 26, 1512.

As soon as his son Süleyman I arrived from Kefe on July 29, Selim marched on to Bursa (December, 1512), where he had five princes put to death. The next victim was Prince Korkud. Sinan Bey, one of Selim's supporters, had him strangled in Teke-ili, where he had taken refuge.

Aftermath

Prince Ahmed, still hoping to succeed to the throne, headed for Bursa via Konya. Selim confronted him at the plain of **Yenişehir** on April 5, 1513, where he was defeated and killed. His son Murad escaped to Iran; his son Alaaddin fled to Egypt. They both died abroad.

Resources

Gibb, H. A. R., et al., eds. *The Encyclopedia of Islam*. Leiden: E. J. Brill, 1986.

Goodwin, Jason. *Lords of the Horizons: A History of the Ottoman Empire*. London: Vintage, 1999.

Wheatcroft, Andrew. *The Ottomans: Dissolving Images*. London: Viking, 1993.

SEE ALSO: Janissaries; Mehmed II; Selim I; Süleyman I; Turkish Wars of European Expansion.

Mehmet Mehdi İlhan

Ottoman-Druze Wars

AT ISSUE: Control over a semiautonomous religious sect within the Ottoman Empire, which supported the Persians in their wars against the Turks

DATE: 1613-1635

LOCATION: Syria and Lebanon

COMBATANTS: Ottomans vs. Druzes

PRINCIPAL COMMANDERS: *Ottoman*, Ḥāfiẓ Ahmed (d. 1632), Mustafa Pasha, Murad IV (1612-1640); *Druze*, Emir Fakhr al-Dīn (c. 1572-1635)

PRINCIPAL BATTLES: Beaufort Castle, Baruk, Beirut

RESULT: Murad IV crushed the Druze influence during the Turko-Persian Wars and severed the group's outside diplomatic and trading ties to the Italian city-states

BACKGROUND

In the early 1600's, Emir Fakhr al-Dīn led the Druze, a religious, nationalistic group within the Ottoman Empire. The sultan received tribute from al-Dīn, who also provided the additional service of restoring law and order in the mountainous region between Syria and Lebanon and protecting the pilgrim route from bandits. As al-Dīn's power grew in the region, competing rulers complained to the sultan about the growing military capabilities of his group, including the repairing of fortresses and the establishment of a large army. The grand vizier who received the complaints had been a rival of al-Dīn and subsequently agreed to send imperial troops to fight against the emir. The Druze leader attempted to negotiate a settlement. When diplomatic efforts failed, he fled the country after making preparations for the defense of the cities. In 1613, he journeyed to Florence, where he remained as a guest of Cosimo de' Medici, until his return in 1618.

ACTION

The first battle of the Ottoman-Druze Wars occurred at **Beaufort Castle** in October, 1613. Imperial and local troops numbering 50,000, under Ḥāfiẓ Ahmed, the *wali* of Damascus, laid siege to the fortress, and for sixty days, cannons bombarded the fortifications. However, the Druze had adequate provisions and the walls withstood the attacks, so the siege was discontinued. The forces then moved on to Shuf, where the Druze repelled them. The imperial troops remained outside Shuf until al-Dīn's son sent his mother with a ransom to lift the siege. The troops withdrew, taking his mother hostage. The imperial troops returned in 1614 and were defeated at **Baruk** and at Tirun Castle. That same year, the grand vizier died, and the new vizier, Muhammad Pasha, a friend of Al-Dīn, immediately offered the exiled leader amnesty. The emir returned to his homeland in October, 1618, and immediately repaid Ḥāfiẓ Ahmed by burning his villages and taking all of the territory encompassing Mount Lebanon, the village of Qab Ilyas, and **Beirut**. By 1623, the Ottoman government granted him possession of Safad, Nablus, and Ajlun before a new vizier, Mustafa Pasha, replaced al-Dīn's friend. The new vizier allied with the *wali* of Damascus, sending 12,000 troops against al-Dīn's four divisions, which surrounded the imperial troops on all four sides before most of the forces fled. With arms from Cyprus and the Ottoman Janissaries in Damascus, al-Dīn forged a strong, highly disciplined army. As the reputation of al-Dīn spread, the Ottoman government became suspicious of his intentions because he controlled more than thirty fortresses, including those at Aleppo and Antioch. When al-Dīn refused to let Ottoman troops quarter for the winter on his land, the sultan responded quickly. Sultan Murad IV, ready to resume the war with Persia, realized the necessity of suppressing the Druze, as they were allies of the Persians. Their presence on his flank created a threat that needed to be eliminated. Al-Dīn realized the need for outside support and dispatched a request to Florence but received no assistance from the de' Medici family. Fighting continued for a number of years, but by 1635, the power of the Druze had been broken.

RESULT

By crushing the influence of al-Dīn, the sultan eliminated a potential rival within his own borders. The Druze had maintained their own diplomatic ties to many of the enemies of the Ottoman Empire, including the Italians and the Persians. The confiscation of Druze lands added much needed wealth to the treasury and solidified control over the interior mountainous regions.

RESOURCES

Abu Izzeddin, Nejla M. *The Druzes: A New Study of Their History, Faith, and Society*. New York: Brill, 1993.

Betts, Robert Brenton. *The Druze*. New Haven, Conn.: Yale University Press, 1988.

Hitti, Philip Khuri. *The Origins of the Druze People and Religion.* New York: Columbia University Press, 1928.

SEE ALSO: Janissaries; Ottoman Empire; Turko-Persian Wars.

Cynthia Northrup

OTTOMAN EMPIRE

DATE: 1451-1922
LOCATION: Istanbul, Turkey
PRINCIPAL MILITARY ACTIONS: Albanian-Turkish Wars, Austro-Turkish Wars, Greco-Turkish War, Hungarian-Turkish Wars, Mamlūk-Ottoman Wars, Ottoman Civil Wars, Ottoman-Druze Wars, Polish-Turkish Wars, Russo-Turkish Wars, Turkish Wars of European Expansion, Turko-Persian Wars
MILITARY SIGNIFICANCE: The Turkish military structure and bureaucratic organization combined to form an empire that stretched from the Atlantic to the Indian Ocean and resulted in armed conflict with European, Asiatic, and North African kings, emperors, and religious leaders.

In 1299, the Turkish ruler Osman founded the Ottoman state, using the military capabilities of his people to consolidate control over Arab lands. In 1326, the sultan Orhan organized the military into three principal contingents. The feudal armed forces received fiefs in exchange for military service and the provision of soldiers, but the land reverted to the sultan if the recipient failed to fulfill his military duties or committed a crime. Janissaries, recruited Christian youths trained in the ways of Islam, served as the standing infantry. Auxiliary troops consisting of scouts, armed nomads, and defenders of outlying fortresses rounded out the military structure.

After establishing administrative control over Anatolia, the Ottomans successfully invaded Europe many times during the next five hundred years. Although the Ottomans achieved many

OTTOMAN EMPIRE IN 1566

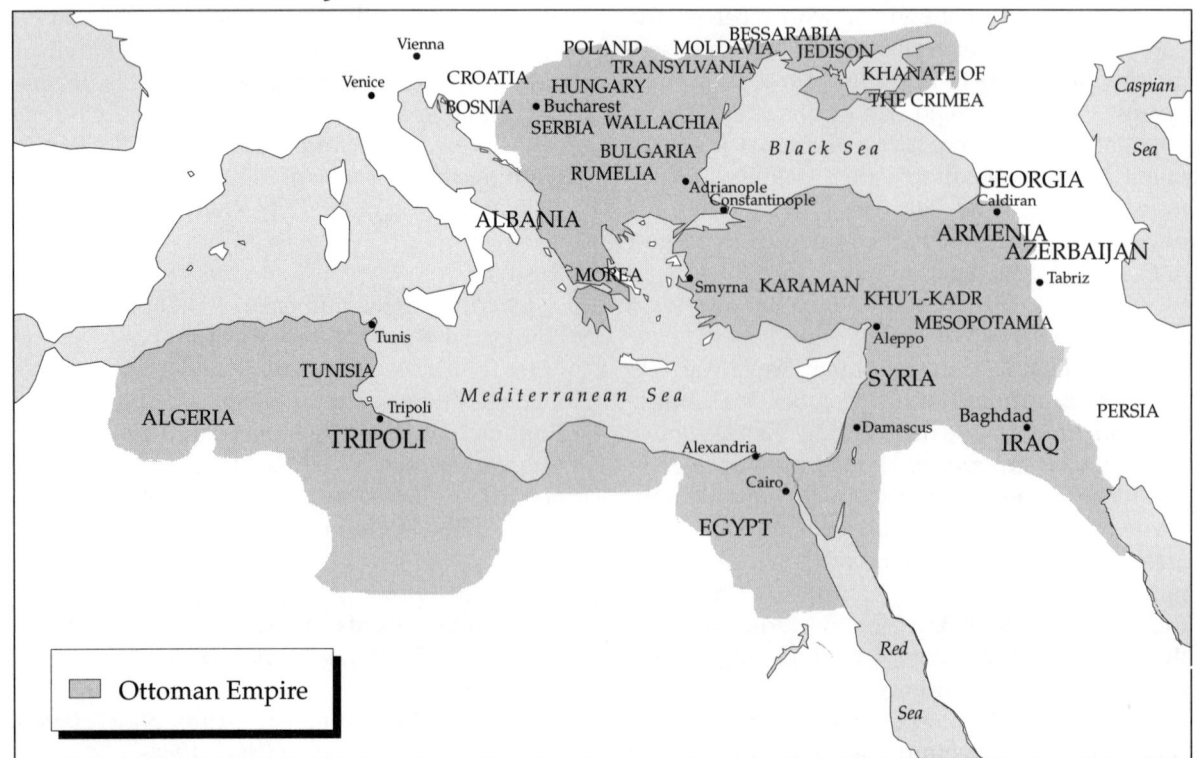

victories and expanded their territory considerably during the fourteenth and early fifteenth centuries, the beginning of the empire period dates from the reign of Mehmed II in 1451. After expanding and improving the army and establishing a navy, Mehmed besieged Constantinople (1453). He was defeated at Belgrade (1456) but occupied Athens, Serbia, Greece, and part of Anatolia. He entered into a war with Venice in 1463, which led to the capture of Dalmatia, Croatia, Negroponte, and Albania. He captured Otranto (1480) in Italy but died before marching on Rome. In 1499, the Ottomans decisively won a naval battle against the Venetians at Lepanto.

The Ottomans turned their attention to the east to deal with the Persian challenge. The Persians, under the Safavids, and the Ottomans waged a series of wars until the eighteenth century that ended in a stalemate. With the Persians checking their advance in the east, the Ottomans shifted their expansionist efforts back to the west.

By 1517, Selim I had conquered Syria and Egypt. In 1521, Süleyman I captured Belgrade and then waged a campaign against the Hungarians and the Austrians. After forming an alliance with the French king Francis I against the Emperor Charles V, Süleyman resumed the war against the Austrians while intermittently halting the campaigns to fight the Persians. By 1562, peace treaties had been signed with both Persia and Austria. After experiencing two major naval defeats in the Mediterranean, Süleyman once again led his army against Austria. Before he could wage war against the forces of Maximilian II, who had refused to pay tribute, Süleyman died. The sultanate passed to his son Selim II, and the military strength of the Ottoman began a rapid decline.

In 1683, the Ottoman forces experienced a crushing defeat at the hands of the Viennese. Recognizing the superiority of European arms after the introduction of gunpowder, the Ottomans attempted to reform their military. Relying on Prussian advisers to train their troops, the Ottomans fell under their sphere of influence. When World War I broke out, the government tried to remain neutral but failed. After the defeat of Germany, the Allies dictated the terms of an armistice to the Ottomans. Several political factions battled over the future of the country, and finally in 1922, Atatürk abolished the sultanate and officially ended the Ottoman Empire.

RESOURCES

Barkey, Karne. *Bandits and Bureaucrats: The Ottoman Route to State Centralization*. Ithaca, N.Y.: Cornell University Press, 1994.

Cook, M. A., ed. *A History of the Ottoman Empire to 1730*. New York: Cambridge University Press, 1976.

Kinross, Patrick Balfour. *The Ottoman Centuries: The Rise and Fall of the Turkish Empire*. New York: Morrow, 1977.

Shaw, Stanford J., and Ezel Kural Shaw. *History of the Ottoman Empire and Modern Turkey: Reform, Revolution, and Republic (1808-1975)*. New York: Cambridge University Press, 1977.

SEE ALSO: Albanian-Turkish Wars; Austro-Turkish Wars; Greco-Turkish War; Hungarian-Turkish Wars; Mamlūk-Ottoman Wars; Mehmed II; Ottoman Civil Wars; Ottoman-Druze Wars; Polish-Turkish Wars; Russo-Turkish Wars; Selim I; Süleyman I; Turkish Wars of European Expansion; Turkish War of Independence; Turko-Persian Wars.

Cynthia Northrup

OUDENARDE

TYPE OF ACTION: Ground battle in the War of the Spanish Succession
DATE: July 11, 1708
LOCATION: Near Oudenarde
COMBATANTS: 80,000 Allies (English, Dutch, and Imperialists) vs. 100,000 French
PRINCIPAL COMMANDERS: *Allied*, John Churchill, first duke of Marlborough (1650-1722), Prince Eugene of Savoy (1663-1736); *French*, Louis-Joseph de Bourbon, duke of Vendôme (1654-1712)
RESULT: Major Allied victory over the French

Having captured Bruges and Ghent, the French under Louis-Joseph de Bourbon, duke of Vendôme, marched toward the Flemish weaving town of Oudenarde, thirty-two miles west of Brussels. This movement led John Churchill, first duke of Marlborough, and Prince Eugene of

Savoy to march fifty miles in sixty-five hours to meet Vendôme in the hilly country immediately northeast of Oudenarde. Crossing the Scheldt below the town, the allies caught the French by surprise. Prince Eugene moved against the French left, as Dutch field marshal Hendrik van Nassau, lord of Ouwerkerk, flanked the French on the right. With Marlborough's forces holding the center of the field, the allies' wings were able to envelop half of the French force by sundown. Vendôme withdrew to Ghent having suffered 6,000 casualties and lost 7,000 prisoners; the allies suffered about 3,000 casualties. Marlborough's high degree of operational control, platoon firing system, and harmonious relationship with Prince Eugene contributed significantly to this victory.

Significance

Although the Battle of Oudenarde and subsequent Battle of Malplaquet regained the allies' strategic advantage in Flanders, the War of the Spanish Succession continued less advantageously elsewhere, leading England to quit the war in 1711 and forcing Austria in 1714 to sign treaties restoring the prewar balance of power.

Resources

Henderson, Nicholas. *Prince Eugene of Savoy*. New York: Praeger, 1965.

Livesey, Anthony. *Great Commanders and Their Battles*. Philadelphia: Courage, 1993.

Parker, Robert. *Military Memoirs of Marlborough's Campaigns, 1702-1712*. Mechanicsburg, Pa.: Stackpole Books, 1998.

Taylor, Frank. *The Wars of Marlborough, 1702-1709*. Cambridge, England: Cambridge University Press, 1921.

Weigley, R. F. *The Age of Battles*. Bloomington: Indiana University Press, 1991.

See also: Denain; Eugene of Savoy; Malplaquet; Marlborough, first duke of; Ramillies; Spanish Succession, War of the.

Randall Fegley

Oudinot, Nicolas Charles

Full name: Nicolas Charles Oudinot, duke of Reggio
Born: April 25, 1767; Bar-le-Duc, France

General Nicolas Charles Oudinot addresses his troops during the French Revolutionary Wars. (Archive Photos/Hulton Getty Collection)

DIED: September 13, 1847; Paris, France
PRINCIPAL WARS: French Revolutionary Wars, Napoleonic Wars
PRINCIPAL BATTLES: Wagram (1809), Berezina (1812)
MILITARY SIGNIFICANCE: Oudinot served as a French officer for forty years including service in the French Revolution, the Napoleonic Wars, and the restoration of the Bourbon government.

Nicolas Charles Oudinot, duke of Reggio, was the commander of the select French line infantry Grenadiers d'Oudinot and from 1813-1814 commanded two divisions of Napoleon's elite Young Guard. He received more wounds in battle than any other of Napoleon's marshals.

At the Battle of Wagram (1809), Oudinot's corps in the center of the battlefield attacked and recaptured the village of Wagram six times, holding it despite severe losses against overwhelming odds. Afterward, Napoleon promoted him to marshal. During the freezing, disastrous retreat from Moscow in November, 1812, Oudinot's 8,000 men held off a Russian force of 27,000 men at the Berezina River for several days, enabling engineers to build bridges and a majority of the army to cross over.

After Napoleon's second abdication in 1815, Oudinot served the Bourbon king's government until 1830. From 1842 to 1847, Oudinot was governor of Les Invalides, the honor society of Napoleon's veteran soldiers.

RESOURCES
Chandler, David. *Napoleon's Marshals*. London: Weidenfeld, 1998.
Elting, John. *Swords Around a Throne: Napoleon's Grand Armée*. New York: Da Capo Press, 1997.

SEE ALSO: Berezina River; French Revolution; French Revolutionary Wars; Napoleonic Wars; Wagram.

Alan Prescott Peterson

P

Pacific, War of the

At issue: Control of the nitrate region of the Atacama Desert
Date: April 5, 1879-October 20, 1883
Location: West coast of South America
Combatants: Chile vs. Peru and Bolivia
Principal commanders: *Chilean*, Arturo Prat, naval captain (1848-1879), Manuel Baquedano, general (1823-1897); *Peruvian*, Miguel Grau, admiral (1834-1879); *Bolivian*, Hilarión Daza, president and general (1840-1894)
Principal battles: Iquique, Cape Angamos, Tarapacá, Tacna, Lima
Result: Chilean victory; Bolivia lost port of Antofagasta; Peru lost provinces of Tarapacá and Tacna

Background

The presence of a valuable mineral within the area of a disputed boundary contributed to the coming of this conflict. Large deposits of sodium nitrate, a rich source for fertilizer and explosives, were located in the Atacama Desert in the Bolivian province of Antofagasta and the Peruvian province of Tarapacá. Chile had claimed portions of Atacama until reaching an agreement with Bolivia in 1874 that gave the territory to Bolivia. In turn, Bolivia agreed not to raise taxes on Chilean nitrate mining companies in the region. President Hilarión Daza decided to ignore this agreement and, in 1878, raised the taxes. The Chilean government responded with a military occupation of key settlements.

Bolivia turned to its neighbor, Peru. These two nations had negotiated a treaty in 1873 that provided for a military alliance against Chile in case of war. Learning that Bolivia and Peru intended to activate this alliance, Chile declared war against both countries on April 5, 1879.

Action

The focus of the conflict, the Atacama Desert, was difficult to reach from Chile except by sea. Naval warfare, therefore, was the first stage of combat. Chile's blockade of Peru's nitrate port of **Iquique** (May 21, 1879) backfired when Peruvian admiral Miguel Grau commanded his nation's two seaworthy ironclads in a surprise attack on two Chilean wooden-hulled ships. As Grau's vessel, the *Huáscar*, bore down on Arturo Prat's hapless *Esmeralda*, the young Chilean naval officer led a heroic but futile and fatal boarding of the Peruvian ironclad. Prat lost his ship and his life, but Chile gained a martyr who inspired patriotic resistance. Grau's *Huáscar* continued to raid coastal shipping until Chile's two ironclads avenged Prat's death off **Cape Angamos** (October 8, 1879). Chile captured the *Huáscar*, and Peru suffered another grievous loss, the death of the resourceful Grau.

With command of the sea, Chile launched a series of invasions along the rugged desert coastline. Chile's forces mastered a difficult beachhead in the province of **Tarapacá** (November 19-27, 1879), but a large Bolivian-Peruvian force threatened to drive them into the sea. Fortunately for Chile, Peru's headstrong and erratic dictator/field commander, Daza, disabled his army by a forced march through the desert and then abandoned his Peruvian allies—leaving them to be defeated at the hands of the invaders.

The fight for Tarapacá had not seen the emergence of a dominant military commander, but the invasion of **Tacna** (May 26, 1880) brought forth such a figure. Chilean general Manuel Baquedano used his 12,000-man force in bloody but effective frontal assaults against the 9,000-man Peruvian-Bolivian army, climaxing with the storming of the city of Tacna. Baquedano next launched the invasion of Peru's capital, **Lima** (January 13-15, 1881), with a force of 26,000. Peru built stout defenses manned by more than 20,000 soldiers and volunteers. Baquedano again used frontal assaults that resulted in heavy casualties (Peru lost 9,000, Chile over 5,000) and the fall of Lima.

Aftermath

The Treaty of Ancón (October 20, 1883) gave Antofagasta and Tarapacá to Chile and left the provinces of Tacna and Arica for later settlement (in 1929 Tacna went to Peru and Arica to Chile). Bolivia lost its coastline and, like Peru, had to endure the humiliation and financial burdens of defeat. Chile, reputed to be the "Prussia of South America," enjoyed the prosperity of nitrate production for several decades.

RESOURCES
Hooker, Terry D. *The Pacific War, 1879-1884*. Cottingham, England: El Dorado Books, 1993.
Ortega, Luis. "Nitrates, Chilean Entrepreneurs, and the Origins of the War of the Pacific." *Journal of Latin American Studies* 16 (1984): 337-380.
Sater, William. *Chile and the War of the Pacific*. Lincoln: University of Nebraska Press, 1986.
Worcester, Donald. "Naval Strategy in the War of the Pacific." *Journal of Inter-American Studies*. 5 (1963): 31-37.

SEE ALSO: Chaco War; Explosives; Warships.

John A. Britton

PACIFISM

The rejection of war as a means of settling disputes. The earliest known instances of pacifism can be traced to Eastern religions and philosophies—including Confucianism and Buddhism—and to ancient Greek theorists who sought to apply the civil order of the *polis* to the war-torn Greek peninsula. While some Western theorists have argued that war deviates from natural law—that it goes against human nature—religious and humanitarian concerns have been the main forces behind pacifism. Mennonites, Quakers, and certain other Christian denominations abhor war, for it denies the biblically justified doctrine of nonresistance. Many more—from eighteenth century intellectuals to young twentieth century activists—have seen war as inhumane, as a great fount of unnecessary suffering. The proliferation of nuclear arms and the looming threat of mutually assured destruction fueled widespread pacifism during the years of the Cold War (1947-1991).

Jeremiah Taylor

PĀNĪPAT, 1399

TYPE OF ACTION: Ground battle in Tamerlane's invasion of India
DATE: December 17, 1399
LOCATION: Pānīpat, near Delhi
COMBATANTS: Mongols vs. Moguls
PRINCIPAL COMMANDERS: *Mongols*, Tamerlane (1336-1405); *Moguls*, Muhammad ibn Tughluq
RESULT: The expansion of Mongol dominion over Hindu India

Tamerlane's goal was to seize the riches of Delhi, the Mogul capital, although his public motive was the city's extreme generosity to non-Muslims. Before besieging Delhi, he launched a battle against Pānīpat, allowing his infantry to take the first shock of combat and restraining his cavalry until the enemy was in total disorder.

Tamerlane's advance guard and right wing, under his grandson Pir-Muhammad, marched into the Punjab to seize Multan in the spring of 1398. The left wing, under another grandson, Muhammad Sultan, marched by way of Lahore. Tamerlane, with a small, special force, crossed the Hindu Kush before turning south to join the main body east of the Indus. After killing and plundering, he advanced on Delhi, engaging in the bloody battle against Muḥammad ibn Tughluq at Pānīpat on December 17, 1399, in which he slew thousands of Indian soldiers.

SIGNIFICANCE
Tamerlane's trail of bloodshed, plunder, and atrocity destroyed vast areas of India. Delhi did not rise from its ruins for more than a century.

RESOURCES
Ahmad ibn Muhammad, ibn Arab'shah. *Timur the Great Amir*. Lahore, India: Progressive Books, 1976.
Bérinstain, Valerie. *India and the Mughal Dynasty*. New York: Abrams, 1998.
Hookham, Hilda. *Tamburlane the Conqueror*. London: Hodder & Stoughton, 1962.
Joveyn, Ala-ed-Dīn 'Ata-Malik. *The History of the World Conqueror*. 2 vols. Cambridge, Mass.: Harvard University Press, 1958.

SEE ALSO: Akbar; Bābur; Bābur, conquests of; Mongul Empire; Pānīpat, 1526; Tamerlane.

Keith Garebian

Pānīpat, 1526

TYPE OF ACTION: Ground battle in the conquests of Bābur
DATE: April 21, 1526
LOCATION: Pānīpat, near Delhi, India
COMBATANTS: 15,000 Moguls vs. 30,000-40,000 Hindus
PRINCIPAL COMMANDERS: *Mogul*, Bābur (1483-1530); *Hindustani*, Sultan Ibrāhīm Lodī
RESULT: Mogul victory

Claiming to be an heir to the great conqueror Tamerlane, Bābur invaded India at the request of rivals for the Hindustani throne in Delhi, held by Sultan Ibrāhīm.

In the spring of 1526, with about 15,000 men, Bābur established a defensive position at the town of Pānīpat, about one hundred miles north of Delhi. He roped together seven hundred wagons into a line, leaving gaps for cavalry forays. Behind the wagons, he placed artillery and matchlock muskets. He anchored his position with Pānīpat on his right and a gully on his left.

Sultan Ibrāhīm arrived from Delhi on April 12, with perhaps 30,000 to 40,000 combat troops. They deployed opposite Bābur's Moguls but did not attack. After a week's inactivity, Bābur tried to provoke an assault. On the night of April 19, he sent 5,000 men toward Ibrāhīm's camp, but at dawn they withdrew in confusion. That encouraged Ibrāhīm to launch his attack on the morning of April 21.

Ibrāhīm's units marched in echelon across Bābur's front toward an increasingly small point of attack on the Mogul right. As the Hindustani troops hesitated before the town, trying to reorganize themselves and launch their assault, Bābur's gunners opened fire. As Ibrāhīm's troops were being massacred, Bābur launched two cavalry attacks that encircled the Hindustanis, striking them from the rear. He then sent infantry and cavalry through the gaps in his own line, resulting in Ibrāhīm's army being crushed from three sides. Between 15,000 and 20,000 Hindustanis died.

SIGNIFICANCE
Bābur marched into Delhi and crowned himself sultan, establishing the Mogul Dynasty in India.

RESOURCES
Bābur. *The Bābur-nama in English*. London: Luzac, 1921.
Foltz, Richard. *Mughal Indian and Central Asia*. Karachi, India: Oxford University Press, 1998.
Habib, Irfan, ed. *Akbar and His India*. Oxford: Oxford University Press, 1997.
Lane-Poole, Stanley. *Medieval India Under Mohammedan Rule*. Reprint. 1903. New York: Krause, 1970.

SEE ALSO: Akbar; Bābur; Bābur, conquests of; Delhi Sultanate, Wars of the.

Paul K. Davis

Parachute troops

Troops deployed from an aircraft by parachute. The Soviets were among the first to develop a corps of airborne soldiers in the interim between World Wars I and II (1918-1939). Parachute troops were not, however, used in combat until 1940, when German *Fallschirmjager* ("parachute light infantry") took part in the invasions of Normandy and the Low Countries. These German airborne troops set the mode of attire for most parachute units to follow: chin-strapped helmet, loose trousers tucked into leather jump boots, and a camouflaged smock. By the end of World War II (1939-1945), paratroopers (as parachute troops are usually called) were considered to be among the elite.

While the deployment of paratroopers is advantageous in that it allows large bodies of armed troops to be quickly deposited near an objective—even in the roughest terrain—it also has marked disadvantages. Wind often disperses parachute infantry, preventing an immediate attack in formation. Moreover, artillery and other heavy arms must be dropped separately. Paratroopers, then, are relatively lightly armed. Nevertheless, parachute operations retain enough tactical significance to assure their continued existence.

Jeremiah Taylor

Parma, Alessandro Farnese, Duke of

FULL NAME: Alessandro Farnese, Duke di Parma e Piacenza
BORN: August 27, 1545; Rome
DIED: December 3, 1592; Arras, France
PRINCIPAL WARS: Dutch Wars of Independence
PRINCIPAL BATTLES: Lepanto (1571), Gembloux (1578), Siege of Antwerp (1584-1585)
MILITARY SIGNIFICANCE: Italian general and governor of the Netherlands, Parma secured Spanish control and Catholicism in what is now Belgium.

Son of Ottavio of Parma and Charles V's illegitimate daughter Margaret of Austria, Alessandro Farnese was born into an aristocratic mercenary family. As a child, he was sent to Philip II's court to guarantee his quarrelsome father's loyalty. Lieutenant to Don Juan de Austria, Farnese fought brilliantly against the Turks at Lepanto in 1571.

In 1577, Don Juan, then governor of the Netherlands, sought Farnese's help in quelling religious disturbances. Farnese routed the Dutch at Gembloux in 1578. When Don Juan died that year, Philip II appointed Farnese governor. His flexibility contrasted with the severity of earlier governors. An astute strategist and charismatic diplomat, he negotiated with Catholic provinces while continuing military operations against the Protestant Union of Utrecht led by William I the Silent of Orange. Promising Spanish withdrawal, the 1579 Treaty of Arras restored peace to the southern Netherlands. His small, poorly trained army captured Maastricht in 1579 and Tournai in 1581. He obtained the recall of Spanish troops in 1582. After taking Diest, Westerlo, Ypres, Bruges, and several coastal towns, he surrounded Antwerp in 1584, starving it into submission thirteen months later. Spanish rule and Catholicism in the southern Netherlands were secure. He succeeded his father as duke in 1586 but never returned to Italy. The Spanish Armada's defeat in 1588 was blamed on Parma, who, exhausted by illness, died at age forty-seven.

RESOURCES

Beeching, Jack. *The Galleys at Lepanto*. New York: Scribner's, 1982

Melegari, V. *The Great Military Sieges*. New York: Thomas Crowell, 1972.
Parker, Geoffrey. *The Dutch Revolt*. London: Penguin, 1990.

SEE ALSO: Antwerp, Siege of; Don Juan de Austria; Dutch Wars of Independence; Lepanto.

Randall Fegley

Parthian Empire

DATE: 247 B.C.E.-226 C.E.
LOCATION: Southwest Asia (roughly Iran, Iraq, and eastern Syria)
PRINCIPAL MILITARY ACTIONS: Parthian-Seleucid Wars, Parthian-Roman Wars, Parthian-Sāsānid War
MILITARY SIGNIFICANCE: Through a series of wars, the Parthians expanded to dominate all of ancient Mesopotamia, Persia, Armenia, and Syria. At the height of its military power, Parthia fought Rome to a stalemate along the eastern frontier of the Roman Empire, allowing Parthia to monopolize the invaluable trade routes to Asia.

Descended from the Scythians, the Parthians moved down from between the Caspian and Aral Seas, filling the void between major empires (Roman, Seleucid Persian, and Mauryan). Through this strategic relocation, the Parthians were uniquely positioned to profit from the give and take between these competing forces but also destined to live and die by the sword.

Military expansion brought Parthia into contact with Rome at precisely the time that internecine struggle and dynastic politics began to weaken the Parthian war machine. Rome's own civil strife, however, offered unique opportunities for Parthian exploitation. Parthia routinely took sides in Roman political warfare, making allies and enemies widely. At Carrhae (53 B.C.E.), the Parthians obliterated the Romans under Marcus Licinius Crassus; total Roman losses approached 75 percent. While the Roman Empire was split between contending claimants, the legions would be unable to consistently defeat the Parthians on the battlefield. Through negotiations, Parthia forced Rome to forego territorial expansion; in exchange, the Parthians returned the captured standards of defeated legions. A humbled Rome became a patient enemy ready to exploit Parthian strategic missteps.

Initial Parthian military success was predicated on three elements: organization, technology, and tactics. Established along feudal lines, the Parthians were able to quickly tap the military potential to defend their society. This was crucial because the Parthians found themselves under attack on virtually all of their frontiers. At the same time, this feudal organization allowed internal rivalries between competing families to weaken Parthian unity.

The military technology, while simple, was very effective. The Parthians combined the bow with the horse. Others had done this effectively. For a time, however, no one did it better than did the Parthians. The Parthian bow was a powerful weapon, capable of sending an arrow completely through the intended target and frequently disabling the next enemy soldier in the ranks as well. Even disciplined troops were unnerved when confronted by Parthian archery. Parthian cavalry proved devastating to the tight ranks of opponents, ripping holes in formations and ready to immediately exploit those holes ruthlessly with mounted troops.

Another effective tactic became known as the "Parthian shot." Parthian cavalry perfected the ability to shoot with deadly accuracy while riding away from their enemy, firing back over the shoulder. This allowed the Parthians, when combat was not going well, to successfully disengage by discouraging pursuit. By feigning retreat, the Parthians could sometimes deceive enemy forces into breaking ranks to pursue, thereby opening themselves to a lethal Parthian countercharge.

Over time, these tactics lost their novelty and their tactical effectiveness. Opponents developed effective countermeasures, and time brought out the many weaknesses in the Parthian system of organization. The Parthian reputation for fierceness lessened considerably. Meanwhile, the Parthians faced pressure from the outside, as other tribes, displaced by the Huns, pushed into Parthia from the East. Fighting at all points of the compass while competing head-to-head with Rome, the Parthian war machine eventually stopped. The Roman army decisively defeated the Parthians at Dura-Europos (163 C.E.) and occupied Mesopotamia. In 227, the Parthians fell to the Sāsānid Persians.

RESOURCES

Goldsworthy, Adrian Keith. *The Roman Army at War: 100* B.C.-A.D. *200*. New York: Oxford University Press, 1996.

Wilcox, Peter, and Angus McBride. *Parthians and Sassanid Persians*. Vol. 3 in *Rome's Enemies*. London: Osprey Books, 1986.

Williams, Derek. *The Reach of Rome: A History of the Roman Imperial Frontier First-Fifth Centuries* A.D. New York: St. Martin's Press, 1997.

Wylie, Graham. "How Did Trajan Succeed in Subduing Parthia Where Mark Antony Failed?" *Ancient History Bulletin* 4, no. 2 (1990): 37-43.

SEE ALSO: Carrhae; Cassius; Mithridatic Wars; Phraates IV; Pompey the Great; Roman Empire; Sāsānid Empire; Trajan.

Michael S. Casey

PATRIOTISM

Devotion to one's native land—a sentiment best conveyed in Horace's famous words: *dulce et decorum est pro patria mori* ("it is sweet and becoming to die for the fatherland"). While pride in one's homeland is an ancient and powerful emotion, it has taken many forms. The Crusades, for instance, arose from loyalty to Christianity, not from any nationalistic concept of patriotism. In fact, fully developed modern patriotism—that associated with the "parent" nation-state and its children-citizens—did not develop until the time of the French Revolution (1789-1792).This was most important in a military sense; leaders who had believed that the mass arming of citizens was no effective way to wage war—indeed, that their loyalty could not be trusted—now found a new impetus for universal service. The resulting mass armies were fundamental to Napoleon's success. If patriotism has often made war possible, so war has given rise to patriotism. The American Civil War (1861-1865) is one of those most illustrative examples: Before that great convulsion, "the United States" was referred to in the plural. In the war's aftermath, the United States was generally spoken of as a single and truly united nation.

Jeremiah Taylor

Patton, George S.

FULL NAME: George Smith Patton, Jr.
ALSO KNOWN AS: "Old Blood and Guts"
BORN: November 11, 1885; San Gabriel, California
DIED: December 21, 1945; Heidelberg, Germany
PRINCIPAL WARS: World War I, World War II
PRINCIPAL BATTLES: St. Mihiel (1918), Meuse-Argonne (1918), Sicily (1943), Normandy Invasion (1944), Bulge (1944-1945)
MILITARY SIGNIFICANCE: General Patton organized a French center for training U.S. tank crews during World War I and championed advanced mechanized warfare during World War II.

George S. Patton was the product of a military family. Both his father and grandfather were graduates of the Virginia Military Institute, which Patton attended as a freshman. He transferred to the U.S. Military Academy at West Point as a sophomore and was graduated in 1909 as a cavalry officer.

George S. Patton. (U.S. Army)

Patton served as General John J. Pershing's aide-de-camp during Pershing's expedition to Mexico in 1917. During World War I (1914-1918), Patton went to France to establish a training center for U.S. tank crews. He was injured during his service in France, which included the Battles of St. Mihiel (1918) and the Meuse-Argonne (1918) and was decorated for his heroism.

In the years between the two world wars, Patton became one of the Army's leading exponents of armored warfare. When World War II (1939-1945) erupted, he commanded the Western Tank Force in Operation Torch, quickly overwhelming the Vichy French forces in Morocco in 1942. He then commanded the U.S. Seventh Army's invasion of Sicily (1943), capturing Palermo in a well-organized armored attack. Here he gained a degree of notoriety for slapping a hospitalized soldier whom he accused of malingering. For this well-publicized act, General Dwight D. Eisenhower relieved him of his command.

Soon Patton was appointed commander of the U.S. Third Army, which broke through the German lines around the Normandy beachhead shortly after D day in 1944. Patton's army then pursued the enemy to the German boundary near Metz, where his vehicles ran out of fuel and could go no farther.

In December, 1944, General Omar N. Bradley ordered the Third Army to strike north against the southern flank in the Battle of the Bulge near Ardennes. Patton, remarkably adaptable, changed the direction of his attack by ninety degrees and, on Christmas Day, 1944, relieved the defenders of Bastogne. Following that, he pushed on into the Rhineland and, without the knowledge or permission of his superiors, crossed the Rhine. Then he began an armored drive to the east and northeast, surrounding half a million Germans in the Ruhr Valley. His army continued moving to the east, pushing into Czechoslovakia and Austria just as the German surrender was imminent. Under his command, these forces had crossed six countries—France, Belgium, Luxembourg, Germany, Austria, and Czechoslovakia—in a little less than ten months.

Despite the unfavorable press General Patton received over the incident in which he slapped a soldier, many people rank him as one of the greatest field commanders the United States has ever produced. After World War II ended, he was appointed to the military governorship of Bavaria in southern Germany. The qualities that made him an effective general worked to his disadvantage as military governor. He was relieved of his duties because of his undiplomatic opposition to official policies regarding the purging of Nazis from Germany. On December 9, 1945, he was injured in an automobile accident near Mannheim, Germany. He succumbed to his injuries in Heidelberg on December 21.

RESOURCES
Blumenson, Martin, ed. *The Patton Papers, 1940-1945*. New York: Da Capo Press, 1996.
D'Este, Carlo. *Patton: A Genius for War*. New York: HarperCollins, 1995.
Farago, Ladislas. *The Last Days of Patton*. New York: McGraw-Hill, 1981.
General George S. Patton. Documentary. Entertainment Distributing, 1996.
Hanson, Victor Davis. *The Soul of Battle: From Ancient Times to the Present Day: How Three Great Liberators Vanquished Tyranny*. New York: Free Press, 1999.
Patton, George S., Jr. *War as I Knew It*. Boston: Houghton-Mifflin, 1995.
Patton. Fiction feature. Twentieth Century Fox, 1970.
Patton: A Genius for War. Documentary. A&E Home Video, 1995.
Sobel, Brian. *The Fighting Pattons*. Westport, Conn.: Praeger, 1997.
Top Command. Documentary. Viewmark, 1996.

SEE ALSO: Bradley, Omar N.; Bulge; Eisenhower, Dwight D.; Meuse-Argonne; Normandy Invasion; Pershing, John J.; Rhine Crossings; St. Mihiel; Tanks; World War I; World War II.

R. Baird Shuman

PAVIA

TYPE OF ACTION: Ground battle in Valois-Habsburg Wars
DATE: February 24, 1525
LOCATION: Pavia, twenty-one miles south of Milan, Italy
COMBATANTS: 33,000 Habsburgs (Imperialists) vs. 26,000 Valois (French)
PRINCIPAL COMMANDERS: *Habsburg/Imperialist*, Charles de Lannoy, viceroy of Naples (c. 1487-1527); *French*, King Francis I (1494-1547)
RESULT: Imperial victory; end of French Siege of Pavia

On January 24, 1525, Charles de Lannoy's imperial army of about 24,000 men left its base at Lodi and set out to end the French Siege of Pavia. However, the French avoided battle, and Lannoy consequently decided to attack the main camp of Francis I, which was located in a large park north of Pavia.

In the early hours of February 24, the imperial army entered the park while the Pavia garrison of about 9,000 men sallied forth from the city to support it. This resulted in fighting between imperial and French forces at various points north of the city. Francis led a cavalry charge that dispersed the imperial cavalry, but the French cavalry then came under heavy fire from imperial arquebusiers. Francis I's cavalry and supporting infantry were quickly outflanked and slaughtered, and the king himself was captured. French losses were about 8,000 dead and wounded, including many prominent nobles. Total imperial losses were about 1,500.

SIGNIFICANCE
The Battle of Pavia temporarily shifted the European balance of power in favor of the Holy Roman emperor Charles V. The battle also demonstrated the decline of heavily armored cavalry and the emergence of infantry with handheld firearms as a decisive factor in European warfare.

RESOURCES
Giono, Jean. *The Battle of Pavia, 24 February 1525*. London: Peter Owen, 1965.
Knecht, R. J. *Renaissance Warrior and Patron: The Reign of Francis I*. Cambridge, England: Cambridge University Press, 1994.
Konstam, Angus. *Pavia, 1525: The Climax of the Italian Wars*. London: Osprey, 1996.

SEE ALSO: Cerisolles; Charles V; Gravelines; Italian Wars; Metz, Siege of; Pavia; Saint-Quentin; Valois-Habsburg Wars.

Thomas I. Crimando

Pax Romana

Latin term meaning "Roman Peace," the Pax Romana was a period of relative calm throughout the Mediterranean from the reign of Caesar Augustus (27 B.C.E.-14 C.E.) to that of Marcus Aurelius (161-180). Under the competent reign of Augustus, who became ruler of the Greco-Roman world after defeating Cleopatra and Marc Antony's forces at Actium in 31 B.C.E., the system of imperial administration and trade that made the Pax Romana possible was established. According to many authorities, a true Pax Romana was not established until the death of the Emperor Domitian in 96 C.E. In the words of the great English historian Edward Gibbon, "If a man were called to fix the period in the history of the world during which the condition of the human race was most happy and prosperous, he would . . . name that which elapsed from the death of Domitian to the accession of Commodus" (96-180). While the era was not nearly as utopian as Gibbon suggests, it did create a respite from major warfare that facilitated the spread of Judaism and Christianity as well as the preservation and eventual transmission of classical culture.

Jeremiah Taylor

Pearl Harbor attack

TYPE OF ACTION: Air and sea battle in World War II
DATE: December 7, 1941
LOCATION: Pearl Harbor, Hawaii
COMBATANTS: Japanese First Air Fleet vs. U.S. Pacific Fleet and U.S. Army, Hawaiian Department
PRINCIPAL COMMANDERS: *U.S. Navy*, Admiral Husband Edward Kimmel (1882-1968); *U.S. Army*, Lieutenant General Walter C. Short (1880-1949); *Japan*, Vice Admiral Chuichi Nagumo (1886-1944)
RESULT: Severe damage to U.S. Pacific Fleet and Army Air Corps; entry of United States into World War II

Following a plan developed at the urging of Fleet Admiral Isoroku Yamamoto, Japanese aircraft struck the U.S. Pacific Fleet at Pearl Harbor on the morning of December 7, 1941. Launched by six aircraft carriers at 6:00 A.M. from a point 220 miles north of Oahu, the first wave of 49 bombers, 40 torpedo planes, 51 dive bombers, and 43 fighters attacked with complete surprise at 7:55 A.M. The second wave of 54 bombers, 78 dive bombers, and 36 fighters, launched at 7:05 A.M., began attacking at 8:40 A.M. and was gone by 9:45 A.M. At a cost of 29 aircraft and 6 submarines, the Japanese destroyed 164 warplanes, damaged 128 others, and sank or severely damaged 18 U.S. warships, including every U.S. battleship. U.S. casualties included 2,403 service personnel and civilians killed and 1,178 wounded. Although virtually every major U.S. military installation on Oahu was devastated by the attack, Japanese vice admiral Chuichi Nagumo retired without striking again. He left intact the Pearl Harbor repair facilities, oil storage tanks, and the U.S. submarine base. Despite the overwhelming Japanese success, some analysts have argued Nagumo should have ordered subsequent attacks to destroy these installations. Without them, the U.S. Pacific Fleet might have been forced to retreat to California. With them, the U.S. recovered and won a stunning victory at Midway only six months later.

Significance

The attack on Pearl Harbor was a pivotal event in world history that decisively altered the course of World War II. In the short run, it paralyzed the U.S. fleet, assisting the Japanese in conquering much of Southeast Asia and the Southwest Pacific. It also led directly to a U.S. declaration of war against Japan and encouraged Italy and Germany to declare war on the United States on December 11, thus bringing the United States directly into the war in both Europe and Asia, and tipping the scales in the Allies' favor. In the long run, the surprise attack united the formerly isolationist American people and filled them with a resolve to fight the war to the bitter end. By 1945, wartime production had ended the Great Depression, created both astonishing U.S. wealth on the home front, and one of the most powerful armies and navies in world history.

The shattering success of the Japanese attack produced a vigorous debate over why U.S. forces were caught so unaware at Pearl Harbor. The commanders of the U.S. Navy and Army in Pearl

Harbor, Husband Edward Kimmel and Walter C. Short, respectively, were both relieved of command after the attack. Some historians have argued that President Franklin D. Roosevelt placed the U.S. fleet at Pearl Harbor to bait the Japanese or that he knew the attack was imminent and did not inform U.S. commanders because he wanted to get the United States into World War II. Others suggest that British prime minister Winston Churchill knew the attack was coming and kept silent for similar reasons. Some believe that the United States deliberately provoked the attack. Although there were mistakes by the dozens on the U.S. side, including a fatal underestimation of the Japanese, thus far, no one has produced conclusive evidence that anything except Japanese skill, American mistakes, and luck account for the outcome of the attack on Pearl Harbor.

The USS Shaw *explodes during the Japanese attack on Pearl Harbor.* (Digital Stock)

Resources
Beach, Edward L. *Scapegoats: A Defense of Kimmel and Short at Pearl Harbor.* Annapolis, Md.: Naval Institute Press, 1995.

Clausen, Henry C., and Bruce Lee. *Pearl Harbor: Final Judgment.* New York: Crown, 1992.

Pearl Harbor: Two Hours That Changed the World. Documentary. ABC News, 1991.

Prange, Gordon W. *At Dawn We Slept: The Untold Story of Pearl Harbor.* New York: Viking, 1991.

Road to Infamy: The Countdown Years. Documentary. Lou Reda Productions, 1991.

Stinnett, Robert B. *Day of Deceit: The Truth About FDR and Pearl Harbor.* New York: Free Press, 2000.

Tora! Tora! Tora! Fiction feature. Twentieth Century-Fox, 1970.

SEE ALSO: Kimmel, Husband Edward; Midway; Nagumo, Chuichi; Short, Walter C.; World War II; Yamamoto, Isoroku.

Lance Janda

Peloponnesian Wars

AT ISSUE: Supremacy of the eastern Mediterranean
DATE: 460-446, 431-404 B.C.E.
LOCATION: Greece and the surrounding area
COMBATANTS: Athenian and Delian League forces vs. Spartan and Peloponnesian League forces
PRINCIPAL COMMANDERS: *Athenian*, Pericles (495-429 B.C.E.); *Spartan*, Lysander (d. 395 B.C.E.)
PRINCIPAL BATTLES: Oenophyta, Sphacteria, Amphipolis, Syracuse, Aegospotami
RESULT: Spartan victory; end of Athenian political hegemony

Background
By the fifth century B.C.E., Athens and Sparta were the two leading city-states of Greece. The two powers generally cooperated when they shared the common goal of stopping a Persian invasion (499-448 B.C.E.). During these years, Sparta was the dominant power because of its leadership of the Peloponnesian League, which included most Greek city-states on the Peloponnesian peninsula and central Greece. A 481 B.C.E. agreement providing that Sparta would direct the land war and Athens the naval war produced the decisive Greek victory at Plataea (479 B.C.E.).

In 478 B.C.E., the Athenians organized the Delian League, which was really an Athenian empire containing most of the islands and coastal regions around the northern and eastern Aegean Sea. Although the ostensible purpose of the league was to fight the Persians, Sparta resented and distrusted the rival empire from its inception. The Spartans had mixed feelings as they observed the Delian League liberating Greek-speaking communities from Persian control on the coast of Anatolia (later Turkey). Spartan resentment grew when Athens suppressed anti-Athenian movements on the islands of Naxos (470 B.C.E.) and Thasos (463 B.C.E.).

Competition for trade and imperial influence was the main source of conflict between the two powers. Because of its large navy, Athens had a distinct advantage in promoting its commercial interests. While sharing a common Greek culture, Athens and Sparta had different political systems that intensified their rivalry. Athens was developing into a limited democracy, with widespread participation of its male citizens. Sparta was a monarchic oligarchy, with less emphasis on individualism and intellectual pursuits.

Action

The First Peloponnesian War (460-446 B.C.E.) was precipitated by the withdrawal of Megara, a small city-state near Corinth, from the Peloponnesian League. When Athens welcomed the strategically located city as a member of the Delian League, Corinth attacked Athens, and the fighting soon spread to the other members of the two leagues.

In Athens, Pericles, then a young general, was the chief political leader and also the commander of the fleets and armies. Because of the superiority of Sparta's heavily armed infantry, the hoplite phalanx, Pericles' strategy was based on Athenian naval power, which meant concentrating on coastal cities such as Argos. When the Spartans crossed the isthmus to invade Boetha, Pericles won a great victory at **Oenophyta** (457 B.C.E.). Overconfident, Pericles then made the mistake of attacking the Persians in Egypt, where the Athenian forces were decimated (454 B.C.E.). After the superior Peloponnesian army, led by the young king Pleistoanax, defeated general Tolmides' forces in Boeotia (446 B.C.E.), the Spartan king inexplicably decided to return home.

In 446 B.C.E., Sparta and Athens agreed to a truce that was supposed to last thirty years. Athens agreed to give up her land possessions in the Peloponnese and central Greece. Sparta agreed to recognize Athenian hegemony over the sea. However, neither side fully carried out the terms of the truce. When Athens allied itself with the Corinthian colony of Corcyra (433 B.C.E.), Corinth and Athens fought proxy battles through their allies and colonies.

The Second Peloponnesian War (431-404 B.C.E.) began when Thebes, an ally of Sparta, attacked Plataea, a close ally of Athens. Athens declared war on Thebes, and the two leagues were again at war. When King Archidamus led the Spartan army into Attica, Pericles' policy was to avoid fighting the superior Spartan army and instead to stay within the city walls and to use Athenian naval superiority to harass the ships and coasts of the Peloponnesian League. With so many people crowded into the city, a terrible plague (430-426 B.C.E.) killed perhaps a third of the city's population, including Pericles himself.

In spite of the plague, the Athenians usually prevailed during the early years of the war. Pericles' successor, Cleon, won a great victory at **Sphacteria** (425 B.C.E.), and he refused a Spartan offer of peace. However, Spartan leader Brasidas surprised Athens in an attack on northeastern Greece, culminating in a decisive Spartan victory at **Amphipolis** (422 B.C.E.), in which Brasidas and Cleon were both killed. The new Athenian leader Nicias persuaded the Athenians to accept Sparta's offer of peace. The so-called Peace of Nicias (421 B.C.E.) only lasted six years.

In 415 B.C.E., the Athenians were persuaded by Alcibiades to invade **Syracuse**, and they assembled some 35,000 troops, the largest Greek expeditionary force until that time. Just before the fighting, Alcibiades was removed on charges of sacrilege, and he deserted to the Spartan side. Nicias, an incompetent strategist, assumed command of the invasion. In 413 B.C.E., Nicias hesitated and was surprised by a Spartan attack. Badly defeated, the Athenian army was forced into a disastrous retreat, losing almost the entire expeditionary force. That same year, Alcibiades, with the aid of the Persians, put together a large Spartan fleet and badly defeated the Athenian navy. Many of Athens's allies left the Delian League.

THE PELOPONNESIAN WARS

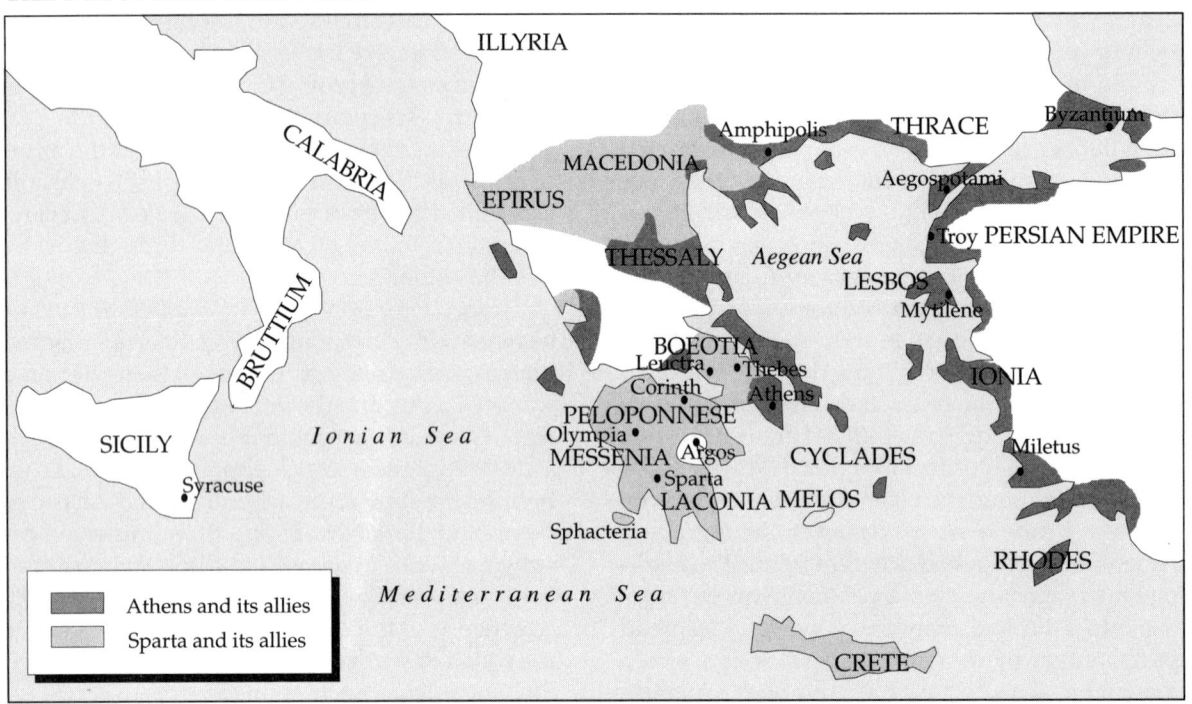

In 411 B.C.E., a civil war between proponents of oligarchy and supporters of democracy further weakened Athens. Despite this internal conflict, the Athenian navy managed to prevail at Cyzicus (410 B.C.E.) and Arginusae (406 B.C.E.). The Athenians, nevertheless, were in a desperate situation, and the talented naval commander Lysander destroyed the Athenian navy at **Aegospotami** (405 B.C.E.). Because the starving Athenians could no longer obtain grain through the Hellespont, they were forced to surrender in April, 404 B.C.E.

Aftermath

Athens lost its empire and never regained its dominant political influence. Lysander installed an oligarchic government in Athens, but a democratic system was restored within a few years. Although Sparta won the war, its heavy-handed policies brought forth new rebellions, and Spartan power declined after the defeat at Leuctra (371 B.C.E.).

There are two interpretations concerning the results of Athens's defeat. Some scholars have argued that Athenian hegemony, without defeat, might have promoted the cause of democracy and united the Greeks so that they would have later been in a stronger position to fight Alexander the Great and the Romans. Others insist that the Greek city-states wanted to maintain their independence, and that Athenian imperialism had threatened the Greek understanding of liberty.

Resources

Cawkwell, George. *Thucydides and the Peloponnesian War*. London: Routledge, 1997.

Henderson, Bernard. *The Great War Between Athens and Sparta*. New York: Ayer, 1973.

Kagan, Donald. *Pericles of Athens and the Birth of Democracy*. New York: Free Press, 1991.

Panogopoulos, Andreas. *Captives and Hostages in the Peloponnesian War*. Amsterdam: Hakkert, 1989.

Peloponnesian Wars. Documentary. Madacy Entertainment, 1995.

SEE ALSO: Aegospotami; Alcibiades; Athenian Empire; Greco-Persian Wars; Pericles; Plataea; Spartan Empire; Syracuse, Siege of.

Thomas T. Lewis